THE FRENCH REVOLUTION AND NAPOLEON

AN EYEWITNESS HISTORY

JOE H. KIRCHBERGER

Facts On File
New York • Oxford

The French Revolution and Napoleon: An Eyewitness History

Copyright © 1989 by Joe H. Kirchberger

Facts On File, Inc.   or   Facts On File Limited
460 Park Avenue South   Collins Street
New York, NY 10016   Oxford OX4 1XJ
USA   United Kingdom

Library of Congress Cataloging-in-Publication Data

Kirchberger, Joe H.
    The French Revolution and Napoleon.

    (The Eyewitness history series ; v. 1)
    Bibliography: p.
    Includes index.
    1. France—History—Revolution, 1789-1799.
2. Napoleon I, Emperor of the French, 1769-1821.
3. France—History—Revolution, 1789-1799—Sources.
4. France—History—Consulate and Empire, 1799-1815—
Sources.   5. France—History—Revolution, 1789-1799—
Personal narratives.   I. Title.   II. Series.
DC148.K56   1989   944.04   89-12058
ISBN 0-8160-2090-6

British CIP data available on request

Facts On File books are available at special discounts when purchased in bulk quantities for businesses, associations, institutions or sales promotion. Please contact the Special Sales Department of our New York office at 212/683-2244 (dial 800/322-8755 except in NY, AK or HI).

Text design by Jo Stein
Jacket design by Keith Lovell
Composition by Facts On File, Inc.
Manufactured by Maple-Vail Manufacturing Group
Printed in the United States of America

10 9 8 7 6 5 4 3 2 1

This book is printed on acid-free paper.

Contents

Preface   vii

1. The Crisis of the Old Regime: 1774 - May 1789   1
2. The Rise of the National Assembly: May 1789 - June 1791   16
3. From the King's Flight to the Second Revolution: June 1791 - August 1792   40
4. The Second Revolution and the End of the Monarchy: August 1792 - January 1793   54
5. Foreign Policy and the War of the First Coalition, Up to January 1793   68
6. Paris and the Provinces: January - September 1793   81
7. The Terror: September 17, 1793 - July 28, 1794   95
8. The Last Months of the National Convention: August 1794 - October 1795   111
9. The War of the First Coalition Up to the Treaties of Basle: January 1793 - July 1795   123
10. Wars Against Austria, England and Switzerland: September 1795 - December 1798   134
11. The Directory: October 1795 - October 1799   145
12. Napoleon's Life Up to the Peace of Campo Formio: 1769 - October 1797   160
13. The Second Coalition and Its War Up to the Peace Treaty of Lunéville: January 1798 - March 1801   175
14. The Egyptian Campaign: February 1798 - August 1801   187
15. Napoleon's Coup d'Etat and Consulate: October 1799 - December 1804   202
16. Napoleon's Conquest of Europe: March 1805 - December 1807   219
17. Napoleon at the Height of His Power: February 1808 - July 1812   235
18. The Russian Campaign: April - December 1812   252
19. The War of January 1813 - May 1814   262
20. Napoleon: From Elba to St. Helena: May 1814 - May 1821   275
21. The Congress of Vienna: September 1814 - November 1815   287

Appendix A, Documents   297
Appendix B, Biographies of Major Personalities   337
Appendix C, Maps   350
Bibliography   357
Index   369

The Eyewitness History Series

Historians have long recognized that to truly understand the past we must relive it. We can only see past eras and events clearly when we free our minds from the knowledge of what unfolded between then and now and permit ourselves to experience events with the fresh vision of a contemporary participant or observer.

To stimulate our powers of historical imagination we must begin by immersing ourselves in the documents of the period, so that we can view events as eyewitnesses. THE EYEWITNESS HISTORY SERIES offers readers and students the opportunity to exercise their historical imaginations by providing in a single volume a large collection of excerpts from what historians call "primary sources," the memoirs, diaries, letters, journalism and official documents of the period.

To give these historical raw materials a framework, each chapter begins with a brief summary of the "Historical Context" followed by a detailed "Chronicle of Events." However, the bulk of each chapter consists of a large selection of quotations from eyewitness accounts of the events of the time. These have been selected to give the reader the widest range of views possible. Each has a specific source in the Bibliography to facilitate further study. To further stimulate the reader's historical imagination, a selection of contemporary illustrations is included in each chapter. Modern maps have been included in an appendix for the convenience of readers.

Rather than interrupt the main text with lengthy official documents, we have included them in an appendix. Another appendix includes brief biographies of the major personalities referred to in the text.

EYEWITNESS HISTORIES are intended to encourage students and readers to discover the powers and the pleasures of historical imagination, while also providing them with comprehensive and self-contained works of reference to significant historical periods.

Preface

What began in Versailles in May of 1789 was certainly the most decisive and portentous event of modern European history. It spread over the whole country within a few weeks and then, within a few years, over a large part of the continent. In the long run, it changed the structure of almost all European states, even where a reaction set in for the years immediately following 1815. The ideas that came to the surface in the French Revolution still dominate a large part of our present political discourse. For one, the concept of revolution as such, as an uprising against one's own or a foreign regime, has inspired, time and time again, nations to rebel and has given them the idealism and optimism without which such ventures cannot succeed.

The French Revolution was not only the most momentous, but also the first revolution of the modern world. The later French revolutions, of 1830, 1848, and 1870 were inspired by the great one of 1789 and were unthinkable without it. It remained the prototype for all later revolutions, all the way to the Russian one of 1917 and the German revolutions of 1918. The uprisings of earlier centuries, on the other hand, were of a different character: The peasant riots of 1525, for instance, were locally limited and never spread over the whole country; also, they had strong religious connotations and aimed only at limited improvements for one particular class of the population. The "great" British revolution of 1640-49 was less a popular uprising than a civil war between the king and the parliament parties, and, again, largely motivated by religion. The second revolution, the "glorious" one of 1688, was hardly more than a change of dynasties, enforced by the parliament. And the American Revolution of 1776-83—which did influence the French Revolution considerably—was nevertheless essentially not an uprising of the people but a separation of colonies from their mother country, fought out as a regular war between the armies of two powers.

The only non-revolutionary events of modern history comparable in magnitude were the two world wars—surely crises of an entirely different nature—and possibly the great reformation movement of the 16th century. The latter presents itself hardly as one single event, but rather as a series of developments; more than 20 years lie between Luther's debut and that of Calvin. But what happened in 1789 and in the following years—actually all the way to 1815—followed in such rapid succession that Europe hardly had a chance to catch her breath during this whole era. The drama of the events, possibly even more than their influence on the years to come, has made them so memorable that hardly any other period of history is so frequently remembered and so heatedly debated, perhaps excepting that of the American Civil War. The French Revolution also brought forward an unusual number of original and impressive personalities who are still on our minds today: Mirabeau, Lafayette, Necker, Sieyès, Danton, Marat, Robespierre, Saint-Just, Talleyrand, Fouché, and, of course, Napoleon and his helpers and adversaries.

What began, or at least came to light, in 1789 was not just the idea of popular revolution. The conception of national sovereignty and self-determination developed out of the struggle of revolutionary France against the Allied powers and stayed alive in most other European countries even where these ideas were again repressed, for a while, after 1815. The principles of the rights of man and the liberty of the individual had been proclaimed in North America years before they were pronounced by the French; but they found their way into European thinking only through the French Revolution. Nationalism and patriotism started in France with the revolutionary wars and in Germany and Italy through the struggle against Napoleon. Universal conscription and mass armies, in contrast to the mercenary armies of earlier centuries, originated with the French *levée en masse* of 1792. One could claim, with little exaggeration, that most of the political principles and ideas of our time began at the time of the French Revolution—even where they contradict each other: The Revolution proclaimed peace and brotherhood for all peoples, yet was constantly at war with England, Austria, and Russia, and some of the time with Prussia, throughout the Napoleonic era; moreover, these wars were conducted much more intensely than the earlier ones fought by mercenaries.

The Revolution proclaimed liberty and equality for all but also produced the first modern dictator, the prototype for all who followed, Napoleon, and actually ended up by getting a small minority of well-to-do bourgeois into power. It also brought about the first socialist and communist ideologies, in the programs of Babeuf, Roux and their followers. It liberated the individual from the arbitrary power of the feudal lord but also produced the first modern reign of terror, which destroyed thousands of its opponents on mere suspicion. To the masses it gave the right of self-determination but soon enough made wealth and possession the basis for the political power of a few privileged individuals. All these ideas and controversies are still our own and, in fact, have been in the center of our political life, at least until 1945 and the dawn of the atomic age.

PERSPECTIVES ON THE REVOLUTION

Naturally, on a subject of such popularity and importance hundreds of books have been written that aim to explain and interpret the various phases and aspects of the Revolution and its equally dramatic and momentous continuation, the era of Napoleon Bonaparte. The French historians dominate the field and have done so ever since Antoine Barnave, one of the revolutionaries, tried to supply an explanation of revolution in general as early as 1792. Since 1885, there has been a special chair for the history of the Revolution at the Paris University. All aspects and facets of the Revolution have been explored from all possible points of view, but as late as our own time one can say that there isn't even an agreement in principle among the experts, neither in the evaluation of the period nor in the explanation of its origins. One of the reasons for this is that statistics in those days were still quite undeveloped; we are ignorant of many basic facts of the time, particularly where life in the French provinces is concerned. Another reason is that so many ideas developed by the Revolution and dominating it at one time or another turned out to be ambiguous. Moreover, the results realized by a given faction often contradicted the faction's original aims.

In the face of so much confusion and in the absence of hard factual data, preconceived points of view have often been decisive in histories of the Revolution. Therefore, we have evaluations of the Revolution from an anti-mob, or liberal, or socialist, or communist point of view; interpretations have been philosophical theories, or power politics, or economics, or national bias or, more often, a mixture of several of these narrow and blinkered views of history. Obviously, a witness like the Anglo-American Thomas Paine, who saw the French Revolution as an outgrowth of the American movement for independence, which he helped to bring about, would hardly see events in the same way as British statesmen such as William Pitt and Edmund Burke, who regarded France as the greatest potential enemy of their country and who lived in a state that, a century before, had anticipated a good part of the liberal and democratic ideas now propagated in France. In Germany and Italy, on the other hand, there was little feeling for nationality yet, as these countries had not existed as unified states for centuries.

So we find, on one end of the spectrum, a completely negative verdict of the French Revolution, as in the writings of Burke, who considered the whole movement superfluous, easily preventable by a few reforms, and taken to extremes thanks to the peculiarities of the French national character. Others saw it as the conspiracy of a few lawyers or freemasons or as the result of unfortunate accidents such as the disastrous harvest of 1788, Louis XVI's weak character, or Mirabeau's early death. Few people still cling to such views, which once attained considerable political importance, particularly in Germany thanks to the political theorist Friedrich Gentz, who translated and popularized Burke's essay on the French Revolution of 1792. Other observers deplore the annihilation of the French aristocracy, which was never replaced by anything of equal refinement and cultural achievement. And certainly many historians claim that whatever was gained by the Revolution was lost again during Napoleon's regime, and that the many bloody wars between 1792 and 1815 were fought in vain.

On the other end of the spectrum there are interpreters who view the Revolution as long overdue and inevitable. From their perspective, the remnants of the Middle Ages and feudalism had outlived their usefulness. With the Revolution, the people, at last, came into their own and have remained there ever since as a result of more progress being made throughout Europe during those 26 years than in any other period of history before or since. In their eyes, modern history began with the Etats Généraux in Versailles and the heroes of the Revolution, most of whom did not survive it, fought not just for the liberation and happiness of the French but for all mankind. Here, the short months of the terror regime and the many occurrences of violence in France are seen as secondary and untypical episodes.

Between these two extremes there are many less one-sided evaluations, of the Revolution as well as of Napoleon as a man and an historical phenomenon. They evaluate the whole era neither as happy nor unhappy but as one of mixed blessing.

Indeed, one could ask if there is such a thing as a blessed or futile, a happy or unhappy period in history. A famous historian once said that in the book of history, the empty pages are the happy ones. Seen this way, our own era certainly was an unhappy one because it was crammed with events. Yet, if we listen to the "Marseillaise," still as popular and alive as ever, we do not get the impression that it was sung by unhappy people. The other great controversy, the question of what brought the Revolution about, lends itself better to a more detailed analysis. In the present context, only a very short and rough outline of this vast subject can be given.

THE CAUSES OF THE REVOLUTION

In the older historical literature, the main causes for the events of 1789-1793 are seen in the philosophical ideas of the 18th century and its political consequences. The great movement of the Enlightenment, which put all emphasis on reason and justice and questioned all traditional values and institutions, had begun in Holland and England in the last quarter of the 17th century and spread from there to France where it took on more radical forms. While the earlier representatives of this movement, such as John Locke in England and Gottfried Wilhelm Leibniz in Germany still saw themselves as Christian thinkers, later French writers such as Francois Marie Arouet Voltaire (1694-1778) and Denis Diderot (1713-84) turned unequivocally anti-church. Neither was any secular authority left unquestioned. In France, it began with Baron Charles de Montesquieu's *Lettres Persanes* of 1721 and especially with his *L'Esprit des Lois* of 1748, which for the first time demanded a strict separation of government into executive, legislative and judiciary, thus guaranteeing the liberty of the individual. While the philosophers of reason, Voltaire, Diderot and many others, fought against superstition and injustice and for the free expression of ideas, Jean Jacques Rousseau (1712-78) undermined the existing order in France from an entirely different angle. His very emotional writings attacked culture (as such) as unnatural, declared private property as the source of all evil, saw in the people the only legitimate sovereign, so that the purpose of government and civil law was to bring about agreement between the will of the state and the wishes of the people. The government, he taught, obtains its sovereignty through society. Again, such an order was hardly compatible with a state ruled by an absolute monarch and a feudally oriented aristocracy.

All these ideas had their effect not just among the up and coming bourgeoisie in France but also among the nobles, who frequently no longer believed in their own privileged position; and there is no question that many of these ideas had a direct bearing on those who took the lead in revolutionary France. In some of Louis Antoine Saint-Just and Maximilien Robespierre's speeches, one can clearly hear the voice of Rousseau, for instance. Yet Voltaire, Diderot and Rousseau had all died years before the Revolution broke out and, in fact, had never much bothered about the realization of their ideas. At best, they would have advocated reforms instead of the violent upheavals that followed their deaths, and though they probably would have approved the first steps taken by the National Assembly, they certainly would have distanced themselves completely from the events of 1792-95. Yet, without their writings, the Revolution surely would have taken a different course. Enlightenment ideas were one of the many causes of the Revolution. Any one particular cause in history carries with it no more than the possibility of a certain effect; nothing that happens is the result of one cause only but is always due to the interplay and meeting of many circumstances, some of which may become obscure and even unobservable to the later analyst.

Later historians have put much more emphasis than their predecessors on the economic and social situation in France during the last decades before 1789 and have arrived at entirely different conclusions. The discussion on what caused the Revolution has never ceased in France since Jules Michelet's *Histoire de la Révolution Francaise* (1847), which represented the traditional, and what one may call the romantic, explanation of the Revolution as the revolt of the oppressed, half-starved masses against the tyranny of a corrupt and greedy government. This historical tradition puts the peasant at the mercy of the usually absent seigneur who exploited him by putting crushing burdens on the peasant while he himself lived in splendor at a luxurious mansion in Versailles or Paris. Michelet paints a gloomy picture of the downtrodden masses, such as we find also described in Charles Dickens' *A Tale of Two Cities* and in the novels of Victor Hugo.

Michelet's history was challenged, only a few years after the appearance of its last volume, by Alexis de Tocqueville, foreign minister during the short-lived Second French Republic (1849-51) and already famous through his brilliant book, *Democracy in America*. His *Histoire*, due to his early death, is limited to an analysis of the Old Regime. The results of his exhaustive research contradict Michelet on almost every point: The French peasants, the vast majority of the population, were considerably better off than in any other European country. Serfdom, still reigning in Eastern Europe, had been abolished almost everywhere in France, and the peasant, unlike the English tenant-farmer, was in many instances a landowner. While it was true that the seigneurial rights still in existence in the 18th century were bitterly resented by the peasantry, they neverthe-less did not constitute a serious financial burden. The spirit of rebellion grew so strong because the lower classes were better off than they had been and because the government was attempting some reforms on its own, thus putting ideas into the people's heads. Hippolyte Taine, a generation younger than Michelet and Tocqueville, was a professor of literature and a philosopher rather than a professional historian, but had been drawn into the discussion by the political events of his day: the French defeat in the 1870-71 war with Germany and the Paris commune. He agreed with Michelet in his evaluation of the misery of the masses but did not share his belief in the people. He detested all revolutions and mass actions, and where Michelet talked of the "people," Taine used "mob"; he made no excuse for the violence and terror. His principal at-titude was anti-democratic and anti-republican.

But the Third French Republic, born in 1870, survived, and Alphonse Aulard, another prominent analyst of the French Revolution, wrote a staunch defense of the republic and of its political forbear, the great Revolution and its ideologies. He showed that outbreaks of violence were actually few and far between, that the seigneurial rights had not become more burdensome under Louis XVI, and that the picture of the utter misery of the masses as painted by Michelet and Taine had been exag-gerated.

A stronger challenge to Michelet and Taine, however, came from the socialist camp, which tried to apply Marxist dogma to explain the causes for the Revolution, first through Jean Jaurès, the longtime leader of the French socialists and advocate of peace, then by his pupil, Albert Mathiez. According to the Marxist theory, the Revolution was brought about not by the poor masses, but on the contrary by the wealthy bourgeois class, which had already attained most of the economic power in the country and now wished to extend that power into the political and social field. So the situation of the peasants had to be presented as quite bearable, and it is interesting to see how closely the results of Marxist research resemble those of the conservative Tocqueville (except that Tocqueville felt the Revolution had not been necessary at all and could easily have been prevented by some appropriate government reforms). Mathiez, on the other hand, points out that the unorganized, illiterate masses were incapable of organizing a full-scale revolution, and that they were used and exploited by the real revolutionaries, the bourgeoisie whose high-sounding tenets and slogans he constantly questions.

But there were other points of view, pronounced by equally respected scholars: Frantz Funck-Brentano paints a rather idyllic picture of the Old Regime, while in the 1920s, Pierre Gaxotte, repelled by the revolutions of 1918-19, sees the great Revolution as one tremendous, unprovoked and unnecessary evil. In substantiating his views, he relies heavily, and ironically, on the evidence presented by his political opposites, the socialists Jaurès and Mathiez. Apparently, the same historical data can be interpreted to demonstrate diametrically opposed political views!

More recent research has concentrated on very exact studies of economic facts and figures. C.E. Labrousse, for instance, has published (1932, 1943) innumerable details on prices, wages, incomes, taxes, etc., during the Old Regime. His conclusions come much closer to those of Michelet than those of Tocqueville and Jaurès: The Revolution arose from the decline of wages and profits, from the misery of the masses and from a number of circumstances that brought together bourgeoisie and proletariat in common opposition.

Finally, Georges Lefebvre (1874-1959), a specialist highly respected by practically all scholars, investigated the role of the peasants and showed their aversion to the introduction of capitalistic and technological methods into the rural economy. He pointed out how vulnerable the temporary alliance between peasantry and bourgeoisie actually was and convincingly demonstrated how it was only the convergence of a number of unconnected and unforeseeable circumstances that caused the cooperation of city and country population and thereby the outbreak of a general uprising in the summer of 1789.

PHASES OF THE REVOLUTION

One can see how much the various evaluations and explanations of the French Revolution diverge, and this is not the forum in which to present new research or theories. But it should be helpful for the understanding of what will follow to cite some of Lefebvre's particularly fertile ideas of dividing the great revolution, which for earlier historians had always been a compact whole, into several revolutions widely differing from one another, with different carriers and aims and which overlapped and influenced each other. It seems to me that by adopting this method, a rapprochement of the various presently existing theories, which contradict each other so vehemently, may become a possibility for the future.

Chronologically, the first revolution was that of the French aristocracy. This may come as a surprise, for the nobility, of course, turned out to be the Revolution's first victim; indeed, the nobles played the part of the proverbial sorcerer's apprentice, who was able to call in the spirits and then could not get rid of them. Since the medieval days of feudalism, the nobility had overwhelmingly dominated the administration and government of France, until it was challenged in the age of absolutism by the growing power of the kings and of the central government. The last great fling of the aristocracy had taken place in the so-called war of the Fronde (1648-53), while Cardinal Jules Mazarin ruled for the young King Louis XIV. After this uprising was crushed by the king's troops, the nobles were pushed back more and more during the long reign of Louis XIV, who brought absolutism to its very peak. Royal intendants taken from the ranks of the bourgeoisie were appointed for all the provinces to check on the feudal lords, and Louis' most important minister, Jean Baptiste Colbert, controller of the finances for over 20 years, was a commoner.

But after the death of the "Sun King" (1715), and under the regency of Philip of Orleans and then the reign of Louis XIV's great-grandson, Louis XV, the aristocracy began to struggle back to its previous dominant position and consistently sought to weaken the powers of the king. Certain institutions left over from previous times helped them in their efforts, in particular the *parlements*, 13 in all, of which the one in Paris was the most prominent. These were courts that derived their rights from the ancient curia regis of the Middle Ages; they had the privilege of registering the laws the king proclaimed—or rejecting them. The parliaments had always been a stronghold of the nobles or, more specifically, of the *noblesse de robe*, which was distinguished from the old *noblesse d'épée*, the noble officers who traced themselves back to knights of the crusades.

The parliaments were, as time-honored institutions, popular with the people. Also, there were provincial representations of the three estates in Flanders, Burgundy, Artois, and Languedoc. In Brittany the Third Estate, the common people, were even represented by a double number of delegates. But since voting was by estate, not by heads, the nobility—in this case the noblesse d'épée, which usually voted with the clergy—had the upper hand. So in the provinces, particularly those with estates, the fight was usually directed against the royal intendant, an outsider from Paris who normally was less popular than the indigenous members of the estates. What the nobility really was striving for was a kind of upper house parliament in Paris modeled after the one in Britain. (Generally, English institutions were greatly admired at the time, by liberals like Montesquieu and Voltaire as well as by the nobility.) The call for *égalité* had originally been the slogan of an aristocracy trying very hard to reduce the king to a primus inter pares once again.

Then, after Louis XVI became king in 1774, when the creeping financial crisis of the state became ever more urgent, the fight between king and aristocracy revolved around the raising of additional taxes, which were sorely needed to put the state back on a sound financial basis. But while Louis XIV had repeatedly reserved the right of imposing taxes for himself, Louis XVI and his ministers (Anne Robert Jacques Turgot, Guillaume Malesherbes, Jacques Necker, Charles Alexandre de Calonne) met with more stubborn resistance from the Paris parliament. Many noblemen considered the huge deficit and the tremendous amounts of debt the state had amassed as their own greatest asset, namely, as a means of forcing the king to give up some of his prerogatives—which the king was unwilling to do.

The aristocracy had further successes: In 1781, a law was passed under which no one could become an officer who could not prove himself to have four noble grandparents, so that a military career was entirely blocked for members of the bourgeoisie. Under Louis XVI, all ministers were noblemen, with the one exception of Necker. Even the royal intendants in the 34 provinces of the country, who were to keep the local nobility under control, were now for the most part noblemen themselves again, so that in case of a conflict with the aristocracy, the king could not expect much help from his intendants. For by now all the nobility stuck together, and the old split between the nobility of the sword and the somewhat less elevated nobility of the robe, whose status was frequently of much more recent origin, had been bridged over. The noblesse de robe quickly became as class-conceited as the noblesse d'épée, whose members were often impoverished, since no more wars were being fought, and who liked to pick their wives from the wealthy nobility of the robe, as well as from the ranks of the rich bourgeoisie.

To sum it up: Under Louis XVI, the aristocracy was well on its way to monopolizing all of the local administration, through the parliaments and other courts, the provincial estates and the intendants, and was still something like a nation within a nation. However, its main contribution to the outbreak of the Revolution was that from 1788 it insisted, together with the bourgeoisie, on the summoning of the Estates-General, again a design intended to reduce the power of the king. That the Estates-General would soon assume the right to turn against the nobility's own feudal privileges could not be foreseen at the time, or at least, was not anticipated. In the summer of 1788, the aristocracy's victory over the king seemed complete, especially since the Paris parliament had immediately decided that the estates would meet separately and vote by estate, not by heads, which automatically put control into the hands of the two privileged estates.

The *bourgeoisie*, which certainly took the lead in the great upheaval from May 1789 on, was not an "estate" under the definition of the Old Regime. Only three estates were recognized in this order: the clergy, the nobility and the "Third Estate," which comprised all the rest, including the bourgeoisie, in our sense of the word, but also peasants, craftsmen, shopkeepers, wage earners, beggars—all in all, about 96 percent of the total population. How many members of the Third Estate could be called bourgeois is hard to say because the borderline between the bourgeoisie and the lower classes was quite vague. The bourgeoisie at the time had assumed the role of spokesman for the rest of the people just because no such clear distinction was ever made.

Within the bourgeoisie there were vast differences. Its upper layers were the beneficiaries of the great progress the French economy had made during the 18th century. They included the great financiers and bankers, who were frequently foreigners, Swiss or Dutch, and therefore Protestants, as well as importers, slave traders, market speculators, rentiers and the entrepreneurs of the textile and iron industries in the large cities like Bordeaux, Marseilles, Lyons, Nantes, Rouen, Orleans. These industries were run by craftsmen; there were as yet few large machines, the steam engine just having been invented. These wealthy people endeavored to imitate the aristocratic style of life in every respect. Frequently, their palaces, were even more splendid than those of the aristocracy. They became just as status- and title-conscious as the noblemen, the main difference being that the bourgeoisie were excluded from careers in the army and the high civil service.

The lower layers of the bourgeoisie consisted of many lawyers, doctors, writers, artists and craftsmen. The latter were organized into guilds and thereby were opposed to the entrepreneurs and employers, who advocated free trade between individuals. Many members of the bourgeois class were intellectuals and had adopted the new ideas of the times. These were discussed and debated in innumerable clubs, which were also frequented by noblemen and clergymen. The Freemason lodges, whose members included princes and where tolerance, freedom of personality and equality before the law were postulated, were particularly numerous.

The historical role of the bourgeoisie in the Revolution began at the moment when the parliament of Paris decided to let the Estates-General convene as it had last done in 1614, thereby ensuring vote by estate, instead of by headcount. At this point the enemy was recognized to be not so much the king as the privileged classes. The party of the "patriots" was founded, but it was also joined by many liberal noblemen such as Lafayette. A huge publicity campaign in favor of equal rights for the Third Estate spread throughout the country; hundreds of pamphlets were written and published, of which one by the Abbé Sieyès became the most famous. It has been claimed that the whole movement was organized by the Freemasons, but this has never been proved. There was also the rather mysterious "Committee of Thirty," which included many prominent personalities such as Honoré Gabriel de Mirabeau, Emanuel Joseph Sieyès and the famous Duke of Orleans, later known as Philippe Egalité. The committee seems to have directed the activities of the Third Estate for a while and probably organized the wave of protests that ran through the country. But that is all we know about it, and there is no reason to believe that it was in the service of the duke.

At any rate, many petitions were sent to the king and the lawyers' associations; the guilds joined in the demand for "doubling" the number of delegates in the Third Estate, a precedent for which already existed in the Provincial Estates of the Languedoc. The clamor for voting by heads started somewhat later; it was the critical point, for the "patriots" knew quite well that they could rely on a number of votes from the liberal noblemen and the lower clergy so that, in a vote by heads, they could secure a majority of votes every time. More and more, the Third Estate began to look upon itself as the representative of the whole nation.

The election method was indirect, and the electors, who then had to vote in the actual delegates, were under obligation to put together a so-called *cahier des doléances* for their respective districts—grievance lists containing the complaints and the wishes of the population. These lists cannot be relied on to give us an exact picture of the mood in the country since, for example, the testimonies of the peasants were formulated by members of the higher classes, lawyers and clergymen who often moderated and changed them to suit their own purposes. Still, they convey a good overall impression of what the people wanted or did not want: All were for the monarch but against absolutism; most of them wished for taxation by the Estates-General, and administration by the Provincial Estates. Many wanted the church reformed, but no one advocated the abolition of religion or the separation of church and state. Though all provinces insisted on administrative independence, the feeling of being one indivisible nation was predominant. The differences of opinion emerged where the interests of the various estates were at stake: The Third Estate demanded complete equality of all before the law; the nobility was, at most, willing to accept equal taxation but deadly opposed to giving up its other privileges. Frequently it was suggested that the king confiscate the income of the monasteries or even sell their landed property, but the real estate of the nobles was never questioned.

In retrospect, it seems that Louis could have accommodated most of the wishes of the majority without meeting open opposition or jeopardizing his own position. Instead, he and the members of his court quickly forgot all their troubles with the aristocracy and rushed to its defense.

But the first great victory of the Third Estate could no longer be prevented. After the Estates-General had finally convened at Versailles on May 5, 1789, some six weeks elapsed during which the nobles and the Third Estate could not agree on the accreditation and voting procedures. After all, there were a great number of lawyers working for both sides. But then the Third Estate took the bold steps of declaring itself to be a National Assembly, rejecting the king's reform plan (which would have left the position of the aristocracy practically unchanged), and refusing to withdraw upon the king's orders. Shortly thereafter, many delegates of the clergy and then also more and more noblemen joined the Third Estate, thus compelling the king to ask the remaining loyal delegates of the First and Second Estates to cooperate with the Third.

But at this moment began, almost simultaneously, the third and fourth revolutions—of the *cities* and *countryside*. When it became obvious that the king would not meekly consent to the high-handedness of the Third Estate but instead began to concentrate troops around Paris, obviously to be used against the Estates-General, and when Louis replaced Necker and the other ministers ready to compromise with a cabinet completely devoted to him, the Parisians rose and stormed the Bastille, the old city fortress built in the 14th century. At this point the ancien régime began to collapse.

The reasons for the dramatic uprising were only partly connected with the struggle between king and National Assembly. The Parisian population had made no move to come to the aid of the assembly in Versailles, which was obviously threatened by the king's troops. The Parisians were motivated rather by the "Great Fear," which seized not just the city population but also the rural peasantry—the fear of a conspiracy of the aristocracy against the common people. The second reason for the uprising was the famine, a result of radically higher bread prices. Once the fall of the Bastille had shown the weakness of the government, the riots spread into most of the nation's cities. Unpopular, even hated, royal intendants were driven out and the municipalities reorganized themselves, defying the royal authority by accepting orders from Versailles only when issued by the National Assembly.

At the same time, the fourth revolution, that of the peasants, had flared up in many parts of the country. We have seen how differently the experts have analyzed the peasants' economic position, but we do know that most peasants owned their land, which amounted to about 30 percent of all the land in the country; in some districts, like the Alsace, Flanders, the Loire Valley and in the South, from half to three-quarters of the land was owned by peasants. The other owners of landed property were the noble feudal lords, with about 20 percent of the total; the church, with about 10 percent; and the bourgeoisie, with about 20 percent. These groups did not cultivate their own soil but had it done by day laborers or the so-called *métayers*, who did all the work and received in exchange one-half of the harvest.

Actually, the social and economic situation of the peasant ran the whole gamut, from the still existing serfs—who, however, had more rights than their fellow sufferers in the East and North of Europe— all the way up to the so-called *laboureurs*, peasants who came up with a surplus that they could sell, thus being the only ones who profited from the increasing market prices. Laboureurs, however, were a small minority. Most peasants did not possess sufficient land to make a living for themselves and their families, and were forced to look for additional work from richer neighbors. The technique of land cultivation was still primitive, hardly changed in France since the 10th century, it has been claimed. A large part of the soil remained untilled, at least for every third, sometimes even every second year. The relation between seed and harvest was only about 1:6, much less favorable than in modern agriculture.

The peasant had many reasons for complaint. The principal tax, the so-called taille, was borne almost exclusively by him and was divided quite unevenly among the various districts. Only he was called up for military duty. There were other taxes, among which the indirect salt tax (gabelle) was especially hated. There were, furthermore, payments to the feudal lord, his hunting and fishing privileges, his monopoly on mills and winepresses, the obligation of the peasants to maintain the roads from which they profited least of all, the payments to the clergy, the so-called "tenth" and many other locally varying burdens.

As a rule, the feudal lord was hated, while there prevailed a naive faith in the goodwill of the king. The news of the summoning of the Estates-General and the invitation to write down all complaints aroused great hopes among the peasantry for a general improvement. When the Assembly did not move forward—or so it seemed to the peasants—they blamed the inaction on a conspiracy of the nobles.

There had been many peasant uprisings in France; they even had a special name, jacquerie, dating back to the 14th century. This time, the rebellions were encouraged by the news of the fall of the Bastille and the riots in the cities. The disastrous harvest of 1788, the "great fear" of the aristocracy, troop movements believed to be directed against the population, and rumors that the rich were hoarding goods, took care of the rest. The violence and the extent of these riots were a tremendous shock to the delegates of the Third Estate. They had thought of themselves as the representatives of the peasants, who hardly appeared in Versailles at all. No one saw that the interests of the bourgeoisie and the peasantry did not run parallel at all. The fact that the Estates decided as early as August 4th to abolish all feudal rights and privileges was surely due to their fear that control over the peasants would otherwise be lost. Yet the alienation of the peasants did not disappear, and after the monarchy had been abolished, huge peasant uprisings against the republic developed in the Vendée and in Brittany.

To summarize, the outbreak of the Revolution of 1789 must be seen as the result of a great number of factors: a financial crisis, which can be traced back to the wars of Louis XIV, and more contemporaneously to the French participation in the American War of Independence; increasing food prices; the terrible harvest of 1788; the great unemployment due to the increase in population; the stubborn and shortsighted attitude of the nobles; and the character of the king and queen.

THE END OF THE REVOLUTION AND NAPOLEON

Another question often asked is: When did the Revolution come to an end? There, too, opinions differ widely. Some believe that with the fall of Robespierre and the end of the Terror (July of 1794), the fervor of the Revolution had ebbed away. Others set the end at the dissolution of the National Convention and the takeover by the Directory in October of 1795. But it seems to me that the essential characteristics of the Great Revolution—the great fervor with which the new ideas of liberty, equality, brotherhood were proclaimed and realized; the violent clash of ideologies; the desperate fight within the country against the royalist reaction on the one side, the ultra-radicals on the other; and, at the same time, the constant fight against practically all surrounding, hostile countries— all these continued almost unabated under the Directory. Even the Terror had not come to a complete end. So, while revolutions certainly do not come to an end because a government so decrees, one may say that in this case Napoleon was not so wrong to pronounce on December 15, 1799, immediately after his coup d'état: "The revolution has come to an end."

This does not mean, of course, that with Napoleon's takover an entirely new era arose having nothing to do with what preceded it. Even the most radical breaks must build on the past. No one knew that better than Napoleon, who always claimed to be the heir and completer of the Great Revolution, who built on many of its achievements and employed many

Jacobins, particularly in the first years of his regime. In his early days he had been a follower of Robespierre, but did he still believe in the principles of the Revolution when he had made himself dictator?

Here again we encounter a great controversy, which has never been completely resolved and probably never will be. Did he, as first consul and as emperor, believe in any ideals or only in his self-aggrandizement? Did he kill the Great Revolution or did he further it? Was he good or bad for Europe? Did he only ride the historical tide, or were the tremendous changes all over the continent his own personal achievement? Finally, a crude but only too obvious question: Can one, should one, compare him to Hitler?

Whole books have been written on these questions, and I cannot hope to contribute anything original. Looking into this man's mind is particularly difficult because he was a past master of self-propaganda, as probably no one before him had been. What he said in retrospect, in the memoirs dictated at St. Helena, differs considerably from what he said when the events took place. But even his on-the-spot proclamations, such as his military bulletins, are quite obviously guided much more by his wish to convey what he wanted people to believe than by the unadulterated facts.

It is easy to point out the negative items on his balance sheet: He was an egocentric of incredible proportions who thought nothing of sacrificing thousands, even hundreds of thousands of people to further his ends. He raced his nation and half of Europe from one war to the next to increase his power, and in the end, in 1815, left the greater part of Europe completely exhausted and France no better off than she had been in 1790. What seemed impossible after the Great Revolution happened: The hated Bourbons came back and with them a reaction that took decades to undo. The people had won the revolution, but it was a few rich bourgeois that Napoleon had left in charge.

All true, but one must also list a few points in Bonaparte's favor:

1. Napoleon did not start the wars in Europe, they were there when he came to power; he only conducted them more successfully than the republic had.
2. While he was fanatically hated and detested by many in the last years of his reign, he also inspired intelligent and discerning men and women of all nations and classes to an almost worshipful adoration, not only during his first campaigns but also when he was at the height of his power.
3. There is no question that he had a unique way of inspiring his armies, and his personal magnetism and charisma must have been quite extraordinary.

4. His energy and intellect were apparently so superior to those of his opponents that it took the whole of Europe, and many years, to overcome him.

5. His reforms in France and in the countries occupied by him were mostly for the good and lasted. The Europe Napoleon left behind was, and has remained to a large extent, the work of Napoleon. No other, single man made such an impression and had such an influence on Europe during the whole of the 19th century.

6. A good case can be made for the theory that he was indeed inspired by an ideal: that of a united, peaceful Europe. This is evident in his frequently repeated allusions to Charlemagne, who had achieved just that and whose successor he claimed to be. That such a Europe would be under French domination or, at least, leadership goes without saying. But was this not justified? France had proven to be the superior military power in Europe; it had also supplied and spread all the new ideals that dominated European political thought from there on. Napoleon's great error may simply have been that he misunderstood the trend of the times. A return to a supernational Europe, such as had existed centuries ago under the medieval Holy Roman Empire and had again become the dream of the early-19th-century Romantics, was not in accord with the trend of history, which was toward nationalism. He probably failed in the end because he did not see that, or did not want to see that.

Of course, it is easy for the later observer to point out mistakes made in the past when the "trend of the times" was not so apparent. All in all, Napoleon undoubtedly had a good instinct for what his times required. His Code Civil, the administrations he set up in the occupied countries, even his sense for publicity, show that. He also had a good, though not unfailing, instinct for the national character of the people he ruled. That he knew how to handle the Italians and was well-liked by them is only natural, as his own roots were Italian; but he was also popular in southern and western Germany. On the other hand, he misjudged the Spanish completely and probably underestimated the stubbornness and fighting capacity of the British.

As one can see, many or almost all of the questions regarding the meaning and underlying causes of the period here under discussion must remain open. The best we can do is to present the facts and let the reader form his own opinion. And one way to help him along is to quote a sufficient number of contemporary eyewitnesses. After all, history can best be understood when seen through the eyes of contemporaries rather than viewed through the prism of what followed.

If history in its boundless abundance of detail and its ambiguity can never be presented exactly as it once happened, then traditional historiography should be complemented by permitting history to speak for itself, by letting the voices of the actual carriers of history, the individuals who lived through it, be heard—not just the prominent actors but also those who observed it, experienced it, who suffered through it. This is why we have included as the centerpiece of each of the following chapters a section of eyewitness accounts— to show how things were seen when they happened.

1. The Crisis of the Old Regime: 1774 to May1789

THE HISTORICAL CONTEXT

The grandson of Louis XV ascended the throne of France as Louis XVI in 1774, at the age of 20. He was a moderately gifted man, full of goodwill and a desire to do the best for his people, neither a despot like Louis XIV nor a wastrel like Louis XV. Yet he was never popular with the people. He was ridiculed for his fondness for good food and drink (and his corresponding corpulence), his love of tinkering in his locksmith's workshop and his shyness. He was no libertine and kept no mistresses, as his predecessors had done, but the public questioned his qualities as a husband and claimed his wife's children were not his.

Marie Antoinette, daughter of the Austrian Empress Maria Theresa and known as *l' Autrichienne*, was even less popular. She had a reputation for pleasure-hunting and irresponsibility, for lacking an understanding of the common people and for trying to influence French politics in favor of her homeland. She never said, "Let them eat cake," when told that the poor had no bread, but the fact that people believed this story shows how they thought about her. Apparently, she was never concerned about the economic crisis of the state. The scandal of the diamond necklace in 1785 was particularly disastrous to her reputation, although she was surely quite innocent in this case. After the scandal and until the outbreak of the Revolution, she never entered the capital; but her personal favorites did much to prevent the reforms her husband was striving to put in motion.

Charles de Montesquieu

Louis was confronted, upon his ascension to the throne, with a prosperous country but a crisis-ridden and practically bankrupt state. France's economy had improved radically since the beginning of the century. Her trade quadrupled between 1700 and 1789. She was Europe's most populous country, with almost 26,000,000 inhabitants, compared to Russia's 24,000,000, Italy's 17,000,000, England and Prussia's 9,000,000 each and Austria's 8,000,000. The upper bourgeoisie had been the main beneficiary of this upswing, but the political power remained in the

1

hands of the aristocracy—about 400,000 persons. Only a few thousand of them, the high nobility, lived in their palaces in Paris or in Versailles, since Louis XIV had moved the government there. The lower nobility lived in the provinces, fighting both the peasants and the royal intendants, with the help of the parlements and the Provincial Estates, wherever these traditional institutions existed. High offices in administration at the court and in the army were for sale and available to all nobles, but at such prices that only the high aristocracy could afford them. Command of a regiment in the army cost between 2,500 and 5,000 livres.

In the official hierarchy, the clergy was the First Estate, consisting of about 130,000 persons. But it was not really an estate. Its higher ranks were filled with noblemen, while the lower clergy often identified with the peasants and supported them frequently in the General Assembly. The clergy was in charge of the schools, all charity and the registration of births, marriages and deaths. Its members paid no taxes but submitted to the king an annual "voluntary" donation. In normal years, this averaged about 12,000,000 livres, but in the crisis year of 1788 it amounted to only 1,180,000. (The "livre," the old monetary unit, was renamed by the Revolution as the "franc," then broken down decimally.)

The clergy was more tightly organized than the nobility and had its own jurisdiction. The overwhelming majority of the population adhered to the Catholic faith. The small Protestant minority, about 600,000 people, had been discriminated against since the revocation of the Edict of Nantes under Louis XIV and had only regained a certain degree of equality through the Toleration Act of 1787. But Protestants were still not admitted as judges. Atheism hardly existed and corruption among the clergy was extremely rare; the case of Cardinal Rohan, the main culprit of the "necklace-scandal," was indeed a rare exception.

Jean-Jacques Rousseau

Only about 16 percent of the population lived in cities. Paris, with 600,000 to 650,000 inhabitants, was by far the largest and most influential, even though the government had been transferred to Versailles. Paris still looked like a semi-medieval city. Almost one-fourth of the buildings were monasteries, former monasteries or convents. The nobility lived in the elegant Faubourg St. Germain; the poor people were concentrated in the faubourgs (suburbs) St. Antoine and St. Denis. There was no class-conscious proletariat. The lower strata consisted of small shopkeepers, craftsmen, journeymen, servants and a huge number of beggars. It has been estimated that there were about 5,000,000 of the latter in France. It seems that these underprivileged groups did not share a common feeling of being exploited, and the protests and demands of the poor were directed not at higher wages but against increasing prices, especially for food. There were no strikes.

When Louis XVI's reign began, there were already many Freemason lodges and other clubs in Paris and, in addition, innumerable coffeehouses. In all of these, new and unsettling political and philosophical ideas were being debated.

Throughout the 18th century, France was recognized as the leading country in Europe, but by 1774 her financial crisis had been lingering on for decades. The endless wars conducted by Louis XIV had exhausted the country, yet by the end of his reign he had lost most of his expensive conquests. There were more wars under his great-grandson, Louis XV, and in the last one, the Seven Years' War against England and Prussia, France had lost her North American possessions. The public debt grew to fantastic proportions during France's intervention in the War of American Independence. While she was on the winning side in that contest, it was a dangerous undertaking for a monarchy to support colonies in rebellion against their legitimate monarch.

Even the lethargic and pleasure-seeking Louis XV had recognized the dire necessity for reforms. His chancellor during his last years, René Nicolas de Maupeou, himself a former president of the Paris parlement, had banished that institution from the city and appointed a more efficient and simple system of courts. But his reforms were unpopular, and Louis XVI dismissed Maupeou and recalled the old parlement to Paris as one of the first acts of his reign.

Then Louis started his own reform program, in the spirit of "enlightened despotism." The Comte Jean Frédéric Phélippeause de Maurepas was made minister of state, and he appointed as controller-general Anne Robert Jacques Turgot, a prominent economist and disciple of the physiocrat school, which assumed that all wealth was derived from the land. Turgot believed in free trade and free competition. His slogan was, "No bankruptcy, no increase in taxes, no borrowing, but economy." In his six edicts, he abolished monopolies, redeemed part of the public debt, restored free grain trade inside France and cut government expenses. He dissolved the old trade guilds and improved the system of farming. Unfortunately, he was blamed for the crop failure of 1775 and the ensuing bread riots, and he encountered the hatred of the guilds and the grain speculators. When he proposed taxation of all the landholders, the parlement resisted and Maurepas suggested his dismissal. Louis let him go, especially as Turgot had also incurred the enmity of the queen by refusing favors to some of her favorites.

Jacques Necker, his successor, was a Swiss banker who had amassed a fortune and was considered a financial genius. Necker was appointed director of the treasury and in the following year, 1777, made director-general of finances. He resumed the policy of borrowing, and the public debt increased further. The 1778 treaty between France and the 13 American Colonies and the subsequent war with England made the situation worse. Necker's reports, in particular his famous *Comte rendu* of 1781, did not render an honest picture of the real financial situation, and, when he asked for greater reform powers, Maurepas suggested his dismissal.

Louis tried other reforms. Serfdom in the royal domains was abolished and, through the reforms of the Comte de St. Germain, the standing army was considerably improved.

There had been an upswing in the economy after the end of the last war in 1763. But prices went up without a proportionate increase in wages, and in the 1770s a general depression set in. Without wars on French soil and the terrible famines of earlier times, the population increased and so did the number of the unemployed and discontent. In the 1780s, the grain prices rose unbearably, the wine industry suffered from over-production, and the treaty of 1786 with England reduced the import tariffs on cheaper English merchandise, a serious blow for the French textile industry in particular.

In 1785, the affair of the diamond necklace became public knowledge and further undermined the reputation of the state and especially the court. Cardinal de Rohan, out of favor with the queen with whom he seems to have been in love, was duped by an adventuress, Comtesse de La Motte, into obtaining an extremely valuable necklace as a gift for the queen, with whom he thought he was corresponding. But the correspondence was a sham; La Motte had even arranged a meeting with a paid prostitute masquerading as the queen. La Motte took the necklace to London where it was sold. When Rohan failed to meet the payments to the jewelers, he was arrested but later acquitted. La Motte was punished but escaped from prison, and popular opinion blamed the whole scandal on the innocent queen.

Necker was succeeded by another physiocrat, Charles Alexandre de Calonne, who first attempted to restore confidence in the finances of the state by a liberal spending program. When this did not work, he changed his policy and, in 1786, suggested a plan for reform: one tax for all, graded by income; the curbing of some privileges; an end to internal tariffs; and the sale of some church property. The aristocracy would still be exempt of the taille. Calonne no longer tried to work with the parlements but arranged for the calling of an Assembly of Notables, an institution that had not been used since 1626. The assembly, again consisting mostly of nobles, resisted him every step of the way and criticized him bitterly. Again, in conformity with his physiocrat tenets he decreed freedom of grain trade, permitting exports from the grain storehouses. This measure contributed importantly to the great famine of 1788-89.

Calonne got himself into further trouble by declaring the national debt to be 80,000,000 and then 113,000,000 livres. He blamed Necker for the deficit; the latter was not given a chance to reply and was exiled from the city. To make matters worse, Calonne claimed that the notables agreed with him, which was not the case at all. Since he got nowhere, he was dismissed, and one of his great critics, Loménie de Brienne, succeeded him and soon dissolved the Assembly of Notables. Brienne, archbishop of Toulouse and a favorite of Marie Antoinette, had nothing new to offer and was now confronted with the parlement of Paris, which rejected his suggestions. Brienne then asked for the convening of the Estates-General, which had not been in session since 1614, claiming that only they had the right to grant new taxes. At this point, the king intervened and in a solemn session (*lit de justice*) ordered the parlement to register the stamp tax proposed by Brienne.

Now the conflict was out in the open. The parlement declared this order to be null and void, and its president, d'Espréménil, became a popular hero. It also indicted Calonne, who fled to England, becoming the first refugee of the Revolution. Louis reacted by sending the parlement to Troyes and trying through his representative, the Comte d'Artois, to have the stamp act registered. This led to a huge demonstration in favor of the parlement, and Brienne finally was forced to withdraw his new tax laws and to recall the parlement to Paris.

By now, the state was practically bankrupt and unable to pay some pensions, so a new loan of 120,000,000 livres was suggested by Brienne, but met with resistance within the royal family. In January of 1788 the parlement proceeded to attack the king by declaring the infamous *Lettres de Cachet* illegal. These were secret documents issued by the king, permitting authorities to throw a person into prison without any further process or hearing. They had been in frequent use since the 16th century. Voltaire had been one of their victims when he was thrown into the Bastille for 11 months, supposedly for having insulted the regent.

Brienne had not yet given up. In March of 1788, he presented the first—and last—budget of the Old Regime. The expenses for 1788 were estimated to be 629,000,000 livres, the income 503,000,000. The royal court's expenses were to be only around 35,000,000, less than 6 percent of total expenditures, but the liquidation of debts ran up to 318,000,000 livres! The declaration of a state of bankruptcy had actually been considered, but the wealthy bourgeoisie as well as the king opposed it.

In May of 1788, the parlement attacked again. Claiming that forcible measures were planned by the king, it put down the "basic laws of the kingdom," declaring, for instance, that judges could not be removed from their offices and that provincial privileges could not be tampered with. The same day, Brienne was trying to restrict the function of the parlements by proposing new registrations with courts to be appointed by the king. The judicial power of the feudal lords was also to be reduced. Two days later, two prominent justices of the Paris parlement held responsible for the declaration of the "basic laws" were arrested.

From this point on, the nobility and bourgeoisie insisted on the summoning of the Estates-General. Revolts in Rennes, Pau, Grenoble and other places emphasized the defiant mood of the country. Against the explicit orders of Brienne, the Estates in the Dauphiné assembled in Vizille, and Brienne had to confirm their actions. His ministers of war and the navy resigned, and he finally had no choice but to promise to convene the Estates-General. Since no loans had been approved, the government had to issue banknotes, thus starting the long line of inflationary steps that would become one of the characteristics of the years to come. In August of 1788, Brienne suspended his new registration courts, set the date for the convening of the Estates and resigned.

Louis recalled Necker, certainly a popular measure, but by September of 1788, things had again taken a turn for the worse. The harvest had been catastrophic, the cost of living in the country had doubled. The reinstituted Paris parlement rejected the "doubling of the Third" demanded by the Third Estate, and there was a sudden, drastic change in the mood of the country. The bourgeoisie began a tremendous propaganda drive for proper representation and even idolized the king, calling for his help against the schemes of the aristocracy, which was equally energetic and active in marshalling all its forces to secure its position at the forthcoming assembly. It, too, appealed to the king, for support against the attacks of the Third Estate. Necker, meanwhile, tried a compromise by recalling the Notables and proposing the doubling of the Third for tax laws only, but to no avail.

The first victory of the bourgeoisie was the decision of the Royal Council to grant the doubling; but nothing was said about the crucial question— voting by estate or by heads. The election procedure pronounced by the king seemed to favor the bourgeois over the peasant; this was probably not intentional, but rather the result of a complex, entirely antiquated election system. During the winter, unemployment increased in many cities, and civil war broke out in Brittany where students led by Jean Moreau, later to become a famous general, defeated gangs hired by the aristocrats. In protest, the Breton nobles refrained from electing any representatives for the Estates-General.

As the election drew nearer, the country was seized by the feverish propaganda of the bourgeoisie and flooded with hundreds of pamphlets. The breakdown of the old order became apparent everywhere, with local peasant riots and uprisings in Paris suburbs and other cities. At the same time, a great wave of optimism and hope swept the country.

CHRONICLE OF EVENTS

1774: Louis XVI succeeds to the throne of France.
He recalls the parlements.
Turgot is made controller-general.

1775: Famine in Paris.

1776: Boncerf's pamphlet condemns feudal privileges.
Turgot's six edicts call for abolition of guilds and *jurandes* and equal taxation of landowners.
Turgot is dismissed and Necker is made director of the treasury.

1777: Necker is made director-general of finances.

1778: Treaty agreed upon between France and the 13 American Colonies.
Britain declares war on France.

1779: Louis abolishes serfdom in the royal domains.

1781: New law limits army officers to those who can show descent from four noble grandparents.
Necker issues *Compte rendu*.
Necker is dismissed.

1783: Calonne is appointed controller-general of finances.
Peace treaty signed between France, Britain, Spain and the U.S. A.

1785/86: The diamond necklace affair blackens the queen's reputation.

1786: Calonne makes new proposal for financial reform.
Commercial treaty signed between Britain and France.

1787: Freedom of grain trade is decreed.
February 22: Assembly of Notables convenes at Versailles (until May) and rejects Calonne's reform plans.
April 8: Calonne is dismissed.
May 1: Loménie de Brienne becomes minister of finance.
May 25: Brienne dissolves the Assembly of Notables.
July 6: The parlement of Paris rejects Brienne's plans and asks for convening of the Estates-General.
August 6: The king orders the Paris parlement to register Brienne's stamp tax. It refuses and indicts Calonne.
August 14: The people acclaim the members of the Paris parlement. The king banishes the parlement to Troyes.
September 19: Brienne withdraws his new tax laws. The parlement is called back to Paris.

Denis Diderot

October 13: The government is unable to pay part of the pensions.

November 19: The king orders the registration of a loan proposed by Brienne. The Duke of Orleans protests and is exiled to his estates.

November 19: Toleration Act for Protestants.

1788: *January 4:* The Paris parlement declares the *Lettres de Cachet* illegal.

March: Brienne presents a budget.

May 3: The Paris parlement publishes a "Declaration of the basic laws of the kingdom." Lamoignon, assistant to Brienne, proposes a reform of the court system, restricting the role of the parlements. The Paris parlement is sent on vacation.

May: Revolts break out in Rennes, Toulouse, Pau and other places.

June 7: "Day of Tiles," a riot in Grenoble.

July 5: Brienne promises the summoning of the Estates-General.

July 13: Hailstorms destroy a large part of the harvest in Western France.

July 21: The Provincial Estates of the Dauphiné assemble in Vizille, defying Brienne's orders.

August 8: The Estates-General are summoned for May 1789.

August 18: The government is issuing banknotes; beginning of the great inflation.

August 24: Brienne resigns.

August 26: Necker is recalled.

September 23: The reinstituted Paris parlement decides that there will be no doubling of the representatives for the Third Estate and voting will be by Estate not by heads.

December 12: Supplication of the high aristocracy to the king: "The State is in peril . . ."

December 27: The "Royal Council" decides that the Third Estate is to have as many delegates as the other two together.

1789: *January 24:* The king determines the election procedure.

End of January: Civil war erupts in Brittany, with students against aristocrats.

January: Abbé Sieyès' pamphlet, "What Is the Third Estate?" published.

February 3: Mirabeau is excluded from the Estates of Provence.

April 27: Riot at the Faubourg Saint-Antoine.
April 30: Riot at Marseilles.
First meeting of the "Club Breton," later the Jacobins, at Versailles.

EYEWITNESS TESTIMONY

The dauphin was with the dauphiness. They were expecting together the intelligence of the death of Louis XV ... This extraordinary tumult informed Marie Antoinette and her husband that they were called to the throne; and, by a spontaneous movement which deeply affected those around them, they threw themselves on their knees; both, pouring forth a flood of tears, exclaimed: "O God, guide us, protect us; we are too young to reign!"

Jeanne Louise Campan, Memoires sur la Vie Privée de Marie Antoinette *(1823).*

Louis XVI who ascended the throne at the age of twenty, brought along a feeling of doubt about his own powers, which is praiseworthy when moderate but quite dangerous when it becomes excessive ... He had been intimidated too much ...

Jean Francois Marmontel, Memoirs *(1805).*

The queen is quite intelligent, but she has enjoyed a rather negative education ... She has never opened a book, except novels ... As soon as the conversation takes a turn for the serious, she looks bored and thereby chills the conversation ... She does not possess natural gaiety and amuses herself instead with the idle stories of the day ... and particularly with scandals found at the court ...

Pierre Joseph, Baron de Besenval, Memoirs *(1821).*

Turgot was commended to the choice of the king by his genius ... he contributed to the administration of finances a spirit and a program of universal beneficence. Louis XVI said, "Only M. Turgot and I love the people" ... Those who benefited from the abuses became alarmed and incited the people against the laws which were to feed them. There were riots in the capital and the adjoining provinces. Storehouses were plundered; all bakehouses pillaged, and there was talk in Paris of marching on Versailles ...

Joseph Weber, Memoirs *(1822).*

At present, things are quiet [in Paris]. Treachery is trembling because it has no power ... The king has managed to drive it to despair by appointing Mr. de Malesherbes as minister, perhaps the only official who is Mr. Turgot's equal in knowledge and virtue. These two men and their young and good master mark the beginning of a renaissance of high morality ... They chase away suspicious persons and force the highest officials who have accepted presents to make reparations. Protection does not help any longer...

Pierre Samuel Du Pont de Nemours, to Markgraf Carl Friedrich von Baden, letter of September 4, 1775, in von Baden's Correspondence with Mirabeau and Du Pont *(1892).*

Only he who has seen the years before 1789 knows what pleasure it can be to live.

Charles Maurice de Talleyrand-Périgord, as reported by Guizot in his History of France.

The great noblemen of France were not particularly well informed, for they had nothing to gain by it. The best way of arriving at honors with the court was to have grace in conversation ... The superficiality of education was one of the causes of their ultimate defeat; no longer were they able to fight against the intelligence

Voltaire in his study

of the members of the third estate whom they should have tried to surpass.

Mme. Germaine de Staël, Selection of Texts (1974).

Inoculation was favored by the court in Louis XV's time; but the *parlement* of Paris passed an *arrêt* against it, much more effective in prohibiting, than the favor of the court in encouraging the practice. Instances are innumerable, and I may remark, that the bigotry, ignorance, false principles and tyranny of these bodies were generally conspicuous; and that the court (taxation excepted) never had a dispute with a *parlement* but the *parlement* was sure to be wrong. Their constitution, in respect to the administration of justice, was so truly rotten ...

Arthur Young, Travels During the Years 1787, 1788, 1789, and 1790 *(1792-94).*

All names are found in it, from the prince to the court usher at the Chatelet [Prison]. Woe to him who is not mentioned in the book! He has no rank, no title, no position. Lucky are the collectors of the "Tenth." They are even richer than the Almanac says. You lose your way through the innumerable personnel of the princely dynasties. What a lot of domestics who try to hide their servitude under high sounding names! Further back you see how many notaries, lawyers, officials and other pen-pushers are fed by the people. They all want to live. What a devastating plague! Figure out how many thousands of livres are taken from the country and the poor peasants by every bishopric year after year—the tremendous amounts procured for the successors of the simple apostles—and you will be appalled ... The titles of the nobles only portend their idleness, and all the gold of the nation belongs to them. How many idle mouths are sucking and gnawing on the state's body—a whole assembly of vampires. Listed in this almanac are neither peasants nor merchants, craftsmen or artisans, but they are the part of the nation who rules the other part completely.

Louis Sébastien Mercier, Tableau de Paris *(1783- 1789).*

In the Faubourg of Saint-Marcel live the poorest, most restless common people of Paris ... One whole family lives in one single room. The walls are bare. All the furniture is not worth 20 thaler. The inhabitants move every three months because they owe their rent and are thrown out. So they wander about, dragging

King Louis XVI

their miserable household equipment from one refuge to the next. You never see leather shoes in these dwellings. In the stairways you hear only the clacking of wooden shoes ... In this suburb, people are more vicious, fiercer, more quarrelsome and inclined to riot than elsewhere. So the police do not dare to push things to extremes. They treat them gently because they are capable of wild excesses.

Mercier, Tableau de Paris *(1783-89).*

He [Calonne] was sworn in as controller-general in November of 1783. In December of 1783, one month after peace had been concluded, 100 million were borrowed on life-annuities to pay for the war expenses. In December of 1784, 125 millions were borrowed ... In December of 1785, 80 millions were borrowed ... In September of 1786, 30 millions were borrowed by the city of Paris ... In February of 1787, after another 50 millions had been borrowed ... an assembly of Notables was chosen ...

Weber, Memoirs *(1822).*

The king told me: "There is Beaumarchais' comedy. You must read it to us ... You will not mention this reading to anyone ..." He interrupted me often ... Most frequently he exclaimed: "This shows his bad taste!" ... At Figaro's monologue where he attacks the various branches of the administration, particularly at the tirades against the prisons, the king jumped up vividly

Marie Antoinette, known as "l'Autrichienne"

and said: "That is disgusting. That should never be performed. One would have to destroy the Bastille on order not to make the performance an inconsistency! This man plays with everything that in a government must be respected." "So it will not be played?" asked the queen. "Certainly not," Louis replied, "you may rely on that." ... day and hour of the opening were announced. The king learned of this only the last morning and immediately signs a "lettre de cachet" prohibiting the performance. When the messenger arrived with the order, part of the hall was already occupied by the spectators and all approaching streets filled with coaches ... The play was not performed, but the king's intervention was considered as infringement on public liberty ...

Campan, about Beaumarchais' Marriage of Figaro in 1784, in Memoirs (1823).

I have seen one of their [the British] latest achievements which is indeed admirable. A grain mill, a very small steam engine ... The grain was taken from the ship, sack after sack, lifted, cleaned by cleverly designed cylindrical brushes, crushed by millstones, separated ... poured back into the sacks and lowered back into the ship—all this in a very short time and all done by the machine. Only one man on the boat ... and one at the mill are required for this complicated process ... All millers in the capital have ganged up to destroy this miracle engine ... but one has used troops to dispel them ... The "Albion Mill" as they call it, has brought down the price for flour even more ... For such an enterprise, enormous capitals are required and they can be brought together only by associations of big capitalists who ... want to get richer still and would not dream of exchanging a lucrative business for a silly public office and a low degree of nobility. If, Sir, we could succeed in correcting the French way of thinking, we would have taken the first large step toward prosperity ...

Count d'Adhémar, to the Count de Vergennes, June 28, 1786, in Cheney's Readings in English History (1908).

The feeling of everybody seems to be that the archbishop [Loménie-Brienne] will not be able to do anything towards exonerating the state from the burden of its present situation; some think he has not the inclination; others that he has not the courage; others that he has not the ability. By some he is thought to be attentive only to his own interest; and by others that the finances are too much deranged to be within the power of any system to recover, short of the States-General ...

Jacques Necker, rector-general of finances

All seem to think that something extraordinary will happen; and a bankruptcy is an idea not at all uncommon ...

Young, Travels *(1792-94).*

His majesty looks forward with pleasure to the moment when he will see the representatives of the noble and loyal nation which he has the good fortune to rule assembled around him ... his majesty entertains high hopes that he will see, after stormy and disquieting days, the arrival of serene and quiet days, the restoration of order everywhere, the consolidation of public debt and a France which continues to enjoy the importance and respect she deserves on account of her size, her people, her prosperity and the character of her population. At the same time, his majesty has considered that the Estates-General should assemble on May 1.

Council of State, announcement of August 8,
1788.

The first cause is the small yield of this year's harvest which in some districts did not even produce the quantities of a normal year; in others, nothing or almost nothing was reaped. Second, the rains and inundations of 1787, the hail and drought of 1788 ... Third, the usury ... the closing of granaries by landed proprietors and tenants. Fourth, private sales from the granaries. Fifth, the lack of supplies at the market places ... Sixth: the peasants do not tresh the grain and do not bring it to the market places. Seventh: Too much export to foreign countries ... One fears further price increases ... All political speculations pale before the clear evidence. Experience teaches us that self-interest prevails over common welfare; no matter how sacred the right is to dispose over one's property, this right can never serve as a lawful pretext allowing the proprietor to lay the whole community under tribute ... Is it possible that there are people cruel enough to speculate on common misery and to increase it to build a house of disgraceful wealth on it? The artificial famines are more to be feared than those caused by the irregularities of seasons and nature ... One may object: Just permit unlimited freedom and the grain will go where there is a sure profit ... There is no lack of grain in France; an insatiable craving for profit hides it, immoderate greed raises its price. The rich speculator wants to get richer at the expense of the poor and needy.

Louis Antoine Séguier, to the Paris parliament, on the increase in grain prices, report of December 13, 1788.

The Assembly of the Notables had only the effect of showing the evil in greater prominence and to emphasize the urgency of rescuing measures ... They began to attack the ministers and the same men who had been chosen and called in by Calonne put him out of office. One of them, the Archbishop of Toulouse [Loménie-Brienne] was chosen as his successor. He had the reputation as a man of talent and ambition, and his choice met with general approval.

Jean Sylvain Bailly, Memoirs of a Witness
of the Revolution *(1804).*

All agree that the States of the kingdom cannot assemble without more liberty being the consequence; but I meet with so few men that have any just ideas of freedom that I question much the species of the new liberty that is to arise. They know not how to value the privileges of the people; as to the nobility and clergy, if a revolution added anything to their scale, I think it would do more mischief than good.

Young, Travels *(1792-94).*

We are having a very severe winter, freezing for 3 weeks ... The river is frozen which hampers the provisioning of Paris, so that they fear a famine; it is also feared in the provinces. There is very little wheat and what there is they cannot grind because of the lack of water, for there has been no rain since August.

Count Hans Axel Fersen, in the winter of
1788-89, Diary and Correspondence to
the Court of France *(1902).*

The fermentation of minds is general; nothing is talked of but the constitution; the women, especially are mixed up in the matter, and you know ... the influence they have in this country. It is all a delirium; everyone is an administrator and talks of nothing but "progress"; in the antechambers the lackeys are busy reading political pamphlets, ten or a dozen of which appear daily; I do not see how the printing offices suffice for them all ...

Fersen, Diary *(1902).*

The plan of this pamphlet is quite simple. We only have to ask ourselves three questions:

1. What is the Third Estate? Everything.
2. What has it been up to now in our state? Nothing.
3. What does it demand? To become something.

... it should suffice here to state that the so-called qualification of a privileged estate for public office is just a chimera; that all the difficult things in this service are taken care of by the Third Estate without the help of the privileged; that the higher offices could be filled infinitely better without them ... Who would dare to claim that the Third Estate does not include everything needed for the culture of a complete nation? It is the strong and powerful man whose one arm is still in chains. If one would remove the privileged estates, the nation would not be less, but a little more ... The Third Estate includes everything that belongs to the nation, and whatever is not Third Estate cannot consider itself part of the nation ... But what would it help if it were represented in the Estates General, if there the interests opposing it had the upper hand? It therefore demands to have as many representatives as the two other estates combined ... Can it ask for less? Can one hope that it will emerge from its political insignificance and become something if it does not have equal rights?

Emanuel Joseph Sieyès, What Is the Third Estate? *(1789).*

One of the most frequent complaints on the "Cahiers" (des doléances) [list of complaints] or the addresses received by the Committee on Feudal Rights was that the seigneurs had increased the size of the measures used for measuring the grain owed by the tenants either for all or part of the "cens," or for "champart," or for the tithe.

Alphonse Aulard, lecture of 1912, in Greenlaw's The Economic Origins of the French Revolution *(1958)*

2. The Rise of the National Assembly: May 1789 to June 1791

THE HISTORICAL CONTEXT

The hopes of the whole nation rested on the 1,200 delegates who assembled at the Hotel des Menus-Plaisirs in Versailles on May 5, 1789. But the beginning was not promising. There was a long procession in which the members of the Third Estate marched right behind the guards, clad in the traditional modest black of the bourgeoisie, followed by the nobility, gilded and plumed. After a mass and some preliminaries, Necker delivered a long speech, partly read by an assistant, in which he only offered advice—to the First and Second Estates to renounce their privileges, and to the Third to show proper gratitude. Nothing was mentioned about a constitution.

There were 46 bishops in the Assembly, among them Charles Maurice de Talleyrand, bishop of Autun; also about 90 liberal noblemen, such as Marie Joseph, Marquis de Lafayette, and Adrien Duport; many lawyers like Maximilien Robespierrre of Arras, Isaac René Guy Le Chapelier and Jean Denis Lanjuinais from particularly radical Brittany. Two of the most influential delegates were defectors from their own ranks. The Abbé Emanuel Joseph Sieyès, author of a celebrated pamphlet, was a great tactician and a skillful drafter of resolutions but a poor orator, who managed to become quite invisible during the time of the Terror and only surfaced again to assume important positions at the time of the Directory. The other was Honoré Gabriel Riqueti, Comte de Mirabeau, probably the greatest orator of them all, a man disfigured by smallpox and with a wild past: He had been imprisoned several times and once even sentenced to death. His own district, Provence, had rejected him as a delegate because in a speech in February he had praised the old Roman Marius for having killed off the nobility of Rome; whereupon he

Abbé Emanuel Joseph Sieyès

had himself elected as a representative of the Third Estate. There were many members of the lower clergy, many lawyers, but hardly any peasants.

To the outside world, very little seemed to happen during the first weeks, but actually a bitter battle was being fought between nobility and Third Estate. The latter refused to convene separately; the former, and with it the clergy, although more reluctantly, decided to do just that. Both felt the right was on their side. The nobles upheld a century-old tradition and as became more obvious every day, also expressed the wishes of the king; they were honestly convinced that maintaining the old order was in the interest of the whole nation and that without the leadership of the aristocracy chaos would break out. On the other side, the delegates of the Third Estate—they now called themselves "commoners"—were for the most part genuine idealists, imbued with the ideas of the Enlightenment, who were resolved to bring up a new era of happiness, liberty and equality not just for the bourgeoisie but for all Frenchmen and in fact for all other nations too. The first plank in the Third Estate's platform was that the First and then the Second Estate must renounce their tax privileges.

The verification of the delegates' credentials, supposedly a mere formality, blocked any progress on substantive issues. Finally, in the middle of June, a number of clergymen accepted an invitation to join the Third, which encouraged the latter to take the bold step of declaring itself to be the National Assembly, with a majority of 491 against 89 votes. Luck was with the Assembly: Louis was out of town just then and in mourning because his eldest son, successor to the throne, had died. But the fight was far from over. The Assembly found its residence, the Hotel des Menus-Plaisirs, locked up, and moved to the Tennis Court (Jeu de Paume), rejecting Sieyès' suggestion to move to Paris and put itself under the protection of the people. Instead, on the advice of the delegate from the Dauphiné, Jean Joseph Mounier, all members swore a solemn oath not to dissolve until a constitution was decided upon.

Gabriel Honoré Riqueti, the Comte de Mirabeau

The use of force by the court was expected; already, on the next day, a royal session rejected Jacques Necker's suggested compromise proposals to make public offices open to everyone and permit voting by heads. Instead, at the third location of the Assembly, in the church of St. Louis, the keeper of the seals, Barentin, acquainted the Assembly, in the presence of the king, with the royal program of reforms: equal taxation, press freedom, decentralization, no more serfdom or compulsion to road maintenance, but no admission of all to public office and voting by heads only in special cases. Louis declared that no king had ever done so much for a nation. His proposals amounted to a constitutional monarchy, where the predominance of the nobles remained practically untouched.

The king then commanded the Assembly to withdraw. The nobility did; the Third Estate and a few of the clergy remained. The president of the Assembly, the renowned astronomer Jean Sylvain Bailly, explained to the royal grand master of ceremonies: "The nation when assembled cannot be given orders," while Mirabeau thundered: "We shall not leave except by the force of the bayonet." When orders were given to clear the hall, some liberal nobles persuaded the guards to withdraw. When thereafter more nobles joined the "commoners," the king gave in, for the time being, and asked the loyal delegates of the two privileged estates to join the Third. At the same time, he ordered the concentration of troops around Paris, which provoked demonstrations against the king and an inquiry of the Assembly as to the meaning of the troop movement. The king's answer was that it was his duty to maintain order and that he would be glad to move the Assembly to Soissons, if it so desired.

The intentions of king, court and high nobility became only too clear when Necker and the other ministers who were willing to compromise were dismissed. Now the masses, driven to despair by hunger and want, began to act swiftly, not only in Paris but in many other cities as well. In Paris, a militia was formed by the 60 city districts, with a twofold purpose: to show that order could be maintained without the intervention of regular troops, but also, in case troops were called in, to resist them. On July 14, the masses, probably organized by some members of the bourgeoisie and inspired by orators such as Camille Desmoulins, proceeded to the Bastille, demanding weapons. The fortress was under the command of the Marquis Bernard René Jourdan de Launay and occupied by only 80 superannuated soldiers and 30 Swiss guards. The French soldiers were reluctant to shoot, but when the crowds forced the drawbridge to be lowered and penetrated the inner court, the commandant ordered them to fire, and 98 people were killed. The rioters managed to bring up cannons, which threatened the main gate, demanded the lowering of the second bridge and then stormed into the fortress. Some soldiers were massacred, and de Launay was pulled out and decapitated in front of the Hotel de Ville. Only seven prisoners were found in the fortress.

The commander of the regular troops at the Champ de Mars, Baron Pierre Joseph de Besenval, had no instructions from his superior, Victor Francois, Duc de Broglie, and in any event chose not to intervene. Five of the six companies of the Gardes Francaises, supposed to protect the king, had gone over to the revolutionaries.

The events of the day showed that the government could not rely on its troops. So the king assured the Assembly of his peaceful intentions and recalled Necker and the liberal ministers. Lafayette was made commander of what was now called the National Guard, and he created the new tricolor cockades (blue-red, the colors of Paris, white, the color of the king). On the surface, there was a great reconciliation, as Bailly, the new mayor, received the king in Paris. But peasant revolts began to flare up all over the country, and the high aristocracy, such as the Prince Louis Joseph de Condé, the Comte Charles Philippe d'Artois, de Broglie and Polignac, began to leave the country. The first terror acts occurred in Paris, and militias were formed in all the provinces.

With half the country in this state of rebellion, the Assembly was pressured into its most momentous resolutions, the "August decrees." In one session lasting until 2 a.m., the abolition of the feudal system was resolved, clergy and nobility renounced all their privileges, the "tenth" payment to the clergy was abolished as were all compulsory labor services.

The nobles do not seem to have protested any of these measures. After these were confirmed, Mirabeau overcame opposition from Sieyès to ensure that no compensation was granted to the clergy for the loss of the "tenth." A few days later, freedom of the press and of religion were declared, and the Assembly advised the king that it had bestowed on him the title of "Restorer of French Liberty."

The most far-reaching step was yet to come: After two weeks of hot debate, the "Declaration of the Rights of Man" was resolved. The principles announced (see Documents, pp. 307) were largely based on the Constitution of the United States of America, which in turn had derived many of them from the "Bill of Rights" of the state of Virginia (June 1776) and English precedents like the Bill of Rights of 1689, the Habeas-Corpus Acts of 1679 and even the Magna Carta of 1215.

These few weeks of activity probably had a greater impact on French history than any other period, except, possibly, the first months of the Consulate. Even without the Anglo-Saxon models for the Assembly's declarations, similar principles, as developed by the English and French philosophers of the 18th century, would have been promulgated in some form during the Revolution.

The "Rights of Man" has been criticized for guaranteeing political liberty to the individal but leaving the right to property untouched, thus promoting economic inequality and the excesses of capitalism. In retrospect, this may appear justified, but in 1789, capitalism in our sense of the word was still in its infancy, and class conflicts, as they had developed by 1840, with increasing industrialization, were hardly foreseeable then. Most of the delegates who were responsible for the "Rights" were idealists and believed in a better future for all classes and all peoples.

At any rate, the August resolutions led to new conflicts, first between monarchists and "patriots," the former demanding that the king should sanction the decrees, while the latter considered this unnecessary. Another source of conflict was the question of a one- or two-chamber system in the constitution under consideration, with the monarchists holding out for the two chambers after the English model. They were defeated, but now a conflict with the king arose. He refused to sanction the resolutions, and in the Royal Council the possibility of transferring the National Assembly to Soissons or Compiègne was seriously considered. Louis decided against it, but demanded a reexamination of the resolutions and secretly ordered a regiment from Flanders to move to Versailles.

The Assembly felt cheated by the king's delaying tactics, and the suspicion of the masses in Paris was again aroused when the Flanders regiment, at a banquet in Versailles and in the presence of the royal family, trampled on the tricolor, distributed white cockades and heard threatening speeches. When the news reached Paris, there was an uprising. It can no longer be determined who the organizers were, quite possibly the Duke of Orleans, and maybe, behind the scenes, Lafayette. Women gathered in front of the Hotel de Ville, shouting for bread. With neither Bailly nor Lafayette present, they decided to march to Versailles with Stanislas Marie Maillard, one of the leaders at the storm of the Bastille, in charge. Lafayette and the National Guard followed only hours later. Louis, who had meanwhile confirmed the August decrees, was off hunting. When he returned and was confronted by the crowd, he refused to commit himself to a return to Paris. In the morning of the following day, October 6th, the crowd turned violent and invaded the royal quarters, disarming the royal guard. When Lafayette finally intervened, the National Guard led the royal family, its guard, the Flanders regiment and about 100 delegates, all surrounded by the crowd, back to Paris, where Louis was greeted by Bailly and taken to the Tuileries, which had stood empty since the days of Louis XIV. The king was now virtually a prisoner of the masses in Paris.

And in Versailles the Assembly heard Dr. Guillotin's proposal for a new form of execution, invented by a German mechanic named Schmitt. On April 25, 1792, it will be used for the first time.

In the capital, the reactions to the new wave of violence were intense. Many foreigners, noblemen and rich bourgeois left the city, increasing unemployment. The Comte d'Artois formed a "shadow-cabinet" in Torino and soon thereafter contacted the Austrian (Holy Roman) emperor, seeking his intervention on behalf of the king. Louis wrote to his cousin, the king of Spain, disavowing all recent decrees forced upon him.

The National Assembly followed the king into Paris and two weeks later established itself in the Riding Academy (Manège), near the Tuileries. During the following months, a great many new laws were decreed. The military privileges of the nobles were abolished. Most religious orders and monastic vows were abolished, the salt tax was discontinued, *lettres de cachet* definitely prohibited, equality of punishment for all decreed, and the Protestants made eligible for office. The administration of the whole country was completely reorganized during this period on the basis of 83 *départements* instead of the old 32 provinces, with the aim of preserving national unity and preventing provincial rivalry. In order to meet its obligations, the government began the issue of the so-called *assignats*, bonds to be covered by the sale of church property; they first carried a 5 percent interest, which was then reduced to 3 percent, and finally they were made into plain paper money. Overissued by the treasury, they caused depreciation of values and inflation. Forgeries launched by the royalists decreased their value even further.

While, all in all, the streets quieted down after the great October upheavals, political activity blossomed, particularly in the clubs representing the various political groups. The radical Jean Paul Marat launched his *L'Ami du Peuple* in which Necker, Lafayette, Mirabeau, Bailly and, of course, the aristocracy were attacked sharply. The anti-revolutionaries founded their *Acts of the Apostles*; the "Monarchiens," who demanded an absolute royal veto over all resolutions of the Assembly, founded their Club des Impartiaux. Most importantly, the first Jacobin Club was founded in December of 1789. It started out as an organization of the radically inclined delegates from Brittany and bore the official name of Society of the Friends of the Constitution, but was commonly called the Jacobins because that was the popular name for the Dominicans in whose monastery they met. Membership cost 24 livres, so the poorer population was excluded. The club spread quickly, and in 1791 no less than 450 of them were in existence throughout the whole country.

Another radical club was the so-called Cordeliers Club, the Society of the Rights of Man and of the Citizen. Cordeliers meant girdle-bearer, a name for the Franciscans whose convent was the club's meeting place. Georges Jacques Danton, Jean Paul Marat and Camille Desmoulins were the main spokesmen here, and it was in this club that the abolition of the monarchy was demanded for the first time. Around the same time, in April of 1790, the aristocrats founded their Salon Français, and two months later, the first issue of *L'Ami du Roi*, a very successful royalist journal, came out. By 1790-91, no less than 150 journals and pamphlets were being published.

Less disturbed by riots and upheavals, the Assembly found time to abolish the hated salt tax, the gabelle that had been in existence since 1383; to abolish the monopoly of the India Company; to organize a special budget for the church and clerics; and to appoint a commission to unify measures and weights throughout the country. Paris was reorganized into 38 districts, the hereditary nobility abolished, together with all liveries and armorial bearings and all titles such as duke, count, marquis, baron, knight, abbot. Feudal courts were terminated shortly thereafter and justices of peace introduced. A civil constitution for the clergy was instituted, clergymen made state officials, the number of dioceses reduced to 83 and thereby coordinated with the number of departments. Priests and bishops were to be elected by active (i.e., tax-paying) citizens, the ordination made independent of the Pope. Strangely enough, all this was sanctioned by the king, while being condemned by the Pope, who had already condemned the Declaration of Rights. Things became even more critical when clerics were required to take an oath of loyalty to the constitution, which the majority of them refused to do.

Still, on July 14, 1790, the nation appeared to be at peace with itself and full of goodwill and optimism. At the great anniversary celebration of the storming of the Bastille, the king accepted the new constitution, which tried to appear as the legitimate heir of the Old Regime and at the same time to secure the achievements of the Revolution. The harvest of 1789 had been good, though poor transportation facilities prevented all parts of the population from benefiting. Lafayette, the fighter for American independence and "hero of two continents," was at the height of his popularity as he vowed loyalty to the king, the law and the nation. Talleyrand, bishop of Autun, was reading mass, and an enthusiastic crowd of 300,000 attended.

The worst crisis seemed over, but new controversies appeared very soon. Aside from the conflict with the priests and the Pope, there were slave uprisings in the colonies, and a heated debate arose between the "friends of the negroes" and the "friends of the colonists" regarding the political rights of blacks and mulattoes. As a result, a Tory party developed that tried to have a rapprochement with the king.

A number of the leading personalities of 1789 left the scene during the following year and a half. Necker had lost much of his popularity and made Mirabeau his enemy. In September of 1790, he was dismissed and retired to his Swiss estate, Coppet. His daughter Germaine, who later became famous as Madame de Staël, left the country two years later. Mirabeau's fortunes declined rapidly too. Since May of 1790, he had been in the pay of the court and since he made no secret of it, he became an object of suspicion to most of his friends— without, however, gaining the full confidence of the court. In December of the same year, he was pushed aside at the Jacobin Club by the up and coming Maximilien Robespierre. Yet, when he died, quite unexpectedly in April of 1791, his body was taken to the Pantheon and many felt that the last chance for the survival of the monarchy had vanished.

There were new clashes between the court and the people. The costs for the court were now controlled by the National Assembly, which forced the abandonment of a number of court offices. The king's trip to Saint-Cloud was stopped by the people and then by the National Guard. More members of his family (*Mesdames*, his aunts) went into exile, while the most prominent émigrés, the Prince Condé and the Comte d'Artois, began to organize armies of emigrants from their headquarters in Worms and Koblenz and tried to persuade the new emperor in Vienna, Leopold II, to intervene in their behalf. All these developments strengthened the position of the anti-monarchists in the Assembly and made the task of the so-called triumvirate (Antoine Pierre Barnave, Adrien Duport and Alexandre Lameth), who as Mirabeau's successors tried to prevent any further progress of the Revolution, very difficult. The main problem in the first half of 1791 was the financial situation: In order to reduce the huge public debt, much of the public lands had been offered for sale. But the indiscriminate issue of the new paper money, the assignats, led to a rapid depreciation of the livre and to widespread discontent among the lower classes. There were bread riots again, and many antirevolutionary uprisings, particularly in the South.

In June 1791, a remarkable law was passed in the Assembly, Isaac René Guy Le Chapelier's, applying the liberal principle of individualism to the economy by prohibiting all meetings and associations of workers or employers; strikes were also forbidden. Strangely enough, there was no protest from the "left," the spokesmen for the lower classes. Neither Marat nor Robespierre objected. This law survived for nearly a century; its last remnants were removed only in 1884 when complete freedom of association was decreed.

CHRONICLE OF EVENTS

Departure of the three estates from Versailles

1789:   *May 5:* Estates-General convene at Versailles.
May 6: The Third Estate refuses to convene separately. Peasant riot at Cambrai.
May 11: The nobles declare themselves to be a separate assembly; the clerics also, but with a bare majority.
May 20: The clergy renounce their tax privileges.
May 22: The nobles renounce their tax privileges.
June 3: Bailly is made dean of the Third Estate delegates.
June 4: Death of the young dauphin (successor to the throne).
June 10: The Third Estate invites the two others to join it for the verification of their credentials.
June 16: At the verification procedure, 19 clerics join the Third Estate.
June 17: The Third Estate constitutes itself as the National Assembly.
June 19: The majority of the clerics and eight noblemen decide to join the Third Estate.
June 20: The National Assembly moves from the Hotel des Menus-Plaisirs to the Tennis Court (Jeu de Paume). All delegates swear not to dissolve until a constitution has been decided upon.
June 21: In a "royal session" Necker's reform proposals are rejected.
June 22: The National Assembly moves to the Church of St. Louis.
June 23: The king's own reform program is announced to the Assembly. The Third Estate refuses to withdraw.
June 25: Forty-seven more nobles join the Third Estate.
June 27: The king orders the nobility and clergy to join the Third Estate.
July 2: Demonstration before the Palais Royal against the concentration of troops around Paris.
July 7: The Assembly appoints a committee on the constitution and declares itself a constituent assembly.
July 8: Mirabeau's stirring speech against the calling of troops and military dictatorship.

Opening of the meeting of the three estates in the Hall of the Menus-Plaisirs, Versailles, May 5, 1789

Allegory of the oath-taking at Versailles

July 11: Necker and three other ministers are dismissed. Riots in Paris.

July 13: Delegates of the 60 districts of Paris form a National Guard.

July 14: The fall of the Bastille.

July 15: The king announces to the National Assembly the withdrawal of his troops. Lafayette is made commander of the National Guard.

July 16: Necker and the other liberal ministers are recalled. Bailly is made mayor of Paris.

July 17: The king is received by Bailly in Paris. First emigrations. Desmoulins' pamphlet, *La France Libre.*

July 17-21: Revolts in Normandy, Strasbourg and other places. National guards are being formed.

July 22: Louis Bénigne de Bertier, the royal intendant of Paris, and his father-in-law, Joseph Francois Foullon, are hanged by the mob (first terror acts).

July 24: The administration of Paris reorganized: 60 districts, 120 delegates.

July 28: First issue of Jacques Pierre Brissot's *Le Patriote Francais.*

Second half of July: Peasant revolts in Alsace, the Saône Valley and the Franche-Comté.

August 4: National Assembly declares abolition of feudal rights and privileges and the sale of offices, and decrees equality of taxation.

August 11: The resolutions of August 4 are confirmed. The tithe of the clergy is abolished without compensation.

August 23-24: Freedom of religion and of the press declared.

August 26: Declaration of the Rights of Man.

End of August: Break between monarchists and patriots on the question of a royal sanctioning of the resolutions of August 4-11.

September 10: The Assembly decides on a one-chamber system.

September 11: The king refuses to sanction the August resolutions.

September 12: Riots in Orleans.

September 16: The first issue of Marat's *L'Ami du Peuple.*

September 18: The king demands a new examination of the August resolutions.

September 23: A regiment from Flanders arrives in Versailles.

Camille Desmoulins

October 1: During a banquet for the officers of the Flanders regiment, the Tricolor is trampled upon.

October 5-6: A Paris mob, mostly women, marches on Versailles and invades the royal quarters. The king and his family are forced to return to Paris.

October 10: Dr. Joseph Ignace Guillotin submits a design of a new machine for executions.

October 12: Secret letter of Louis XVI to the king of Spain, retracting all concessions forced upon him. The Comte d'Artois requests military intervention from Emperor Joseph II.

October 19: The National Assembly moves to Paris.

November 2: Church property is nationalized. First issue of the *Acts of the Apostles*, a strongly royalist journal.

November 7: The National Assembly forbids any member to accept office under the king.

November 9: The Assembly moves from the Archbishop's Palace to the Manège (Riding Academy).

November 19: A special fund is created, fed from the sale of church property.

December 1: Equality of punishment for all citizens is decreed.

December 12: Marat is arrested and acquitted.

December 17: Resolution to use the sale of church property for payment of the national debt.

December 19: Introduction of assignats (paper currency).

December 24: Protestants are made eligible for office.

December: The first Jacobin Club founded in Paris.

1790:   *January 7:* Bread riots in Versailles.

January 18: Marat publishes his "Denunciation of Necker."

January 28: Jews of Spanish-Portuguese descent become citizens.

February 13: Abolition of monastic vows and of most religious orders.

February 19: The Marquis Thomas de Mahy Favras is executed.

February 26: Names, sizes and borders of the 82 new *départements* are established.

February 28: Reorganization of the army; all monopolies of the aristocracy are abolished.

March 16: Abolition of the lettres de cachet (secret arrests by the king).

The Storming of the Bastille, July 14, 1789

March 21: The gabelle (salt tax) is abolished.

March 29: Pope Pius VI condemns the "Declaration of the Rights of Man."

April 3: The monopoly of the East India Company (Compagnie des Indes) is abolished.

April 5: Antirevolutionary riot at Vannes (Brittany).

April 13: Special budget for expenses of church and clerics is introduced.

The Assembly refuses to recognize the Catholic faith as state religion.

April 17: The assignats are made the official currency; their interest rate is reduced to 3 percent.

April 18-20: Counterrevolutionary demonstrations at Toulouse and Nîmes (southern France).

April 27: Founding of the Society of the Friends of the Rights of Man and of the Citizen, or the Cordeliers Club.

April: The Salon Francais is founded as a meeting place of the aristocrats.

May 8: The principle of uniformity in weights and measures is established.

May 10: Mirabeau is being paid by the royal court.

May 21: The 60 districts of Paris are reorganized into 48 sections.

May 28: Officers must wear the tricolor cockade.

June 1: First issue of the royalist journal, *L'Ami du Roi*.

June 11: A counterrevolutionary rebellion at Avignon is defeated. Avignon demands reunion with France.

June 19: Hereditary nobility, titles, military decorations, liveries and armorial bearings are abolished.

July 3: Secret conversation between Mirabeau and the queen. Condorcet advocates women's right to vote.

July 13: Civil constitution of the clergy. The number of dioceses is reduced from 130 to 83.

July 14: Huge feast of the "Fédération" at the Champ de Mars, emphasizing the unity of the nation and its revolutionary principles.

July 23: Louis XVI sanctions the civil constitution of the clergy but receives on the following day a letter from the Pope condemning it.

July 26: Marat demands the execution of 500 to 600 aristocrats.

July: The Salon Francais tries to organize the escape of the king to Lyons.

Portrait of Lafayette, commander of the National Guard

August 7: The royal secretariat (Maison du Roi) is taken over by the ministry of the interior.

August 16: Feudal courts are abolished; justices of the peace are established.

August 31: Military revolt in Nancy suppressed.

September 4: Necker dismissed.

September 7: The National Archives are organized.

September 16: Naval mutiny in Brest.

September 29: Interest payment on assignats discontinued.

October 12: The legality of slavery in San Domingo is confirmed.

October 21: The Tricolor is made the official national flag.

October 29 and November 25: Negroes and mulattoes riot in San Domingo.

October 31: All internal tariffs are abolished.

November 23: A general land tax is introduced.

November 27: Clerics are required to take an oath of loyalty to the constitution.

December 15: All purchasable and hereditary offices are abolished.

December 26: The king sanctions the decree of November 27.

December 29: In *L'Ami du Peuple*, Marat vigorously attacks the king.

1791:   *January 4:* Most clerics refuse to take the oath on the constitution.

February 19: Mesdames, the daughters of Louis XV and aunts of Louis XVI, go into exile.

February 28: Four hundred armed aristocrats gather at the Tuileries and are arrested by Lafayette. They are released on March 13.

March 2: Corporations and *jurandes* (meetings of the guildmasters) prohibited. Protection by patent created.

March 10: Pius VI, in his brief "Quot Aliquantum," condemns the civil constitution of the clergy.

April 2: Mirabeau dies. His body transferred to the Panthéon on April 14.

April 18: The king is prevented by a riot and soldiers of the National Guard from going to St.-Cloud.

April 21: Lafayette resigns as commander of the National Guard but returns the next day.

May 6: Assignats now available in 5-livre notes. Value of the livre has declined by 15 percent.

May 7-15: Great debate at the Assembly about the rights of negroes and mulattoes in the colonies. Patriots split between "friends of the negroes" and "friends of the colonizers."

May 30: Voltaire's ashes are transferred to the Panthéon.

June 14: Le Chapelier's Law: Meetings and associations of workers or employers, as well as strikes, are prohibited.

EYEWITNESS TESTIMONY

The procession is splendid ... Neither the king nor the queen seem to be particularly happy. Everywhere, the king is greeted with shouts: "Vive le Roi," but no one is cheering the queen. She is looking at the scene with contempt ... and seems to be saying: "I will accept this for the moment, but my hour will come." ... The king is displeased because the Duke of Orleans is attending as a deputee, not as a royal prince and also because the queen was not cheered in public. The queen feels deeply offended ... Madame de Chastellux repeated to me a clever answer of Madame Adelaide, the king's aunt. In a fit of bad mood the queen had said of the French people: "Oh, these shocking French!" She replied: "You should rather say: 'These shocked French,' Madame!"

Gouverneur Morris, at Versailles, May 4, 1789, Diary of the French Revolution *(1939).*

The various deputees enter and occupy their seats according to their districts. The entrances of Necker and the Duke of Orleans are greeted with long applause ... An old man who refused to wear the suit prescribed for the Third Estate and instead wears a peasant's dress is also cheered loudly ... Finally, the king appears and takes his seat; the queen sits at his left, two rows below. He reads a report on the situation, short, but well expressed ... Then Necker rises. He tries to play the experienced orator, but with little success. The applause is long and loud. When the speech is finished, the king rises to leave the hall; long and heart-warming shouts: "Vive le Roi." The queen rises and much to my satisfaction, you hear shouts "Vive la Reine," for the first time in many months. She bows her head graciously ...

Morris at Versailles, May 5, 1789, Diary *(1939).*

Huge masses of people were watching us in respectful silence ... The cries of "Vive le Roi," accompanied by muddled and unending applause, plunged the soul into a state of profound intoxication ... France, my homeland, showed herself in all her splendour ...

The king delivered a noble and wise address ... Necker explained the present state of the finances. His speech took three hours. I thought it very mediocre and by far not living up to what should have been expected from a man who enjoys such great esteem.

Marquis Charles Elie Ferrières, letter of May 6, 1789, to his wife, Memoirs *(1822).*

The clergy tried to achieve a meeting of the Estates by surprise and sent the Archbishop of Aix to the deputees of the Third Estate; he delivered a passionate speech on the misery ... in the open country. He produced a piece of dark bread that even animals would have rejected, but on which the poor depended ... A deputee spoke up and surpassed the Archbishop's speech for the needy yet managed cleverly to raise some doubts on the intentions of the clergy: "Go and tell your colleagues they should, if they are so impatient to better the plight of the people, join the friends of the people here in this hall; tell them not to hinder our initiative by artificial delays ... As servants of religion and worthy disciples of their master renounce the abundance surrounding you, the splendor which insults poverty ... Sell those proud coaches and convert this contemptible luxury into food for the poor!" There was no applause for this speech which fit so well into the passion of the moment ... but rather a muddled murmur which was even more flattering. Everybody wanted to know who the speaker was ... only after some search a name was passed around in the hall and on the galleries which within three years would make all of France tremble: Robespierre.

Etienne Dumont, at Versailles, early June 1789, Recollections of Mirabeau and the First Two Assemblies *(1833).*

Festival of the "Fédération" at the Champ de Mars, July 14, 1790

Do not believe that the people participate in the metaphysical discussions which have excited us here. They are of greatest importance ... but the people are still far from contemplating the system of their rights or a sound theory of liberty. The people want relief because they have no longer the strength to suffer. They shake off tyranny because they can no longer breathe under the burden which is crushing them. They only ask not to have to pay more than they are able to and to bear their misery in peace.

Honoré Gabriel Riqueti Mirabeau, speech at the Assembly, June 15, 1789.

If you abandon me in this great enterprise I shall work alone for the welfare of my peoples ... I shall consider myself as their only true representative ... None of your plans and proceedings may become law without my express approval ... I order you to separate at once and to proceed tomorrow morning each to the hall of his own order to renew your deliberations ... Never has a king done so much for any nation.

Louis XVI, to the National Assembly, June 23, 1789.

Yes, Sir, we have understood the idea one has prompted to the king, and you who can never be part of the Assembly of the Estates General, who has neither a seat nor a voice nor the right to speak, are in no position to remind us of his speech. But in order to remove any ambiguity and prevent any delay, I declare to you, that in chase you have orders to drive us away from here, you will have to obtain authority for the use of force, for we shall be dispersed from our places only by the force of bayonets.

Mirabeau, to Marquis de Brèze (king's messenger), at the National Assembly, June 23, 1789, Works (1912-21).

The delegates of the nation have the queen of events acting in their favor: Necessity. It is hastening towards the sound goal they have staked out and will overcome any obstacles by its own power. But its power is its reason; nothing is more alien to it than tumults, shouts of disorder, aimless, confused agitation. Reason will be victorious with its own weapons.

Mirabeau, speech at the Assembly, July 1, 1789, Works (1912-21).

At present, there are in the city and its surroundings more than a million people who depend exclusively on the alertness and care of the government to obtain bread; but even the greatest efforts will hardly suffice to meet the various needs.

Morris, July 9, 1789, Diary (1939).

At the first news of M. Necker's dismissal, all of Paris was upset, the Palais-Royal was shaken, the Bourse closed, and theater performances were called off ... The tocsin sounded, some houses were ransacked. The shopowners did not dare to open up their stores ... ten thousand armed robbers roamed through the streets. Workshops were abandoned ... the city was becoming uninhabitable when the bourgeois suddenly armed himself, instead of having recourse to the king as the born defender of the state.

Comte de Rivarol (Antoine Rivaroli), Memoirs (1824).

When I take my leave, he [Marshall de Castries] takes me aside and advises me that Necker is no longer in office. This upsets him very much, and me too ... I tell him it is not too late to warn the king of the danger he is in which is infinitely greater than he believes; that his soldiers would not fight the people, and if he would follow the advice to use force the nation would undoubtedly turn against him. He had not noticed that the sword had slipped out of his hand, and the National Assembly is master of the nation. He did not answer, but is deeply moved ... The people are invading the shops of arms dealers, and soon a large detachment of the Palace Guard arrives with fixed bayonets. The masses move in between, some of them armed too. These poor fellows apparently have crossed the Rubicon. Now their slogan must be: "Victory or the hangman's rope." I think the court will give in some more ... if it does not, a civil war will be more than likely.

Morris, July 12 1789, Diary (1939).

The scarcity of bread and the uncertain future spread fear and panic and increased the general anxiety. There were riots at some market places, and government transports into the neediest districts were intercepted. This forced me to divide the troops at my disposal ... in order to maintain order, safeguard the grain shipments and restore peace where bold outlaws committed acts of violence. Until July 12 when the revolution erupted I had the satisfaction to maintain the peace within my command ...

Pierre Joseph, Baron de Besenval, Memoirs (1821).

Precious blood would be shed on both sides, without helping the public order. Almost under my eyes they pressed my troops hard, trying to persuade them … I received warnings which made me worry about their loyalty.

Considering all this I thought it best to withdraw the troops and leave the city to its own devices.

Besenval, about July 13, 1789, Memoirs *(1821).*

Martin, my servant, comes home and reports that the Hotel de France was stormed and all prisoners freed … They help themselves to arms wherever they can find them; 600 barrels of gunpowder were confiscated on a boat on the Seine river. They entered the monastery of St. Lazare and discovered a grain depot started by the monks. The supplies are put on carts to take them to the market places; they place one monk on every cart.

Morris, July 13, 1789, Diary *(1939).*

The court thought it [the Bastille] impregnable … but the man to whom it was confided, the Marquis de Launay, would not, or dared not or could not use the means he had of rendering its resistance murderous; and this populace that so vilely assassinated him, owed him thanks and praises … He had 15 pieces of cannon on the towers; and whatever calumny may have been said to palliate the crime of his assassination, not one single cannon shot was fired from these towers. There were besides, in the interior of the castle, three cannon loaded with case shot, pointed in front of the drawbridge. These would have made great slaughter … The small number of Swiss soldiers that had been sent to him were sure men and well disposed to defend themselves; the Invalides were not so, and he must have known that … Too inferior to his situation, and in that stupor with which the presence of danger strikes a weak mind, he looked on it with a steadfast but troubled eye; and rather motionless with astonishment than with resolution. Unhappily, not a man in the council supplied the foresight that he wanted.

Jean Francois Marmontel, July 14, 1789, Memoirs *(1805).*

"Citizens, you know the nation had demanded that Necker stayed on … they have thrown him out! Can one defy us more insolently? After this coup they will dare anything, and maybe they are planning for this night a night of St. Bartholomew for all patriots. Take up arms!" … The Bastille could have lasted 6 months, if anything

could persevere French impetuosity … Taken by citizens and leaderless soldiers, without a single officer!

Camille Desmoulins, to his father, how he spoke to the people on July 14, letter of July 16, 1789, in Collection of Memoirs Relating to the French Revolution *(1820-26).*

The Marquis de Launay could have put up more resistance to the occupation of the first drawbridge; but this miserable handyman of the tyrants, more worthy of a jailer than of a commander of a fortress, lost his head when he saw himself surrounded by the enraged people and fled hastily behind the huge mass of his bastions … The defenders signalled they were ready to surrender, hoisting the white flag on the Bazinière tower. But it is too late. The people, furious because of the cowardly treason of the governor who let them fire at his own delegates suspects … only a new trick and under constant shooting advances to the inner drawbridge. The Swiss officer … requests safe conduct. "No, no" they shout at him. Now he shoves a piece of paper through the opening … this is what it said: "We have twenty thousand pounds of gunpowder; we shall blow up the garrison and the whole section of the city unless you accept our capitulation." … But at the word "capitulation" the people protest violently and have three cannons brought up … Those who came in first treated the defeated men humanely and embraced the officers … but when some soldiers on the platforms who did not know the fortress had capitulated fired a few salvos the enraged masses hurled themselves at the invalids and maltreated them … The last words of the governor of the Bastille were: "Oh, my friends, kill me, kill me on the spot, do not let me suffer long!" The mob cut his throat at the steps of the City Hall, fearing one could take their victim from them … The whole fury of the people was directed against the invalids who where less guilty than the Swiss. They had not lost a man; only one was killed later, accidentally the same one who had aimed the heavy cannon which had caused so much destruction …

T.M. Kerversau (a lawyer), in Two Friends of Liberty's History of the French Revolution of 1789 *(1790-93).*

When the besiegers saw that their artillery had no effect they reverted to their original plan to break open the doors. For this they brought their cannons into the court … aiming at the door. When de Launay saw these preparations from the tower he let his drummer call for a rally, without consulting his staff or notifying the garrison. Whereupon I ran ... to the embrasures to arrange a cease-fire. The mob came closer and the governor declared his willingness to capitulate.

... the streets and houses, even the roofs were filled with people abusing and cursing me. Daggers, bayonets, pistols were constantly pointed at me. I did not know how I would be killed but was sure my last hour had come. Those who had no arms were throwing stones at me, the women wrenched their teeth and threatened me with their fists. Two soldiers behind me had already been killed by the furious mob and I am convinced I could not have reached City Hall had not one officer ... escorted me ... I defended myself as well I could, said that I had occupied a low rank and if I had caused any casualties it was because of the orders I had to obey ... As I saw no other way out to save myself and the unfortunate remaining soldiers under my command I declared I wanted to join the cause of the city and the nation. I do not know if they had gotten tired of killing or if I convinced them, but there was applause and shouting, "bravo, bravo, brave Swiss!" Instantly, wine was brought up and we had to drink to the health of city and nation ...

Ludwig von der Flühe (Swiss officer), in his "Reports of the Taking of the Bastille, July 14, 1789, by One of Its Defenders" (1834).

Intoxicated with success one had forgotten the unfortunate prisoners in the fortress ... Seven prisoners were found who were led to the Palais Royal ... Soon they saw the bloody head of the governor on that fatal pike to which was fastened a sign reading: "de Launay, Governor of the Bastille, false and treacherous toward the people." At this sight, tears of joy came out of their eyes and they raised their hands to heaven to bless their first moments of freedom.

Kerversau, History (1790–93).

July 1789: The 13th: Nothing. The 14th: Nothing.

Louis XVI, his diary, in the National Archives, Paris.

This is the greatest event that ever happened in the world! And the best!

Charles James Fox, upon hearing about the storming of the Bastille, Memorials and Correspondence (1970).

Tell him that we are surrounded by alien hordes who yesterday received visits from princes and princesses and their favorites, their caresses, exhortations and presents; tell him that this night these alien minions replete with gold and wine, announced in their wicked songs the defeat of France, that their brutal desires have prayed for the destruction of the National Assembly.

Mirabeau, to members of a delegation sent to the king to ask for withdrawal of the troops, July 15, 1789, Works (1912-21).

We met about 300 deputies who came to Paris escorting the king. He arrived. I presented him with the keys and said: "Sire, I am handing over to you the keys of your loyal city of Paris; they are the same which were once delivered to Henry IV. He won back his people; now the people have won back their king." ... The king replied that he was accepting, with pleasure, the homage of the city of Paris ... they suggested to me to present the king with the three-colored cockade which the Parisiens wear as a sign of recognition since the revolution broke out. I did now know how he would take this and if such an offer would not be unsuited ... When the king emerged from his carriage I went up to him, walked next to him and handed over the cockade, saying: "Sire, I have the honor to present your majesty with the badge of the French. He took it graciously and put it on his hat. Then he went up the stairs [of City Hall] ... surrounded only by some citizens, all with swords in hand, forming above his head a roof of crossing blades ... It would not have surprised me if he had felt some fear at this moment. But ... he strode up with the assurance of a good king in the midst of good people ... When he had occupied the throne prepared for him, a voice from the assembly ... cried: "Our king, our father!" At this, the applause doubled ...

Jean Sylvain Bailly, events of July 17, 1789, Memoirs of a Witness of the Revolution (1804).

One hundred and fifty chateaux in Franche-Comté, Mâconnais and Beaujolais have already burned! ... What should I say about the atrocities, the murders committed against the noblemen? M. de Barras, cut to pieces in front of his wife ... M. de Montesson was shot after he saw his father-in-law's throat cut! A nobleman who was paralyzed, was left on a funeral pile! They burned the feet of another one so that he would give up his title-deeds! They told the peasants the nobles were against the king; they [deputies of the commons] sent supposed orders to burn down the chateaux and to kill the feudal lords ...

Ferrières, July 1789, Memoirs *(1822).*

Waiting for my carriage, I go for a walk under the arcades of the Palais Royal. A mob triumphantly accompanies the head and body of Mr. Foullon, the head is mounted on a pike while the body is dragged over the ground naked ... His crime had been to have occupied a seat in the ministry. The mutilated remains of the 70-year-old man are dragged to his son-in-law, Berthier, intendant of Paris who also is killed and hacked to pieces. The mob carries the shapeless parts around, wild with joy. Oh God, what kind of people!

Morris, July 22, 1789, Diary *(1939).*

Yesterday, the artillery followed the French Guards, subdued the sentinels and joined the patriots at the Palais-Royal ... The people surround any soldier and ... take him to the nearest inn and make him drink to the health of the Third Estate.

Desmoulins, letter of July 1789, Collection *(1820- 1826).*

The following day was horrible. We saw the palace guards ... at the Rue Royale, together with the people, shouting and dancing, dragging women along who were dressed as nuns; men were dressed as capuchin monks ... and all shouted and sang: The aristocrats to the lantern ...

Duchesse de Gontaut, July 1789, Memoirs *(1891).*

Several times today, more than one hundred delegates were on their feet at the same time, and Ms. Bailly was absolutely powerless to keep order.

Arthur Young, at the National Assembly in the summer of 1789, Travels During the Years 1787, 1788, 1789, and 1790 *(1792-94).*

Today is the day when I will bless liberty which has ripened such beautiful fruit in the National Assembly. Let us fortify our work by declaring the delegates of the Estates-General as inviolable.

Mirabeau, speech of July 23, 1789, Works *(1912-21).*

After a few hours, the venerable constitution of the French State, collapsing thunderously under the blows of an indefatigable group of savages ... is nothing more than a formless heap of ruins and shambles.

Ferrières, on the end of the session of August 4, 1789, Memoirs *(1822).*

I well remember the long debate on the subject which lasted several weeks, as a period of mortal ennui. There were silly disputes about words, much metaphysical trash, and dreadfully tedious prosing. The Assembly had converted itself into a Sorbonne, and each apprentice in the art of legislation was trying his yet unfledged wings upon such puerilities ... "Men are born free and equal"—that is not true. They are not born free; on the contrary, they are born in a state of weakness and necessary dependence. "Equal!" how are they so, or how can they be so? ... It would require volumes of argument to give any reasonable meaning to that equality proclaimed without exception ... Mirabeau, on presenting the project, even ventured to make some objections to it and proposed to defer the declaration of rights until the constitution should be completed.

Dumont, about "The Rights of Man," in Recollections *(1833).*

Dont let anybody take us for a ride! If it was charity that inspired these sacrifices one must understand that it hesitated a little too long to reveal itself. What? By the blazing light of their burning castles they discover their magnanimity to renounce their privilege to keep people in chains who have fought and won their liberty with the sword in their hand!

Jean Paul Marat, after the abolition of feudal rights on August 4, 1789, Selected Texts *(1963).*

Paris is the focus of trouble, and nearly every one is in haste to leave it. Vagabonds and deserters are taking refuge there ... They are received into the militia which is being raised under the command of the Marquis de La Fayette; they have better pay than our regiments and there are no means not employed to entice them ... The king's authority is totally annihilated, and so is that of the parlements and the magistrates; the States-General tremble before Paris and this fear greatly influences their deliberations ... all bonds are broken; and how can they be reestablished?

Count Hans Axel Fersen, August 1789, Diary and Correspondence to the Court of France *(1902).*

The king would not have the right to oppose the establishment of a constitution; he has to sign and ratify it, both for himself and his successors ... he might insist on some changes, but if these were contrary to public liberty the Assembly could resort to two recourses: it may refuse to grant taxes, or it could turn to its constituents, for the nation has surely the right to use any means necessary to its liberty.

Jean Joseph Mounier, in the National Assembly, September 4, 1789.

The constitution does not require royal approval, for it is older than the monarchy.

Mounier, in the National Assembly, September 11, 1789.

The sloth of the Assembly (unavoidable from their number) has done the most sensible injury to the public cause. The patience of a people who have less of that quality than any other nation in the world is worn threadbare. Time has been given to the aristocrats to recover from their panic, to cabal, to sow dissensions in the Assembly, and to distrust out of it.

Thomas Jefferson, in a letter to John Jay, September 19, 1789, Writings (1854-56).

... the sources of income for the state are exhausted, the treasury is empty ... and tomorrow, nay today, at this moment, your intervention is necessary. Under these circumstances, gentlemen, it seems impossible to suggest a plan to the minister of finance [Necker] or to examine the one he has submitted to us ... Checking of the figures alone would take months ... Two hundred years of robbery and loot have torn open an abyss in which the kingdom is about to perish. This horrible abyss must be filled up. Well, here is the list of the wealthy French. Pick among the richest in order to sacrifice less citizens. But choose; for must not a small number go down so that the mass of the people will be saved? Indeed, these two thousand privileged possess enough to cover the deficit ... Throw them in the abyss and it will close ... Do you not see that if you declare bankruptcy, or, even worse, make it inevitable without declaring it, you will soil yourselves with an action a thousand times more criminal ... Do you believe that the thousands and millions of people who at this moment, through the terrible explosion ... will lose everything, their only comfort in life and perhaps their only means of subsistence will permit you to enjoy the fruits of your crime? ... No, you would perish ... Therefore,

approve this extraordinary loan which, we hope, will be sufficient ... Beware of asking for time to reflect! Our misfortune does not permit it!

Mirabeau, speech of September 26, 1789, Works (1912- 21).

It is proven that the orgy took place; also that there is general unrest. We have no proof to assert with assurance that there is an actual conspiracy. But ... who would doubt that, should the enemy appear before our gates today, he would find us unprepared? ... All good citizens must arm and assemble ... The National Guard has enough sense to know that it must never isolate itself from the rest of the citizens and that, should their commanders forget themselves far enough to issue anti-citizen orders, they, instead of obeying them, should take care of them. After all, in case of a threatening danger we shall be lost if the people do not appoint a tribune and transfer to him the command over the armed forces.

Marat, to the editor of L'Ami du Peuple, about the "orgy" of the Flanders regiment, letter of October 4, 1789.

We received orders to prevent the people to go to Versailles, and shortly thereafter about 60 awful women appeared, all shouting they wanted to visit the king and asking everyone to join them ... Only at six in the evening an adjutant of M. de Lafayette arrived ... Immediately, our right half-bataillon started to march to Versailles while 20,000 men should have been sent 8 or 10 hours sooner to take possession of the forest of Meudon and the gates of Sèvres and Saint-Cloud ... At the break of dawn, they woke us up ... At this moment, the mob stormed in through an open door and up to the queen's rooms, and the bodyguards started attacking who were later saved by the palace guard ...

Moving the king to Paris, announced as a triumph and considered a victory, sufficed to restore peace for the time being. The first concern was to get these horrible gangs back to Paris. During the whole trip the mob announced ... the arrival of the king whom they called "the baker," alluding at the abundance which would now prevail in Paris. The heads of two unfortunate bodyguards served as banners.

General Thiébault, October 5, 1789, Memoirs (1898).

I came to the National Assembly around eight o'clock in the evening and saw a strange spectacle. The people from Paris had come in … the galeries were occupied by men and women armed with halberds, pikes and sticks. The session had been interrupted … When we finally got back into the hall where the president [Mounier] tried in vain to establish some order, Mirabeau raised his powerful voice, drowning out everyone else and asked the president to create some respect for the asssembly and ask all outsiders to disappear. Because of his popularity he was successful and the people retired by and by … Around midnight, an adjutant of Lafayette's announced his arrival at the head of the Paris National Guard, and now one believed to be safe under his protection … and the masses began to quiet down on account of the assurances the king had given which had been distributed solicitously … When I awoke I received a confused account of what had happened: the invasion of the castle and the disarming of the guards.

Dumont, October 5, 1789, Recollections *(1833).*

Around six in the morning, armed men and women assemble at the square [before the castle] … then they form several columns, as if they were obeying different leaders. There are outbursts of fury against the Palace Guard … Another column invades the open gate of the chapel; a soldier of the Versailles militia shows them the way to the stairs leading to the king's rooms … Then the conspirators turn to the rooms of the queen, shouting: "We want to cut off her head, tear out her heart, hack up her intestines." Miomandre runs up to the door of the first antechambre, tears it open, shouting: "Save the queen, they want to kill her. I am alone against 2000 tigers. My comrades had to leave the room." … Miomandre is left behind, dead. The conspirators storm into the great hall. The Duke of Orléans, in a grey tailcoat … a little cane in his hand walks between the various groups with a cheerful face … smiling at some, talking freely to others. There are repeated shouts: "Our father is with us! Long live the king of Orléans!" The Duke, encouraged by these demonstrations, follows this group for a while; but on top of the stairs he does not dare to take the last step which separates the intention from the crime; he is content to identify, with a gesture, the rooms of the queen, then turns to the king's rooms and disappears …

The queen reaches the hidden staircase connecting to the king's rooms … Finally the door is opened. Entering, she bursts into tears and cries: "Friends, dear friends, save me!" The conspirators … run up to her bed and

pierce it several times with pikes. Seeing that the queen has escaped they storm the antechambre of the king … But now grenadiers of the former palace guard rush forward.

… the courts of the castle present an even more horrible spectacle of popular fury. Groups of women and men, armed with pikes and rifles, pursue the bodyguards everywhere. M. des Hutes and M. de Varicourt are led to the royal gate, thrown to the ground; a man with a long beard cuts off their heads with an axe. The barbarian hordes shout triumphantly, some dip their hands into the blood of the murdered guards and smear on their faces, others dance around the bodies, singing … Some demand the king should live in Paris. The crowd repeats, shouting: "The king to Paris! The king to Paris!"

Lafayette sees that the riot can be calmed down only if the king complies with the wish of the people … The king promises to go to Paris the same day if the queen and his family will follow. He requests leniency for his bodyguard … The king started out around noon. The

Contemporary caricature of Marie Antoinette as an arsonist.

heads of des Hutes and de Varicourt are carried ahead on two pikes. Forty to fifty bodyguards followed, disarmed, escorted by men armed with sabres and pikes … Their rifles are decorated with oak leaves as a sign of their victory, there is constant rifle fire and shouting: "We are bringing the baker, the baker's wife and the little baker's boy!", also gross insults against the queen, threats against priests and noblemen: This was the disgraceful, barbarian escort accompanying the king, the queen and the royal on their six hour trip to the Paris City Hall.

Ferrières, October 6, 1789, Memoirs *(1822).*

It is impossible to be more gracious and courageous than the queen has been during the last eight days. Everything is quiet here. I like it better than among the people of Versailles. M. de Lafayette behaved excellently, the National Guard too … There is plenty of bread. Court is held almost as in the past: There are parties every day, on Sunday, Tuesday and Thursday there is gambling, suppers in high fashion on Sunday and Thursday …

Madame Elizabeth, sister of Louis XVI, to a friend, Angelique de Bombelles, letter of October 13, 1789, Correspondance de Elisabeth de France *(1867).*

Up to the age of forty, he [Sieyès] had led a solitary life, contemplating political questions, with a great proficiency in abstraction; but he was not well equipped to communicate with others … Still, since he had a superior mind and a concise and laconic way of expressing himself, the Assembly showed him customarily an almost religious respect … They thought that Sieyès, the man of mystery, knew of all the secrets of constitutions … Many of the young people, even those with a mature mind, expressed their admiration for him and praised him higher than anyone else. This was because he never committed himself completely on any question.

Mme. Germaine de Staël, October 1789, Selection of Texts *(1974).*

Mirabeau … never quite freed himself of his childhood's prejudices; he always stood up for the nobility and the monarchy. "Do you believe," he said to some noblemen, "that the nobility would have given in so promptly if I had been their deputy?" … To his natural rhetorical talents Mirabeau added a thorough study of the art of oratory. He realized that a man of genius will appeal more to feelings than to reason … His

eloquence, full of bold images and striking metaphors, dominated the contemplations of the Assembly. His style … resembled a heavy hammer in the hands of a skillful artist …

Ferrières, Memoirs *(1822).*

It seems illegal to me that an authority is being used to remove barriers which it has not created. Without the approval of the church, people are granted a freedom who have voluntarily limited it by solemn oaths. Barnave answered: The fact that the existence of monks is incompatible with the needs of society is sufficient reason to suppress them.

The bishop of Clermont, to the National Assembly, on the abolition of monastic vows on February 13, 1790.

Let us not defame the people! I am calling all of France as a witness, and leave it to her enemies to exaggerate the acts of violence and to claim the revolution to be a series of barbarisms. I call all good citizens, all friends of virtue as witnesses that never a revolution has caused so little bloodshed and cruelties.

Maximilien Robespierre, on the riots in the country, speech of February 22, 1790, Complete Works *(1910-67).*

But I see, that we are in a state of anarchy and are sinking deeper into it every day; the thought that I should have contributed to this destruction enrages me, and the fear to see another head at the top than the king is so intolerable to me …

Mirabeau, to Auguste, Comte de la Marck, letter of May 10, 1790, Works *(1912-21).*

In the council of state, M. Necker was the only one to advise the king against sanctioning the decree which annihilated the nobility … The king had decided to sanction all of the Assembly's decrees, considering himself, since October 6, to be in a state of captivity; and only because of his religious scruples did he not consequently sign his name to the decrees proscribing the priests who submitted to the power of the pope.

Mme de Staël, June 1790, Selection of Texts *(1974).*

At the other end of the square there was an altar where Talleyrand, then bishop of Autun, celebrated Mass. After Mass—M. de La Fayette—swore loyalty to the nation.—A limited monarchy had always been

France's cherished desire; the federation ceremony of 1790 was the climax of this great surge.

Mme de Staël, letter about the Feast of Federation, July 14, 1790, Selection of Texts (1974).

At a time of anarchy and confusion it would be the height of stupidity to oppose the vile conspirators who trample on the laws and only wait for the day when they will be strong enough to shed blood, solely with the arms of the law.

Marat, in L'Ami du Peuple, *July 30, 1790.*

The private communications which were still kept up between the court and Mirabeau procured him an interview with the queen in the gardens of Saint-Cloud. He left Paris on horseback, on pretense of going into the country ... but stopped at one of the gates of the gardens of Saint-Cloud, and was led to a spot situated in the highest part of the private garden where the queen was waiting for him. She told me she accosted him by saying: "With a common enemy, with a man who had sworn to destroy monarchy ... I should at this moment be guilty of a most ill-advised step; but in speaking to a Mirabeau," etc. The poor queen was delighted at having discovered this method of exalting him ... and in imparting the particulars of this interview she said: "Do you know that those words, 'a Mirabeau,' appeared to flatter him exceedingly?" On leaving the queen he said to her with warmth: "Madame, the monarchy is saved!" It must have been soon afterwards that Mirabeau received considerable sums of money. He showed it too plainly by the increase of his expenditure ... Mirabeau forgot that it was easier to do harm than good, and he thought himself the political Atlas of the whole world.

Mme. Jeanne Louise Henriette Campan, Mémoires sur la vie privée de Marie Antoinette *(1823).*

What is meant by "foundations of the constitution?" A hereditary monarchy of the dynasty of the Bourbons. A legislative body, periodically elected and permanent whose authority is limited to the drawing up of laws. Unity and extreme liberty of the highest executive power concerning everything connected with the administration of the kingdom, the enforcement of the laws, control of state power. Exclusive assignment of taxation to the legislative body, new subdivisions of the kingdom. Free administration of justice, freedom of the press, responsibility of the ministers. Sale of royal domains and estates of the clergy. Introduction of a civil list. No political differentiation of estates, no privileges, exemption from taxes, no feudal system, no parlements, no nobility or clergy as a political body, no provinces with their own estates or corporations.

That is what I would consider the basic principles of the constitution. They limit royal power only to make it stronger. They are entirely compatible with monarchic government ... Why shouldn't one elect a few ministers from the ranks of the Jacobins, and some others from a different section of the popular party? Equal participation in power is an effective way of rapprochement, and they surely would soon understand one another. This cooperation would improve the one side through the other, and the uniting of the various parties would turn entirely to the advantage of the royal power ...

Mirabeau, to the Court, memorandum of October 14, 1790, in Grab's The French Revolution *(1973).*

Recognize the fundamental principle for the organisation of the National Guard: that all resident citizens have a right to be accepted in the ranks of the Guards, and resolve that they may have themselves entered in the registers of the community where they are living. It would be futile to oppose these inviolable rights by asserting so-called disadvantages and imagined horrors ... You are unjust and spoiled, and so are the wealthy classes to whom you want to grant this power—the people are good, patient, magnanimous.

Our revolution and the crimes of its enemies show it; a thousand bold, heroic traits which are in their nature prove it. The people demand only peace, justice and the right to live—the powerful, the rich are hungry for honors, treasures, pleasures. The interest, the wishes of the people are those of nature, of humanity ...

Robespierre, in the National Assembly, December 5, 1790.

Right after the king will have crossed the border the enemy armies will advance on our homes, with rivers of blood running ... Nobody will escape, men, women and children, and your delegates will be the first victims ...

Marat, in L'Ami du Peuple, *February 1791.*

Finally, is the nation sovereign if the greatest numbers of its individuals is deprived of its political rights which make it sovereign? ... The example of England and those peoples assumed to be free, these are brought up as proofs used against what is reasonable. I should answer just with one word: The people, these multitudes of human beings whose cause I am defending, have rights of the same origin as your own rights. Who gave you the authority to take them away from the people? England! Well, what do you care about England and its faulty constitution which may have looked to you as free when you had sunk to the lowest depths of slavery, but which one should stop praising out of stupidity or habit? The free peoples? Where are they? … But the people, but corruption—oh, cease, cease to abase this touching and sacred name of the people by associating it with the idea of corruption …

Robespierre, about the division of the people into active (tax-paying) and passive citizens, April 20, 1791, Complete Works *(1910-67).*

3. From the King's Flight to the Second Revolution: June 1791 to August 1792

THE HISTORICAL CONTEXT

From October of 1789, when the royal family had been forced to move to Paris, attempts to free the king from his "captivity" had been organized from the centers of emigration, like Koblenz, Worms and London, and also by the loyal nobles in the provinces. As early as February 1790, the Marquis Thomas de Mahy Favras had been accused of plotting against the National Assembly and planning to abduct the king; he was executed at the Place de Grève. A few months later, the Salon Francais tried to arrange for the escape of the king to Lyons, and in February of 1791, 400 armed nobles, the *chevaliers du poignard* had met at the Tuileries, only to be arrested by the Marquis Marie Joseph Lafayette.

Caricatures of "The National Assembly Petrified" and "The National Assembly Revivified"

In early 1791 another, more elaborate plot to free the king and his family was already in preparation. Its main managers were the Baron Louis Auguste de Breteuil who had established contact abroad, the Marquis Francois Claude de Bouillé who tried to secure a route to the Eastern border, and the Count Hans Axel Fersen, a Swedish diplomat and favorite of Marie Antoinette who had secret doors installed at the Tuileries. Fersen drove the coach with the royal family out of the city, with Louis disguised as a valet. One door of the castle had been left unguarded by the National Guard, so it is possible that Lafayette was involved in the plot. Relief horses had been provided for the whole journey to Montmédy near the Luxembourg border; but there were delays, some horses were withdrawn, and the king's flight ended ingloriously at Varennes in the Argonne forest. There he was stopped by soldiers and peasants because he had been recognized in Saint-Menehould. Louis denied that he had intended to leave the country, but a proclamation to the French people he had composed and his previous secret letters to the king of Spain and other monarchs made it quite clear that he had planned to move on an join the Austrian army and then attempt a return to Paris to restore his absolute regime. Instead, he was led back to Paris as a prisoner.

Despite the evidence of Louis's complicity in the escape attempt, the committee appointed by the Assembly found the king innocent and claimed he had been "abducted." Apparently, the moderates were much less afraid of Louis' power than of new mass violence. When the Jacobins demanded, instead, the immediate deposal of the king, the monarchists broke away, formed their own party and, as the Feuillants, were still to play an important role in the following months. They succeeded in saving the monarchy, although, with the abolition of the royal veto power, the country looked more and more like a republic.

The masses of Paris were indignant over the acquittal of the king, and the Cordeliers and Jacobins organized a great demonstration on the Champ de Mars. When the National Guard shot into the crowd and killed 30 to 50 people, the "triumvirate" (Barnave, Duport, Lameth) suppressed all radical activities in the city; even the Cordeliers Club was closed for a while. Lafayette's popularity declined rapidly after the bloodshed, and his next role, as a mayor of Paris, was brief.

The National Assembly, during its last months, issued a number of laws aimed at forcing the emigrants to return to France. They failed to achieve their purpose; even when the king had finally ordered his brothers to return, they refused to obey him, claiming that Louis had acted under compulsion. On the other hand, the Duke Louis Philippe Joseph of Orleans, who now called himself Philippe Egalité , a descendant of a brother of Louis XIV, had remained in the country and in fact had joined the Jacobins. He had been in opposition to the king ever since the days of the Notables and had been one of the main agitators during the march on Versailles in October of 1789.

Jacques de Warville Brissot

The constitution, decided upon and accepted by Louis in September of 1791, was based on liberal-monarchic principles. The king was to have a suspensive veto only; there was to be one parliament, which would hold the ultimate decision over war and peace. None of the delegates of the National Assembly were eligible for the new Legislative Assembly, but since only tax-paying citizens were entitled to vote, the new assembly again represented primarily the middle classes. On its right were the royalists, Feuillants and constitutionalists, their influence rapidly decreasing. The left, the majority, was composed of the Plain, an unorganized and often undecided group, swayed in turn by two other groups: the Girondists, who included some brilliant orators such as Pierre Vergniaud, Jacques Pierre Brissot and Marguerite Elie Guadet, and the radical democrats, the Montagnards, the champions of a united, indivisible republic, inclined to grant the provinces much less power than the Girondists wanted. Under the new constitution, the old parlements were finally abolished, each département was granted its own assembly, and priest and bishop were made elective positions.

A major source of conflict between right and left was the question of war versus peace. The Feuillants, about one-third of the total number of delegates (260 out of 745), wanted to avoid an armed conflict with Austria and Prussia, whose hostility grew from one day to the next, while the left—with the one exception of Robespierre—fervently hoped that a victorious France could spread her revolutionary ideas over all Europe. The king, too, favored war, but for the opposite reason. He was convinced that the French army, deprived of most of its noble officers, would be no match for the well-organized German armies. So Louis affronted his own followers by appointing the pro-war General Charles Francois Dumouriez as foreign minister.

A real reconciliation between king and assembly turned out to be impossible, not only because of the ever more stringent measures against emigrants and opposing priests, to which the king would not agree, but also because of the economic situation. Since July of 1791, when they still represented 87 percent of their nominal value, the assignats had depreciated rapidly, provoking the lower classes to demand, ever more stridently, the fixing of maximum food prices. Most of the Assembly's delegates, belonging to the upper classes, wanted to maintain the status quo and avoid any further radicalization of the Paris masses. Food riots and pillaging in the capital and other cities were the result.

In the long run, the monarchy and the Feuillants were fighting a losing battle, and one moving toward a climactic confrontation as a consequence of revolutionary France's poor relations with the rest of Europe. The Revolution had aroused great enthusiasm in many parts of the continent when it broke out. Poets such as William Blake, Samuel T. Coleridge and William Wordsworth in England and Friedrich Hoelderlin, Friedrich Gottlieb Klopstock and Ludwig Gleim in Germany, as well as such prominent statesmen as Charles James Fox and William Wilberforce in England sympathized with the revolutionaries. But the heads of the "legitimate" monarchies observed the development in France with increasing concern, fearing similar outbreaks in their own countries. For a while, any joint action by the monarchies was delayed because of disagreements over the Polish question. However, their Pillnitz declaration in August of 1791, which stated their intent to restore the absolute monarchy in France (see chapter 5), was seen in France as a challenge.

As the Gironde had hoped, French national pride and readiness for war was aroused, and there was little opposition when France entered into war against Austria and Prussia. Yet the country was woefully un-prepared, not only because so many trained officers had left the country—and, often enough, were fighting against France by then—but also because the remaining generals were not up to the task. So the War of the First Coalition started out with a number of defeats for the French armies, after which the generals in the field were unwilling to continue. Yet the Paris government conducted the war with great energy, while the king abandoned his Gironde ministers (Jean-Marie Roland and General Dumouriez) because he opposed their anticlerical legislation, and so lost more and more of whatever reputation he had left in the country. While the new Feuillant ministers were unpopular, the Gironde, too, was in a dilemma. The Girondists were afraid of the mas-ses whose mobilization for the war they themselves had instigated; but neither could they work with the king, who played the patriot but wanted military defeat and who was not trusted by the people.

The great demonstrations of June 20, 1792, during which the Parisian mob invaded the Tuileries, brought the monarchy to the edge of dis-aster. Louis was saved by the Girondist Mayor Jérôme Pétion and by his own tenacity. But when things got worse at the front, when the homeland was officially declared to be in danger and above all, when the manifesto of the Duke Charles Guillaume Ferdinand of Brunswick, which threatened to lay Paris in ruins should any harm be done to the royal family (see chapter 5), became known in the capital, there was no one left in Paris to defend the king. An explosion became inevitable; par-ticularly since the patriots from the provinces, the Fédérés, began to march into the capital, making common cause with the radical democrats and the aroused population.

CHRONICLE OF EVENTS

1791:   *June 20-25:* The king and his family's flight from Paris. He is recognized and stopped at Varennes and returned to Paris. His powers are suspended.

June 23: Duke Phillipe of Orleans (Philippe Egalité) is received as a member of the Jacobin Club. On June 28 he renounces his rights as a regent.

July 9: The Assembly orders all emigrants to return within two months.

July 15: The fact-finding committee of the Assembly absolves the king and claims he had been abducted.

July 16: The suspension of the king is maintained until he has ratified the constitution. The Jacobins demand the deposal of Louis. The moderate members break ranks and form the Feuillant Club.

July 17: The "Champ de Mars Massacre": Lafayette lets the National Guard shoot at a crowd protesting the acquittal of the king. State of emergency declared in Paris.

August 17: The emigrants are asked again to return to France within one month.

August 22: Beginning of mass riots by the black slaves in Haiti.

August 28: First issue of Jean Lambert Tallien's *L'Ami des Citoyens.*

September 3: The National Assembly ends the discussion of the proposed constitution.

September 9: Danton, who had fled to England after the Champ de Mars Massacre, returns to Paris.

September 13: The king accepts the constitution.

September 14: After a favorable plebiscite, Avignon and Venaissin are incorporated into France.

September 15: A penal code is promulgated.

September 27: All people living in France are declared free and all Jews become French citizens, but slavery in the colonies is maintained.

October 1: The Legislative Assembly convenes.

October 8: Lafayette is elected mayor of Paris and resigns as commander of the National Guard.

The king is stopped at Varennes, June 22, 1791.

The royal family returns to Paris, June 25, 1791.

October 20: Brissot and his friends begin their campaign in favor of war.

November 9: Ultimatum issued to all emigrants. It is vetoed by the king on November 11.

November 14: Pétion is elected mayor of Paris over Lafayette. The great majority of the voters does not participate.

November 29: Priests who refuse to swear the oath on the constitution are declared "suspect."

December 3: The king's brothers refuse to obey his order to return to France.

December 19: Louis vetoes the decree of November 29.

December 30: Maximin Isnard pleads for war as indispensable for the completion of the Revolution.

1792: *January 23:* Riot in Paris forces shopkeepers to reduce sugar prices.

February 14: Pillaging of food shops in Paris.

March 3: Mayor Jacques Guillaume Simoneau of Etampes, south of Paris, is killed by a mob demanding fixed prices.

March 10: Louis appoints General Charles Francois Dumouriez, who wants war with Austria and Prussia, as foreign minister.

March 23: Jean-Marie Roland de la Platière of the Gironde is made minister of the interior.

March 24: All colored peoples of the Antilles are granted equal rights.

April 21: Assignats sink to only 50 percent of their nominal value.

April 25: "La Marseillaise" is sung for the first time at Strasbourg.

May 17: First issue of Robespierre's *Défenseur de la Constitution.*

May 27: All opposing priests are to be deported.

May 29: The protective guard of the king is to be dissolved. A crowd of sansculottes, singing "Ça ira," demonstrates at Faubourg Saint-Marcel, demanding fixed food prices.

June 8: The Assembly decides to station 20,000 troops outside of Paris to pressure the king in favor of a continuation of the war, which the generals want to end.

June 11: The king vetoes the decrees of May 27 and June 8. Roland protests the veto.

June 12-15: The king dismisses the Gironde ministers (Roland and Dumouriez) and appoints Feuillants instead.

June 20: Huge demonstrations of the sansculottes, led by Antoine Joseph Santerre, who invade the Tuileries. The king does not withdraw his vetoes of June 11.

June 28: Lafayette arrives in Paris and demands the dissolution of the radical clubs.

July 2: The National Assembly and the provincial administrations decide to ignore the royal veto of June 11.

July 11: The homeland is declared to be in danger ("La patrie en danger"). New battalions are called in.

July 15: Lafayette speaks for the king in the Assembly and considers a coup d'état. The Cordeliers club asks for a national convention, and Robespierre begins his campaign for the removal of the king. The patriots from the provinces (Fédérés) demand suspension of the king.

July 27: The property of the emigrants is confiscated.

July 29: Robespierre supports the demands of the Fédérés.

July 30: Battalions of Fédérés from Marseilles march into Paris, singing Claude-Joseph Rouget de Lisle's "Marseillaise." Non-taxpaying (so-called *passif*) citizens are admitted in the National Guard.

August 3: Forty-seven out of 48 sections of Paris demand the deposal of the king.

EYEWITNESS TESTIMONY

Departed from Paris at midnight, arrived and stopped at Varennes in the Argonne region, at 11 o'clock in the evening.

June 22: Departure from Varennes at 5 or 6 o'clock in the morning, breakfast at St.-Menehould, arrived in Chalons at 10 o'clock, had supper there, spent the night at the old office of the intendant.

June 23: Interrupted Mass at 11.30 to hasten the departure, breakfasted at Chalons, lunch in Epernay, met with delegates of the National Assembly at the port of Buisson, arrived at Dormans at eleven, dined there, slept on an easy-chair for three hours.

June 24: Departure from Dormans at 7.30, lunch in la Ferte- sous-Jouarre, arrived in Meaux at 11 o'clock, had supper there and slept in the bishop's residence.

June 25: Departure from Meaux at half past six, arrived in Paris at 8 o'clock without stopping.

June 26: Nothing at all, Mass at the Galerie, talk with the delegates of the National Assembly.

June 28: I drank buttermilk.

Louis XVI, journal entries of June 21-28, 1791, ms. in National Archives, Paris.

We were supposed to leave during the night from Sunday to Monday, June 20; but fear that a chambermaid of the Dauphin who was on duty that day and was known to be a follower of Lafayette, might betray the departure ... caused the delay to the next day, the 21. On this day, the chambermaid was replaced by another, reliable one. M. de Bouillé was notified, and if the Duke de Choiseul had been less careless and surer in his appearance the delay would not have mattered. In order not to to arouse any suspicion, the queen personally took the children for a walk in Tivoli ... and at her return instructed the commander of the bataillon on the next day's excursion. I did the same for the Dauphin ... Count Fersen played the part of the coachman perfectly, he whistled and talked to a so- called colleague and took some tobacco from his box. I was on pins and needles, but did not show my excitement when the princess [the 13 year old "Madame Royale"] remarked: "Here comes M. de Lafayette." I hid the Dauphin under my clothes and assured everybody that all was fine, but I was not calm at all ...

The king arrived only after midnight. Bailly and Lafayette ... had started a conversation and in order not to arouse suspicion he did not want to appear to be in a hurry ... The king told us how he had walked very calmly through the great gate of the Tuileries, feeling completely secure because of the precautionary measure to have the Knight de Coigny walk through the same gate whose appearance was so much like his own. Thus the guards had been so used to see him that they let him pass this evening in complete safety ... There were several small incidents which proved that the most unimportant circumstances can influence great events ... Then we met a wedding party, but fortunately

Pierre Victurnien Vergniaud

we were not recognized and got through without difficulty …

… When the king left him [Count Fersen] he showed him his gratitude in the most cordial way, mentioning that he would soon be able to express this better than in mere words … I was posing as the mistress, under the name of a Baroness Korff, the king acted as my valet, the queen as my lady-in-waiting … When we had passed the gates [of Paris] the king began to believe in the favorable outcome of his trip and started to talk about his plans. He intended … to travel through several border cities to arrive more safely at the French town where he wished to stay permanently, for he did not want to go abroad even for a moment. "Now I am," the good king said, "outside of Paris where I had to swallow so much bitterness. You may be sure that, once I am firmly established again, I shall be quite different from the way you have seen me." … He anticipated the good fortune he hoped to bring to France: the return of the princes, his brothers, and the chance to restore religion and to compensate for all the suffering …When he looked at his watch which showed 8 o'clock he said: "Lafayette is not feeling very comfortable right now." …

We passed Chalons without being recognized, and were now quite calm and had no inkling that our good fortune was coming to an end and would be followed by the most horrible disaster … In Varennes and all of its surroundings the tocsins were ringing and it was impossible not to realize we had been recognized. For a long time, the king refused to step out of the carriage to make himself known …

Louise Elizabeth, Duchesse de Tourzel (governess of the king's children), Memoirs *(1883)*.

In the coach, a woman was sitting, and I thought I recognized the queen; a man sat on the left front seat and I was struck by his resemblance to the king whose picture was shown on the assignat bill I carried with me. At the inn near my house [in Saint-Menehould] there was a detachment of about 50 dragoons whose commander approached the coach, talking softly to the couriers accompanying it. I noticed the couriers were very anxious to let the coachmen depart … My suspicion increased … When we rode down the road, we came upon an inn where people had not yet gone to bed; I took the innkeeper aside and asked him: "Are you a good patriot?" "Indeed," he answered. "Well," I said, "the king is up there at Varennes and wants to get away. Run and get all good citizens together, so we can stop him!" He ran off at once.

We ran to the mayor and the commander of the National Guard; in less than 5 minutes 8-10 armed men had assembled. We all went up to the coach as it came down the road … While the passport was being checked I told the ladies that I could not believe that the Baroness [Tourzel] were a foreigner. If this were the case she would not be given an escort of dragoons and hussars; and that I suspected the king and the queen were in the coach. The mayor … asked them to get off … The king said: "This is my wife, these are my children; we implore you to treat us with the respect the French have always shown to their king!" … The commander of the hussars … wanted to talk to the king and take him into custody; he was told he would not be surrendered to him … and I added that if he intended to take him away from us he could only rob us of his dead body … The commandant of the National Guard brought up two small cannons on top of the road and two below … The hussars consulted one another and a moment later they defected to the National Guard; their commander escaped. They were very stupid to give in so easily; the cannon we threatened them with were not loaded.

Jean Baptiste Drouet, subsequent report to the Paris Commune, Mémoir Justificatif *(1796).*

They were discussing how to treat the king. All thought: "This fat pig is becoming a nuisance." "Will they put him in prison?" "Will he still reign?" "Will they give him a counsellor?" Lafayette made jokes and smiled sneeringly … Maubourg [the third delegate] said: "… he is a stupid fellow and in a bad spot; and can feel sorry for him." Barnave [the second delegate] remarked one could indeed consider him an imbecile … [Near Epernay] the king's coach stops, we advance. As soon as they see us, they shout: "Here are the delegates of the National Assembly!" Everybody rushes to make room for us … I thought: What tremendous reputation the Assembly is enjoying! … How great would be its responsibility should it not justify this boundless confidence, this touching love! …

"No, gentlemen," the king said glibly, "I did not want to go abroad, I have stated that already, it is the truth." … [In Dormans] I must admit I was not sorry that the court got acquainted with an ordinary inn … No one shouted: "Vive le roi," they kept on shouting: "Vive la nation! Vive l' Assemblée Nationale!" and sometimes: "Vive Barnave, vive Pétion!" … at our feet flowed the Marne river. I cried: "What a beautiful country! ... No kingdom in the world that one could compare with France!" I uttered this intentionally, watching what impression it would make on the king, but his face remained always cold and dismally in-animate. To tell the truth, this mass of flesh is quite insensitive. He wanted to talk to me about the English, their industry, the commercial genius of this nation. He completed one or two sentences, then his tongue slipped, he noticed it and blushed; the effort it takes him to express himself makes him so bashful.

Those who do not know him may be inclined to interpret this as dullness, but they would be mistaken. He rarely makes an inappropriate remark and I have never yet heard him say anything stupid ... The queen chatted ... about the education of her children ... but it did not take me long to notice that all she said was quite superficial. She expressed no vigorous or independent thought. She did in no way possess the character nor the attitude which would have been appropriate to her position.

But when the foot soldiers of the National Guard joined us, above Pantin, there was a turmoil which threatened to get serious. The grenadiers pushed back the horses, the riders resisted, bayonets whirled around the coach. Malicious people could have given the queen a few stabs with the bayonet in this riot. Some soldiers looked very angry and gave her mean looks. Then there were cries: "The whore, the harlot! It is no good that she shows us her child. Everybody knows it's not his!" The king heard all this clearly ... The young prince cried a few times, the queen clung to him, tears rolled from her eyes ...

Jérôme Pétion, report to the Assembly on his trip as one of three delegates to meet the returning king, Memoirs *(1866).*

The mud, the ... monsters with human faces, the royal family shamefully dragged along, surrounded by guards; it all amounted to so frightful a spectacle ... that even today I cannot think of it without feeling complete-ly overwhelmed. The queen was at times in a state of passivity hard to describe. Her son, on her knees, suf-fered from hunger and asked for food. As Marie An-toinette could not help him, she pressed him to her heart and wept, exhorting him to bear it in silence ...

Joseph Weber, the return to Paris, Memoirs *(1822).*

Now, people, look at the honesty, the honor, the religion of your kings! ... Beware of royal oaths! In the morning of the 19th, Louis XVI was laughing at his oaths and gloated in advance over the terror his flight would cause you. The Austrian woman has seduced La Fayette last night ... Louis ... has stolen away ... now he is laughing at the stupidity of the Parisians, and soon he will bathe in their blood ...

Jean Paul Marat, proclamation after the king's flight from Paris, June 21, 1791.

During the whole journey, Barnave was silent and respectful. Pétion, impertinent and garrulous, asked Madame for something to drink whenever he was thirsty, with a most appalling familiarity. He kept on talking about America and how happy the republics were. The king said to him, "We all know of your desire to establish one in France." He answered insolently: "France is not yet ripe for one, and I will not have the good luck of seeing one founded during my lifetime."

Duchesse de Tourzel, returning from Va-rennes, Memoirs *(1883).*

The National Assembly committed never so great an error as in bringing back the king from Varennes. A fugitive and powerless, he was hastening to the frontier, and in a few hours would have been out of French territory ... Clearly they should have facilitated this escape and thus have avoided the infamy of a regicide government and attained their great object of republican institutions. Instead of which, by bringing him back, they encumbered themselves with a sovereign whom they had no just reason for destroying and lost the inestimable advantage of getting rid of the royal family without an act of cruelty.

Napoleon, about Varennes, in Gourgaud and Montholon's Memoirs *(1823-25).*

I do not wish to investigate whether nowadays people take still the position that kings are being ab-ducted like women ... whether the King's departure was just a trip without significance, or if it must be associated with all preceding events ... The king is inviolable, he cannot be punished ... You are defaming yourselves; no, you have never resolved that one person should be above the law ... It is not enough to shake off the yoke of one despot if one is to fall into that of another despot. England freed herself from the yoke of one of her kings only to bow under the more humiliating yoke of a small number of her citizens ... We have to protect the nation from an oligarchic regime which stays in power too long.

Maximilien Robespierre, speech on the king's flight, July 14, 1791, Complete Works *(1910-67).*

Gentlemen, today everyone must realize that in the interest of all the revolution must come to a halt; those who have lost must understand that it is impossible to make it undone and that the only question can be how to domesticate it. Those who wanted the revolution, and made it, must understand that it has reached its last goal and that the happiness of the nation and their own fame require that it is not perpetuated any longer. We are all interested in the same thing ... the kings must understand that, if we stop now, they will remain kings ...

Antoine Barnave, speech of July 15, 1791.

A great crime is committed: Louis XVI flees. He leaves his station, undignified; only two steps separate the state from anarchy ... The population of the capital implores you not to decide anything about the fate of the guilty until you have heard the explicit wishes of the other 82 *départements*. You are stalling. Vast numbers of petitions are pouring in. All sections of the country demand simultaneously that Louis is put on trial. You, gentlemen, have stated in advance that he is without guilt and inviolable by declaring in your decree of the 16th that the Constitution should be submitted to him as soon as it is completed. Gentlemen, this was not the wish of the people and we thought you would consider it your greatest glory and even your duty to be the servant of the public will ... Al this obliges us to request from you in the name of all of France to reconsider this decree once more; to remember Louis XVI's crime has been proven and that this king has abdicated; accordingly, to accept his abdication and to call in a new Constituent Assembly ...

Petition of the sections of Paris at the Champ de Mars, July 17, 1791.

A wonderful change has taken place since the disturbances of the 17th compelled the majority of the Assembly to be sensible of its power. It is calculated that 200 people have been imprisoned since that event, upon suspicion of fomenting sedition ... Danton is fled, and M. Robespierre, the great dénonciateur and by office

"Accusateur publique" is about to be "dénonce" himself.

Earl Granville Levinson, Lord Gower, after the Champ de Mars massacre, dispatch of July 22, 1791, Despatches *(1885).*

A king must use all means which will help to maintain the monarchy. All other thoughts are more than alien to him. Today, his Majesty can rule the nation only with the help of a legislative body proceeding from the people.

Antoine Rivaroli, Comte de Rivarol, letter to M. de la Porte, September 4, 1791, Memoirs *(1824).*

I think he [the king] has virtue, but a weak king cannot be good. He cannot ward off the people's misfortune.

Charlotte Corday, as reported by a friend, September 29, 1791 in Furet and Richet's The French Revolution *(1970).*

The free people are essentially good. When the danger is over, they will finally forgive even their fiercest enemies. Have you not seen that the American royalists who devastated their own country with fire and sword, that they were called back even by the most ardent patriots ... I have already indicated that all laws against emigrants, rebels and their leaders will be to no avail if you do not combine them with a drastic provision which alone can guarantee success; it concerns the attitude you will assume against the foreign powers who encourage and support these emigrations and revolts.

Jacques Pierre Brissot de Warville, speech of October 20, 1791, Correspondence and Papers *(1912).*

These blockheads [the Girondists]! They do not understand that in doing that [striving for a war against Austria and Prussia] they are playing right into our hands!

Marie Antoinette, to Count Fersen, letter of December 14, 1791, in Soboul's Summary of the History of the French Revolution *(1962).*

After two years, France has exhausted all her peaceful means to bring the rebels back into her fold; all attempts, all exhortations were fruitless, they insisted on their rebellion, the foreign princes insist on supporting them therein; can one hesitate if one should attack them? … Would not France be dishonored if she continued to suffer insults which a despot would not tolerate for two weeks? Louis XIV declared war on Spain because his ambassador had been insulted by the Spanish ambassador; and we, free as we are, should hesitate even for a moment?

Brissot, speech of December 16, 1791.

So, finally the moment has come when France must reveal herself before the eyes of Europe as a free nation willing to defend and maintain her freedom … At this point, war will be a national blessing and the only misfortune we have to fear is that there may be no war … The exclusive interest of the nation recommends war!

Brissot, before the Legislative Assembly,
speech of December 29, 1791.

The most extravagant idea which may originate in the head of the politician is that it would suffice for a people to invade another one with the force of arms in order to make it accept its own laws and constitution. Nobody likes armed missionaries; and the first advice nature and caution will give to people is to beat back invaders as enemies. I have said that such an invasion would much rather reawaken memories of the pillage of the Palatinate [under Louis XIV] and the last wars than inspire thoughts of a constitution … Trying to give liberty to others before we have gained it for ourselves would mean to unite our own servitude with that of the whole world …

Do we not have enough enemies in our country? No, you know none, you know only Koblenz. Have you not said that the source of all evil is sitting in Koblenz? Not in Paris, then? There is, then, no connection between Koblenz and another place not far from here (the royal castle)? … War is good for army officers, for ambitious people, for stock market operators, for those ministers whose enterprises it will cover with an even thicker veil … good for the court, the executive whose authority, reputation and influence will increase, good for the coalition of noblemen, plotters and moderates who are ruling France … The destruction of the party of patriots is the great goal of all conspiracies of this group … You claim I am discouraging the nation? No, I am enlightening the nation; to enlighten free men means to encourage them.

Robespierre, at the Jacobin Club, anti-war
speech of January 2, 1792, Complete Works
(1910-67).

The Parisian mob invades the Tuileries, June 20, 1792.

People were—quite unsatisfied. They had not seen anything. The whole thing was over too fast.

Chronique de Paris, *reporting on the first*
use of the guillotine, April 25, 1792.

Since, as you know, we have to receive many people and always try to get some variety into the conversation, my husband had the idea of having a special song composed. The captain of the engineer's corps Rouget de l'Isle, a gracious poet and composer, quickly set the war song ["La Marseillaise"] to music. My husband has a fine tenor voice and he sang it; it has a sweeping and rather special quality. It is like an improved Gluck, more vivacious and cheerful. I … have arranged the voices for piano and other instruments …

Luise Dietrich (wife of Strasbourg's mayor),
to her brother, letter of May 1792, in Tiersot's
Rouget de l' Isle *(1892).*

The executive is not in accordance with you. No further proof for that is necessary. The dismissal of the patriot [Gironde] ministers is sufficient. Should the fortune of a free people thus depend on the whims of a king? And is this king permitted to have a will other than that expressed in the law? The people want it, and their heads are worth at least as much as the crowned head of a tyrant … We complain, gentlemen, that our armies are idle. We demand that the reason for this is investigated. If it is found in the executive, away with it! The blood of patriots must not flow just to satisfy the arrogance and ambition of the treacherous Tuileries … We are complaining, finally, about the tardiness of the High National Tribunal … Will one force the people to act as on July 14th and to take the sword in its own hands? … No, gentlemen, you see our fears, our concern, and you will dispel them … The people are here and are silently awaiting an answer which is worthy of its sovereignty. Legislators, we demand that our arms shall not rest until the constitution is put into practical use. Not only the inhabitants of the Faubourg Saint-Antoine stand behind this petition, but all sections of the capital and the surroundings of Paris.

Petition of the Paris Section, addressed to the National Assembly at the uprising of June 20, 1792.

Up to this time, the six ministers had been on good terms, dining together on council days … But there was no friendship, respect or mutual confidence in this group, and it did not last. Lady Roland who actually ran the ministry in her husband's name, wished to be present at these discussions. This desire let a coolness arise between the ministers … Dumouriez grew tired of this despotism [of the Gironde ministers] and waited impatiently for a chance to throw off this yoke … He was happy to notice that the king showed less repugnance towards him than the other ministers. He was resolved to profit from this situation … but, since he was hated by the court, and even more so by the constitutionalists he felt that he could not do without the Girondists … He did not desire a break with them before he could be sure of a party strong enough to support him against their intrigues.

Marquis Charles Elie Ferrières, on the Gironde ministers, May/June 1792, Memoirs (1822).

The king was tired of their bickerings and decided to dismiss the three ministers … Roland, Servan and Clavière received the dismissal, hiding their fury under a semblance of contentment, pretending to congratulate each other … on leaving a cabinet where nothing good could be achieved because one had to struggle continuously against the perfidious intrigues of the counterrevolutionary court.

Ferrières, June 1792, Memoirs (1822).

Legendre arrives and presents a red cap to the king. It is pushed away by one of the grenadiers. The king says: "Let him do what he wants, if he wants to be rude, what of it?" He received the cap and put it on his head. They cheer in triumph. Somebody comes up with a bottle, asking Louis to drink to the health of the nation. Looking for a glass, they find none. The king takes the

bottle and drinks … "Bread and meat are too expensive," some workers shout, "We don't want any more vetos!"

Ferrières, events of June 20, 1792, Memoirs (1822).

"Let us follow the mob," Bonaparte said to me. We … went to walk on the terrace next to the water, and there he observed the shameful scenes … It would be difficult to describe the feelings of amazement and disgust they excited in him. He was unable to understand such weakness and patience. But when the king showed himself at one window … with a red cap … Bonaparte could not hold back his indignation any longer. "Che coglione," [roughly, "What blockheads!"] he cried, "how could they allow this rabble to enter? They could have mowed down four or five hundred with cannon, the rest would still be running!"

Louis Antoine Fauvelet de Bourrienne, with Napoleon in Paris, June 20, 1792, Memoirs of Napoleon (1829-30).

… they were united in their hope for an invasion and in their efforts at all foreign courts … they were firm in their belief that the certain result [of a foreign invasion] would be the counterrevolution. M. de Calonne, the main agent of the princes was known to have said publicly at Brussels: "Should the powers hesitate to make war, then we will know how to induce the French to declare it." The aristocrats at the court shared this feeling. The king and the queen vacillated between the parties. The queen above all, who would have agreed to owe her deliverance to Austrian, even Prussian arms, was held back by her unwillingness to lay herself under obligations to Monsieur, whom she had always disliked, and to the Count of Artois whom she liked no longer. She exclaimed with bitterness: "Then the Comte d'Artois will become a hero!"

Marquis de Lafayette, about the emigrants, Mémoires publiés par sa famille (1837).

Gentlemen, in which awkward situation does the National Assembly find itself? … At the very moment when our armies of the North obviously make progress and flatter our courage by the prospect of victory, they are suddenly drawn back from the enemy; they abandon favorable positions they had conquered and are led back into our territory, thus carrying the spectacle of war into our own country and leaving nothing with the unfortunate Belgians but the memory of the conflagrations illuminating our retreat! ... Why is it that at the moment of the gravest crisis, at the verge of an abyss threatening to devour the nation the movements of our armies are restrained; that by a sudden dissolution of the cabinet ... the ties of confidence are torn and the welfare of the nation is put into the hands of inexperienced men picked at random? Why is it that the administration impedes its own actions, that the army forgets that obedience is its very essence and that misled citizens try to guide the action ... of the highest executive? Do they want to restore a military government? One grumbles about the court—who dares to say that it is not justified? One suspects it of treacherous plans; but how can one dispel this suspicion?

Pierre Victurnien Vergniaud, speech of July 3, 1792.

You know what happened on June 20; our position has become more dangerous since then ... On the one side, violence and rage, on the other weakness and indecision. Neither the National Guard nor the army are reliable ... It is high time for the powers to speak up forcefully. Everything is lost if the rioteers cannot be put under control by fear of forthcoming punishment. They want a republic at all costs and in order to get it decided to assassinate the king ...

Marie Antoinette, letter of July 4, 1792, in Furet and Richet's The French Revolution *(1970).*

The nation is in danger; it is not in danger because we lack men who can bear arms, not because our fortresses are in poor condition, but because our strength has been paralyzed. And to whom do we owe this disastrous lethargy? To one single man whom the nation has made its head and whom vile courtiers have made the enemy of the nation. To act against the Tuileries means to hit all traitors with one blow; for the court is the place where all threads of the conspiracy converge.

Brissot, speech of July 9, 1792, Correspondence and Papers *(1912).*

We do not wish to describe to you again Louis XVI's whole attitude since the first days of the revolution, his bloodthirsty designs against Paris, his preference for noblemen and priests, his distaste for simple people ... but we must remind you, legislators, very briefly of the benefits Louis received from the nation and the ingratitude of this prince. For how many reasons could he have lost his throne at the moment when the people regained their sovereignty ... The nation, true to its character, wished to be magnanimous rather than calculating; the despot of a nation of slaves became the king of a free people; after he had tried to flee from France to rule in Koblenz he was again put on his throne, perhaps against the will of the nation one should have asked first ...

And soon we saw how all these good deeds of the nation turned against it. The power transferred to Louis so that he may preserve liberty took on arms to destroy it. ... Two enemy armies threaten our land from abroad. Two despots publish an impertinent and stupid manifesto directed against the French nation. Infamous Frenchmen, led by the brothers, relatives and allies of the king prepare to thrust the dagger into their home country ... And while the enemy advances in forced marches noblemen command our republican armies, our generals leave their stations in face of the enemy, allow the army to get involved in discussions, come here to announce their demands to the Legislative Assembly ... and slander a free people which they have a duty to defend.

The head of the executive power is the first link in the chain of the counterrevolution ... As long as we have this king, liberty cannot be secure, and we wish to remain free. We should have preferred to be lenient and to ask you only to suspend Louis XVI temporarily, as long as the nation is in danger; but the constitution does not permit this. Louis XVI constantly refers to the constitution; now we, for our part, refer to it and demand his deposition.

Pétion, petition in the name of a delegation representing 47 Paris sections, August 3, 1792.

4. The Second Revolution and the End of the Monarchy: August 1792 to January 1793

THE HISTORICAL CONTEXT

August and September 1792 saw the bloodiest mass actions of the entire revolutionary period. On August 10th, the fighting between the masses and the Swiss Guards resulted in over 1,000 Swiss and almost 400 rioters dead or wounded. Many of the latter came from provincial bourgeois ranks. The sympathies of the National Guard, which now admitted passive, non-taxpaying citizens, were with the crowd. The Assembly, to whom the king and his family had fled, treated him as a king as long as the fighting remained undecided. But when the crowd had won, the Assembly immediately suspended the king, replacing him with an executive council led by Georges Danton as minister of justice. Under the pressure of the crowd, the Assembly decided not only to dissolve itself and hold an election for a National Convention to give the country a republican constitution but also to make radical changes in the election method. Universal suffrage was introduced, with only servants excluded.

Louis XVI imprisioned at the Temple

The downfall of the monarchy was also that of the Feuillants, who had been comprised of the rich bourgeoisie and the liberal nobility. The winners were the Montagnards, who from here on sought the support of the lower classes, the sansculottes, and the war advocates, whose spokesman was Georges Jacques Danton. When a criminal court organized to deal with the opponents of the war worked too slowly it antagonized the people, contributing to a new outbreak of violence in the following month.

The Dauphin, Louis XVII

Before this happened, a remarkable ceremony took place that showed the idealistic belief of the French revolutionaries in international goodwill, as well as their naivete. The Assembly made 18 citizens of foreign countries, who were considered friends of the Revolution, honorary citizens of the nation and asked them to become candidates at the forthcoming elections of the National Convention. Among this group were Americans George Washington, James Madison and Alexander Hamilton; Englishmen Thomas Paine, Joseph Priestley and William Wilberforce; the Swiss Johann Heinrich Pestalozzi; and the Pole Tadeusz Kosciousko. Only Paine, famous for his pamphlet "Common Sense," which pleaded for the independence of the American Colonies, and the German Baron Jean-Baptiste (Anacharsis) Cloots became members of the National Convention; but during the terrorist regime, Paine, who also had written a pamphlet in defense of the French Revolution and against Edmund Burke, was imprisoned for 11 months. Cloots was guillotined.

The indiscriminate slaughter of suspects, royalists, resistant priests and common criminals, known as the September massacres, was the result of military setbacks, of the constant agitation on the part of the radicals on the left, such as Jean Paul Marat and his *L'Ami du Peuple*, of the suspicion of the lower classes that they were being sold out to the enemy, and of their impatience with the measures taken by the government against the traitors and collaborators. Thousands of innocent people in Paris and other cities were slaughtered by the mob, and the government did nothing or could no do nothing to stop the killing. The effect of the September days on the rest of Europe was devastating, and a great part of the sympathy abroad for the revolutionary movement was lost.

The same fateful month of September saw the first session of the new National Convention. Its composition revealed the tremendous shift to the left that had taken place: There were no royalists, and the Gironde, about 200 delegates out of a total of 750, was now the "right." The Montagnards, about 100 delegates, were outnumbered at first, since the uncommitted "plain" sided with the orderly and law-minded Gironde, in reaction to the violence that had taken place. The abolition of the monarchy and the introduction of the new republican calendar were announced immediately. At the same time, the first wholesale riot in the Western provinces flared up. The Chouans, so named after their leader, Jean Cottereau, nicknamed Jean Chouan, rose against the Paris government. They received support from Royalist agents from England but developed into a real danger only in 1793 when they combined with the rioters in the Vendè who rose after the execution of the king.

Georges Danton, who had been the soul of the fanatical resistance against the enemies abroad and its main organizer, lost much of his popularity because of apparent irregularities during his administration.

Meanwhile, the break between Gironde and Montagnards, who could not agree on how to proceed against the imprisoned king, became ever more apparent, with the Jacobin Club siding with the Montagnards. The trial of Louis XVI became inevitable in November, when documents were discovered in the Tuileries that proved his association with the counterrevolution and revealed his correspondence with foreign rulers. The last attempt by the Gironde to take the decision on Louis' fate to the people was defeated by the left, led by Louis Saint-Just and Robespierre; the sentence of death by a very close vote and the execution of the king in January 1793 aroused a great amount of indignation and protest not only abroad but also in the provinces and in the capital.

The main purpose of the Convention—to put a stop to the counter-revolution by eliminating its potential head—had been achieved. Yet for decades to come, the "regicides" who had voted for Louis' death were regarded as murderers; after the restoration of 1815, those who were still alive were banished from the country. A conciliation with the "legitimate" powers abroad was no longer thinkable in 1793. Revolutionary France had to be victorious or would perish.

The few months between August of 1792 and January of 1793 marked the downfall not just of the king, the Royalists and the Feuillant party. Lafayette, too, who had been the darling of the people two years ago, was ruined. He had tried to march his troops against Paris during the crises in August, but since the National Guard now included "passive" citizens from the lower classes, he lost his control over them. After he was threatened with indictment, he defected to the enemies of a regime he himself had helped to establish. The Austrians imprisoned him for several years.

The National Convention, the longest-lasting parliament revolutionary France was to have, was lucky in that it convened just when the first military successes occurred at the front: The Prussian army had been stopped and was eventually thrown back at Valmy. The great crisis, during which the minister of the interior, Roland de la Platière, had suggested that the government leave the capital, had been overcome. For the time being, the Gironde, which included in its ranks most of the intellectuals and the best orators, kept the lead in the Assembly. But the center of gravity had actually moved from the parliament to the Paris Commune, which did not intend to abandon the dominant role it had played during the August rebellions, and to the political clubs, particularly the Jacobins, where the new triumvirate of Robespierre, Marat and Danton dominated. The last great success of the Gironde was the reintroduction of free trade in December of 1792, a measure in the interest of the upper classes. Yet the radical measures required for the conduct of the war were always blocked by the legal-minded Girondins.

CHRONICLE OF EVENTS

1792:   *August 10:* General insurrection: Mobs from the Faubourg Saint-Antoine, supported by Fédérés from Marseilles and Brest, invade the Tuileries. The commandant of the National Guard is killed and replaced by Antoine Joseph Santerre. Almost the whole Swiss Guard is killed. The king seeks protection at the Assembly, which decides to suspend the monarchy and to call in a National Convention. The king and his family are imprisoned at the Temple. All citizens will have the right to vote, except servants.

August 11: A temporary Executive Council is elected by the Assembly, including Danton, Roland, Etienne Clavière and Pierre Marie Lebrun-Tondu.

August 14: The property of emigrants and of the communes is offered for sale.

August 17: A special criminal court to deal with the opposition against the war effort is instituted.

August 18: The last religious orders are dissolved.

August 21: First use of the guillotine by the criminal court.

August 26: Eighteen citizens of foreign countries are made honorary citizens of France.

August 30: Wholesale persecutions and arrests of suspects in Paris (about 3,000 imprisoned).

September 2-5: The September massacres. The mob enters the prisons, killing political suspects, resistant priests and ordinary criminals—in Paris alone, about 1600 die. Similar actions in Lyons, Reims, Orleans, Versailles.

September 14: Duke Philippe of Orleans changes his name to Philippe Egalité.

September 20: Last session of the *Assemblée Legislatif.* Law about marriage and divorce is passed.

September 21: First session of the National Convention. Royalty is declared abolished and the republic is proclaimed.

September 22: First day of the new Republican Calendar.

September 22-24: French troops enter Savoy and Chambéry.

Georges Jacques Danton, minister of justice

Maximilien Robespierre

September: First revolts of the Chouans, who later unite with the rioters in the Vendée.

October 9: Danton replaced by Dominique Joseph Garat as minister of justice, after he cannot account for some money he had received.

October 10: Brissot excluded from the Jacobin Club; definitive break between Girondists and Jacobins. The convention forbids the use of *Monsieur* and *Madame*, replacing them with *Citoyen* and *Citoyenne*.

November 20: Secret documents are discovered at the Tuileries showing the king's correspondence with foreign rulers.

November 27: Savoy and Nice are annexed.

November 29: The criminal court instituted on August 17 is dissolved.

November 30: Pétion is replaced by Chambon-Montaux as mayor of Paris.

December 1: Great speech of Jacques Roux at the Observatory District and beginning of the propaganda campaign of his "Enragés."

December 5: The Convention decides that the trial of the king will take place before the Convention.

December 8: The Gironde brings about the restoration of free trade. All laws concerning the storing up of grain are rescinded.

December 11: The king before the Convention.

December 26: Romain de Sèze speaks before the Convention in defense of the king.

December 27: The delegate Jean Baptiste Salles proposes to the Convention an appeal to the people regarding the fate of Louis XVI. Robespierrre and Saint-Just are against; the Gironde leader Vergniaud favors this plan, which is finally rejected by the Convention.

1793: *January 11-12:* Demonstrations in Paris and Rouen for the benefit of the king.

January 15: The Convention finds Louis guilty of conspiracy against liberty, with a vote of 707 against 0.

January 17: Louis is condemned to death, by a vote of 361 for, 360 against. Of the latter, many voted for imprisonment, exile or a suspended death sentence.

January 19: The Convention rejects a delay of the execution: 383 for, 310 against.

January 20: Louis Michel Le Peletier de Saint-Fargeau, a former marquis who voted for the king's death, is assassinated by a royalist. Some time later, he is declared a "martyr of the revolution."

January 21: Louis XVI is decapitated at the Place de la Révolution (now the Place de la Concorde).

EYEWITNESS TESTIMONY

These disgusting allies, the scum of Marseille, arrived in Paris on July 30 … One cannot think of anything more revolting than these 500 insane men, three quarters of them drunk, almost all with their red caps, in rags, with naked arms … constantly growing in numbers by the influx from Saint-Antoine and Saint-Marceau, fraternizing with gangs just as fearful as they are … They came down the Boulevards, dancing the Farandole … We left them when they turned to the Champs-Elysées where satanic dances preceded the orgy to which they had been invited by Santerre [chief of the National Guard] … If Paris became sadder each day after June 20, it turned into a place of horror after this hellish crowd appeared on the scene. They did their murderous work while yelling "a ira" and the Marseillaise, songs of which the first was meant for dancing, the second for more dignified purposes.

General Paul Baron de Thiébault, Memoirs *(1898).*

Jean Paul Marat, "L'Ami du Peuple"

Gentlemen, I have come here to prevent a horrible crime. I am convinced I could not be in safer hands.

The president answered: Sire, you may count on the firmness of the Assembly whose members have sworn to die for the protection of the rights of the people and its constitutional representatives.

Louis XVI, before the National Assembly, August 8, 1792.

The Place Vendôme was filled with a crowd which followed those scoundrels who carried heads on their pikes. With horror I saw how very young people, children even, played with heads, throwing them up in the air and catching them with the ends of their sticks. This happened shortly before one heard the cannon fire accompanying the storming of the Tuileries. At the first cannon shot the crowd dispersed … The bodies of the poor Swiss guards they had pursued … and then massacred, were undressed, insulted and examined by women. My pen cannot repeat such atrocities …

Comte Guillaume Mathieu Dumas, delegate of the nobility, on the storming of the Tuileries, August 10, 1792, Memoirs of His Own Time *(1839).*

Soon the news came that the Swiss had fired at the mob … I could not believe this. But then one could hear cannon shots … Good friends warned me and my six soldiers to hide … fortunately, I had civil clothes I put on immediately … I could not show myself, but saw heavy smoke rising up to the clouds, and heard horrible shouting and crying in the streets … Now … comes and reports that they were batting about torn pieces of the Swiss in the streets, and that they were carrying their torn-out hearts at the ends of their sabres. Every time a torn piece of a killed Swiss was passing by, I heard shouts "ho-ho, bravo, bravo" which set my teeth on edge. O cruelty and indescribable pain—every time I heard the shouting in the street I cried in my room: Oh God, they are hurling around another part of my co-patriots and comrades … Even if I get away this time, it won't be for long … there is no hope, no consolation left for me ... I cannot even show myself to my best friends ...

J. Bonifaci Good, sub-lieutenant, Swiss Guard, letter to his family, August 10-September 10, 1792, Neue Züricher Zeitung *(Aug. 1, 1916).*

Some [of the Swiss Guards] wanted to join the people, but too late; others who did not want to shoot were thrown out of the windows by their own comrades. The king who had fled into the Assembly showed, displayed only a dull, inhuman indifference. He asked for a piece of bread and ate it with a carefree and cold expression. The queen showed a sad face, but full of impudence and arrogance. One has to admit, the people were cruel, but many circumstances aggravate the crime of the Court. If you knew them, you would realize that the people deserve the highest praise. There was no looting or robbery. The gems, the porcelain and the minted gold were taken to the National Assembly.

A student, his report on the storming of the Tuileries, August 10, 1792, in Two Friends of Liberty's History of the French Revolution of 1789 *(1790-1793).*

A group of citizens stormed up, claiming the Swiss had attacked them after they had lured them to come closer. They demanded the deposition and condemnation of the king, and asked for his death. The frenzy had come to a climax. "We demand the deposition" the invaders shouted [which meant: we shall be satisfied with the dethronement], "but swear that you will save the nation." The Assembly shouted back: "We swear it!" From this moment on it was no longer free and no longer master over the king's fate.

Pierre Louis Roederer, Chronicle of the 50 Days Between June 20 and August 10, 1792 *(1832).*

Louis XVI, seated in a stenographer's box, had to listen to all these discussions about himself. He was ... so to speak, present at his own obsequies. The queen was not as submissive ... and suffered much more. Commissioners of the municipality ... advised that the Luxembourg had many exits, making it easy for the king to get away ... If the Assembly persisted in keeping the king at the Luxembourg, the municipality could not be responsible for his person. They proposed the Temple ...

Marquis Charles Elie Ferrières, August 10, 1792, Memoirs *(1822).*

Louis de Saint-Just

My dear fellowmen: A man who for your sake has suffered ostracism for a long time is leaving his underground hideout today to help bring victory to your side by his efforts ... He has predicted that your armies would be led to the slaughterhouse by treacherous generals and three disgraceful defeats have marked the beginning of the campaign ... I repeat to you: Beware of the reaction! Your enemies will not spare you after the dice have fallen in their favor ... No one abhors bloodshed more than I; but in order to prevent bloodbaths I implore you to spill a few drops ... Above all: Hold the king, his wife and his son as hostages and see to it that he is shown to the people four times a day until his verdict is spoken. And since it depends only on him to remove our enemies forever, explain to him that, unless the Austrians and Prussians will be outside our boundaries ... within two weeks, never to be seen here again, his head will roll before his feet ... All counterrevolutionary members of the Paris general staff must be executed, all officers hostile to their country must be expelled from the bataillons ... Let the dissolution of all foreign and Swiss regiments be decreed as they have shown to be enemies of the revolution.

Jean Paul Marat, in L'Ami du Peuple, *August 10, 1792.*

I could have found a high position in this new order of things … but my feelings would not permit me to think along such lines. I voiced opposition to the Jacobin tyranny, but you are familiar with the feebleness of our *honnêtes gens*. They abandoned me … and there was nothing left for me than to leave France. We were … detained by an Austrian detachment which violates the *droits des gens* … I am an American citizen, an American officer and no longer in the service of France.

Marquis de Lafayette, to a friend, letter after August 10, 1792, in Mémoires publiés par sa famille *(1837).*

We hear that at present in all theaters the song "Allons enfants de la patrie" is asked for … The Fédérés have brought it along from Marseille where it has been in high fashion … The part where all wave their hats and sabres and shout in unison: "Aux armes, citoyens!" can actually make you shiver … It is often sung at the Palais Royal, sometimes also in the theaters between the plays …

Chronique de Paris, *August 20, 1792.*

Because of my brother's health, we went for walks in the garden every day, and almost every time my father was insulted by the guards. Rocher [the doorkeeper] tried to molest my father in every way: he sang the "Carmagnole" and other horrors, and in passing blew smoke into his face, knowing that my father was

The execution of Louis XVI at the Place de la Révolution, January 21, 1793

bothered by the smoke. My father suffered all this very gently.

One other day, they sounded alarm during dinner; one thought the foreigners [the Allied army] were coming; this awful Rocher seized his big sabre and told my father: If they come, I will kill you! … Simon [the cobbler to whom her little brother was entrusted] abused my brother when he wept because of the separation from us; the child became disturbed and no longer dared to shed any tears. Simon put a red cap on his head and put a Jacobine's coat on him. … Several soldiers of the city guard and officers of the National Guard appeared and the latter ones insisted that my father should show himself at the window; the former were against it, rightfully. When my father asked what was going on, one young officer told him: "Well, Monsieur, if you want to know, they want to show you the head of the Princess de Lamballe [a close friend of the queen]." My mother was petrified with horror.

Marie-Thérèse Charlotte de France (Madame Royale), daughter of Louis XVI and Marie Antoinette, August 1792, Memoirs of the Captivity *(1892).*

You know that Verdun is not yet in the hands of your enemies. You know the garrison has vowed to kill the first one who talks of surrender.

One part of the people is on the way to the borders, another one is busy digging ditches, a third one will, armed with pikes, defend the centers of our cities …

At this moment, gentlemen, you may declare that the capital is serving all of France well. The National Assembly, at this moment, is turning into a regular war committee. We demand that anyone refusing to serve in the war personally or to hand over his arms … be punished by death. The sounding of the tocsins which will start now is no sign of alarm but marks the general attack against the enemies of the nation. To defeat them, we need courage, gentlemen, courage and again courage; then France will be saved.

Georges Danton, speech to the Legislative Assembly, September 2, 1792.

I had hardly put down my pen [writing his last will] when I saw two more uniformed men. One of them whose arm, coat and sabre were full of blood said: "For two hours I have been hacking off limbs right and left … I am more tired than a mason who has stirred plaster for two days." Then they talked of Rulhière [a knight of the order of St. Louis] to whom they promised all degrees of the most cruel pains; they swore with hor-rible oaths to cut off the head of anyone who would give him the coup de grace ... then hit him with their flat sabres which soon lacerated his intestines ... I took off my coat and dressed in a rough, very dirty shirt and a poor overcoat, without a vest which I had asked to be sent to me out of fear of what was to come ... I thought that clad in this way I would not be suspected to belong to the educated classes who were slaughtered like traitors. It turned out that this precaution was helpful indeed ...

So I went through the Rue des Ballets, and there were three rows of people on either side ... Arriving at the end, I turned around in horror as I saw a huge heap of naked bodies in the brook, besmirched with dirt and blood. Upon those, I had to swear an oath ... I said the words demanded from me and then was recognized by one of my clients who, undoubtedly by mere accident, was passing by. He vouched for me, embraced me a thousand times and even persuaded the murderers to have pity on me ...

Maton de la Varenne (lawyer), imprisoned at the time of the September Massacres, The Crimes of Marat and the Other Throat-cutters *(1795).*

... we hasten to advise our brothers in all départements that some of the imprisoned malicious conspirators have been killed by the people; an indis-pensable act of justice aimed to keep under control the innumerable traitors hiding in their houses at a time when we have to march against the enemy. No doubt the whole nation will not hesitate, after the long se-quence of treacheries which have brought us close to the abyss to apply the same method so necessary for the public welfare, and like the Parisiens all Frenchmen will exclaim: We are marching against the enemy, but we will leave no criminals behind who would slaughter our wives and children!

Paris Commune, circular sent to the departments after the September massacres.

I have told you that I consider most of the delegates of the Convention as honorable ... But I have also advised you that ... some of the men in this assembly are bad citizens and plotters ... I say that there are men here who had themselves elected by intrigue ... You all know the letters of Brissot, Lasource, Guadet, Vergniaud which were distributed in the departements

Sketch of Marie Antoinette on her way to execution

The commune, trying to give this terrible slaughter the appearance of popular justice, has hastily organized a tribunal in each prison. The president has a long sword at his side, sitting at a table littered with papers, pipes and bottles ... Three cut-throats bring in a prisoner. Their sabres are across his breast and he receives warning that he will be pierced if he moves. Two monsters with bare swords ... and bloody shirts are guarding the door ... In the middle of the table, a candle ... reflects its flickering light on the sinister faces of the judges, revealing their savage and ghastly fea-tures ... No plea will save the designated victim. A man, 60 years old, is led in ... two national guards show up to testify in favor of the accused ... insisting that he has always been a good citizen. The president says only "Recommendations are useless in the case of traitors." The man cries "This is horrible, this trial amounts to an assassination." The president replies "My hands are washed of it" and then: "Conduct the gentleman." He is dragged out of the court and butchered.

Ferrières, on the September massacres, Memoirs *(1822).*

before the elections … It seems very strange that you are not willing to listen to a political denunciation, and that is all I am doing; I did not permit myself to utter abusive remarks, after I had to listen to all those abominable curses pronounced against me here …

Marat, against the Gironde, speech of October 4, 1792, Selected Texts (1963).

Do you want to meet the spirits of destruction? Read Marat, listen to Robespierre, Collot d'Herbois, Chabot. Look at the posters defacing the walls of Paris; dig out the dead bodies of September 2; remember the sermons of the apostles of murder in the Départements! The impunity of the second of September has made Europe doubt our principles … The disorganizers are those who want to equalize everything, property, prosperity, the food prices and the services to society …

Jacques Pierre Brissot de Warville, anti-Jacobin proclamation of October 1792, Correspondence and Papers (1912).

In the midst of this general commotion the approach of the foreign enemies awoke feelings of disgust and revenge and the hearts were boiling with rage against the traitors who had called them in. Before the citizens, the victors of the Tuileries left their homes, wives and children, they wanted the punishment of the traitors which had been promised to them; so one rushes into the prisons … Could the magistrates hold them back? It was an uprising of the people, and not, as some have ridiculously assumed, an isolated riot of a few villains paid to murder their fellow citizens … They claim that one innocent man was killed—one chose to exaggerate their numbers, but even a single one is far too much— Citizens, deplore this cruel misunderstanding … deplore even the guilty victims felled by the sword of the people's justice … but your grief must come to an end, as do all human things. Let us save a few tears for a more touching misfortune. Cry for the 10,000 patriots sacrificed by tyranny …

Maximilien Robespierre, on the September Massacres, speech of November 5, 1792, Complete Works (1910-67).

I claim the king must be punished like an enemy; we must fight him, not put him on trial … What kind of law could exist between mankind and a king?

Louis de Saint-Just, to the Convention, speech of November 13, 1792.

But man, struggling with his lot on earth, is seeking his pleasures in delusions. Seeing how a rich man pursues all his pleasures … he believes that in another world his own joys will be all the greater … Do not condemn his error, but enlighten him. Explain to him that it is the declared intention of the Convention not to destroy but to create better conditions … Tell the people clearly and distinctly: You will keep your priests as long as you think you will need them for your happiness. The ci-devant [formerly called] king will be sentenced in the near future, and the Convention is ready to make all necessary sacrifices to secure your subsistence, but will hit all those with all the severity of the law who dare to violate it. Show confidence, circumspection, resolution—and you will save the republic.

Danton, speech of November 30, 1792.

The king has been dethroned by his crimes. He conspired against the republic; he will be condemned, or the republic will not be acquitted … If the king is not guilty, then those who deposed him, are. To put him on trial would amount to a court investigation where a case is submitted for decision by a higher court.

Robespierre, speech at Louis XVI's trial, end of November 1792.

Kings deserve to die from the moment they come to this world. What punishment is sufficient for him, whose wickedness surpasses that of a Medici or Nero, if one only thinks of the massacres at Nancy, Montauban and Nîmes, in the colonies and at the Champ de Mars … Either Louis' head will fall or we will be buried under the ruins of the republic. The kings have cemented despotism with the unjustly spilled blood of the people. It is time to cement the liberty of the peoples by the lawful spilling of the impure blood of the kings. England did not hesitate to lead Charles Stuart to the scaffold. Rome even punished Brutus' son with the hatchet of the consuls … Sternness and justice are the main virtues of a republican … Put Marie Antoinette on trial … let us cleanse the earth of the monsters who defile it! Moderation will ruin the public weal and will, gradually, dig the grave for the slaves. Holland has lost her liberty by hesitation.

Jacques Roux, speech at Louis XVI's trial, December 1, 1792.

The decree stated "Louis Capet should be brought before the National Convention." The king answered: "Capet is not my name, but the name of one of my ancestors … I shall come with you, not obeying the Convention, but because my enemies are using force." … A large crowd awaited him at the gate of the Temple.

Jean-Baptiste Antoine Cléry, Journal of the Events at the Temple during Louis XVI's Captivity (1798).

One has tried to seduce the patriots to take rash measures by suggesting the death of the tyrant should be decided by acclamation … In order to determine who the traitors are—for there are traitors in this assembly—and to be certain about them, I propose an infallible method: To decide on the death of the tyrant by roll-call and to publish the result.

Marat, on Louis XVI's trial, December 6, 1792, Selected Texts (1963).

The king is coming; he who applauds him will be beaten up; he who insults him will go to the lantern.

The king has aimed at the nation; the rifle did not go off; people, now you shoot!

Posters at the Convent during Louis XVI's trial, September 1792 to January 1793, in Victor Hugo's 1793 (1874).

I have no illusions: These ungrateful ones who dethroned me will not stop halfway; they would have to blush too much if they had to look at their victim. The lot of Charles I awaits me, and my blood will flow to punish me because I never shed any.

Louis XVI, to his counsel, Chrétien Guillaume de Malesherbes, letter of December 1792, Works (1864).

The king is not a coward … but he is overwhelmed by a strange shyness and self-distrust … He lived like a child … till the age of 21.

Marie Antoinette, in 1792, as reported in Mme. Campan's Memoirs (1823).

He slept on a bed which had not been made in six months, for he did not have the strength to do it himself. It was full of fleas and bugs, and they were in his clothes and on his body too. His feces stayed in the room. He did not remove them, nor did anyone else. The window was never opened and the evil smell in the room was intolerable. By nature he was not very clean, and lazy, and he could have done more for his person. He often

had no light, and the poor boy almost died with fear, but he never asked for anything …

Marie-Thérèse Charlotte de France (Madame Royale), about her brother, the Dauphin, December 1792, Memoirs of the Captivity (1892).

The people have promised Louis inviolability, and only the people can declare that they want to make use again of a right they had renounced … If you are true to your principles you do not have to fear criticism, and if the people wish Louis to die, they will so direct. But if you violate these principles you expose yourselves to criticism … to have left the path of duty. And what awful responsibility will you burden yourselves with by neglecting your duty!

Pierre Victurnien Vergniaud, speech to the Convention, December 31, 1792, Parliamentary History (1847).

Augustin Robespierre: I do not know that pity which strangles the people and pardons the tyrants: Death.

Lavicomterie: As long as the tyrant is breathing, liberty is suffocating: Death.

Foussedoire: I detest shedding blood, but royal blood is no human blood: Death.

Gentil: I vote for imprisonment: A second Charles Stuart will get us a second Cromwell.

Paganel: Death penalty: A king is useful only when he dies.

Tellier: One should mold a cannon for the head of Louis XVI, to shoot it against the enemy.

Chaillon: He may live: I do not want the dead to be declared a saint by Rome.

Sieyès: I have voted for death, without mincing words [*sans phrase*].

Saint-Just: Personally, I do not see a middle way: Either this man should reign, or he should die.

Robespierre: It is better that Louis dies than hundreds of thousands of good citizens. Louis must die so that our country may live.

Delegates of the Convention, votes and comments on the verdict of Louis XVI's trial, as reported in Victor Hugo's 1793 (1874).

The king made no motion showing surprise or excitement; he only seemed moved by the pain of the venerable old man [Malesherbes, who had reported the death verdict to him] … The king ordered me to bring him the volume of English history dealing with the death of Charles I. I learned that his majesty had read 250 books during his stay at the Temple.

Jean-Baptiste Cléry, valet and barber to Louis XVI, Journal of the Events at the Temple during Louis XVI's Captivity (1798).

We went to the Temple and advised the tyrant that the hour of execution had come. He requested to have a few minutes with his father confessor. He wanted to give us a package to be forwarded to you. We replied that we had only the order to take him to the scaffold. His answer: "That is correct." He wanted his family to be remembered and requested that his valet Cléry become the queen's valet, then corrected himself and added "my wife's." He then said to Santerre [the chief of the National Guard]: "Let us go." He walked across the court, then entered his carriage. On the way, there was complete silence and there was no incident. We never took our eyes off Capet up to the guillotine. He arrived ten minutes after ten o'clock. He wished to speak to the people, but Santerre did not permit this. His head fell. The citizens dipped their pickaxes and their handkerchiefs into his blood.

Jacques Roux, to the general council of the Paris Commune, on the execution of the king, report of January 21, 1793.

At the scaffold, he looked at the deadly machine with firmness … The drumroll meant to prevent the people from asking for mercy was interrupted by Louis' gesture, as if he wanted to speak to the people. But upon further orders … the drummers resumed their work so that … one could only hear a few words like "I forgive my enemies" … The adjutant of the general ordered the executioner to do his duty and Louis was bound to the fatal board and his head was cut off before he had time to suffer … Most people went away with mourning in their hearts to cry in the bosoms of their families … In his last talk with his father, the former Dauphin had requested urgently to be allowed to accompany him so that he could ask the people for mercy. A naive trait which very much speaks for the child …

Philippe Pinel, physician and witness of the execution, Letters (1859).

Finally, we have landed at the isle of liberty and burnt the boat that brought us here!

Cambon, at the Convention after Louis XVI's execution.

Among all the horrors of political cataclysm even the assassination of a monarch is not the gravest one; for one could imagine it was done out of fear … It is the formal execution which instils a terror into a soul steeped in the ideas of human rights, which one will feel time and again thinking of such scenes as connected with the fates of Charles I and Louis XVI.

Immanuel Kant, German philosopher, in "Metaphysical Principles of Law," part one of Metaphysics of Morals (2nd, augmented ed., 1798).

5. Foreign Policy and the War of the First Coalition, Up to January 1793

THE HISTORICAL CONTEXT

While the ideas of the Revolution had met with much sympathy, even enthusiasm among large parts of the European population, the reaction of the European governments was different, though not uniform. While Catherine II of Russia would have been happy to lead a counterrevolutionary crusade against France, and the king of Sweden shared her views, the governments in London and Vienna were much more cautious.

William Pitt

In London, the government of William Pitt pursued the traditional British policy of neutrality and preserving the existing balance of powers. While Pitt himself, personally, and Edmund Burke were violently opposed to the principles proclaimed in Paris, other prominent politicians such as Charles James Fox saw in the Revolution the rise of a new age. In Vienna, Emperor Leopold II, by nature a cautious man, was not in principle opposed to constitutional reforms and, since Austria was the traditional, main rival of France, was pleased about the weakened position of the French monarchy. Moreover, he was preoccupied with problems within his own country, especially on its eastern borders. On the other hand, the monarchs of Prussia, Sardinia and Spain were much more inclined to interfere in France in the interests of legitimacy. This was partly the result of Louis XVI's own secret requests for interference, and partly due to the activities of the prominent emigrants who agitated in all countries surrounding France: Charles Alexandre de Calonne, in London, worked on Prussia; the Count Charles Philippe D' Artois tried to obtain intervention by Spain to support the rebellions in the south of France; and the Prince Louis Joseph Condé organized an emigrant army in Koblenz.

Lazare Hoche, a brigadier general at the age of 25

But there were other areas of conflict. The Pope had protested the anticlerical measures taken in Paris and was further embittered by the loss of Avignon, which had been ruled by papal legates ever since the "Babylonian Captivity" of the Popes in the 14th century, but now after a plebiscite, was incorporated into France. There were also violations of feudal rights in Alsace, which antagonized the emperor and other German rulers, and when the archbishop of Trier felt threatened by France, the emperor declared his intention to defend him.

As early as February of 1790, the National Assembly had solemnly declared that it would never conduct any wars of conquest, and it repeated the statement in August of 1791. But the mood of the country changed with the Declaration of Pillnitz in which the Emperor Leopold and King Frederic William II of Prussia announced their intention to take action in France to restore the rights of the sovereign, if the other powers, including England, would consent unanimously.

While the wording of the statement was quite careful in accordance with the position taken by the emperor, it was taken by the patriots as a provocation and an interference in internal affairs, particularly since it mentioned the emigrant brothers of Louis. France began to prepare for war. New generals were appointed, and an army of volunteers created to complement the regular troops. The patriots saw Austria, a symbol of the old feudalistic regime, as the main enemy. Yet after the alliance between Austria and Prussia in February of 1792, it was clear that the war would have to be conducted against both powers; that, considering the state of the French forces, seemed foolhardy. More than half of the 12,000 officers had emigrated since 1789; the combined strength of regular and volunteer troops was only around 150,000 men, and there were considerable conflicts within the army between the patriotic soldiers and the aristocratic commanders. The generals leading the three field armies were quite inadequate: Jean-Baptiste, Marquis de Rochambeau, in the north, had played an important part in the American War of Independence but was now an old man and not highly regarded by his troops; Marshal Nicolas von Luckner, leading the Army of the Rhine, was 70 years old and had fought for many years in the services of Austria, Bavaria and Hanover. And Lafayette, the third commander, was more of a politician in uniform than a soldier at heart. None of the three, nor their king, believed in a French victory, and they acted accordingly when war was declared.

This became inevitable when Emperor Leopold died and his son Francis proved to be even more recalcitrant than his father. When the Gironde government, through Foreign Minister Dumouriez, issued an ultimatum to Austria, demanding the reduction of her armaments in Belgium, it remained unanswered. So war was declared—only against Austria—and Dumouriez ordered a general offensive that resulted in the temporary occupation of Belgium, as the Austrians could not muster sufficient troops at first. But when the Austrians confronted them in force, the French commanders withdrew, blaming their defeat on the lack of discipline in the army and on the government that tolerated it. Lafayette, in the Ardennes, had not moved at all, and in May, the three commanding generals decided on their own to cease hostilities. This was obviously a political, not a military decision, and all the more dangerous as Prussia now entered the war (July 6).

But the Paris government reacted quickly and effectively. New regular and volunteer troops were called up, and the patriotic response was excellent. In Paris alone, 15,000 volunteers were recruited in one week. And again, as with the Pillnitz declaration, the enemy helped to strengthen French resistance. The manifesto of the Allied commander, the Duke Charles William Ferdinand of Brunswick, which threatened terrible revenge on the city of Paris and its population should any harm befall the king or the queen, had the opposite effect from the one intended. New commanders, Dumouriez and Francois Etienne Christophe Kellermann, took over at the front. Lafayette was indicted and fled. And while the fortresses of Longwy and Verdun were taken by the Allies, thus opening the way to Paris, their advance was stopped at the great artillery duel of Valmy (in the Argonne hills). Here, the Duke of Brunswick attacked with all the Prussian, Austrian, Hessian and émigré troops he could bring up, to no avail; it was the first time that the Prussian army, feared since the days of Frederick the Great, had been beaten back. The Allies retreated and, due to weather and epidemics, this retreat turned into a disaster. The French armies followed the enemy up to the Rhine and the Alps and occupied Belgium. Even more impressive than Valmy was Dumouriez' victory over the Austrians at Jemappes, after which he occupied the Austrian Netherlands.

The question arose, however, as to whether these occupations had to be taken as conquests or, as the French government claimed, as liberations of the people. The National Convention, convinced it was fighting for the liberty and happiness of all the people of Europe, decided to establish revolutionary administrations in all occupied territories, which led to stubborn resistance and open rebellion on the part of the native populations.

These very successes set the stage for French setbacks. The orthodox Catholic monarchies in Madrid and Naples were antagonized by the French conflict with the Pope, and their devoutly religious populations had an antipathy for the new, liberal ideas spreading from Paris, which had already brought about a pro-revolution uprising in parts of Switzerland. The decisive change, however, took place in England. British policy could never accept the occupation of Belgium, in particular Antwerp, one of the major European ports, and Pitt finally abandoned his policy of neutrality.

Anti-French agitation spread over England, and when Louis XVI was executed, the British court went officially into mourning, apparently forgetting that it had been England that had pioneered in the decapitation of kings; in fact, the precedence of Charles I's execution 140 years before had been constantly referred to in the Convention's debates preceding Louis' condemnation.

So, while England's motives to take arms against France were essentially determined by economic and geopolitical reasons, a large part of Europe began to see in France not a liberator, but a godless, brutal conqueror.

CHRONICLE OF EVENTS

1790:   *February:* Edmund Burke condemns the French Revolution in British Parliament while Charles James Fox welcomes it.

February 22: The National Assembly proclaims that it will never conduct any wars of conquest.

July 27: Convention of Reichenbach between Austria and Prussia. First indication of a joint action against France.

August 26: The National Assembly declares the pact between the French and Spanish dynasties to be null and void.

November: Burke publishes his *Reflections on the French Revolution.*

December 3: Letter of Louis XVI to the king of Prussia, asking for a European congress to help him restore his authority.

December 14: Emperor Leopold II protests the violation of feudal privileges in Alsace.

1791:   *February 23:* In Worms, the Prince Condé organizes an army of emigrants.

March 15: Diplomatic relations between the Vatican and France are broken off.

June 15: The Comte d'Artois establishes his headquarters at Koblenz (Rhineland).

July 14: Three students in Tübingen, southwest Germany—Georg Friedrich Wilhelm Hegel, Friedrich Hoelderlin and Friedrich Wilhelm Joseph Schelling—plant a "Tree of Liberty."

August 5: The National Assembly again denounces all wars of conquest.

August 27: By the declaration of Pillnitz, Saxony, Austria and Prussia declare their readiness to intervene in France with the consent of other powers.

December 3: Another letter of Louis XVI to the king of Prussia, asking for intervention by the European powers.

December 21: Emperor Leopold advises the French government that he will defend the elector-archbishop of Trier against military attacks by France.

December 27-28: Generals Rochambeau and Luckner are made marshals and commanders of the armies of

Soldiers of the Revolution

the North and the Rhine. New battalions of volunteers are established.

1792:   *January 25:* The National Assembly sends an ultimatum to Emperor Leopold. Talleyrand goes to London to attempt a rapprochement with England.

February 7: Treaty of Berlin between Austria and Prussia, against France.

March 1: Death of Emperor Leopold who is succeeded by his son, Francis II, last emperor of the Holy Roman Empire.

March 7: The Duke of Brunswick is appointed commander of the allied Austrian and Prussian armies.

March 27: In an ultimatum, the Gironde government asks Austria to reduce its armaments in Belgium.

April 20: France declares war against Austria.

April 25: French troops under Rochambeau invade Belgium.

April 28-29: First French defeats. General Dillon is killed by his troops.

May 17: Lafayette offers an armistice to the Allies.

May 18: Rochambeau, Luckner and Lafayette decide to discontinue hostilities and advise the king to ask for immediate peace.

July 12: Fifty-thousand additional regular army troops and 42 volunteer battalions are called in.

July 25: Manifesto of the duke of Brunswick: The authority of the French king must be restored.

August 20: Lafayette, accused of treason, goes over to the Austrians.

August 23: Longwy capitulates to the Prussian army.

August 29: Dumouriez suggests a new invasion of Belgium to divert the Prussians but is ordered to join Kellermann instead.

September 2: Verdun capitulates.

September 20: Cannonade of Valmy. Dumouriez and Kellermann force the Prussians to retreat.

September 30: The French under Custine take Speyer (on the Rhine).

October 14 and 19: The Prussian armies evacuate Longwy and Verdun.

October 21-23: Custine occupies Mayence and Frankfort.

November 6: Dumouriez defeats the Austrians at Jemappes (southern Belgium) and occupies the Austrian Netherlands.

November 7: The German naturalist, world traveller and writer Georg Forster founds a Jacobin club in Mayence.

November 14: The French armies occupy Brussels.

November 19: The Convention offers brotherhood and support to all peoples fighting for their liberty.

November 28 and 30: French armies take Antwerp and Liège.

November 29: The English government protests the French proclamation of November 19.

December 5: In Geneva, Switzerland, a revolutionary group guided by the events in Paris, puts the people's party into power.

December 7: A demonstration in Brussels demanding the independence of Belgium is suppressed by the French Army.

December 15: Pierre Joseph Cambon, financial expert of the Convention, introduces a revolutionary administration in the occupied countries. Feudal privileges are abolished, clerical property confiscated, the rich are taxed heavily.

December 16: Aix-la-Chapelle occupied by the French.

December 17: The French fleet approaches Naples in order to put pressure on King Ferdinand IV.

December 18: The English radical Thomas Paine is tried in absence for publishing his *The Rights of Man*, a reply to Burke's condemnation of the French revolution.

1793: *January 13:* The French ambassador in Rome killed by a mob hostile to the Revolution.

January 24: Diplomatic relations between Britain and France are broken off.

EYEWITNESS TESTIMONY

… one cannot know if you are still alive … in the den of bandits who have taken over the government of France and will bring about a Gaul of the time of Caesar. But a Caesar will subdue them! You may be sure he will come. If I were M. d'Artois or M. de Condé I would know how to handle those 300,000 French cavaliers … These thoughts are for you and no one else; I do not wish them to prejudice Paris against the king and queen.

Empress Catherine II of Russia, to Grimm, letter of January 13, 1791, in Brückner's
Catherine II *(1883).*

The advantages the inner situation of France offer to such an action stem from the disagreement between her various parties, and the cooling off of the initially fanatical adherence to the principles of the people's liberty. The surest way to lose these advantages, to reincite the earlier enthusiasm of the whole nation, to unite all parties for the defence of the constitution … would be to threaten the nation with a total overthrow of the constitution …

Emperor Leopold II of Austria, to Catherine II, about a proposed joint action against France, letter of August 11, 1791, in Beer's
Leopold II, Francis II and Catherine, Their Correspondence *(1874).*

"The Marseillaise," composed by Rouget de L'Isle, was first heard at Mme. Dietrich's salon in April 1792.

I have always enjoyed the affection the English nation has for me and I confess my own predilection for it. I agree completely with Edmund Burke's opinion regarding the French anarchy. Immortal glory could be gained by its suppression, and undoubtedly this is reserved for the king of Prussia; if he wants to, he can gain it and thereby do a very great service to humanity.

Catherine II, to J.G. Zimmermann, letter of September 16, 1791 in Brueckner's
Catherine II *(1883).*

Do not believe our present situation would prevent us from striking the decisive blows! A people in the midst of a revolution is invincible! The flag of our liberty is the flag of victory! … Our enemies are opposed to the constitution; they want to reinstate the parlements and the nobility into their old positions … to strengthen the privileged rank of the king, of a man whose will can paralyze the will of a whole nation, who alone consumes 30 millions while millions of citizens suffer privation … Let us say to Europe that if the cabinets of the kings will involve them in a war against the peoples, we shall involve the peoples in a war against the kings … Finally, let us tell Europe that 10 million Frenchmen, inspired with the fire of liberty and armed with a sword, a pen, with reason and eloquence will be able, all by themselves, to change the face of the earth and to make all tyrants tremble on their thrones of clay …

Maximin Isnard, delegate from Departement Var, speech of November 29, 1791.

… there never was, nor is, nor ever will be, the least rational hope of making an impression on France by any Continental powers if England is not a part, is not the directing part, is not the soul of the whole confederacy against it … England, except during the eccentric aberration of Charles II (his alliance with Louis XIV against Holland, in 1670), has always considered it as her duty and interest to take her place in such a confederacy. Her chief disputes must ever be with France.

Edmund Burke, December 1791, Thoughts on French Affairs.

When we passed Sasbach we wanted to kiss the ground where a hellish shell put an end to the life of this famous commander [Turenne] ... besides, the news from France are so sad that we are afraid to learn them ... If the French who are faithful to the king think of us sometimes, they should worry about how most of those who have no money can make ends meet. By and by, lack of money is becoming the fate of everyone, no one is excepted. Unfortunately, none of us had foreseen that his absence would be such a long one ... But, dear father, I am glad not to have followed your advice by leaving my servant behind, particularly since I am so young ... I wish I had decided on that sooner ... I had no idea then that a man like I could live on 10-12 sous per day without running the risk of getting too thin ... This active and simple life is very healthy ... but one cannot help being touched and feeling pity for some comrades to whom it must be extremely arduous.

Comte Felix de Romains, to his father about life as an émigré officer in the Palatinate, letter of January 1792, Reminiscences of a Royalist Officer *(1824).*

Leopold [the Emperor] and Gustav [of Sweden who had just been assassinated], one a supporter, the other one the instigator of the alliance against the liberty of France, do no longer exist, and we have declared war on the head of the Austrian dynasty. Our enemies are amazed at our energy and frustrated by our fast action and will need some time to agree on what to do. Will Catherine II stick to the secret agreements she had made with Gustav and Leopold? Will the Swedish regency continue the project of the late king? And will Frederick William [II of Prussia] feel obliged to support Austria?

General Charles Dumouriez, dispatch of April 27, 1792, in Two Friends of Liberty's History of the French Revolution *(1790-93).*

I am unable to understand how we could ever get into a war without the slightest preparation!

Marquis de Lafayette, to the minister of war, letter of May 6, 1792, in Furet and Richet's The French Revolution *(1970).*

It is easy to see what confidence these armies gave us. He [the Count of Provence] received the following letter from Paris: "Everything works out as you wished it. The declaration of war saves you; one last effort and you will complete the great work ..." The Duke of Brunswick himself spoke of the campaign with incredible flippancy: "Monsieur I see with regret that we will not have any obstacle to overcome. In the interest of all I should have wished the Allies would meet with some resistance, for the French deserve a lesson such as will never be extinguished from their memory." Monsieur resented these words and answered, alluding to the defeat the Duke had suffered under Louis XV: "Take care, prince, not to get into an unforeseen rut! I fear the

During the great artillery duel of Valmy, Dumouriez and Kellermann force the Prussians to retreat.

French will contend with you for the terrain. They have not always been beaten."

Madame la Duchesse de Gontaut, on the émigré armies in Koblenz, Memoirs *(1891).*

Count d'Artois has come out and spent one quarter of an hour to talk to everybody and to show people what he felt. He said he was not dissatisfied with his trip ...there was some hope. He looked phantastic. Everybody said: "He is really our prince, our hope, the grandson of Henry IV." ... Everybody wanted to touch him. He had this charming grace which appeals to the French and, as the older ones assured us, the eyes of Louis XV ... No one thought of bad news, all regained their courage looking at him ... De Esterhazy has been sent to Russia, Baron d'Escard to Sweden; Baron de Roll follows the king of Prussia, M. de Flaslande will stay, I believe, in Vienna, the Duke de Havre in Spain. The emperor had misinterpreted England's answer ... M. de Calonne has used all his eloquence to clarify this ... The king of Prussia is reliable ... They say that at the consultations the Count d'Artois spoke with energy and eloquence which came from his heart ...

Marquise de Lage de Volude, on the émigrés in Koblenz, letter of summer 1792, in Daudet's History of the Emigration *(1904).*

England was eager to get her revenge for the loss of America and the Dutch alliance France had taken away from her. Seeing the poor state of the royal finances and the disorder prevailing in the kingdom she thought the moment for an important move had come. Her minister to the Porte, therefore ... persuaded the Turks to declare war on Russia exactly at the time when we tried very hard to guarantee them against an invasion as had been planned by the Empress of Russia and the [Holy Roman] Emperor for a long time ... The Porte, our ally, was induced to this action in order to make us suspect to Russia.

Pierre Joseph, Baron de Besenval, of England in 1792, Memoirs *(1821).*

Some of the German courts have emissaries here [in Paris]—all apostles of liberty—preaching equal rights and assuring the giddy multitude that their example will be followed by the whole world! Prussia for intrigue takes the lead. She pays court to each party as appearances may seem to favor. The Tuileries she disregards. All her agents vociferate against the house of

Austria as plotting with the queen for the purpose of destroying the Revolution.

William Augustus Miles, on Germany in 1792, Correspondence on the French Revolution, 1789-1817 *(1890).*

To emigrate had become a regular fashion. Every day, new coaches arrived at Koblenz, cabs and carriages of the court which were known as "pots de chambres." The elegant ladies of Paris played along. Publicly, they abused noblemen and military people who were disinclined to go abroad, proposing that they should settle down at the distaff.

Marquis de Bouthillier, summer of 1792, in de Broc's Ten Years in the Life of an Emigrant Woman *(1893).*

Since Monday night we are in France, 2 1/2 miles outside of Thionville. The village we are occupying is quite large, the inhabitants very patriotic and though they are quiet right now, not particularly intimidated by us. Thionville has not surrendered, the citizens seem determined to defend themselves. Heavy artillery will be moved up ... The former ministers have been reinstated. The police officers are passing by, bringing along a constitutional minister, handcuffed and gagged who is supposed to be one of the worst scoundrels. I talked to him. He claims that he swore the oath in good faith because the king had sanctioned the (civil) constitution. He refused to recant ... If we are victorious, nothing can stop us to march onto Paris, and to be there soon ... How sorry I am our parents are in Paris. May God inspire them to leave the city! Adieu. The trumpet is sounding. That means to get ready to march on.

Marquis de Falaiseau, to his wife, letter of summer 1792, in De Broc's Ten Years *(1893).*

When the armies withdrew, we were in Luxembourg ... The confusion after the defeat was awful. After each toilsome day we were looking for shelter ... the disappointment was great when we read the harsh words at the gates of the small towns: Entrance forbidden to jews and emigrants.

Duchesse de Gontaut, August 1792, Memoirs *(1891).*

I saw Monsieur de Boishue, father of my slaughtered comrade, as he marched lonely and mournfully through the mud, with bare feet, carrying his shoes on the tip of his bayonet in order to preserve them ... saw wounded soldiers ... and a chaplain ... kneeling and commending their souls to Saint Louis whose heir they had endeavoured to defend.

Vicomte Francois René de Chateaubriand,
August 1792, Memoirs from Beyond the
Tomb *(1849-50).*

The Prussians may get as far as Paris, but they will never leave from there.

Le Moniteur, *September 3, 1794 (as reported*
by Goethe in his 1822 work Kampagne in
Frankreich*).*

I returned to report d'Artois this change [Dumouriez' retreat]; he was with the Duke of Brunswick and had no doubts that he was informed, and greatly surprised that the Duke knew nothing about it ... He replied that I must be in error; Dumouriez would not be so stupid as to give up his position ... When he saw that he could not deceive anyone about the little success he had gained at such a favorable moment, he changed his tone and showed his displeasure, indignant that M. de Clerfayt had not cut off the enemy's retreat. But nobody was fooled ... I have been around him for too long and watched him too well not to realize that his capabilities were greater than those of the people who criticized him; if he showed lack of decision, foresight and skill it must be charged to his conscience, not his military talent.

He always entertained the idea in his soul to play the part of the mediator; but he thought too highly of the cause of the revolution to wish to dominate it as its conqueror. He believed that through his manifesto he could throw dust into the eyes of the brigands ... convinced he could succeed in a war of fanaticism ... by enlightening, without having to strike hard blows. The defeat of the Duke of Brunswick in this campaign must be seen as the result of the skill of his enemies, not of their superiority ...

Comte R. de Damas, before the battle of
Valmy, Memoirs *(1912).*

Our men were burning with desire to attack the French: Officers and ranks wished ardently the Supreme Commander would attack at this moment, and our fierce advance seemed to indicate this, too. But Kellermann had positioned himself too advantageously, and now the cannonade began of which much has been told but which, in its immediate violence one cannot describe, not even recall in one's imagination ... Cannon balls flew at us wildly while we did not grasp where they were coming from ... I kept sideways and had the most marvelous view: the shells hit the ground by the dozen, right in front of the squadron, but fortunately did not ricochet burrowing themselves into the soft ground. Yet muck and dirt splashed over men and horses; the black horses, kept together as much as possible by their excellent riders, panted and roared.

Finally the order came to retreat and descend ... only one horse was killed where all of us, particularly those at the extreme right wing, should have perished ... So the day had passed: The French stood unmoved, Kellermann had occupied a more comfortable position. Our men were pulled back from the firing line, and it all looked as if nothing had happened. There was general consternation spreading through the army. In the morning, we still had thought to spear all Frenchmen and devour them, and I myself had been lured into participation in this dangerous expedition by my complete confidence in such an army and the Duke of Brunswick. Now ... we did not look at each other, and when one did it was to curse ... We happened to close a circle when night fell in; no fire could be started this time. Most of us were silent, some talked, but no one seemed to be able to meditate or pass judgment. At last they asked for my opinion, for I had usually entertained the group with short aphorisms; this time I said: From here on, a new epoch in history begins, and you may say you have been there! [These last words were written down by Goethe only decades later.]

Johann Wolfgang von Goethe, at the begin-
ning of the battle of Valmy, September 20,
1792, Kampagne in Frankreich *(1822).*

... when we woke up, the mutual greetings were not at all cheerful; because we were aware of a hopeless, shameful position ... One had to admit that an armistice was desirable for even the most courageous, passionate person had to realize after thinking a little that an attack would be the most desperate undertaking ... For honor's sake we maintained the same position as at the beginning of the bombardment; only in the evening it was somewhat adjusted ... The wooded Argonne mountains from St. Menehould to Grandprée were occupied by the French, and their hussars conducted the boldest, most malicious little war from there. We had learned yesterday that a secretary of the Duke of Brunswick and other noble persons of his staff had been captured ... Where the bombardment had hit one looked at great misery. Men lay there, unburied and the badly wounded animals could not die ...

Goethe, September 21, 1792, Kampagne in Frankreich *(1822).*

The Prince von Hohenlohe proposed to attack the enemy at night, but the Duke refused. He was to spend the night in one room of the two houses of the farm; the other, less dirty one was reserved for the King of Prussia who had not slept nor eaten for two days ... The Duke fell into a deep sleep and while I heard him snore and ... watched him, I asked myself: How can a man sleep so quietly who missed such a favorable opportunity for a battle and who should be concerned with awaiting the next day, the suffering of his troops, the groaning of the wounded next door?

Damas, after the cannonade, Memoirs *(1912).*

We took the first row of earthwork with the bayonet; but the enemy doubled his efforts to defend the rest of the entrenchments. Canister shots, rifle salvos, cavalry attacks were used, but all failed before the courage of the French ... The most difficult part was the taking of the last entrenchments which were defended by the elite of the imperial troops, Hungarian grenadiers ... The undaunted Dumouriez, the generals Bournonville, Egalité [son of Philippe; later, King Louis-Philippe] and I have led the attacks at the head of the squadrons ... Soldiers from Paris and other cities of the republic have been living through incredible hardships, spending their nights in bivouacs, frozen stiff and drenched from the rains.

I cannot end without mentioning the bravery of the veteran Jolibois, my former comrade. He learned a few days before the battle that his son had deserted from his Paris bataillon. He arrives in the morning of the battle, taking over his son's station and tears ran from his eyes while he fired shot after shot at the slaves of despotism. He cried: "Oh my son, is it possible that so beautiful a day will be soiled by the thought of your cowardice." ... I recognized him after the battle for it had been my honor to serve with him, embraced him and shed tears of admiration. I wrote to the bravest of the brave, general Dumouriez, asking him to demand an officer's commission for this brave veteran.

Brigadier General Auguste Picot, Marquis de Dampierre, battle of Jemappes, November 6, 1792, "Report on the Conduct of the Troops of the Belgian Army," in Jonquière's Battle of Jemappes *(1902).*

The French emigrants have deceived our good king and all foreigners infamously. They had assured us there would be a counterrevolution as soon as we showed ourselves, that the regular troops were low riffraff and that the National Guards would run away after the first shot. Nothing of that is true. The emigrants have contributed nothing and the French troops resemble in no way the picture they had drawn for us. We have encountered good looking men and a very well trained cavalry. Their discipline is as good as that of our own troops. We have seen them execute manoeuvers which our generals could only admire. Their artillery is handled excellently; we learned that on September 20 for they killed many of our brave men.

Moniteur Universel, from a letter found on a dead Prussian officer, November 14, 1792.

For some hours, the Panisel ... and Jemappes, which protected Mons were shelled, but little damage was done to the enemy behind his huge fortifications. General Dumouriez called together all his grenadiers and addressed them as follows: "Comrades, we are fighting for the liberty of the peoples; you know the soldiers of the despots are afraid of the drawn sword. I have called you to ask if we can take this post [Mont Panisel] in hand-to-hand combat; if we can take it, we shall soon be the masters of Mons." The general had hardly finished when the grenadiers shouted: "Yes, general, let's go!" They took off their rifles, pouches and belts, and with sabres in their hands climbed heroically up the high fortifications, penetrated them and started a massacre such as history has rarely seen. After this position was taken, the two others and Mons were soon evacuated.

Moniteur Universel, on the fighting around Mons, November 14, 1792.

I would need the pen of Jeremy, my dear Vaudreuil to give you an idea of the situation since your departure ... I admit that I am desparately unhappy ... The emperor's silence embarrasses us immensely. M. de Metternich ... have advanced an amount of 87,000 francs ... but since we did not receive a Thaler from anyone else and the king of Prussia did not pay us the 100,000 francs he promised a month ago we were forced to spend part of the money on the most miserable of our companies to save them from starving and to pay the bakers and butchers ... We have knocked on so many doors where we had a right to hope for some money! But the defeat of the Austrians and their retreat to the

Meuse river caused all sources to dry up … We will not and cannot declare the dissolution of our army until we know the intentions of the court in Vienna and receive the money from the king of Prussia. But every thing is falling to pieces, involuntarily and dies of hunger … I have written to poor Calonne and asked him for resources; instead, I found out that the poor man was imprisoned because he had signed a promissory note for us …

Comte d'Artois (the future Charles X), to Marquis de Vaudreuil, letter of November 19, 1792, Intimate Correspondence *(1889).*

We should never rest until all of Europe is in flames. We should issue manifestoes in French and Spanish. We should inspire every mind to revolt or to accept the revolution.

Jacques Pierre Brissot de Warville, speech in November 1792, Correspondence and Papers *(1912).*

The further we penetrate into an enemy country, the more ruinous the war becomes for us, particularly because of our philosophical and generous principles … We declare incessantly that we are bringing freedom to our neighbors. We are also bringing them our ready money and our food; but they do not want to have anything to do with our assignats.

Pierre Joseph Cambon, speech of December 10, 1792, in Soboul's Summary of the History of the French Revolution *(1962).*

… while the French are doing all in their power to make the name of liberty odious to the world the despots are conducting themselves so as to show that tyranny is worse.

Charles James Fox, to his nephew, from a letter of December 1792, Memorials and Correspondence *(1970).*

I am charged to notify you, Sir, that, since the character and functions with which you were invested at this court are today entirely annulled by the Death of His Most Christian Majesty, you have no longer any public character here, and His Majesty has judged it proper to order that you quit this kingdom within a week's delay.

Lord William Wyndham Grenville, Britain's foreign secretary, to the French ambassador, letter of January 1793, in Thompson's English Witnesses to the French Revolution *(1938).*

6. Paris and the Provinces: January to September 1793

THE HISTORICAL CONTEXT

Immediately after the execution of the king, the country faced major crises at home and abroad. The economy took a turn for the worse, the conflict between Gironde and Montagne intensified into a life or death fight, and in the provinces, particularly in the West, civil war raged. Foreign powers, in a frenzy over the king's execution, threatened intervention.

In spite of the warnings of Louis Saint-Just, more and more assignats had been issued by the government to pay off public debts. The peasants rightfully distrusted the paper money, which decreased in value from day to day, and held back their merchandise, so that food prices in the cities increased to such a level that people were starving. Radical measures against hoarders and war profiteers proposed by the extreme left were rejected by the leadership of the Gironde, which was violently attacked by Jean Paul Marat and his friends for not doing anything to combat the famine or the food riots and armed uprisings, which flared up in many parts of the country. Jean-Marie Roland de la Platière, the minister of the interior, an orthodox liberal who had been inspector of manufacture during the Old Regime, had to resign. Marat and the other Montagnards opposed the open endorsement of rioting and pillaging by Jacques Roux and his *enrags*, but their main target was the Gironde. Pushing aside the Girondists, the more energetic and reckless Montagnards and Jacobins took radical action—establishing the Revolutionary Tribunal, closely supervising departmental administrations through delegates from Paris, and organizing the Committee of Public Safety.

The greatest danger for the republic arose in the Vendée, the section of western France along the Bay of Biscay, particularly the wooded areas, which for years would become the center of resistance against the

Charlotte Corday on her way to execution

republican regime. The execution of the king had infuriated the devoutly religious, loyal peasants, supported and led by their local priests and clerics from other parts of the country who had refused to swear the loyalty oath to the republic. The huge conscriptions ordered in Paris met with violent opposition from the Vendéans, who also received help from England. Although largely led since April of 1793 by militarily trained aristocrats, the peasants also produced a number of fanatical and capable leaders of their own, such as Jacques Cathelineau, Gaston Bourdic and Jean-Nicholas Stofflet.

Until October of 1793, the Vendéans seemed invincible, and they continued their armed rebellion for several years, never quite being subdued until the very end of the republic. So bitter and merciless was the fighting in the Vendée that it resulted in many more deaths than in all the Reign of Terror. Right in the beginning, at Machecoul, a small town on the lower Loire loyal to the republic, victorious rebels massacred almost 600 republican officials, National Guardsmen and priests loyal to the government. In this section of the country the alliance of 1789 between peasants and the middle class seems never to have materialized; rather, the peasants went with the nobility against the bourgeoisie in the cities, partly because they apparently felt that the middle classes had obtained too large a share of the public property put on sale by the government.

New trouble developed with the military commanders. The republic had never shown much gratitude to them, probably adhering to Robespierre's dogma that one honors generals only after a war is over. Charles Francois Dumouriez, who had won important victories for the republic, lost at Neerwinden and was indicted immediately. Like the Marquis Joseph Paul Lafayette, he defected to the Austrians, taking along the son of Philippe Egalité, who in 1830 was to become king of France under the name of Louis-Philippe (the "bourgeois-king"). This act of treason not only undermined the reputation of the Gironde but also marked the downfall of Philippe Egalité, who despite his avowed devotion to the principles of the Revolution, fell under suspicion, was arrested and, in November of 1793, was guillotined.

The newly created Committee of Public Safety, at first dominated by Georges Danton, acted quickly. All army headquarters were taken under strict control by government agencies who, in a way, were the precursors of the red commissars of the Soviet army. Danton, thinking of the events of the previous September, declared: "We must learn from previous mistakes: We must be horrible, so that the people do not have to be." Meanwhile, the Girondists in Paris were fighting for survival as the majority of the radical Paris section demanded the removal of their leaders. The Gironde succeeded in putting Marat, their deadly enemy, before the Revolutionary Tribunal, but since its members were Montagnards, he was acquitted and triumphantly carried back to the Convention by the people. A similar attempt to have the radical leftists Jacques René Hébert and Jean Varlet arrested and to investigate the activities of the Paris Commune also failed. The establishment of maximum prices for food on May 4th was an important victory of the sansculottes, as was the loan enforced on the rich on May 20, 1793.

The end came for the Gironde in Paris with the uprising that began on May 31st and lasted for several days. On the first day, demonstrations by the masses resulted only in the dismissal of the Gironde investigating committee of 12 men. But on June 2, the Convention was surrounded by 80,000 National Guardsmen commanded by Francois Hanriot who prevented the delegates by force from coming out and pressured them finally into giving in to the demand of the Commune—the arrest of the Gironde leaders. This was a serious defeat of the idea of parliamentarism, and it finished the Gironde, but only in Paris.

In all the big cities of the south, the Gironde took over and organized armed resistance against the republic. Lyons, Bordeaux, Marseilles, Toulon, Nîmes and many other cities were temporarily lost to the central government. At the end of June, no less than 60 of the 83 departments were in the hands either of the Gironde or the Royalists, and by July of 1793 the democratic republic was teetering. One of its most radical and popular spokesmen, Jean Paul Marat was assassinated on July 13th. Charlotte Corday, who stabbed him in his bath, was of aristocratic background but had sympathized with the Revolution at first, until the actions of the Jacobins horrified her and reports about the Terror in Paris reached her through the Girondins, who had fled the capital and gathered at Caen in Normandy.

But the republic hit back and, in the long run, won out. A new, genuinely democratic constitution, designed to secure the central position of the parliament for all time, was quickly drafted and ratified, although its actual implementation was delayed until peacetime—which turned out to mean never. The last remnants of feudalism were abolished. Disobedient generals such as Comte Adam Philippe Custine were recalled, put on trial and executed, and on August 23, the *levée en masse*, compulsory military service, was introduced and organized by Lazare Nicolas Carnot. New, young generals like Mathieu Jouve Jourdan and Louis Lazare Hoche were promoted. In the south, Marseilles was reconquered and punished terribly: Hundreds of royalists and moderates were executed, and the city was renamed Ville-sans-Nom, city without a name. Toulon and Lyons were retaken too. In Paris the radical rioters under Jacques Roux were repulsed and he himself arrested, while at the same time the destitutes were appeased with a daily allowance.

Though the radicals Hébert and Roux considered themselves the legitimate heirs of Marat, the actual leadership by the end of July was firmly in the hands of Robespierre, who, as president of the Convention and of the Committee of Public Safety, exercised an ever-tightening dictatorship, supported by Saint-Just, Jacques Nicolas Billaud-Varenne, Jean-Marie Collot d'Herbois and Lazare Nicolas Carnot. Terror was now declared a legitimate means of government and the systematic devastation of the Vendée officially decreed.

CHRONICLE OF EVENTS

1793:

January 22: Roland retires as minister of the interior and is replaced by Dominique Joseph Garat.

January 28: Louis, the Comte de Provence, declares the imprisoned son of Louis XVI to be the new king, Louis XVII.

February 1: The value of the assignats sinks to 55 percent of their nominal value.

February 14: Jean-Nicolas Pache, former Girondist, now a Montagnard, is elected mayor of Paris.

February 21: Jacques Roux demands the death penalty for war profiteers and racketeers.

February 25: Food rioting breaks out in Paris. Foodstores are looted. The Convention decides to call 300,000 more men to arms.

March 3: A royalist insurrection breaks out in Brittany.

March 4: At Cholet (Departément Maine-et-Loire) riots occur against the levy of "volunteers" for the army.

March 10: In Paris, another riot organized by Roux's *enragés* is suppressed. A Revolutionary Tribunal is created whose decisions are irrevocable. Antoine Quentin Fouquier-Tinville becomes public prosecutor.

March 11: The Convention sends representatives to all departments to supervise their administrations. Royalist insurrections begin in the Vendée: Peasants, noblemen and priests against the urban bourgeoisie.

March 14: The Vendée rebels conquer Cholet.

March 18: The Convention decrees the death penalty against all those engaged in enterprises directed against private property. This is directed mainly against the enragés.

March 19: Death penalty is decreed against all mutineers in the Vendée. Republican troops at Pont-Charrault in the Vendée are defeated.

March 21: Supervising committees against foreigners and suspects are instituted in all communes and sections.

March 28: New, more rigorous laws against the emigrants are enacted.

The death of Jean Paul Marat

A revolutionary committee

April 1: The value of the assignat drops to 43 percent. In order to indict Marat, the Gironde has the immunity of delegates suspended.

April 5: Dumouriez, who is being investigated because of his defeat at Neerwinden, defects to the Austrians, and with him goes Philippe Egalité's son, the future King Louis Philippe. Egalité is arrested the next day.

April 6: The Committee of Public Safety (*Comité du Salut Public*) is created as executive organ of the Convention. It has almost unlimited powers. Danton dominates it.

April 9: Government agents with unlimited authority are attached to all army headquarters.

April 11: The assignats are made compulsory.

April 13: The Vendéans are victorious at Aubiers.

April 15: Pache, the mayor of Paris, demands in the name of 35 of the 48 sections the removal of 22 leading Girondists.

April 16: Conscripts at Orléans revolt.

April 22: The Vendéans win two victories under Charles Melchior Bonchamp and Maurice Joseph Louis d'Elbée.

April 24: Marat is acquitted before the Revolutionary Tribunal.

April 29: In Marseilles, an anti-mountain-party committee is founded.

May 1: Demonstration at Paris's Faubourg Saint-Antoine demands maximum prices and an enforced loan upon the rich.

May 4: Maximum prices for grain and flour are decreed.

May 5: Republican general Quétineau surrenders to the Vendéans under Comte Henri de La Rochejaquelein at Thouars. Another 1,200 million assignats are issued.

May 10: The Convention moves from the Manège to the old theater in the Tuileries.

May 20: A loan of 1,000 million livres is enforced on the wealthy.

May 24: The Gironde, through the Committee of Twelve that investigates the Paris Commune, has Hébert and Varlet arrested. They are acquitted on May 27.

May 25: Fontenay is taken by the Vendéans.

May 26: Rebellion breaks out in Corsica under Pascal Paoli.

May 29: Revolt begins in Lyons. Royalists and moderates upset the Mountain party administration. Mayor Joseph Chalier is executed in July and is declared a "martyr of liberty" in Paris.

May 31: Paris rises against the Gironde. The Convention is besieged but does not give in.

June 2: The masses enforce the arrest of 29 Girondists, including Jacques Pierre Brissot, Pierre Vergniaud and Jérôme Pétion.

June 6-7: In reaction to the overthrow of the Gironde, revolts begin in Marseilles, Nîmes, Toulouse and Bordeaux.

June 9: The Vendéans conquer Saumur (Maine-et-Loire). Revolt begins in the Calvados Département.

June 10: The last remnants of feudal institutions in the provinces are abolished.

June 13: Fugitive Gironde leaders meet at Caen (Departément Calvados) and decide on civil war against the Paris regime. At this time, about 60 of the 83 departments are hostile to Paris.

June 18: The Vendéans take Angers (Maine-et-Loire).

June 24: The new, entirely democratic constitution, inspired by the Mountain Party, is accepted. It will never come into effect.

June 25: Jacques Roux reads his *Manifesto of the Enraged* to the Convention. He is booed.

July 3: Republican troops under Francois Joseph Westermann take Chatillon, which is reconquered by the Vendéans two days later.

July 4: Marat violently attacks the Committee of Public Safety, also Roux and the enragés.

July 10: Danton resigns from the Committee of Public Safety.

July 13: Marat is assassinated by Charlotte Corday. A Paris volunteer corps defeats the Gironde troops in Normandy.

July 17: Charlotte Corday is given the death penalty.

July 18: The Vendéans win a major victory at Vihiers.

July 22: The arrest of Custine is ordered by the Convention.

July 24: Jean Antoine Rossignol is made commander of the government troops in the Vendée.

July 26: The property of emigrants is offered for sale.

Sweeping price controls prevented a catastrophic fall of the assignats.

July 27: Maximilien Robespierre presides over the Committee of Public Safety; beginning of his dictatorship.

August 1: The Convention decrees the systematic devastation of the Vendée. The decimal system is adopted in France.

August 4: The new constitution is ratified.

August 8: General Francois Etienne Kellermann begins the siege of rebellious Lyons.

August 14: The Vendéans are beaten before Lucon. Carnot and Claude Antoine Prieur enter the Committee of Public Safety.

August 22: Temporary arrest of Jacques Roux.

August 23: After a speech of Bertrand Barère, the *levée en masse*, compulsory military service applying to all males between 18 and 25, is introduced; to be organzied by Carnot. Hoche and Jourdan are made generals.

August 24: The "Great Book of Public Debts" is created.

August 25: Marseilles is taken by government troops before the British can come to help. Terror under Barras and Fréron begins.

August 28: Custine is condemned to death and executed.

September 5: Masses of sansculottes demonstrate and invade the Convention, demanding stricter measures against the opposition. The arrest of suspects and the levying of new troops is decreed, as well as another loan enforced. Jacques Roux is again arrested. Convention and Committee of Public Safety acknowledge the Terror as a legitimate means of government. The Vendéans are victorious at Chardonnay.

September 6: Collot d'Herbois and Billaud-Varenne join the Committee of Public Safety to supervise the government representatives in the departments.

September 9: A revolutionary army is organized and put under the command of General Charles Philippe Ronsin, an Hébertist. The destitute in Paris are granted a daily allowance of 40 sous.

September 11: The law regarding maximum prices for grain is extended over the whole of France.

September 16: The Vendéans under François Athanase Charette are defeated at Montaigu.

EYEWITNESS TESTIMONY

But citizens, let us be generous. Le Peletier's life was beautiful; even in his death he serves the republic! Generous citizen, I envy you for your death … One has demanded the Pantheon for him. Certainly, already he has won the palm of liberty. Yes, I also vote in favor of the Pantheon.

Georges Danton, speech after the January 21, 1793, assassination of Le Peletier.

The uprisings which took place in Paris yesterday are the work of this criminal faction [the Right] and its agents. They are the ones who sent secret messengers into the sections to stir up unrest. You have seen how 5 or 6 days ago seditious citizens … arrived here to demand fatal measures. And when the patriots wished to report these intrigues to you the messengers of the Roland faction kept them away from you; and because I, in my indignation, said the shops of the usurers should be ransacked and they should be strung up on their doorframes as the only effective means to save the people … one dares to demand an indictment against me … [His speech was constantly interrupted by exclamations of disgust and horror.]

Jean Paul Marat, on the riots, speech to the Convention of February 26, 1793.

The grocers have only been forced to return to the people what, by their high prices, they had taken from them for a long time.

Jacques Roux, speech after the Paris food riots of February 1793, Writings and Documents (1969).

The general reflections [by Robespierre] you have heard, are quite correct, but right now the main thing is to investigate the reason for the events before we apply remedies hastily. When a house is on fire I do not throw myself at the scoundrels who want to ransack it, but I first extinguish the fire. I am telling you, citizens, that

Dumouriez' dispatches must convince you that not a moment should be lost to mobilize all resources of the nation … Dumouriez has not lost courage. He has taken Gertruydenberg. He has war material everywhere. All he needs is soldiers, and France is full of them …

Where is the center of our enemies' activities? It is in the English cabinet. Pitt knows well that there will be no mercy since he has everything to lose … Citizens, this is not the time to contemplate but to act. You have a decree [on appointing commissioners for special missions with the armies]; this decree must carry our determination everywhere. The commissioners must start out at once, they must leave this very night … France has been in a similar situation once before when the enemy had invaded France. Then I told those who called themselves patriots: Your quarrels hurt liberty. Leave me, you all are traitors. Let us beat the enemy, we can have debates later. I said: What do I care if they defile my name, if only France is free! … Beware! The rich should hear this: Our conquests must pay for our debts or else the rich must pay them, and soon !

Danton, speech of March 10, 1793.

Let us learn from the mistakes of our predecessors. Let us do what the Legislative Assembly did not do: Let us be terrible so that the people do not have to be terrible; let us organize a tribunal, not a good one, that is impossible, but no worse than necessary, so that the people may know that the sword of the law is hanging above the heads of all its enemies.

Danton, speech in the evening of March 10, 1793.

I ask for permission to speak [Marat interrupts: "… to waste our time!"] … On the day when the instigators of the first food riots were left unpunished new conspiracies were started, at the expense of the republic … So, proceeding from crime to amnesty, from amnesty to crime a great number of citizens began to confuse the seditious riots with the great uprising for liberty … A tyrant of antiquity had an iron bedstead on which he laid his victims: those taller than the bed were mutilated, those who were smaller had their limbs stretched to bring them up to size. This tyrant was a friend of equality and the equality of the scoundrels is the one which will tear you to pieces. For the members of a society, equality is only the equality of rights.

Pierre Victurnien Vergniaud, speech of
March 13, 1793.

A great nation in the middle of a revolution is like the ore seething in the smelting furnace: The statue of liberty has not yet been cast … If you do not know how to handle the smelting furnace, it will devour you all … Roland—I just want to mention this one fact and ask you to forget it then at once—has written to Dumouriez in a letter he showed to me and to Delacroix: "You have to join up with us to destroy that party in Paris, and above all Danton." [Shouts of indignation.] Judge yourselves, citizens, whether a brain which can produce such thoughts, whether a man who is right at the center of the republic has exercized an evil influence or not. … Our enemies have had some successes; while we have contemplated, the despots have gathered their strength and driven us back. But a Frenchman who retreats and stands again on his country's soil, is gaining new power, like that mythical giant …

Danton, speech of March 27, 1793.

Beurnonville received another letter from Dumouriez, complaining again about the cowardliness of his soldiers and the plundering they indulged in. He praised the moderation and decency of the Austrians. He claimed that the Convention exercised no authority, and that the country would be in extreme danger as long as the country remained under the control of certain people … the forts were deprived of garrisons … the enemy could easily take them and march on Paris. He called France a "kingdom." There was a great outburst of indignation at this recital. No longer could there be a doubt that Dumouriez was either a traitor or insane; some thought he was both.

Antoine Claire Thibaudeau, Dumouriez's
treason, March 29, 1793, Memoirs of the Convention and the Directory (1824).

Misery is one of the reasons which can compel a people to long back to servitude. [some voices: "you are slandering the people."] No, I do not slander it at all, but bread is needed above all other things. I propose

that in view of the misery in the provinces devastated by the civil war people there will be released of their overdue taxes. [Many deputees shout: "Only the rich would profit from that."]

Marat, speech of April 2, 1793.

The only men then worthy of having their place in history were the Girondists. No doubt that deep in their hearts they felt repentance over the way they had overthrown the monarchy; when the same methods were used against them, whereby they recognized their own weapons in the wounds they now received, they must have contemplated the quick justice of revolutions.

Mme. Germaine de Staël, in April 1793, The Reasons for the Principal Events of the French Revolution (1818).

One used to assume that man was wild and murderous by nature, in order to claim the right to enslave him. Thus the principle of slavery and misery of man … has even been declared to be sacred; according to the belief of the tyrants, he considered himself a savage and in his gentleness he tolerated … being tamed. Only in the judgment of their oppressors men are savage, they never were so to one another … The French monarchy has perished because the rich class instilled the other classes with hatred against work.

Antoine Louis Léon de Saint-Just, speech of April 24, 1793, Works (1834).

The great masses of the people have more instinct and genius for the revolution than those who think of themselves as great men. In a nation, great men account for no more than tall trees in a vast forest … The rich! If contributions are demanded of them, they can only benefit from that. For the large proprietors, the big capitalists, it is a real advantage to sacrifice so that the enemy cannot invade our territory. The greater the sacrifice, the more property will be respected and maintained … Just see the tremendous resources which will all at once be at the disposal of France: Paris has innumerable riches: Well, by the decree you have issued this sponge will be squeezed dry … There will be enough advantages left to those who are privileged by fate …

Danton, speech of April 27, 1793.

Scarcely a day passed on which Danton did not come to see me … I looked into this cruel and ugly face; and though I kept on reminding myself that one should not judge without investigating, that I could not be certain of anything against him, and that even the most honest of men may, at a time of such political turmoil, have conflicting reputations, and, finally, that one must not trust appearances, I still could not imagine an upright man with a face like his.

Mme. Jeanne Manon Roland de la Platière,
April and May 1793, in Beugnot's Memoirs
(1866).

A sansculotte, my rascally gentlemen? That is one who always walks on foot, who does not possess millions as you would love to possess, no castles, no lackeys to serve him, and who lives, with his wife and children, if he has any, very simply on the 4th or 5th floor. He is useful for he knows how to plow a field, to forge, to saw, to rasp—and how to shed the last drop of his blood for the welfare of the republic. And since he is working, you may be sure not to meet him at the Café Chartres, nor in the gambling joints where the conspirators sit ... In the evening, he joins his section, not nicely made up, powdered and in high boots hoping that all women in the galeries notice him—no, rather to support with all his strength the good proposals and to kill all those hailing from the pitiful clique of the ruling politicians. By-the-way: A sansculotte always keeps his sword drawn to cut off the ears of all enemies of the revolution. At times, he walks calmly, carrying his pike; but at first beat of the drum you will see him march into the Vendée, or join the army of the Alps or of the North.

Vingternier, spokesman for the sansculottes,
draft for a publication, April 1793, in Two
Friends of Liberty's History of the French
Revolution of 1789 (1790-93).

Citizens, the fact that the conspiracy of May 10 remained unpunished, has brought disorder in your sessions and has exposed you to the plots of the rioters. If this conspiracy that just misfired will not be punished, then it will produce new ones until you and liberty have been devoured by the horrors of anarchy.

Vergniaud, speech of May 24, 1793.

May 31 was the day they had set for the uprising, on which the National Convention would be dispersed and the victims would perish under the murderers' swords ... Drums were beating the general alarm, couriers were stopped, barriers closed, letters intercepted. From the tribunes of the popular societies cruel proposals were shouted and repeated ... There was no doubt that the 31st was the fatal date set by the leaders

because they had seals engraved in advance showing the words: "The Revolution of May 31."

Jérôme Pétion, Memoirs (1866).

Lafayette and his faction have quickly been unmasked: today, the new enemies of the people have given themselves away: they fled; they changed their names and stations, they secured forged passports for themselves. This Brissot, leader of the villainous sect which will soon be extinguished, this man who emphasized his courage and modesty by accusing me of having my pockets filled with gold, today he is but a miserable creature who cannot escape the sword of the law ... This constitution [of 1793] is a battery which fires its canister shot against the enemies of liberty and will destroy them all; form some armed forces, but against the enemies in the Vendée. Wipe out the rebellion in this part of France and you will have peace. Once the people have been informed about this latest phase of the revolution, one will no longer be able to take it by surprise. There will be heard no more calumnies against a city which has created liberty and which will not perish, but triumph and gain immortality with liberty.

Georges Danton, speech of June 13, 1793.

In the last four years, the rich have harvested the fruits of the revolution ... It is time that the fight for death and life between the workers and the profit-makers comes to an end ... Yours is not a democracy, for you permit riches. The rich have reaped the fruits of the revolution during the last four years ... It is time that the death struggle between the workers and the profiteers should come to an end ...

Roux, speech to the National Convention,
June 25, 1793.

... time and time again you have promised us to annihilate the bloodsuckers of the people. Now the constitution is to be presented to the sovereign people for approval; have you, in it, outlawed stock exchange speculation? No! Have you defined what freedom of trade consists of? No! Have you set the death penalty against hoarders? No! Have you prohibited the sale of coined money? No! Well, so we declare that you have not done everything for the happiness of the people. Liberty is but an empty illusion as long as one class can let the other starve. Equality is but an empty illusion as long as the rich, by means of his monopoly, decides over life and death of fellowmen. The republic is but an empty illusion as long as the counterrevolution is working day and night, escalating all food prices which three quarter of the citizen can pay only with tears in their eyes …

For four years only the rich have profited from the advantages of the revolution. The aristocracy of the merchants, more horrible than that of the nobles and priests, have made a cruel game out of snatching the private fortunes and finances of the republic for themselves … Delegates of the mountain, why have you not climbed up to the upper floors, from the third to the ninth, of the houses in this revolutionary city? Your hearts would have softened, seeing the tears and sighs of a vast population without bread or clothes which fell into this abyss of misery through the fault of the speculators and hoarders, for the laws were cruelly against the poor, as they were made only by the rich and for the rich … Admit that in your faintheartedness you approve of the devaluation of the assignats, that you favor state bankruptcy by tolerating encroachments and crimes that despotism in the last days of its brutal power would have been ashamed of.

Roux, June 25, 1793, from "The Manifesto of the Enraged," Writings and Documents (1969).

You have described representatives of the people … as instigators of civil war in your reports. Instead I denounce you to France as impostors and murderers, and will prove it. Impostors: If you had believed the accused member to be guilty, you would have reported that at once and asked for impeachment … Murderers: You did not dare to bring them before the tribunal where their innocence and your disgrace would have been revealed, but subjected them to the vilest suspicion and extreme danger of the people's revenge … Impostors: If all you say were true you would not be afraid to recall them … Murderers: You strike at them only from behind. Impostors: You accuse them of instigating troubles … which you yourself and other members of your committee have incited. [Remarks directed against Barère and Lindet.]

Vergniaud, speech to the Committee of Public Safety, June 28, 1793.

They were further displeased by the new oath demanded of the priests. As they found themselves deprived of the curates they had been accustomed to, who knew their habits and their way of speaking, who with few exceptions belonged to the country and whom they had known and respected, and now found them

replaced by strangers, they no longer attended mass at their parishes. The sworn-in priests were deserted or insulted … This war was not, as has been claimed, instigated by the nobles and priests … The uprisings began at the spur of the moment, without a plan, without concert, almost without a hope, for what could such a small group of men, with no means at their disposal, achieve against the arms of the whole of France? Their first victories went much beyond their own expectations.

Mme. Marie Louise de La Rochejaquelein, on the peasants of the Vendée, Memoirs (1817).

The fighting began on March 12, 1793. The peasant rose up at La Bretière. Then they spread to the neighborhood parishes and approached M. Sapinaud de Bois-Huguet who was better known as La Verrie. "We make you our general and you must lead us," they said. He told them, "My friends, this is an earthen pot against an iron pot, weak against strong. How much can we do, one department against eighty-two? We will be beaten …" But these honest peasants were far from accepting his reasons, remonstrating that they would not obey a government which had deprived them of their priests and put their king in prison. "We have been abused. Why are they sending us constitutional priests? " they said. "These are not the ones who stood at the deathbeds of our fathers, and they should not be blessing our children." My brother-in-law … hesitated to endanger these good people and himself to an almost certain death. But he finally gave in to their pleadings, putting himself at their head …

Mme. de Sapinaud, Historical Memoirs of the Vendée (1824).

… the once so modest … [leader of the Vendée rioters] Charette could hardly be recognized: His violet clothes were embroidered with green silk and silver … and some pretty young women followed his entourage … The rearguard was less glamorous: Many women from the quarters of poverty, most of them barefoot … in rags, as were their little children; their men had been killed, their huts burnt down … they had no other refuge but the army …

Mme. de Sapinaud, May 1793, Memoirs (1824).

… different people, a complete adherence to their cause, unlimited confidence in their leaders, a fidelity to their promises which made any further discipline unnecessary, and an incredible courage in all kinds of dangers and miseries: These made the Vendéans such formidable enemies and makes them one of the greatest fighting people in history. The Vendéans were, in short, French, inspired by the twofold fanaticism of religion and royalty. They were victorious for a long time and would have been unconquerable, except by French republicans.

Baron Louis-Marie de Linières Turreau,
Memoirs to Serve the History of the War in
the Vendée (1824).

A method of fighting hitherto unknown and probably inimitable as it can only be practiced in this part of the country and probably has something to do with the special disposition of its inhabitants ... Their attack is a terrible, sudden and almost always unforeseen bursting forth because good reconnoitering is difficult in the Vendée ... to prevent any surprises ... Before there is time to orient yourself one is under such rapid firing that it cannot be compared at all with what is set forth in our own firing regulations ... They disperse, escape over fields and hedges, through forests and bushes since they know all the paths. When they are victorious, they surround you, cut off every way of escape and pursue you with incredible fury, tenacity and speed ... Let them [the officers] tell you if they would not rather fight for a year at the borders than for a month in the Vendée.

Turreau, Memoirs (1824).

The attempt of the French people to reinstate their sacred human rights and to obtain their political freedom, has only revealed its ineptitude and unworthiness, and has thrown back into barbarism and slavery a great part of Europe and a whole century.

Friedrich von Schiller, letter of July 13, 1793,
Works (1825).

Last night at eight o'clock, Marat was assassinated by a woman who for several days had asked for him under the pretense of pleading for mercy on behalf of the citizens of Orléans. He was taking a bath when the murderess thrust a dagger into his chest. He was dead on the spot. The woman did not attempt to flee. She stayed quietly in her carriage and waited to be arrested. "Do what you want," she cried, "the deed is done, the monster is dead."

Gazette Francaise, July 14, 1793.

... I have avenged many innocent victims, and prevented numerous other miseries; some day, the people will recognize this and be happy for having been freed from a tyrant ... I hope you will not be persecuted ... Forget me, or, even better, rejoice over my lot ... You know your daughter; she would not have been motivated by unworthy causes ... and do not forget the verse of Corneille: "The crime is shameful, not the scaffold."

Charlotte Corday, to her father, letter of July
16, 1793, in La Varende's Mademoiselle de
Corday (1946).

... a certain Legros, one of the executioner's assistants, grasped her head to show it to the people and took the liberty to slap it several times; this barbarian deed was disapproved by the people ... He [Marat] was too great to have consented to such a base action; he knew, and everyone should know that the law has been complied with when the crime has been punished.

Citizen Roussillon, on the execution of Char-
lotte Corday, letter to Chronique de Paris
(July 16, 1793).

On August 2 [1793] they woke us up at two in the morning to read a decree of the Convention to my mother ... she was brought to the Conciergerie to be put on trial ... When she arrived, they put her in the dirtiest, dampest, unhealthiest room of the whole building. She was being watched constantly by a gendarme who never left her, day or night ... They elaborated on all those disgraceful ... the very idea of these things could only have occurred to people of this kind. Her answer to all these shameful accusations was : "I appeal to all mothers." The people were touched. The judges ... hurried to send her to her death. My mother listened to the sentence with great composure.

Marie-Thérèse Charlotte de France (Madame
Royale), Memoirs of the Captivity (1892).

The enemies in our midst have yet to be punished, those you have already arrested and the ones you still have to capture. The Revolutionary Tribunal must be divided into a sufficiently great number of sections ... so that every day one aristocrat, one criminal will pay with his head for his crimes.

Danton, speech of September 5, 1793.

Where the cannon does not help, gold should do the work; and when Pitt's guineas attack the fundaments of freedom, why not undermine the enemy likewise? It makes no sense to let only the enemy apply such means. Fifty millions are at the disposal of the committee. I claim that with only three or four millions we could already have reconquered Toulon for France and hanged the traitors who turned it over to the English

... One must fight the enemy with all available means, must even use his own; one even must exploit the vices of individuals. Consider, at last, these new methods which can help to bring the cause of the people to triumph.

Danton, speech of September 6, 1793.

7. The Terror: September 17, 1793 to July 28, 1794

THE HISTORICAL CONTEXT

The ideological groundwork for the Reign of Terror was laid on September 5 when the National Convention and the Committee of Public Safety declared terror measures as admissible and necessary means of government. But the Terror began in earnest on September 17, 1793, when the law of suspects was passed, its definition of "suspect" being so vague that it left practically everyone at the mercy of the government and its prosecutors.

The period now beginning, which ended quite abruptly with the fall of Maximilien Robespierre, is certainly the most dramatic of the Revolution and has been described most often by historians and fiction writers. The Reign of Terror is usually associated with the name of one man, Robespierre, who, in the beginning of 1794 achieved almost limitless power. Yet he was not a dictator in the modern sense of the word but ruled by the strength of his convictions, his personal integrity and absolute incorruptibility and his skill as a tactician. A pupil of Jean-Jacques Rousseau, whom he liked to quote, he was a strange mixture of dogmatist and compromising parliamentarian. He was not a great orator like the Comte de Mirabeau or Georges Danton, but his power of persuasion in committees and clubs must have been extraordinary.

For one year he had to keep the balance among left extremists, atheists and sansculottes on the one side and antirevolutionaries, royalists, war profiteers and reactionaries on the other. In the process, his application of the Terror in Paris became increasingly more extreme. In the provinces and reconquered cities, it was even worse. Jean Baptiste Carrier at Nantes, Guislain Francois Le Bon at Arras, Jean Lambert Tallien at Bordeaux, Georges Auguste Couthon, Joseph Fouché and Jean Marie Collot d'Herbois at Lyons, a city that suffered probably more than any other,

Detailed drawing of a true guillotine

95

Antoine Quentin Fouquier-Tin-ville, "l'Accusateur public"

exterminated the "Enemies of Liberty" with ruthless efficiency. In the meantime, more assignats were issued and the new Republican Calendar was officially introduced. Sweeping price controls covering many commodities and wages helped to prevent a catastrophic fall of the assignats and ensured the provisioning of the armies.

New dangers loomed for the regime of the Committee of Public Safety, which by now had been given almost unlimited authority. One was the anti-Christian movement of the left, headed by Jacques René Hébert, the Jacobin and journalist. It considered all priests as monarchists and enemies of the people, advocated the recasting of church bells into cannons and tried to replace the saints of the Catholic Church with heroes of Greek and Roman history. Robespierre, a convinced deist, saw that this philosophy would never be accepted by the people and would further antagonize foreign countries. To combat Hébert's radical worship of Reason, he needed and obtained Danton's help. While in November the church of Notre Dame had been converted into a Temple of Reason, the National Convention confirmed the freedom of religion and worship one month later. Worshipping the Supreme Being was also promoted by Robespierre, and culminated in the great festival of June 8, 1794, at which he acted as the high priest.

Another conflict had developed in October of 1793. A sudden fear of a "conspiracy of foreigners" focused on Thomas Paine, Anacharsis Cloots and a number of foreign businessmen, who were accused of tempting the republic into ultra-extreme measures and thereby deliberately ruining it. This suspicion originated with the sansculottes, who were inclined to be hostile to strangers, and was probably furthered by a case of financial corruption in connection with the old East India Company in which a number of foreign bankers and members of the Hébertist faction had been involved. Some Dantonists were also implicated. Danton himself had come out of retirement and, together with his friend Desmoulins, started on a campaign of "indulgence," a policy of conciliation, under the motto: Enough blood has been spilled. Unfortunately, the winter of 1793-94 was particularly hard on the Paris population, and the indulgents could not overcome Robespierre's resistance, who consistently pursued his Reign of Terror.

Throughout these controversies, the Committee of Public Safety remained in full control, with Robespierre in command. In March of 1794, he managed to get rid of his last remaining rivals: First, with Danton's support, Hébert and his Cordeliers, then Danton and his followers also. After the fall of the Hébertists, Danton had apparently assumed he could get back into his former position of power, but Robespierre wouldn't let Danton take the reins out of his hands. Danton's oratorical abilities were so feared that, during his trial before the Revolutionary Tribunal, he was silenced by the Committee of Public Safety, upon Louis Saint-Just's proposal, because he had "shown no respect for justice."

Danton's trial was a farce; but his personality and merits are as controversial as those of Robespierre. Alphonse Aulard saw him as a great patriot and statesman, while Albert Mathiez considered him an unscrupulous demagogue. There is no doubt that his energy and powerful voice, which always called for unity, did much to save France in such critical situations as September of 1792.

While the form of parliamentarism remained unchanged, Robespierre ruled through the committee for four more months. The mass executions of suspects went on. An even stricter and more comprehensive terror law was enacted on June 10, permitting condemnations without the hearing of any evidence. As a result, during the last six weeks of the regime the number of death sentences surpassed those of the whole preceding year. The pretext for this law had been the discovery of assassination attempts against Robespierre and his colleague Collot d'Herbois, former terrorist at Lyons.

No historian has yet provided an exact explanation of what actually happened on July 27th, the Ninth of Thermidor, and what caused the sudden fall of Robespierre. These events may never be reconstructed completely because the written testimony of witnesses capable of giving us a reasonably complete view of these tumultuous events does not exist. The conspirators—Tallien, Billaud-Varenne, Collot d'Herbois, Barère and probably Fouché and Carnot—had been close collaborators of Robespierre's until almost the last day. They did not constitute a uniform faction, but they all probably felt imperiled by Robespierre's last speech against "traitors," whose names he did not mention. Moreover, the revolutionary fervor of the masses had receded in recent months; Saint-Just had remarked that the revolution had "frozen."

There was also a general feeling that enough or too much blood had been shed. Many were indignant about the way Danton, a national hero, had been treated, and during the wild session of the Convention on July 26, some delegates had shouted at Robespierre: "Danton's blood is choking you!" Another underlying reason may have been that after the military successes of Jean Baptiste Jourdan and Jean Charles Pichegru, the general situation of the country had sufficiently improved to make so oppressive a regime unnecessary. At any rate, the Paris Commune, on whose support Robespierre and his friends had relied, was slow to rally to him and lacked proper leadership, so that Paul Francois Barras, until recently one of the most feared terrorists and now directed by the Convention to uphold law and order, had no trouble in gathering some troops and preventing any interference on the part of the population.

Both Robespierre and his friend and aide Saint-Just, who had done a tremendous job in activating and inspiring the armies in the field and who was partly responsible for the recent French victory at Fleurus, were unusually talented and self-sacrificing men, idealists who realized, however, that "he who rules cannot remain innocent," as Saint-Just himself had declared during the trial of Louis XVI. Neither of them knew or cared much about the laws of economy, and their bourgeois background and belief in a free economy could not be reconciled either with the wishes of the masses, with whom they wanted to work, or the necessities of the war situation, which strained the resources of the country to the utmost. With the Ninth of Thermidor, the Revolution did not come to an end, but the chances for a genuinely democratic republic built on equality had been dealt a deadly blow.

CHRONICLE OF EVENTS

1793:

September 17: Reign of Terror begins when Couthon, member of the Committee of Public Safety, introduces the law of suspects. Whole groups of people are declared as suspect, and a tremendous number of trials and death sentences follow.

September 18: Republican power is reestablished at Bordeaux. Terror begins under Tallien and Isabeau.

September 21: By decree of the Convention, all women must wear the tricolor cockade.

September 26: First issue of Robespierre's *l'Anti-Fédéraliste* published.

September 28: Another 2,000 million assignats are issued.

September 29: General maximum law enacted: Upper limits set for food and other commodities but also for wages. Reporting of storages made mandatory.

October 1: The Paris prisons now hold 2,400 suspects.

October 3: Brissot and 44 other deputies brought to trial, bringing the total number of indicted deputies to 136. Marie Antoinette is indicted.

Transfer of René Descartes' ashes to the Panthéon is decided. The Convention starts on an anti-Christian policy.

October 5: The new republican calendar of September 22, 1792, comes into effect.

October 9: Lyons is taken by the republican forces, after a two-month siege. Many people are killed; part of the city, which is renamed Ville-Affranchie, is demolished.

October 10: A Revolutionary Government is sanctioned for the duration of the war. The Committee of Public Safety obtains additional dictatorial powers.

October 16: Marie Antoinette is condemned and executed.

October 17: Generals Jean-Baptiste Kléber and Francois Séverin Marceau are victorious over the Vendéans at Cholet.

October 23: The Vendéans take Laval and unite with the Chouans under Jean Cottereau.

July 27th (9th Thermidor) marked the sudden fall of Robespierre.

The execution of Robespierre and his accomplices, Saint-Just and Couthon

October 25: Vendéans win again at Entrammes.

October 31: Twenty-one prominent Girondists, among them Brissot and Vergniaud, are guillotined. Saint-Just imposes a tax of nine million on the rich at Strasbourg. The Committee of Public Safety now addresses people officially with "thou" (*tu*), instead of *vous*.

November 6: The Convention recognizes the right of communities to renounce the Catholic cult and to replace local saints by heroes of antiquity etc.

November 7: Philippe Egalité is guillotined. Manon Jeanne Roland, wife of Jean Marie Roland de la Platière, is guillotined. He had escaped the tribunal but at the news of her death commits suicide. Antoine Pierre Barnave is guillotined.

November 10: At Notre Dame in Paris, now called the Temple of Reason, a ceremony celebrating liberty and reason, as promoted by Hébert and his friends, is conducted.

November 11: Jean Sylvain Bailly, astronomer and former mayor of Paris, is executed. Saint-Just charges the rich at Nancy with a five million tax.

November 14: The Vendéans who had taken Avranches are defeated and are being pushed back to the Loire. The Convention decides to transfer Marat's remains to the Pantheon. Robespierre has a number of deputies close to the Hébertists arrested for speculations with shares of the East India Company.

November 17: Robespierre has some Dantonists arrested.

November 20: Danton, who had retired to Arcis-sur-Aube since October, returns to Paris and begins his campaign for moderation, tolerance and national unity. Camille Desmoulins supports him.

November 22: National lands are offered for sale.

November 25: Mirabeau's ashes are removed from the Pantheon.

December 4: Additional powers are given to the Committee of Public Safety, establishing a wartime dictatorship.

December 5: First issue of Desmoulins' *Vieux Cordelier* is published, starting his campaign against the Hébertists. The radical Anacharsis Cloots, honorary citizen, is excluded from the Jacobin club.

December 6: The Convention confirms freedom of religion, counteracting Hébert's radical cult of reason.

December 13: La Rochejacquelein, now supreme commander of the armies of the royalists, who have just taken Le Mans, is beaten decisively by the government troops.

December 15: Desmoulins' third issue of the *Vieux Cordelier* challenges the Terror and Robespierre.

December 19: The English are driven from Toulon. Major Napoleon Bonaparte plays a decisive role in their defeat. The city is looted and many "enemies of the republic" are killed.

December 21: The Paris prisons how hold 4,525 suspects.

December 23: Bonaparte is made brigadier general. The Vendéans are defeated at Savenay.

December 25: Robespierre delivers famous speech on the principles of revolutionary government.

December 31: Hébert attacks Desmoulins as a moderate, beginning the battle between Citras (moderates) and Ultras, with Robespierre and Saint-Just mediating.

1794:   *January 8:* Robespierre attacks Philippe Francois Fabre d'Eglantine at the Jacobin club.

January 9: The Vendéan leader Maurice Joseph d'Elbée is taken prisoner and shot.

January 12: Fabre d'Eglantine is arrested and shortly thereafter guillotined.

January 16: Marseilles is officially renamed Ville-sans-Nom (city without a name).

January 17: General Louis Marie Turreau organizes the *colonnes infernales* for the systematic destruction of the Vendée. Thousands of natives are killed.

January 19: The English, called in by Paoli, land in Corsica.

January 29: La Rochejacquelein, leader of the Vendéans, is killed in battle.

End of January: The Convention decrees that the Basque, Flemish and Catalan languages are to be excluded from all schools and courts.

February 1: Nicolas Stofflet becomes commander of the Vendéan army.

February 4: All blacks are proclaimed to be free, and slavery in the colonies is abolished by the Convention.

February 5: Robespierre delivers speech at the Convention on the principles of political morality, praising virtue and terror.

February 6: Jean-Baptiste Carrier, terrorist at Nantes and originator of the infamous *noyades* (mass drownings), is recalled.

February 10: Jacques Roux commits suicide in jail.

February 26: Saint-Just pushes through the confiscation of property owned by suspects, which is to be given to the poor, thereby preventing even more radical measures by the Hébertists.

March 2-4: Attempts of the Hébertists to start a general insurrection fail.

March 13-14: After Saint-Just's report at the Convention, the leaders of the Cordeliers Club, Hébert, Ronsin, Vincent, Cloots and others, are arrested.

March 24: Hébertists are executed.

March 27: Jean Antoine Nicolas Marquis de Condorcet, mathematician, philosopher and educator, suspected as a moderate, is arrested and commits suicide.

March 30: Danton, Desmoulins, Jean Francois Delacroix and Pierre Nicolas Philippeaux arrested.

April 2-4: The Dantonists are put on trial.

April 5: Danton, Desmoulins and their friends are condemned to death and guillotined.

April 10: Trial begins of the "conspirators of Luxembourg": Pierre Gaspard Chaumette, Jean Baptiste Gobel, the widows of Hébert and Desmoulins. They are executed on April 13.

April 14: On Robespierre's motion, the remnants of Jean Jacques Rousseau are transferred to the Panthéon.

April 22: Guillaume Chrétien de Malesherbes, the former counsel for Louis XVI, and the deputies Isaac René Guy Le Chapelier and Jacques Guillaume Thouret are executed.

April 26: Lazare Nicolas Carnot and Louis Saint-Just clash at the Committee of Public Safety, the former being accused of contacts with aristocrats.

May 7: The Convention recognizes the Supreme Being. In its honor, four great festivals are created: July 14, August 10, January 21 and May 31.

May 10: Jean Nicolas Pache, mayor of Paris, is arrested and replaced by a partisan of Robespierre. Madame Elizabeth, sister of Louis XVI, is guillotined.

May 22: Thérésa Cabarrus, mistress of Tallien, is arrested. This will become one of the motives for the conspiracy against Robespierre.

June 4: Robespierre is unanimously elected president of the Convention.

June 8: Festival of the Supreme Being held at the Champ de Mars, presided over by Robespierre, announced by the painter Jacques Louis David.

June 10: New terror law against suspects enacted, increasing the power of the Revolutionary Tribunal and permitting condemnations without hearing evidence. Between June 11 and July 27, 1,376 death verdicts are pronounced, more than during the entire preceding year.

June 19: 1,200 millions in new assignats are issued.

June 29: Violent fights at the Committee of Public Safety. Carnot, Billaud-Varenne and Collotd'Herbois call Robespierre a dictator. He leaves the committee, returning only on July 23.

July 4: Bertrand Barère defends the Terror before the Convention.

July 14: On application of Robespierre, Joseph Fouché is excluded from the Jacobin club.

July 23: Alexandre Beauharnais, general and first husband of Josephine, later the wife of Napoleon, is held responsible for the capitulation of Mayence and condemned to death.

July 25: André Chénier, one of the great French poets of the 18th century, first enthusiastic about the Revolution, but then opposed to it because of its excesses, is guillotined.

July 26: Robespierre delivers speech at the Convention, accusing "the traitors" but refusing to mention names. Many feel menaced, and during the following night a conspiracy against him is prepared by Tallien, Billaud-Varenne, Collot d'Herbois and maybe Fouché.

July 27: Robespierre, Saint-Just and Couthon's arrest ordered by the Convention. They are temporarily freed by their partisans, but the population fails to come to their rescue. They are outlawed on the following day and executed.

July 29: A total of 106 Robespierrists are guillotined while the spectators cry: "Down with the maximum law!" At the same time, the infamous "last wagon" carries 45 more people condemned by the terror regime to the guillotine.

EYEWITNESS TESTIMONY

She was ... dressed in white; this gesture was noticed and made people smile; the color symbolizing innocence did not suit Marie Antoinette very well ... When she saw the cart, she showed ... surprise and indignation. She had been convinced she would be picked up in a coach, like her husband ... The people remained rather quiet ... for a moment, the misfortune this woman has brought to France, seemed to be forgotten.

Louis Marie Prudhomme, on the queen's execution, in Les Révolutions de Paris, *October 27, 1793.*

Our early victories were attributed to the terror ... The people, victims or instruments of the tyranny which tore up the country, were bitterly opposed to being ruled by emigres or foreigners. They believed they had controlled the trouble at home by putting suspects into prisons and marched to the frontiers, with noble devotion ... The mercenaries of Europe were beaten by its armies of citoyens, and famous generals defeated by simple soldiers who had risen from the ranks. The Republic had the good fortune to have a very extraordinary man in the committee of public safety. Free of any intrigue or ambition ... incorruptible, skilled in the art of war and an ardent supporter of the liberty, glory and independence of the Republic ... like one of the heroes of antiquity ... This man was Carnot who had become the dictator over the armies and justified it ...

Antoine Claire Thibaudeau, Memoirs of the Convention and the Directory (1824).

By now the Convention was a representative body only by name. The hideous dictatorship of the famous committee of public safety rose on the ruins of the Convention's independence ... Its majority did not want the terror any more than the majority of the nation wanted it. It had not ordered the noyades of Nantes nor the mitraillades of Lyons. In its weakness and timidity it did not utter any open criticism ... and kept a mournful silence. Its sessions which used to be long and excited, were now mostly calm and formal, and lasted hardly longer than an hour. The little freedom they had left was only for unimportant matters. They left all important problems to the committee of public safety. They were kept waiting for members of the committee or its reporters as one waits ... for a head of state ... When military triumphs were announced, his [the committee's reporter] arrogant attitude seemed to say: "Not you, or the army, or the people are victorious; no, it is the committee of public safety!"

Thibaudeau, at the height of the Terror, Memoirs *(1824).*

Indeed, the order of the day is terror, and should be for the egotists, the federalists, the heartless wealthy, the crooked opportunists ... the unpatriotic cowards ... Rivers of blood have been shed for the gold of Peru ... Well, should not liberty have the same right to sacrifice lives ... and even, for some time, some individual liberties? In the midst of the battle, is there foolish crying over the fallen warriors? ... Is the French Revolution not such a ... war to the death between those desiring to be free and those satisfied to remain slaves? ... There can be no middle ground: France must be completely free or will go down in the attempt, and all methods are justified in the fight for such a great cause.

Les Révolutions de Paris, *October 1793 (#212).*

For the friends of liberty, the terror was more devastating than for its enemies. The latter had emigrated ... but the dutiful and patriotic friends of the revolution were faithful to the country which annihilated them. More plebeians than priests and noblemen perished ... The nobles and priests had many avengers, but the names of the others were forgotten. Patriots ... were persecuted as federalists and moderates. Most of those who opposed May 31 had to pay with their lives for their generous attitude.

Thibaudeau, Memoirs *(1824).*

Coupé has tried to poison public opinion against me. It is certain that I never attempted to cut the sinews of the revolution when I said the constitution would have to stay at rest as long as the people were busy to beat its enemies. The principles I have represented are founded on the independence of the people's societies from any kind of authority ... When I appeared on the rostrum there were demonstrations of disapproval. Have I lost those features which characterize the face of a free man? Am I not the same who stood by you in times of danger? ... I was one of the most intrepid defenders of Marat; I conjure up the shadow of the "ami du peuple" for my defense. If I describe my private life to you, you will find out with amazement that the huge fortune which my and your enemies ascribe to me is limited to that little property which has always been my possession.

Georges Danton, speech of December 3, 1793.

In the meantime, these daily executions began to weary even that portion of the people who were in the pay of the tyrants ... The theater of his assassinations became deserted, notwithstanding all the efforts of the infamous Le Bon to attract a crowd thither ... Based and hardened as he was, he could not disguise from his own thoughts that the continuation of his atrocities might sooner or later incite a general revolt, of which he might infallibly be the first victim.

Anonymous, Horrors of the Prisons of
Arras, *December 1793 (1826).*

As for myself, I am completely encouraged again; and as long as I am breathing, I shall know how to protect my liberty-loving republican pen from being disgraced. After this #3 of the "Cordélier," let Pitt come and say I had not uttered my opinion as freely as the "Morning Chronicle"! Let him claim there is no longer

The infamous "last cartload" of 45 more condemned people

a freedom of the press in France! ... Undoubtedly it is the maxim of republics: Better to leave a few guilty ones unpunished than to hit one innocent one. But is it not true that in revolutionary times this maxim, born out of the spirit of reason and humanity, helps to encourage the traitors of the nation, because the law ... asks for unmistakable evidence and helps the guilty one, if he is clever enough, to escape punishment? This way a free people is forging weapons against itself ... In contrast, the maxim of despotism is: Rather let a few innocent perish than have a guilty one escape ... The Committee of Public Safety has sensed this correctly, and believed that, in order to build up the republic, one could for a short while not do without the jurisdiction of despotism. Thus, it has thrown a veil over the statue of liberty for a limited time. But ... is it permissible to equate the constitution, the creation of the montagnards, with Pitt's monstrosities, the errors of patriotism with the crimes of the foreigner's party?

Camille Desmoulins, in the Vieux Cordélier,
December 15, 1793.

Lyons exists no longer; Marseilles and Bordeaux have returned to the fold of the republic. There is no longer a Vendée. Valenciennes and Toulon's turn will come soon. Federalism is dying, morals have risen ... equality is no longer just a word. Punishment does no longer allow crime to breathe ... The civic spirit has improved ... the theaters have turned into schools for patriotism. Courage, you worthy legislators ... Unity and tenacity, you good sans-culottes; since the revolution was made by you, it was also made for you ...

Les Révolutions de Paris, *October 1793*
(# 212).

... and instead of this merry bustling of the excited crowds, the imposing splendor, there reigns now the silence of the grave over all the streets of Paris; all shops are closed, everybody is barricading himself in his house and one could imagine a black crape was spread over all that breathes. Since sansculottism was praised and in order not to show any luxury people had adopted the opposite extreme of poverty and misery; these fellows [the city officials] also pretended misery. To appear dirty was some kind of a passing permit in those days ... "Whom are you calling 'you?' One can see they are not up-to-date in your community; only Pitt and Coburg say 'you' to one another; first learn to say 'thou' in a free country!" ... I asked where her husband was … he had gone to the Place de la Révolution to see 30 aristocrats "sneeze into the sack" … this is what Hébert in his dirty journal "Père Duchèsne" called the cutting off of the heads.

Citizen L., returning to Paris after an 18-month absence, end of 1793, in Two Friends of Liberty's History of the French Revolution of 1789 *(1790-93).*

… The friend of kings and the great advocate of humanity can get along. A fanatic in a monk's robe and a fanatic atheist have much in common. The democratic barons are the brothers of the marquis of Koblenz; and sometimes the red cap of the sansculottes resembles the red caps of the aristocrats more than one would think … As a result of 5 years of treason and tyranny, of carelessness and credulity … Austria, England, Russia, Prussia and Italy had time to form a secret government in France which competes with the official government … the foreign courts are sending all their paid scoundrels into our country for some time. Their agents undermine our armies, even the victory of Toulon proved this: All the bravery of our soldiers, all the loyalty of our generals and the heroism of the delegates were needed to defeat treason … Fear of terror should not dwell in the hearts of the patriots and the poor, but in the hideouts of the foreign brigands, where they divide the loot and drink the blood of the French people.

Maximilien Robespierre, speech to the Convention, December 25, 1793.

… on the way [to the guillotine] I would have thrown myself at her [the queen's] feet, and no executioner nor devil could have stopped me … [to the condemning judge who confiscated her property] … you thief … I congratulate you on my property! You won't overeat yourself, I promise you …

Eglé, a young Parisian streetwalker condemned as a royalist, January 1794, in Beugnot's Memoirs *(1866).*

It can be stated with a great amount of certainty that the majority of the French people detest the Convention, the Jacobins, the regime and the rulers; this majority includes six-eighths of the nobility, the middle classes and the small proprietors …further the majority of money-jobbers, merchants, manufacturers, businessmen, lawyers … and artisans, the farmers and

people living by their labor who still have some principles of religion and decency …

Jacques Mallet du Pan, on the Terror, Memoirs and Correspondence *(1852).*

When I stepped out of the carriage … the crowd shouted with joy. Applause, … wild laughter showed the savage joy of these cannibals over the arrival of new victims … I saw Bailly, who should have commanded the greatest respect … reeling from being pushed, then brutally pulled up again by others—This spectacle made me sadder than his death would have done …

Jacques Claude Beugnot, a deputy on his way to prison during the Terror, January 1794, Memoirs *(1866).*

We want a new order in which any low and cruel passions are unknown, and all beneficiary and noble inclinations are encouraged by the laws … We wish, in one word, to fulfill the wishes of nature, to reach mankind's destination and to keep the promises of philosophy … France, once so prominent among the enslaved peoples, should from now on obscure the glory of all free peoples that ever existed and become the paragon of nations, the terror of the oppressors and the gem of the earth! … Only in a democracy the state is really the homeland of all its individuals; therefore it can count on as many defenders interested in its cause as it has citizens. This is why free people are superior to all others. This is why Athens and Sparta defeated defeated the tyrants of Asia, and the Swiss the tyrants of Spain and Austria …

A nation becomes rotten when it loses its character and liberty and changes from democracy to aristocracy or monarchy … In vain did Demosthenes thunder against Philip, who found more eloquent defenders in the vices of Athens than Demosthenes had been … As in peacetime, the mainspring of popular government is virtue, so it is both virtue and terror in revolutionary times; virtue without which terror is disastrous, terror without which virtue is helpless … Certain people are crying: Mercy for the scoundrels! No! Mercy for innocence, for mankind! … The slowness of the verdicts amounts to absolution; the uncertainty of punishment encourages all criminals …

He who asked France to conquer the whole world had no other intention than to bring about the conquest of France [referring to Brissot] … That hypocritical foreigner [Anacharsis Cloots] who for 5 years has loudly proclaimed Paris the capital of the earth, only translated the curses of those low federalists who wanted to turn Paris over for destruction [the Girondins], into a different gibberish. To preach atheism is a way to absolve superstition and to accuse philosophy. And the declaration of war against God was only a diversion for the benefit of royalty [said against the Hébertists] ... Two types of evil can topple democracy: the aristocracy of those who have the government in their hands; and the disdain of the people for the authority it has established itself ...

Robespierre, speech of February 5, 1794.

What is the first principle of democracy? ... I am speaking of the high virtue which produced so many miracles in Greece and Rome, and will produce even more astonishing miracles in republican France ... therefore, one may say that the people do not require any high virtue in order to love justice and equality: It suffices if they love themselves ... Terror is nothing but justice, prompt, sure and unbending. It is a revelation of virtue.

Robespierre, to the Convention, speech of February 7, 1794.

We have been flooded with degenerate literature; one is proclaiming an intolerant and fanatical atheism; one could think that the priests had become atheists and the atheists priests. It would be better not to talk about it any more. For while we need energy, they are seducing us to insanity and weakness ... Look at Europe! There are 4 million prisoners in Europe whose anguished cries you do not hear, while our suicidal moderation allows the enemies of your government to triumph ... Your Revolutionary Tribunal has put to death 300 scoundrels within one year. Did not the Spanish Inquisition sacrifice more people? ... There is a sect in France which is on good terms with all parties [referring to the Dantonists]; it is walking slowly. If you talk about terror, they talk about leniency ... In the beginning of the revolution, there were indulgent voices in favor of those who fought against it. This indulgence ... has in the meantime cost the lives of 200,000 men in the Vende ...

How long will we be deceived by our foreign and domestic enemies whose intentions we are promoting by our weakness? Our enemies cannot resist us for long, they are waging war against us in order to destroy each other. Pitt wants to bring down the Austrian dynasty, Austria, Prussia, all of them Spain, and this contemptible, false alliance wants to destroy all European republics.

Louis de Saint-Just, on the Ventôse Decrees, speech of February 26, 1794, Works (1834).

... So, every party is criminal because it involves isolation from the people and society, and independence from government. Thus, every faction is criminal because it is striving to split up the citizens ... Factions were good for isolating tyrannism and to diminish the influence of despotism; today they are a crime ... The reports we have obtained have shown us that the Allies will not start the campaign in order not to divert the people ... from developments which are being prepared domestically and in Paris ... It is a campaign of crimes, of riots, of corruption and famine which is being prepared against us.

Saint-Just, against the Hébertists, speech of March 13, 1794, Works (1834).

I dream of a Republic admired by the whole world. Never would I have thought that men are so bloodthirsty and unjust ... My Lucile ... My tied-up hands embrace you ... my dying eyes will rest upon you when my head is separated from my body!

Desmoulins, his last letter form prison, April 6, 1794, in Collection of Memoirs Concerning the French Revolution (1820-26).

[When advised to flee]: You cannot carry the soil of your country on the soles of your shoes ... There has been enough bloodshed. It is better to be guillotined than to guillotine.

[After being sentenced by the Tribunal]: Vile Robespierre! You will follow me!

[On the way to the guillotine, to Desmoulins, who cried for help]: Quiet! Do you think you can mollify this rabble?

[At the scaffold]: You must pick up my head and show it to the people. They won't see anything like it for a long time. My home will soon be nothingness; but my name will live in the pantheon of history!

Danton, April 4-6, 1794, Writings (1867).

Danton ... was always his natural self and often gracious. While on the rostrum, his face was ferocious, but elsewhere it was calm, even amused ... His speeches were fierce to the point of fury, yet in his private life he was pleasant, free and cynical, fond of enjoying himself and contemptuous of life ... He was ideally equipped to act as the tribune of the people, the Mirabeau of his period … If I had to decide between them, I would have chosen Danton [over Robespierre] … One day, I told him: "I am amazed at your indifference … Do you not see that Robespierre is planning your downfall? Will you do nothing to prevent him?" He answered, with a movement of his lips which showed anger and contempt: "If I thought he had the slightest idea of this kind, I would tear out his intestines!" Five or six days later, this awful man let himself be arrested like a child and slaughtered like a sheep …

Thibaudeau, on Danton, Memoirs *(1824).*

The assembled crowd recognized her soon, watched only her and increased her suffering by abusing her which she endured patiently. "So there she is, the great lady who used to show up so splendidly, riding in beautiful coaches; now she is on the cart, like all the others!" There is nothing as hurtful for a sensitive person as this cannibalistic shouting. Unfortunate ones should be sacrosanct … One must admit, the execution was made much easier, be it because of some semblance of humanity, or of habit or the desire to finish up faster, by the speed with which all was carried out and because one saw to it that the condemned descended and stood with their backs to the scaffolds so that they could not see anything. Up to a degree, I was grateful to the executioners, also for the decency they maintained and their earnestness … there was no hint of laughter or an insulting gesture.

Abbé Carrichon, accompanying Mme. de Noailles and daughter to the scaffold, April 1794, La Nouvelle Revue *(January-February 1888).*

For the legislator all that is useful and good is also true. The idea of a Supreme Being and the immortality of the soul reminds us always of justice. This is why the idea is social and republican.

Robespierre, against atheism, speech of May 7, 1794, Complete Works *(1910-67).*

When Robespierre descended to light up the pyre, 7 or 8 delegates followed him who no doubt were devoted to him. That started a murmur among the members of the Convention and they whispered in each other's ears: "These are his lictors!" … When the procession turned toward the Champ de Mars, Robespierre obviously saw to it that he marched at the head of the Convention. No doubt he had given corresponding orders to the servants, and they tried very hard to make

the Convention march in a military manner. But nobody complied with it …

Jacques Joseph Francois Cassanyès (a deputy), the June 8, 1794, Festival of the Supreme Being, memoirs in Vidal's History of the French Revolution *(1885-89).*

When I arrived at the Hall of Liberty, I met Robespierre wearing the costume of a people's representative and carrying a bouquet of cereal plants and flowers. For the first time, I saw joy radiating from his face … His eyes rested upon the splendid spectacle, one could see him revelling in enthusiastic rapture. "The universe has assembled here. O nature, how lofty and precious is your power! How the tyrants must pale at the thought of this festival!" This was the whole conversation. Who would not have been deceived by the mendacity of the tyrant?

Joachim Vilatte, a member of the Revolutionary Tribunal, at the Festival of the Supreme Being, Causes Secrètes de la Révolution du 9 Au 10 Thermidor *(1825).*

Soon thereafter, one heard of an amnesty for the Vendéens; at first it was declared to include only the common soldiers; yet the hopes these reports created were soon reduced when we heard that a man who had been inquiring in our behalf was arrested … and thrown into a prison at Blain … The prisons opened and a general amnesty was announced … It was even prohibited to call them [the liberated Vendéens] brigands. In the strange language of those days, it was ordered that we should be called "frères égarés" [misled brethren].

Mme. Marie Louise de la Rochejacquelein, the summer of 1794, Memoirs *(1817).*

The tyranny of these monsters was not the only evil … famine was pressing on with hasty strides. The law of the maximum had not only driven away the foreign merchant, but also kept at a distance the dealer who was accustomed to provide for the daily returning wants of the inhabitants. The grazier no longer drove his oxen to Paris where the "maximum," on entering the barriers, diminished half their value … One wag more indignant than the rest expressed well the state of want and cruelty to which Paris was then abandoned, by writing on the pedestal of the statue which was placed on the spot of the public execution: "Il n'y a de boucherie à Paris que sur cette place!" [There is no butcher shop in Paris except upon this square!]

Helen Maria Williams, famine under
Robespierre, Letters Containing a Sketch ...
during the Tyranny of Robespierre *(1795).*

Even aside from his words and actions, his person was repellent to me ... Though the leader of the sans-culottes, faultlessly dressed and using powder when others had discontinued its use ... He was uncommunicative and kept even his close friends at a distance, a vain pontiff, flattered by the cult his Janissaries and followers had erected around him. There was something of a Mohammed, and something of a Cromwell in him, but without their genius.

Thibaudeau, on Robespierre, Memoirs *(1824).*

I have talked to Robespierre twice. He had something uncanny, never looked into my face, his eyes had a constant, unpleasant twinkle ... He said that he was bashful like a child, and would tremble every time he went to the rostrum ...

Pierre Etienne Louis Dumont, June of 1794,
Recollections of Mirabeau and of the First
Two Assemblies *(1833).*

He was but one step from becoming the absolute master of the revolution which he so daringly endeavored to control; but he needed 30 more heads and had marked them out ... He realized I had an inkling of this, and thus I had the honor of being on his deathlist ... He had me expelled from the Jacobins where he was the high priest, and this meant for me, practically, the death warrant. I started to save my life by having secret talks with those colleagues who were likewise threatened ... such as Légendre, Tallien, Danou and Chénier ... Tallien, Barras ... began to display some energy ... I disclosed to Collot d'Herbois, Carnot and Billaud-Varenne the projects of this modern Appius ... I said to them, "Count the votes in your committee and you can see that if you take the initiative he will be limited to a helpless minority with Couthon and Saint-Just."

Joseph Fouché, the conspiracy against
Robespierre, Memoirs *(1824).*

What crimes were Danton, Fabre, Desmoulins accused of? That they had supported the enemies of the nation and conspired with the intent to obtain an amnesty for them which could have been disastrous for liberty ... Hébert, Chaumette and Ronsin tried to make the revolutionary government unbearable and ridiculous while Camille Desmoulins attacked the government in satirical pamphlets and Fabre and Danton intrigued for his defense. The first pronounced the calumnies, the others created the pretexts for these calumnies. This same method is being continued today publicly. Why is it that those who once indicted Hébert are now defending his accomplices? ...

I promised some time ago to leave a horrible testament for the suppressors of the people; I shall publish it at this moment, without any restraint, as befits my situation! I leave to them the awful truth and death ... The traitors must be punished, the offices of the Security Committee must be newly filled, the Committee itself must be cleaned up and subordinated to the Committee of Public Safety; the Committee of Public Safety itself must be cleansed ... The time has not yet come when honest people can serve the nation in safety; as long as a horde of scoundrels is ruling the defenders of liberty will be outlawed.

Robespierre, his last speech to the Convention,
July 26, 1794 (8th Thermidor).

O my God! What a scheme to aim at the downfall of innocent men! ... I testify that Robespierre declared himself a firm supporter of the Convention, and that he spoke at the Committee ... with caution in order not to attack any of its members. Collot and Billaud have not participated in the discussions for some time, they seem to devote themselves more to private interests ... Billaud attends all sessions without saying anything ... unless there is something to say against Paris, against the Revolutionary Tribunal, against those men whose downfall he now seems to desire ... Billaud-Varenne and Collot d'Herbois are the instigators of this conspiracy ... I am happy when victories are announced, but I do not want them to be turned into disguises for vanity. The victory of Fleurus was proclaimed loudly, but others who participated in it personally, did not speak about it [namely Saint-Just himself] ... I am not drawing any conclusions against those I have mentioned, but I wish that they may justify themselves and that we may become smarter and wiser.

Saint-Just, in defense of Robespierre, speech of
July 27, 1794.

I have armed myself with a dagger and I will pierce this man's [Robespierre] breast if the Convention does not have the courage to order his arrest.

Jean Lambert Tallien, during the Convention session of July 26, 1794.

… At these words [of Billaud-Varenne] Robespierre whose fury can be easily imagined rushes to the rostrum in the belief he could overwhelm them with his imperious tone of voice which had always succeeded in the past. But the charm was broken. Everybody was convinced and they shouted at him from all sides: "Down with the tyrant!" Overwhelmed by these outcries, he drops his head and steps down …

Durand de Maillane, debates at the session of the 9th Thermidor, in de Maillane's History of the National Convention *(1825).*

Robespierre tried his best to be heard. He finally shouted: "I demand to die!" and looked around in fury and desperation. He called the delegates who had talked against him villains, scoundrels, cowards and hypocrites. The turmoil grew worse. The president put on his hat. Robespierre still wanted to speak, but one did not let him. "With what right," he cried, "does the president protect murderers?" More turmoil, and the president covered his head a second time. All asked for a decree of arrest, and finally it was approved, under general applause and shouts, "Long live the Republic!"

Vossische Zeitung (Berlin), 1794 (#97).

… I reached the door of the Committee while they hit me … I recognized Robespierre … jumped at him, pointed my sabre at his chest and shouted: "Surrender, you traitor." He raised his head and replied: "You are the traitor, I will have you shot." At this point, I took one of my pistols with my left hand … and fired. I meant to hit his chest, but the bullet smashed his lower jaw; he fell from his easy-chair … the pistol shot had so scared his brother that he jumped out of the window … Saint-Just and Dumas were led to the Conciergerie … a moment later. Saint-Just looked at the large table of Human Rights which stood there, pointing at it and saying: "This, after all, is my work."

Charles André Méda, a gendarme on 9th Thermidor (July 27), 1794), Précis historique *(1825).*

Hanriot [the military commander] had actually advanced with some hired assassins into the court of the Tuileries … But, after the first shock, the members of the Convention gathered enough courage … and decided to bring this disgraceful struggle to an end by outlawing Robespierre and his followers. This decree was adopted with cries of "Long live the Republic" … When the decree was made public at the Place de l'Hotel de Ville, the battalions of the National Guard disbanded, and the citizens returned to their homes …

Thibaudeau, the Commune in support of Robespierre, Memoirs (1824).

The tyrant had his whole head including his face in bandages … All who surrounded him had lost their arrogant behavior, as had he. Their subdued attitude only increased the general indignation. One remembered that the conspirators who preceded these at least had known how to die. Curses of any kind could be heard from all sides … The people took their revenge for all the flatteries to which they had been compelled during the reign of terror …

Journal de Perlet, *on the July 28 executions, July 30, 1794.*

8. The Last Months of the National Convention: August 1794 to October 1795

THE HISTORICAL CONTEXT

The main and most immediate reaction to the overthrow of Robespierre was a feeling of relief and the desire to do away with the most brutal institutions of the Terror. The law against suspects was abolished, the prisons opened and hundreds of prisoners were released almost immediately. Public opinion welcomed joyously the removal of the triumvirate of Robespierre, Saint-Just and Couthon, and hundreds of congratulatory messages were sent to the Convention. But the coup d'état had been carried out by disparate elements, and the Thermidoreans, as they were called, did not agree among themselves on who was to rule and what measures were to be taken. The revolt had been directed more against Robespierre's personal regime than against the Terror itself. Some of the leading Thermidoreans had been prominent terrorists themselves, and, as further popular uprisings and the possibility of civil war were greatly feared, the Jacobins, still a strong and influential group, did not want to drop the terror policy altogether. But as the political atmosphere relaxed and public opinion became more moderate, the Jacobins lost many of their followers during the subsequent months, and the antirevolutionary groups in the country grew in strength.

It was fortunate for the government that these groups were split into several sections. The Catholic Church, still a great power in France, was divided between Ultramontanists, who accorded the Papacy complete authority, the Gallicanists, who advocated an almost independent French church, and the Jansenists, who were more democratically oriented and to whom most of the "constitutional" lower priests belonged. The other large opposition group, the royalists, were split into

Madame de Staël, whose salon was a center for political and literary activity

111

"Jeunesse dorée" patrolled the streets and intimidated any utterances of revolutionary opinion

the followers of the Comte de Provence, later to become King Louis XVIII, and those of Louis XVI's other brother, the Comte d'Artois, later to become King Charles X. Both factions were subsidized by British money, and this alone made them quite unpopular. Yet, the landing of an army of 3,000 emigrants at Quiberon Bay in Brittany, organized and financed by England and the Comte d'Artois, could have developed into a real danger to the republic as the emigrants threatened to join up with the rebels in the Vendèe. The quick intervention of General Louis Lazare Hoche prevented this and doomed the whole expedition.

But even without strong or united leadership, the royalist movement kept growing, particularly in the South. Assassinations and other acts of revenge against Jacobins and those who had purchased national land (and who were especially detested by the returning emigrants) became almost daily occurrences. In the north, the reaction to the Terror manifested itself in the so-called *Jeunesse dorée* (Gilded Youth), young, mostly wealthy people, recognizable by their long locks of hair and square collars, who armed themselves with sticks, patrolled the streets and intimidated any utterance of revolutionary opinion. They gained influence in the sections of Paris and for a while dominated the Convention, partly because the middle classes, and even the lower classes after the last great riot of May 1795, had grown apathetic.

In the Convention, the Montagnards lost more and more of their former power, and the most prominent Thermidoreans left the committee within five weeks. The Assembly itself had forfeited much of its popularity. The people felt it had been in power for too long and that a new constitution was needed, since the democratic one of 1793, rather hastily drafted, had never gone into effect and no longer expressed the mood of the country. Still, in the 15 months it had left, the Convention accomplished a good deal: The separation of church and state was carried through, the whole school and education system was reorganized, the National Institute for Arts and Sciences was founded. In the Vendée, where the republican armies had been more and more successful since the end of 1793, armistices were concluded with the rebel leaders, which brought at least a provisional peace to the region. Revolts attempted by the right (*Jeunesse dorée)* and the left (Francois Noël Babeuf's first plot) had to be suppressed.

After the harsh winter of 1794-95, the contrast between the rich and poor became worse. There were hunger riots in Paris, and the ostentatious displays of the wealthy—who, after the long period of austerity and fear, openly visited concerts, operas and theaters in their new and extravagant fashions—provoked further uprisings in the spring of 1795, culminating in the great insurrection of the sansculottes on May 20-23. It was finally suppressed, and the results were further persecutions of former terrorists, Jacobins and Montagnards. Some historians have considered the insurrection of May 1795, as the last revolutionary spasm of the whole era.

While the old republican clubs were closed, elegant salons became the meeting places of the new upper class, which combined the remnants of the old ruling class with the nouveaux riche, the speculators in assignats, war profiteers and new owners of national lands. They no longer addressed each other as *citoyen* and *citoyenne*, but again as *monsieur* and *madame*; the republican *tu* gave way to the old *vous*; and the repeal of the maximum-laws increased the misery of the poor even further. During these turbulent months, the Convention had worked out a new constitution that featured special precautionary measures against dictatorship and terror-regimes. It provided two chambers, and the executive was entrusted to a Directory.

The National Convention, which held its last session in October of 1795, had been the center of government for over three years. While it had vacillated and acted ambiguously on many vital questions, it had always been consistent on one point: It had always fought the aristocracy and done everything in its power to prevent the return of the Old Regime. Even during its very last weeks, it attempted to secure a republican majority in the new chambers, in the face of a threatening royalist majority. This resulted in the last major uprising of the Revolution, that of the royalists under Louis Michel Danican on October 5, which was quelled, under Paul Francois Barras' direction, by young General Napoleon Bonaparte.

CHRONICLE OF EVENTS

1794   *August 1:* The law of June 10, 1794, against the suspects is rescinded. Antoine Quentin Fouquier-Tinville, the public prosecutor, is put on trial.

August 5-10: 478 prisoners are released, among them Thérésa Cabarrus, Jean Lambert Tallien's mistress. She marries him and later becomes the mistress of Barras.

August 9: Napoleon Bonaparte is arrested at Nice, as a partisan of Robespierre. He is released on August 20.

August 10: The Revolutionary Tribunal is reorganized.

August 24: The government is reorganized into 16 commitees.

August 29: First anti-Jacobin demonstration of the *Jeunesse dorée* on the Paris boulevards.

September 1: Thermidoreans Billaud-Varenne and Collot d'Herbois resign from the Committee of Public Safety. Tallien is forced to resign.

September 3: First issue published of the *Journal de la Liberté* of Francois Noël (*Gracchus*) Babeuf, later renamed *Le Tribun de Peuple*.

September 13: Report of Henri Baptiste Grégoire on the revolutionary vandalism.

September 18: By decree of the Convention, church and state are separated.

September 21: Jean Paul Marat's remains are brought to the Pantheon.

October 1: Clashes occur in Paris between partisans and opponents of the Terror.

October 3: Bertrand Barère, Billaud-Varenne and Collot d'Herbois are attacked in the Convention. Some sansculotte leaders are arrested.

October 11: Rousseau's remains are brought to the Panthéon.

October 13: Carrier, terrorist of Nantes, is arrested and put on trial. He will be executed in December.

October: The value of the assignat sinks to 20 percent of the metal livre.

November 12: At the instigation of the *Jeunesse dorée*, the Convention orders the closing of the Paris Jacobin

Caricature of royalists promenading in the Boulevard des Italiens

club through Louis Legendre, a former Jacobin.

November 26: Import controls, except from hostile countries, are rescinded.

December 2: The amnesty requested by Lazare Nicolas Carnot for the Vendée rebels is confirmed by the Convention—for those who lay down their arms within one month. Freedom of religion is guaranteed for them. Similar agreements with other royalist groups in February and April 1795.

December 8: Seventy-three surviving Girondists, excluded since May 31, 1793, return to the Convention.

December 24: The maximum law is rescinded. This is popular with the people, but artisans and wage earners are to suffer because the assignats are sinking further.

1795: *January 10:* A yearly festival of January 21, commemorating the "just punishment of the last king of the French," is decreed.

January 19: For the first time, "Le Réveil du Peuple," antirevolutionary hymn of the *Jeunesse dorée*, is being sung.

February 2: Clashes between the *Jeunesse dorée* and sansculottes in Paris. The former begin to remove busts of Marat from theaters and public squares.

February 4: The conspiracy of Babeuf is easily suppressed. He is arrested and imprisoned until September. Carnot intentionally exaggerates the danger of this plot.

February 5: Upon insistence of the *Jeunesse dorée*, the remains of heroes of the Revolution not yet dead for 10 years are removed from the Pantheon, including those of Marat. Jacques Louis David's painting commemorating Marat is removed from the assembly hall of the Convention.

February 14: Beginning of assassinations of Jacobins in the streets of Lyons.

February 21: Freedom of worship is proclaimed in France.

February 24: Central schools are being created in all departments, three of them in Paris.

March 2: Barère, Collot d'Herbois, Billaud-Varenne and Marc Guillaume Vadier are indicted. Vadier manages to escape.

March 17: Hunger riots erupt in Paris.

March 19: The value of the assignats is down to 8 percent of their nominal value.

Thérésa Cabarrus, Tallien's mistress, became Madame Tallien and then the mistress of Paul Barras.

March 21: New hunger riots and demonstrations for the constitution of 1793 in Paris. As proposed by Emanuel Joseph Sieyès, the Convention passes a law providing the death sentence for anyone threatening violence against a deputy.

March 28: Beginning of Antoine Quentin Fouquier-Tinville's trial.

April 1: A crowd gathers at the Temple of Reason (Notre Dame) and then invades the Convention for 4 hours. Jean Charles Pichegru, supported by Barras, suppresses the insurrection, but there are further riots the next day. Barère, Billaud-Varenne and Collot d' Herbois are banished to Cayenne, without formal completion of their trial.

April 1 and 5: Sixteen deputies of the Montagnard party are arrested as having been participants in the tyrannical regime before the Ninth of Thermidor.

April 10: Further actions against former terrorists who lose their civil rights. In Paris, about 1,600 persons are involved.

April 23: The Convention appoints a committee of 11 members who are to draft a new constitution.

May 4: Imprisoned Jacobins are massacred in Lyons, also in Marseilles.

May 7: After a long trial, Fouquier-Tinville and 14 members of the Revolutionary Tribunal are condemned and executed.

May 20-23: Insurrection of the sansculottes starts in the Faubourg Saint-Antoine. The Convention is taken over by the masses shouting "bread and the constitution [of 1793]." The deputy Jean Bertrand Feraud is killed. The crowd is finally dispersed by the National Guard, then by the regular army, where Joachim Murat appears for the first time. The resistance is finally broken by a corps of volunteers under General Jacques Francois Menou. The result is additional arrests of Montagnards.

May 31: The Revolutionary Tribunal is dissolved.

June 8: Death of the Dauphin, Louis XVII, is announced. The Comte de Provence, younger brother of Louis XVI, is now calling himself Louis XVIII.

June 17: Six deputies, arrested and condemned for participation in the insurrection of May 20-23, commit suicide.

June 23: About 3,000 emigrants from England land at Quiberon Bay in Brittany, trying to join up with the

Vendéans. England supplies ships. General Hoche, blocks off the invaders, 751 of whom are captured. Tallien has 748 of them shot, marking a final break between Thermidoreans and royalists.

July 4: First reading of the proposed new constitution.

July 27: At the first anniversary of the Ninth of Thermidor, both the "Marseillaise" and "Le Réveil du Peuple" are sung.

July: As a revenge for the execution of royalists at Quiberon Bay, the Vendée commander, Francois Athanase Charette, has 1,000 captured republicans shot.

August 9: The Convention decrees the arrest of 10 Montagnard deputies, among them Joseph Fouché.

August 15: The franc becomes the official standard of currency, replacing the livre.

August 22: The Convention adopts the new (third) constitution: Two assemblies, the Council of Ancients and the Council of 500. The executive is a directory of five. One-third of the deputies and one director to be exchanged every year.

August 22 and 31: Attempts of the Convention to secure in advance a two-thirds majority for themselves are very unpopular with the royalists and moderates.

September 23: The election results for the directorial constitution are announced. The constitution is accepted by a large majority, the two-thirds provisions of August 22 and 31 by a small majority.

September 23-October 5: Riots of the *Jeunesse dorée* against the Convention, which, they fear, will again appoint Jacobins and terrorists.

Oct 3: The Convention appoints a special committee for its protection against riots. Barras organizes three battalions, called the "patriots of 1789," and entrusts the army to three new generals: Guillaume Marie Brune, Jean Baptiste Carteaux and Bonaparte.

October 5: The last great insurrection occurs in Paris: Royalists, under Danican, attack with 20,000 to 25,000 men and occupy the left bank of the Seine. They are dispersed by the troops of the Convention. Three-hundred are killed and wounded. Bonaparte, acting under Barras, plays a decisive role.

October 16: Bonaparte is made major general.

October 21: The election results for the two assemblies show great successes for the royalists. Tallien tries to cancel the elections.

October 23: The assignats are down to 3 percent of their nominal value. There are twenty billion assignats in circulation.

October 25: Last laws of the Convention are enacted. Relatives of emigrants are excluded from public office. New terror laws against priests. There is strong opposition from the monarchists.

October 26: Last session of the Convention declares amnesty for all deputies sent to prison and the Place de la Révolution is renamed Place de la Concorde. Napoleon Bonaparte is appointed commander of the Army of the Interior.

EYEWITNESS TESTIMONY

... I think it a very good event in ... that it will serve to destroy an opinion that extreme severity and cruelty are the means of safety and success ... Whoever comes in Robespierre's place cannot be worse than he was in these respects ...

Charles James Fox, on the 9th of Thermidor,
Memorials and Correspondence *(1970).*

People were embracing each other in the streets; they were so surprised to be still among the living that their rejoicing turned almost into madness.

Charles de Lacretelle (a Parisian), reaction to
fall of Robespierre, in Furet and Richet's The
French Revolution *(1970).*

The dancing craze was very sudden, spontaneous and frightening. The scaffold had hardly been toppled ... and the ground was still soaking in human blood which had been shed onto it for two months, when public dancing was being organized all over the capital ... The merriest tunes of clarinets, violins ... called upon the survivors of the reign of terror to indulge in the pleasure of dancing.

Georges Duval (a clerk) after 9th Thermidor,
in Furet and Richet's The French Revolution *(1970).*

Luxury, amusements and arts are recovering in the most amazing way; yesterday, they played "Phaedra" at the opera, and since two o'clock there was an innumerable crowd though the prices had tripled. Coaches and elegant people appear again, or rather it seems like a dream to them that they had ever ceased to sparkle ... And how could one remain a prophet of doom in all this extravagance of spirit and vivacious hustle?

Napoleon Bonaparte, to his brother Joseph, let-
ter from Paris after Robespierre's fall, in
Joseph's Memoirs *(1853).*

Those who had participated brought forth excuses of the most incredible sophistry one could imagine. Some claimed they had been forced ... others explained that they sacrificed themselves to the common good, when one knew they had only thought of saving themselves. All were blaming a few, and—amazing in a country known for its military bravery—several political leaders mentioned their fear as a sufficient excuse ...

Mme. Germaine de Staël, after the Terror,
The Reasons for the Principal Events of
the French Revolution *(1818); in* Choix de
Textes *(1974).*

Not to have suffered persecution during the tyranny of Robespierre is now to be disgraced; and it is expected of all who have escaped that they should assign some good reason or offer some satisfactory apology for their suspicious exemption from imprisonment ... Paris once more assumes a gay aspect; the poor again have bread and the rich display the appendages of wealth. The processions of death ... are now succeeded by carriages, elegant in simplicity ...

Helen Maria Williams, Letters Containing a
Sketch ... during the Tyranny of
Robespierre *(1795).*

Billaud-Varenne who was as sullen and ill-disposed as Robespierre, flattered himself in believing he should be his proper successor. When he was interrupted one day by indications of opposition, he looked at the Convention threateningly and remarked: "I think I am hearing some murmurs." ... Such impertinent threats no longer impressed the Convention. It had recovered its power completely after the 9th of Thermidor, and remembering its recent suppression made it quite jealous of its barely regained independence.

Antoine Claire Thibaudeau, after
Robespierre's fall, Memoirs of the Convention and the Directory *(1824).*

There are only two parties now in France: One in favor of maintaining the Robespierre-government, the other one in favor of reinstituting a government based exclusively on the imperishable human rights.

Francois Noël Babeuf, in his own Journal de
la liberté de la presse, *September 22, 1794.*

Grace and laughter, banished by the reign of terror, have returned to Paris; our beautiful women with their blond whigs are adorable; the concerts, whether in public or in a small circle, are delicious … The butchers, the Billaud, Collot and the whole gang of madmen call this turnabout in public opinion the "counterrevolution" …

Messager du soir (Paris), November 22,
1794.

Why all this barbarian slowness?
Hurry up, you sovereign people
To surrender to the monsters
All those who drank human blood …

"The Counter-Marseillaise," a song written
by Souriguères and sung by the Jeunesse
dorée in January 1795, in Furet and Richet's
The French Revolution *(1970).*

What are you waiting for to rid the earth of these cannibals? Do not their pallid skins and deep-set eyes show clearly enough by what kind of fathers they were raised? Arrest them … the sword of the law will deprive them of the air they have poisoned for too long.

Montreuil section of Paris, against the former
terrorists, proclamation of March 1, 1795, in
Soboul's Summary of the History of the
French Revolution *(1962).*

Under Robespierre's rule blood was flowing but there was no scarcity of bread; today blood is not longer flowing, but there is no bread. Therefore, blood should flow again, so that there will be bread again!

Slogans spread among the people during the
famine in the spring of 1795—(as repeatedly
reported by the Paris police), in Soboul's
Summary *(1962).*

… the people decided as follows:

Article I: The citoyens and citoyennes of Paris will proceed to the National Convention today, without delay, to demand:

1. bread;
2. the dismissal of the revolutionary government all of whose members have, one after the other, abused their power to ruin the people, to starve and enslave them;
3. the immediate proclamation and enactment of the democratic constitution of 1793 …

5. the immediate release of all citizens who are held in captivity because they demanded bread and uttered their opinion freely;
6. the calling in of all constituents for the 25th Prairial of this year for new elections of all magistrates;
7. the calling in of a Legislative National Assembly to succeed the Convention, for the 25th Messidor of this year …
10. The people's slogan is: Bread and the democratic constitution of 1793! Anyone who during this uprising does not carry this slogan, written on his hat with crayon, will be regarded as a starver of the people and enemy of liberty. All flags, banners and battle standards must also show this slogan …

Rioters of May 20, 1795 (1st Prairial), Decla-
ration, in Grab's The French Revolution, a
Documentation *(1973).*

The lowest part of the Populace indulged in every possible excess in the dismal days of Prairial (end of May 1795). At this time, the Convention was magnificent. The quiet attitude of its president, Boissy d'Anglas, and the dignified bearing of the assembly which sat in silence, just two steps away from those who had come to kill them, equalled all heroic deeds history has to offer. The factions of 1793 were thrown back, after several attacks. It is in the month of Prairial that the Thermidor revolution came to an end.

Lucien Bonaparte, a brother of Napoleon,
Memoirs *(1836).*

… the young prince was left to the brutal treatment of that monster Simon, a former shoemaker and drunkard … One time, in a drunken stupor, he almost knocked out his eye, who was … to serve him at table. He, the descendant of so many kings was always exposed … to obscene songs … Simon asked him one day: "Capet, if those Vendéens free you, what will you do?" The young king replied: "I shall pardon you." … During the winter, my brother suffered several attacks of fever; he was always close to the fire … He grew weaker and weaker and died in agony … I do not believe he was poisoned …

Marie-Thérèse Charlotte de France (Madame
Royale), the death of the Dauphin, Memoirs
of the Captivity (1892).

This civil war is a figment of the mind, and the remedy of a foreign war is just as threadbare; nothing can equal the contempt one has in France for the arms and the policy of the Allies, except possibly the equally widespread hatred they have provoked.

Jacques Mallet du Pan, on royalist hopes for English help, June 21, 1795, Memoirs and Correspondence (1852).

At last you must guarantee the property rights of the rich ... Equality of the law is all a reasonable man can ask for. Absolute equality is a chimera; in order to make it possible, there would have to be total equality of intellect, virtue, physical strength, education, and even of possession of all men ... We must be ruled by the best; the best are those who are most thoroughly informed and most interested in the preservation of the laws; aside from very few exceptions you will find such men only among those who possess property and are fond of the state, the laws which protect it and the quiet it maintains ...

Comte Francois Boissy D'Anglas, to the Convention, introducing the draft of the new constitution, speech of June 23, 1795.

If you grant to people without means unlimited political rights and if they sit on the benches of the legislators they will create unrest, or tolerate it, because they do not have to fear the consequences. They will burden trade and agriculture with disastrous taxes, or tolerate them since they have not recognized nor feared nor foreseen the terrible consequences, and finally they will throw us right back into those tremendous convulsions from which we have just escaped.

D'Anglas, to the Convention, speech of June 23, 1795.

It is obvious that the property owners, without whose consent nobody in the country would either have food or lodging, are the leading citizens of this country. They are sovereigns by the grace of God, of Nature, of their work, of their progress and of the work and progress of their ancestors.

Pierre Samuel Dupont de Nemours, constitutional monarchist, before the Convention, June 23, 1795.

The castastrophe of Quiberon (subject of ineffaceable shame to the English government at that period, if it is true that it abandoned its victims, and for the French government which had the atrocious courage to immolate them, with or without capitulation)—the catastrophe of Quiberon raised the public indignation.

The royalists were equally skillful in appropriating to themselves the fruits of the heroism and the errors of the conventional party. The counterrevolutionary spirit was not calmed.

Lucien Bonaparte, July 1795, Memoirs (1836).

He who proves by his own strength that he is able to do or earn as much as four others is nevertheless conspiring against society ... Social education must reach a point where it will deprive everyone of any hope to get richer or more powerful or more prominent because of his ... talents.

Babeuf, in Tribune du Peuple, 1795, and in Selected Texts (1950).

These resolutions violated the tacit understanding between the Convention and all decent people ...

Mme. de Staël, on the Convention resolutions of August 22 and 31, 1795, designed to secure former deputies a two-thirds majority in the new chambers, Selection of Texts (1974).

Wherever the Revolutionary Committee had settled down one was under the impression of seeing traces of devastations by an army of Huns or Vandals ... One could at that time buy many of those houses for a few millions, that is for a piece of bread ... Since the 9th of Thermidor one may again see a few private carriages, at least during the day ... The extent and activity of general bargaining surpass all imagination ... One could believe that all of Paris was up for bankruptcy sale ... There is such fear of buying or selling not early enough ... Anyone who with his pockets full of assignats would go out every day, just with the intention of buying anything that could be had cheaply, could quickly acquire an immense fortune ... What struck me most in Paris was this particular insecurity on almost all faces, this distrustful, tormented, often ... disturbed expression ...

Henri Meister, Memories of My Last Trip to Paris - 1795 (1910).

... to me the ease of this victory was nothing short of a miracle; our enemies were, after all, Frenchmen, and outnumbered us at least five to one. The attack was done in a ridiculous way, for if the section-troops had used the streets and houses around the Tuileries better, they could have finished off the few defending soldiers. Instead ... they came forward in close, deep columns.

This gave an unestimable advantage to the artillery and sharpshooters fighting for the Convention …

Thibaudeau, the 13th Vendémiaire (October 5, 1795), Memoirs *(1824).*

And the thirteenth Vendémiaire could not, unfortunately, assure the triumph of the patriot party except at the price of the blood of too many Frenchmen … Named commissioner of war, I departed for the capital to rejoin my brother. It will naturally be imagined how much I reflected at that moment upon what he had said to me at Antibes, scarcely two years before: "Have patience; in a little time I shall command Paris."

Lucien Bonaparte, October 5, 1795, Memoirs *(1836).*

If the royalists are not removed from the administration and the judiciary system, the counterrevolution will have won its victory by legal means within three months.

Jean Lambert Tallien, to the Convention, speech after October 1795 elections.

9. The War of the First Coalition Up to the Treaties of Basle: January 1793 to July 1795

THE HISTORICAL CONTEXT

From March of 1793, France was at war with all of Europe, with the exception of Switzerland and the Scandinavian kingdoms. While she had expanded deeply into her neighboring countries, annexing Nizza, Monaco and Belgium, a setback was inevitable, given the overwhelming odds. Moreover, the patriotic volunteer corps, which had played a role in the victories of 1792, lost much of their strength during the following year when many of the volunteers took their leave, as was their right to do. New conscriptions turned out to be more difficult to gather than before and met with strong resistance, particularly in Brittany and the Vendée and in the south of the country.

General Charles Francois Dumouriez

So Belgium was lost again, the British entered the war and took Toulon, and Spanish troops advanced in the Pyrenees. But the government in Paris was quick in taking drastic countermeasures. General conscription, the famous *levée en masse* was decreed; and instead of the old, aristocratic commanders who had believed neither in their own troops nor in the cause they fought for, an amazing number of young and capable generals arose and put themselves at the disposal of the republic. In addition to the many already mentioned, there were Jean Charles Pichegru, Jean Baptiste Kléber, Jean Victor Moreau, and later, Jean Etienne Championnet and Charles Pierre Augereau. And while in the past the commanders had acted quite independently and even, like Marquis Marie Joseph de Lafayette and Charles Francois Dumouriez, had been free to defect to the enemy, the command of the army was now put under strict political control. Louis Saint-Just took over the organization or this control, travelling tirelessly from one army headquarters to the next. Disobedient generals like Adam Philippe de Custine and Jean Nicolas Houchard were removed and put on trial.

The soldiers were thoroughly indoctrinated with the democratic spirit. Journals like Jacques René Hébert's *Le Père Duchesne* and other Jacobin publications were distributed by the sansculotte minister of war, Jean Baptiste Noël Bouchotte. The troops elected their own corporals and fought against the counterrevolutionaries, the emigrants and the oath-resisting priests as much as against the English, the Austrians, the Prussians and the Spanish. While their weapons were hardly different from those of the Old Regime, new fighting tactics were developed, the echeloned columns replacing the spread-out lines. The soldiers were trained to take full advantage of the terrain and to attack relentlessly, especially using the bayonet. The manufacture of arms was stepped up. By November of 1793, in Paris alone 1,000 rifles were made every day. No less than 600 weaponmaking firms were founded in Paris, Autún, Moulins and elsewhere.

The tide of war had turned in favor of the French by October of 1793, when the first victories over the Allies were won and the danger of an invasion was averted.

During the first months of 1794, the French armies were mostly victorious, and by July, Brussels, Antwerp and Liège had been retaken. In the fall, the Rhineland was occupied, and by January of 1795, all of Holland was also occupied by the French and made into a satellite state under the name of the Batavian Republic. The fact that the French had captured the Dutch navy, while it was frozen in at Helder, was considered a disaster in London and strengthened British resolve to resist France at all costs.

Other developments in Europe had improved the French situation. Pro-revolutionary uprisings had taken place in Switzerland. And the Prussian-Austrian alliance fell apart, when Poland was divided among the three great powers bordering it, because Empress Catherine of Russia's understanding with Austria had left Prussia with the least desirable part of the Polish lands. Prussia, angered and, moreover, financially exhausted by military operations in France, in the Rhineland and in Poland, decided to leave the alliance and so concluded the Basle peace treaty with France, ceding the west bank of the Rhine in return for guarantees of compensation on the right bank. This eliminated Prussia as a potential enemy of France for the next 11 years and also kept the smaller states in Northern Germany out of the war.

Even before this date, peace had been concluded with the grand duchy of Tuscany. The states of central Germany (Saxony, Hesse) followed Prussia's example. By July of 1795, after the Spanish armies had also been defeated and Bilbao in northern Spain occupied, Spain was ready for peace, too. By the time the second treaty of Basle was signed, the potentially dangerous Quiberon Bay invasion had also been overcome and the situation in the Vendè greatly improved. France was now surrounded by occupied satellite states, and only two major enemies remained at war: Austria and England.

CHRONICLE OF EVENTS

1793:   *January 31:* The Convention announces the annexation of Nizza. Georges Danton also claims the annexation of Belgium.

February 1: The Convention declares war on England and Holland.

February 14: France annexes Monaco. Coalition against France formed by England, Austria, Prussia, Holland, Spain and Sardinia.

February 17: The French armies under Dumouriez invade Holland.

February 21: The volunteer battalions and the regular army are integrated into one unit. Soldiers now elect their corporals. Another 300,000 men are called to arms.

March 1: The Convention decrees the annexation of Belgium. Austrian General Duke Frederick de Coburg forces the French armies to retreat in Belgium.

March 7: France declares war on Spain.

March 17: The Rhenisch National Convention opens in Mayence, proclaiming the first republic on German soil. This convention requests France to annex the territories of the Rhine.

March 18: The Austrians under Coburg defeat Dumouriez at Neerwinden. Brussels recaptured by the Austrians.

March 25: English-Russian alliance formed against France.

March 26: The Holy Roman Empire declares war on France.

March 27-April 1: Dumouriez criticizes the Convention and refuses to appear after being summoned to Paris. He surrenders to the Austrians the Convention's commissars and War Minister Pierre de Beurnonville, who were sent to his headquarters. The Rhineland is lost to the Allies as Custine remains inactive. The French garrison in Mayence is under siege.

April 3-4: Dumouriez fails to persuade his army to march against Paris. He is declared an outlaw by decree of hte Convention. He and Philippe Egalité's son (King Louis Philippe, later) desert to the Austrians. Egalité is arrested.

pril 9: Diplomats of the coalition meet at Antwerp.

July 10: The Austrians conquer the fortress Condé-sur-Escaut.

July 12: Adam Philippe de Custine, suspect because of his inactivity, is deposed by the Committee of Public Safety.

July 23: The besieged French troops at Mayence surrender. They are allowed to return home if they will not take up arms again in the foreign wars. Most of them will fight in the Vendée. The Jacobins in Mayence are cruelly mistreated.

July 28: Valenciennes falls to the Dutch-English armies.

August 23: The Dutch-English armies besiege Dunkirk.

August 27: Toulon surrenders to the British.

September 8: French troops defeat the British and Dutch at Hondshoote.

September 12: The Austrians take Quesnoy.

September 22: Spanish troops capture Truillas, in the eastern Pyrenees.

October 16: French defeat Austrians at Wattigny, thereby reducing the danger of an invasion.

December 27: At Landau, with French victory over the Allies, the danger of immediate invasion is averted.

1794:   *January 19:* Upon Pascal Paoli's request, British troops land on Corsica.

April 19: Treaty signed at the Hague by Britain, Prussia and Holland against France. England will pay for 62,000 Prussian troops to fight against France.

April 30: Jean Charles Pichegru beaten by Coburg at Landrecies.

May 1: The Spanish are beaten at Boulou.

May 18: Pichegru wins at Turcoing.

May 20: The Mont-Cenis pass on the Grenoble-Torino road is occupied by the French Army of the Alps.

May 26: After a report of Bertrand Barère to the Convention on the "crimes of Britain against the French people," the Convention forbids taking of any English or Hanoverian prisoners.

May 28: The Army of the Pyrenees retakes three mountain towns.

June 2: In a naval battle about a grain shipment from the United States, the French lose seven ships to the British.

June 8: Saint-Just unites the armies of the Moselle and the Ardennes under the command of General Jean Baptiste Jourdan.

June 25: Charleroi taken by the French army. After a 14-hour battle, the French under Jourdan defeat the Austrians under Coburg at Fleurus.

July 10: Jourdan and Pichegru join up and take Brussels.

July 19: Successful pro-revolutionary rebellion occurs at Geneva, Switzerland.

July 27: Pichegru takes Antwerp and Jourdan, Liège.

August 5: Trèves (Trier), on the Moselle, is taken by the French.

August 30: The fortress Condé-sur-Escaut is retaken, and all of France liberated from foreign troops.

September 17: Kléber begins the siege of Maastricht, southeast Holland.

September 23: Jourdan occupies Aix-la-Chapelle.

October 1: The annexation of Belgium is proclaimed, in spite of violent protests by the population. It is divided into nine departments.

October 6: Cologne is occupied by the Army of the Sambre-et-Meuse.

October 8: Bonn is occupied by French troops, Koblenz shortly thereafter.

October 31: Prussian troops have evacuated the west bank of the Rhine.

November 19: Treaty in London, between England and the United States, against French corsairs and for a blockade of the French coastline.

November 20: Spanish army defeated at Montagne-Noire.

December 14:: Kléber begins the siege of Mayence.

December 27: Pichegru crosses the Meuse (Maas) River.

1795: *January 5:* Pichegru begins the invasion of the Netherlands. He occupies Amsterdam on January 19.

January 8: Third division of Poland, by treaty between Russia and Austria and with Prussia joining in. The latter obtains Warsaw and "New-East Prussia," but is dissatisfied with the policies of Russia's Empress Catherine, and starts peace negotiations with France.

January 19: Pichegru occupies Amsterdam.

January 22-23: The French cavalry at Helder, Holland, captures the Dutch fleet, which is frozen in. Thus Belgium and Holland become satellites of France, and England becomes France's mortal enemy.

February 3: Holland is made the Batavian Republic.

February 9: Peace treaty negotiated between France and the grand duchy of Tuscany.

April 5: Peace treaty agreed upon at Basle between France and Prussia. While Lazare Nicolas Carnot and Balthazar Francois Barthélemy wanted only the Meuse border, popular patriotism insisted on the Rhine as boundary line. Prussia gives in, ceding the west bank of the Rhine but is secretly guaranteed compensation on the east bank. All northern German states remain neutral from here on.

May 7: Jourdan occupies Luxembourg. Pichegru, disgruntled because his achievements have not been appreciated by the Convention, does not move his troops.

May 16: Peace Treaty of the Hague agreed upon between France and Holland, which as the Batavian Republic is put under French protectorate. Flanders and Maastricht are annexed. France will receive a payment of 100 million guilders; Holland remains occupied by 25,000 French troops.

May 17: A demarcation line is set between France and Prussia, keeping the other northern German states out of the war.

July 17: General Bon Adrien de Moncey defeats the Spanish and occupies Bilbao on July 19.

July 22: Peace treaty of Basle agreed upon between France and Spain. France is to evacuate Catalonia and the Basque country and is ceded the Spanish part of San Domingo.

EYEWITNESS TESTIMONY

For the honor of human nature it were necessary to banish such an action from our memory, efface it from the pages of history and hide it from the eyes of the present and future world. But whatever be our sentiments on the subject, since it is not possible, alas! to prevent our time being soiled by this crime, since it is not possible to prevent the voice of tradition from carrying its remembrance to posterity, it is a duty which we are bound to fulfil to protest solemnly, in the name of all the principles of honorable and upright men, against the most atrocious crime recorded in history.

William Pitt, after the execution of Louis XVI and the dismissal of the French ambassador, January 1793, in Guizot's History of France.

You can hope for victory not just because of the numbers and the discipline of our soldiers; you will win it only through the progress the republican spirit will make in the armed forces ... The unity of the republic requires the unity of the army, the fatherland has but one heart.

Antoine Louis Léon de Saint-Just, February 12, 1793, Works *(1834).*

War causes misfortunes to the nations for the moment, but they are well recompensed by the establishment of liberty and equality. Holland still continues to tax bread and beer, that beer that is so necessary to the brave fellows of the poorest class. To be free we need only bread, beer and iron. You will give to the Batavians of the poorest class the means of dancing round the tree of liberty. In a short time Amsterdam will become your business center; the Dutch will have their country houses at Paris and their banking houses at Amsterdam.

Pierre Joseph Cambon, minister of finance, on the occupation of Holland, February 1793, Guizot's History.

You must conquer the army, if you wish it to conquer in its turn. If you leave nominations in the hands of the generals or the executive power, you render them powerful against yourselves, you reestablish the monarchy. I only consider here the liberty of the people, the right of the soldiers, the subversing of all authority before the genius of popular independence. As soon as

a man is appointed, he ceases to interest me; I consider him in a state of dependence. Command is an improper word; we observe the law; we do not command.

Saint-Just, to General Dumouriez, February 1793, in Guizot's History.

You are the representatives of the nation in the Assembly; the soldiers are the country's representatives in face of the enemy. Its safety depends on their glory or disgrace; therefore they have the right of telling you the truth and demanding what they require in order to act with success. Armed Europe is not capable of making them afraid, but they have need of clothes, arms, horses and provisions. I fought in Champagne with a handful of men, and that formidable Prussian army vanished before the courage and resolution of the republican soldiers. All branches of service seconded me, and I have nothing but praise to give them. The same army has just taken Belgium from the Austrian despot; yet it is in need of everything because they have thrown the administration into disorder. The war office has become a club, and a club is no place for the despatch of business.

General Charles Francois Dumouriez, to the Convention, February 1793.

If the Convention approves of such crimes, so much the worse for it and for our unhappy country; but observe this, that if it were necessary to commit a crime to save the Convention, I should not commit it. The delegate Camus answered: "General, they accuse you of being Caesar; if I thought so, I should be Brutus and should stab you." Dumouriez laughed and replied: "My dear Camus, I am not Caesar and you are not Brutus, and if I am to perish by your hand, it is a patent of immortality."

General Dumouriez, to Convention delegates protesting his dismissal of a delegate for arresting the bishop of Antwerp and robbing some churches, March 1793.

If within three weeks I do not make peace, the Austrians will be at Paris. The Convention has not so long to live. I cannot agree to Condorcet's constitution [constitution of 1793], it is too stupid; that of 1791 is preferable ... with a king. There must undoubtedly be one, called Louis or James ... My army will be well able to insist on having a king; my Mamelukes, as you call them. More than half of France desires it. Then I shall bring about peace quickly and easily ... Even should the Convention decree my accusation, I defy them to put their decree in execution in the midst of my army. Besides, I have always the resource of a gallop towards the Austrians.

General Dumouriez, to emissaries of the Convention, after his defeat at Neerwinden, March 1793, Guizot's History.

I cannot at present leave the army. I must restore it to order. You are masters of my fate; I am quite ready to resign ... After, I shall do as suits me. I shall not carry my head to the tigers who are now asking it ... The Romans neither had a Jacobin club nor a Revolutionary Tribunal. I shall not imitate Curtius by throwing myself into the chasm.

General Dumouriez, when asked to resign, end of March, 1793, Guizot's History.

It would be doing you a wrong to conceal the great measures demanded in the name of the Republic in danger. The coasts of both seas blockaded by Spanish and English squadrons; Austria and Prussia laying waste the territory of the Northern provinces, besieging the fortresses, some of which have already fallen into their hands; England purchasing treason, the royalists gaining partisans, fanaticism redoubling its efforts, the Vendeans rending the bosom of the country, the Federalist administrations shaking new firebrands of civil war, Corsica surrendering to the English ... where, then, is the Republic in the midst of so many dangers and crimes? Where is she? In a Constitution solemnly sworn, in the firmness of her representatives, in the courage of her soldiers, in the patriotism of the men sent by the sovereign people to meet in this chamber.

Bertrand de Vieuzac Barère, report to the Convention, summer 1793.

The majority of the leaders were, if not ready to betray the Republic, at least but little disposed to make great sacrifices for that form of government. Few generals had sprung from the ranks of the people, and there was no doubt that a certain number of them

regretted the constitutional monarchy under which they thought themselves destined to the highest offices ...

René Levasseur, Convention delegate, on France's military leaders in the summer of 1793, in Guizot's History.

The most remarkable sight was that of the riflemen riding up on their horses; they had been very quiet, until their musician started the Marseillaise march. This revolutionary Te Deum has some sad and ominous quality anyway, even when played very aggressively; but this time they took it very slowly, as suited the slow walk at which they proceeded. It was touching and awesome, a solemn sight as the riders, tall haggard men, approached, their facial expression corresponding to the music. As individuals you could compare them with Don Quixote, as a mass they appeared to be most venerable.

Johann Wolfgang von Goethe, the French withdrawal from Mayence, July 23, 1793, "The Siege of Mayence," in Collected Works *(1854).*

I have no more defenders; they have disappeared. My conscience charges nothing against me. I die calm and innocent.

Adam Philippe, General Comte de Custine, after condemnation as a traitor in July 1793, in Guizot's History.

There is a general wish to promote those of equal rank according to their seniority; but the soldier of the longest service is often an illiterate man, about to occupy a post of which he is unable to fulfill the functions; and soon none of your officers will be able either to read or write.

Calès (a Convention delegate), report in fall of 1793, in Guizot's History.

It has become generally known that the policy of the London cabinet contributed much to the first impulse of our revolution. Pitt's design was an ambitious one: In the midst of our political wounds he wanted the exhausted and divided France to change its government and to put the Duke of York on Louis XVI's throne. This plan would have been favored by the intrigue of the house of Orléans whose head was hostile to the French court and had been in close contact with the British court for a long time ... Carrying out this plan was to secure for England three great objects of her ambition and jealousy: Toulon, Dunkirk and our colonies ...

Pitt—like a child whose weak hand is hurt by a burning vessel it touched carelessly, wanted to play with the French people and was smashed … We have already explained the political phenomenon of the alliance between the king of Prussia and the head of the Austrian dynasty … However, behind this appearance of unity is hidden a real disunity between the two powers. In this case, though, Austria is being cheated by Prussia whose cabinet is basically controlled by Russia, even though this fact is not generally known … Even the little king of Sardinia is being deluded by the hopes of becoming king of the Dauphiné, the Provence and of the countries bordering his former possessions … England also threatened Denmark with her navy to force her joining the league, but Denmark, governed by a clever minister, rejected with dignity these impertinent attacks … By-the-way, even if all of Europe should turn against us, we are stronger than Europe … They say that to complete our happiness you intend to starve us, and you have started a blockade with one hundred ships—be careful! A great nation, by-the-way, which they dare to threaten with starvation, is a terrible enemy; if she has nothing left but iron, she still would not accept food and bread from her oppressors, and at the end will kill them … At the end of this campaign the rotten cabinet in London will see its league almost annihilated by its criminal machinations, the English arms disgraced, its fortune tottering.

Maximilien Robespierre, to the Convention, speech of November 17, 1793.

If France can extricate herself from this situation she will have more strength than ever before; she will be obedient and tame like a lamb; but that would require a man who would have to be skilful, courageous and superior to his contemporaries and to his whole century. Does he exist? Will he appear soon? Everything depends on it.

Empress Catherine II of Russia, letter of February 1794, in Brueckner's Catherine II *(1883).*

France must be seen as totally subservient to the National Convention, and any effort to break the accord … would be illusory. Equally, the soldier could not be separated from the cause of the Convent. He could not find abroad what he has in France …

Mercy d'Argenteau, Austrian ambassador in Paris and Brussels, to his foreign minister, report of spring 1794, in Fisher's Six Summers in Paris *(1966).*

That's their business. Send them to the delegates, and let them kill them and eat them, like the savages they are.

Sergeant (in Netherlands), to officer who said that Convention's delegates would have several English soldiers shot according to decree of May 26, 1794, in Guizot's History.

It is not a scrap of paper that I want; it is the town I ask. Yesterday you might have been listened to; today you must surrender at discretion. That is my last word. I reckon on the assistance of the army.

Saint-Just, to the governor of the besieged Charleroi, June 1794, Works (1834).

According to the report of … general Kléber that the second battalion of la Vienne fled ignominiously before the enemy yesterday while the banners of the other battalions waved victoriously, and in view of the fact that this crime cannot be the fault of the whole battalion because bravery and hatred against the tyrants are alive in the hearts of all Frenchmen and that, if a soldier leaves his post … the fault is with the cowardice of the officers and their failure to maintain discipline and to educate the soldiers under their command to strive for glory which consists of defying the dangers of war and at the post entrusted to them by the nation to be victorious or to die: We order that the leaders and all captains of the second batallion of la Vienne be removed and arrested.

Saint-Just, as commissioner with French Army of the Rhine, summer 1794, Works (1834).

Remember that so far we, though victorious, have always spared the peaceful dwellings of the inhabitants of a country we are trying to liberate from the hateful slavery into which it was thrown by the regicidal Convention … In spite of the atrocities and abominations perpetrated by the scoundrels of this Robespierre who without bearing this name is your king or rather you tyrant, we ourselves have always rejected the thought of just retaliation, convinced that the people of the country were innocent … Therefore, if we in spite of these sentiments … followed the call for just revenge yesterday … do not be surprised!

May the residents of this village [Tiercelet] blame themselves for the misery which has befallen them. Why did they shoot at us? Why did they defend themselves to whom we had done no harm? May this example be a lesson to you! May it prove to you that, if

Robespierre's arsonists can wage war only with torches in their hands, Austria's brave soldiers know how to take their revenge ... We swear that we, tired of he atrocities your soldiers commit every day, will no longer restrain ourselves; every time and as many times as these villains burn down just one of our villages, we shall burn to the ground ten others in your country; and we shall burn to ashes any village through which we pass peacefully and where we are being shot at.

Austrian soldiers to the French living near the Luxembourg border, summer 1794, in Grab's The French Revolution *(1973).*

The present war has never had for its object conquest or glory, it does not aim at commercial advantages, or the establishment of a form of government. The struggle is for the security, tranquillity and existence even of Great Britain, as well as of all established governments and of all the nations in Europe. Every hour the necessity and justice of this are more clearly demonstrated.

Pitt, to the House of Commons, summer 1794.

Do you wish to wage a perpetual war with Europe? Then tell the people that they will be soon brought to ruin by having too many demagogues ... We shall trace with a sure hand the natural limits of the Republic. We shall make sure of the rivers which, after watering several of our departments, take their course toward the sea, and limit the countries now subject to our arms.

Jean Jacques Régis de Cambacérès, to the delegates of Prussia, at the peace negotiations in Basle, April 1795, in Guizot's History.

10. Wars Against Austria, England and Switzerland: September 1795 to December 1798

THE HISTORICAL CONTEXT

After the great military successes of late 1793 through the first half of 1795, the spirit of the French armies began to change again. Their provisions and equipment had deteriorated ever since the free market system had been reintroduced. After the downfall of the Robespierre/Saint-Just regime, the control over the generals had relaxed. There were many deserters now, and the gap between army and people was widening. The soldier now looked down upon the civilians whom they called *pékins* (philistines). After annexing so many non-French countries and imposing her will on them, France was no longer just patriotic but had become extremely nationalistic, dominating her surrounding "sister-republics" of Belgium and Holland and parts of Switzerland and Italy.

When the Directory took over in October of 1795, Lazare Nicolas Carnot, its leading man, planned a threefold attack against Austria and England: The Sambre-Meuse army under Jean Baptiste Jourdan and the Rhine-Moselle army under Jean Victor Moreau were to march through Germany toward Vienna; Louis Lazare Hoche was to organize a landing in England from his base at Brest; and in Italy, Barthélemy Louis Joseph Scherer was to invade the Austrian-held states of Piedmont and Lombardy.

Jourdan's first attempt to invade Germany by crossing the Rhine at Düsseldorf miscarried because he received no support from the disgruntled Jean Charles Pichegru, who was then replaced by Moreau. After the Austrians counterattacked and occupied the Palatinate, an armistice with Austria was concluded, but the French policy of annexation induced Austria to terminate it soon. And when Jourdan tried a second invasion of Germany, he was confronted with the best general the Austrians had produced so far, the Archduke Charles.

Eventually, both Moreau and Jourdan operated in Germany and occupied Frankfort, Würzburg and Nürnberg, but since Charles succeeded in keeping their armies separated, they had to retreat across the Rhine before the end of 1796. The only gain for France had been the cession of some territories of Württemberg and Baden on the west bank of the Rhine.

France's operations against England were even less successful. Hoche's first attempt of an invasion, in December of 1796, was frustrated by a storm that dispersed his fleet. During the following spring, there were mutinies in the British navy operating in the North Sea, and in May of 1798, the Irish began to revolt against English rule, hoping for a French invasion. But when, in August and September of 1798, two expeditions were finally launched by France and landings effected in Ireland, they met with disastrous defeat.

Switzerland, too, became involved in a conflict with France. There had been pro-revolutionary uprisings, and emigrant Swiss democrats had urged the Directory to intervene in their country against the antiquated canton system in which the aristocracy ruled. France, on the other hand, was interested in holding the militarily important Alpine passes. So, against the will of a majority of the population, the Helvetian Republic was proclaimed in February of 1798, the state treasury in Berne confiscated, Swiss resistance suppressed and Geneva annexed by France. During 1799, Switzerland became a battleground for the wars between France and the Austrian and Russian allies. The Helvetian Republic, organized along the lines of the Paris Directory, never became popular, but, due to the presence of French troops, lasted until 1803 when Napoleon reorganized it into a looser federation of cantons.

Conflicts arose even with the United States. In March of 1797, the Directory had decreed the confiscation of all ships bearing the American flag, because it regarded John Jay's treaty with England as evidence of a pro-British policy by the United States. When President John Adams sent a commission to France, consisting of later-chief-justice John Marshall, Charles Pinckney and Elbridge Gerry, to negotiate a treaty on neutral trade and against privateering, the French negotiator, Charles Maurice de Talleyrand, tried to detach the pro-French Gerry from the other two and bribe him. When this became public knowledge in April of 1798, the two other commissioners left France, but Gerry remained because Talleyrand demanded a bribe of $250,000 and a loan of $10,000,000. The

United States was put on a war footing, but war was not declared and the matter was finally settled in 1800. A naval war had developed in the meantime, however, and in the treaty of 1800, the old alliance between France and the United States was abrogated. This incident, known as the XYZ Affair, after the names used by the French agents, was responsible for the creation of a navy department in Washington.

Of the prominent generals employed by the government up to this time, quite a number were no longer fighting for France. Marquis Marie Joseph de Lafayette, Charles Francois Dumouriez, Jean Charles Pichegru, Adam Philippe Custine had disappeared, and Louis Lazare Hoche, one of the most promising young officers and a general at the age of 31, died suddenly in 1797, during the German campaign, possibly of poisoning. But new leaders had come up: Louis Charles Desaix in Germany, Championnet in Italy, and, in the great Italian campaign of 1796, Napoleon Bonaparte, whose star soon outshone all the others.

CHRONICLE OF EVENTS

1795:   *July 27:* The reconquest of Belgium is completed.
September 6: Jourdan, fighting the Austrians, crosses the Rhine at Düsseldorf but receives no support from Pichegru and must retreat again on October 1.
December 31: Armistice established between Austrians and French at the Rhine.

1796:   *March 14:* Moreau replaces Pichegru as commander of the Rhine and Moselle army.
May 20: Austria terminates the armistice with France.
May 31: Jourdan again crosses the Rhine but is beaten back by the Austrian Archduke Charles.
June 24: Moreau crosses the Rhine.
July 4: Moreau beats the Austrians at Rastatt and occupies Munich.
July: Jourdan occupies Cologne and Frankfort but cannot join up with Moreau.
July 9: The English occupy the isle of Elba.
July 25: Jourdan takes Würzburg.
August 11: Jourdan occupies Nürnberg.
August 16 and 25: Peace treaties signed between the Directory and Württemberg and Baden, who cede their possessions on the western bank of the Rhine to France.
September 3: Jourdan is defeated near Würzburg. During the following weeks, the armies of Jourdan and Moreau retreat and recross the Rhine into France.
October 22: English evacuate Corsica.
October 31: Boats of neutral countries are no longer permitted to introduce British merchandise into France.
November 5: Admiral Louis Thomas de Villaret, who opposes an expedition into Ireland, is replaced by Justin Bonaventure Morard de Galles.

December 17-24: Expedition from Brest toward Ireland, led by Hoche, who is separated from part of his fleet by a storm and is forced to return.

1797:   *March 2:* The Directory decrees, as a revenge for the Anglo-American alliance, the confiscation of all ships bearing the American flag.
March 18: The British evacuate the isle of Elba.

Conquest of the Dutch fleet, January 1795

April 16: A number of mutinies begin in the British fleet on the North Sea, encouraging French invasion plans.

April 17: Championnet defeats the Austrian army at Altenkirchen.

April 18: Hoche defeats the Austrian army at Neuwied.

Napoleon, after marching from Italy through Tyrol, occupying Klagenfurt and apparently on his way to Vienna, concludes an armistice with Austria at Leoben; Austria's Belgian provinces are ceded to France, who in turn makes some concessions in Italy at the expense of neutral Venice.

June 10: Austrian troops occupy the Venetian part of Dalmatia.

September 19: General Hoche, only 31 years old, dies at Wetzlar, Germany.

September 23: Augereau, who supported the Directory in its coup d'état of September 4, is made supreme commander of all troops in Germany.

October 10: Napoleon takes the Veltlin district away from Switzerland and adds it to the Cisalpine Republic. Beginning of the XYZ diplomatic incident between France and the United States.

October 17: Peace treaty of Campo Formio, between Austria and France, is arranged by Napoleon. A conference at Rastatt is to settle peace conditions with the Holy Roman Empire and the question of compensation for the ceded west bank of the Rhine. Austria recognizes the French-controlled Cisalpine Republic and obtains Istria, Dalmatia and Venetia. The ancient Republic of Venice ceases to exist. Napoleon, who conducted the negotiations quite independently, sends two delegates to Paris where the Directory ratifies the treaty on October 26.

October 26: The Directory declares war on England. Napoleon is made supreme commander of the army against England.

October 27: Napoleon is made France's plenipotentiary for the congress at Rastatt.

November 4: The annexed west bank of the Rhine is divided into four departments.

November 16: Prussian King Frederick William II dies and is succeeded by his son Frederick William III.

November 28: The Rastatt Congress opens; attended by Napoleon only until December 2.

December 25: Napoleon discusses an expedition into Ireland with the Irish exile Wolfe Tone.

December 29: The fortress of Mayence is turned over to the French.

1798:   *January 12:* Napoleon submits to the Directory a plan to invade England.

January 18: A new French law provides that any neutral ship carrying British merchandise or having landed at a British port may be seized. This provokes the United States, which cancels former treaties and sends privateers against French ships. The Austrians occupy Venice.

February 9: France declares Switzerland as the Helvetian Republic, to be organized entirely on the French pattern.

March 5: Switzerland declares war on France, and her troops defeat the French general Guillaume Marie Brune at Laupen, but the French General Baron Alexis de Schauenberg beats a second Swiss army. Berne surrenders and is looted.

April: Five Swiss-Catholic cantons, under Aloys von Reding, revolt against the French. A compromise is finally found, and they accept the new Helvetian constitution.

April 21: At Aarau, the "United, Indivisible Helvetian Republic" is proclaimed, which replaces the old, loose federation of cantons led by patricians.

April 26: Geneva is annexed by France.

May 23: Revolts begin in Ireland where people believe that the fleet Napoleon prepared against Egypt will come to free the Irish.

July 14: The Irish revolts are suppressed by the British.

August 18: Three Swiss cantons of Uri, Schwyz and Unterwalden revolt; suppressed within a few days.

August 19: An alliance between France and Switzerland is concluded, making the latter completely dependent on France.

August 22: A French expeditionary force under General Jean Joseph Humbert lands at Killala, northwest Ireland.

September 15: After some initial successes, the French corps under Humbert is confined at Ballynamuck and must surrender.

September 16: A second French expedition is sent to Ireland.

October 11: French expeditionary fleet is defeated in the Bay of Donegal. Six of its eight ships are captured.

October 12: Belgian peasants revolt against military conscription.

October 25-27: A Russian-Turkish fleet conquers the Ionian islands, occupied by the French since June of 1797.

December 4: The revolting Belgian peasants are massacred by French troops at Hasselt, province of Limbourg. This is the end of the Belgian riots.

December 6: The Directory sends an ultimatum to the Rastatt Congress, demanding the bridgeheads of the east bank of the Rhine. It is accepted on December 9.

EYEWITNESS TESTIMONY

Dumouriez' "Life" let us look deeper into the particular events the general aspects of which were, unfortunately, sufficiently known; some characters were explained to us and the man for whom we had always felt much sympathy, appeared in a clear and favorable light.

Johann Wolfgang von Goethe, 1795, "Annalen," in Collected Works *(1854).*

In my travels through several departements of the republic I observed that deserting troops are walking along the roads as undisturbed as I, and nobody felt obliged to arrest them or to use the laws on desertion against them. More than that: I have learned that in many cases the parents of these deserters were mayors or municipal officials.

V. Dupuis, report to the Directory on the state of the army, November 1795, in Military Operations on the Sambre in 1794 *(1891).*

The retreating Austrians crossed the Lahn river but intend to hold on to Frankfurt while the French approach. The town is being bombarded, part of the Jewish quarter burns down, otherwise little damage … whereupon the town surrenders … My good mother brings her belongings into fireproof cellars and flees to Offenbach, crossing the Main bridge which was kept open … the Austrians, once again, get the upper hand. Moreau retreats, and all royalists regret their previous haste. The rumors unfavorable to the French increase. Moreau is being pursued … they already claim him to be surrounded. Jourdan also retreats and people are in despair for having saved themselves prematurely.

Goethe, 1796, "Annalen," in Collected Works *(1854).*

You will grant a general pardon to all those who have merely been led astray, but arrest and try by court-martial the four deputies who handed over the crown to the King of England, the members of the government and the leaders of the infamous treason.

Napoleon Bonaparte, to his General Gentile, after the British evacuation of Corsica, October 1796, in Guizot's History of France.

The emperor is to be put in possession of all the states which he possessed before the war. Italy will be evacuated by the French troops, with an engagement not to interfere in her internal affairs. Peace will be concluded with the empire.

Lord Malmesbury, foreign minister, presents England's peace demands to France, December 1796, Guizot's History.

You yourself, have you not pointed out to me that the Republic was no longer in a state of monarchical decrepitude? I can agree with you that France, by her change of government, has acquired a power and authority much superior to what she could gain by an increase of territory. France, when under a monarch, already attracted the attention, not to say suspicion, of the European states, and by her republican constitution she is now more powerful. Thus she can cause more inquietude, and every addition to her territory may alarm Europe.

Malmesbury, to French Minister of Foreign Affairs Delacroix, December 1796, in Guizot's History.

After exhausting all the means of evasion and delay, Lord Malmesbury has at last been forced to express himself categorically. His proposals were all contrary to the constitution, laws and treaties. He proposed to France disgrace and perfidy; and has been ordered to depart.

Journal Officiel (Paris), December 19, 1796.

… am now so near the shore that I can see distinctly two old castles, yet I am utterly uncertain whether I shall ever set foot on it.

Theobald Wolfe Tone, adjutant general of a French invasion army off the Irish coast, December 21, 1796, "Journals," in MacManus' The Story of the Irish Race *(1946).*

Our first idea was it might be an English frigate lurking in the bottom of the bay … for it seemed incredible that an admiral [Bouvet] should cut and run in this manner without any previous signal … to warn the fleet.

Tone, off the Irish coast, as fleet is ordered to depart, December 25, 1796, "Journals," in MacManus' Irish Race (1946).

Every effort and every resource should be called into action which cannot be done unless there is a formal declaration of war. To me, there appears no alternative between actual hostilities on our part and national ruin.

President John Adams, on the XYZ Affair, March 1797, in Smith's The Shaping of America (1980).

The Jacobins in Senate and House were struck dumb and opened not their mouths, not having their cue, not having received their lesson [from Jefferson and Madison].

Abigail Adams, to her sister, on the XYZ Affair, letter of March 1797, in Smith's The Shaping of America (1980).

General-in-chief, the brave soldiers make war and desire peace. Has this war not lasted six years? Have we killed men enough, and inflicted upon humanity woes enough? She protests on every side … Is there, then, no hope of our coming to an understanding, in spite of the intervention of the court of London? Shall we continue to cut each others' throats for the interest of a nation which is a stranger to the evils of war? You, M. General-in-Chief, who by your birth approach so near the throne, you who are above the little passions which frequently animate ministers and cabinets, are you decided to deserve the title of benefactor to humanity, to be the real savior of Germany? … As for me … if the overture which I have the honor of making you can save the life of a single man, I shall feel prouder of the civic crown which I shall have gained, than of the sad glory of military triumphs.

Napoleon, at Klagenfurt, letter to Archduke Charles, April 1797.

Certainly, M. General-in-Chief, whilst making war … like you I desire peace for the good of the people and humanity … as I am not furnished on the part of his majesty the Emperor with any power to treat, you will consider it natural … that I wait for superior orders on a subject of such great importance … But whatever may

be the future chances of war, I beg of you, general, to be convinced of my esteem and high regard.

Archduke Charles of Austria, to Napoleon, in reply, April 1797, in Guizot's History.

We renounce, it is true, all Lombardy, but shall we not have drawn from our success all the advantage possible when we shall have the Rhine for boundary, and shall have established in the heart of Italy a Republic, which in Carrara will be found quite close to us, will give us the commerce of the Po, of the Adriatic; and which will increase as fast as the power of the Pope is destroyed?

Napoleon, to the Directory, on the armistice at Leoben, April 1797.

The Republic does not require to be recognized, it is the sun at noonday; so much the worse for those who will not see it. Questions of etiquette and precedence have not been arranged, that concerns the diplomats.

Napoleon, at Leoben, after Austrian offer to recognize French Republic, in Guizot's History.

This city [Newburyport, Massachusetts] … has become one military school and every morning the sound of the drum and the fife lead forth.

Abigail Adams, to her son, John Quincy, on war preparations over XYZ Affair, letter of May 1797, in Smith's The Shaping of America (1980).

These will be more important to us than the whole rest of Italy put together. They are essential to the wealth and prosperity of our commerce. If we wish to destroy England effectively we must get our foot into Egypt. The vast Turkish Empire, dying a little more every day, forces us to get ahead of developments and to take prompt measures to preserve our commerce in the Levant.

Bonaparte, to the Directory on Ionian islands taken from Venice, letter of August 16, 1797.

The Frenchman is not quiet for a moment, he walks, gossips, jumps, whistles, sings and makes so much noise that … one always expects a greater number in a town or village than are actually present; while the Austrian goes his way quietly and calmly … They get irritated if one does not understand their language, they seem to expect that from the whole world … but if one knows how to talk to them and treat them they show themselves at once as bons enfans and rarely continue to be nasty or brutal. Yet one tells of various bribing manoeuvers under all sorts of pretexts ... When they left a place where their cavalry had been stationed, they are supposed to have asked for payment of the manure. When that was refused, they set out to requisition as many carriages as were needed to transport the manure to France; whereupon, naturally, one decided to rather pay the compensation ... They praise the excellent order and work done in the offices of their generals, and the public spirit of their soldiers.

Goethe, occupation of Frankfurt by the French, August 1797, Journey to Switzerland *(1797).*

Finish the peace, but an honorable peace; let the Rhine be our limit; let Mantua belong to the Cisalpine republic and Venice to the house of Austria.

Paul Francois Barras, to Napoleon, instructions for the peace negotiations at Campo Formio, October 1797, in Guizot's History.

The Directory will not ratify the treaty passed with the king of Sardinia; one of the articles guarantees to this prince the safety of his kingdom; now we cannot give to kings a guarantee against peoples; such an engagement would lead us to make war against the principles for which, up to the present time, we have been fighting. Piedmont will become what it can, between France and Italy, both of which are free.

Charles Maurice de Talleyrand-Périgord, to Napoleon, at Campo Formio, October 1797, Guizot's History.

You do not know the Italians; they do not merit that forty thousand Frenchmen should be killed for them ... you imagine that liberty will cause great things to be done by a people who are effeminate, superstitious, haughty and cowardly. You wish me to do miracles. I do now know how.

Napoleon, to the Directory, pleading for peace with Austria by ceding them Venice, October 1797.

The Emperor is irrevocably resolved to expose himself to all the chances of war, and even to fly from his capital rather than consent to such a shameful peace. Russia offers him her troops; they are ready to hasten to his succor; it will be seen what the Russian troops are.

You do not wish for peace; all the blood shed in this new war will be on your head; I set out tonight.

Jean Phillipe de Cobenzl, Austrian plenipotentiary, to Napoleon, October 16, 1797, Guizot's History.

Well, the truce is then broken, and the war declared; but remember that before the end of autumn I shall have crushed your monarchy like this porcelain. [Cobenzl signed the following day.]

Napoleon to Cobenzl, while dropping a set of porcelain on the floor, October 1797, in Guizot's History.

... you and the constitution of the year III, together, have triumphed over all obstacles. Religion, feudalism and royalty have successively, during twenty ages, governed Europe, but the peace you have just concluded begins the era of representative governments ... The peace secures the liberty, the prosperity and the glory of the Republic ...

Napoleon, to the Directory, December 10, 1797.

Why, then peace is accomplished—a peace à la Bonaparte. The Directory are satisfied, the public enchanted, everything is for the best; we shall hear, perhaps, some grumbling from the Italians, but that is of no consequence. Adieu, general peacemaker, adieu! Friendship, admiration, respect, gratitude; one does not know where to stop in this enumeration!

Talleyrand to Napoleon, letter of October 1797, Guizot's History.

We should abandon any serious attempts to invade England, and be satisfied with the mere appearance of it, while we are devoting all our attention and resources to the area of the Rhine ... We should not keep a large army at a distance from Germany ... Or we may prepare an expedition into the Levant and thus threaten England's commerce with India.

Napoleon, to the Directory, letter of February 23, 1798.

It is an admirable thing that troops who have not made war for two centuries should have been able to sustain five consecutive combats, and that they should be with difficulty driven from one post, only to be found holding and defending another.

General Baron Alexis Henry Antoine Balthasar de Schauenberg, fighting the Swiss, letter of March 1798, Guizot's History.

… no ghost of Poland, of Venice is going around to …announce … their resurrection. But what vitality is pulsing in the defeated, but virile and strong body of Helvetia! … an overwhelmingly powerful neighbor brought her this spark of Prometheus on the tip of a bayonet … Here, for the first time, there was no artificiality as on the Po and Tiber rivers … there was chaos, but heralding not dissolution, but a new strength to live.

Neueste Weltkunde (Stuttgart), after France had forced its revolutionary system on Switzerland, March 1798.

11. The Directory: October 1795 to October 1799

THE HISTORICAL CONTEXT

In August of 1795, the Convention had accepted the new, third constitution, which was preceded by a declaration of the rights and duties of the French citizen. It provided for two chambers, the Council of Ancients, with 250 members, and the Council of 500. The latter proposed the laws, the former decided on them. The five directors were selected by the Council of Ancients from a list submitted by the other chamber. Every year, one director and one-third of both chambers had to retire and were then replaced. Voting was indirect and secret.

This constitution attempted to recreate a government of the liberal bourgeoisie, the kind the country had in 1791, but without a monarchy. The rights of man were defined even more precisely than in the original proclamation of August 1789, which had become part of the constitution of 1791. This time, equality was clearly understood as equality before the law, not economic equality. The strict centralization of administration as practiced during the rule of the Jacobins and Montagnards was loosened somewhat. The cleverly contrived system of government, designed to prevent the rise of a dictatorship of the right or the left worked quite well for some time, and the directors maintained the upper hand against the plots of the Neo-Hébertists, Francois Nöel Babeuf's egalitarian revolutionaries and military conspirators such as Charles Brottier.

The Vicomte Paul Francois de Barras

Yet basically the Directory was supported only by a small minority of the population and could not rely on either the lower classes or the aristocrats, or even on all of the bourgeoisie. It never became popular, and its leading personalities did not enjoy the confidence of the masses. Lazare Nicolas Carnot, at first the central figure, had changed from terrorist to conservative. The Vicomte Paul Francois de Barras, who took over from him around the beginning of 1797, was a skillful politician who managed to be on good terms with the left and the right but had no convictions of his own and obviously was open to bribery.

Francois Noël Babeuf

The extremely harsh winter of 1795-96 resulted in a dangerous breakdown of law and order. The government reacted by creating a special ministry of police, and it finally did away with the assignats, which had become almost totally worthless. But the new paper money, the *mandats territoriaux* lost value just as radically, within six months, as the old assignats had done in five years. Since they were to be used for the purchase of public lands, national property was thus squandered away, and inflation was worse than ever. Only the large amounts of metallic money, flowing in from the conquered territories from 1796 on, enabled the Directory in February of 1797 to abandon the paper money system altogether and to reintroduce metal coins. The success of the armies, where the revolutionary spirit had survived much more vividly than in the rest of the country, had once again saved the nation.

During 1796, the main political opposition had come from the left, in particular Francois Nöel (Gracchus, as he now called himself) Babeuf and his partisans, the so-called Conspiracy of the Equals. Babeuf has been called the first communist in modern history. He demanded not only common ownership of land, the right of all men to work and to share in the products of the economy, but his secret committee had also worked out a plan for a popular dictatorship, temporary until the people had been sufficiently enlightened and opponents eliminated. His teachings were never entirely suppressed, even after his conspiracy was finally crushed, and there is no doubt that his ideas anticipated much of what Marx and Lenin were to proclaim later, except that he did not envision a sharing of the means of production but only of the distribution of goods.

But by the beginning of 1797, the main danger seemed to come from the opposite camp. First, there was the attempted military coup of Abbé Brottier, which was easily suppressed. The second and more threatening development was the great royalist wave that swept through the south and brought about anti-republican majorities in both houses. The Directory, now dominated by the new triumvirate of Barras, Jean Francois Reubell and Louis Marie de La Revellière, reacted with a coup d'état, well-prepared and executed with great skill and precision, after the decisive military leaders, in particular Lazare Hoche and Napoleon Bonaparte, had been won over and then participated in the action. The result was a military dictatorship that sent emigrants and resisting priests into exile, put down the press and got rid of undesirable politicians, above all Carnot, by sending them to Guyana—a practice known as the dry guillotine (*guillotine sèche*).

In short, a new terror system was enacted, little less brutal than that of Robespierre. Only this time, a number of generals were behind it, especially the victor of the 1796 Italian campaign, Bonaparte, whose prestige grew from day to day. The Directory was apparently less afraid of the generals than of the royalists—partly because by 1797 peace was finally achieved on the continent, diminishing some of the generals' glory, and partly because in the south, where the Jacobin terror was only too well remembered, the Catholic Church and British money worked hand in hand with the royalist opposition.

The so-called Second Directory, which ruled the country for another two years after the coup of September 1797, stood on shaky grounds and managed to survive only by means of another coup d'état, this time against the radical left, which in turn had been encouraged by the antiroyalist terror. The spring elections of 1798 were dominated by a lively neo-Jacobin agitation. When, as a result, both chambers were filled with Jacobins, the Directory did not hesitate to revise the election results by law, excluding a number of elected leftists and replacing them with supporters of the government. Thus, a pro-Directory majority was forcibly achieved in both chambers, and a number of important reforms could be carried through. The public debt was cut by two-thirds in an entirely arbitrary way, with the government paying off debt in bonds usable only for the purchase of land taken from the nobles and the clergy. The tax system was reorganized and general conscription reintroduced. The first international exhibition took place on the Champ de Mars in the fall of 1798 and was a great success. The first population census was taken, and welfare institutions were organized in all communities. New uprisings in the Vendée and by the Chouans were, after some initial successes, finally and decisively put down.

Yet the lingering crisis in the country had never been resolved completely, and this became very obvious in the year 1799. Complete control of the economy or even an effective reduction of the profits of the great entrepreneurs could not be achieved, since the government lacked the authority to carry out the necessary measures. A third attempt to start a new non-Christian cult, La Revellière's "Théophilantropes," was based on belief in God, virtue and immortality and bore some resemblance to the tenets of Freemasonry; it was even less successful with the people than the "Cult of Reason" and the "Worship of a Supreme Being" had been and failed to pacify the devoutly Catholic south. Economically, France was living off its conquests in the surrounding countries. When they were lost again, in 1799, the economic crisis created a political one. One of the great revolutionaries of 1789, Emanuel Joseph Sieyès, a fanatic enemy of the directorial constitution, was elected a director and supplanted Barras as the leading spirit in the Directory. The time for a thorough reorganization of France seemed to be at hand.

By 1799, 10 years after the outbreak of the Revolution, France had been transformed. Tremendous changes had taken place, as uprisings and civil wars had destroyed whole sections in the cities, and hundreds of villages and whole areas in the Vendée were ruined. Churches and monasteries had suffered terribly. A modern traveller through France will notice that most of the destruction and vandalism in churches does not go back to the time of the English-French dynastic wars or the great religious wars but to the Great Revolution. In Paris in 1799, many monasteries and churches had fallen into ruin and were up for sale. The giant palace of Versailles, which for so long had been the splendid center of royal government, stood empty, with grass growing in its courtyards. Even the old royal castle in Paris, the Tuileries, was deserted, for the Directory had settled in the smaller Palais de Luxembourg, built for the widow of Henry IV, which had served as a prison in the days of the Terror.

Great ladies dominated Paris society, which met in their salons, such as that established by Thérésa Cabarrus, former Marquise de Fontenay, then friend and later wife of the Thermidorean Jean Lambert Tallien. Called *Notre Dame de Thermidor*, she had escaped the guillotine during the Terror only by the skin of her teeth. Among the other influential women were Madame Jeanne Francoise Récamier, friend of Benjamin Constant, Francois René de Chateaubriand and Madame Germaine de Staël; and Josephine de Beauharnais, whose husband had been guillotined in 1794 and who was a friend of Barras and later became the wife of Napoleon Bonaparte. All these society ladies had lived with different men; this had now become generally acceptable.

Many of the old feudal estates stood empty now or had been taken over by land speculators. Yet many of the emigrants had returned. Though in principle the Directory was anti-emigrant, because it feared nothing but trouble from these circles, its directives were not as strictly obeyed as they had been in Robespierre's time, for the regime was so much less respected. Madame de Staël, as an example, managed to bring back to Paris her friend Charles Maurice de Talleyrand, former bishop of Autun who had lived in British and American exile since 1792. Similar to Sieyès, he became part of the government during the last period of the Directory and then continued to play an important, even decisive role in French and European politics under Napoleon.

It is estimated that during the time of the Revolution about 150,000 people emigrated from France and that about 20,000 were executed for political reasons. In spite of this and the enormous bloodletting in the Vendée, France, with about 28 million inhabitants, was still the most populous country in Europe, and her armies were superior to those of any European nation. They fought simultaneously in Belgium, on the Rhine, in Switzerland, Italy and Egypt, and they spread the ideas of 1789 all over Europe.

With all these fundamental upheavals, it is astonishing to observe how little the artistic styles and tastes of the country had changed in those years. When the theaters were reopened after the 9th of Thermidor, they again played Corneille, Racine, Voltaire and Molière as they had done in the days of Louis XV and Louis XVI. The neoclassical style, which followed the rococo, had its origins in the years before 1789. Returning to simpler, more classic forms appealed to the historical conceptions of the revolutionaries, whose great inspiration was classical antiquity and whose heroes were Gracchus and Brutus. Jacques Louis David, the most prominent painter of the revolutionary period and later court painter to Napoleon, influenced decisively not only the painting but also the interior decoration and fashions of his time by building his style completely on Greek and Hellenistic models.

State-church relations, on the other hand, had changed radically since 1789 and would never be the same, in spite of the restoration under Napoleon. The old alliance between state and church was dissolved. At first the Revolution had limited itself to the secularization of the state and the establishment of a civic constitution for the church. But during the time of the National Convention, mutual hostility grew, mostly because of the attitude of the priests who refused to take the oath of loyalty to the government. Marriages of priests and divorces were now permitted. The new republican calendar and the introduction of the *décade*, the tenth day as a day of rest instead of the old Sunday, were antichurch measures, as were the three attempts to substitute new cults for Christianity.

Under the Consulate, a religious restoration was quickly accomplished, but the church remained subordinated to the state, and a certain indifference to religious matters became a permanent characteristic of French government. To cite just one example, the abbey of Cluny, center of the Cluniac movement and order—in the 11th and 12th centuries the largest and one of the most beautiful churches in the world—was sold to a building contractor in 1798 who started to demolish it. Of the giant complex of buildings, only a small part still stands today, for the demolition was continued through the consular and imperial and even deeply into the restoration period and was not stopped until 1823!

CHRONICLE OF EVENTS

1795:   *October 31:* The five directors are elected, all of them "regicides": At the left, the Vicomte Paul Francois de Barras (diplomacy, finance, justice). The most moderate is Lazare Nicolas Carnot, former Jacobin (ministry of war), also Louis Francois Letourneur (navy); while former Girondist Louis Marie de La Revellière-Lepeaux (education, arts, industry) takes a position at the center. Emanuel Joseph Sieyès declined the post since his plan for a constitution had been rejected. Leading in the Directory are first Carnot and from spring of 1797, Barras, the Thermidorean.

End of October: System of education reorganized. Upon Pierre Claude Daunou's initiative, the National Institute for Sciences and Arts is founded in Paris.

November 30: In Francois Nöel Babeuf's *Tribune of the People*, his "Manifesto of the Plebeians" is published. He demands happiness for all by sharing of goods and even distribution of work.

December 5: Babeuf's arrest is decreed. He stays in hiding.

December 18-26: Madame Royale, daughter of Louis XVI, is released in exchange for a number of republican prisoners (Pierre de Beurnonville, Jean Baptiste Drouet and others).

December: The poor harvests of the last two years result in the worst winter of the Revolution. Highway robberies and murders occur every day, huge numbers of beggars crowd the streets. This starts a new wave of agitation through the Jacobins and in the Paris Pantheon Club (Babeuf).

1796:   *January 2:* A ministry of police is created, headed by Philippe Antoine Merlin de Douai, the originator of the law against suspects.

February 19: The issue of new assignats is discontinued. Thirty-one billion are in circulation.

February 23: Chouans' leader Nicolas Stofflet, who had taken up arms again upon the instigation of the Comte Charles Philippe d'Artois, is captured and shot.

February 28: On orders of the Directory, General Napoleon Bonaparte closes the Pantheon Club.

Lazare Nicolas Carnot

March 18: Instead of the assignats, a new type of paper-money, called *Mandats territoriaux* is issued. Within a few weeks, it loses two-thirds of its value. Since it is accepted for the purchase of public lands, a great number of estates change ownership within a very short time.

March 23: General Louis Lazare Hoche defeats the Vendée leader, Francois Athanase Charette, who is taken prisoner and shot at Nantes.

March 30: Since the Pantheon Club is closed, Babeuf and his friends, Pierre Sylvain Maréchal and Philippe Michel Buonarotti found the Secret Committee of Conspiracy for Equality.

April 6: Babeuf and his friends publish their *Manifeste des Egaux.*

April 27: Benjamin Constant's brochure on the power of the government supports the Directory.

End of April: The rebellion in the Vendée is finally suppressed, and the Army of the West is dissolved.

May 10: Carnot alarms the Directory and the public about the danger of Babeuf's plots and has him and his coconspirators arrested.

July 5: Pius VI recognizes the French republic, but further negotiations fail because he will not accept the civic status of the clergy.

July 31: The experiment of the *Mandats territoriaux* is discontinued; payment for national lands from now on will be based on the metal value of the franc. This comes too late to prevent the dissipation of public lands.

September 9: An uprising of Babeuf-partisans at Paris's Grenelle district, apparently provoked by the police, is suppressed.

October 10: A military commission condemns to death 32 Babeuf-conspirators and Montagnards from the Grenelle district.

December 4: Laws against uncooperative priests are mitigated.

1797:   *January:* Conspiracy of Abbé Charles Brottier for a military coup against the Directory is betrayed by Colonel Malo; Brottier and his accomplices are sent to prison for 10 years. In the Directory, the influence of Barras is increasing at Carnot's expense. Le Revellière founds the *Secte des Théophilanthropes* in Paris, which shows similarities to the Freemasons.

February 4: The experiment of paper money is abandoned altogether. Future payments are permitted only in metal currency. This was made possible through the vast amounts of foreign money obtained by the armies in Germany and Italy.

February 20 : Trial of Babeuf and his friends begins.

February 25: Because the Directory fears election victories of the royalists, 120,000 former emigrants are deprived of the right to vote.

February 26: Hoche takes over the command of the Sambre-et-Meuse army.

March: In spite of all the measures taken by the Directory, the royalists are victorious in the election of one-third of the delegates to both councils.

May 20: Because of the election results, three monarchists obtain leading positions: Jean Charles Pichegru is made president of the Council of 500; Francois Barbe-Marbois, president of the Council of Ancients; and Balthazar Francois Barthélemy, a diplomat, replaces Letourneur in the Directory.

May 27: Babeuf and his follower Darthé, after being condemned to death and unsuccessfully attempting to commit suicide, are taken to Vendôme and executed.

June 4: The Circle of Constitutionals (*Cercle constitutionel*) convenes, consisting of moderate, non-terrorist republicans: Talleyrand, Sieyès, Tallien, Dominique Joseph Garat and others.

June 14: The councils transfer complete control of public finances to the ministry of finances, in order to restrict the authority of the Directory.

June 27: The harsh law of October 25, 1795, against recalcitrant priests and emigrants is rescinded.

July 1: Hoche, the only reliably pro-Directory army commander, who has a secret understanding with Barras, sends 9,000 troops to Paris, while the other commanders, Jean Victor Moreau on the Rhine and Bonaparte in Italy, do not commit themselves in view of the developing conflict between Directory and royalists.

July 14: The Directory's republican triumvirate, Barras, Reubell and La Revellière, appoint Talleyrand as minister of foreign affairs and Hoche as war minister, thereby reducing the influence of the royalist directors Carnot and Barthélemy.

July 17-20: Hoche's troops, presumably called in for the expedition against Ireland, camp close to Paris,

Jean Francois Reubell

Reubell

Napoleon Bonaparte

which is forbidden by the constitution. The royalists protest.

July 20: Barras accuses Pichegru of having contact with Louis XVIII. Carnot sides with the republican directors.

July 22: Hoche is dismissed and replaced by Barthélemy Louis Scherer.

July 27: Bonaparte sends Charles Pierre D'Augereau to Paris to take Hoche's part in the forthcoming coup d'état.

August 7-8: D'Augereau arrives in Paris and is put in command of the troops around the city.

August 25: La Revellière replaces Carnot as president of the Directory.

September 3: To counteract the manipulations of the republican directors, the councils decide to indict Barras, Reubell and La Revellière, but it is too late.

September 4 (18th Fructidor): Coup d'état of the triumvirate against the councils. D'Augereau arrests Pichegru and Barthélemy and the leading royalists. Carnot hides and escapes. Remaining directors proclaim the reintroduction of terror laws. Anyone advocating the monarchy or the constitution of 1793 will be shot. Fifty-three deputies are exiled to Guyana. The elections in 49 departments are declared invalid. The last terror laws of the Convention of October 25, 1795, are reintroduced. The two councils are demoralized and approve all measures.

September 8: A new law establishes control of the press by the police. The editors and journalists of 42 royalist journals are deported.

September 14: Philippe Antoine Merlin de Douai and Nicolas Louis Francois de Neufchateau replace Carnot and Barthélemy as directors. The military dictatorship is now fully established.

September 19: Hoche dies in Wetzlar, Germany.

September 23: D'Augereau is made commander of both armies operating in Germany.

September 30: Dominique Vincent Ramel, minister of finances, introduces a law to annul two-thirds of the public debt. The government pays, but only in bonds usable for the purchase of lands taken from the nobles or the clergy.

December 17: Another 16 royalist journals are prohibited.

December 25: Bonaparte is elected a member of the Institut National, instead of the outlawed Carnot.

1798: *January 27:* General Guillaume Marie Brune is made commander of the French troops in Switzerland.

April 18-19: Elections are held for one-third of the deputies of both councils.

May 11: The *Coup d'Etat du 22 floréal*: The two councils revise the election results, which favored the Jacobins, and exclude 106 Jacobins, replacing them by moderate deputies.

June 17: Francois de Neufchateau leaves the Directory, becomes minister of the interior and carries out a number of liberal reforms in industry during the next year.

August 4: The *Décadi*, every tenth day, become the official days of rest. A regular cult for these days, to be performed in schools etc., is determined by law on September 9.

September 5: On instigation of General Jean Baptiste Jourdan, general conscription for all men between 20 and 25 is reintroduced.

September 24: 200,000 men are called to arms, but only one-third comply.

October 15: Neufchateau holds first National Exhibition of manufacturers in Paris.

November 23: A real estate tax is introduced, also one on doors and windows.

1799: *April 9-18:* The elections for one-third of both councils reinforce the left opposition against the Directory. Sieyès, who is radically opposed to the directorial constitution, is made director, replacing Reubell.

June 16-20: Conflict within the government: The Directory is held responsible by the councils for recent military setbacks. Merlin de Douai and La Revellière are dismissed, and Barras and Sieyès enforce a more radical-republican course.

June 28: A loan of 100,000,000 francs is enforced upon the rich to finance the conscription of new troops, causing a panic among the capitalists.

July 2: Jean Baptiste Bernadotte is made war minister.

July 6: The *Réunion d'amis de la Liberté et de L'Egalité* is founded, a resurrection of the Jacobin club. Upon Sieyès' insistence, it is closed again on August 13.

July 12: The hostage law is enacted. Relatives of emigrants or Chouans can be taken as hostages, of which four will be deported every time a "constitu-tional" priest or a buyer of public lands is assas-sinated. Former directors La Revellière, Reubell, Jean Baptiste Treilhard and General Scherer are indicted by the Council of 500.

July 20: Sieyès puts through a number of appoint-ments of personalities agreeable to him: Jean Jacques Cambacérès as minister of justice, Joseph Fouché as minister of police, Robert Thomas Lindet as minister of finances, Charles Frédéric de Reinhard as foreign minister. Sieyès dominates the Directory from here on.

August 6: Royalist revolt in Bordeaux.

August 18: By a very close vote, the indictments against La Revellière, Reubell etc, are dropped.

September 14: Jourdan's demand to have the mother-land declared to be in danger is rejected by the Coun-cil of 500. Bernadotte, accused by Sieyès of preparing a pro-Jacobin coup d'tat, is dismissed.

September 15: The surviving royalist leaders in the Vendée and of the Chouans unite to prepare a new revolt.

October 14: Moreau, approached by Sieyès, refuses to participate in a coup d'état. The Chouans take Le Mans but must evacuate it three days later.

October 19: The Chouans, led by Chantillon and d'Andigne, occupy Nantes.

October 29: In spite of some further successes, the Vendée rebels are beaten back at Cholet, and the revolt subsides from here on.

EYEWITNESS TESTIMONY

... We shall determine the limits of property rights. We shall prove that the land and the soil do not belong to individuals, but to all. We shall prove that whatever anyone appropriates for himself beyond what he needs for his subsistence is theft from society ... We shall prove that the law of inheritance by the family is no less of a monstrosity because it divides the members of society and turns every household into a small republic which is forced to conspire against the great republic ... that the superiority of talent and diligence is just a fairy tale, a dazzling deception which has always supplied a semblance of justice to the plots of the conspirators against equality ... that it is totally unjustified to evaluate a day's work of a clockmaker twenty times as high as that of a man who ploughs his acre ... that it is senseless and unjust to demand a higher reward for him whose work requires a higher degree of intelligence, more diligence and a greater intellectual effort; because these do not in any way increase the capacity of his stomach ... that the value of intelligence is likewise only a question of personal judgment, and that one should perhaps investigate if the value of natural, purely physical strength is not just as great ...

Francois Nöel (Gracchus) Babeuf, "Manifesto of the Plebeians," November 1795, in Selected Texts *(1950).*

People of France! You have lived in slavery for 15 centuries, which means in misery. For the last six years, you have breathed a little more freely, expecting independence, happiness and equality ... Therefore, we demand that from now on we should live and die as equals, as we were born equals. We want real equality, or death. And we shall have this real equality, whatever it may cost ... The French Revolution is but a forerunner of another, much greater, much more serious revolution which will be the last one ... We declare that we will no longer tolerate that the overwhelming majority of men work and sweat serving the whims and desires of a tiny minority ... The moment has come to found the republic of equals, the great home open to all people. The days of thorough restitution have come.

Pierre Sylvain Maréchal, "Manifesto of the Equals" (coauthor), January 1796, in Lefèbvre's The Thermidorians and the Directory *(1964).*

I have now travelled one hundred fifty miles in France and I do not think I have seen one hundred fifty acres uncultivated, the very orchards are under grain. All the mills I have seen were at work, and all the chateaux' shut up without exception.

Theobald Wolfe Tone, Irish Revolutionary, upon returning to France from America, February 12, 1796, in Thompson's English Witnesses to the French Revolution *(1938).*

1. Nature has bestowed on every man an equal right to the enjoyment of all goods ...

3. Nature has imposed on every man the obligation to work ...

7. In a free society there should be neither rich nor poor.

10. The purpose of the Revolution is to abolish inequality and establish common happiness.

Babeuf, selected propaganda articles posted in working- class quarters, April 11, 1796, Selected Texts *(1950).*

Will you consider it beneath you, citizen directors, to treat me as between one power and another? ... You hold nothing, although I am in your power. I am not the whole plot, I am but one link of the chain. Is it for your interests, or the interests of the country, to give notoriety to the conspiracy you have discovered? I think not. What will happen should the affair be openly published? Such a trial would be not one of justice, but one of the strong against the weak, of the oppressors against the oppressed and their magnanimous defenders ... You have even been genuine republicans, and why not be so again? Declare that there has been no serious conspiracy. Five men, by proving themselves generous, can save the country. I can assure you that for the future the patriots will defend you with their bodies, and you will no longer have need of an army to protect you.

Babeuf, to the Directory after his imprison-
ment, letter of May 1796, Texts *(1950).*

… no matter how determined your will, it is impossible not to be influenced by the company you keep. First you agree out of politeness, then you feel too self-conscious to retrace false steps, and finally you will accept the opinion of others, in spite of yourself. In this way the republican party produced many traitors: Some were just making concessions here and there, but others surrendered completely to the royalists …

Antoine Claire Thibaudeau, Paris in 1796,
Memoirs of the Convention and the Directory *(1824).*

We all are chained to the throne of the Supreme Being by an elastic band which holds us without enslaving us … In revolutionary times, this chain is suddenly shortened, the elbowroom is getting smaller … The French revolution led the people, rather than being led by them … Those who established the republic did it without wanting it or knowing what they were doing … they were the instrument of a power who knew more than they did.

Joseph de Maistre, French diplomat and con-
servative philosopher, Considérations sur la
France *(1796).*

Each drop of Louis XVI's blood will cost torrents to France; possibly four million Frenchmen will have to pay with their lives for the terrible crime of an antireligious and antisocial rebellion which was crowned by regicide.

De Maistre, Considérations *(1796).*

I have been running about Paris just as formerly [i.e., before the revolution] … how dull, how gloomy Paris is! All its hurry and crowds seem concentrated round the focus of this neighborhood. The rest of the town is deserted. The Fauxbourg Saint-Germain can never recover. I had been told by English republicans and Americans that wonderful things had been done, and magnificent works undertaken. I see many things pulled down, but except a repair on the roof of the Luxembourg, the alteration of the Palais Bourbon and the finishing of the bridge I have not seen one new stone put upon another. There are wood and plaster statues where brass and marble stood, dead poplar trees of liberty and the word "Proprit nationale" upon more than half the houses.

Henry Swinburne, English traveler and
plenipotentiary of the British Government, let-
ter of November 17, 1796, in Thompson's
English Witnesses *(1938).*

I have been at the site of the Bastille, now a timberyard. As there have been 57 new prisons instituted in Paris I think I may say that the Parisians have uselessly destroyed an ornament of their town … The complexion of the women seems to me much improved, and there is not such a quantity of rouge used as formerly.

Swinburne, letter of November 17, 1796, in
Thompson's English Witnesses *(1938).*

No winter in Paris has ever been so joyful. All over France, the pleasures of life were being enjoyed without restraint. A long famine had come to an end, money reappeared and with it an abundance of all things … Nobody talked any more about informers and the police … Even on the large streets masks were being worn … life was like one single big carneval.

Mme. de Chastenay, young Burgundian lady
of noble birth who returned to Paris after the
Terror, 1796-97, in Furet and Richet's The
French Revolution *(1970).*

What a contrast between the Paris of the [Directory] Constitution and that of the revolution! The revolutionary committees and the prisons have disappeared, instead there are dances, entertainments, fireworks … The ladies of the royal court have disappeared, but their places are being taken by the ladies of the newly rich, and as their predecessors, they are being followed by the whores who try to imitate their luxury and extravagance. Around these dangerous sirens swarm hordes of those brainless creatures … they now call "merveilleux"; while dancing, they talk about politics, they long for the return of the monarchs while they are eating their ice, and they yawn with boredom while watching the fireworks.

Charles Maurice de Talleyrand-Périgord,
shortly after his return to France, letter of
July 5, 1797, Memoirs *(1891-92).*

Every since the new third [of delegates] has been elected, the government has been shaken in its foundations … everywhere, the buyers of national estates are being murdered or ransacked …

Benjamin Constant, on the "royalist" March
elections, letter of August 1, 1797, in Works
(1957).

The émigrés were now beginning to return to France, after their resources had been spent, unwilling to endure the humiliation of depending on foreign help. They were ready to face all sorts of dangers, hoping to find some remnants of their property …

Etienne Denis Pasquier, chancellor under the future King Louis Philippe, 1797, in Furet and Richet's The French Revolution *(1970).*

The revolution was carried out to insure liberty and equality for all while leaving the property of each inviolate … all the government's powers … must aim of maintaining it … surrounding it with a sacred barrier … Whoever outlaws wealth conspires against mediocrity!

Constant, to property owners at the Constitutional Club and on behalf of the Directory, February 27, 1798, Works *(1957).*

You must exclude from your teaching all things relating to any dogmas or rites of any religion or sect whatsoever.

The Directory, to all teachers, October 8, 1798.

The Cisalpina should confine herself to serving exclusively the interests of the French Republic and to aid her in becoming the arbiter for all political controversies on the whole peninsula; she must get strong enough to be of use to us, but not so strong to enable her to do us damage.

The Directory, instructions to plenipotentiary Trouvé in Milan, June 1798.

No more brigands in office, no more scoundrels in power … Would you like to see the Law of the Maximum restored? Would you like to see the murderers of Féraud reappear, carrying his bleeding head on a pike?

Francois de Neufchateau, former director and administrative expert for the Directory, in a circular before the election of March 1799, in Lefèbvre's The Thermidorians and the Directory *(1964).*

Frenchmen, you have been victorious against Europe which conspired against us; all that is left is to defeat the enemies in our midst … Citizens, no hatred, no revenge, and above all no reaction! … Citizens of all classes, the same interest unites you to exclaim in unison: Stop the anarchy in France!

The Directory, slogans for the elections of March 1799, in Soboul's Summary of the History of the French Revolution *(1962).*

You have destroyed civic virtue, gagged liberty, persecuted the republicans, suppressed the newspapers and suffocated the truth … In the year VI, the French people had elected men for public office who were worthy of its confidence; you have dared to claim that the elections were the result of an anarchistic conspiracy, and you have mutilated the representation of the nation.

H.G. de Bertrand, member of Council of 500, attacking the Directory, speech of June 18, 1799.

Some want the people to be used to repel the barbarians; others are afraid of using this omnipotent force, in other words they are more afraid of the mass of republicans than of the hordes from the North.

Francois Lamarque, member of Council of 500, during election campaign of 1799, in Lefèbvre's Thermidorians *(1964).*

No, no, that will never rise again. There is not one of us who would not die fighting any factionists who tried to bring it [the terrorist regime] back.

Boulay de la Meurthe, member of Council of 500, defending the Directory, June 1799, in Lefèbvre's Thermidorians *(1964).*

Since the 13th Thermidor [July 31] people make every effort to conceal their wealth, while the previous trend was to present and even exaggerate it. Therefore, there is no more luxury. This has become a necessity for many people, in particular the owners of estates. Others are trying to avoid the enormous taxes they are afraid of. Again others go into bankruptcy to show their misery convincingly.

Le Publiciste, *on the compulsory loan imposed on the rich in July of 1799, in Sciout's* Directory *(1895-97).*

Italy has been subjugated, the barbarians from the North are standing at France's gates, Holland is occupied, the navies have been lost through treachery, Helvetia is devastated, royalist gangs are committing all possible outrages in many departments, and the republicans are being denounced as Terrorists and Jacobins. One more setback, and the tocsin of royalism will ring on all French soil.

General Jean Baptiste Jourdan, at the Council of 500, proposing a declaration of a national emergency, September 13, 1799.

We have come to a point where it is no longer possible to recover anything, neither liberty, nor property, nor the Constitution which guarantees both. The rapacious law of the compulsary loan ruined our finances, the hostage law brought us civil war, part of the income of year VIII has been used up by the seizures, and all the credit is lost.

Le Moniteur *November 10, 1799.*

I was so convinced that in this event [a Jacobin plot and victory] one could expect the cruelest persecution that I collected all the money I possessed at the time, with my business friends in order to divide it between two of my best friends and myself, so that we would be able to go abroad immediately. Every quarter of an hour, I received news from Saint-Cloud, and depending on what news I received I hastened or delayed my departure.

Mme. Germaine de Staël, fears at the time of 18th Brumaire, 1799, The Reasons for the Principal Events of the French Revolution *(1818).*

In this French revolution everything was planned in advance, thought out, calculated, decided and established; everything was the fruit of utter wickedness, for everything, even the most abominable crimes, was prepared and arranged by people who, in their secret societies, pulled all the strings of conspiracy and who could select and accelerate the various trends favorable to their plots [referring to the freemasons].

Abbé Barruel, a royalist journalist for Actes des Apôtres *1799, "Memoirs," in Sciout's* The Directory *(1895-97).*

12. Napoleon's Life Up to the Peace of Campo Formio: 1769 to October 1797

THE HISTORICAL CONTEXT

Napoleone Buonaparte came from a Corsican family of the petty nobility and was born one year after Louis XV had purchased the island from Genoa. Both his parents were fervent Corsican patriots and resented the French occupation, but his father eventually made his peace with the new masters and sent Napoleon and his older brother Joseph to school in Autun, France. At this time, Napoleon hardly spoke any French, and throughout his life, despite all the lessons he took, his conversational French remained poor.

From Autun, he went to the military schools of Brienne and Paris where, in the final examination, he was rated as only the 42nd among 58 pupils. He never felt any loyalty toward the Old Regime but remained a Corsican patriot. From 1786 on he visited his home country repeatedly, interrupting his military career, and at one time heading the revolutionary party at Ajaccio, and later the National Guard. But in 1793, when Pascal Paoli, the head of the Corsican independence movement, broke with the Convention and called on the British for help, the Buonapartes were considered francophiles and had to leave the island in a hurry.

Josephine Bonaparte

Napoleon had been in Paris during the violent mob scenes of 1792. They had disgusted him, and he had only contempt for the weakness of the royal regime. So, in June of 1793 he rejoined his regiment, having spent only 30 months on duty in the course of seven and a half years of service. But he had made up his mind. He sided with France, once and for all. By now a captain commandant, he became an admirer of Robespierre and wrote a pamphlet completely in the spirit of the Mon-

160

tagnard ideology. His great chance came when Convention Commissioner Christophe Saliceti ordered him to assist in the siege of Toulon, then occupied by the British. He succeeded brilliantly, but with Robespierre's fall, his career seemed to have come to an end: Saliceti denounced him as a terrorist; he was relieved of his duties and actually imprisoned for a few weeks. Then an investigation cleared him.

Still, for months his future career was extremely uncertain. An expedition against Corsica in which he participated failed, and he refused several commands offered to him. Then he met Josephine Beauharnais, close friend of Paul Francois Barras, and it was probably her help that later allowed his plan for an Italian campaign to be presented to the Convention. Barras used him at a crucial point in the fight against the royalist uprising in October of 1795. At the age of 26, he was appointed general of division and commander of the Army of the Interior. But what he wanted was the command of the Italian army, and since General Barthélemy Louis Scherer refused to accept his plan for a campaign, Napoleon was given the desired command, probably again with Josephine's help. Before he left for Nice, he married Josephine and changed his name to "Bonaparte."

He found a starved and ragged army, demoralized and distrustful of the "political officer." But he transformed his army into a first class fighting force within a short time: by introduction of a supply system independent of the financially exhausted Directory, permitting the troops to live off the land; by his reliance on speed and surprise attacks; and by his magic influence over the morale of his soldiers. He managed to keep the troops opposing him separated and forced the king of Sardinia to sign a separate peace after only four weeks of fighting. The duke of Parma followed soon after. Some of the battles against the Austrians that followed were not as easily won as Napoleon—or his propaganda machine—would have it, particularly the one at Lodi on May 10. But they were won. And he delivered to the Directory what it most urgently needed—money and gold. He promised riches to his soldiers, which they got, and liberty and independence to the Italian peoples, which they did not get, at least not in the form they had hoped for.

The Directory was distrustful of the Italian Jacobins, and Napoleon himself preferred an "aristo-democratic republic" wherever he set up new Italian satellite states. So there were revolts that were brutally suppressed by the French. After Napoleon had succeeded in signing armistices with Naples and Pope Pius VI—always without consulting his superiors in Paris—he forced the Austrians to retire into the great fortress of Mantua. Its siege had to be interrupted when the Austrians sent another army, under General Dagobert Sigismund de Wurmser, across the Alps. After the French victories of Castiglione, Roveredo, Bassano, Arcola and Rivoli, the Austrians were hopelessly beaten; Mantua surrendered and Napoleon was in control of virtually all Italy. The newly established Lombardic and Cispadane republics, soon to be followed by the Cisalpine Republic, all showed the main features of Napoleon's ideal of government: an administration of distinguished men under the strict control of the executive power.

After imposing the treaty of Tolentino upon the Pope, Napoleon marched north into the Alps and against the Austrians under Archduke Charles, brother of the emperor. No doubt this is what the Directory wanted, since it considered the war in Italy secondary to that against Austria and England. But after occupying Klagenfurt, he surprisingly offered an armistice to the archduke. The reasons for this are not entirely clear. It is true that there were uprisings against the French in several Italian cities, which may have threatened his rear. But the armistice was against the wishes of the Directory, since, while Belgium was ceded to France, its terms left open the question of the west bank of the Rhine. This had been the principal aim of the Directory; Jean Francois Reubell, in particular, had always been a strong proponent of France's "natural borders," first proclaimed by Georges Danton, which were to consist of the Rhine, the Alps and the Pyrenees.

The Paris government, however, needed the support of its generals because of the growing danger from the royalists behind whom were not only England but also Austria, both apparently expecting better peace terms from a restored royalist government. So Napoleon proceeded with his own plans, promising a completely neutral Venice to the Directory. In September of 1797, when the coup d'état of the "triumvirate" against the royalists was carried out—with Napoleon and his sub-general Charles Pierre Augereau's help—the republic had little choice but to follow, by and large, Napoleon's ideas in the peace treaty of Campo Formio, which confirmed the arrangements of the Leoben armistice. In the meantime, Napoleon had annexed the ancient republic of Venice and proclaimed the Cisalpine and Ligurian republics.

In conducting the negotiations with Austria and the Holy Roman (German) Empire almost independently, Napoleon had shown himself to be not just a brilliant general but also a superior diplomat, and it is indeed astonishing what this one man accomplished within a mere 18 months. He may have been lucky in some of his battles and undoubtedly owed much of his military success to his generals, especially Augereau and André Masséna. But by presenting himself as not only a victorious general but also a peacemaker, he dazzled many of his contemporaries, and his fame began to grow inside and outside of France.

CHRONICLE OF EVENTS

1769:   *August 15:* Napoleone Buonaparte is born at Ajaccio, Corsica. In June, his father Carlo had sworn fealty to King Louis XV and had thus become a French subject.

1771:   *September 13:* A declaration is issued by the French government stating that the nobility of the Buonaparte family is established.

1779:   *January 1:* Napoleon and his older brother Joseph are taken by their father to Autun, France, and enter school there.

April 25: Napoleon enters the Royal Military College in Brienne (Champagne).

1783:   *June:* Napoleon abandons the navy for the army, choosing the artillery.

1784:   *September:* Napoleon is selected to go to the Ecole Militaire in Paris.

1785:   *September:* Napoleon is commissioned as second lieutenant of artillery.

November: He serves garrison duty at the regiment La Fère in Valence (Dauphiné).

1786:   *September:* Napoleon arrives at Ajaccio after an absence of almost eight years.

1787:   *September:* Back in France, he applies for extended leave to assist at the deliberations of the estates of Corsica.

1788:   *June:* After spending five months at Ajaccio, Napoleon rejoins his regiment at Auxonne.

1789:   *July 19:* Napoleon's regiment takes part in rioting and looting before the officers can restore order.

September: Napoleon heads the revolutionary party at Ajaccio.

1790:   *April 16:* Napoleon asks for extended leave for health reasons.

1791:   *February:* Back at his regiment at Auxonne, he is welcomed by his colonel.

June 16: Napoleon is transferred to the 4th Regiment at Valence (Rhone).

September: Having obtained a new leave, over the objections of his colonel, he returns to Corsica where Pascal Paoli, who is cool toward the Buonapartes, is now in full control.

1792:   *February-April:* Napoleon is now considered an emigrant by the French authorities. He is appointed lieutenant-colonel of the Corsican Volunteers, forfeiting his French commission.

May 28: Napoleon is back in Paris as a private person.

July-August: He is reinstated in his regiment and promoted to captain. Napoleon witnesses the Second Revolution.

October: He arrives at Ajaccio and is appointed commander of the National Guard.

1793:   *April:* The Convention orders the arrest of Paoli, the Corsican national hero who had taken up contact with the British. Napoleon writes an eloquent defense of Paoli.

May: Split develops between the Paolists and the Buonaparte family.

June: Napoleon flees with his family to France. After a long absence, he rejoins his regiment at Nice and is made captain commandant.

July: Napoleon publishes a pro-Jacobin pamphlet, *Le Souper de Beaucaire*, and participates in an attack on antirevolutionists at Avignon.

September: He assists General Jean Baptiste Francois Carteaux in besieging Toulon, held by the British.

December 19: Toulon falls. Napoleon strongly objects to the reprisals on the inhabitants. He is made brigadier general.

1794:   *February:* He is assigned to the Army of Italy.

July: His plans of a campaign for the armies of the Alps and of Italy are approved by the Committee of Public Safety. Napoleon undertakes a secret mission in Genoa.

August 9: As a follower of Robespierre, Napoleon is suspended and put under arrest.

August 20: He is released and reinstated.

1795:   *February:* Napoleon, in Toulon, prepares an expedition against Corsica, occupied by the British.

March: The expedition is scattered by the British fleet. Napoleon is without a post. He evades a command of artillery in the Vendée.

June: Napoleon evades the command of a brigade of infantry in the Army of the West.

July: He holds a minor job at the War Office. He meets Josephine Beauharnais.

August 31: His plan for the campaign in Italy is read by the Convention.

October 1: Napoleon is appointed second in comand, under Barras, of the Army of the Interior.

October 4: He confers with Barras, Lazare Nicolas Carnot and others regarding the threatened royalist insurrection.

October 5: He suppresses the insurrection of 13th Vendémiaire, dispersing the royalists and the National Guard.

October 16-26: Napoleon is made major general, then commander of the Army of the Interior. He applies for command of the Army in Italy.

November 1: Sir Gilbert Elliott is appointed viceroy of Corsica and opens parliament.

1796:   *January 19:* Napoleon submits his plan for this year's campaign in Italy, providing for an attack in Piedmont and an invasion of Lombardy. Carnot informs Scherer, general of the Army of Italy, who rejects it.

February 4: Scherer is dismissed as commander of the Army of Italy.

February 23: The Directory appoints Napoleon to command the Army of Italy.

March 9: Napoleon marries Josephine, née Tascher de la Pagerie, widow of Alexandre de Beauharnais, from whom she had two children and who had been guillotined in 1794. She herself had been imprisoned during the Reign of Terror. Napoleon signs his name, for the first time and from here on, as "Bonaparte."

March 27: Napoleon joins his army in Nice and finds the troops in deplorable condition.

April 4: He makes a stirring proclamation to his troops.

April 12: Napoleon defeats the Austrian general J.P. Beaulieu at Monto Notte in the Apennines.

April 14: He defeats the Austrians at Millesimo in Liguria.

April 15: He defeats the Austrians at Dego.

April 22: He defeats the Sardinians (Piedmontese) at Ceva and Mondovi.

April 24: Napoleon dispatches an indignant letter to the Directory about the condition of the Army of Italy.

April 28: The king of Sardinia signs an armistice, yielding his fortresses to France.

May 7: Napoleon crosses the Po at Piacenza to attack Beaulieu.

May 9: He arranges an armistice with the duke of Parma.

Napoleon at the siege of Toulon

The French enter Milan on May 15, 1796.

May 10: Napoleon, on his way to Milan, forces the crossing of the Adda at the bridge of Lodi, with the help of his generals Louis Alexandre Berthier, Masséna and Cervoni, beating the Austrian General Sebottendorf. Lombardy is now in French hands. Napoleon, for the first time, is called "the little corporal" by his troops.

May 14: In a letter to the Directory, Napoleon refuses to share his command with General Francois Etienne Kellermann. The Directory gives in.

May 15: Napoleon enters Milan. In Paris, peace is concluded between France and the king of Sardinia. Savoy and Nice are ceded to France.

May 16: Lombardic Republic is established.

May 19: Napoleon issues proclamation in Milan, promising independence to all Italians.

May 26: Pavia revolts and, upon Napoleon's orders, is to be pillaged for 24 hours; but he stops the looting after three hours. Brescia is occupied.

May 30-31: Napoleon defeats the Austrians at Borghetto and drives Beaulieu into the Tyrol.

June 5: Napoleon arranges armistice with the king of Naples.

June 18-19: Modena and Bologna are taken by the French.

June 23: Armistice of Foligno is arranged between Pope Pius VI and Napoleon. Bologna and Ferrara are ceded to France, which is also to receive 21,000,000 lire and 100 works of art.

July 13: Napoleon meets Josephine in Milan.

July 29: At Verona, Napoleon and Josephine are nearly captured by the new Austrian army under Dagobert Sigismund de Wurmser.

July 30: Napoleon raises the siege of the fortress at Mantua to meet Wurmser.

August 3: French are victorious at Lonato.

August 5: At the battle of Castiglione (SW of Brescia), Napoleon, supported by Augereau, defeats Wurmser and drives him back into the Tyrol. In the Five Days' Campaign Verona and Brescia are reoccupied and the siege of Mantua is resumed.

September 4: Napoleon, pursuing the Austrians, beats Wurmser at Roveredo (south Tyrol).

September 8: Wurmser is again beaten at Bassano. He retreats into Mantua.

October 10: Peace treaty with Naples is signed.

October 16: In Bologna, Napoleon proclaims the Cispadane Republic, comprising the province of Emilia, later to become part of the Cisalpine Republic.

October 22: Corsica is abandoned by the British. The inhabitants declare for the French.

November 2: Two new Austrian armies invade Italy via Friuli and the Tyrol.

November 15-17: After a desperate battle, Napoleon decisively defeats the Austrian General Josef Alvinzi at Arcola.

November 18: Napoleon reenters Verona.

November 23: Wurmser tries an unsuccessful sortie from besieged Mantua.

1797:   *January 14:* With Masséna's help, Napoleon defeats Alvanzi at Rivoli, thus deciding the fate of Mantua.

January 26: Masséna is victorious at Carpenedolo.

February 2: Wurmser surrenders Mantua.

February 12: Napoleon invades the Papal States.

February 19: Treaty of Tolentino is negotiated between the Pope and Napoleon. Pius VI cedes the Romagna, Bologna and Ferrara to the Cispadane Republic.

March 12-16: Napoleon, marching north against the Austrian Archduke Charles, crosses the Piave and the Tagliamento.

March 21-22: Napoleon occupies Trieste and Bressanone (Brixen), on the Brenner road, and Bolzano.

April 13: Having marched through Friuli and Carinthia and occupied Klagenfurt, Napoleon offers an armistice to Archduke Charles, since he feels threatened in his rear by revolts in Verona and Venice.

April 18: Armistice is signed at Leoben.

May 2: Because of the uprisings in Venice and Verona, Napoleon declares war on Venice. The city and its islands along the Dalmatian coast are occupied by French troops during the month.

June 14: In Genoa, Napoleon founds the Ligurian Republic.

June 28: The island of Corfu is occupied by French troops.

July 9: Cisalpine Republic, which included Milan, Modena, Ferrara, the Romagna and Carrara, is established. Here and in the Ligurian Republic Napoleon puts moderate, well-to-do republicans in charge.

An English caricature of Bonaparte in Rome

September 13: Napoleon writes a letter to the Directory, suggesting the seizure of Malta, in preparation for his schemes for the conquest of Egypt.

October 17: Peace Treaty of Campo Formio is agreed upon.

EYEWITNESS TESTIMONY

I lived separately from my schoolmates. I looked for a corner in the school garden and retired there to dream undisturbedly. When the others tried to penetrate my little corner I defended myself with all my strength. I felt instinctively that my will would subdue the will of others and that all things I liked would have to belong to me. I was not loved at school: it takes time to acquire people's love, but I had, even when I did nothing, the vague feeling I should not lose any time.

Napoleon Bonaparte, as told by Claire Elisabeth Rémusat, Comtesse de Vergennes, Memoirs 1802-1808 *(1881).*

M. de Bonaparte ... excellent health ... obedient, friendly, honorable, grateful; behavior excellent; distinguished himself by his diligence in mathematics, possesses very good knowledge of history and geography; quite poor in belles lettres. He would make a fine sailor and deserves to be accepted in the Paris school.

Brigadier General de Keralio, superintendent of military schools, his testimonial concerning Napoleon, 1784, in Mereschkowskij's Napoleon *(1928).*

I have no diversions here, except work. I wear the new uniform [that of a lieutenant of artillery] but once a week. I sleep incredibly little: I go to bed at ten and get up at four; I eat only once a day which is very beneficial to my health.

Napoleon, to his mother from Valence, letter of 1785-86, in Lévy's The Intimate Napoleon *(1893).*

What will I dream of tonight? Of death. At the dawn of my life, I should hope for a long life ... and happiness. What insanity makes me wish for the end? ... Yet, what am I to do in this world? ... How far have men removed themselves from nature! How common, low and contemptible they are! What will I see when I return home? Trembling people, burdened by their chains, kissing the hand of their oppressor ... When the patriot has no longer a fatherland, he must die ...

Napoleon, in Valence, Diary, *1786.*

I have thought thoroughly about our situation. We are on the verge of committing great stupidities. Of course, the Convention has committed a great crime, and I deplore that more than anyone else; but Corsica must be united with France, no matter what happens.

Napoleon, to the commissioner of the National Convention, after Louis XVI's execution.

To the list of patriots I have submitted to you I should like to add the name of Citizen Buonaparte, Commanding General of the Artillery, a man of extraordinary merit. He is a Corsican. The only guarantees he can offer are those of a Corsican who resisted Paoli's enticements, and of one whose property has been plundered by this traitor.

Augustin Robespierre, to his brother, Maximilien, letter of April 5, 1794, in Lévy's Intimate Napoleon *(1893).*

Was I not devoted to the revolution from the very beginning? I ... have sacrificed everything for the republic. I deserve the name of a patriot ... Lend me your ears ... But if my enemies are after my life—I do not think highly of it and have often despised it. Indeed, only the thought that my life could be of use to the nation makes me carry its burden courageously!

Napoleon, to the Convention from the prison at Antibes, letter of August 1794.

His gloomy looks made you think of a man you would not like to meet in a forest after dark ... His worn uniform looked so pitiful that I could not believe in the beginning that I was talking to a general. But I soon discovered that he was a very intelligent or at least an unusual man ... If he had not looked so haggard to the point of looking sick one could have seen that he had extremely fine features. He sometimes talked a lot and became lively when he described the siege of Toulon, and then again he sank into sinister silence ...

A Parisian lady, on Napoleon in 1795, as reported by Stendhal in his Life of Napoleon *(1843).*

Thank God it is all over … We have killed many people and disarmed the sections … Everything is quiet now. As always, I was not hurt. Fortune smiles upon me.

Napoleon, to his brother Joseph after 13th Vendémiaire, letter of October 1795.

His short stature and sickly-looking face did not make a favorable impression on us. He was holding in his hand a portrait of his wife which he showed to everybody, his extreme youth … all these facts made us believe that his appointment had been the result of an intrigue.

General André Masséna, at Napoleon's arrival in Italy, March 1796, in Castelot's Bonaparte *(1967).*

When a soldier has no bread, he will behave in such a way that one is ashamed to be a human being. I shall set terrible warning examples and restore order, or I shall give up the command over this gang of brigands.

Napoleon, to the Directory at beginning of Italian campaign, letter of April 1796.

Soldiers, you are badly clad, badly fed. The government owes you much and can give you nothing … Your patience and courage which you show in the midst of these rocks are admirable, but they bring you no glory … I wish to lead you into the most fertile plains in the world. Rich provinces, large towns will be in your power. It is up to you to conquer them. You wish to do it and you can do it … Soldiers of the army of Italy, will you fail in courage or constancy? So, let us go ahead!

Napoleon, to his soldiers at beginning of Italian campaign, proclamation of April 1796.

Soldiers, in fifteen days you have gained six victories, taken twenty-one flags, fifty-five cannon and several strongholds. You have conquered the richest part of

Napoleon defeats Alvanzi at Rivoli, January 1797.

Piedmont. You now rival the armies of Holland and the Rhine. You have won battles without cannons, crossed rivers without bridges, you have made forced marches without shoes, bivouacked without brandy and often without bread. Only soldiers of liberty were capable of undergoing all that you have undergone. But you have done nothing, since there remains something for you to do: Milan has not been taken … Some say that some of you are losing courage: I cannot believe it. The conquerors of Montenotte, Millesimo, Dego and Mondovi burn to carry further the glory of the French name.

Napoleon, to the Army of Italy, proclamation of April 26, 1796.

Peoples of Italy! The French army is coming to break your chains; the French people are the friend of all peoples. So, come to receive it! Believe us, we have no grudge except against the tyrants who oppress you … We are your friends, the descendants of a Brutus, a Scipio, of all the great men of antiquity. To restore the Capitol, to set up new statues of the heroes, to wake up the Roman people who have slept in slavery for centuries … that will be the fruit of our victories.

Napoleon, to the Italians, proclamation of April 26, 1796.

If you do not come to terms with the king of Sardinia, I shall keep the strongholds and march upon Turin. Meantime, I advance tomorrow against Beaulieu, force him to recross the Po, and pass immediately after. I take possession of all Lombardy, and hope to be within a month on the mountains of Tyrol, to join the army of the Rhine and wage war upon Bavaria. This scheme is worthy of the army and destinies of France.

Napoleon, to the Directory, letter of April 1796.

Neither the day of Vendémiaire [October 5, 1795] nor Montenotte had suggested to me the idea that I was a man of superior station. This thought occurred to me only after Lodi [May 10, 1796]. After that, the first spark of high ambition was kindled.

Napoleon, memoirs as dictated to Comte Emanuel de Las Cases, Memorial of St. Helena (1823).

How happy I was in those days! This enthusiasm, these shouts: "Long live the liberator of Italy!" And I was twenty-five! I could feel what I would be some day.

The world was vanishing from under me, as if I were flying through the air.

Napoleon, on the Italian campaign of 1796, in Montholon and Gourgaud's Memoirs (1823-25).

I think it very unadvisable to divide the army of Italy into two. It is against the interest of the Republic to place over it two different generals. I have done the campaign without consulting anyone; and should have done nothing so well if I had been obliged to adapt my plans to the opinions of another. I gained several battles over superior forces when we were absolutely in want of everything, because from my assurance of your confidence in me, my advance was as rapid as my thought. If you impose upon me checks of every kind, if I must refer at every step to commissioners of the government, if they can change my movements, deprive me of troops or send more, then expect nothing good. If you weaken your means by dividing my forces, if you break in Italy the unity of military idea, then I tell you with sorrow, you have lost the fairest opportunity of imposing laws upon Italy … Kellermann will command the army as well as I. Victories are due to the courage and boldness of the army, no one is more convinced of that than I. But to join together Kellermann and me is the way to ruin everything. One bad general is better than two good ones … Whether I wage war here or elsewhere, I care not: To serve my country, to deserve a page in our history, to give the government proofs of my devotion, is my whole ambition; but I eagerly desire not to lose in one week the toil, suffering and dangers of two months.

Napoleon, to the Directory, letter of May 14, 1796.

You ought not to reckon upon a revolution; it will come, but the mind of those peoples must be disposed for such an event. If in order to protect the principles of liberty, one sets on fire a civil war, if one excites the people against the nobles and priests, one becomes responsible for the excesses which invariably accompany such a struggle. When the army is mistress of all the Austrian states in Italy, and the papal states on this side of the Apennines, it will be in a position to proclaim liberty and excite Italian patriotism against foreign rule …

Napoleon, to the Directory, on its suggestion to incite riots in Piedmont, letter of May 1796.

Non tutti Francesi sono ladroni, ma buona parte! [Not all the Frenchmen are robbers, but a good part are!]

Popular Italian saying after Napoleon imposed a heavy tax on Lombardy in May of 1796, in the Durants' Age of Napoleon *(1975).*

Scholars in Milan have not enjoyed the appreciation they have deserved … they considered themselves happy if no king or priest did them any harm. This is no longer the case … There is no more Inquisition, intolerance, no more tyranny. I invite all scholars to meet and to advise me what measures should be taken … to give sciences and the fine arts a new life.

Napoleon, to astronomer Barnaba Oriani, letter of May 1796 (after the occupation of Milan).

The signing of the Treaty of Leoben, April 17, 1797

At first glance, his face did not seem beautiful, but his very pronounced features, the lively, searching eye, his quick, buoyant motions showed a bold character, and his broad, worried forehead betrayed a profound thinker … His way of speaking was concise, and at that time still full of mistakes. He said that, as long as we did not hold Mantua, nothing was decided; only then could one call oneself the master of Italy. No doubt, Austria would bring up another army to come to the help of so important a fortress, but that would take time, and therefore we had one more month … I soon recognized that he did not care much about Toscana and was already thinking of occupying Livorno … "The commissioners of the Directory have nothing to do with my politics, I do as I please; they should concern themselves with the administration of public income— the rest is not their business …" I did not notice any indications of confidentiality between him and his comrades which I had observed elsewhere and which was encouraged by the republican égalité. He had already defined his position and made the difference quite perceptible …

Comte Mio de Melito, Florentine envoy, conversation with Napoleon in Brescia, June 1796, Memoirs (1858).

Since our parting, I have been very sad at every moment. I know of no happiness except when I am with you … Shall I ever be relieved of worries and responsibilities, free to spend all my time with you? … A few days ago I imagined I loved you, but since I have seen you again I love you a thousand times more … Come quickly to meet with me …

Napoleon to Josephine after her visit to Milan, letter of July 1796.

The siege [of Mantua] is impracticable before January. I have 19,000 men in the army of observation, 9,000 in the besieging army. I leave you to consider if without receiving assistance it is possible for me this winter to resist the Emperor who will have 50,000 men in six weeks. Our position in Italy is uncertain and our political system very bad. Rome is arming the people and exciting their fanaticism; coalitions are formed against us on every side. They are waiting for the moment of action, and it will be favorable to them as soon as the emperor's army is reinforced. Peace with Naples is essential, alliance with Genoa or the court of Turin necessary. Make peace with Parma. Declare that France takes Lombardy, Modena, Reggio, Bologna and Ferrara, under her protection … Diminish the number of your enemies. The influence of Rome is incalculable, and it was badly done to break with that power. If I had been consulted, I should have delayed the negotiation. So often as your general in Italy is not complete master, you will run very great danger. This language must not be attributed to ambition: I have only too many honors. My health is so shattered that I almost feel compelled to ask you for a successor: I cannot ride on horseback. All that is left me is courage which is not sufficient in a post like my present one.

Napoleon, to the Directory after the battle of Bassano, letter of September 1796.

The Roman legions are supposed to have marched twenty-four miles in a day; our half-brigades, however, are marching thirty miles, and during the rest periods they fight.

Napoleon, to the Directory, on the forced marches to Mantua after the battle of Rivoli, letter of January 1797.

Bonaparte did not stretch to appear as tall as the others; already, one saved him that trouble. Nobody he talked to seemed to be taller than he. Berthier, Kilmaine … even Augereau waited in silence until he addressed them, a favor not everybody enjoyed this evening. Never did a headquarters resemble a court as much as Bonaparte's did in Milan in those days.

Antoine Vincent Arnault, poet, a conversation with Napoleon in Milan, 1797, Les souvenirs et les regrets (1861).

Meanwhile, I was lying on a mattress in Verona, resting. But Jourbert who thought he was being attacked by superior forces … kept on sending his adjutants to me, begging me to come and judge the situation by myself and take measures … I let them talk, turned around on my mattress and fell asleep again. One did not understand how I could be so calm. But as soon as I received the news of the enemy's maneuver which could leave no doubt about his intentions, I shouted: To Rivoli! All my divisions will march there, and I myself will also go there in the middle of the night. From this moment on, the battle had been won in my head. You know the rest.

Napoleon, as told by Arnault, before the battle of Rivoli, January 1797, Les souvenirs … (1861).

I do not love the men of this government; still, I prefer it to the one preceding it or the one they want to replace it with. This government, controlled by a constitution, is more to my liking than the despotism of the Committee of Public Safety, or that of Louis XIVth, although this had been alleviated during Louis XVI's regime. But I doubt that one can get out of this without surrendering to the power of one single man … But this one man, where is he?

Napoleon, as told by Arnault, on the Directory, 1797, Les Souvenirs … (1861).

With few exceptions, the most numerous army can be sure of victory. Therefore, the art of war consists of being superior wherever you want to attack. If your army is smaller than that of your enemy, do not allow him the time to unite his forces … Turn quickly against the various army corps which you prudently have kept apart … In this way, I have destroyed, by and by, the armies of Beaulieu, Wurmser, Alvinczy and the Archduke Charles … Further, one must never be afraid to make the necessary sacrifices demanded by the circumstances. I owe the victory of Castiglione to such a

sacrifice. I … did not hesitate for a moment to abandon the siege of Mantua so that I could operate against him [Wurmser] with all my forces. For that I had to abandon all my siege artillery, 140 cannons had to be left behind. When I announced this decision to the division commanders, they could not calm down. Berthier was crying. Let us go, I said, we shall reconquer all of it, here and over there, pointing at the city. And have I been wrong?

Napoleon, as reported by Arnault, on strategy, 1797, Les Souvenirs … (1861).

If he had only a fortnight's provisions and spoke of surrendering, he would not deserve an honorable capitulation. Since he sends you, it is because he is reduced to extremity. I respect the age, the bravery and the misfortune of the marshal. If he opens the gates tomorrow, if he delays a fortnight, a month, two months, he will still have the same conditions … [Wurmser capitulated the following day.]

Napoleon, to the envoy of the besieged General Wurmser, who claimed Mantua was still amply provisioned, February 1, 1797, in Guizot's History of France.

I shall leave, but I request that the golden book be brought to me in which is written the name of my family, that I may erase it with my own hand. I ask also that the armour of my ancestor Henry IV be given me which he presented to the Republic as a pledge of friendship.

Comte de Provence (later, Louis XVIII) on quitting Venetian territory at urging of the Venetian government, February 1797, in Guizot's History.

I have not concealed from the inhabitants that if the pretended king of France had not evacuated their town before I crossed the Po, I should have set fire to a city presumptuous enough to think itself the capital of the French Empire.

Napoleon, to the Directory, his negotiations with the Republic of Venice regarding the presence of the Comte de Provence at Venice and Verona, April 1797.

If it is your intention to draw five or six millions from Venice, I have arranged for you this quarrel on purpose; if you have any more decided intentions, send me instructions … in order to watch for the proper opportunity … The emigrants are escaping from Italy, and more than 1,500 left two weeks before our arrival. They run to Germany, to carry there their remorse and misery.

Napoleon, to the Directory, April 1797.

The republic of Venice shall be treated as a neutral power, and not in any sense as a friendly power. She has done nothing to deserve our respect.

The Directory, instructions to Napoleon, May 1797.

She was a Maiden City, bright and free,
No guile reduced, no force could violate;
And when she took unto herself a Mate,
She must espouse the everlasting Sea.

And what if she had seen those glories fade,
Those titles vanish, and that strength decay
Yet shall some tribute of regret be paid
When her long life has reached its final day
Men are we, and must grieve when even the shade
Of that which once was great is pass'd away.

William Wordsworth, "On the Extinction of the Venetian Republic" (1802).

We are separated from France by mountains, but if necessary we shall go across them with the speed of an eagle to defend liberty and to protect the government and the republicans!

Napoleon, to his army, in support of the Directory against growing royalist pressure, proclamation of July 14, 1797.

13. The Second Coalition and Its War Up to the Peace Treaty of Lunéville: January 1798 to March 1801

THE HISTORICAL CONTEXT

After the the treaty of Campo Formio, there was peace in Europe, except between France and England. A peace settlement with England would have been very unpopular, so on October 26, 1797, the Directory issued a violent declaration of war, appointing Napoleon as general-in-chief of the Army of Britain. Before he could concentrate on his new assignment, he had, however, to act as France's plenipotentiary at the Congress of Rastatt, where he spent only a few days. The congress was to decide upon compensation to those German princes who had lost territories on the west bank of the Rhine, territories that had secretly been ceded to France at Campo Formio. These negotiations led nowhere, and the congress dissolved in April of 1799.

Archduke Charles of Austria

To sail against England, the government decided to concentrate a fleet of 63 men-of-war and 50 frigates at Brest; they were to be joined by a Mediterranean squadron under Admiral Francois Paul Brueys.

There had been no sea battles with the British navy for five years, and while previous confrontations in the 18th century had always shown British superiority, French hopes rose because mutinies had occurred of late aboard some British ships. On the other hand, the English blockade had effectively prevented the French navy from obtaining supplies from abroad; also, through years of emigration the French navy had lost even more officers than the army. The battle of Camperdown in October of 1797, in which the British had destroyed the Dutch fleet allied with France, had been a severe setback; and after a thorough inspection of the Brittany and Normandy ports, Napoleon and his advisers came to the conclusion that an attack on England would be foolhardy because mastery of the sea could not be obtained. He suggested that France either make peace with England or attack it elsewhere.

Meanwhile, the continent did not remain peaceful. The Italians, who had been promised liberty and independence, found themselves again divided into small satellite states. Anti-French riots ensued, particularly in Rome, but only made things worse: Rome was occupied, a Roman Republic declared and the Pope taken prisoner. Then Naples came to the rescue; its troops, under an Austrian general, reoccupied Rome. So France declared war against Naples. By the end of 1798, the French under Jean Etienne Championnet and Barthélemy Catherine Joubert again had the upper hand, and the Helvetian Republic had joined the ranks of French satellite states. The Parthenopean Republic was proclaimed at Naples and the Congress at Rastatt was pressured into yielding all important bridgeheads over the Rhine to France. So, while Napoleon had left for Egypt, France's position on the continent seemed as secure as ever.

However, rebellions against the French regime constantly flared up in the occupied countries. To complicate matters, the Directory's anti-Jacobin coup d'état of May 1798 caused many of the Jacobins ruling the satellite states to turn against their homeland. Finally, England succeeded in bringing together Naples, Turkey, Portugal and, above all, Russia in a new coalition against France, which seemed to threaten them all. When Austria joined the coalition in March of 1799, France was threatened by overwhelming forces. The first eight months of 1799 saw a series of crushing defeats for the armies of the republic. Austrian troops under General Michael Melas and Russian armies under Alexander Wassilievitch Suvorov invaded Italy, defeated the French and occupied Milan and Turin. A few months later the French garrisons in Naples and Rome had to surrender. In all these cities, the new satellite republics were dissolved and many French partisans massacred. In Siena and Florence, the republicans were driven out and often massacred, and the French commander in Italy, Joubert, was decisively beaten and killed in the battle of Novi, on August 15.

In the north of Holland an English army landed on August 27 and joined up with a Russian corps. At the beginning of September, General Mathieu Jourdan proposed that the Council of Five Hundred declare the

General André Masséna

homeland in danger once more. But then the English-Russian invaders were beaten, and Suvorov was called back from Italy to support the Russian troops under Korsakov operating in Switzerland. There, General André Masséna held the Russians and Archduke Charles at bay, until the erratic Czar Paul withdrew from the coalition. When the British evacuated their troops from Holland, the immediate danger to France passed.

By this time, Napoleon had returned from Egypt and made himself First Consul. His peace offers to England and Austria were rejected. In the spring of 1800, the French Army of Italy was beaten by the Austrians and General Masséna was besieged in Genoa. All of Napoleon's conquests of 1796 seemed lost, but by May he had crossed the Alps, repeating Hannibal's exploit of 2,000 years before—not proudly, on a prancing horse, as shown in David's painting, but mounted on a mule. He arrived too late to save the starving French troops at Genoa, but he recaptured Milan, restored the Cisalpine Republic and, at Marengo, defeated the Austrians decisively. The lightning campaign ended on June 16 in a truce.

The hostilities in Germany continued until General Jean Victor Moreau occupied Munich after a series of Austrian defeats and concluded an armistice. The war was resumed in November, but after Moreau's December 3 victory at Hohenlinden, Austria was threatened by two additional French armies under Etienne Jacques Macdonald and Guillaume Marie Brune, the victor in Holland. Austria had to sue for peace, and, in the treaty of Lunéville, the arrangements of Campo Formio were reestablished. The War of the Second Coalition came to an end on the continent, but a settlement with Britain had to wait until France had evacuated Egypt.

CHRONICLE OF EVENTS

1797:   *December 27:* Riots break out in Rome. French General Maturin Léonard Duphot is killed by a mob. The Pope's apologies are rejected by the Directory.

1798:   *January 11:* General Louis Alexandre Berthier, replacing Napoleon in Italy, is ordered by the Directory to occupy Rome.

January 18: The Austrians occupy Venice, according to the provisions of the treaty of Campo Formio.

February 4: The annexed territories on the left bank of the Rhine are divided into four departments.

February 11-15: The French Army of Italy under Berthier occupies Rome. He proclaims the Roman Republic. Pope Pius VI is taken prisoner and brought to Siena, then to Florence and Turin, and in the following year to Grenoble and Valence where he dies later that same year.

November: Ancona in central Italy capitulates.

November 27: The army of Ferdinand IV, king of Naples, commanded by the Austrian General Karl von Mack, invades Rome, which is only feebly defended by French General Jean Etienne Championnet. Jews and Jacobins are massacred.

December 5-6: France declares war on the king of Naples. The new commander of the Army of Italy, General Joubert, occupies Piedmont, and Championnet defeats the Neapolitan army near Civita Castellana.

December 12: Championnet forces Mack to abandon Rome.

December 21: French launch offensive against Naples; King Ferdinand escapes on Admiral Horatio Nelson's flagship.

December 29: Second Coalition organized against France by England, Russia and Naples, who are later joined by Portugal and Turkey. Coalition plans provide for occupation of the English island of Jersey by Russian troops for an attack on Brittany, and for further attacks in Holland, Germany, Switzerland and Italy.

Crossing the St. Bernard Pass, May 14, 1800

1799:   *January 23:* After prolonged street fighting, Championnet occupies Naples.

January 26: The Neapolitan Republic, called *République parthénopéenne*, is proclaimed.

January 27: The French occupy Ehrenbreitstein, German fortress opposite Koblenz.

February 3: Conflict erupts between Championnet and the government commissioner, Guillaume Charles Faipoult. Championnet expels Faipoult from Naples but is called back to Paris and replaced by Macdonald.

March 3: After a four-month siege, the French troops at Corfu surrender to the Russian-Turkish fleet. Thus the last Dalmatian coast island taken from Venice is lost. General Jean Baptiste Bernadotte crosses the Rhine near Speyer.

March 12: The Directory declares war on Austria and Tuscany.

March 21: Tuscany is invaded by French troops.

March 23: Masséna's advance is stopped near Feldkirch in western Austria.

March 25: Archduke Charles of Austria defeats Jourdan at Stockach in the upper Rhine Valley. Jourdan retreats across the Rhine and resigns his command. His and Bernadotte's troops are joined together under the supreme command of Bernadotte.

March 27: The Austrians occupy Verona.

April 5: Austrian General Paul Kray von Krajova defeats the Army of Italy at Magnano.

April 14: The Austrian troops under Melas and the Russians under Suvorov join up at the Mincio River in Lombardy.

April 23: The Rastatt Congress, in session since November 1797, is dissolved because of the new outbreak of war. Two of the French delegates, while leaving the town, are murdered by Austrian hussars.

April 27: Suvorov and Melas defeat Moreau, the new commander of the Army of Italy, at Cassano. Russian troops occupy Milan two days later. The Cisalpine Republic is dissolved.

May 19-20: The English land near Ostend, Holland, but withdraw the following day.

May 24: Naples besieged by peasants rising against the French.

May 26: Russians and Austrians occupy Turin. The remnants of Moreau's army are surrounded in Genoa.

The Austrians are defeated by Napoleon at the battle of Marengo, June 14, 1800.

June 4: Battle of Zurich fought between the Austrians under Archduke Charles and the French under Masséna. Masséna withdraws the next day.

June 19: Suvorov defeats Macdonald in the battle of the Trebbia. The French garrison at Naples capitulates. King Ferdinand returns and dissolves the Parthenopean Republic. Many republicans are massacred in ruthless acts of revenge. The same occurs in Rome as the Roman Republic is toppled.

June 28: Siena is retaken by the king of Naples. Many republicans are killed by the peasants of Tuscany.

July 5: General Joubert is appointed commander of the Army of Italy and Championnet of the Army of the Alps.

July 7: Antirevolutionary Tuscan troops occupy Florence.

July 30: The French garrison in Mantua surrenders.

August 15: In the battle of Novi, Joubert is beaten decisively and killed by the Prussians and Austrians under Suvorov and Melas.

August 27: An English army lands in Helder, Holland, and is joined by a Russian army.

August 29: Championnet is appointed supreme commander in Italy.

September: Suvorov crosses the Alps by the St. Gothard Pass in order to join up with a second Russian army under General Alexander Korsakov, operating in Switzerland.

September 19: General Guillaume Marie Brune defeats the English-Russian armies at Bergen in Holland.

September 26: Korsakov is defeated and driven out of Zurich by Masséna. Suvorov is also forced to withdraw. Masséna takes Constance and threatens the flank of Archduke Charles, who is preparing an invasion of France from the Rhine.

October 6: Brune again defeats the Russian-English forces at Castricum. Brune and Masséna's successes greatly reduce the chances of a Jacobin uprising.

October 18: At the Convention of Alkmar, the British surrender all prisoners taken in Holland in return for unobstructed evacuation.

October 22: Czar Paul I withdraws from the coalition, displeased with the conduct of his allies, particularly the Austrians.

December 26: With the concerted attack on France beaten back, Napoleon, now First Consul, writes "Letters of Peace" to the king of England and the emperor of Austria. His offers are rejected.

1800: *April:* The Austrian army defeats Masséna at Voltri and takes Nice. Masséna and Nicolas Soult retreat to Genoa.

May 6: Napoleon starts his second Italian campaign.

May: The French army of 40,000 men crosses the Alps at the Great St. Bernard Pass.

June 2: The French take Milan, and Napoleon restores the Cisalpine Republic.

June 5: After a stubborn defense and a horrible famine in Genoa, Masséna gives up the city.

June 9: The French under Generals Jean Lannes and Claude Victor defeat the Austrians at Montebello.

June 14: At the battle of Marengo (near Alessandria in Piedmont), the Austrians under Melas are defeated by Napoleon after a desperate battle that is finally decided by General Louis Charles Desaix, who is killed. General Jean Baptiste Kléber is assassinated in Cairo by a Moslem fanatic.

June 16: Truce arranged between Napoleon and Melas. All fortresses west of the Mincio and south of the Po are surrendered to the French, ending the Campaign of Thirty Days. Napoleon offers to the Austrian emperor to renew the treaty of Campo Formio.

July: Moreau, having beaten the Austrian army at Hochstadt, crosses southern Germany and takes Munich. Napoleon gives Malta to Czar Paul, but the British refuse to recognize his claim when Malta surrenders, after a two-year blockade. The czar then joins the Armed Neutrality League, which is directed against England.

September 15: Armistice agreed upon between France and the Austrian emperor.

September 30: Treaty of Mortefontaine between France and the United States ends the "XYZ" diplomatic incident between the two nations.

October 7: Under secret agreement between France and Spain, Louisiana is returned to France, which sells it three years later to the United States.

November 12: Hostilities in Italy and Germany are renewed.

December 3: At the battle of Hohenlinden, Moreau completely defeats Archduke Johann and advances to

Linz. A second army, under Macdonald, advances into the Tyrol.

1801:   *January:* A third French army, under Brune, crosses the Adige and penetrates Austria from the south. Peace negotiations begin.

February 9: Peace of Lunéville agreed upon between France and Austria. The concessions of Campo Formio are confirmed and the Grand Duchy of Tuscany is ceded to Parma; Tuscany is transformed into the kingdom of Etruria. The princes who lost territory by the cession of the west bank of the Rhine to France are to be indemnified inside Germany. This means, practically, the destruction of the Holy Roman Empire. The Second Coalition dissolves.

March 28: Peace treaty between France and Naples. Britain remains at war.

EYEWITNESS TESTIMONY

The fortress was bursting with prisoners; during the last six weeks, over one hundred officers of the guard had been thrown into the prison ... When Paul read the last line [of Voltaire's *Brutus*]: "Rome is free, that is enough ... Let us give thanks to the gods," a spasm of anger came over his face. Without saying a word, he returned to his apartment, took from the library a Life of Peter the Great, opened the page which described the torture and death of the Czarevich Alexis who had disobeyed his father, and asked Kutaissov to take the book to the Grand Duke and ask him to read this instructive passage.

Princess Charlotte de Lieven, about the reign of Czar Paul I (1796-1801), in Daudet's "La Princesse de Lieven" (1901).

I have predicted this to you. If you had not received in your house the revolutionists whom I have constantly driven from mine, all this would not have happened. It is his own fault that General Duphot was killed. After all, we wanted a pretext against Rome, and now we have one.

Jean Baptiste, Baron Cacault, French minister, to the French ambassador in Rome who had left the city, end of December 1797, in Guizot's History of France.

As a favor, I am asking you to withdraw me from my command; I only accepted it because you proposed it to me and under the supposition that it would only last a month. I have always told you that I wanted to stay away from revolutions; four years in America and ten in France are quite enough. I shall fight as a soldier as long as my country has enemies, but I do not wish to mix myself up with revolutionary politics. ... The troops are barefoot, I have not a half-penny and the generals are thinking of nothing but getting back to France; the result is a disorganization disastrous to important operations. However, I shall act in such a way that our vengeance shall be without blemish, that is to say without pillage.

General Louis Alexandre Berthier, to Napoleon, upon receiving orders to march on Rome, letter of January 1798, in Lacroix's Directory, Consulate and Empire (1898).

I reached Rome this morning. I find in this country nothing but the most profound consternation and not a glimmer of the spirit of liberty. One solitary patriot has presented himself to me and has offered to set at liberty 2,000 convicts; you may judge how I received him. I think that military operations have become superfluous and that there is more need here of negotiators. I consider my presence useless.

General Berthier, to Napoleon, letter of February 10, 1798, in Lacroix's Directory ... (1898).

The French army showed itself, and Rome is free. The assembled people of this great capital have declared their independence and resumed their rights. A deputation waited on me and at the Capitol; I recognized the Roman Republic in the name of the French Republic. The deputies presented me with a crown in the name of the Roman people. I told them ... that it belonged to General Bonaparte whose exploits had paved the way for liberty and that I received it for him.

General Berthier, to Napoleon, letter of February, 1798, in Lacroix's Directory ... (1898).

The peace of the world will have begun on the 26th Pluviôse of the year VI; on this day, fanaticism which is at the root of every war, has been extinguished.

Roger Ducos, Director, on the occupation of Rome, February 15, 1798.

The so-called capitulation with reference to the Pope, decreed by General Berthier, is annulled. General Berthier will at once arrest the Pope and his household ... He will likewise send away ... all cardinals and priests who formed part of the Roman government ... He will form at once a provisional government and will take measures, in concert with the commissioners of the Directory, to establish a definite government without delay.

The Directory, decree of February 1798.

I know no other insignia than those with which the Church has decorated me; my body is at your mercy, my soul belongs to God. I acknowledge the hand which strikes down the flock and the shepherd; I worship it and am resigned. You offer me a pension; I have no need of it. A sack to cover myself, and a stone upon which to rest my head, are all I need. It is enough for an old man who wishes to end his days in penitence ... I cannot forsake my people and my duties; I wish to die here.

Pope Pius VI, refusing to choose a residence and to hoist the tricolor cockade, February 1798, in Guizot's History.

Our resources are almost nothing. Rome is poor in cash and we must have money to provide us with food and to sustain its new government. There are fifty thousand beggars in the city.

General Berthier, commanding the entire Army of Italy, to the Directory, letter of February 1798.

The French sick in the hospital of Rome will be considered as hostages. Every cannon shot that comes from the castle will cause the death of one of them who will be abandoned to the just anger of the people.

General Baron Karl von Mack von Leiberich, to French occupation forces besieged at Castel St. Angelo, proclamation at end of November 1798, in Guizot's History.

... the greatest enemies, meanwhile, were not the Austrians, nor the Russians, nor the bands of Piedmontese brigands. It was the scarcity of money, of provisions, of clothing ... and often of ammunition. Never had an army been so forsaken by the government, and never had one suffered more privations.

Laurent, Marquis de Gouvion-Saint-Cyr, commander Army of Rome, summer 1799, Memoires pour servir a l'histoire militaire sous le directoire, le consulat et l'empire *(1831).*

A battle of fifteen days, upon a line sixty leagues in extent, against three combined armies conducted by generals of great reputation, occupying positions deemed impregnable, such have been the operations of Helvetia.

General André Massena, to the Directory, of his victory at Zurich, report at end of September 1799.

Guided by my honor, I hastened to come to the help of humanity, and I have sacrificed thousands of men for its benefit. But when I decided to destroy the French colossus it was not my intention to permit another one

to take its place and to become, in its stead, the terror of the neighboring princes. [Referring, apparently, to the emperor in Vienna and the king of Naples.]

Czar Paul I, his disillusionment with the Second Coalition, autumn 1799, Troyat's Alexandre I *(1980).*

Called by the will of the French nation to be first magistrate, I deem it expedient on entering upon my charge to communicate directly with your Majesty. Must the war which for eight years has ravaged the four quarters of the globe be eternal? Is there no other means of arriving at a mutual understanding? How can the most enlightened nations of Europe, powerful and strong beyond what their security and independence require, sacrifice the interest of commerce, the prosperity of their people and the happiness of families to the ideas of vainglory? These sentiments cannot be foreign to the heart of your Majesty who governs a free nation with the sole aim of rendering it happy ... France and England by their abuse of their power, may for a long time yet retard its termination; but I dare to say that every civilized nation is interested in the close of a war which embraces the whole world.

First Consul Napoleon Bonaparte, to King George III, letter of December 26, 1799.

When was it discovered that the dangers of Jacobinism cease to exist? When was it discovered that the Jacobinism of Robespierre, of Barère, of the five directors of the triumvirate has all of a sudden disappeared because it is concentrated in a single man, raised and nurtured in its bosom, covered with glory under its auspices, and who has been at once the offspring and the champion of all its atrocities? ... It is because I love peace sincerely that I cannot content myself with a vain word. It is because I love peace sincerely that I cannot sacrifice it by seizing the shadow when the reality is not within my reach. Cur igitur pacem nolo? Quia infida est, quia periculosa, quia esse non potest! [Why do I not want peace? Because it is unreliable, and dangerous, because it cannot be.]

William Pitt, prime minister, in Parliament during the debate on French peace overtures, January 1800.

Did I not drive before me hordes of Sardinians and Austrians and clean up the face of Italy four years ago? We will do it again. The same sun shines upon us that shone at Arcole and Lodi. I am relying on Masséna and hope he will hold out in Genoa. But if hunger forces him to surrender, I shall retake Genoa and the plains of the Scrivia. With what pleasure will I then return to my dear France …

Napoleon, to Bourrienne, letter of March 17, 1800, in Bourrienne's Memoirs of Napoleon *(1829-30).*

Keep firmly together. If an emergency occurs, do not be alarmed by it. I shall return like a thunderbolt, to crush those who are audacious enough to raise a hand against the government … This poor M. de Melas will pass by Turin, he will fall back upon Alessandria. I shall pass the Po and come up with him again on the road to Piacenza, in the plains of the Scrivia; and I shall beat him there …

Napoleon, to co-consuls Cambacérès and Lebrun, early May 1800.

We were all proceeding along the goat paths, men and horses, one by one. The artillery was dismounted, also the guns, and put into hollowed-out tree trunks which were drawn on ropes … After we reached the summit, we sat down on the snow and slid downward.

Louis Antoine Fauvelet de Bourrienne, traversing the St. Bernard Pass, May 1800, Memoirs of Napoleon *(1829-30).*

We await with impatience the announcement of your success. M. de Kray and I are groping about here—he to keep his army around Ulm, I to make him quit the post. It would have been dangerous, especially for you, if I had carried the war to the left bank of the Danube. Our present position has forced the Prince of Reuss to remove himself to the passes of the Tyrol … Thus he is no longer dangerous for you. If M. de Kray comes towards me, I shall still retreat as far as Meiningen; there I shall join General Lecourbe and we shall fight. If M. de Kray marches upon Augsburg, I shall do the same. If he will quit his support at Ulm, we shall see what will have to be done to cover your movements. We should find more advantages in carrying on the war upon the left bank of the Danube … but that would not suit you, as the enemy would be able to send detachments down into Italy … Give me, I pray you, some news of yourself and command me in every possible service I can render you.

General Jean Victor Moreau, to Napoleon, in southern Germany, letter of May 27, 1800, in Guizot's History.

Yes, the battle is lost. But it is only three o'clock. There is still time to win another one. [Other reports say these words were spoken not by Desaix, but by Napoleon.]

General Louis Charles Antoine Desaix de Veygoux, before attacking at Marengo, June 4, 1800, in Thiers' History … *(1893).*

Go and tell the First Consul that I am about to charge, I need to be supported by cavalry … I have been too long making war in Africa, the bullets of Europe know me no longer … Conceal my death—it might unsettle the troops …

General Desaix, at Marengo, June 4, 1800, in Thiers' History … *(1893).*

To so much virtue and heroism I want to pay homage such as no other man ever received. Desaix's tomb will have the Alps as its pedestal and the monks of Saint Bernard for its guardians.

Napoleon, Desaix's death in the great victory at Marengo, in Herold's Bonaparte in Egypt *(1966).*

Sir, my conditions are irrevocable … Your position is as well known to me as to yourself. You are in Alessandria, encumbered with the dead, the wounded and the sick, and destitute of provisions; you have lost the elite of your army. You are surrounded on all sides. I could exact everything, but I only demand of you what the situation of affairs imperatively requires …

Napoleon, to Austrian General Melas, loser of Marengo, June 1800.

I could not help wishing that Bonaparte might be defeated as that seemed the only means of stopping the progress of his tyranny.

Mme. Germaine de Staël, on the battle of Marengo, 1800, The Reasons for the Principal Events of the French Revolution *(1818).*

On the battlefield of Marengo, surrounded by the sufferers and in the midst of 15,000 dead bodies, I implore your Majesty to hear the cry of humanity, and not to allow the offspring of two brave and powerful nations to slaughter one another for the sake of interests of which they know nothing … The recent campaign is sufficient proof that it is not France which threatens the balance of power. Every day shows that it is England— England who has so monopolized world commerce and the empire of the seas that she can withstand singlehanded the united fleets of Russia, Sweden, Denmark, France and Holland …

Napoleon, to the Emperor Francis II, after
Marengo, 1800.

My intention is to have neither arches of triumph nor any species of ceremony. I have too good an opinion of myself to hold such bauble in much estimation. I know of no other triumph than public satisfaction.

Napoleon, to his brother, Minister of the Inte-
rior Lucien Bonaparte, about his impending
return to Paris after Marengo, June 1800, in
Guizot's History.

It is from France that we have received persecution for the last ten years. Well, it is from France that will perhaps come in future our succors and our consolations. A very extraordinary young man, and even more difficult to be judged, rules there today. There is no doubt he will soon have reconquered Italy. Remember that he protected the priests in 1797, and that he recently rendered funeral honors to Pius VI. Let us not neglect the resources which offer themselves to us on this side.

Ercole Consalvi, secretary of the Sacred Col-
lege in Rome, to Pope Pius VII, about French
overtures for friendly relations, June 1800, in
Guizot's History.

Without any doubt, it would be a fine thing to enter Vienna. But it is a much finer thing to dictate peace.

General Moreau, when pressed by his
lieutenants to advance after the great victory
at Hohenlinden, December 1800, in Castelot's
Bonaparte *(1967).*

[after enumerating all recent French victories] … the plenipotentiary of the Emperor at Lunéville has declared himself ready to open negotiations for a separate peace. Thus Austria is freed from the influence of the English Government. The Government, faithful to its principles … confides to you and proclaims to France and entire Europe the intentions which animate it. The left bank of the Rhine shall be the limit of the French Republic; she claims nothing on the right bank. The interests of Europe will not permit the Emperor to cross the Adige. The independence of the Helvetic and Batavian Republics shall be assured and recognized. Our victories add nothing to the claims of the French people. Austria ought not to expect from its defeats that which it would not have obtained by victories … it will be the happiness of France to restore calm to Germany and Italy; its glory to enfranchise the continent from the covetous and malevolent influence of England. If our good faith is still deceived, we are at Prague, at Vienna, at Venice.

Napoleon, to the Corps Legislatif, message of
early February 1801.

… as the termination of the war was favorable to France, the house of Austria ought to expect the valley of the Adige [i.e., the borderline] on the crest of the Julian Alps. There is no power in Europe which did not see with pleasure the Austrians expelled from Italy.

Joseph Bonaparte, brother of the first consul,
to Cobenzl, Austrian plenipotentiary, on the
morning of the treaty of Lunéville, February
9, 1801, Memoirs (1853).

14. The Egyptian Campaign: February 1798 to August 1801

THE HISTORICAL CONTEXT

It is not clear why Charles Maurice de Talleyrand, usually an advocate of good relations with England, suggested an expedition against Egypt. Some have suspected that he wanted to do his English friends a favor by thus taking the edge off a possible direct attack on the British Isles. The fact that the Directory promoted the Egyptian plan as soon as it had Napoleon's support can also be explained by its desire to get rid of the ambitious young general who had become so popular and whose ultimate intentions were anything but clear. Crucial elections were coming up, and Napoleon's presence in Paris could have had unpredictable consequences. He himself had entertained thoughts of conquests in the Orient for some time, as shown by his annexation of the Venetian-held islands along the Dalmatian coast. At any rate, the idea was a popular one. France had never forgiven England for the loss of her American colonies in the Treaty of Paris in 1763; France longed to build up an eastern colonial empire to replace the lost one in the west, particularly if it could be done at the expense of her great rival across the Channel.

General Louis Charles Desaix

Preparations for the expedition were made at a fast pace and in great secrecy. The English were not fooled, but the Irish were; they rose once more against England, anticipating an invasion. Amazingly, the huge French fleet managed to avoid an encounter with the much faster British fleet under the experienced Admiral Horatio Nelson, who was lying in wait for them. They slipped by him, first upon leaving Toulon, then at Malta, which surrendered without resistance, and finally at the landing in Alexandria, where Nelson had been only two days before them! Four days before their landing, the French had, in fact, sighted Nelson's fleet,

General Jean Baptiste Kléber

but weather conditions prevented the British from, in turn, discovering the French.

Egypt had been a province of the Ottoman Empire since 1517 and was ruled by a pasha appointed by the Sublime Porte ["Sublime Gate," the government at Constantinople]. But the Mameluke beys, the Egyptian ruling class, had reattained a genuine sovereignty, which gave Napoleon the chance to present himself as the restorer of the sultan's rights. Later, he himself called his proclamation a piece of "charlatanism." He had no trouble beating the Mamelukes and occupying Cairo, and his General Louis Charles Desaix, sent to Upper Egypt to pursue the Mameluke troops, finished their military power for good. But in the meantime, Nelson had discovered the French fleet off Aboukir and managed to surround and destroy it completely. This changed the situation overnight. England was now the undisputed master of the Mediterranean; Napoleon and his army were cut off. Also, Napoleon could not deceive the sultan for long. His intentions became clear when he organized a French protectorate in Cairo and tried to incite the Albanians and the Greeks in the Morea (the Greek Peloponnesus) against their Turkish masters. The sultan responded by joining the great coalition against France.

Napoleon, anticipating a Turkish attack, marched to Suez and from there to Jaffa. It was taken by storm and then 1,200 prisoners were slaughtered upon his orders; he claimed he had no other way of dealing with them. In Jaffa, the plague was raging and spread into his army, killing hundreds of soldiers. Proceeding to the little coastal fortress of Acre, he was stopped by the stubborn resistance offered by a former comrade at the Paris Military School, the emigrant Louis Phélipeaux, and by the arrival of a British fleet. He was forced to retreat to Egypt where he defeated a large Turkish force that had been landed by the British at Aboukir. But his army, weakened by battles, sickness and the fierce climate, could not expect any reinforcements.

Napoleon transferred command to General Jean Baptiste Kléber and left Egypt in great secrecy, accompanied by only a small staff. Again, he was extremely lucky to escape the British warships and land, after a nerve-wracking six-week voyage, in France. Kléber, informed of his new command only by a written note left by Napoleon, managed to defeat the Turks once more. But after Kléber was assassinated by a Moslem fanatic in June of 1800, the remnants of his army finally had to surrender to the British.

The Egyptian expedition concluded in complete failure, serving only to strengthen the British position in the Near East. Napoleon must have been aware of the tremendous risks he was taking, in view of the clear superiority of the British fleet. Whether his plans were really as far-reaching as he later claimed, whether he actually intended to follow the example of Alexander the Great by conquering India and subduing one-half of Asia, is rather doubtful. It seems more likely that, as Johann Wolfgang von Goethe presumed, he felt that the time was not yet ripe for a coup d'état; also, he was loath to jeopardize his popularity by inactivity. In any case, it is remarkable how well he succeeded in maintaining his prestige of invincibility, after this clear-cut defeat. Public opinion in France still saw in him the conqueror of Italy and the peacemaker of Campo Formio.

It is also remarkable that in the midst of all these military and administrative operations he found time for cultural affairs. A group of no less than 187 scientists, artists and writers accompanied him to Egypt, and through their work the ancient Egyptian culture was revealed to the European public for the first time. The famous Rosetta Stone was found during his expedition, enabling Jean Francois Champollion and others to eventually decipher the ancient hieroglyphics. When Napoleon came across the remnants of the old Pharaonic canal, he developed a plan to build a modern one between the Mediterranean and the Red Sea; the plan later inspired Ferdinand de Lesseps to build the Suez Canal. And only a month after Bonaparte had entered Cairo, he founded there the Egyptian Institute for Sciences and Arts.

CHRONICLE OF EVENTS

1798:   *February 14:* Talleyrand sends a memorandum to the Directory proposing the conquest of Egypt.

February 23: Napoleon reports to the Directory that he considers an invasion of England impossible and recommends an expedition into Egypt.

March 5: Napoleon's plan is adopted, and he is appointed supreme commander of the expedition.

April 12: The Army of the Orient is created.

May 19: The French fleet, consisting of 48 men of war and 280 transports carrying about 36,000 men, including a number of scientists and scholars, sails from Toulon. Additional units from Genoa and other ports subsequently join the expedition.

June 11-12: Malta is occupied.

June 28: The British fleet, under Admiral Nelson, which did not catch sight of the French, reaches Alexandria. Nelson believes the French to be farther east and leaves.

June 30: Napoleon reaches Alexandria and occupies it.

July 3: The French fleet anchors across the bay of Aboukir.

July 10 and 13: The Mamelukes are beaten at Ramanieh and Chebreis.

July 20: Nelson, searching for the French fleet, lands in Syracuse, Sicily, which he leaves after five days.

July 21: In the battle of the Pyramids, Napoleon decisively defeats the Mamelukes under Murad Bey.

July 24: Napoleon enters Cairo and proceeds to organize Egypt as a French Protectorate.

August 1: Nelson locates the French fleet under Admiral Francois Paul Brueys at Aboukir, east of Alexandria. The French fleet is surrounded and, except for two ships, completely destroyed. Brueys goes down with his ship. The French army is now isolated.

August 30: Because Napoleon has been inciting the Greeks in the Morea (Pelopponese) and the Albanians to rise against the Sultan at Constantinople, the latter concludes a military alliance with Czar Paul I. Napoleon founds the Egyptian Institute for Sciences

Malta is taken by the French fleet in June 1798.

Napoleon captures Cairo, July 1798.

and Arts in Cairo. General Desaix is sent to Upper Egypt to pursue the Mamelukes.

September 2: Malta revolts against the French. Their garrison is besieged in the fortress of La Valetta.

September 12: Turkey declares war on France.

October 7: Desaix beats the Mamelukes at Sediman in Upper Egypt.

October 21-22: Napoleon suppresses a general insurrection in Cairo against the French.

December 24: Napoleon leaves Cairo and marches toward Suez.

December 30: Napoleon develops a plan to have a canal dug between the Mediterranean and the Red Sea.

1799:   *February 1:* Desaix defeats the last remnants of the Mameluke army at Aswan and completes the conquest of Upper Egypt. Napoleon invades Syria.

February 15: French defeat the Turks at El-Arich.

February 25: Napoleon occupies Gaza in Palestine.

March 4-7: Napoleon invests Jaffa and takes it by storm; 1,200 prisoners are shot on his orders.

March 11: Plague breaks out in the French army. Napoleon inspects the hospitals.

March 19: Napoleon invests Acre, already supported by a small British fleet under Sir Sidney Smith.

April 16: Napoleon interrupts the siege to defeat the Turks at Mont-Tabor, near Nazareth.

May 17: After several unsuccessful attempts to take Acre, he raises the siege and begins a retreat to Cairo.

June 14: Napoleon reenters Cairo.

July 17: A large Turkish force, transported by the British, lands at Aboukir.

July 25: Napoleon defeats the Turkish army at Aboukir.

August 23: Napoleon secretly embarks for France in two small frigates, which manage to avoid the British fleet. He leaves, naming General Kléber as his successor in Egypt.

October 9: Napoleon lands in the bay of Fréjus, France.

1801:   *March 8:* The British land at Aboukir.

March 21: In the battle of Alexandria, the British under Abercromby defeat the French under Jacques Francois Menou, the successor of the assassinated Kléber.

June 7: The French evacuate Cairo.

August 31: In the second battle of Alexandria, Menou surrenders to the British commander Hutchinson. Cairo is occupied by the British.

EYEWITNESS TESTIMONY

All chances were against, not a single one was in our favor. With a light heart we walked into almost certain doom. One must admit, it was an insane gamble, and even its success would not have justified it.

General Auguste Frédéric Marmont, the
Egyptian campaign, Memoirs *(1856-57).*

Soldiers, you are one of the wings of the army of England. You have waged war amongst the mountains, on the plains and in besieged cities. It remains for you to wage war upon the seas. The Roman legions that you have imitated many times, but not yet equalled, fought against Carthage, time after time, upon the sea and on the plains of Zama. Victory never forsook them because they were constantly brave, patient to endure fatigue, well disciplined and united amongst themselves. Soldiers! The eyes of Europe are upon you. You have great destinies to fulfill ... you will do more than you have yet done for the prosperity of your country, the welfare of mankind and your own glory ... be united! Remember that in the day of battle you have need of one another. Sailors ... you have been hitherto neglected! Today the greatest solicitude of the Republic is for you; you will be worthy of the army of which you form part ... [The soldiers were still ignorant of their destination.]

Napoleon Bonaparte, to the expeditionary
force at Toulon, proclamation of May 1798.

A few months, or six years. It will all depend on how things run. I will colonize this country, import artists, workmen ... We are only twenty-nine, and shall be thirty-five then. That is still young. Six years will be sufficient for me to go to India, if all goes according to plans.

Napoleon, to Bourrienne, in May 1798, on
the time required for the expedition's pur-
poses, in Bourrienne's Memoirs of
Napoleon *(1829-30).*

When you are apprized that the appearance of a British Squadron in the Mediterranean is a condition on which the fate of Europe may at this moment be stated to depend, you will not be surprised that we are disposed to strain every nerve, and incur considerable hazard in effecting it ... the task should be entrusted to Admiral Horatio Nelson whose acquaintance with that part of the world, as well as his activity and disposition seem to qualify him in a peculiar manner ...

Earl Spencer, First Lord of the Admiralty, to
Admiral Jervis, May 2, 1798, in Warner's
The Battle of the Nile *(1960).*

I shall believe that they are going on their scheme of possessing Alexandria and getting troops to India, a plan ... by no means so difficult as at first be imagined ... Be they bound for the Antipodes, your Lordship may rely that I will not lose a moment in bringing them to action, and endeavor to destroy their transports.

Admiral Viscount Horatio, Lord Nelson, to
the Lord of the Admiralty, dispatch ca. June
18, 1798.

Even for officers and civilians, things were becoming a little rough; there was hardly any livestock left to supply their table with fresh meat. There was no more fuel to heat our fetid water. The useful animals were disappearing while those which were eating us multiplied a hundred-fold.

Baron Dominique Vivant Denon, with the
French fleet, approaching Malta, 1798,
Travels in Upper and Lower Egypt in
1798 and 1799 *(1807).*

It would be difficult to convey an exact idea of what we felt as we approached the inner sanctum of power, dictating its orders amidst 300 sail, in the mystery and silence of the night, with only the moon lighting the spectacle just enough to let us take it in. We were about 500 of us on deck; one could have heard the buzzing of a fly.

Baron Denon, aboard frigate La Junon, *recon-*
noitering before Alexandria, June 27, 1798,
Travels ... *(1807).*

Soldiers! You are about to undertake a conquest whose effects on the world's civilization and trade are incalculable. You will inflict on England a blow which is certain to wound her in her most sensitive spot, while waiting for the day when you can deal her the death blow ... The people with whom we shall live are

Mohammedans. Their chief creed is: 'There is no God but God and Mohammed is his prophet.' Do not contradict them. Act toward them as in the past you have acted towards the Jews and the Italians. Respect their muftis and imams as you have respected the rabbis and the bishops. Show the same tolerance toward the ceremonies prescribed by the Koran … The Roman legions used to protect all religions. You will find here customs quite different from those of Europe; you must become used to them. The people of the countries where we are going treat their women differently … but in all countries, the man who rapes a woman is a monster. Looting enriches but a few. It dishonors us, it destroys our resources and it turns the people we want to befriend into our enemies.

Napoleon, to his troops just before reaching Alexandria, proclamation of June 28, 1798.

When I arrived before Alexandria and when I learned that the English had passed by there with superior forces a few days before, I decided to land my troops, despite the horrible storm … I recall that just at the moment when the manoeuvres preparatory to the landing began, a warship was sighted on the horizon. As it turned out, it was [the frigate *La Justice*] coming from Malta. I cried out: 'Is my luck leaving me? All I need is five days!'

Napoleon, the landing near Alexandria, 1798, in Copies of Original Letters … *(1798).*

I can assure you in all confidence that what inspired our soldiers in the capture of Alexandria was … thirst. At the point the army had reached, we had the choice only between finding water or dying.

Lieutenant Louis Thurman, to his family, letter of June 1793, Bonaparte in Egypt *(1902).*

Nelson destroys the French fleet at the battle of Aboukir Bay, August 1-2, 1798.

We already thought that the city had surrendered and were quite surprised when a volley of musketry was being fired at us just as we were passing a mosque … A general who happened to be on the scene ordered us to force the gate and to spare no one we found inside. Men, women and children … lost their lives under our bayonets. But, since human feelings are stronger than revenge, the slaughter ceased when they were crying for mercy, and about one third of them was saved.

P. Millet, the capture of Alexandria, July 2, 1798, Memoirs of the Egyptian Campaign *(1903).*

People of Egypt, they tell you that I came to destroy your religion. Do not believe it. Answer them that I came to restore your rights, to punish the usurpers, and that I respect, more than the Mameluke, God and his prophet and the Koran. Were we not the ones who destroyed the Pope, who said it was necessary to wage war against the Muslims? Did we not destroy the Knights of Malta because these madmen believed that God willed them to wage war against the Muslim? Thrice happy those who are on our side! Happy even those who remain neutral. But woe, threefold woe to those who shall arm for the Mameluke and fight against us! God has cursed them as usurpers and tyrants … Is there a beautiful slave, a fine horse or a grand house, it belongs to the Mamelukes … God is just and pities the people. He has ordained that the Empire of the Mamelukes should end!

Napoleon, after his entrance into Alexandria, proclamation of July 2, 1798.

Perhaps you Parisians will laugh when you see the Mohammedan Proclamation of our commander-in-chief. He is ignoring all our joking about it, and it will surely produce an enormous effect.

Pierre Amadée Emilien Probe Jaubert, navy commissioner, to the minister of marine, on Napoleon's proclamation of July 2, 1798.

The soldiers are accusing the generals of the incredible sufferings through which they have gone ever since they left the ships. They are crying, they keep asking what wrongs they have done to be sent into the desert to perish in this way …

Baron Nicolas Philibert Desvernois, march to the pyramids, July 1798, Memoirs *(1898).*

Some Arabs on horseback came provokingly close to our headquarters. Bonaparte watched from the window and became furious. He turned to his young aide-de-camp Croisier who was on duty and ordered him to take a few men and drive this rabble away … A skirmish followed, as we watched the fight from the windows … our manner of attack showed a hesitation the supreme commander could not tolerate. He shouted … as though he could be heard—"Forward, dammit!" Our men retreated every time the Arabs counterattacked. Finally, the Arabs withdrew unchallenged; they had not lost one man.

The general flew into a wild rage which he wreaked on the returning Croisier … so brutally that Croisier went out with tears in his eyes. Bonaparte then told me to follow him to calm him down, but it was no use. Croisier said "I will never survive this … I cannot live dishonored." Bonaparte had called him a coward. Only at the siege of Acre Croisier found the death he had sought.

Louis Antoine Fauvelet de Bourrienne, at Damanhur en route to the Nile, July 1798, Memoirs of Napoleon *(1829-30).*

When they saw the Nile, the soldiers broke ranks and threw themselves onto it, some with their clothes, even their weapons on. Others undressed first, then dove into the water and stayed in it for several hours. Many of them drank too greedily and died of it.

Desvernois, July 1798, Memoirs *(1898).*

It was generally assumed … that once the landing was accomplished, we should sail to Corfu where we would have been reinforced by our battleships from Malta, Toulon and Ancona so as to be prepared for any eventuality. The general decided differently. The luck that makes all his operations succeed will attend this one [to leave the navy at Aboukir] also. Incidentally, all of us here are propelled by the wind of fatalism, which begins to affect even my convictions a little.

Jaubert, navy commissioner, to the minister of marine, July 9, 1798.

At sunrise, military music suddenly burst upon us. The supreme commander had ordered the Marseillaise to be played, knowing its effect on the soldiers. This marvellous song incites the soldiers' courage, inflames their patriotism and makes them realize that the time for complaints has passed and that their job is to be victorious.

Captain Vertray, before the battle of the pyramids, July 21, 1798, Journal of an Officer of the Army of Egypt *(1883).*

Bonaparte visits plague victims at Jaffa.

Soldiers, forty centuries are looking down upon you … [The authenticity of these words has been questioned.]

Napoleon, before the battle of the pyramids, in Mereschkowskij's Napoleon *(1928).*

… before us were the beautiful Arabian horses, richly harnessed, neighing, snorting, prancing … their martial riders covered with splendid arms, inlaid with precious metals and stones. They wore very colorful costumes, egret feathers on the turbans, some wore gilded helmets. They were armed with spears, sabres, lances, battle axes and daggers and each wore three pairs of pistols. Their sight, in its novelty and richness, left a vivid impression on our soldiers. From now on, their thoughts dwelt on booty.

Desvernois, battle of the pyramids, July 21, 1798, Memoirs *(1898).*

When general Reynier ordered "form your ranks" we formed our squares instantly to absorb the shock, ten men deep. This was carried out with excellent precision and control … We fired so calmly that no cartridge was wasted, waiting for the very moment when their riders were about to break in to our squares. The number of bodies around our square grew rapidly, the clothes of the wounded and dead Mamelukes burnt like tinder.

Vertray, the battle of the pyramids, July 21, 1798, Journal … *(1883).*

When I saw them [the French ships] I could not help popping my head every now and then out of the window (although I had a damned toothache) … I knew what stuff I had under me so I went into the attack with a few ships only, perfectly sure that the others would follow me, although it was nearly dark and they might have had every cause for not doing it, yet they all in the course of two hours found a hole to poke in at.

Nelson, the battle of Aboukir Bay, August 1-2, 1798, in Warner's The Battle of the Nile *(1960).*

Although the blazing *L'Orient* presented a most awful and grand spectacle, such as formerly would have drawn tears down the victor's cheeks, pity was stifled as it rose by the remembrance of the numerous and horrid atrocities their unprincipled and blood-thirsty nation had and were committing.

Captain Miller, commander of the British Theseus, *at Aboukir Bay, August 1, 1798, in Warner's* Battle of the Nile *(1960).*

Nelson owed his victory to the ineptness and the negligence of the captains of *Le Guerrier* and *Le Conquérant*, to the accident of *L'Orient* and the poor conduct of Admiral Villeneuve … It was in Villeneuve's power to turn the battle into a French victory as late as daybreak.

Napoleon, on the disaster of Aboukir Bay, in Correspondence of the French Army in Egypt *(1799-1800).*

Nelson's conduct … cannot be held up as a model, but he and the English crews displayed the utmost possible skill and vigour, whereas half of the French squadron showed as much ineptness as pusillanimity.

Napoleon, the defeat at Aboukir Bay, in Correspondence … in Egypt *(1799-1800).*

The soldiers were rebelling, and so were the generals. It is an awful thing to say, but perhaps it was our good fortune that the fleet was destroyed at Aboukir; otherwise the whole army would have taken it upon itself and embarked!

Napoleon (as reported by Gourgaud), on the destruction of his fleet at Aboukir Bay, in Mereschkowskij's Napoleon *(1928).*

One thing I observed in these Frenchmen quite different from anything I had ever before observed: In the American war, when we took a French ship … the prisoners were as merry as if they had taken us, only saying "Fortune de guerre,"—"you take me today, I take you tomorrow." Those we had on board [after Aboukir]

were thankful for our kindness, but were sullen and as downcast as if each had lost a ship of his own.

John Nicol, on the prisoners taken at Aboukir Bay, August 1798, The Life and Adventures of John Nicol, Mariner *(1822).*

All the trade in the Mediterranean must be led into French hands … It is the secret wish of the Directory and will also be the necessary result of our present position there … France has always coveted Egypt and it must belong to the Republic. Luckily, the impertinent and insulting attitude of the beys and the weakness of the Porte permitted us to penetrate Egypt … The Directory is determined to position itself in Egypt by all means at its disposal.

Charles Maurice de Talleyrand-Périgord, to Pierre Jean Marie Ruffin, after battle of Aboukir Bay, confidential letter of August 4, 1798, in Correspondence … in Egypt *(1799-1800).*

If I was King of England, I would make you the most noble, puissant Duke Nelson, Marquis Nile, Earl Alexandria, Viscount Pyramid, Baron Crocodile and Prince Victory, that posterity might have you in all forms.

Emma, Lady Hamilton, in Naples, to Nelson, letter following the battle of Aboukir Bay, in Herold's Bonaparte in Egypt *(1966).*

By gaining the support of the great sheiks of Cairo one gains the public opinion of all Egypt. Of all the leaders that nation could have, none are less dangerous to us than the sheiks who are timid and incapable of fighting and who, like all priests, inspire fanaticism without being fanatics themselves.

Napoleon, to General Kléber, letter of August 1798.

He cut such a poor figure, wearing a turban and caftan, and in this unfamiliar attire looked so self-conscious and awkward, that he left the room very soon thereafter to take them off; he never felt the temptation to repeat this masquerade.

Bourrienne, Napoleon dons Turkish garb to impress the divan (council), September 1798, Memoirs … *(1829-30).*

The native population were very slow in understanding what this assembly of grave and studious people [the scientists] was about who neither governed nor administered nor served any religious function.

They thought they were making gold. Eventually, however, they formed a correct opinion of them. Not only the sheiks and notables but even the lowest class of people held the savants in high esteem.

Napoleon, Egypt, September 1798, in Correspondence … in Egypt *(1799-1800).*

When you wrote that letter, Citizen General, you forgot that you were holding the graver of History in your hand and that you were writing to Kléber. I expect … to receive by the next courier your order suspending me, not only as governor of Alexandria, but from all my functions in the army until you are more thoroughly informed …

General Jean Baptiste Kléber, to Napoleon, after being criticized by Bonaparte, September 1798, in Correspondence … in Egypt *(1799-1800).*

He was always … wrapped up in war and glory … always badly dressed, sometimes even ragged, and despising comfort … When in Egypt, I made him a present of a complete field-equipage several times, but he always lost it. Wrapped up in a cloak, Desaix threw himself under a gun and slept as contentedly as if he were in a palace … He was intended by nature for a great general.

Napoleon, on General Desaix, in O'Meara's Napoleon in Exile *(1822).*

One of our men, stretched out on the ground, crawled toward a dying Mameluke and slit his throat. An officer asked him: How can you do such a thing in the state you are in? "It's easy for you to talk," the soldier answered, "but me, I have only a few minutes to live, and I want to have fun while I may!"

Baron Denon, with Desaix, fighting Murad Bey near El Lahun, October 7, 1798, Travels … *(1807).*

I had occasion to notice that, while they never refused to pay, there was not a single ingenious device they did not resort to in order to postpone by a few hours their parting with the money [they owed].

Baron Denon, on the Egyptians, Travels … *(1807).*

I would be glad to continue the pursuit of them [Murad's troops], but … the inundation which cuts me off from the villages, would make it impossible for me to feed the troops … The eye disease is truly a horrible

plague, it has deprived me of 1,400 men. In my last marches, I have dragged with me about a hundred of these wretches who were totally blind … We are practically naked … The troops really need a rest. Give us the supplies … [Napoleon agreed.]

Desaix, to Napoleon, from El Lahun, letter of October 1798, in in Correspondence … in Egypt *(1799-1800).*

From Herodotus' time on, all travellers were satisfied to sail up the Nile quickly and dared not to leave their boats out of sight. Since General Desaix received me so cordially and since I was helped by all officers who shared my love for the arts, I had nothing to fear except that I may not have time, pencils, paper and talent.

Baron Denon, in Egypt, Travels … *(1807).*

The following morning, hostilities were resumed. We [in the Institute] had been given arms; all the savants got ready for combat. The leaders were nominated, everybody had his own plan, but nobody felt obliged to obey.

Baron Denon, the great insurrection in Cairo, October 22, 1798, Travels … *(1807).*

… you must, at least for some time, manage to manoeuver by yourself … all you have done to bring the native to our cause, conciliate the Arabs and to win partisans … merits our approval. As we cannot send you any help, the Directory knows better than to issue any orders or even instructions to you … Since it would be difficult, at the present time, to arrange your return to France, you have three choices open: To remain in Egypt … or to march to India where … you undoubtedly will find men ready to join in your fight against English domination. Or to march on Constantinople and to meet there the enemy who is threatening you. The decision is yours and that of the brave and excellent men who surround you.

Talleyrand, to Napoleon, letter of instructions, November 1798.

If I chose, I could call each of you to account for the most hidden feelings of his heart, for I know everything, even what you have told no one. But the day will come when all men shall see beyond all doubt that I am guided by orders from above and that all human efforts avail nought against me. Blessed are they who in good faith are the first to choose my side.

Napoleon, after giving a full pardon to all Cairenes, proclamation of December 21, 1798.

You will have the goodness, Citizen General, to order the commandant of Cairo to have the heads of all prisoners, who were taken arms in hand, cut off. They will be taken to the banks of the Nile … after dark; their headless corpses will be thrown into the river.

Napoleon, to General Berthier, after suppression of the Cairo insurrection.

Wherever a village rises in rebellion, the general in command of the province, by way of punishment, will seize all boys between twelve and sixteen years old. A report will be sent to the commander-in-chief who will issue orders concerning their subsequent disposition.

Army of the Orient, order of the day, December 28, 1798.

Citizen Boyer, surgeon of the hospital of Alexandria, has been cowardly enough to refuse to treat those wounded soldiers who had been in contact with patients allegedly suffering from contagious disease. He is unworthy of being a French citizen. He will be dressed in women's clothes and led, on a donkey, through the streets of Alexandria, with a sign on his

A contemporary caricature of Bonaparte leaving Egypt

back reading: "Unworthy of being a French citizen; he is afraid of dying."

Army of the Orient, order of the day, after plague had broken out in the ranks, January 8, 1799.

Although its dimensions are enormous, those contours which have survived are as subtle as they are pure. The face has a soft, graceful and serene expression … The mouth shows thick lips and has a sweeping and refined sensuality which is admirable indeed. It is like living flesh.

Baron Denon, the Great Sphinx, Travels … (1807).

I went from one object to another, pencil in hand, drawn from one to the next … I did not have sufficient eyes nor hands, my head did not suffice to see, draw and identify all the objects which struck me. My inadequacy to draw these sublime objects made me feel ashamed.

Baron Denon, at Tentyra (Dendera), January 1799, Travels … (1807).

I received eighteen minor wounds, the enemy had chosen me as his main target. The tendons of my right forearm were cut by a sabre, forcing me to grab the sword with my left hand which put me in a dangerous position … I shouted to Savary to come and help me and he shot back "help yourself as well as you can" …

Desvernois, fighting Murad Bey near Dendera, January 19, 1799, Memoirs (1898).

Although no order had been given, the men fell into ranks and presented their arms, accompanied by the drums and the bands.

Desvernois, the army's first, unexpected sight of the temples of Luxor and Karnak, January 27, 1799, Memoirs (1898).

We are in mud and water up to our knees. The weather and the cold are about the same as in Paris at this time of the year. You are lucky to be enjoying the sunshine of Cairo.

Napoleon, in Gaza, to General Dugua, in Cairo, letter of late February 1799, in Correspondence … in Egypt (1799-1800).

The soldiers' fury was at its height: everybody was put to the sword. Being sacked, the town experienced all the horrors of a city taken by storm.

Napoleon, the March 7 slaughter of the in-
habitants of Jaffa, letter of March 1799, Correspondence ... in Egypt *(1799-1800).*

When the commander-in-chief ordered us to conquer Upper Egypt, he was concentrating entirely on his own campaign and gave us absolutely nothing. My division ... has received no pay for one month longer than the rest of the army ... We are exhausted ... but will continue beating the Meccans, the Mamelukes and peasants. I have requested from the chief commander the many things we need, but I am giving up, for I never get anything out of him.

Desaix, to General Dugua, commanding at
Cairo for the absent Bonaparte, letter of
March 9, 1799, in Correspondence ... in
Egypt *(1799-1800).*

Men, women and children threw themselves into the Nile. True to their ferocious character, mothers were observed drowning those children they could not take along or mutilating their daughters to protect them from being raped ... I found a girl, seven or eight years old, sewed up in a way ... to prevent her from satisfying her most urgent needs which caused her terrible convulsions. I was able to save her life by a counteroperation and a bath ...

Baron Denon, the occupation of Philae,
March 1799, Travels ... *(1807).*

We would have been happy to exchange the little bread we had for bullets and gunpowder. There was no time to eat, but even if there had been we could not have used it since we were so exhausted from thirst and fatigue that we could not even speak. Close by, there was a lake but our division was not able to reach it ... We were wading up to our waists in water which we had craved to drink only a short while ago. But now we though no more of drinking, but of killing and dyeing the lake with blood of these barbarians who only a moment ago had hoped to cut off our heads and drown us in the same lake where they were drowned themselves now, and which was filling up with their dead bodies.

P. Millet, battle at Mount Tabor, April 16,
1799, Memoirs of the Egyptian Campaign
(1903).

... I did not want to ask you the question "Are the French willing to leave Syria?" before you had a chance to match your strength against ours, since you could not be persuaded, as I am, of the impractibility of your enterprise. But now ... that you can see [this fortress] becomes stronger each day instead of being weakened by two months of siege, I do ask you this: "Are you willing to evacuate your troops from the territory of the Ottoman Empire before the intervention of the great Allied army changes the nature of this question?"

Admiral Sir William Sidney Smith, com-
manding the British fleet at Acre, to
Napoleon, letter of May 8, 1799, in Barrow's
Life and Correspondence ... *(1848).*

The Providence of Almighty God has been wonderfully manifested in the defeat and precipitate retreat of the French army ... The Plain of Nazareth has been the boundary of Buonaparte's extraordinary career.

Admiral Smith, to Nelson, on his victory at
Acre, report of May 1799, in Barrow's Life
and Correspondence ... *(1848).*

The city is not, and never has been, defensible according to the rules of art. But, according to every other rule, it must and shall be defended. Not that it is in itself worth defending, but we feel that it is by this breach Buonaparte means to march to further conquest.

Admiral Smith, to Lord Vincent, on the siege
of Acre, report of May 1799, in Barrow's Life
and Correspondence ... *(1848).*

After having maintained ourselves in the heart of Syria for three months, with only a handful of men, after capturing 40 guns and 6,000 prisoners, after razing the fortifications of Gaza, Jaffa, Haifa and Acre[!], we shall return to Egypt. I am obliged to go back there when hostile landings may be expected. Only a few days ago you could still hope to take [Djezzar] Pasha prisoner in his palace; but at this point the capture of the castle of Acre is not worth wasting even a few days. The brave men I might have lost in that enterprise are needed now for more important operations. Soldiers, there are more hardships and dangers facing us ... You will find in them new opportunities for glory ...

Napoleon, to his troops at Acre, proclamation
of May 17, 1799.

A grain of sand has put a stop to my career. If Acre had been taken, the French army would have thrown itself at Damascus and Aleppo, and within a short time would have reached the Euphrates river. 600,000 Christian Druses would have joined us and who can say where that would have led us? I would have gone to Constantinople, to India …

Napoleon (as told by Bourrienne), on the siege of Acre, Bourrienne's Memoirs … *(1829-30).*

I saw with my own eyes officers who had limbs amputated being thrown out of their litters [by their bearers] … amputated men, wounded men, plague-stricken men, or people merely suspected of having the plague, being abandoned in the fields … We were surrounded by nothing but dying men, looters and arsonists …

Bourrienne, retreat from Acre, Memoirs … *(1829-30).*

Citizen General, only you yourself will be in a position to judge if you can safely leave behind part of your army, and the Directory is authorizing you, that, in this case, you entrust your command to anyone else you find qualified.

Talleyrand, to Napoleon, letter of May 1799.

The occasion seemed to favor the capture of Acre, but our spies, deserters and prisoners all reported that the plague was ravaging the city … they would have brought back into camp the germs of that horrible evil which is more to be feared than all the armies in the world.

Napoleon, to the Directory, report of May 27, 1799.

Under these untoward circumstances, we have the satisfaction of observing the enemy's losses to be such that a few more victories like this will annihilate the French army … I am sorry to have to acquaint your lordship of the entire defeat of the first division of the Ottoman army.

Admiral Smith, to Nelson, after Bonaparte's victory over the Turks, at Aboukir, August 2, 1799, in Barrow's Life and Correspondence … *(1848).*

If, because of unforseeable events … you will have received no help or news by the month of May [1800] and if in this year the plague will strike in Egypt in spite of all precautionary measures and you lose over 1,500 men, I feel that you should not risk the next campaign, and you have the authorization to make peace with the Porte, even if the main condition for that should be the evacuation of Egypt.

Napoleon, to General Kléber, his successor in Egypt, end of August 1799.

The sun was setting and the enemy was standing against the sun. We could see them clearly, but since the evening fogs were enveloping us, we were hardly visible to them and they could not recognize the way our sails were set. This saved us. It was a fateful moment. Ganteaume proposed to Bonaparte to return to Corsica, but he, after thinking it over for a moment, decided to entrust himself to Providence and merely to change our direction—toward St. Raphael- Fréjus. The English thought our two frigates had come from Toulon and chased after us into the open sea while we were heading straight for the coast.

Marmont, aboard the frigate Muiron *off the south coast of France, October 7, 1799,* Memoirs *(1856-57).*

What I like in Alexander the Great is not his campaigns … but his political methods. He was right in ordering the murder of Parmenion who like a fool objected to Alexander's giving up Greek customs. It was most politic of him to go to Amon: it was thus he conquered Egypt. If I stayed in the Orient, I probably would have founded an empire like Alexander's by going on a pilgrimage to Mecca.

Napoleon (as told by Gourgaud and Montholon) on his Egyptian policy, Memoirs … *(1823-25).*

I do not now what would have happened to me if that happy idea of going to Egypt had not come to me. I did not know, when I embarked, whether I was saying farewell to France forever; but I had no doubt that she would call me back. The fascination of the Oriental conquest pulled my thoughts away from Europe, more than I ever would have thought possible.

Napoleon (as told by Mme. Rémusat) in 1803, Memoirs 1802-1808 *(1881).*

One can see, he had started this campaign [into Egypt] only to fill out a period when he could do nothing in France to become the master … Napoleon treated the world as Hummel treated his piano …

Johann Wolfgang von Goethe, to Eckermann, on Napoleon, April 1829, in Eckermann's Conversations with Goethe *(1902).*

15. Napoleon's Coup d'Etat and Consulate: October 1799 to December 1804

THE HISTORICAL CONTEXT

During the final two years of its existence, the Directory survived only with the help of two coup d'états: the 18th Fructidor (September 4, 1797), directed against the royalists, and the 22nd Floréal (May 11, 1798), against the Jacobins. But its position remained precarious. In the spring elections of 1799, only 71 out of 143 candidates "recommended" by the executive had been elected, and a radical foe of the Directory, Emanuel Joseph Sieyès, had become its central figure. The military defeats administered by the Second Coalition had inspired a new wave of patriotism in the country, which identified itself with the radical revolutionary ideas of the old Jacobin days. Since Danton's time, patriotism and Jacobinism had gone hand-in-hand in times of emergency.

Lucien Bonaparte, Napoleon's brother

The yearly elections for both chambers prescribed by the constitution perpetuated political unrest, despite the great longing for stability not only among the governing classes, the upper bourgeoisie and businessmen, but also among the peasants, many of whom had become wealthy by the purchase of national lands. The Jacobins, for their part, felt that the true upholders of the Revolution, the masses in the cities, had gotten the worst of the deal and had lost most of their influence since the great May insurrection of 1795. The weakness of the government was revealed also in the new advances of the Chouans, who once again occupied Le Mans and Nantes. There was a growing call for strengthening the executive, but any change of the constitution by constitutional means involved a very complex procedure requiring years to accomplish. It seems that Sieyès was toying with the idea of a coup d'état as early as the summer of 1799. Though he was known as the

Bonaparte, Cambacérès and Lebrun

deadly enemy of the old aristocracy, he was now suspected of planning the reintroduction of a constitutional monarchy, either with the Duke of Orleans or a German prince. In any case, the cooperation of the military was essential to any such plan. Sieyès may have thought of General Barthélemy Catherine Joubert (who was killed in August of 1799) or Jean Victor Moreau, whom he approached around the time of Napoleon's return and who is alleged to have answered Sieyès: "This is your man!"

In view of the tremendous popular acclaim that greeted Napoleon, Sieyès realized that nothing could be done without him. Relations between the two men were slow to develop, but they shared the same moderate accomplices: Charles Maurice de Talleyrand, Jean Jacques Cambacérs, Benjamin Constant and, in particular, Napoleon's younger brother Lucien, now president of the Council of Five Hundred, who had informed his brother in full detail of the proposed coup d'état and the constitution Sieyès had in mind. When the two met at Lucien's house, Napoleon insisted on the establishment of a provisional consular government, which would then draft the new constitution. Sieyès had to give in. The rest of the preparations were comparatively easy: Barras agreed to everything; Joseph Fouché, as minister of police, promised to keep out of it; the president of the Council of Ancients was won over.

Everything went smoothly on the first day of action, the 18th Brumaire, one month after Napoleon had landed. But on the following day the conspiracy was nearly foiled. On the first day, under the pretext of a terrorist plot, both chamber were transferred to Saint-Cloud—this was constitutionally correct—and Napoleon put in charge of the transfer. The directors who refused to resign were taken into custody. But on the second day, the chambers stubbornly demanded proof of a plot. When Napoleon, who could command armies but was no popular speaker, tried to address the delegates, he was shouted down and, in the Council of 500, even bodily attacked. Without Lucien's quick-witted and energetic help, the day could have ended in utter disaster for Napoleon, since the soldiers surrounding the castle of Saint-Cloud were barely persuaded to intervene. Finally, Joachim Murat cleared the hall, dispersing the 500, who left shouting, "Long live the republic." The intimidated Ancients then recognized the new provisional government, and in the evening Lucien and Sieyès managed to make the action legal by reassembling a minority of delegates, who dissolved the Directory and appointed Bonaparte, Sieyès and Jean Francois Ducos as provisional consuls. This last session, masterfully conducted by Lucien, was a farce, and Napoleon was quite displeased with the way things had gone. But he was in charge now.

He appointed his ministers within two days, and within five weeks the new Constitution of the Year VIII was proclaimed—but considerably altered from Sieyès's original design. The other two consuls were Cambacérès and Charles Francois Lebrun, who had only advisory capacities. Sieyès played only a minor role thereafter. The proclamation of the new consuls ended with the words: "Citizens, the revolution holds up the principles which prompted its beginning. It is finished." There was no declaration of human rights in the new constitution. The legislative bodies it provided for were mere tools to execute the will of the first consul, Napoleon.

In February of 1800, a plebiscite was held on the new constitution; of 3,000,000 voters, only 1,500 reportedly disapproved. The vote was not secret; yet a secret vote would hardly have yielded a different result. Even before the voting, Napoleon had imposed a tight control over the press, prohibiting newspapers from becoming "instruments in the hands of the republic's enemies." The 13 publications allowed to continue were warned that they must, "respect the sovereignty of the people and the glory of our armed forces." The *Moniteur* was established as Napoleon's instrument for informing the public and forming public opinion.

The most urgent problem was to put order into the nation's finances, as the Directory had left the Treasury empty. The currency was stabilized and, with the help of financial experts, the Bank of France was founded. The administration was then reorganized and centralized into a system of prefects and sub-prefects, all chosen by the central government. The court system and the tax laws were reformed, and Napoleon began to put the whole legal system on a new basis. A commission of four appointed by Napoleon, together with the second consul, Cambacérès, worked out a codification of the entire French civil law, which was promulgated in 1804 as the *Code Civil*, or *Code Napoléon*. Based on Roman principles and Germanic laws, it secured the civic achievements of the Revolution, in particular equality before the law. Napoleon supervised the final draft of the Code, which turned out to be his most enduring accomplishment. It was also adopted in Northern Italy, Holland and some German states occupied by France, and influenced legislation all over Europe throughout the century.

The tremendous activity of his first year of dictatorship— interrupted only for the three months of his lightning Italian campaign—changed the inner structure of France more than any other such brief period in her history, excepting only the first months after the Estates General had convened in 1789. This burst of activity also served to establish Napoleon's authority and image in the public eye. One of his first acts had been to move into the old royal castle, the Tuileries. Shortly after his triumphal return from the Marengo campaign, he began negotiations with the Holy See; after some trying months of bargaining, the Concordat was concluded in 1801. Napoleon himself was a sceptic, but he considered the Catholic Church the most perfect instrument to keep the masses under control. More specifically, he also hoped thereby to create a permanent peace in the Vendeé, which had never been entirely pacified. At the same time, he was always careful to present himself as the heir and executor of the Revolution. As late as 1814, when the Allied armies were invading France, he declared: "One must put on the riding boots of 1793 once again," and when he returned from Elba in 1815, thousands of people greeted him in Lyons shouting: "Vive l'empereur, vive la révolution!"

Napoleon met with fanatic opposition from the two extremes: the old revolutionaries and the royalists. The suggestion of the Comte de Lille to abdicate in favor of the Bourbons was declined by Napoleon, who argued that the reinstitution of a Bourbon would lead to a bloody civil war. Then followed the Nivôse plot, in which Napoleon was almost blown up on his way to the Opera. He blamed the conspiracy on the Jacobins to whom he became increasingly hostile, although Georges Cadoudal and the royalist Chouans were actually to blame, and Fouché persecuted them accordingly. But Cadoudal did not give up. In the summer of 1803, he was back in France and involved men like Jean Charles Pichegru and even Moreau in his plan to assassinate Napoleon. When the plot was discovered, Napoleon overreacted again, this time against the royalists. The Duke Louis Antoine d'Enghien, whom he abducted, brought to France, and shot, was innocent of the plot. This incident was extremely damaging to Napoleon's reputation in Europe.

In foreign politics, Napoleon tried to get on friendly terms with Czar Paul I of Russia, who had formed an armed neutrality league to counteract British interference with neutral shipping. But the league was dealt a blow when the British destroyed the Danish fleet and forced Denmark to withdraw from the league. Paul himself, a very erratic ruler, was assassinated, with the knowledge of his son and successor, Alexander I, who desired to come to terms with England.

Benjamin Constant

After a failed attack on the French fleet at Boulogne, and some economic setbacks, England was ready to make peace with France. At Amiens the 10-year-old war between the two countries was brought to a temporary end. Once again British tourists flocked to the French capital; the malicious cartoons in the British press that had lampooned Napoleon seemed forgotten, and the past and future prime minister, Charles James Fox, forever the promoter of peace between the two countries, was given an interview by Napoleon, who by this time had been made First Consul for life.

Napoleon's policies, however, remained as expansionist and aggressive as those pursued by the Directory, jeopardizing the peace. His attempt to extend France's empire by establishing a colony on San Domingo (Hispaniola) was short-lived, partly because the native rebels received help from the American President Thomas Jefferson, who feared that Napoleon might make the island a base for an invasion of Louisiana. Jefferson's fears may or may not have been justified. Napoleon acquired the huge Louisiana territory from Spain in a secret treaty, but as soon as it had been ceded to France, he sold it to the United States—perhaps perceiving that British domination of the seas could easily cut off France from its colonial possessions.

Nevertheless, Napoleon's ambitions for France seemed to make conflict inevitable. During the year of peace following the treaty of Amiens, which ended the British blockade of French ports, France imposed high import dues on competitive British products. To consolidate his position in Europe, Napoleon founded the Ligurian Republic, annexed Elba, Piedmont and Parma in Italy, increased his influence in Switzerland, and, by arbitrating the indemnification of German princes under the treaty of Lunéville, enhanced his position within Germany. Thus he upset again the delicate balance of power on the continent that was all-important to the British. Consequently, the British refused to honor their obligation to restore Malta to the Knights Hospitalers until France withdrew from Holland, Italy and Switzerland. After that, both sides again prepared for war, which broke out in May of 1803. England was again threatened by a French invasion from the port of Boulogne; the Irish rebelled in vain; Toulon was blockaded by the British navy; and William Pitt took over the government in London. In May of 1804, the Senate at Paris proclaimed Napoleon Emperor of the French. The office was made hereditary, with the emperor having the right to adopt the children of his brothers.

Emperor Napoleon I established a brilliant court at once. Grand dignitaries of the empire and 18 marshals of France were created. In eight years, he named four princes, 30 dukes, hundreds of counts and about 1,000 barons. A new nobility arose, based, however, on achievement rather than on birth.

Pope Pius VII, who had come to Notre Dame to crown Bonaparte as emperor, protested after the ceremony that Napoleon had taken the crown from him and put it on his own head. He complained that popes for a thousand years had upheld their right to place the crown on the head of emperors. Upon Pius VII's request, the episode was not mentioned in the *Moniteur*; but by this act of effrontery Napoleon had established his supremacy.

The new emperor had deceived himself on one important point. He had assumed that this coronation would gain him admittance to the ranks of legitimate sovereigns. But the Austrian, English and Russian aristocracies still saw in him only the usurper and parvenu. He had to gain their respect by defeating them in battle.

CHRONICLE OF EVENTS

1799:   *October 17:* Napoleon, back in Paris, is received by the Directory.

October 23: His younger brother Lucien is elected president of the Council of 500.

November 1: Napoleon and Sieyès hold crucial talks at Lucien's house. Sieyès is forced to drop his own plan for a new constitution and agree to Napoleon's design for a temporary government of three consuls.

November 3: Fouché, minster of police, agrees not to interfere with the coup d'état.

November 9 (18th Brumaire): Napoleon stages his coup d'état. The Council of Ancients is alerted to a "terrorist plot" and decides that both councils should move to the suburb of Saint-Cloud. Napoleon, appointed commander of the army in Paris, is entrusted with the transfer of the councils. He speaks to the Council of Ancients. Barras, Sieyès and Ducos resign as directors; the other two directors, Gohier and Moulin, refuse and are kept under custody by General Moreau.

November 10 (9th Brumaire): In the councils there is strong resistance, particularly by the Jacobins who dispute the existence of a plot. Napoleon's speech to the Ancients is ineffective; at the Council of 500 he cannot make himself heard; the Jacobins demand that he be outlawed and attack him. Lucien pacifies the deputies, and finally Napoleon has the hall cleared with the help of Murat, wherupon the Council of Ancients recognizes the provisional consular government. Lucien reassembles about 100 deputies who are persuaded to make the action look legal. Three provisional consuls are elected: Bonaparte, Sieyès and Roger Ducos.

November 11-12: Napoleon appoints his ministers: Berthier, Fouch, Cambacérès. Ten days later, Talleyrand is made foreign minister.

December 15: The Constitution of the Year VIII is promulgated. Napoleon is elected as First Consul for 10 years; the other two consuls, Cambacérès and Lebrun, have only advisory capacities. The constitu-

The 18th Brumaire, the beginning of Napoleon's coup d'état to impose a new constitution

tion also provides for a senate of 80, a tribunate of 100, and a legislative chamber of 300 members.

December 27: The *Moniteur* is made the sole official journal.

1800:

January 17: Sixty out of 73 newspapers are suppressed, the publication of new ones forbidden.

February 7: France is ordered into mourning for George Washington.

February 13: The Bank of France is established.

February 19: Napoleon takes up residence in the Tuileries. Departmental prefectures are created.

February 20: The Comte de Provence (later, Louis XVIII) writes to Napoleon asking him to abdicate in Louis' favor. He receives a polite but negative answer.

March 3: The lists of emigrants are closed.

March 18: The court system is reorganized.

April 5: Theater censorship is established and three more journals suppressed.

July 2: Napoleon returns to Paris after the Italian campaign.

December 24: In the "incident of Nivôse," Chouan rebels attempt to blow up Napoleon while he is riding to the Opera. He escapes unscathed, while a dozen people are killed by the explosion, 28 are wounded and 46 houses are damaged. Fouché rounds up the guilty ones.

1801:

February: William Pitt resigns.

March 24: Czar Paul I is assassinated. His son Alexander I succeeds him.

March 28: France and Turkey agree on peace terms. Egypt is restored to Turkey. Peace treaty of Florence between France and Naples bars British ships from Neapolitan ports.

April 2: Admiral Horatio Nelson bombards Copenhagen. Denmark, an ally of Russia, is forced to withdraw from the Northern Convention of Armed Neutrality.

July 15: Napoleon concludes Concordat with the Pope.

August: Nelson launches two unsuccessful attacks against Boulogne.

October 1: Preliminary peace treaty agreed upon between France and England.

December 13: A French fleet, under General Victor Emanual Leclerc, husband of Napoleon's sister

An explosion in the Rue Saint-Nicaise on December 24, 1800, is an attempt to assassinate Napoleon.

Duke Louis Antoine d'Enghien, falsely accused of plotting to assassinate Napoleon, is ordered shot.

Pauline, sails from Brest against San Domingo (Haiti, at this time in control of all Hispaniola).

1802: *January 25:* Napoleon makes himself president of the Italian Republic.

February 3: The French expedition lands in San Domingo.

March 27: Peace treaty of Amiens agreed upon between France and England. England returns most of her overseas conquests to France but obtains Trinidad and Ceylon. Europe is completely pacified.

May 17: Francois Dominique Toussaint L'Ouverture, Haitian patriot, surrenders to French forces.

May 19: Order of the Legion of Honor is created.

July 29: A new government of the Ligurian Republic is established. The senate announces the result of a plebiscite to make Napoleon First Consul for life: Of 3,570,259 persons voting, only 8,374 reportedly vote against it.

August 1: New (fifth) constitution is promulgated. The powers of the senate are enlarged, those of the legislative bodies and the tribunate are reduced. Elba is annexed by France.

September: Piedmont is annexed by France. Charles James Fox, liberal British statesman, is received by Napoleon. Napoleon interferes in Switzerland, which is torn with civil dissension.

October 9: Upon the death of the Duke of Parma, the Duchy of Parma is annexed by France.

1803: *February 19:* By the Act of Mediation in Switzerland, the independence of the separate cantons is restored. Enactment of the delegates of the Empire in Regensburg settles the indemnification of the larger powers as provided by the treaty of Lunéville. Many small German states and practically all ecclesiastical regimes are dissolved; of the 48 free imperial cities, only six are left. The indemnified princes gain considerably more than they had lost. The foundations of the old German Empire are destroyed. The French occupy Hanover.

February 26: Napoleon offers a pension of 2,000,000 francs a year to Louis XVIII (the Comte de Provence) if he will renounce all claims to the throne of France.

March 8: The king of England asks parliament for new war supplies. Napoleon, in return, makes instant

Napoleon's coronation as Emperor of the French

preparations for war. The encampment at Boulogne threatens England with an invasion.

April 30: France sells Louisiana to the United States for 60,000,000 francs.

May 18: Britain declares war on France.

May 22: Napoleon orders the arrest of all British subjects in France. About 10,000 are made prisoners of war.

June 1: At Boulogne, Napoleon prepares for the invasion of England.

July 8: Nelson blockades Toulon.

July 23: A rebellion in Ireland under Robert Emmett fails.

August 23: Georges Cadoudal, a royalist conspirator financed by England, lands on the coast of Normandy. His plan: to assassinate Napoleon.

September 27: Press censorship established by Napoleon.

October 3: Madame Germaine de Staël is expelled from France.

November 30: The French evacuate San Domingo.

1804:   *January:* Jean Charles Pichegru arrives from London and joins Cadoudal. They try to bring Jean Victor Moreau into the plot.

February 14-15: The plot is revealed by a Chouan prisoner sentenced to death, and Moreau is arrested.

February 28: Pichegru, who had been in British service since his escape from Cayenne, is arrested.

March 9: Cadoudal is arrested.

March 15-20: Louis-Antoine de Bourbon-Condé, the Duc d'Enghien, one of the commanders of the émigré army—whom Napoleon suspects to be the prince the royalists plan to put in his place—is abducted from his residence on the right bank of the Rhine, brought to Vincennes and, on Napoleon's orders, shot. It is almost certain that he was innocent of Cadoudal's plot. There is great indignation throughout Europe.

March 21: The new Civil Code (Code Napoléon) is passed by the Corps Legislatif.

April 6: Pichegru is found strangled in his cell.

May 10: William Pitt is again prime minister of England.

May 18: By decree of the senate, Napoleon is created emperor.

June 24: Cadoudal is executed.

June 25: Moreau is released and sails for America.

August 28: Pierre de Villeneuve is made admiral of the French fleet at Toulon.

October 2: The British admiral, Sir Sidney Smith, unsuccessfully attacks the French flotilla assembled at Boulogne.

October 8: Jean Jacques Dessalines, black independence fighter of Haiti, is crowned emperor.

November 6: Secret convention agreed upon between Russia and Austria.

November 23: Pope Pius VII enters France to crown Napoleon and is met by him near Fontainebleau.

December 2: Napoleon is crowned emperor at Notre Dame. He places the crown on his own head. The imperial office is made hereditary.

EYEWITNESS TESTIMONY

The victory which followed Bonaparte everywhere has in this case preceded him—Oh Mr. Pitt, what terrible news for you—To lose three battles would have been better for you than Bonaparte's return!

Le Moniteur, October 13, 1799.

You wish it, but I know the lot that awaits me. When he has succeeded he will remove his colleagues, and cast them behind his back like that!

Emmanuel Joseph Sieyès, to Cabanis and Joseph Bonaparte, upon being urged to meet with Napoleon, end of October 1799, in J. Bonaparte's Memoirs *(1853).*

You are one of the supporters of the republic, Lefebvre, you will not allow us to perish in the hands of these lawyers? Stay—here is the sword which I bore at the pyramids. I give it to you as a token of esteem and confidence.

Napoleon Bonaparte to General Lefèbvre, commander of the division of Paris, November 9, 1799, in in Guizot's History of France.

… the Republic was perishing. You perceived it and your decree [moving to St. Cloud and entrusting the command to him] has just saved it. Woe to those who desire trouble or disorder! Aided by General Lefebvre, General Berthier and all my former companions in arms, I will prevent them. Let no one seek in the past for examples with which to hinder our progress. Nothing in history resembles the end of the 18th century …

Napoleon to the Council of the Ancients, November 9, 1799.

In which situation have I left France, and do I find her now? I left you peace, and upon my return I am finding war! I left you conquests, and now the enemy is crossing our borders! I left you full storehouses and now I find them empty. I left you the riches of Italy; I return to a scene of legal spoliations and misery everywhere. What has become of the 100,000 men who have disappeared from the soil of France? They are dead, and they were my companions in arms. Such a state of things can

last no longer. In less than three years it would conduct us through anarchy back to despotism.

Napoleon, to Bottot, Barras' secretary, November 9, 1799, in Castelot's Bonaparte *(1967).*

My precautions are taken. The first who stirs will be thrown into the river. I will answer for Paris. You keep watch over St. Cloud. Otherwise, the gowns will get the better of the bayonets.

Joseph Fouché, to Napoleon, November 10, 1799, Memoirs *(1824).*

"Caesar! Cromwell!" They have given me these names. It is a calumny. I could have done as they did on my return from Italy. I did not wish it. I do not wish it today. You demand the Constitution? You broke it on the 18th of Fructidor. You broke it on the 22nd of Floréal. You broke in on the 20th of Prairial. It can no longer be a means of safety since it is respected by no one; we cannot restore its position. May every citizen again find that liberty which is his due …

Napoleon, to the Council of 500, St.-Cloud, November 10, 1799.

If some orator in the pay of foreigners dares to propose to place me outside the law, let him beware, or he may bring his sentence upon himself. If he speaks of putting me outside the law, I shall call upon you, my brave comrades in arms—upon you, grenadiers whose bearskin I see here—upon you, brave soldiers with your bayonets. Bear in mind that I march under the protection of the God of Fortune and the God of War!

Napoleon, to the Council of 500, November 10, 1799.

Terrorists in this council, insolent brigands bribed by England, have revolted against the Council of Ancients and want to outlaw the Supreme Army Commander [Napoleon] … I declare that only those are France's true legislators who with me get out of this assembly, the others will be dispelled by force … I swear to you that I shall kill my brother with my own hands if he should ever dare a plot against the liberty of France.

Lucien Bonaparte, speaking as president of the Council of 500, November 10, 1799.

It seems, Bourrienne, I have said a lot of stupidities? ["Quite a number, general."] I speak much rather to soldiers than to lawyers. These fools have confused me completely. I do not have the experience to speak in assemblies. But that will come ... Oh, yes, I meant to say: Tomorrow, we shall be sleeping at the Luxembourg!

Napoleon, as reported by Bourrienne, November 10, 1799, Memoirs of Napoleon *(1829-30).*

Since 1790, the 36,000 local bodies have been like 36,000 orphans. As heiresses of the old feudal rights, they were neglected and exploited ... by the trustees of the Convention and the Directory. A new set of mayors ... or councilors has usually resulted only in a new form of robbery ... If this system would last ten more years, what would become of the municipalities? They ... would be so bankrupt ... they would ask for charity of the inhabitants ...

Napoleon, to Lucien Bonaparte, letter of December 25, 1799, in the Durants' Age of Napoleon *(1975).*

The ministers of a God of peace will be the first promoters of reconciliation and concord. Let them speak to all hearts the language which they learn in the temple of their Master! Let them enter temples which will be open to them and offer for their fellow-citizens the sacrifice which shall expiate the crime of war and the blood which has been made to flow [referring to the Vendéans].

Napoleon, to priests returning to their provinces, appeal of December 28, 1799.

Without doubt harmony is desirable amongst the authorities of the Republic. But the independence of the Tribunate is no less necessary to that harmony than the constitutional authority of the government. Without the independence of the Tribunate, there will be no longer either harmony or constitution, there will be no longer anything but servitude and silence, a silence that all of Europe will understand.

Benjamin Constant, against the new censorship, January 1800, Oeuvres *(1957).*

Washington is dead. This great man has fought against tyranny. He consolidated his country's liberty. His memory will forever be precious to the people of France and to all free people of the two worlds, and above all to those French soldiers who, with him and the American soldiers, fought for equality and liberty.

Napoleon, proclamation of February 7, 1800.

... You have accepted an eminent place and I am thankful for it. Better than anyone you know how much force and power are needed to make the happiness of a great nation. Save France from her own madness and you will have accomplished the first desire of my heart. Restore to her her king, and future generations will bless your memory. You will always be too much a necessity of the State for me ever to discharge by the highest appointments the debt of my forefathers and my own.

Comte de Provence (later, Louis XVIII), to Napoleon, letter of February 20, 1800.

For a long time, general, you must have been convinced that you have won my esteem. If you have any doubts about my gratitude, fix your reward and mark out the fortune of your friends. As to my principles, I am French, merciful by character and still more so by reason. No, the victor of Lodi, Castiglione and Arcole, the conqueror of Italy and Egypt, cannot prefer a vain celebrity to real glory. But you are losing precious time. We can ensure the glory of France. I say "we," because I require the help of Bonaparte, and he cannot do anything without me. General, Europe is watching you, glory awaits you and I am impatient to restore peace to my people.

Comte de Provence, to Napoleon, letter of summer 1800.

Sir, I have received your letter. I thank you for the kind words about myself. You ought not to desire your return to France. You would have to march over 100,000 dead bodies. Sacrifice your private happiness to the peace and happiness of France. History will not forget you ... I am not insensible to the misfortunes of your family. I shall contribute with pleasure to render your retirement pleasant and tranquil.

Napoleon, to the Comte de Provence, letter of September 7, 1800.

We must make the numbers convicted equal to the number of their victims ... The action of a special tribunal will be slow, it will not get hold of the truly guilty. This is not a question of judicial metaphysics. There are in France 10,000 miscreants who have persecuted all honest men ... They are not all culpable in the same degree, far from it. Strike the chiefs boldly, and the soldiers will disperse. There is no middle course here. It is necessary to pardon all, like Augustus, or else there must be a prompt and terrible vengeance proportionate to the crime. It is necessary to shoot 15 or 20 of these miscreants and transport 200 of them ... It is not myself I seek to avenge here. I am as ready to die as First Consul as to fall upon the field of battle. But it is necessary to reassure France who will approve my policy. [Exiled to Guiana were 133 Jacobins—for this royalist plot!]

Napoleon, after the assassination attempt upon his life of December 24, 1800, in Guizot's History.

He was right, his opinion was better than that of the others. The returned emigrants, the royalist plotters and people of that sort ought to be closely watched. I am pleased, however, to be rid of the Jacobin staff.

Napoleon, after Fouché had exposed the real assassination conspirators, Fouche's Memoirs *(1824).*

... to bolster the manufacture of Lyons and stop the payment of tributes to England, the First Consul forbade us to wear chiffon. Everything he thought was made in England he threw into the fire. When mother and I cam in, elegantly dressed, his first question was always: "Is that chiffon that you are wearing?" We often answered it was linen, but our smiles gave us away, and then he immediately ripped off the part that was foreign made.

Hortense de Beauharnais, Josephine's daughter, letter of 1801, in the Durants' Age of Napoleon *(1975).*

You can easily imagine that a person ... without being told beforehand, without knowing anything of the habits, customs and dispositions of those before whom he appeared, and who was in a measure considered responsible for the bad success of the negotiations so far as they had been carried, must, at the sight of such grandeurs, as imposing as it was unexpected, have felt not only profound emotion, but even a too evident embarassment.

Cardinal Ercole Consalvi, Pope Pius VII's emissary, on his arrival in Paris, July 1801, in Guizot's History of France.

I know the object of your journey to France. I wish the conferences to be opened immediately. I leave you five days time. And I tell you beforehand that if at the expiration of the fifth day the negotiations are not finished, you must return to Rome. As for me, I have decided what to do in that case.

Napoleon, to Cardinal Consalvi, July 1801.

I have no need of Rome! I have no need of the Pope! If Henry VIII who had not the twentieth part of my power was able to change the religion of his country, I am much more able to do so! By that change of religion I shall change the religion through nearly the whole of Europe, wherever the influence of my power extends. Rome will be sensible of the losses she brings on herself. She will lament them, but there will be no remedy. You wished to break ... Very well! Let it be so, since you wished it. When do you set out? [Consalvi stayed for dinner—and a compromise.]

Napoleon, to Cardinal Consalvi, at a last minute disagreement, July 1801.

Fifty emigrant bishops, paid by England, manage all the French clergy, and their influence must be destroyed. The authority of the Pope is necessary for that. He deprives them of their charge, or obliges them to resign ... The First Consul nominates the fifty bishops; the Pope institutes them. They name the curés, and the State pays their salaries. They take the oath: the priests who refuse to submit are removed, and those who preach against the government are referred to their superiors. After all, enlightened men will not rise against Catholicism. They are indifferent.

Napoleon, on the Concordat of July 1801, in Lacroix's History of Napoleon *(1902).*

We have conceived esteem for you and we are pleased to recognize and proclaim the services which you have rendered to the French people ... Assist the general by your advice, your influence and your talents. What can you desire? The liberty of the negroes? You know that in every country in which we have been we

Napoleon ratifies the Concordat and the clergy of France take the oath of allegiance on April 8, 1802.

have given it to the peoples who had it not … Consider, general that if you are the first of your color who has arrived at so great power and is distinguished by his valor and military talents, you are also before God and before us the most responsible for their conduct. Count without reserve on our esteem and let your behavior be that which becomes one of the principal citizens of the greatest nation of the world.

Napoleon, to Toussaint L'Ouverture, about General Leclerc's Haiti expedition, letter of December 1801.

He who is fated to treat with the First Consul must bear always in mind that he is treating with a man who is arbiter of the affairs of the world—who has paralyzed, one might say, all other powers of Europe, who has conceived projects the execution of which seemed impossible and who has conducted them with a success which astonished the whole world … When the First Consul is against us, things proceed with a frightful rapidity.

Cardinal Jean Baptiste Caprara, papal legate in Paris, to Cardinal Consalvi, letter of April 1802, Guizot's History.

People of Helvetia [Switzerland], you have been disputing for three years without understanding each other. If you are left any longer to yourselves, you will kill each other in three years without understanding each other any better. Your history, moreover, proves that your civil wars have never been finished unless by the efficacious intervention of France. I shall therefore be mediator in your quarrels, but my mediation will be an active one such as becomes the great nation in whose name I speak. All the powers will be dissolved. The Senate alone, assembled at Berne, will send deputies to Paris; each canton can also send some. And all the former magistrates can come to Paris, to make known the means of restoring union and tranquillity and conciliating all parties. Inhabitants of Helvetia! Revive your hopes!

Napoleon, proclamation of September 1802.

... the resolution of the First Consul is irrevocable. He will not have Switzerland converted into a new Jersey ... With what war would they threaten us? With a naval war? But our commerce has only just started afresh and the prey that we afford the English would scarcely be worthwhile. Our West Indies are supplied with acclimatized soldiers! ... They might blockade our ports, it is true. But at the very moment of declaration of war England would find herself blockaded in turn. The territory of Hanover, of Holland, of Portugal, of Italy down to Tarento would be occupied by our troops ...

And what would happen if the First Consul ... collecting all the flat-bottomed vessels of Flanders and Holland and preparing the means of transport of 100,000 men, should plunge England into the agonies of an invasion—always possible, almost certain? Would England stir up a continental war? But where would she find her allies? The First Consul is only 33 years old; he has as yet only destroyed States of the second rank. Who knows but that he might have time enough (if forced to attempt it) to change the face of Europe, and resuscitate the Empire of the West?

Charles Maurice de Talleyrand-Périgord, on
English threats, letter of February 1803, in
Guizot's History.

In view of the military preparations which are being made in the ports of Holland and France, the king has believed it to be his duty to adopt new measures of precaution for the security of his States. These preparations are, it is true, officially intended for colonial expeditions. However, as there exist important differences of sentiment between his Majesty and the French Government, his Majesty has felt it necessary to address his Parliament, counting on its concurrence in order to assure all the measures which the honor and interests of the English people require.

George III, to Parliament, message of March
8, 1803.

It is an astonishing and sorrowful fact that in a moment like this all the eminent men of England are excluded from its government and its councils. For calm weather an ordinary amount of ability in the pilot might suffice; the storm which is now brewing calls for men of greater experience. If the vessel founders, we shall all perish with her.

Sir Philip Francis, a Pitt adversary, calls for
his return, March 1803, in Cheney's Readings in English History *(1908).*

He [Napoleon] reproaches us above all with not having evacuated Egypt and Malta. "Nothing will make me accept that," he said to me. "Of the two, I would sooner see you master of the Faubourg St.- Antoine than of Malta ... Every wind that blows from England bears to me the evidence of its hatred and ill-will. If I wanted to take back Egypt by force, I could have had it a month ago by sending 25,000 men to Aboukir ... Sooner or later Egypt must belong to France, either by the fall of the Ottoman Empire, or by some arrangement concluded with it.

"What advantage should I derive from making war? I can only attack you by means of a descent upon your coasts ... I know very well that there are a hundred chances to one against me. But I shall attempt it if I am forced to it, and I assure you that such is the feeling of the troops that army after army will be ready to rush forward to the danger. If France and England understand each other, the one, with its army of 480,000 men which is now being got in readiness, and the other with a fleet which has rendered it mistress of the seas, and which I should not be able to equal in less than ten years—they might govern the world. By their hostility they will ruin it ... Now we have arrived at this point: Do you want peace or war? It is upon Malta that the issue depends."

Napoleon, as reported to London by Ambassador Lord Whitworth, April 1803, in
Wilson's William Pitt the Younger *(1930).*

If General Bonaparte does not accomplish the miracle that he is preparing at this moment, if he does not pass the straits, he will throw himself upon us and will fight England in Germany.

Emperor Francis II, May 1803, in Guizot's
History.

I have passed these three days in the midst of the camp [of Boulogne] and the port. I have seen from the heights of Ambleteuse the coasts of England, as one sees the Calvaire from the Tuileries. You can distinguish the houses and the movements going on. It is a ditch which shall be crossed as soon as we shall have the audacity to attempt it.

Napoleon to Cambacérès, letter of November
16, 1803.

Poor man! He also has his ambition and wishes to have a turn at governing France. He would not be her master for twenty-four hours!

General Charles Pichegru, on General Moreau, his coconspirator, January 1804, in Lacroix's Directory, Consulate and Empire *(1884).*

I know that he [Pichegru] has desired to see me. I am thankful not to have known him, after the vile means of which it is said he has desired to make use, if it is true … On the contrary, I have never seen him [Dumouriez] … I earnestly entreat to have a private audience with the First Consul. My name, my rank, my way of thinking and the horror of my situation make me hope that he will not refuse me my request.

Duc d'Enghien, when cross-examined after his kidnap and arrest, March 1804, Guizot's History.

Pitt: Bonaparte had done himself more mischief than we have done him since the last declaration of war.

Talleyrand: If while England was planning the murder of Paul I, the conspirators had been known to be hiding at a stone's throw from the borders, would they not have been arrested as quickly as possible?

Fouché: This is more than a crime, it is a mistake.

Comments on the March 1804 execution of the Duc d'Enghien, in Fouché's Memoirs *(1824).*

… certain people, closely associated with politics, were starting to assert that in France the need of absolute right in the governing forces was growing. Both political courtiers and honest supporters of the revolution saw that the stableness of the nation depended upon one life and were debating the precariousness of the Consulate. By and by, the thoughts of all people were once again tending in the direction of a monarchy.

Mme. Claire Elisabeth Rémusat, Comtesse de Vergennes, in 1804, Memoirs 1802-1808 *(1881).*

In this head there is more knowledge and in these two years more great deeds have been accomplished than under a whole dynasty of French kings.

Pierre Louis, Comte de Roederer, on the Civil Code, March 1804, in Stendhal's Life of Napoleon *(1843).*

All is over! The monarchy is reestablished. But I have a presentiment that what they are now constructing will not be durable. We made war upon Europe to give it republics which should be daughters of the French Republic. Now we shall have to give to Europe monarchs, sons and brothers of ours. And France, exhausted, will soon succumb to such fatal attempts.

Jean Jacques Regis de Cambacérès, to Charles Lebrun, May 1, 1804, Guizot's History.

16. Napoleon's Conquest of Europe: March 1805 to December 1807

THE HISTORICAL CONTEXT

By the end of 1804, the monarchs of England, Sweden and Russia had yet to recognize Napoleon as "Emperor of the French," and his peace offer to George III, addressing him as "Sir and Brother," had remained unanswered. Instead, British diplomacy and British gold were busy forming a new alliance on the continent.

Austria had good reason to fear French expansion in Italy, especially since Napoleon had received the Iron Crown of Lombardy at Milan in May of 1805 and had shortly thereafter accepted the request of the doge of Genoa to incorporate the Ligurian Republic into France. No doubt Napoleon was in a position to absorb the Papal States and the kingdom of Naples and then swallow the rich province of Venezia, which contributed substantially to Austria's revenues. So Austria accepted, when England offered her subsidies.

Entry through Berlin's Brandenburg gate

Prussia had been neutral in all the conflicts since 1795, though it was anxious to take over the province of Hanover, which Napoleon had occupied in 1803. But Prussia was reluctant to agree to his offer of alliance as a condition for recovering Hanover, as it feared British warships cruising off its coast. Alexander of Russia had designs on Turkey in the East and aspired to establish Russia in the Mediterranean by occupying the Bosporus and the Dardanelles. He was keenly interested in keeping England, certain to oppose such a move, occupied in her war with France. So he, too, promised troops to the coalition in return for English subsidies and allied himself with Sweden, which was already allied with England.

219

Against this powerful alliance, France had the support of only a few minor German states and the Spanish and Dutch fleets. As usual, England prevailed at sea. Against Napoleon's orders, the French admiral, Pierre de Villeneuve, failed to elude Nelson's fleet and kept his ships too long at Cadiz on Spain's southwestern coast, thereby frustrating Napoleon's plans to cross the English Channel. When the invasion plans had failed, once and for all, Villeneuve was ordered to attack Nelson head on, which he did at Trafalgar, near Cadiz. The English captured 20 French ships and lost none. Nelson was killed in this, his greatest victory. Villeneuve was captured, later released, and then committed suicide.

In the meantime, the Austrian General Karl von Mack had been outmaneuvered by Napoleon's generals Louis Nicholas Davout, Joachim Murat, Michel Ney and Nicolas Jean Soult. After Mack's surrender at Ulm, Napoleon had no difficulty entering Vienna on November 14, but the real test was yet to come. Exactly one year after his coronation, he met the Russian and Austrian armies at Austerlitz in Moravia—and celebrated with one of his greatest triumphs. When William Pitt, near death at the time, heard the news, he asked for the removal of the map of Europe from his wall—so Talleyrand says in his memoirs.

The peace treaty that followed not only left Austria at the victor's mercy, it also gave Napoleon practically all of Italy, except for Sicily. French art connoisseurs raided Austrian galleries and palaces for art treasures, and Austria paid France an indemnity of 40,000,000 francs, part of which had just arrived in Vienna from England. Napoleon's two brothers became kings of Naples and Holland, and a triumphal column was raised in the Place Vendôme, coated with metal taken from cannon captured at Austerlitz.

With the formation of the Rheinbund (Confederation of the Rhine), the Holy Roman Empire was broken up, and Prussia, the only central power left, was completely isolated. She was forced to cede some territory in southern and western Germany and received, in turn, Hanover—which Napoleon did not hesitate to offer to England a short time later. When Prussia was compelled to enter into an alliance with France, her Baltic seaports were blockaded by the British, and Sweden declared war on her. At this point, Prussia's only ally, Russia, withdrew her armies. In spite of her isolated position, the war party won out in Prussia after much internal discussion, and an ultimatum was sent to Napoleon demanding the evacuation of all French troops east of the Rhine. This was a grave mistake; Prussia, still basking in the glory her troops had gained under Frederick the Great, vastly overestimated her military strength. Napoleon succeeded in keeping the two Prussian armies separated and beat them thoroughly before the Russians could arrive on

A caricature of the European balance of power in the aftermath of Austerlitz

the scene. The Prussian supreme commander, the old Duke Karl Wilhelm of Brunswick who in 1792 had threatened to destroy Paris, was mortally wounded. Saxony, Prussia's ally, made peace with the emperor and by so doing became a kingdom, increasing the number of German kings to four (Prussia, Bavaria, Württemberg and Saxony)—a state of affairs that lasted until 1918.

It took two more bloody battles to get Napoleon and Czar Alexander to the conference table. After Eylau and Friedland, both armies were decimated and exhausted; the French, in particular, were not used to the harsh northern climate. The peace treaty of Tilsit gave both parties what they wanted most. Napoleon obtained Alexander's recognition of the Confederation of the Rhine and of his own and other newly-minted royal houses. Above all, he obtained a secret alliance with Russia (should England refuse to accept the proffered peace). Alexander gained land from New East Prussia, and the newly founded Grand Duchy of Warsaw was limited to land previously acquired by Prussia, with no attempt to restore the greater Poland that existed before the partitions of 1772, 1793 and 1795. Alexander was free to take Finland from Sweden in return for leaving Napoleon a free hand in the Iberian Peninsula in trying to complete his blockade of English merchandise along the whole European coastline.

It seems that the two rulers got along well with each other at Tilsit and that Napoleon's generosity stemmed from his belief that he had won a real ally and friend. Such was not the case with Prussia, which, in spite of the beautiful Queen Luise's attempts to soften his demands, was brutally crippled and burdened with an indemnification of 120,000,000 francs, later increased to 140,000,000. Although her size had been reduced from 89,000 to 46,000 square miles, Prussia was forced to support 150,000 French occupation troops.

When Napoleon returned to Paris, his report to the nation was one of his proudest: Austria was subdued, Prussia crushed, Russia won as a new ally, England cut off from commerce with the continent. Some 123,000 captives had been taken, and all expenses for his wars were to be paid for by defeated enemies.

Talleyrand, who had rendered invaluable service to Napoleon in his negotiations preceding the Concordat and elsewhere, was made Prince of Benevento and therefore could no longer hold the position of minister of foreign affairs. It was evident that Napoleon distrusted Talleyrand's loyalty, since in 1805 he had disregarded Talleyrand's advice to deal leniently with Austria after Austerlitz. In the following years, Napoleon concluded that Talleyrand was beginning to have Austria's interests more at heart than those of his master. Yet Napoleon did not wish to antagonize the higly respected, experienced and skillful diplomat and kept using him for special missions.

A pacified Europe as envisioned at the Tilsit treaty was not to last for long. Before the year was over, the French invaded Portugal in order to enforce their Continental System. It was the beginning of one of the emperor's most frustrating military campaigns.

CHRONICLE OF EVENTS

1805:

March 13: Napoleon is proclaimed king of Italy.

April: Treaty arranged between England and Russia, as a result of Alexander's policy of reconciliation with Britain. The Northern Convention, directed against Britain, is dissolved.

May 26: Napoleon is crowned king of Italy in Milan.

May 30: The Ligurian Republic is annexed by France.

June: The Code Napoléon is extended to Italy.

July: Austria enters into the treaty between Russia and England.

July 22: English defeat the French fleet at Cape Finisterre (northwestern Spain).

August: War begins against the Third Coalition: England, Austria, Russia and Sweden.

September: Napoleon hastily breaks camp at Boulogne. The French armies, under generals Lannes, Davout, Soult and Ney march to the Rhine to engage the Austrian armies under Archduke Ferdinand and General Mack.

September 27: Napoleon joins the army at Strasbourg, crosses the Rhine and marches into Bavaria, which has been invaded by the Austrians. Bavaria and the other southern German states side with the French.

October 17: General Mack is surrounded at Ulm and surrenders with 30,000 men.

October 21: In the naval battle of Trafalgar (south-western coast of Spain), Nelson defeats the French and Spanish fleets under Villeneuve. Nelson is killed during the battle. Thereafter, British seapower is unchallenged.

November 14: Napoleon, having marched down the Danube, enters Vienna with little resistance.

November: In Italy, General André Masséna drives Archduke Charles' army back into Germany. Two Russian armies, under Mikhail Kutusov and Czar Alexander, come to the aid of the Austrians.

December 2: Battle of Austerlitz (Battle of the Three Emperors): The combined Austrian and Russian armies are defeated by Napoleon. Austria agrees to a truce; the Russian armies retreat.

Meeting little resistance, Napoleon and the Grand Army triumphantly enter Vienna on November 13, 1805.

December 15: Treaty agreed upon between Prussia and France. Prussia, which had remained neutral, cedes Ansbach and Neuchatel in return for Hanover.

December 26: Treaty of Pressburg agreed upon between Austria and France. Austria cedes Venetia, Istria and Dalmatia to Italy, recognizes Napoleon as king of Italy, acknowledges the electors of Bavaria and Württemberg as kings and cedes the Tyrol and other territories to Bavaria, Württemberg and Baden. Austria receives Salzburg and Berchtesgaden. The Bourbons at Naples are dethroned by proclamation of Napoleon. Genoa is annexed by France.

1806:   *January 23:* William Pitt dies, and Charles James Fox becomes prime minister.

March: Napoleon makes his elder brother, Joseph, king of Naples. The Bourbons withdraw to Sicily where they are protected by the British navy. Murat is made grand duke of Berg (western Germany); Louis Alexandre Berthier is made prince of Neuchatel; Louis, third brother of Napoleon, becomes king of Holland (the former Batavian Republic).

July 12: The Confederation of the Rhine (Rheinbund) is founded under Napoleon's protection. All of southern and most of central Germany come under French domination.

August 6: Holy Roman Empire ends as the Austrian Emperor Francis II lays down the imperial crown, having already assumed the title of Francis I, Emperor of Austria.

August 26: The publisher Johann Philipp Palm, who had published an anti-Napoleon pamphlet and refused to reveal the name of the author, is shot at Braunau, on the Inn River.

September 13: Prime Minister Fox dies.

October 9: War begins between France and Prussia, which had been provoked by Napoleon's policies on Hanover and the Rhineland. Prussia's outmoded army, concentrated in Thuringia and commanded by the Duke of Brunswick, advances and is defeated at Saalfeld on October 10.

October 14: Napoleon defeats one Prussian army, at Jena, and Davout the other, at Auerstedt.

October 27: Napoleon enters Berlin. Another Prussian army surrenders at Prenzlau.

Caricature of the Fleet of Boulogne

November 7: General Gebhard Leberecht von Blücher, after a stubborn defense of Lübeck, surrenders, as do most other Prussian fortresses.

November 21: Napoleon's Berlin Decree announces a blockade of Great Britain and closure of the continent to British trade.

December 11: Saxony, Prussia's ally, concludes a separate peace with France. The elector becomes king and joins the Confederation of the Rhine. The French invade Silesia and instigate a Polish revolt.

December: War begins between Russia and Turkey (lasting until 1812). Dalmatia and Ragusa are taken over by France. Venice is added to the kingdom of Italy.

1807: *January:* The Russian army advances to aid Prussia.

February 7-8: Battle of Eylau (in East Prussia), near the Polish border) ends indecisively.

February 17: A British squadron enters the Dardanelles and appears before Constantinople but is then forced to withdraw.

March: George Canning becomes Britain's foreign secretary.

May 26: Danzig capitulates to the French army.

June 14: Napoleon defeats the Russians and Prussians at Friedland. Königsberg is occupied. Napoleon advances to the Niemen River.

June 25-26: Napoleon has conference with Czar Alexander on a raft in the Niemen.

July 8-9: Peace treaties of Tilsit agreed upon among France, Russia and Prussia. A Grand Duchy of Warsaw is formed under the king of Saxony and Danzig is restored as a free city. Russia recognizes the Confederation of the Rhine and all kingdoms under Napoleon's protectorate. Napoleon is to mediate between Russia and Turkey, and Alexander between France and England. Prussia cedes all lands between the Rhine and Elbe and all lands taken from Poland since 1772 and joins the anti-British blockade. Prussian fortresses are occupied by the French, until payment of the war indemnifications.

August: Napoleon, back in Paris, suppresses the Tribunate. Kingdom of Westphalia (capital at Kassel) is founded, with Napoleon's brother Jérôme as king.

September: Because Denmark has agreed to join the Continental Blockade, an English fleet bombards

Copenhagen and seizes the Danish fleet, resulting in a Danish/French alliance. Russia declares war on England.

October 4: Baron Karl vom Stein becomes Prussian minister of home affairs. Edict of Prussian serfs' emancipation issued. Military reforms in Prussia are organized by Gerhard Johann von Scharnhorst.

November: Because Portugal refuses to join the Continental Blockade, it is invaded by a French army under General Andoche Junot. Lisbon is occupied. Royal family flees to Brazil.

December: Napoleon occupies Tuscany.

December 17: Napoleon's Milan Decree reiterates the blockade against British trade. Since Spain has also joined the blockade, the entire European coastline, theoretically, is now closed to the British.

December: Slavery is abolished in British dominions.

EYEWITNESS TESTIMONY

Once my turn comes, then it will be essential to work, little by little of course, for a way of representing the nation ... this by means of a free constitution, after which my own authority will come to an absolute end. And if Providence will support our efforts, I shall retire ... and live contentedly and blissfully, looking at the good fortune of my country and enjoying it.

Crown Prince Alexander of Russia, to
Frédéric César de La Harpe, letter of October
8, 1797, Palmer's Alexander I *(1974).*

Sire, the French nation has just erected one of the most beautiful monuments of love and gratitude by presenting your Imperial Majesty the title of Emperor, a rank exactly cut out for him who so much resembles the first of Caesars by the superiority of his genius and by his actions ... My gratitude is as great as your majesty's fame; it will be unique and will pass into posterity ...

The Field Marshal Count of Hesse-Rothen-
burg (Austria), to Napoleon, letter of June 1,
1804, in Kircheisen's Princes' Letters to
Napoleon *(1929).*

... one has to admit the General Mortier maintained a strict discipline—that is why the French do not like him and complain about him, the generals and even Bonaparte ... It is very strange that the French corporals and privates observe, without exception, the rule of thieves and crooks, not to know one another, when one asks them about the names of their generals and officers.

Major August H. Bohnsack, Hanover Artil-
lery, after French occupation of Hanover,
diary entry of June 5, 1803, in Mundhencke's
Hannover, A Diary *(1960).*

I dislike the complete absence of respect that privates and corporals show for their officers ... They pass a general at close range without seeming to notice him. A grenadier enters the room of his captain with his hat or cap on his head, does not put away his two-inch-long pipe—the jacket he has taken off he puts on a chair next to the captain ...

Bohnsack, Diary entry of June 5, 1803, in
Mundhencke's Hannover, A Diary *(1960).*

My great and dear friend! For two years we have given each other proofs of our mutual confidence ... Today, for the first time it seems that our respective interests would be beclouded. The less I believed in such a possibility, the more am I saddened by its probability ... Many of our patriots got excited. I alone have kept my faith ... If I shall find in your answer the assurance that after the occupation [of Hanover] your sense of justice will keep all other consequences of this unfortunate war away from the North ... that you will reject any measure apt to provoke the arms of the British navy against the liberty of the rivers and thereby to destroy neutrality, security and trade, I could feel not to have neglected my duties ... Your word would mean more to me than a solemn treaty for others ...

King Frederick William III of Prussia, to
Napoleon, letter of July 3, 1803, in
Kircheisen's Princes' Letters *(1929).*

Without any doubt, I do consider the preservation of a good friendship and ... of all good relations between our two states as very important. I feel that the alliance between Prussia and France is particularly suited to prevent new disasters for Europe.

Napoleon, to Frederick William III after he
had complained about arrest of English chargé
d'affaires in neutral Hamburg, letter of
November 10, 1804.

I believe neither the Russian, nor the clumsy action of the English, but Bonaparte: War will break out because he wants it. Hence ... the bold usurpation of a royal title associated with the crown of Germany for 950 years [Napoleon's title of emperor and king of Italy], hence Russia is no longer spared, the arrogance, the pressure, the robbery are getting more apparent and bolder ... You will have seen from my lecture of January 24 that I believe in a system of closest cooperation between Austria and Prussia ... Only in that way the preservation of a European equilibrium is possible; but one would need the backing of Russian power and English resources ...

Johannes von Mueller, Swiss historian, to
Friedrich Gentz, letter of April 10, 1805,
Gentz & von Mueller, Correspondence
(1840).

I must take sides either against France, which means that I would be deluged by troops, treated as an enemy within 3 days, or must join up with France against the Emperor—disdaining all laws of the Empire, my most sacred obligations …

The elector of Württemberg, to his sister, letter of August 29, 1805, Kircheisen's Princes' Letters *(1929).*

Between two fires, they could not all make up their minds right away. The Archduke of Bavaria who had retreated with his army toward Würzburg, still hesitated … We sent General Mouton to the Archduke of Württemberg through whose territory we had to march. At the same time, Ney marched to the capital and had already forced the gates when Napoleon's adjutant approached our ambassador: "Your mission will be very difficult. The archduke will shout. He is, a rare combination, both irate and firm; he will make a lot of noise." "Not more than a cannon," the adjutant said, "and to that I am used." … After his first words, the archduke interrupted him, crimson with rage: "What do you want? Your troops are overrunning my country, they are violating my neutrality! That is treason! What does your Bonaparte seek here? A newly made prince, an upstart wants to force me, a prince of pure blood … But I am the master here … I reject blackmail!" … The archduke was still boiling with rage, but the contrast between excitement and [the adjutant's] calm assurance amazed him. He changed his tone of voice … and then, as if talking to himself, he let the words slip out … that by making a kingdom out of his archdukedom everything could be arranged. When the adjutant … submitted this suggestion to Napoleon, he laughed and replied: "Fine! I can ask for no more. If that is all he wants, then let him become a king!"

Comte Louis Philippe de Ségur, the outbreak of war, September 1805, Memoirs *(1827).*

Soldiers, the war of the third coalition has commenced. The Austrian army has passed the Inn, broken the treaties, attacked our ally … You yourselves have been compelled to hasten, by forced marches, to the defence of our frontiers … We will have no more peace without a guarantee. Our generosity shall not again deceive our policy. Soldiers, your emperor is in the midst of you; you are only the vanguard of the great people …

Napoleon, to his troops at Strasbourg, address of September 27, 1805.

… By now, we are so used to all that, so that cannons and powder wagons do not frighten us any longer. About 20 years ago Mephisto [actually, the student, Frosch] sang in *Faust*: "The Holy Romish empire now / How does it hold together?" Now one can really ask this question. The archduke and princes are running to and fro, back and forth … everything goes in circles, one does not know whom to hold on to. But it will all straighten out, for our good father above the firmament does not let the trees grow into the sky …

Katharina Elisabeth von Goethe, to her son Johann, from Frankfurt, letter of October 10, 1805, Koch's Letters of the German Romantics *(1938).*

A courier from Berlin has advised me of the unpleasant impression this passing of French troops … has made on the king … One can be convinced that Prussia's declaration of war would drag along all other Northern states …

Maximilian Joseph, Archduke of Bavaria, to Napoleon, after French troops had marched through Prussia's neutral Anspach, letter of October 13, 1805, in Kircheisen's Princes' Letters *(1929).*

I desire that the place capitulate. If I take it by assault, I shall be compelled to do what I did at Jaffa, where the garrison was put to the sword. It is the sad law of war. I desire that the necessity for such a frightful act should be spared to me, as well as to the brave Austrian nation. The place is not tenable.

Napoleon, to emissary of General von Mack, before Ulm, October 16, 1805, Guizot's History of France.

… I translated the [Dutch] article as well as I could, and I saw very clearly the effect … in spite of the efforts he made to hide it. This was the last time I saw him … his manners and countenance were so altered. I conceived from it, in spite of myself, the sad presentiment of the misfortune which threatened us.

Lord Malmesbury, Pitt learns of Mack's surrender, journal entry of October 1805, in Wilson's William Pitt the Younger *(1930).*

England expects that every man will do his duty.

Admiral Horatio, Lord Nelson, to the fleet at Trafalgar, signal of October 21, 1805, in Guizot's History.

The battle of Trafalgar was Nelson's greatest victory.

You need not wait for signals from the admiral … each one ought to listen only to the voice of honor, and throw himself into the place of greatest danger. Every captain is at his post if he is under fire.

Admiral Pierre de Villeneuve, to his officers at Trafalgar, October 21, 1805, in Guizot's History.

What a blessing that I have no child to receive my horrible inheritance and to live under the weight of my name!

Admiral Pierre de Villeneuve, to his wife, before committing suicide at Rennes, letter of April 22, 1806, in the Durants' Age of Napoleon *(1975).*

Public opinion, led by half-wits and narrowminded people, is still as bad as possible, and there is hardly any party where you don't have to stand up for the cause. It is much better in Germany. I am receiving the warmest, most passionate letters. The peoples, and many of their rulers are ready for anything … just courage, sense of the moment, a quick war with all our strength, and a salvation is still possible.

Mueller, to Gentz, after von Mack's surrender at Ulm, letter of November 9, 1805, Gentz's Selected Works *(1836-38).*

Meanwhile, everybody is reading here the Apocalypse of John, finding everything about Bonaparte prophecied in all details … I laughed for half an hour that the stupid people clearly recognize Napoleon in Apollyon [Apocalypse 9:11].

Friedrich Meier, painter, to Wilhelm V. Ger-
lach, from Dresden, letter of November 11,
1805, in Schoeps' From the Years of
Prussia's Peril, 1805-1820 *(1963).*

[Prussia] maintains, with considerable expenses, a large military apparatus, but permits the lapse of time to corrode the springs which can be kept intact only by military motion.

Count Hauterive (Council of State), to Tal-
leyrand, Paris, November 27, 1805, in Lettow-
Vorbeck's War of 1806 and 1807 *(1891).*

In three months this third coalition has been vanquished and dissolved. Soldiers, when all that is necessary to insure the happiness and prosperity of France shall be accomplished, I shall lead you back into France. There you will be the object of my most tender solicitude. My people will see you again with joy, and it will suffice for you to say: "I was at the battle of Austerlitz" to receive the reply: "There is a hero!"

Napoleon, to his troops, after Austerlitz,
December 2, 1805.

Instead of … taking sides and issuing a vigorous declaration, we are groping around cautiously and do not dare to mention the word war.

Prince Louis Ferdinand of Prussia, to his
sister, letter of December 20, 1805, in
Kircheisen's Princes' Letters *(1929).*

I still have no certain knowledge about the actual peace conditions, but the main thing is: Germany, head and members, are finished. Bonaparte can dispose of anything. His empire extends from Brest to the Bukowina. It is of little interest if this or that province belongs to the prefecture of Francis II or a new king or a French general. The West and South are lying at his feet.

Mueller, to Gentz, letter of January 9, 1806,
in Gentz's Selected Works *(1836-38).*

Roll up this map of Europe. In ten years time, there will be no further need for it.

William Pitt, after the battle of Austerlitz,
January 23, 1806, (on his deathbed), in
Wilson's William Pitt the Younger *(1940).*

The German people, the old Germany, degraded and almost destroyed, and venerable old dynasties are

pushing to get under that tyrannical yoke, without shame or a feeling of the scorn they arouse in every noble soul … And Prussia, what role has she played and is still playing, and will play? She will finally repent and end up as the duped one.

Duchess Louise of Saxe-Weimar, to Prince
Christian of Hesse, letter of February 14,
1806, in in Kircheisen's Princes' Letters
(1929).

The French soldier, among all those of Europe, is the only one who has made incredibly rapid progress in the art of war … in him, there rules and lives an esprit de chevalerie … let us pass on to the armies of the North! Almighty God! What a treatment of human beings! Being thrashed like animals, all sense of honor is killed in them.

Minerva, *a Hamburg journal, March 1806.*

The impression he makes is not unpleasant, not at all imposing; I do not like his laughter … at our tête-tête he had such a good and trusting expression that I had to hold back in order not to say more than I intended …

Countess Amalia of Baden, to her sister, after
meeting Napoleon, letter of February 24,
1806, in Kircheisen's Princes' Letters *(1929).*

Letter from Munich, March 31: One cannot imagine how low this [Prussian] government has sunk in public opinion here, and I believe in all of Germany, by its spineless way of acting.

Letter from Stuttgart, April 9: While the French take all liberties in Bavaria, they show forbearance in Württemberg …

Letter from Stuttgart, April 12: They have a caricature here—Hardenberg, standing on one side, is handing a drawn sword to the king [of Prussia] who pushes it back, reaching in the most friendly manner for the night-cap offered to him by Haugwitz; the caricature is not very subtle, but one could not express it more clearly.

"Meyer," code name of an Austrian agent in
southern Germany, in 1806, in Lettow-
Vorbeck's War *(1891).*

Regrets are useless, but if the great man whom you serve could see with the same eye with which I behold it, the true glory which would accrue to him from a moderate and just peace, what good fortune would not result from it for France and for all Europe?

Prime Minister Charles James Fox, to Talleyrand, letter of April 10, 1806.

Reports of the proclamation of the Rhine League and the Protectorate. Reflections and discussions. Fight between the servant and the coachman, which excited our passions more than the splitting of the Roman Empire.

Johann Wolfgang von Goethe, August 6-7, 1806, Annalen *(1830).*

One may assume that ... of the foreign conscripts, one half, at best, were careless, but not completely depraved people, while the other half consisted of good-for-nothings who made a profession out of deserting, but in the meantime tried to increase their pay by fraud and theft ... In all our cantonments, for instance, there were prowling around many well-dressed, clever wine merchants ... who, as we learned later, were French officers in disguise.

Hermann von Boyen, on the Prussian army, September 1806, Memoirs *(1899).*

I saw the French Army—all infantry officers on foot, with the knapsack on their backs—while our batallions required 50 luxury-horses! ... General Ruechel ... replied to me: "My friend! A Prussian nobleman does not walk!"

Friedrich C.F. von Mueffling, at Ansbach, September 1806, in Lettow-Vorbeck's War *(1891).*

O dear mother how I bless the day that made me a soldier. I shall vent my revenge on that monster, the Emperor Napoleon, and by my exhortations enrage the already embittered soldiers ...

Cadet Frederic W.M. von Eberhardt (age 15), to his mother, letter of October 2, 1806, in Schoeps' Prussia's Peril *(1963).*

The officers were ... on the whole a worm-eaten society. Most of them were elderly, worn-out men ... Cane-beatings, whippings, running the gauntlet were still in full swing; besides, the soldiers' clothing was poor beyond description ... so, in the cold autumn nights, the troops had to get along with those thin linen trousers.

Ludwig von Reiche, a staff officer at the outbreak of war, October 1806, in Schoeps' Prussia's Peril *(1963).*

Meanwhile, the terrible confusion gets worse, it is a man-to-man fighting. Suddenly I notice with horror that the prince is reeling. He had received a wound in the neck, and immediately afterwards a blow with a sabre across his chest ... Weakened by the loss of blood he fainted and fell heavily over the saddle.

Karl von Nostitz, adjutant to Prince Louis Ferdinand, battle of Saalfeld, October 10, 1806, Diary of General Count von Nostitz *(1908).*

I sincerely regret that one has made you sign such a document. I am replying to you only to assure that I will never hold against you personally the insults it contains, as they are at variance with your character ... If, in your note, you had asked for anything humanly possible, I would have granted it; this way, however, you are asking for my dishonor and must have anticipated my answer ... I do not value a victory bought with the lives of so many of my children ... But, Sire, your Majesty will be defeated! You will have sacrificed the peace of your days, the life of your subjects without being able to produce the slightest excuse ...

Napoleon, to Frederick William III, answering the king's September 25 ultimatum, letter of October 12, 1806.

I saw the Emperor, this soul of the world, riding through town ... indeed it is a wonderful sensation to see such an individual, concentrated at one point, sitting on a horse, taking over and dominating the world ... everyone's sympathies are with the French army which, indeed, cannot fail to win, considering the huge dif-

Napoleon with Louise, Queen of Prussia

ference of their leaders and common soldiers as compared with those of their enemies …

*Georg Wilhelm Friedrich Hegel, philosopher,
to Friedrich Immanuel Niethammer,
theologian, letter of October 13, 1806, in
Schoeps'* Prussia's Peril *(1963).*

… he [Napoleon] found all of Lannes' artillery stuck in a ravine … and took over in person the job of an artillery officer by providing light for the gunners who, under his order, widened the ravine … I shall always remember the faces of the gunners who saw the emperor, holding a lantern in his hand …

*General Anne J.M.R. Savary (later,
Napoleon's minister of police), before battle of
Jena, October 13, 1806, Lettow-Vorbeck's*
War *(1891).*

Soon, around 8 or 9 o'clock, appeared the first obvious deserters in this chaos which got wilder and more confused all the time … Their faces showed consternation and despondency, hardly any of them answered questions … Base characters discharged their rifles to increase terror and haste, or threw away their arms … upset carriages, particularly those containing food or beverages, were pillaged …

*Lieutenant Johann Friedrich Ernst von
Borcke, at Jena, October 14, 1806, Lettow-
Vorbeck's* War *(1891).*

The following day, Napoleon spoke to the assembled Saxonian officers … He went so far as to intimate that he was fighting Prussia only to see Saxonian independence maintained.

*Karl Heinrich von Einsiedel, Saxony army of-
ficer, taken prisoner at Jena, in Lettow-
Vorbeck's* War *(1891).*

Many houses have been pillaged empty … and then the awful humor of this nation, their wild songs: "Mangeons, buvons, jouons, brulons tous les maisons." … Wieland received an escort, Herder's widow had to escape into the castle; at her place, everything was destroyed … all posthumous manuscripts of the great Herder … Goethe lost nothing …

*Johanna Schopenhauer, to her son, Arthur,
from Weimar after the battle of Jena, letter of
October 1806, in Lettow-Vorbeck's* War
(1891).

… Davout's Corps moved into the city, and the infantry at once to the market place. Their appearance was not very inviting, though, as they wore their rather dirty capots … There was nothing left but to put up some of the troops in the Thomas Church … By-the-way, the billeting of the troops gave little cause for complaint. In particular, the officers, if one was able to converse with them, were, as a rule, quite modest, and made less demands than they were entitled to, by their rules.

*J.C. Gross, Leipzig, memoirs of October 18,
1806, Lettow-Vorbeck's* War *(1891).*

How everything came true that we foresaw a year ago! One could have written then the newspaper of today … It would be horrible if this tyrant should found his empire. We are the peoples enslaved by the Romans. The intention is to plunder all of Europe …

*Heinrich von Kleist, dramatic poet, to his
sister, from Königsberg, letter of October 24,
1806, in Schoeps'* Prussia's Peril *(1963).*

… one was whispering questions into one another's ears … how it was possible that these thin, small men had beaten our proud warriors … Again something new! A soldier, running in rank and file … that made the strangest impression on the Berliners. Our soldiers, of course, how could they ever run, in their tight ankle boots, pressed uniforms and narrow trousers … the French sold clothes, merchandise, food for a song … the heavier the item, the cheaper it was … and never have so many bargains been concluded than on Oct. 26, 1806.

*Canvas George, French army marches into
Berlin, October 25, 1806,* Memoirs of a
Prussian *(1840).*

… these braggarts have no qualms about staring into one's face constantly … Vienna is less beautiful than Berlin, but the Viennese are more decent than the Berliners … I just come from the theater. They played "Iphigenia in Tauris." … Prussia has been conquered, the king … has fled, yet the theater was sold out, and nobody seemed to think of his fatherland … the ballet was charming. I doubt that it can be done better in Paris.

*Pierre Francois Percy, French army surgeon,
October 26, 1806,* Campaign Journal *(1903).*

"All your money, or you die" was the usual formula … Many unhappy ones were killed because they did not obey fast enough … I don't know how it happened that there was no conflagration on all four corners of the city … In short, there happened abominations of such savage, impudent debauchery that I, Madame, may not even hint at them …

C.F.D. de Villers, French artillery officer, the taking of Lübeck, November 6, 1806, in Schoeps' Prussia's Peril *(1963).*

… the capitulations … of fortresses surpassed anything one would have thought possible … A Prussian officer had meant the incarnation of honor, brave pride and excellent military efficiency; now the name meant bragging cowardice …

Varnhagen von Ense, after capitulation of Magdeburg, November 8, 1806, Memoirs *(1843).*

… our billeting hosts were ordered to give a bottle of wine per day to every soldier. But the poor people could not afford this … and asked us to be content with canned beer … Our officers persuaded us, saying that the beer was good … We lived in peace and harmony with these friendly people.

Grenadier Jean-Roch Coignet, Berlin, notebook entry of November 1806, in Schoeps' Prussia's Peril *(1963).*

… I must say that the wide range of his knowledge, the subtlety of his observations, the genuine intelligence … the all- embracing view filled me with admiration, and his way to talk to me, with love for him … Since my audience with Frederick the Great I never had a more diversified conversation, at least not with a prince … I must grant superiority to the Emperor; Frederick was somewhat Voltairian.

Johannes von Mueller, to his brother, from Berlin after an interview with Napoleon, letter of November 20, 1806, in Gentz and Mueller's Correspondence *(1840).*

The noncommissioned officers and soldiers may not ask their host for anything but: Half a pound of good meat, one and a half pounds of bread, vegetable or rice, a bottle of beer, one ration [glass] of brandy … per day.

The Grand Army, order of the day, Hamburg, November 22, 1806.

All amusements, all wretchedness is going on in the old way. One looks at the war as a subject for conversation, reviles the English as being responsible for all

discord … and in particular the Russians who, it is true, act a little asiatically in our country …

Barthold Georg Niebuhr, Prussian diplomat, to Dore Hensler, from Königsberg, letter of December 22, 1806, Letters *(1926).*

Surely, one could almost believe in the fairy tale going around that the horseman in the grey coat, with the clubfoot, was riding next to Bonaparte and his generals, invisibly bewitching his enemies; this huge disgrace was just so inexplicable.

Ernst Moritz Arndt, poet, 1806, Geist der Zeit *(1806-18).*

Even the amusements are overheard by the watchful eye of the government, through a thousand spies. All silly and foolish things may be discussed openly, but no word is said about serious and important matters. That is how slaves are made.

Arndt, 1806, Geist der Zeit *(1806-18).*

Write to General Lagrange [in Kassel] that it is my intention to have the two small towns of Eschwege and Hersfeld burnt down or have 60 of the guiltiest people … shot …

Napoleon, to General Berthier, after riots in Hesse, January 19, 1807. His orders were not carried out.

… What a picture of destruction! From Uderwangen on, there was not a single village left, no tree … no living creature. One saw not even ruins of the buildings, everything was burnt or covered with filth … This confirmed, as was claimed by the peasants that the Russians had caused this devastation.

F.A.L. von der Marwitz, in East Prussia, April 15, 1807, A Nobleman of Brandenburg *(1908).*

Is vengeance worthy of him who can wield it without resistance? A woman may tell you what a man would hesitate to utter … I know we will have to make sacrifices, but at least one should not separate Prussia from provinces which belonged to her for centuries … should not take away subjects she loves like favorite children.

Queen Luise of Prussia (as reported by Swedish ambassador von Brinckmann), her talk with Napoleon, July 6, 1807, in Schoeps' Prussia's Peril *(1963).*

I really had to defend myself, as she wanted to compel me to make some additional concessions to her husband; but I ... stuck to my policy! ... She is very charming ... When you read this letter, peace with Prussia and Russia will be concluded. [Afterwards, to Czar Alexander: "The king of Prussia entered at the right time; a quarter of an hour later I would have promised anything to the queen."]

Napoleon to Josephine, his talk with Queen Luise, July 7, 1807.

Prussia will have to buy salt abroad, and her wonderful porcelain manufacture will not be able to continue ... One resents the king's lack of skill. Manufacturers and artists are desperate and are talking about going abroad ...

General Henri Jacques Guillaume Clarke, governor of Berlin, to Napoleon, July 24, 1807, Reports from Berlin's French Period, 1807-1809 *(1913).*

Two days ago I got into some shooting ... A broad street, full of people. "Damned Frenchman!" By this they mean my uniform. 20 people surround me ... because a soldier had stabbed a civilian. They wanted to storm the hospital where the dead man was lying, but 150 dashing soldiers opened fire at this mob.

Stendhal (Marie Henri Beyle), French war commissioner, to his sister, from Brunswick, letter of September 6, 1807, Selected Letters *(1922).*

17. Napoleon at the Height of His Power: February 1808 to July 1812

THE HISTORICAL CONTEXT

Between 1808 and 1811 Napoleon ruled the European continent, except for the northern, Russian sphere, and the southwest corner, Spain. For this, he engaged the help of men and women he believed he could rely on under all circumstances—his immediate family and in-laws. The results were not always satisfactory.

Joseph, Napoleon's older brother, assisted him in his negotiations with England and Austria. He has been described as well-meaning and gentlemanly, but not particularly capable. Later, as king of Naples, he tried to win the loyalty of the Italians by a mild and benevolent government but was unable to defend himself against an insurrection instigated by the Bourbons. Napoleon had to send an army under André Masséna to rescue him. When made king of Spain, he was equally unable to defend his throne. Napoleon judged his brother to be a very good man and blamed himself for raising Joseph to positions for which he was not suited.

Popular leaflet of Napoleon

Lucien, six years younger than the emperor, had unquestionably saved the day for him on November 9 and 10, 1799. But he was critical of Napoleon's policies and married a commoner, against his brother's wishes. He then lived in Italy under the protection of the Pope, and when Pius VI was dethroned, he tried to escape to America. But Lucien was captured by the British and interned in England; he became reconciled with his brother during his stay in Elba. Surely the most gifted of Napoleon's brothers, he was the only one who did not serve the emperor in any high capacity.

Louis, born in 1778, accompanied Napoleon to Egypt, and in 1802, pressured by Josephine and Napoleon, reluctantly married Hortense,

Letizia Bonaparte, Napoleon's mother

Josephine's daughter. Hortense's first son was rumored to be Napoleon's; her third son, Charles Louis Napoleon, would be the future Emperor Napoleon III. Louis was made king of Holland, but his sympathies were with his new subjects rather than the empire; he incurred the displeasure of his brother by tolerating violations of the Continental Blockade. Napoleon finally moved troops into Holland, and Louis had to abdicate. He retired to Granz and became an author of prose and verse. Hortense separated from him and in 1814 joined her mother at Malmaison. When Napoleon returned from Elba, she secretly gave him a very valuable diamond necklace, which after Napoleon's death was restored to her by General Charles Tristan de Montholon; it saved her from poverty.

The youngest brother, Jérôme, went to the West Indies with the navy and, while still a minor, married Elizabeth Patterson in Baltimore. Their grandson, Charles Joseph Bonaparte, served under Teddy Roosevelt as secretary of the navy. Napoleon saw to it that the marriage was dissolved, and Jérôme, by marrying Catherine of Württemberg, became king of Westphalia. Jérôme showed little understanding for his brother's problems, and instead lived a life of luxury. After the battle of Leipzig, he had to flee to France and later fought for his brother at Waterloo. He lived long enough to receive honors at the court of his nephew, Napoleon III.

Of Napoleon's sisters, Elisa was made princess of Piombino and grand duchess of Tuscany and seems to have been a good ruler. Her younger sister Pauline was one of the most beautiful women of her time. She accompanied her first husband, General Victor Emmanuel Leclerc, to San Domingo and upon her return married the Prince Borghese. As duchess of Guastalla, she led a rather scandalous life, and at one time Napoleon banished her from Paris to Italy. There she presided over a famous salon in Rome. She never got along with her brother's second wife, Marie Louise, but when Napoleon's fortunes fell, she proved more loyal to him than his other brothers and sisters. Caroline, the youngest sister, married Joachim Murat when she was only 17, became duchess of Clèves and Berg and later queen of Naples. Her hopes for her son Lucien as imperial heir were destroyed when Marie Louise bore Napoleon a son. After Murat's execution, she fled to Austria.

Josephine's other child, Eugène, first resented his mother's marriage to Napoleon but then became his admirer and close friend, often acting as intermediary when relations between his mother and Napoleon became strained because of the former's infidelities. He distinguished himself at Marengo and other battles, and in 1805, when he was only 24, Napoleon made him viceroy of Italy. He seems to have heeded Napoleon's advice much better than Jérôme ever had done. He held a brilliant court, was an able administrator, and, after Napoleon's fall, finished his life in Munich as duke of Leuchtenberg.

Napoleon's mother Letizia never participated in the glamor and luxury surrounding her. She saved most of her allowance of 500,000 francs a year and continued living with the frugality she had been used to all her life. She accompanied her son to Elba and, in 1818, appealed to the great powers to release him—to no avail. Stoically, she survived Napoleon, Elisa and Pauline, dying in 1836 at the age of 86.

Since he had conquered more territories than he had relatives to place over, Napoleon conferred some minor dependencies on his generals and ministers. Louis Alexandre Berthier was given the province of Neuchatel, taken from Prussia; Cambacérès was made prince of Parma; Charles Francois Lebrun became duke of Piacenza; Louis Jacques Savary was made duke of Rovigo; and Joseph Fouch, duke of Ontranto.

The most unusual career of Napoleon's generals was that of Jean Baptiste Jules Bernadotte, who had distinguished himself in the Italian campaign of 1796-97 and at Austerlitz. Napoleon made him marshal of the empire and prince of Ponte Corvo. He negotiated for Napoleon in 1809 with the Swedes, who were impressed by his generosity. When Gustav IV abdicated, Bernadotte was adopted by his successor as the crown prince—with Napoleon's approval—and for a while controlled Swedish foreign affairs. But then he threw in his lot with Russia and England against Napoleon and Denmark, and his Swedish contingent played an important part in Napoleon's defeat at Leipzig. He became king in 1818 and founded the present Swedish dynasty.

Joseph Fouché

Peace never reigned for any length of time in the Napoleonic empire. Only three months after Tilsit, Napoleon felt compelled to invade Portugal, which traditionally had been allied with Britain and refused to close her ports to English goods. At the same time, he took advantage of the discord in Spain's ruling Bourbon family and the unpopularity of the prime minister/dictator, Manuel de Godoy. Napoleon chose his brother Joseph as king of Spain, instead of Murat, whose troops occupied Madrid and who had hoped to become king. Yet, neither Joseph's acceptance of Catholicism nor the hastily designed, half-liberal constitution Napoleon introduced could suppress the growing insurrection all over the peninsula, which was fanatically supported by the clergy and encouraged by the landing of British troops under Sir Arthur Wellesley (later, the Duke of Wellington) in Portugal.

Napoleon felt uneasy about leaving his best troops in Spain, thousands of miles away from a possible uprising in Austria or Prussia. So, at the great Congress at Erfurt (in Thuringia), mainly conceived to reinforce the Franco-Russian alliance, he surrounded himself with all his satellites and all the splendor he could muster up. The Comédie Francaise, including the great Francois Joseph Talma, was brought over to produce the classic French tragedies. Napoleon even interviewed the German poets Johann Wolfgang von Goethe and Christoph Martin Wieland, overawing both of them. It seems that Napoleoln considered further strengthening his friendship with Czar Alexander by proposing marriage to his sister Anna, but the wily Talleyrand secretly advised the Czar against it. At any rate, Napoleon felt free to turn against Spain, where his troops expelled the English—but not for long. Meanwhile, trouble arose in central Europe.

Both Prussia and Austria had used the time since their defeats to modernize and strengthen their inner structures. In Prussia, Karl, Baron von Stein, and after him Karl August von Hardenberg reorganized the town governments, abolished hereditary serfdom, reformed the financial and tax systems and liberated industry from burdensome restriction. August Neidhardt von Gneisenau, Gerhard Johann von Scharnhorst, Karl von Clausewitz and others reorganized the military system; the University of Berlin was founded; and a wave of patriotism, expressed by writers like Johann Gottlieb Fichte, Ernst Moritz Arndt and Heinrich von Kleist, pervaded the country. In Austria, similar, though less extensive, reforms were carried out by Count Johann Phillip von Stadion and Archduke Charles. An Austrian uprising took place in 1809 while Napoleon was again running into difficulties in Spain. Archduke Charles appealed to the whole German nation to join in a war of liberation, but only the Tyrol, under Andreas Hofer, followed his call. Napoleon hurried back from Spain, retook Vienna, but suffered his first major defeat at Aspern. Eventually, however, he was victorious, and the poor Tyrolese were abandoned by Vienna. Once more, the empire seemed invincible: Austria and Sweden both joined the Continental System.

Napoleon finally succeeded in marrying into the high nobility after divorcing Josephine, who could not bear him any children. His second wife, the daughter of Emperor Francis of Austria, must have disliked intensely this destroyer of the great Hapsburg empire in the beginning, but she seems to have grown quite fond of Napoleon after she met him. She bore him the son he had so longed for, and Napoleon II was baptized as "King of Rome" at the age of 10 weeks.

The succession to the throne seemed secure, but the emperor's position in Europe began to deteriorate. Pius VII refused to join the Continental System, Rome was occupied and Napoleon excommunicated. In Spain, the British gained the upper hand, and Napoleon could prevent neither a peace agreement between Turkey and Russia, nor the Czar's quiet sabotage of the continental blockade. While as a person Napoleon was still greatly admired inside and outside of France, opposition to his regime grew in his homeland: In the salon of Madame Claire Elisabeth de Rémusat and in the writings of Benjamin Constant, of Vicomte Francois René de Chateaubriand and Madame Germaine de Staël. Liberal and nationalistic feelings— first stirred up by the Great Revolution— were on the rise inside and outside of France and wanted only a spark to burst into flame.

CHRONICLE OF EVENTS

1808:   *February 2:* Rome is occupied by French troops.

February: Spain is invaded by 100,000 French troops, under the pretext of guarding the coasts against the English.

March 19: Charles IV of Spain abdicates, in favor of his son Ferdinand, because of a popular uprising against Prime Minister Godoy, the queen's lover and virtual dictator of the country.

March 27: The Pope excommunicates Napoleon.

March: Joachim Murat occupies Madrid. A new nobility of France is created.

May 2: Great insurrection in Madrid (*Dos de Mayo*) is suppressed by Murat's Mamelukes.

May 6: At Bayonne, Ferdinand VII is forced to abdicate.

June 6: Napoleon makes his older brother Joseph king of Spain (Don José I).

June 15: New insurrections erupt in Spain. The French force at Cadiz surrenders to the Spanish.

July 4: Peninsular War begins when the British land in Portugal, under the command of Sir Arthur Wellesley, later known as the duke of Wellington.

July 15: Napoleon makes Murat king of Naples and Sicily.

July 20: After the battle of Medina del Rio Seco, Joseph enters Madrid.

July 22: General Dupont capitulates at Bailen with 20,000 men, one-third of the French forces.

August 21: At Vimeiro, Wellesley defeats the French under Andoche Junot.

August 30: At the Convention of Cintra, Junot agrees to evacuate Portugal. A general insurrection forces the French to retreat behind the Ebro.

September 8: Convention of Paris held between France and Prussia.

September 27-October 14: At the Congress of Erfurt Napoleon negotiates with Alexander I, whose "friendship" with Napoleon had cooled off since the Tilsit treaty. Four kings and 34 princes also attend. Talleyrand negotiates with the Czar behind Napoleon's back to frustrate further measures against

Napoleon's sister, Princess Pauline Borghese, was one of the most beautiful women of her time (seen here in Canova's reclining sculpture).

Austria. Finally, Alexander is given a free hand in Finland and the Danubian provinces, and he leaves Napoleon free to conquer Spain.

October 26: Napoleon proceeds to Spain with 150,000 men to help Joseph, against whom the whole country has risen.

November 10-11: The Spanish are beaten at Burgos and Espinosa.

December 4: Napoleon enters Madrid, receives its capitulation and abolishes the Inquisition.

December: The British, under Sir John Moore, invade northwestern Spain from Portugal.

December 22: Napoleon leaves Madrid and delegates the command against the British to Marshal Nicolas Jean de Soult.

1809:   *January 16:* At battle of Corunna Soult defeats Moore, who is killed. The British evacuate Spain.

January: Treaty of the Dardanelles agreed upon between England and Turkey.

January 27-28: Napoleon arrives back in Paris and raves against Fouché and Charles Maurice de Talleyrand, who have made plans behind his back and contacted ambassador Clemens Wenzel, prince of Metternich, while Austria is rearming. Archduke Charles reorganizes Austria's army.

April 12: Austria declares war and appeals to the German people to join her in a war of liberation. Only the Tyrol under Andreas Hofer rises in revolt. The Austrians invade Bavaria with 170,000 men.

April: England unites with Austria against France.

April 19-23: Napoleon defeats the archduke in quick succession at Abensberg, Landshut, Eckmühl and Ratisbon (Regensburg). Charles retires into Bohemia.

May 12: After a bombardment, Napoleon enters Vienna.

May 21-22: In his attempt to cross the Danube, Napoleon is defeated by the archduke at Essling and Aspern. Marshal Jean Lannes is killed.

May 31: Major Ferdinand von Schill killed at Stralsund.

June 10: Since the Papal States have been annexed by Napoleon's decree from Vienna, the Pope again excommunicates him.

July 5-6: Napoleon, reinforced by troops from Italy, recrosses the Danube and defeats the archduke at

The family Bonaparte

Joachim Murat, King of Naples

Wagram. Wellesley expels Soult from Portugal. The Pope is arrested.

July 28: At battle of Talavera in central Spain, the English and Spanish under Wellesley defeat the French. He is made Lord Wellington. The French push on to conquer the south of the peninsula.

October 12: Attempt on Napoleon's life by Friedrich Staps fails. Staps is executed.

October 14: Peace treaty between France and Austria signed at Schönbrunn. Austria loses vast territories to Russia, Bavaria and the duchy of Warsaw. Austria cedes its Illyrian provinces to France, which organizes them into a new state under Auguste F.L.V. de Marmont, duke of Ragusa. Austria joins the Continental System and breaks with England.

November: The Tyrolese, fighting alone against the French and Bavarians, are subdued. Andreas Hofer is captured and shot in Mantua.

November 4: Napoleon sends a formal proposal to the Czar to marry his youngest sister, Grand-duchess Anna. Alexander stalls.

December 16: Napoleon divorces Joséphine.

1810:   *January:* Treaty of Paris agreed upon between Sweden and France. Sweden receives Swedish Pomerania and joins the Continental System. The French conquer Andalusia.

March 11: Upon Metternich's initiative, Napoleon marries Marie Louise, daughter of the Austrian emperor and grandniece of Marie Antoinette, by proxy at Vienna. His marriage to Josephine is declared null and void.

April 1: Official wedding ceremony is held at Saint-Cloud.

May: The Swedish estates elect Marshal Bernadotte as prince.

July 1: Napoleon's brother Louis abdicates as king of Holland and flees—the consequence of his refusal to join the Continental System.

July 9: Holland is annexed to France.

July 10: In Spain, the French take Ciudad Rodrigo, the British fall back toward Lisbon.

August: France annexes Westphalia, Berg, East Friesland and the Hanseatic cities. The empire now consists of 130 departments and extends along the entire channel and North Sea coast, but is ineffective in blocking the smuggling of British goods. Masséna invades Portugal.

September 6: Napoleon authorizes Bernadotte's election as crown prince of Sweden.

September 27: The British, who have been holding the lines of Torres Vedras in Portugal, defeat the French in the battle of Bussaco.

October: The Fontainebleau Decrees step up enforcement of the continental blockade against Britain.

December: The Russians throw up earthworks on the Dwina and Dneister.

December 31: Czar Alexander closes his ports to ships carrying French merchandise.

1811: *February 28:* Napoleon writes to Alexander complaining about Russia's secret agreement with Great Britain.

March: The Russians, in their war against Turkey, cross the Danube and advance into Bulgaria.

March 20: Napoleon's son is born. He is baptized as king of Rome at Notre Dame on June 2.

April: General André Masséna falls back from Portugal into Spain. The British advance and besiege Badajoz and Almeida. Masséna is defeated in the battle of Fuentes de Onoro.

May 16: British general William Carr Beresford defeats Soult in the battle of Albuera. During the following months, tension between Napoleon and Alexander rises. The latter does not cooperate in the establishment of the Continental System and resents the deposition of the duke of Oldenbourg, his close relative, by Napoleon.

June 17: Council of the bishops under Cardinal Joseph Fesch tries to find a compromise between the Pope and Napoleon over the investiture of bishops.

December: Napoleon studies detailed accounts of the campaigns of Sweden's Charles XII in Poland and Russia.

1812: *January:* The French occupy Swedish Pomerania and Rügen and thereby alienate the Swedes. Napoleon forms alliance with Austria and Prussia, who are to furnish 30,000 and 20,000 men each in the forthcoming campaign. In Spain, the British retake Ciudad Rodrigo.

April 6: The British take Badajoz, in southwest Spain, after bitter fighting.

April: Peace treaty signed at St. Petersburg between Russia and Sweden. Sweden is promised the annexation of Norway, which had belonged to Denmark, to be indemnified elsewhere.

May 28: In spite of French efforts to keep Turkey fighting against Russia, a peace treaty is concluded at Bucharest in which the province of Bessarabia is ceded to Russia.

June: England makes peace with Russia and Sweden.

July 22: Wellington defeats the French under Marshal Marmont at Salamanca. Joseph Bonaparte abandons Madrid and falls back behind the Ebro River. An advanced, democratic constitution, drawn up by the first national cortes in Cadiz, is promulgated for the freed part of Spain.

EYEWITNESS TESTIMONY

So he too is no more than an ordinary man. Now he will step on all human right, just to satisfy his ambition, will become a tyrant! [The composer then tore up the dedication of his *Eroica* to "Buonaparte."]

Ludwig van Beethoven (as reported by
Wegeler and Ries in 1838), Napoleon making
himself emperor, in Mereschkowskij's
Napoleon *(1928).*

He neither knew how to enter a room nor how to leave. He had no idea as to how to greet a person, how to get up or how to sit down. He was walking this and that way and did not know what to do or to say.

Mme. Claire Elisabeth Rémusat, Napoleon as
a novice emperor, Memoirs 1802-1808
(1881).

At half past twelve, both shores of the river are occupied by troops, the emperors board their boats, Napoleon's is decorated with leaves. He arrives first, Alexander five minutes later. They greet cordially. Napoleon goes toward the Russian Emperor, embraces and kisses him. The Imperial Marshals and some Russian high dignitaries accompany their masters. The talk lasted for an hour and a half. The two rulers were all by themselves … They parted at two o'clock … Our emperor seemed highly satisfied … It seems Alexander and Napoleon understand and love each other. Everything is in motion and everybody is figuring out the way to take, in order to get to France as fast as possible.

Pierre Francois Percy, on the Niemen River
after battle of Friedland, June 25, 1807, Campaign Journal *(1903).*

The Prince Regent of Portugal loses his throne … influenced by the intrigues of the English … for not having been willing to seize the English merchandise at Lisbon. What does England do—this ally so powerful? She regards with indifference all that is passing in Portugal. What will she do when Portugal is taken? Will she go to seize Brazil? No; if the British make this attempt, the Catholics will drive them out. The fall of the house of Braganza will remain another proof that the fall of whatever attaches itself to the English is inevitable.

Le Moniteur, *a French army arrives at Lis-*
bon, November 13, 1807.

Your people must enjoy a degree of liberty, equality and affluence that is unknown to the rest of Germany. Such a liberal government must cause the healthiest developments for the politics of the Confederation of the Rhine and the power of your state. For you, it will be a mightier barrier against Prussia than the Elbe River.

Napoleon, to his brother, Jérôme, November
15, 1807.

… Nevertheless, while desiring to avoid disturbance and to leave things in status quo, I am prepared to take strong measures the first time the Pope indulges in any bull or manifesto; for a decree shall be immediately published, revoking the gift of Charlemagne and reuniting the states of the church to the kingdom of Italy, furnishing proofs of the evils that religion has suffered through the sovereignty of Rome, and making apparent the contrast between Jesus Christ dying on the cross and His successor making himself a king.

Napoleon, instructions upon the occupation of
Rome, February 2, 1808, Guizot's History of
France.

We must recommence the work of Louis XIV … The present circumstances do not permit your Majesty to

Napoleon divorces Josephine, who cannot bear him children.

refrain from intervention in the affairs of this kingdom … Thus your Majesty, compelled to undertake the regeneration of Spain, in a manner useful to her and useful to France, ought neither to reestablish at the price of much blood a dethroned king, nor to sanction the revolt of his son, nor to abandon Spain to herself; for in these two last cases it would be to deliver it to the English who by their gold and their intrigues have succeeded in tearing and rending this country, and thus you would assure their triumph. I have set forth to your Majesty the circumstances which compel you to come to a great determination …

Jean Baptiste Nompère de Champagny,
France's foreign minister, to Napoleon, letter
of March 1808, Guizot's History.

The surroundings of Berlin are an ocean of sand. Whoever built a city there, must have been ridden by the devil … As good-looking as the women are, as ugly are the men: savagely distorted and mostly base features. At twenty paces, a young German officer may look attractive … but at close sight he becomes less so … One can laugh one's head off about German soldiers exercising, they re so awkward and clumsy. No inkling

Marie Louise, daughter of Emperor Francis of Austria, became Napoleon's second wife and bore him a son.

The duke of Reichstadt, Napoleon II, baptized king of Rome

of the light, elegant marching of the Imperial Guard. In the civilians, I always found and still find something military … I am not a competent judge, but I think them to be more daring horsemen than we are … I do not doubt that their intellectual structure would change if every man would drink a bottle of Languedoc per day. Generally, men are more like domestic animals than in Italy or France.

Stendhal (Marie Henri Beyle) diary entry of
April 18, 1808, Selected Letters *(1923).*

It would be blasphemy to say that God is with him [Napoleon]; but evidently he is a tool in the hand of the Almighty to bury the old which no longer has a right to live …

Queen Louise of Prussia, to her father, letter
of April 1808, in Granier's Reports from
Berlin's French Period, 1807-1809 *(1913).*

You owe the treasury 2 million. Your drafts were not honored— no honorable man lets this happen. I shall not tolerate that you break your word. Sell your diamonds, your tableware! Do not indulge in this insane wastefulness that makes you the mockery of Europe and will finally incite the indignation of your people. Sell your furniture, your horses, your jewelry, but pay your debts! Honor above all!

Napoleon, to his brother Jérôme, July 16, 1808.

It would take 200,000 Frenchmen to conquer Spain and 10,000 scaffolds to maintain the prince who should be condemned to reign over them. No, sire, you do not know this people; each house will be a fortress, and every man of the same mind as the majority ... Not a Spaniard will be on my side if we are conquerors; we cannot find a guide or a spy ... Everyone who speaks or writes differently either lies or is blind.

Joseph Bonaparte, king of Spain, to Napoleon, letter of August 11, 1808, Guizot's History.

The affairs of Spain are making a vivid impression. It would be very helpful to circulate them with caution. Here, people think the war with Austria is inevitable. It would decide the fate of Europe and therefore of our own, too. [Letter intercepted by French police; Napoleon declares Stein an enemy of France.]

Heinrich Friedrich Karl, Freiherr vom und zum Stein, Prussian statesman, to a confidant of King Frederick William III, letter of August 15, 1808, Granier's Reports *(1913).*

... In Vienna, one has seen with regret your Majesty's enterprise in Spain.

Napoleon: Surely, they cannot be angrier than I myself, for it is the greatest stupidity I have committed in my life.

Vincent: Could one not say, in this case ... that the shortest stupidities are the best and that it would be smart to give them up?

Napoleon: And how, dear general? ... I am an usurper. In order to get where I am I had to have the best

The arrest of the Pope, July 5-6, 1809

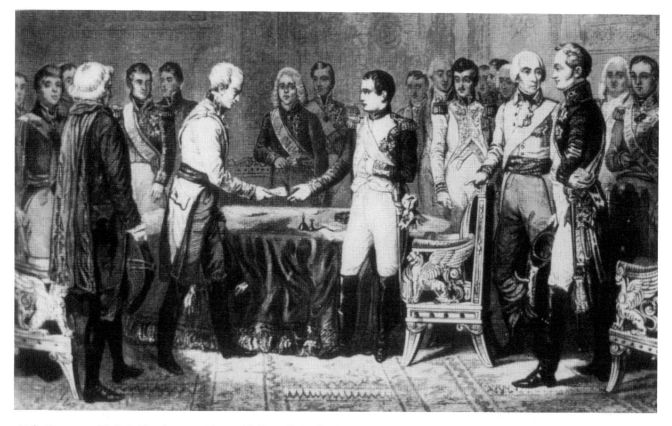

At the Congress of Erfurt, Napoleon negotiates with Czar Alexander I.

sword and the best head in Europe. And to keep myself there, everybody must still be convinced of this. I ... cannot step in front of the universe and say I made a serious mistake and will retreat, with a beaten army. Judge yourself: Is that a possibility?

Baron de Vincent, Austrian ambassador, and
Napoleon, talk of September 1808, in
Souvenirs du Baron de Barante *(1890-95).*

A tremendous crowd filled the streets ... everybody wanted to see the man as well as possible who distributed crowns and thrones and who held in his all-powerful hand the destinies of Europe, joy and hope, poverty and misery. Three men on this earth have been celebrated more than anyone else: Augustus, Louis XIV and Napoleon. Each of them differently, according to the times and circumstances, but basically in the same manner. The ovations he received, the sincere as well as the enforced and simulated ones were almost monstrous ... I can think of no other word. Flattery bordering on worship and a low mentality coming close to being nauseating tried to outdo each other. How often did I notice in those days that particularly those

who had suffered most under Napoleon and had all reasons to be filled with hatred and exasperation were most anxious to cheer him and to praise his fortune ... I did not see one single man in Erfurt who would have dared to touch the mane of the lion fearlessly and freely.

Charles Maurice de Talleyrand-Périgord,
Napoleon's arrival at Erfurt, September 27,
1808, in Orieux's Talleyrand *(1970).*

The Spanish people, having shaken off the yoke of authority, aspired to govern. The intrigues of the agents of the Inquisition, the influence of the monks who are so numerous ... and who dreaded reform, have at this critical moment occasioned the insurrection of several Spanish provinces ... We have seen frightful anarchy spreading over the greater part of Spain. Will your Majesty allow England to be able to say that Spain is one of her provinces and that her flag, driven from the Baltic, the northern seas, the Levant and even the Persian coasts, rules over the gates of France? Never, sire. To avoid so great a disgrace and misfortune, there are two million of brave men ready, if need be, to cross the

Pyrenees, and the English will be driven out of the Peninsula.

Champagny, France's foreign minister, to
Napoleon, letter of October 1, 1808, in
Guizot's History.

With your help ... a lot has been accomplished. The last remnant of slavery, serfdom is destroyed and the unshakable pillar of every throne, the will of free men, is established. The unlimited right to acquire real estate has been proclaimed. The towns have been declared of age ...

Stein, farewell to his officials upon his own
dismissal, letter of November 24, 1808,
Granier's Reports *(1913).*

Never have I seen such keen determination ... I have seen women come to be killed in the breach. Every house has to be taken by storm, and without great precaution we should lose many soldiers ... In spite of all the orders I have given to prevent soldiers from rushing forward, their ardor getting the better of them has given us 200 wounded more than we ought to have.

Marshal Jean Lannes, to Napoleon, the
Spanish resistance at Saragossa, January 27,
1809, Guizot's History.

Their misfortune has not changed the military. They have not lost any of their vanity ... At present, the reason for all commotion is the ordinance of the government that everyone has to turn in his silver ... Those who have not hidden it have sold it cheaply to the Jews ... Nothing can describe the disorder in the administration. Who can say where the center is? There is none ...

Captain Flolard (France), from Berlin, report
of March 31, 1809, Granier's Reports *(1913).*

We were sometimes received with pleasure, but people were reluctant to show their feelings ... a peasant answered him [Schill]: You are right, things must change. Just let us wait till the harvest is in!

Neigebauer, a member of Major von Schill's
Prussian volunteer corps, near Magdeburg on
about May 8, 1809, in Granier's Reports
(1913).

The English are not to be feared. All their forces are in Spain and Portugal ... As to Schill, he is of little moment and has already put himself out of the question by retreating towards Stralsund ... Experience will show you the difference there is between the reports spread by the enemy and the reality ... you have nothing to fear ...

Napoleon, to his brother Jérôme, after his
defeat at Aspern, letter of June 9, 1809.

I have a sorrowful mission to accomplish ... I know that the emperor is under many obligations to your holiness ... but I must inform you that I am ordered to take you away with me ...

General Radet (France) to Pope Pius VII, July
6, 1809, Guizot's History.

The confidence which all of Germany once had in Prussia's sway toward genuine enlightenment and higher cultivation of the spirit has not waned on account of the recent unhappy events; on the contrary, it has increased ... A good part of this confidence is based on the plan of founding a universal educational establishment in Berlin.

Wilhelm von Humboldt, Prussian statesman,
to King Frederick William III, July 1809, in
Granier's Reports *(1913).*

I saw French officers and soldiers, even women disemboweled ... Some men were put between two board and sawed asunder ... others were buried alive up to their shoulders, or hung up by their feet over fireplaces, so that their heads burned.

Captain Francois, atrocities of the Spanish
war, letter of 1809, in in Lacroix's Directory,
Consulate and Empire *(1884).*

Your majesty has not entire confidence in me and meanwhile, without that, the position is not tenable ... I give all my faculties to business from 8 o'clock in the morning to eleven o'clock in the evening ... I am the goal of all complaints ... My power does not extend beyond Madrid, and at Madrid itself I am daily thwarted ... I am only King of Spain by the force of your arms. I might become so by the love of the Spaniards; but for that it would be necessary to govern in my own manner. I have often heard you say: Every animal has its instinct and each one ought to follow it! I will be such a king as the brother and friend of your Majesty ought to be, or I will return to Mortefontaine, where I shall ask for nothing but the happiness of living without humiliation ...

Joseph Bonaparte, king of Spain, to Napoleon,
letter of February 17, 1810, Memoirs (1853).

You will not succeed in Spain except by vigour and energy. This parade of goodness and clemency ends in nothing. You will be applauded as long as my armies are victorious; you will be abandoned if they are vanquished. You ought to have become acquainted with the Spanish nation in the time you have been in Spain … Accustom yourself to think your royal authority as a very small matter.

Napoleon, to Joseph Bonaparte, letter of
March 1810.

Misery in the whole kingdom [of Westphalia] has grown so much— nobody can be paid—that one cannot continue for more than 2 months, as I had already the honor of reporting to your Majesty … in spite of all care I do not believe it possible to maintain the government any longer and I am asking your Majesty for permission to return to Paris.

Jérôme Bonaparte, to Napoleon, letter of September 20, 1809, in Goodrich's Court of Napoleon *(1857).*

The journals and other recent news may already have informed you that I am the wife of Emperor Napoleon. You may well imagine, dear grandmother, how difficult a step this was, and only the obedience I owe to my father and the unanimous wish and hope of two nations have persuaded me to make this sacrifice … Oh, I feel only too well the full extent of the task I am setting for myself and wish nothing more than to be able to accomplish it … The whole thing happened so fast that it still seems like a dream to me. Actually, I can see it only as a trial by divine providence, and thus I yield in submission.

Princess Marie Louise, to her grandmother,
before departing for France, letter of March
1810, Goodrich's Court of Napoleon *(1857).*

Ever since I arrived here I have been with him constantly and he loves me very much. I am grateful to him and respond to his love sincerely. I feel he becomes much more likable on closer acquaintance. There is something quite charming and very eager about him that one cannot resist …

Empress Marie Louise, to her father, on
Napoleon, letter of late March 1810,
Goodrich's Court *(1857).*

My son just brought me your letter. How eagerly I have read it! Not one word is in it that does not make me cry, but these are very sweet tears … I understand the reasons for your silence … Be happy, be happy, you deserve it, I say that with all my heart. You, too, have given me my share of happiness …

Josephine, to Napoleon, a month after their
divorce, letter of April 21, 1810, in Lévy's
The Intimate Napoleon *(1893).*

It is astonishing that the feudal law has continued almost without modification among such enlightened people … The separation of classes, in Germany much more distinct than it ever was in France, was bound to smother the military instinct of the citizen … The stoves, the beer, the tobacco smoke surround the common man in Germany with a kind of hot and heavy atmosphere from which he does not like to rise … Love of liberty has not been cultivated by the Germans; neither by enjoying nor by missing it have they learned its value.

Mme. Germaine de Staël, on Germany in
1810, Selected Texts *(1974).*

The restlessness has reached its zenith … if war should break out [with Russia], extended and spirited riots would take place in all regions between Rhine and Oder … The despair of the people who have nothing to lose because everything has been taken from them is much to be feared.

Jérôme Bonaparte, to Napoleon, letter of
December 5, 1811, in Goodrich's Court
(1857).

You must not suppose that the order I sent you was motivated by your failure to mention the Emperor in your last book [*De l'Allemagne*] … he could find no place in it that would be worthy of him … It seemed to me that the air of this country did not agree with you …

Louis Jacques Savary, minister of police, to
Mme. de Staël, after she was asked to quit
France, letter of October 3, 1810, in de Staël's
Selected Texts *(1974).*

I am convinced that the honor and the interest of the country require us to remain here to the latest possible moment … I shall not seek to relieve myself of the burden of responsibility by causing the burden of defeat to rest upon the shoulders of ministers. I will not ask from them resources which they cannot spare … If the Portuguese do their duty, I can maintain myself here; if not, no effort in the power of Great Britain to make will suffice to save Portugal.

Duke of Wellington, to the Government at London, from Spain, letter of October 1810, in Longford's Wellington *(1969).*

Believe me, my views are not based on passion. I respect and esteem very much of the new management, and very little of what our princes and governments have done in the past. There are some very capable men among the higher French officials and the new court system is a great step forward.

Friedrich Christoph Perthes, Hamburg bookseller, after the city was declared French, letter of January 1811, in in Schoeps' From the Years of Prussia's Peril *(1963).*

18. The Russian Campaign: April to December 1812

THE HISTORICAL CONTEXT

Imperfectly as it was carried out, the great blockade was having an effect on Britain's economy. Her total exports fell by over 12 percent between 1806 and 1808, and in 1810-11 her exports to northern Europe declined by 20 percent. Swedish iron and Russian lumber needed for British industry and ships became unavailable. Corn prices were rising, strikes occurred, and the country seemed on the verge of bankruptcy. On the continent, the great ports—Amsterdam, Hamburg, Lübeck—were suffering, but domestic industry and trade flourished. The damage done by a great depression, which swept through France in 1811, was recouped by the excellent harvest of 1812. So Napoleon could dedicate himself to the preparation of his last great campaign, which would enforce the blockade and bring Britain to her knees—the war against Russia.

By adding West Galicia to the Grand Duchy of Warsaw, Napoleon had aroused Alexander's suspicion that a resurrection of the old, pre-partition Poland was intended. The Czar was further offended by Napoleon's annexation of the north German state of Oldenburg, whose duke was his close relative. The French ambassador to Russia, Duke Armand de Caulaincourt, was recalled by Napoleon in February of 1811. Impressed as he was by Alexander's personality, he failed to convince the emperor of Russia's peaceful intentions. Both sides were looking for allies, Russia to Sweden, Napoleon to Austria.

Alexander had no difficulty in arousing his nation against the "infidels." The peace treaty of Tilsit had always been condemned by Russian patriots, and this opposition was now turned into fervent religious support for Holy Mother Russia. Also, 200,000 men were stationed along the border rivers, the Dnieper and the Dvina, separating the Polish and Lithuanian territories from Russia.

Napoleon, meanwhile, organized the greatest army ever assembled up to that time, originally about 420,000 men, later about 600,000, which in-

Madame Juliette Récamier

252

Baron Karl Vom Stein, one of Czar Alexander's advisers

cluded large contingents of Poles, Dutch, Swiss, Prussians, Austrians and soldiers from the Confederation of the Rhine. But France's own response to the conscription drive showed how much popularity the army had lost. Of 300,000 men called, 80,000 failed to show up, and many of the new recruits were unwilling and unreliable soldiers. Napoleon's appeal to his generals also fell on barren ground; they had grown rich and would have preferred to enjoy their lives. Some of the emperor's close advisers even dared to speak openly against his plans, whereupon he advised them of his idea of a united Europe, even of his plan to march through Moscow to India. On his way to join his *Grande Armée*, he was greeted by the emperor of Austria (his father-in-law), the king of Prussia, and all the minor German potentates. Probably, many of them were secretly praying for his defeat at this time.

It took the French armies less than three months to reach Moscow. The Russian armies retreated time and again, offering resistance only at Smolensk, which was set on fire, and then under the new supreme commander, Mikhail Kutuzov, at Borodino. After an extremely bloody battle, the French won, but only about 100,000 men were left to reach Moscow, the rest having been lost through disease, desertion and battle. The city was almost deserted, except for a few lower-class inhabitants. The deserted palaces and estates were sacked, and Napoleon moved into the Kremlin, expecting a peace move from the Czar. But on that same evening, September 15, 1812, fires broke out in the city. It is not certain whether the departing governor of the city had given orders to burn it. Some fires were certainly started by looting Russians, released prisoners and French soldiers. About 11,000 wooden houses burned down; most of the 340 churches, built of stone, survived.

The capture and burning of the holy city shocked all Russians, who were convinced that Napoleon was a savage atheist. While some Russian nobles, fearing that Napoleon might offer freedom to their serfs, were inclined to compromise with him, the great majority urged Alexander to fight on, and so did the prominent foreigners who had become part of his entourage: Baron Karl vom Stein, Madame Germaine de Staël and many others. He began to see himself as the leader of civilized Europe and Christianity against the devil incarnate; he left unanswered the messages that reached him from Moscow. Napoleon, for a while, acted as the victor in Moscow. Concerts and plays were presented, and by daily courier he kept in close touch with Paris, even finding time to reorganize the Comédie Francaise in Paris. But as time went by and winter drew near, he had to conclude that there was but one thing to do—retreat.

When the retreat began, the army carried provisions for about 20 days, after which Napoleon hoped to reach Smolensk, where new supplies awaited him. With the severe weather setting in, no more than 50,000 men reached that city, only to find that most of the food and clothing had been lost through Cossack raids and embezzlement. Neither was a long rest possible, because Kutuzov was approaching with an army by now greatly superior to the remaining French forces. Napoleon reached the Dnieper River at Orsha, after great losses, and was finally joined by Ney who brought up the rear. When the Berezina River was bridged, the plight of the remaining troops was desperate. To make matters worse, some bridges collapsed and thousands of soldiers and noncombatants were lost.

The news of Brigadier General C.F. de Malet's attempt to depose Napoleon, which had almost succeeded, convinced the emperor that his presence in Paris was indispensable. He left the army, putting Joachim Murat in charge—not his most able general, but a king in rank. In the bitter cold, only about 30,000 men reached Kovno, where, in June of the preceding year, 400,000 men had crossed the Niemen on the march to Moscow. There, Murat followed Napoleon's example and left the army, worried about his own throne. The 30-year-old Eugène Beauharnais took charge to lead the ragged, frozen and half-starved remnants to the Elbe River. On December 16, the famous bulletin No. 29 told Parisians the truth for the first time: The *Grande Armée* had been destroyed. Two days later, the emperor arrived back in Paris, after travelling incognito through Poland on a nonstop journey of 13 days and nights.

CHRONICLE OF EVENTS

1812:   *April 8:* Russia presents ultimatum to Napoleon, demanding the evacuation of Prussia, Swedish Pomerania and all points east of the Elbe River. Napoleon declares war.

May 9: He leaves Paris to join the *Grande Arme* encamped on the Vistula River. The largest army ever assembled up to this time: originally about 420,000 men, ultimately about 600,000 with reinforcements including large contingents from the Confederation of the Rhine as well as Austria and Prussia. The Austrians under Prince Karl Philipp Schwarzenberg form the right wing, the Prussians under General Johann David von York the left.

June 24: The army crosses the Niemen River.

June 28: Vilna is occupied. Napoleon sets up a provisional government. The Russian armies, about 150,000 men, under Mikhail Barclay de Tolly and Pëtr Bagration, use scorched-earth tactics and retreat.

July: Napoleon's Prussian contingent besieges Riga; the Austrians penetrate into Volhynia.

July 27: Napoleon reaches Vitebsk. Barclay's army slips away again.

August 12: The French attack heavily fortified Smolensk. Barclay resumes the retreat, having ordered the city to be burned.

End of August: Barclay is replaced by Prince Mikhail Kutuzov.

September 7: Battle of Borodino is fought on the Moskova River with horrible losses on both sides. Napoleon refuses to send in the Guard; 40,000 Russian and 20,000 French soldiers are killed. The Russians retreat farther and abandon Moscow. The French army is by now reduced to slightly more than 100,000 men.

September 14: Napoleon enters Moscow, which has been deserted by most inhabitants, and establishes himself in the Kremlin.

September 15: The great fire of Moscow begins, and looting breaks out in the city. Hundreds of incendiaries are shot by the French. Napoleon must escape

The surrender of Madrid, December 4, 1808

The bombardment of Vienna, May 13, 1809

from the Kremlin and moves to the Petrovsky Palace. His truce offer to Alexander remains unanswered.

October 19: He begins to retreat toward Smolensk.

October 23: In Paris, General de Malet announces the emperor's death in Moscow and almost succeeds in taking his place.

November: Very severe weather sets in. Kutuzov's army and swarming Cossacks attack the invaders. Separate corps of the French army fight at Jaroslavetz, Viazma, Krasnoi and other places.

November 14: Napoleon is forced to leave Smolensk. Most of his army has changed into a disorderly crowd desperately trying to survive the hunger, the bitter cold and the constant enemy attacks.

November 26-28: French forces cross the Berezina, a tributary of the Dnieper, while fighting superior Russian forces. Thousands drown or are massacred by the Cossacks, but Charles Nicholas Oudinot, Michel Ney and Claude Victor manage to avoide complete annihilation.

December 5: At Molodechno, Napoleon leaves the army, entrusting its command to Murat.

December 16: The *Moniteur* issues the first detailed report on the disaster of the *Grande Arme*. Murat has also abandoned the army, whose remnants are brought back across the Niemen by Ney, Louis Alexandre Berthier and Victor.

December 18: Napoleon arrives back in Paris. He is informed by Berthier that the *Grande Arme* no longer exists.

December 30: Prussian General York concludes the Convention of Tauroggen, an agreement of neutrality, with the Russian General Hans Karl von Diebitsch.

EYEWITNESS TESTIMONY

If Napoleon wages war against us, it is possible, even likely that he will beat us ... but that will not give him the peace. The Spanish have been beaten repeatedly but are neither defeated nor subdued. The emperor needs quick successes, as his thoughts are quick; he will not have them with us. I shall learn from his teachings which are those of a master. We will leave it to our climate, our winter to conduct the war against him. The French are brave but not as hardened as our soldiers, and easier discouraged. Miracles happen only where the emperor happens to be; but he cannot be everywhere.

Czar Alexander I (as reported by Caulaincourt to Napoleon), June 5, 1811, in C.'s Memoirs *(1933).*

Are you relying on Austria? You made war upon her in 1809, and deprived her of a province during peace. Is it Sweden from whom you took Finland? Is it Prussia whose spoils you accepted at Tilsit after being her ally?

Napoleon, to Prince Alexander Borisovitch Kourakin, Russian ambassador, August 15, 1811, Guizot's History of France.

As was his custom, he walked in front of the ranks. He remembered what wars each regiment had fought with him. Stooping in front of the oldest soldiers, he would mention the battle of the Pyramids to one, to another Marengo, or Austerlitz, Iena or Friedland, tapping them on the shoulder ... The veteran who thought the Emperor had recognized him seemed to grow in size and glory before his less experienced, envious comrades.

Comte Louis Philippe de Ségur, Napoleon reviewing his troops in East Prussia in spring of 1812, Memoirs *(1827).*

Those where no longer the frivolous French of 1806 who marched with conspicuous carelessness ... The

French of 1812 obviously followed their flags under more compulsion than one had seen before.

Canvas George, French troops entering Berlin, March 28, 1812, Memoirs of a Prussian *(1840).*

Everything will be against us in this war. On their side, love of their country and independence; all private and public interests, even the secret wishes of our allies. On our side, against so many obstacles, glory alone, even without any hope of plunder, since the frightful poverty of those regions renders it impossible.

Napoleon, to Caulaincourt, at the outset of the Russian campaign, C.'s Memoirs *(1933).*

The reports from East Prussia can really make you despair: It had not really recovered from the last war

Austrian Foreign Minister Metternich

when this new misery began. Being forced to supply for the needs of an innumerable army, or at least of two-fifths of it, in the midst of general impoverishment and a very poor harvest, all this is causing indescribable misery. Everywhere, most of the horses are transported off to bring up food supplies, and so are the cattle, for slaughtering ...

Barthold Georg Niebuhr, letter of June 30, 1812, Letters *(1926)*

The army has only marched a hundred leagues since the Niemen. I saw it before crossing and already everything is changed. The officers, arriving ... from the interior of France are frightened at the sight which meets their eyes. They had no conception that a victorious march without battles could leave behind it more ruins than a defeat.

General Jean Rapp, to Napoleon, August 1812, Guizot's History.

And you, too, are you one of those who wish to stop? As you are only an old woman you may go back to Paris. I can do very well without you.

Napoleon, to General Berthier, end of August, Guizot's History.

By chance, the Emperor had received from Paris a portrait of the King of Rome [his 2-year-old son] the very same day [of the battle of Borodino]. Since his day of birth Napoleon had been at his son's side every day, showing his tender feelings toward him ... The picture was set up outside the imperial tent and he called his officers and even soldiers of the Old Guard so that he could share his feelings with these battle-hardened soldiers ... and present this symbol of hope at a time of grave danger.

Ségur, September 7, 1812, Memoirs *(1827).*

When he caught a glimpse of the fighting it was without alarm or impatience ... When informed of the loss of one of his best generals, as happened repeatedly, he just gestured sadly in resignation ... His staff members were staring at him, amazed. In all important battles, he had always shown a composed, cool activity; but today he was slow, indifferent and inactive.

Ségur, Napoleon at Borodino, September 7, 1812, Memoirs *(1827).*

You [the war council] are afraid of retreating through Moscow. I, however, look at it as a gift of Providence, because that will save the army. Napoleon is like a

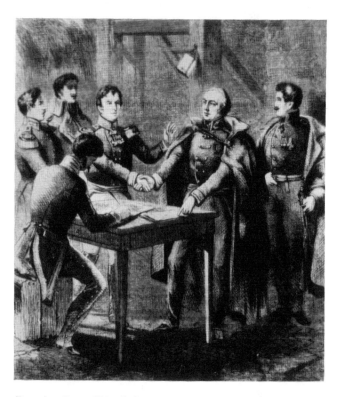

Prussian General Yorck signs an agreement of neutrality with the Russians at the Convention of Tauroggen, December 30, 1812.

torrent which we have not as yet been able to stop. Moscow will be the sponge to absorb him.

Marshal Mikhail Kutuzov, after Borodino, September 7, 1812, the Durants' Age of Napoleon *(1975).*

Smolensk may have cost a lot, but it was worth the price and decided the war, as I thought right away ... The strategy of retreating could be justified as far as Smolensk, but if one could not make a stand there and was not permitted to fight a battle it was senseless to get involved in the war. The weather is incredibly favorable to the Emperor. Since the beginning of the war, nothing has happened as strange as the Emperor's declaration in today's papers that the campaign would be finished on October 10. That must be calculated certainty of peace. I believe it, but the miraculous part is to predict it to the very day.

Niebuhr, to Friedrich Christoph Perthes, letter of September 15, 1812, Letters *(1926).*

One last hill had to be climbed. It was close to Moscow and overlooking it, called "The Mount of Greetings" [Poklonny Hill], because the inhabitants always knelt down at the sight of the city and crossed themselves ... The sun made the tremendous city shine in innumerable colors. Our scouts had soon climbed to the top ... Everyone quickened his step ... and the whole army was clapping their hands and shouting deliriously "Moscow, Moscow" as sailors shout "Land" after a long sea voyage ... We stood there quietly and proudly. This was the day of our glory. It would always be the finest, most magnificent memory of our entire lives. At this moment, we felt the eyes of the amazed universe resting upon us ...

Ségur, first sight of Moscow, September 14, 1812, Memoirs (1827).

... we blamed ourselves. Most of us thought that lack of discipline and the drunken stupor of our soldiers had caused the beginning of the catastrophe which the storm had completed. We did not dare to think of the outcry of horror which would come from all of Europe ... We had sunk to be an army of criminals ... But then reports began to arrive which accused only the Russians of this disaster ... Bombs, surreptitiously placed in several houses, had exploded, wounding soldiers who had gathered there for warmth ... All officers had ob-

Napoleon meets Czar Alexander I

served savage-looking men and women wandering around in the blazing streets ... who did not try to hide themselves but ran in triumph through the flames. They were caught when spreading the fire with torches they held in their hands, and our soldiers had to cut off their hands to make them lose their grip on the torches ... One said they were criminals released by Russian leaders from their prisons to burn Moscow ...

Ségur, the burning of Moscow, Memoirs (1827).

For eight years I have been improving this estate and lived here happily ... The inhabitants of this estate, numbering 1,720, leave it at your approach and I set fire to my house that it may not be polluted by your presence ... I left you my two houses in Moscow, with contents worth half a million of rubles. Here you find nothing but ashes.

Governor Feodor Vasilyevich Rostopchin (of Moscow), to the French, message left at his estate at Voronovo, September 1812, Guizot's History.

The beautiful and magnificent city of Moscow no longer exists. Rostopchin [the governor of Moscow] burnt it down. 400 arsonists were taken in the act, and, having all declared that they had lighted the fire by order of the governor and the director of police, they were shot. The fire at last seems to have ceased. Three fourth of the houses are burnt ... Such a conduct is atrocious and served no purpose. Was the intention to deprive us of some resources? But those resources were in the cellars which the fire could not reach. Besides, why destroy one of the finest cities of the world ... to accomplish so paltry an object? ... Humanity, the interests of your Majesty and this great city demanded that it should be entrusted to my keeping since it was deserted by the Russian army ... That was done at Vienna twice, at Berlin and Madrid ... If I thought such things were done by your Majesty's orders, I should not write you this letter ... While carrying away the fire-engines from Moscow, they left 150 field cannon, 60,000 new muskets ... I made war upon your Majesty without animosity. A letter from you before or after the last battle would have stopped my march, and I should have been ready to forego the advantage of entering Moscow. If you Majesty still retains aught of your former sentiments, you will take this letter in good part. In any case, you must feel indebted to me for giving an account of what is taking place in Moscow.

Napoleon, to Czar Alexander, from Moscow, letter of September 20, 1812.

All the opinions which you have received from me, all the determinations expressed in the orders addressed to you by me—everything ought to convince you that my resolution is immovable and that at the present moment no proposal of the enemy can make me think of terminating the war, and so failing in the sacred duty of avenging our outraged country.

Czar Alexander, to Marshall Kutuzov, October 21, 1812, Guizot's History.

The whole of France [is my accomplice], and you, too, if I had succeeded. A man who has undertaken to be his country's defender needs no defence: he triumphs or he dies. I die, but I am not the last of the Romans. I die, but I have made the enemy of the republic tremble.

Brigadier General C.F. de Malet, to his judges, after failure of his anti-Bonaparte plot, October 23, 1812, Guizot's History.

Everywhere famine showed itself by the sight of dead horses whose flesh had been eaten to the bone. Doors and windows of the houses had been broken and ripped off, to be used as fuel for the bivouacs. There were no shelters, no winter quarters, no wood. The sick and wounded had been left in the streets …

Ségur, retreat to Smolensk, November 1812, Memoirs *(1827).*

There will be no way out this time, except for the brave. I shall master the situation if we can cross the river: We, with the Guard and two fresh corps of Victor and Oudinot will be strong enough to beat the Russians. If we cannot cross over, we shall break ranks … We have to arrange in advance to destroy everything and leave no trophy for the enemy. I should rather eat with my fingers from here on than to leave one fork with my crest on it to the Russians.

Napoleon (as reportd by Caulaincourt), after the Russians captured the bridge over the Berezina, November 20, 1812, in C.'s Memoirs *(1933).*

When we came to Borisov, completely exhausted and in extreme disorder, we could hear loud shouting from the road ahead of us … Our catastrophe had been carefully hidden even from their officers. So, when they saw, instead of the columns of splendid fighting men, conquerors of Moscow, a crowd of tattered ghosts in Napoleon's wake, wrapped in women's coats, pieces of carpets … their feet wrapped in all types of rags, they were stunned with utter dismay. As these skeletons of soldiers passed by, their haggard, gray faces covered with ugly beards, without weapons, marching … out of step, their heads lowered, silent, like a horde of convicts, they stared at them in horror. What struck them most was to see so many straggling colonels and generals, isolated, paying no attention to anyone but themselves … walking along with the soldiers who hardly noticed them … The officers [of Victor and Oudinot], with tears of compassion on their cheeks, seized any of their comrades they could recognize …

Ségur, the retreating army, Memoirs *(1827).*

A few lines from Werner, written at the battlefield of Smolensk on a drum … He writes that they have to fight not only the great superiority of a colossal nation, but also ignorance of the country, the elements, hunger … lack of strength and food … Yet the "Moniteurs" talk of victory upon victory which have paved their way to Moscow.

Philippine von Griesheim, letter of December 2, 1812, Letters of a Bride during the Wars of Liberation *(1905).*

… after Molodechno and the emperor's departure, winter closed down on us with terrible severity. As we all were attacked all associations against calamity collapsed and nothing was left but a crowd of individual agonies. The best soldiers lost all their self-respect and stopped at nothing … There was no longer any fraternity of arms, no … human relations … The strong despoiled the weak, crowding around the dying, robbing them often before they expired … When a horse fell, the men threw themselves on it and tore it to pieces …

Ségur, December 5, 1812, Memoirs *(1827).*

The army was in good condition on the 6th November … The cold began on the 7th, and from that time we lost every night several hundred horses which died during bivouac. Soon 30,000 had succumbed and our cavalry were all on foot. On the 14th, we were almost without cavalry, artillery and transports. Without cavalry we could gain no information beyond a quarter of a league. Without artillery we could fight no battle nor keep positions steadily. It was necessary to march to avoid a battle. Some men … seemed staggered … and thought of nothing but disaster …

The enemy, seeing on the roads traces of the frightful calamity which struck the French army, tried to take advantage of it. Our columns were surrounded by Cossacks who, like Arabs in the desert, carried off the trains … The enemy, however, had reason to repent of every attempt of importance … Nevertheless, the enemy held all the passages over the Beresina, a river 80 yards wide and carrying much ice, with its banks covered with marshes … The Duke of Reggio [Oudinot] crossing, attacked the enemy in a battle lasting for two hours; the Russians withdrew … during the whole of the 26th and 27th the army crossed … Rest is its principal want. Supplies and horses are arriving …

Throughout all these operations, the emperor has always marched in the midst of his guard … Their [the cavalry's] generals acted as captains, the colonels as under-officers … The health of his Majesty has never been better.

Grande Armée, *29th Bulletin, dispatched on December 5, 1812, in Guizot's* History.

The road which we followed was covered with [French] prisoners who required no watching and who underwent hardships till then unheard of. Several still dragged themselves mechanically … with their feet naked and half frozen. Some had lost the power of speech, others had fallen into a kind of savage stupidity, and wished, in spite of us, to roast the dead bodies in order to eat them. Those who were too weak to go to fetch wood stopped near the first fire they found, and sitting upon one another they crowded closely round the fire … the little life left in them going out at the same time as it did. The houses and farms which the wretches had set on fire were surrounded with dead bodies, for those who went near had not the power to escape the flames which reached them …

A Russian officer of the advance guard, December 1812, Guizot's History.

When Murat reached Gumbinnen [East Prussia] he met Ney there who, at his surprise, had arrived before him from Kovno without a rear guard. The Russian advances had, fortunately, slowed down as soon as they had won back their own territory. It seems they hesitated to cross the Prussian border, not knowing whether they should enter as friends or enemies.

Ségur, the retreat, December 1812, Memoirs *(1827).*

As large as the loss of human lives must be, as wrong would it be to imagine, as many may do at your end as they do here, that the army is almost completely exterminated … between December 8 and 22, 118 generals, 220 colonels … and 1,119 officers of captain or lower rank have arrived at Koenigsberg … One should believe that horses must become extinct in the world; for this campaign surely 300,000 have paid with their lives.

Niebuhr, to Dore Hensler, Königsberg, letter of December 27, 1812, Letters *(1926).*

I have to report to your Majesty that the regular army is in utter disorder, and so is the Guard which consists of no more than 400-500 men. The generals and officers have lost all their property, most of them are frostbitten. The roads are littered with dead bodies, the houses filled with dying soldiers. The entire army now consists of no more than a column stretched out over a few leagues. It starts out in the morning and stops in the evening; it receives no orders. The marshals are walking along with all the others. The army exists no longer.

General Louis Alexandre Berthier, to Napoleon, final report on the Grande Armée, end of December 1812, Guizot's History.

19. The War of January 1813 to May 1814

THE HISTORICAL CONTEXT

The great uprising against the Napoleonic regime that followed the Russian disaster was not quite as automatic and spontaneous as it may seem in retrospect. Mikhail Kutuzov, the victorious Russian supreme commander, advised not to pursue the enemy across the Russian border. The Prussian king refused to approve the unauthorized pact between his General Johann David, Count York, and the Russians; and the Austrians, afraid of being the first ones to be attacked by the French, chose to remain faithful to their alliance with France. Also, Emperor Francis could not ignore the fact that he had a daughter on the French throne. But Czar Alexander I overruled Kutuzov, put himself at the head of his armies, advanced across East Prussia and urged the people and the king of Prussia to join him. Public pressure became so great that Frederick William III had no choice but to call his people to arms. The response was tremendous, the result of the patriotic rebirth that had taken place in the nation during the years of humiliation.

Prince Kutuzov, the victorious Russian supreme commander

Yet, after the first great advances that brought the Allies to Dresden and Hamburg, it appeared that Napoleon and his seasoned troops and generals were anything but beaten. In May of 1813, the French were generally victorious; the king of Saxony rejoined Napoleon; Hamburg and Dresden were again in French hands. At this point, Clemens Prince Metternich, the Austrian foreign minister, suggested an armistice and offered to mediate. Napoleon accepted, hoping to get reinforcements and fearing to antagonize his father-in-law Francis, thus driving him into the Allied camp. Later he declared that accepting the armistice had been his greatest mistake. He seems to have been willing to accept the gist of the Allied demands, the restoration of France within its "natural borders." But England reserved the right to make further conditions, and in the meantime the British armies had been victorious in Spain. Also, the Swedes, up to that point busy occupying Norway, now joined the Allies in strength.

262

Napoleon's counterproposals reached Vienna too late, war was resumed, and while Napoleon was victorious in Bohemia and Dresden, the advances of his generals on Berlin were defeated and his southern German allies began to forsake him. To prevent the three large Allied armies from uniting and cutting him off from France, he had to give up Dresden and give battle at Leipzig. There, the century's highest number of combatants had gathered, and during three days of incessant fighting, Napoleon was outnumbered and thoroughly defeated. He retreated to the Rhine, and his German and Dutch dependencies collapsed. Joachim Murat, the king of Naples, who had fought with Napoleon at Leipzig, now plotted with Metternich to save his kingdom and promised the Allies a contingent of 50,000 men. Napoleon, hearing this, raged at the treason of his brother-in-law, calling him the "Bernadotte of the Midi." By the beginning of 1814, the Allied armies were in France. For a few weeks Napoleon attacked and repeatedly beat Gebhardt Leberecht von Blücher and the cautious Prince Karl Philipp Schwarzenberg. But his troops were exhausted and outnumbered, and when the combined Allied forces marched on Paris, there were insufficient troops available to prevent the storming of the capital.

The empress-regent Marie Louise finally left Paris. She was not permitted to join her husband after he had abdicated unconditionally. Before she and her three-year-old son, the king of Rome, left for Vienna, it seems that Napoleon had unsuccessfully tried to commit suicide by taking the poison his doctor had given him on his return from Russia. A few days later, on April 16, he wrote a farewell letter to Joséphine, saying: "Never forget him who never forgot you and never will forget you." Josephine died a month later.

Four hundred of the Old Guard chose to accompany him to Elba, where he was exiled by the Allies. As he passed through the strongly Catholic Provence, he had to be protected from the crowds who hurled insults at him. Near Arles, he saw himself hung in effigy and disguised himself from there on. But at Fréjus, he was received on board the British *Undaunted* with a 21-gun salute.

Louis XVIII, the former Comte de Provence, was installed on the French throne, but he could never be popular as a king. The French remembered that he had sworn in February of 1791 never to leave the country— and had left it four months later. He had fought with the Prussians against the French at Valmy, had lived in exile in Poland, Prussia and Italy, always retreating from the advancing Napoleon, and, during his last years in England, had begun to look like a gouty, enormously fat English country squire. Neither he nor his much more fanatical and reactionary brother and successor, the Comte Charles Philippe D'Artois, knew anything of the needs of the country they had not seen for 25 years. Louis, in dealing with the Allies, had to rely on the experience and skill of his foreign minister, Charles Maurice de Talleyrand, who had been for most of this time in the forefront of French history. In his efforts, Talleyrand was helped by the desire of the victors to strengthen the weak regime against the one they had just toppled and also by the difficulty the four great powers had in agreeing with one another. Russia wanted Poland; Prussia wanted Saxony; Austria wanted a free hand in Italy; and England, as always, wanted a balance of power on the continent. The chances for a beaten France getting off cheaply at the forthcoming great peace conference improved from month to month.

CHRONICLE OF EVENTS

1813: *January 3:* General York, who had concluded the neutrality agreement with Russia without authorization, urges King Frederick William III to use the opportunity to gain independence from Napoleon.

February 3: The Prussian king appeals to his people, calling on them to form volunteer corps.

February 28: Treaty of Kalisch between Russia and Prussia forms a defensive and offensive alliance. In case of victory, Prussia is promised as much territory as she possessed in 1806. Austria and England are invited to join.

March 3: England and Sweden conclude a treaty under which England will pay subsidies to Sweden and not interfere with her union with Norway. Sweden joins the Allies with 30,000 men, under Crown Prince Jean Baptiste Bernadotte.

March 16: Prussia notifies France that their alliance is broken off.

March 17: King Frederick William III declares war on Napoleon and issues an appeal "to my people." All able-bodied men between 17 and 40 are called to arms (*Landwehr* and *Landsturm*); the order of the Iron Cross is founded.

March 18: Russian forces occupy Hamburg.

March 25: Russian Supreme Commander Kutuzov appeals to the German princes for support.

March 27: The Russians and Prussians under General Ludwig Adolf Peter Wittgenstein and Blücher occupy Dresden. General Louis Nicolas Davout withdraws; the king of Saxony flees.

April 28: Napoleon reaches Weimar. His army consists of 180,000 men, but many are inexperienced conscripts, the German contingents are by now of doubtful loyalty, and he is short of cavalry.

May 2: French are victorious at battle of Gross-Görschen (Lützen), but with great losses on both sides. Dresden is reoccupied. French achieve alliance with Saxony, whose king has returned.

May 20-21: In the battle of Bautzen (near Dresden), Napoleon defeats a Russian-Prussian army. The allies retreat beyond the Oder River in Silesia.

French troops are shown the portrait of the king of Rome.

Moscow aflame

May 30: Hamburg is reoccupied by Davout.

June 4: Armistice of Poischwitz begins. It is to last until July 26, but is then prolonged to August 16.

June 15: In the treaty of Reichenbach, England promises subsidies to Russia and Prussia.

June 26: Last, decisive conference is held between Metternich and Napoleon.

June: In Spain, Arthur Wellesley, Duke of Wellington, decisively defeats the French under Jean Baptiste Jourdan. The French abandon most of the country.

July 5-August 11: Congress of Prague held between the Allies and the French, with Austria mediating. But no agreement is reached.

August 12: Austria declares war on France.

August 21: In Spain, the British storm San Sebastian and besiege Pampeluna. The Allies put three armies into the field: The Bohemian army under Schwarzenberg, the Silesian army under Blücher and the Northern army under Bernadotte.

August 23: The Prussians defeat a French corps at Grossbeeren.

August 26: At the battle at the Katzbach, Blücher defeats a French corps under General Etienne Jacques MacDonald.

August 26-27: Napoleon defeats the army of Bohemia at battle of Dresden.

September 6: In the battle of Dennewitz, the Prussian generals Friedrich Wilhelm von Bülow and Bogislaw Emanuel Tauentzien defeat Marshal Michel Ney and prevent him from taking Berlin.

September 9: In agreement of Teplitz, Russia, Austria and Prussia promise mutual support, guarantee their respective territories and pledge no separate peace or armistice with France. In secret articles, Prussia and Austria guarantee each other their territorial status of 1805.

October 3: York forces a passage across the Elbe at Wartenburg. The Northern Army also crosses the Elbe.

October 9: Treaty between Austria and Bavaria guarantees the latter's possessions. Bavaria withdraws from the Confederation of the Rhine and joins the Allies. The British under Wellington enter France from Spain.

The remains of the Grand Army cross the Berezina, November 26-28, 1812.

October 16-19: Battle of Leipzig (Battle of the Nations) fought. On the third day, the Allies, who outnumber Napoleon almost three to one, nearly surround the city and storm it the next day. The Saxon and Württemberg corps go over to the Allies; the Hessians start shooting at the French. Napoleon withdraws after heavy losses. The kingdom of Westphalia and the grand duchies of Berg and Frankfort collapse. The king of Saxony is taken prisoner.

November 2: Napoleon crosses the Rhine at Mayence. The members of the Confederation of the Rhine join the Allies. Most, but not all, fortified cities surrender to the Allies, during the next few weeks.

November 9: In Paris, Napoleon rejects an Allied peace offer, which would give him the boundaries of the Alps and the Rhine. He restores Spain to King Ferdinand. The Cortes agrees.

November 15: The Dutch revolt and expel French officials.

December 1: The Allies decide to invade France.

December: Bernadotte invades Holstein and forces Denmark to cede Norway to Sweden, in the treaty of Kiel, while Sweden cedes western Pomerania and Rügen to Denmark. Wellington, in southern France, invests Bayonne. Schwarzenberg crosses through Switzerland, in violation of her neutrality.

1814:   *January 1:* Blücher crosses the Rhine at Mannheim and Koblenz; 200,000 Allied troops advance in France.

January 29: Napoleon attacks Blücher at Brienne and drives him back.

February 1: Blücher defeats Napoleon at the battle of La Rothière.

February 10-15: Blücher advancing separately along the Marne, is attacked by Napoleon and defeated in four battles: Champaubert, Montmirail, Chateau-Thierry and Vauchamps.

February 17-18: Napoleon turns on Schwarzenberg and defeats him at Nangis and Montereau.

February-March: At Congress of Chatillon, Napoleon is offered the borders of 1792. He rejects the offer.

February 27: Schwarzenberg defeats generals Oudinot and MacDonald at Bar-sur-Aube.

March 9: Treaty of Chaumont between the Allies is arranged by the British foreign minister, Lord Robert Stewart Castlereagh. The alliance is confirmed, barring a separate peace for any member.

March 9-10: The Allied armies, now combined, defeat Napoleon at Laon.

March 12: The British under Wellington capture Bordeaux.

March 20-21: Napoleon, defeated again at Arcis-sur-Aube, throws himself into the rear of the Allies who, however, ignore this move and march toward Paris.

March 25: Marmont and Mortier are defeated at La Fère-Champenoise and rush back to defend the capital.

March 30: The Montmartre is stormed by the Allies and the city of Paris is forced to capitulate. Napoleon's marshals refuse to join him in an assault on the capital.

April 4: Napoleon proposes to abdicate in favor of his son. This is rejected by the Allies.

April 10: General Nicolas Soult is defeated by the British in the battle of Toulouse. The campaign in southern France is ended.

April 11: At Fontainebleau, Napoleon abdicates unconditionally.

April 19: Napoleon takes his leave of the Imperial Guard at Fontainebleau. The Allies grant him the island of Elba as a sovereign principality. France is to pay him 2,000,000 francs annually. Both he and Marie Louise retain the imperial title. She receives the duchies of Parma, Piacenza and Guastalla.

May 30: In the First Treaty of Paris, Louis XVIII, brother of Louis XVI, is put on the throne of France, thanks to Talleyrand's maneuvering. He issues a constitution (*charte constitutionelle*) somewhat similar to the British, with a chamber of deputies, a chamber of peers appointed by the king, and various guaranties of religious and civil liberty. The Allies want to strengthen the new regime and offer lenient peace conditions. The boundaries of 1792 and the independence of the Italian and German states and of Switzerland are recognized by France. Most of her colonies (but not Malta) are restored by England. France promises to abolish the slave trade; the Allies drop all claims for indemnity. The settlement of the reconquered territories is to be decided by a general congress, to be held in Vienna.

In the battle of Bautzen, Napoleon defeats a Russian-Prussian army.

EYEWITNESS TESTIMONY

It will now become the privilege of your Majesty ... to become the saviour and protector of your own and all German people. It is quite apparent that Providence is guiding this great enterprise; but the moment must be used quickly. Now or never is the time to recover liberty, independence and greatness without having to make excessive sacrifices ... The timid needs an example to follow and Austria will proceed on the path which your Majesty will prepare. You know me as a calm, cool man who does not mix in politics ... But the circumstances have changed the situation, and it is our duty to exploit the unique constellation. I am speaking the language of an old, faithful servant. We shall fight like the old, genuine Prussians and your Majesty's throne will stand fast and unshakable in the future.

General Count Hans David Ludwig York von Wartenburg, to King Frederick William III, from Tilsit, letter of January 3, 1813, in Königswald's Prussian Reader *(1966).*

If the great army had been drowned to the last man recrossing the Niemen, such is our martial superiority that we should not be any the less in a situation to recommence the campaign in the spring.

Hugues Bernard, Duke of Bassano, French ambassador to Metternich, January 1813, Guizot's History of France.

The emperor was thus retrograding towards the revolutionary practices which the public treasury used to indulge in at the time of his advent to power, when no scruple was felt at substituting mere promises to pay for the real payments which had been guaranteed. His method of defining credit was this: "Credit is a dispensation from paying ready money," forgetting that the first condition of credit is a free agreement between borrower and lender.

Count Mollien, minister of the treasury, Napoleon's financing of his new campaign, January 1813, Guizot's History.

Little does it matter under what banner they have served. I see in them only my children. I commend them to your Imperial Majesty. May they learn that the con-queror is the friend of their father! Your Majesty could not give me a more touching proof of your sentiments for me.

Comte de Provence (later Louis XVIII), to Czar Alexander, from exile in England, on 100,000 French prisoners-of-war, letter of January 1813, Guizot's History.

I trust that you are not one of those who believe the lion is dead. Since the time I left Vilna you have done all in your power to do me damage [by leaving the *Grande Armée*]. It is the title of king which made you lose your head. If you wish to keep it—I mean the title—you will have to behave quite differently from the way you have up to now.

Napoleon, to Marshal Murat, letter of January 26, 1813.

The agents of England are propagating amongst all our neighbors the spirit of revolt against the sovereigns. England wishes to see the whole continent a prey to civil war and all the terrors of anarchy ... Four times since the rupture which followed the treaty of Amiens I have offered peace formally. I shall never make peace except an honorable one—one suited to the interests and greatness of my empire. My policy is not in any way mysterious. I have declared what sacrifices I could make. So long as this murderous war continues, my people ought to be ready to make sacrifices of every kind; for a bad peace would cause us to lose everything, even hope itself ...

Napoleon, to the legislative body, February 14, 1813, in Bourrienne's Memoirs of Napoleon *(1829-30).*

... we were crushed by France's superior strength. The peace which deprived me of half of my subjects did not bring us its blessings; it inflicted deeper wounds than even the war. The country's blood was sucked ... its agriculture paralyzed, the freedom of trade impeded ... We saw only too clearly that the emperor's treaties would slowly destroy us, even more than his wars. Brandenburger, Prussians, Silesians, Pomeranians, Lithuanians! You know how you have suffered for almost seven years, you know the sad lot that will be yours if we do not end this war honorably. Think of your past, the great Elector, the great Frederic! Remember the blessings for which our forefathers fought … freedom of conscience, honor, independence, commerce, industry, arts and sciences. Think of the great example of our mighty Allies, the Russians, remember the Spanish, the Portuguese. Even smaller nations have gone to war for these ideals and were victorious against more powerful enemies. Think of the heroic Swiss and Dutch.

Frederic William III, "to my people,"
Proclamation of March 17, 1813, in
Königswald's Prussian Reader *(1966).*

I know how favorably disposed towards peace are both the Emperor Alexander and the cabinet of St. James. The calamities of the continent call loudly for it, and your Majesty ought not to put obstacles in the way. Possessor of the grandest monarchy on earth, ought you desire ceaselessly to extend its limits and to bequeath to an arm less powerful than your own the inheritance of never-ending wars?

Jean Baptiste Bernadotte, Crown Prince of
Sweden, to Napoleon, letter of March 23,
1813, Guizot's History.

In what way do you expect me to negotiate with England? Your emperor proclaims that the French dynasty reigns and will reign in Spain. How would you have me negotiate with Russia and Prussia when you say that the constitutional territories or dependencies of these allies—that is to say the Hanseatic towns and the grand duchy of Warsaw—must remain inviolably alienated from them? Why be so positive on points that are impossible to defend? For even in gaining victory— and you will need to gain many to make Europe what you would have it to be—the force of public opinion is not always to be resisted … As for us, we shall merely have to choose; we are offered everything … but we shall only desire those things which cannot be refused to us. We wish for an independent Germany and for peace.

Prince Clemens Mettternich, to French Mini-
ster Otto, at Vienna, March 1813, Guizot's
History.

I wish to have fewer people about me, fewer cooks, fewer plates and dishes … In camp and on march, the tables, even my own, shall be served with a soup, a boiled and roast joint and vegetables, with no dessert …

I wish to take no pages with me, they are of no use … Diminish in the same way the number of canteens; instead of four beds, only have two, instead of four tents, let there be only two, and furniture in proportion. We must be lightly equipped, for we shall have many enemies to fight against; and in order to achieve success, we shall have to march quickly.

Napoleon, to marshal of the palace at Saint-
Cloud, April 15, 1813, Guizot's History.

By knowing the Emperor Alexander's views we shall at last come to an understanding. My intention, moreover, is to make him a golden bridge, to save him from Metternich's intrigues. If I must make sacrifices, I prefer to do them for the advantage of Alexander who is an honorable foe, and the King of Prussia in whom Russia takes an interest, than for that of Austria who has been a false ally and who, under the title of mediator, wishes to arrogate the right of disposing of everything, after having done what suited herself. By treating now, all the honor of the peace will belong to the Emperor Alexander alone; whereas by making use of the mediation of Austria, the latter power, whatever be the result of peace or war, should seem to have weighed in the balance the fate of Europe.

Napoleon, to Caulaincourt, after Metternich
had suggested an armistice, May 1813,
Caulaincourt's Memoirs *(1933).*

What kind of peace can come from this armistice? Will Austria's mediation help, now that we saw she hesitated at the decisive moment and avoided war? Will she show resolution if Napoleon does not give in anywheres, since the fortunes of war are turning against the Allies? And even in the best possible case, would war not be resumed with a great disadvantage? I am trying hard not to give up all hope … World domination has advanced so far, arbitrary power organized so masterly into the smallest ramifications, the art of war is being conducted by such huge masses that a popular uprising can form only under the protection of large armies … Peace and enslavement have become synonyms.

August Wilhelm Schlegel, German Romantic
poet, letter of June 10, 1813, in Koch's Letters of the German Romantics *(1938).*

N: Thrice I have restored his throne to the Emperor Francis. I have even made the mistake of marrying his daughter … Under the pretext of mediation you have been arming; and now … you pretend to dictate to me conditions which are those of my enemies. The Russians and Prussians ... I have beaten them ... although they have told you the contrary. Do you therefore wish to have your turn also? Very well ... you will have it. I make an appointment with you in Vienna for October ... You Austrians wish for the whole of Italy, your friends the Russians wish for Poland, the Prussians for Saxony, the English for Holland and Belgium ... All right, I am willing to negotiate ... I have offered Illyria if you stay neutral ... How much did England pay you to persuade you to play this role against me?

M: I have seen your soldiers, you have nothing left but children. You have caused an entire generation to be wiped out. When these have vanished also, what will you do?

N: You are not a soldier. You do not know what is going on in the heart of a soldier. I grew up on the battlefield and do give a damn for a million lives ...

M: Let us open the doors, sire, open the windows, that the whole of Europe may hear you.

N: Now I see how great a mistake my marriage was. It may cost me my throne, but I shall drag the whole world down with me ... You are not really going to wage war against me?

M: Sire, you are lost. I thought so when I was on my way here, but now I know it.

Napoleon and Metternich, their last discussion, at Dresden, June 26, 1813, in Thiers' History of the Consulate and the Empire of France *(1893).*

We shall not be neutral, let him not flatter himself as to that. Should we remain neutral which is what he really desires, the Allies would be beaten. But after their turn, ours would come—and we should well deserve it ... The Emperor my master has not taken this resolution lightly, for he is a father and loves his daughter. But we prefer everything, even the chance of defeat, to dishonor and slavery.

Metternich, to the French ambassador, before expiration of the armistice, August 10, 1813, Guizot's History.

As liberators of the German fatherland we are respected everywhere, even loved in some places, yet as Prussians we are hated throughout. An indestruc-

tible prejudice prevails against this name. To all Germans, Prussia is something alien. As soon as there is talk about uniting with Prussia, everybody is frightened.

F.A.L. von der Marwitz, to Baron Hardenberg, Prussian state chancellor, letter of summer 1813, A Brandenburg Nobleman *(1908).*

I should write about war and peace? Oh my dear, it is war, wicked, evil war. The emperor and his guard left last Sunday, and since that time the street is always filled with troops—artillery, cavalry, infantry are coming up on the road from Silesia like an eternal procession. We do not know if a battle has taken place, but everybody is extremely tense and God knows what will happen to us. We completely entrust ourselves to fortune and Napoleon's arms ...

E.T.A. Hoffman, German Romantic writer, from Dresden, letter of August 19, 1813, in Koch's Letters of the German Romantics *(1938).*

... we could no longer doubt that it was Seifertshain which went up in flames before our very eyes. Only someone who has met with the same fate ... can quite realize the painful thoughts which overwhelmed me. I ... burst into hot tears. Then a young Prussian, his arm bandaged up, came across the field and asked me solicitously: "Why are you crying, young lady?" I showed him the cause of my tears and he replied, solemnly: "It is true, your fate is a cruel one, but mine ... is worse yet! Today, I have seen my three brothers fall beside me and I could not even assist them in their last hour. I am the last son of my parents and should be their consolation and support but this day has made a cripple out of me also." He showed me the stump of his right arm ... we could only express our deepest sympathies to the unfortunate one and show him the way to Naundorf where he would find a surgeon.

Auguste Vater, of Seifertshain (near Leipzig), an eyewitness to the battle, October 16, 1813, in Schmidt's Reports from the Battle of Leipzig *(n.d.).*

In the course of the afternoon, my father went back to Albrechtshain once more to see what the situation was. Some Russian stragglers had started a little looting, but then had returned some items goodnaturedly which our courageous servant maid took from their hands ... There was no light and after dark the looters took torches from the kitchen and ran through the house ... looking everywhere where they had searched ten times already ...

Vater, October 16, 1813, Schmidt's Reports *(n.d.).*

One half of the night between October 16 and 17 had not yet passed when the grainhouse, with 6,000 wounded, the greatest number one could possibly accommodate, was already overcrowded. Wounded who arrived later simply lay down in the street, exhausted, and on both sides of the New Market, the Grimma Lane all the way to the stock exchange ... the wounded lay so closely together that there was only a very narrow path left for the pedestrians. On Sunday October 17 the sight was truly horrible. The wounded who could still crawl, tried to get away to find accommodations. But the heavy casualties weltered in their own blood and several dead bodies lay in veritable pools of blood. We were not yet used to such horrible sights and our most urgent concern was to remove them and have the streets cleaned. But we had to get used to such degrees of heartlessness from then on ...

Werner, town clerk of Leipzig, the city during the battle, October 16-17, 1813, in Schmidt's Reports *(n.d.).*

Even Napoleon spent the night in town, at the Hotel de Prusse. But even this overpowerful ruler could not change stones into bread, and neither could his terrifying guards and proud courtiers provide it. He and his large staff had to be satisfied with the small quantities scraped together from the various bakeries ... There can hardly be a more convincing proof of the scarcity of bread at Leipzig ...

Werner, Leipzig during the battle, in Schmidt's Reports *(n.d.).*

On October 19 at 10 o'clock Napoleon had left the city and at twelve our troops moved in. Though I did not arrive from the side where the main fighting had taken place, the fields were covered with wounded and dying men. Some wounded had dragged themselves to the ditches along the roads. One could hear the rattling of their weakening voices. In between these groups, Cossacks wandered about the country to find some loot. In the city proper, behind the gate, corpses lay upon corpses ...

Schlegel, to Mme. de Staël, letter of October 29, 1813, in Koch's Letters of the German Romantics *(1938).*

I foresaw the outcome, and that was my agony; my star was setting, the reins slipped from my hands, and I could do nothing about it.

Napoleon, the battle of Leipzig, in his Memoirs ... *as edited by Gourgaud and Montholon (1823-1825).*

Do not believe that I am indifferent to the great ideas of liberty, nation, fatherland. They are in us, are part of our existence and no one can shed them. I have often felt bitter pains thinking of the German nation which in its individuals is so respectable and as a whole so miserable. The German mission, to quote Napoleon, has not yet been completed.

Johann Wolfgang von Goethe, to Heinrich Luden, conversation of November 1813, in Königswald's Prussian Reader *(1966).*

Surely, when we have to drive the enemy from our frontiers, it is not the time to ask me for a constitution. You are not the representatives of a nation, you are merely the deputies sent by the departments. I alone am the representative of the people. After all, what is a throne? Four pieces of gilt wood covered with velvet? No, the throne is a man, and that man is myself. It is I who can save France and not you! If I were to listen to you I would surrender to the enemy more than he is demanding. You shall have peace in three months, or I shall perish.

Napoleon, to the legislature, message of January 1814, in Thiers' History *(1893).*

I do not fear to acknowledge that I have made war too long ... I wished to secure to France the empire of the world. I was mistaken: Those projects were not proportioned to the numerical force of our population. I should have been obliged to put them all under arms, and I now perceive that the advancement of society ... are not compatible with converting an entire people into a nation of soldiers ... Go then, gentlemen, announce to your departments that I am about to conclude a peace, that I shall no longer require the blood of Frenchmen for my enterprises, for myself ... but for France and to maintain the integrity of our frontiers. Tell them that I ask only the means of repelling a foreign foe from our native land. Tell them that I call upon Frenchmen to come to the aid of freedom.

Napoleon, to senators, shortly after his message of January 1814, in Thiers' History *(1893).*

I am pained to see that you have spoken to my wife about the Bourbons and the opposition which might be made by the Emperor of Austria. I beg of you to avoid such conversations. I have no wish to be protected by my wife … Let her live as she has lived … The Emperor of Austria can do nothing because he is weak and led by Metternich who is in the pay of England—that is the secret of the whole … You always write as if the peace depended on me … If the Parisians wish to see the Cossacks, they will have cause to repent.

Napoleon, to his brother Joseph, letter of March 12, 1814, in Guizot's History.

The only opinion I can form is that twenty years have elapsed since the princes of the houses of Bourbon left France; they are as much, and perhaps more unknown there than the princes of any other royal family in Europe; that the allies should agree among themselves to propose to France a sovereign in place of Napoleon, who must be get rid of before Europe can ever enjoy peace; but that it matters little whether it be a prince of Bourbon or of any other royal family.

Duke of Wellington, to Lord Henry de Bathurst, March 1814, in Longford's Wellington *(1969).*

I knew that the empress did not trust me and that, if I had spoken in favor of her departure, she would have stayed. So I spoke in favor of her remaining, in order to make her leave.

Charles Maurice de Talleyrand-Périgord, when the Council of Regents wanted Marie Louise and her son to stay, March 28, 1814, Memoirs *(1891-92).*

It is not my intention to do the least harm to the town of Paris. It is not upon the French nation that we are waging war, but upon Napoleon.

Czar Alexander, March 30, 1814, Guizot's History.

I forgive Talleyrand, for I mistreated him. He would not have remained in France if I had triumphed. The Bourbons will do well to use him. He loves money and intrigues, but he is capable. I have always liked him … My enterprises flourished while Talleyrand was in charge … He is better acquainted with France and Europe than anybody else. He can persuade the émigrés without irritating the new people …

Napoleon, on Talleyrand, the day of his abdication, April 11, 1814, in Orieux's Talleyrand *(1970).*

Soldiers, I bid you farewell. For twenty years we have been together, your conduct has left me nothing to desire. I have always found you on the road to glory … Be faithful, then, to your new king, be obedient to your new commanders and do not desert your beloved country. Do not lament my lot. I shall be happy when I know that you are so … if I consent to live it is still to promote your glory. I shall write down the great things we have achieved. I cannot embrace you all, but I embrace your general. Come, General Petit, that I may press you to my heart. Bring me the Eagle [the Guard's standard] that I may embrace it also … Adieu, my children. The best wishes of my heart shall always be with you. Do not forget me!

Napoleon, to the Old Guard, at Fontainebleau, parting words of April 20, 1814, in the Durants' The Age of Napoleon *(1975).*

The entire human race indicts you and calls for revenge in the name of religion, liberty and morality. Where have you not spread despair … is there a family so obscure that has escaped your devastations? You have murdered the sons of Spain, Italy, Austria, Germany … The judgment of the world pronounces you the greatest criminal that ever appeared on earth … You wanted to reign by Attila's sword and Nero's maxims in the center of civilization, in the age of enlightenment. Surrender now your iron scepter and descend from the mountain of ruins on which you have throned. We are casting you out …

Francois René, Vicomte de Chateaubriand, in "De Buonaparte et de Bourbons" (1814), in C.'s Memoirs *(1849-50).*

The people have achieved what was asked of them; they are waiting that now will be done what was … promised at the time of danger. Germany wants a constitution which will closely bind together prince and people … this is the only reward for which they have fought.

Joseph von Goerres, German political writer, in Der Rheinische Merkur *(Cologne), August 8, 1814.*

The defeated emperor had to leave the world stage. That is the destiny of defeated usurpers. But once France was overrun, the odds against her were very heavy … For a number of years I had felt it [to look for a successor] my right to do … Neither was I betraying Napoleon nor conducting a conspiracy against him, though he had claimed several times that I was. I have conspired only when the majority of France was my accomplice.

Talleyrand, 1814, in his Memoirs *(1891-92).*

20. Napoleon: From Elba to St. Helena: May 1814 to May 1821

THE HISTORICAL CONTEXT

When he landed at Portoferraio, Elba, Napoleon was greeted with wild acclaim by the same population who only a week earlier had hanged him in effigy and declared him a man madly in love with war. His welcome was based in part on the belief that he was bringing millions to spend on the island. Actually, he brought with him about 3,500,000 francs in gold and silver, which he used to surround himself with all the trappings of majesty—a royal guard, court servants, musicians and uniforms. Besides the 400 members of the Old Guard, volunteers joined him from Italy, until eventually he had some 1,600 men in arms around him.

Without his promised pension, which never was paid, he could not maintain such pomp for long. Moreover, he had reason to fear for his life; his brother Joseph warned him of assassination plans and Talleyrand repeatedly had uttered: "that man on the island of Elba must be got rid of." It is also clear that he soon became bored with ruling a tiny island of 86 square miles and 12,000 inhabitants. By February of 1815, when the congress in Vienna was nearing its end and the Allied troops were beginning to go home, he had decided that it was the time to act. On March 1, Napoleon landed in the Gulf of Juan, near Cannes, with 1,000 men.

Prussian Marshal Prince Blücher

Crossing from Elba to southern France was almost as dangerous as his voyage to Egypt had been. His tiny flotilla could easily have been discovered and captured. But again his luck held, and continued to hold during the 20-day march from his landing in the Gulf of Juan to his entry into Paris. These were probably the most dramatic days in his eventful life. He later said that he had never been so happy. In Grenoble,

Arthur Wellesley, Duke of Wellington

his life hung on a thread: If just one of the hundreds of royal soldiers ordered to fire on him had obeyed, there would have been no Waterloo.

In spite of his triumph over the Bourbons, things could not be as they had been before. After Louis XVIII had offered a liberal constitution to the French, Napoleon could do no less, which hampered his style. But it is remarkable how many of his old adversaries now offered their support, including: Benjamin Constant; Lazare Nicolas Carnot, the old revolutionary whom he made minister of the interior; his brother Lucien, who had opposed him since his consular days; and even Joseph Fouché, the feared minister of police, probably appointed just to keep him under surveillance. Fouché, always a man of questionable morality, is supposed to have predicted, while serving the emperor again, that his second regime could not last longer than three months.

Constant's constitution was accepted by a huge majority of the voters, and many of his old Jacobin enemies now supported the emperor, but there remained a great deal of opposition in the country, particularly in the south. The army, of course, was for Napoleon, and most of his former marshals were still, or again, with him.

He later regretted that he had wasted so much precious time on the constitution, since he was resolved to dissolve the parliaments as soon as he had been victorious in the field. At any rate, the parliaments were not as obedient as he had hoped for. The Comte Jean Denis Lanjuinais, his declared enemy, was elected president, and the chamber convened because the Marquis Marie Joseph Lafayette, whom Napoleon had liberated from the Austrians in 1797 and who had come out of retirement, insisted on a meeting before the emperor's departure to the battlefield. Still, Napoleon won over both chambers when he addressed their combined session in a very conciliatory and modest manner.

He left Paris on June 12 at 3 o'clock in the morning for his last campaign. By advancing swiftly, he succeeded in keeping the Russians away from the ensuing battles. Against the 213,000 men led by Arthur Wellesley, Duke of Wellington, and Gebhard Leberecht von Blücher, he had only about 125,000 men at his disposal. But Wellington had to cope with the inexperience of many of his troops and the fact that large contingents were Dutch, Belgian and German and did not understand their English commanders.

Following his old principle of keeping his enemies separate, Napoleon attacked Blücher's army at Ligny, and a desperate battle followed. Although he did not get the support he expected from his General Drouet D'Erlon, who instead tried to help Marshal Michel Ney against Wellington, Napoleon finally beat Blücher by reluctantly committing his Old

Guard. His soldiers were exhausted, he himself ill, and on the following day, June 17th, heavy rains prevented his artillery from moving against Wellington. General Emanuel De Grouchy, directed to pursue Blücher but content with having defeated a small part of the Prussian force, rested that day at Wavre. That day of rest may have decided the outcome of the battle of Waterloo, which, in turn, decided the fate not only of Napoleon but also of all Europe for several decades to come. Blücher and his chief of staff, August Neidhardt von Gneisenau, on the other hand, managed to move their slightly groggy army up to Waterloo to arrive just when Wellington's stubborn English and Scot troops began to retreat under Napoleon's last, desperate attack, into which he threw even his beloved Old Guard. Blücher's arrival broke the French. Wellington lost 15,000 men, and Blücher 7,000, while Napoleon lost 25,000 dead and wounded and about 8,000 prisoners.

He and France knew he was finished, and his demand for dictatorial powers found almost no response in Paris, Lucien and Carnot being two of the few exceptions. What followed seemed inevitable: his second abdication and surrender to the British, his transfer as a prisoner of war to St. Helena, and the second Peace Treaty of Paris, in which France was dealt with much more harshly than in the first.

Some historians have seen in these "Hundred Days"—from March 1, Napoleon's landing near Cannes, to July 7, the second occupation of Paris—a meaningless, hopeless postlude, asserting that the fate of the Napoleonic Empire had been decided at Leipzig in October of 1813. But after that decisive defeat he repeatedly came close to gaining the upper hand again, and while it is impossible to imagine him continuing his regime for any great length of time against a Europe united in its determination to get rid of him, he did actually come very close to winning at Waterloo. Those who believe that there is logic in history will point out that Napoleon had to lose because he stood in the way of the coming age of the nation-state. All we can say with certainty is that, after his downfall, Europe was blessed with several decades of peace, after 23 years of incessant warfare.

Napoleon surrenders to the English on board the Bellerophon, *July 15, 1815.*

Meanwhile, during the six years he spent in St. Helena, Napoleon's legend was established in his memoirs, in which he presented himself as the apostle of the revolution, the liberator and martyr of democracy. His death in 1821 passed almost unnoticed, but the legend lived on and is still alive today.

CHRONICLE OF EVENTS

1814:   *May 4:* Napoleon lands on Elba. Marie Louise is prevented by her father from joining him. Only his mother, his sister Pauline, and his former Polish mistress Marie Walewska, with his little son, visit him. He sets out to improve conditions on the island, building roads, a hospice and the theater. He learns that he is still considered dangerous in Vienna and of plans, furthered by Talleyrand, to remove him to the island of St. Helena. He also learns of the discord of the Allies at the congress and the unpopularity of the Bourbons. The pension promised him is held back by Louis XVIII.

May 29: Josephine dies at Malmaison.

1815:   *March 1:* Napoleon lands with about 1,000 men in the Gulf of Juan, near Cannes. He marches via Digne and Sisteron toward Grenoble, pursued by André Masséna, who is loyal to the king, coming up from Marseilles, and the Comte d'Artois, marching up from Lyons.

March 6: At Grenoble, troops disobey orders to fire and go over to Napoleon's side. D'Artois is forced to leave Lyons.

March 13: The Allies in Vienna ban Napoleon and declare him liable to public prosecution. Napoleon leaves Lyons for Macon. As more and more troops go over to Napoleon, the king relies on Ney, who has declared he will bring Bonaparte to Paris "in an iron cage," but who also switches sides after receiving Napoleon's note to meet him at Chalons.

March 18: Napoleon arrives at Auxerre.

March 19: Louis XVIII and his bodyguards and personnel leave the Tuileries, on their way to Ghent.

March 20: Napoleon enters Paris in triumph.

March 25: New alliance of Austria, England, Russia and Prussia formed against Napoleon. Over a million men begin assembling in Belgium under the command of Wellington and Blücher. Sweden keeps away, while undertaking the conquest of Norway. Napoleon pledges a liberal constitution, which is drawn up by Benjamin Constant.

The execution of Murat, October 13, 1815

The battle of Waterloo

May 3: Joachim Murat, king of Naples, who again sides with Napoleon, is defeated by the Austrians at Tolentino.

May: Eighty Bonapartists, 30 to 40 Jacobins and around 500 Liberals elected to the Chamber of Representatives.

May 22: The Austrians take Naples, and Murat flees to France; the Bourbon Ferdinand is restored to his throne.

June 1: Great imperial festival is held at the Champ de Mars. Napoleon appears in his coronation robes.

June 15: Napoleon crosses the Belgian frontier and attacks the Prussians at Charleroi.

June 16: Wellington occupies Quatre-Bras before Ney arrives. Napoleon attacks Blücher at Ligny and beats him back. Blücher is wounded. Grouchy is sent to pursue the Prussian army.

June 18: At the battle of Waterloo (Belle Alliance), Napoleon attacks Wellington's army. Grouchy misunderstands new orders and lets Blücher slip away; Blücher arrives just in time to decide the battle for the Allies. The French army is pursued by Gneisenau, Blücher's chief of staff.

June 21: Napoleon, back in Paris, demands dictatorial powers and is supported by his brother Lucien, but the Chamber of Representatives is unwilling to go along. Marshal Louis Nicolas Davout, his minister of war, rejects his suggestion to send grenadiers into the Chamber.

June 22: Napoleon abdicates for the second time, proclaiming his son to be Emperor Napoleon II.

June 25: He leaves for Malmaison and travels from there to Rochefort. He rejects the possibility of going to America.

July 7: Paris is occupied by the Allies, and Louis XVIII returns to the throne.

July 15: Napoleon surrenders to Captain Maitland on board the British warship *Bellerophon*. By unanimous decision of the Allies, he is treated as a prisoner of war and exiled to St. Helena, a British island dependency in the South Atlantic, 1,200 miles off the African coast.

August 8: Off the English coast, he is transferred to H.M.S. *Northumberland*, which arrives at St. Helena on October 15.

October 13: Murat lands in Calabria to recover his kingdom but is captured and shot.

November 20: In the Second Peace of Paris, France gives up several fortresses and part of Savoy; is restricted to the boundaries of 1790; and is ordered to pay 700,000,000 francs for war expenses. Art treasures taken by the French are to be returned to their owners. Seventeen fortresses are to be garrisoned by Allied troops for up to five years.

December 7: Marshal Ney is shot as a traitor.

1816:   *April:* Sir Hudson Lowe assumes charge at St. Helena.

June: Napoleon begins dictation of his memoirs to his aides, Gaspard Gourgaud and Charles Jean Tristan Montholon.

1821:   *May 5:* Napoleon dies of cancer of the stomach. A recent claim that he died of arsenic poisoning, due indirectly to arsenic contained in the wallpaper of his house in St. Helena, has not been generally accepted.

EYEWITNESS TESTIMONY

Recalled by the love of our people to the throne of our fathers, enlightened by the misfortunes of the nation which we are destined to govern, our first thought is to invite that mutual confidence so necessary to our power and their happiness ... Resolved to adapt a liberal Constitution ... The representative government will be maintained as it at present exists, consisting of two bodies ... Taxation will be by free consent, public and personal liberty secured, the liberty of the press respected ... the liberty of religious worship guaranteed. Property will be inviolable and sacred; the sale of what belonged to the nation irrevocable ... The public debt will be guaranteed ... the Legion of Honor shall be maintained ... every Frenchman will be eligible for civil and military service. Finally, no person will have need to be anxious on account of his opinions or his votes.

Louis XVIII, proclamation of May 3, 1814,
Guizot's History of France.

Napoleon on the beach at St. Helena

England: Napoleon's fate is sealed; he will be exiled to St. Lucia ... the climate there will, within a short time, free the world from the Corsican monster.

France: It was a great mistake to let Bonaparte live. As long as he is not lying six feet under the ground, one cannot quiet down. Banishment is a good thing, but the grave is better.

Public opinion (as reported by Houssaye),
Napoleon at Elba, 1814, Napoleon's First
and Second Abdications *(1905).*

I shall live here like a justice of the peace ... The emperor is dead; I am nothing, and I am thinking of nothing any more than my little island, nothing occupies me, except my family, my little house, my cows and mules.

Napoleon, upon his arrival at Elba, May
1814, in Houssaye's Abdication *(1905).*

They want to kill me—so be it!—I am a soldier ... I myself will bare my breast. But I do not want to be sent away.

Napoleon to Sir Neil Campbell, English
delegate, Elba, 1814, in Mereschkowskij's
Napoleon *(1928).*

Let me be a mother for a while, and then I shall give you my opinion ... Go on, my son and fulfill your destiny.

Letizia Bonaparte, to her son Napoleon, visit-
ing Elba in February 1815 and learning of his
plans, in Thiers' History of the Consulate
and the Empire of France *(1893).*

They plotted openly, even at the corners of the streets, and everybody, except perhaps the ministers, knew what was going on.

Anne Jean Savary, Duke of Rovigo, France in
1814, in Guizot's History.

As the advocate of collective demands against the sacred rights of the individuum, Napoleon changed right into wrong, wrong into right ... Bonaparte's appearance was necessary. The good he caused is new, the evil he did is in its essence anything but new.

*Johann H. Pestalozzi, Swiss educational
reformer, Ein Wort der Zeit (1814).*

Soldiers! You have not been conquered! Two men from your ranks betrayed our laurels, their prince, their benefactor ... Shall we suffer them to inherit the fruit of our glorious labors, to take possession of our honors and property, to slander our glory? ... In my exile I heard your voices, and I have come through all obstacles and dangers. Your general, summoned to the throne by the prayer of the people and raised upon your shields, is now restored to you; come and join him. Tear down those colors which were proscribed by the nation and around which for 25 years all the enemies of France have rallied. Display the tricolor ... Get back those eagles which you had at Ulm, Austerlitz, Iena, Eylau ...

Do you think that that handful of Frenchmen, today so arrogant, could bear the sight of them? They would return whence they came ... Come, soldiers! Stand by the banners of your chief. Victory will march at full speed. The eagle, with the national colors, will fly from steeple to steeple, even to the towers of Notre Dame ...

*Napoleon, to the army, after landing in
France, proclamation of March 1, 1815,
Guizot's History.*

We were beginning to be happy and tranquil. Now you will trouble everything.

*Mayor of Antibes, to Napoleon, after
Bonaparte's landing on March 1, 1815, in
Gourgaud and Montholon's Memoirs ...
(1823-1825).*

Officers, sub-officers, soldiers! The cause of the Bourbons is lost forever. The legitimate dynasty which

The Allies in Paris

Napoleon taking leave of his troops at Fontainebleau

France has adopted is about to remount the throne. To the emperor Napoleon, our sovereign, belongs alone the right to rule over our beautiful country. Whether the Bourbon nobility choose to return to exile or consent to live among us, what does it matter to us? The times are gone when the people were governed by suppressing their rights. Liberty triumphs in the end, and Napoleon, our august emperor, comes to confirm it. Soldiers, I have often led you to victory. Now I would escort you to join this immortal legion which the Emperor Napoleon conducts to Paris, and which in a few days will reach the capital …

Marshal Michel Ney, to his troops, at Lons-le-
Sonier, March 14, 1815, in Guizot's History.

The Tiger has broken out of his den/The ogre has been three days at sea,/The Wretch has landed at Fréjus/The Buzzard has reached Antibes,/The Invader has arrived in Grenoble,/The General has entered Lyons,/Napoleon slept at Fontainebleau last night/The Emperor will proceed to the Tuileries today/His Imperial Majesty will address his loyal subjects tomorrow.

Paris broadsheets, comments on Napoleon's
march from the Riviera coast to Paris,
throughout March 1815, in Longford's Wellington *(1969).*

I fear nothing for myself, but I fear for France. He who comes among us to light the torch of civil war, brings us also the plague of foreign war. He comes to place our country once more under his iron yoke. He comes to destroy this constitutional charter I have given you—my best title in the eyes of posterity—this charter which all French cherish—may it be our sacred standard!

Louis XVIII, when leaving Paris on March
19, 1815, Guizot's History.

Well, he is back again! It is no illusion, liberty is now lost. Poor France, after so much suffering, and despite vows so ardent and unanimous! Since he prevails, I go away from this country. Ah! if the Bourbons had the power of will, if they had listened to us! But no matter: I love them, I sorrow for them. They are honest men, and they alone are able to give us liberty.

Mme. Germaine de Staël, Napoleon's return,
Selection of Texts *(1974).*

There are two kinds of loyalty, that of dogs and that of cats. You, gentlemen, have that of cats who never leave the house.

Napoleon, to the Comte de Ségur and others
who had reassured him of their loyalty, in
Paris, in Ségur's Memoirs *(1927).*

… three months ago circumstances and the confidence of the people reinvested me with an unlimited power. Today the most urgent desire of my heart is fulfilled: I am about to begin the constitutional monarchy … I aspire to see France enjoy all the liberty possible …—I say possible because anarchy always brings back absolute government. A formidable coalition of kings have a spiteful hatred against our independence, and their armies are arriving on our frontiers …

Napoleon, to the newly instituted chambers,
June 7, 1815.

The excitement of the troops is not that of patriotism, or enthusiasm, but an actual madness to fight for the emperor and against his enemies; no one thinks there is any question about the triumph of France.

General Maximilien Sébastien Foy (France),
writing in his military journal in Belgium,
June 14, 1815, Guizot's History.

We fought a desperate battle on Friday [at Quatre-Bras] in which I was successful though I had but very few troops. The Prussians were very roughly handled and retured last night which obliged me to do the same to this place yesterday. The course of the operations may oblige me to uncover Bruxelles for a moment … for which reason I recommend that you and your family should be prepared to move to Antwerp at a moment's notice.

Duke of Wellington, to Lady Frances
Webster, from Waterloo, letter of 3 A.M.,
June 18, 1815, in Longford's Wellington
(1969).

Pursue the Prussians with only one detachment, if they are on the road to the Rhine. Do the same if they are marching upon Brussels. If they are posted in front of the forest of Soignies, keep them together and occupy them while you detach a division to take the left wing of the English in rear.

Napoleon, to General Grouchy, June 17,
1815, Guizot's History.

May the pens of the diplomats not spoil what the people have achieved with such great effort!

Marshal Blücher, toast offered after the vic-
tory at Waterloo, in Königswald's Prussian
Reader *(1966).*

That campaign was begun by Buonaparte himself. He had not, for this time at least, to blame the elements. He had not to accuse the seasons, nor the defection of those from whom he expected support … He had the choice of the time, of the place and of the adversary with whom he might be desirous to contend. Under these circumstances he had begun the battle, and he failed. His attacks were repulsed; the order was reversed—he was attacked in his turn. His boasted genius shrunk under the ascendency of the mightier genius of him [Wellington] whom he was opposed and the result was the complete rout and overthrow of the French army.

Lord Bathurst, to the House of Lords, speech
of June 23, 1815.

The duke of Wellington has greatly raised the military character of England. In India his conduct obtained for him the approbation of his country; he had been praised as the saviour of Spain and Portugal. One thing only was wanting to complete his own glory and that of his country—a triumph over him who was said to have conquered every other general to whom he had been opposed. That object was gained. It was reserved for his last triumph to supply all that was wanting to the consummation of his glory. Many had heretofore doubted what would be the result of a contest in which he and Buonaparte fought hand to hand; that doubt was gone forever. We now saw renewed the splendid days of Crécy and Agincourt, and this we owed to the duke of Wellington …

Sir T. Acland, to the House of Commons,
speech of June 23, 1815.

Prince, you are calumniating the nation. It is not for having abandoned Napoleon that posterity will be able to reproach France, but, alas, for having followed him too far. 600,000 Frenchmen sleep by the banks of the Ebro and the Tagus. Can you tell us how many have fallen on the banks of the Danube, the Elbe, the Niemen and the Moskawa? Alas! Had she been less constant, France would have saved 2 millions of her children. She would have saved your brother, your family, us all, from the abyss into which we are being dragged today, without knowing if we shall be able to extricate from it.

Marquis de Lafayette, to Lucien Bonaparte, in the chambers and in reply to a defense of Napoleon, June 21, 1815, in Lafayette's Mémoires publiés par sa famille *(1837).*

Our paper of today will satisfy the sceptics, for such there were beginning to be, as to the capture of that bloody miscreant who has so long tortured Europe, Napoleon Buonaparte … The cruelty of this person is written in characters of blood in almost every country in Europe and in the contiguous angles of Africa and Asia which he visited … this wretch has really lived in the commission of every crime so long that he has lost all sight and knowledge of the difference that exists between good and evil, and hardly knows when he is doing wrong, except he be taught by proper chastisement. A creature who ought to be greeted with a gallows as soon as he lands …

The London Times, Napoleon's surrender, June 25, 1815.

After being aimed at both by the factions which divide my country and by the enmity of the great powers of Europe, I have finished my political career and now come, like Themistocles, to sit down by the hearth of the English people. I place myself under the protection of their laws which I claim from your Royal Highness as the most powerful, the most steadfast and the most generous of my enemies.

Napoleon, to the Prince Regent of England, letter of July 13, 1815.

His manners were extremely pleasing and affable. He joined in every conversation, related numerous anecdotes and endeavoured in every way to promote good humour. He admitted his attendants to great familiarity … though they generally treated him with

much respect. He possessed, to a wonderful degree, a facility in making a favorable impression upon those with whom he entered into conversation.

Captain Maitland, HMS Bellerophon, *after Napoleon's surrender to his ship, July 15, 1815, in Cheney's* Readings in English History *(1908).*

Farewell to thee, France! when thy diadem crowned me, I made thee the gem and the wonder of earth,-/But thy weakness decrees I should leave you as I found thee,/Decayed in thy glory and sunk in thy worth …

Farewell to thee, France!- but when Liberty rallies/Once more in thy regions, remember me then,-/The violet still grows in the depth of thy valleys;/Though wither'd, thy tear will unfold it again.

George Gordon, Lord Byron, "Napoleon's Farewell," July 25, 1815, in Byron's Complete Poetical Works *(1905).*

Oh, bloody and most bootless Waterloo!/Which proves how fools may have their fortune too,/Won half by blunder, half by treachery:/Oh, dull Saint Helen! with thy gaoler nigh-/Hear, hear Prometheus from his rock appeal/To earth, air, ocean, all that felt or feel/His power and glory, all who yet shall hear/A name eternal as the rolling year.

Byron, "The Age of Bronze" (April 1, 1823).

Is it not touching to see the master of kings so far reduced at last that he has to wear a turned uniform? And yet, if we consider that this was the end of a man who trampled on the life and fortune of millions the fate he met was still a very mild one; a nemesis which cannot help to be a little chivalrous, in view of the hero's greatness. Napoleon shows us how dangerous it is to rise into the absolute and to sacrifice everything to the realization of an idea.

Johann Wolfgang von Goethe, to J.P. Eckermann, in Eckermann's Conversations with Goethe *(1902).*

I closed the gulf of anarchy and cleared the chaos. I have purified the revolution, dignified nations and enthroned kings. I incited all kinds of ambitions, rewarded all merits and extended the limits of glory … The dictatorship was absolutely necessary … Will I be blamed for having been too fond of warfare? It could be demonstrated that I always received the first attack …

will I be accused of too much ambition? Undoubtedly, I must be allowed to have possessed this passion but ... it was of the highest and noblest kind—that to establish and consecrate the empire of reason and the full exercise and enjoyment of all the human faculties.

Napoleon, to Comte Emanuel de Las Cases, on St. Helena, in Las Cases' Memorial of St. Helena *(1823).*

When I am gone, there will be a reaction in my favor ... It is my martyrdom that will restore the crown of France to my dynasty ... Ere twenty years have elapsed, when I am dead and buried, you will see another revolution in France.

Napoleon, to Barry Edward O'Meara, on St. Helena, in O'Meara's Napoleon in Exile *(1822).*

21. The Congress of Vienna: September 1814 to November 1815

THE HISTORICAL CONTEXT

The Congress of Vienna, whose work was all but concluded before Napoleon was finally vanquished at Waterloo, saw an assembly of monarchs and prominent statesmen and politicians such as the world had never seen, and would not see again until the Versailles Conference of 1919. But in contrast to the later Versailles, no serious attempt was made by the victors to reduce the defeated power to a second-rate status. While the Big Four (Russia, England, Austria and Prussia) dominated the Congress, France was soon considered a near-equal. This relatively benevolent attitude toward the vanquished was thanks, in part, to Charles Maurice de Talleyrand's skillful tactics and in part to Prince Clemens Metternich's principle of "legitimacy." He used this to justify the suppression of all political newcomers and the reversal of all the changes wrought by the French Revolution. The Bourbons were certainly considered the most legitimate of all monarchs represented at Vienna.

King Louis XVIII's second return

The dominating personality was Czar Alexander I, and Russia certainly emerged as the greatest power on the continent and would remain so until the Crimean War, 40 years later. Russia made heavy inroads into central Europe, and the Napoleon-created Duchy of Warsaw became a Russian dependency. England, on the other hand, no longer had any rivals at sea and it had acquired, during the Napoleonic era, Malta, Helgoland, Ceylon and the Cape Province. Austria retreated from the Rhine and the Netherlands and moved the empire's center of gravity to Italy and the southeast of Europe. Compared to these three powers, Prussia was still the smallest. Moreover, she had not borne the brunt of

Napoleonic aggression as long as the others and had put up the least resistance. She never recovered what she had lost in the East, but gained considerable territory in the Rhineland where a thoroughly Catholic population had been quite happy under French rule; they would never quite integrate with the territorially unconnected, less easygoing Protestants of old Prussia, ruled by the sober, Calvinist Hohenzollern dynasty.

The two problem children of continental Europe were Germany and Italy. The Germanic Confederation, which replaced the old Empire, was dominated by Austria whose chief interest was to maintain the status quo and to prevent rival Prussia from gaining further power. This new confederation was, to say the least, a rickety structure. On the one hand, large parts of Austria and Prussia did not become part of the Confederation—the Polish, Hungarian and Italian territories of Austria and the Prussian provinces of East and West Prussia and of Posen. On the other hand, members of the Confederation included the king of England (as king of Hanover), the king of Denmark (as the duke of Holstein and Lauenburg), and the king of the Netherlands (as the archduke of Luxemburg).

Italy, where a strong movement for national unity also had arisen, fared even worse, and Metternich rightly if condescendingly referred to her as "a geographical term only." Austria dominated the north with her provinces of Lombardy and Venetia; the Papal States were restored, through the skill of the Papal Delegate Ercole Consalvi; all the dynasties of central Italy and Sardinia were reestablished; and all of the rulers of those states bitterly opposed unification of the country. It would take another 45 years and the interference of another Napoleon to bring about the unification of Italy. Only the Swiss obtained approximately what the population wanted. The revolutionary and Napoleonic interferences with her independence were the last ones the country had to suffer; her neutrality, now guaranteed by the great powers, was respected, even during the two world wars.

All in all, it would be fair to say that in Vienna there was no attempt to restore the pre-Napoleonic Europe. Never in history has there been any genuine restoration of a bygone age, for history cannot stop or go back. Rather, Napoleonic Europe was divided up among the powers.

In all that was decided at the great Congress, the people of the various countries were shuffled around by the great powers but were never consulted. Still, the idea of the sovereignty of the people, born with the French Revolution, lived on. After the Great Revolution and the age of Napoleon, a system created without regard to the nationality or the views of the population could not last. The only reason that major upheavals didn't come sooner than they did was that, after so many years of revolution and war, the great majority of the European population wanted peace and quiet. Nevertheless, the system instituted in Vienna and watched over by the Holy Alliance and the Quadruple Alliance began to fall apart soon enough in France, where the reaction had been the most rigorous, in 1830; in many European countries, in 1848-49; in Russia, in 1855; in Italy, in 1861. In England, the country least touched by the French Revolution, the industrial age had already begun, and on the continent the liberal ideas of 1789 took on new forms and a new meaning in the age of bourgeois capitalism and imperialism.

CHRONICLE OF EVENTS

1814:   *September:* The Congress of Vienna convenes. Most European rulers attend in person, joined by a large number of lesser potentates and ministers. The chief negotiators are for Great Britain, Robert Stewart Castlereagh and the Duke of Wellington; for Russia, the Czar and his advisers, among them Karl Freiherr vom Stein; for France, Talleyrand; for Austria, Metternich; for Prussia, Karl August von Hardenberg, Stein's successor, and Wilhelm von Humboldt. The main decisions are made by the four great powers of the Alliance; the lesser members—Sweden, Spain and Portugal—are only occasionally consulted. The Congress never convenes in its entirety.

1815:   *January:* There is critical dispute and deadlock between the Allies over the fate of Poland and Saxony, with Russia and Prussia opposing England and Austria. Talleyrand mediates and improves France's position by supporting the anti-Russian side.

March: The negotiations are interrupted by Napoleon's return from Elba.

June 8: All agreements are combined in the Act of the Congress. The Germanic Confederation (Deutscher Bund) is created as the successor of the old Holy Roman Empire. It is a loose confederacy dominated by Austria in which all liberal and German-nationalistic movements are suppressed. Only 39 states and four free cities become members; all others remain subordinate. A kingdom of the Netherlands is formed, including the Austrian Netherlands (Belgium) and the Republic of Holland. England returns most of the former Dutch colonies, except for the Cape of Good Hope and Ceylon. Austria receives Lombardy and Venetia, the Illyrian provinces, Galicia and the Tyrol. Prussia receives part of the Duchy of Warsaw (Posen), Swedish Pomerania and a large part of Saxony and Westphalia. Most of the Grand Duchy of Warsaw is given to Russia and is made a Polish kingdom, the Russian czar being its king. Alexander grants Poland a rather liberal constitution; Cracow is made a free state under the protection of Russia, Prussia and Austria. England retains Malta and some

Napoleon arrives on Elba.

Wellington is introduced to the statesmen at the Congress of Vienna.

French and Dutch colonies. Sweden retains Norway, and Denmark is indemnified with Lauenburg. Switzerland is restored as an independent confederacy of 22 cantons, including Geneva, Wallis and Neuchatel. The legitimate dynasties in Spain, Tuscany, Modena, Sardinia (including Genoa) and in the Papal States are restored; also in Naples, later in the year.

July-August: After Louis XVIII's return, the fanatical royalists start a "White Terror" against Bonapartists, revolutionaries and especially the regicides of 1793. The ultraroyalists obtain a large majority in the parliament and are opposed by the prime minister, the Duke Armand Manuel de Richelieu.

September 26: The Holy Alliance is founded and signed by the rulers of Russia, Austria and Prussia and eventually by all other European rulers, except the English king, the Pope and the Turkish sultan. The Alliance pronounces the upholding of Christian principles as its goal but is soon suspected to be an "alliance" against the liberties of the people.

November: England assumes a protectorate over the Ionian Islands.

November 20: The Quadruple Alliance among England, Russia, Austria and Prussia is renewed in the Treaty of Paris. They pledge to support each other in the event of a violation of the treaty by each providing 60,000 troops. Future meetings to carry out the provisions of the treaty are arranged. This alliance, later to be joined by France, was responsible for the reactionary policies pursued by the great powers in the following decades. In popular opinion, however, those policies were identified with the Holy Alliance, which became a symbol of Metternich policy—a policy of implacable opposition to any progress or any change in the balances achieved in the international treaties of 1815.

EYEWITNESS TESTIMONY

For Russia: The duchy of Warsaw. In the worst case, I agree to yielding only Posen up to a line drawn between Thorn and Peysern ... This is just because my subjects should be compensated for all their sacrifices, and that a military border should protect them from any future invasion.

Czar Alexander, personal notes upon entering Vienna, September 25, 1814, in Troyat's Alexander I *(1980).*

Emperor Alexander is simple, noble, splendid and polite. His penchant for women is very pronounced ... The king of Prussia always looks like resentment and fury ... The king of Bavaria looks like a rude, bad-tempered coachman ... The old Duke of Weimar keeps on living his free and easy life as he always did ... Among the diplomats, Talleyrand is the most important though he stays in the background with his increasing indolence, and possibly also out of principle. As a consequence, no end for the congress is in sight, due to the illiberal principles and inflexibility of the minds ... It will probably come to an end somehow by some exterior event which will take care of those things that reason cannot master.

Johann, Count von Nostitz, Prussian, then Russian diplomat, at the Congress of Vienna, Diary of the General Count von Nostitz *(1908).*

Have I understood correctly? Allies? Against whom? No longer against Napoleon: He is on the island of Elba. No longer against France: we are at peace. Or against the king of France, for he is a guarantor of the peace.

King Louis XVIII fleeing the Tuileries.

Caricature of Napoleon's return from Elba

Gentlemen, let us speak frankly. If there are still allied powers, then I do not belong here ...

Charles Maurice de Talleyrand-Périgord, to Metternich and Nesselrode, after their use of the expression "allied powers," Vienna, end of September 1814, in Orieux's Talleyrand *(1970).*

All that Metternich is interested in is the arrangement of entertainments and Tableaux vivants for the court. He thinks nothing of keeping a number of ambassadors waiting while watching his daughter dance and chatting with the ladies amiably. To him, only trifles are serious; serious business he treats as trifles.

Wilhelm von Humboldt, to his wife, from Vienna, letter of September 1814, in Grunwald's Life of Metternich *(1938).*

Your Prussians are passionately fond of Bonaparte's doctrine of usurpation. They detest only its successful applications. They are dreadful, especially M. de Humboldt ... They intend to destroy Saxony as if it were their

right, as if conquest alone conferred sovereignty. I protest all such notions.

Talleyrand, to duchess of Courland, letter of October 1814, in Orieux's Talleyrand *(1970).*

I believed that France owed me something. You are always talking about principles. But your public law does not mean anything to me. I do not know what it is. What do you think all your old documents and treaties mean to me? ... The king of Prussia will be king of Prussia and of Saxony, and I shall be emperor of Russia and king of Poland. The degree to which France will support me on these two points will be the measure of the degree to which I myself will support her on everything which may be of interest to her.

Czar Alexander, to Talleyrand, Vienna, October 1814, in Orieux's Talleyrand *(1970).*

"I shall keep what I occupy," said the Czar. "Your Majesty surely cannot wish to keep that which is not yours." "I am in agreement with the great powers." "I do not know whether your Majesty considers France one of those powers." "Yes, of course I do. But if you would not have each one pursue his own expedients, then what are you after?" "I rank legality before expedients." "Europe's expedients are legal." "This is not your language, Sire; it is unlike you and denies your true feelings." Then I turned toward the wall near which I stood, leaned my head against it and pounding on the paneling, moaned: "Europe! Europe! Poor Europe! Shall it be said that you destroyed her?" "There will be war before I give up what I occupy," the barbarian thundered ...

Talleyrand, a conversation with Czar
Alexander about Poland, November 1814, in
Orieux's Talleyrand *(1970).*

We learn from high sources a project is made,/How Vienna's grand Congress the Christmas will spend./Since public affairs have so long been delayed/They may very well wait till the holidays end.

Morning Chronicle *(London), in December*
1814.

The way public affairs are going is discouraging, not because, as in the past, heavy and terrifying clouds are hanging over our heads, but because almost all the public figures are mediocre and quite incapable.

Friedrich Gentz, diary entry at end of Decem-
ber 1814, in Königswald's Prussian Reader
(1966).

Not only does France no longer stand alone in Europe, but your Majesty has already a federation system such as it seemed that fifty years of negotiation could not have provided for her. France is in concert with two of the greatest powers and three states of the second order, and she will soon be in concert with all the states which are guided by other than revolutionary principles and maxims. Your Majesty will be in reality the head and the soul of that union ... So great and happy a change is only to be attributed to that special favor of Providence which was so visibly marked by the restoration of your Majesty.

Talleyrand, to Louis XVIII, letter of January
4, 1815, Memoirs *(1891-92).*

It was quite strange; I have contributed almost nothing to the general conversation. Metternich and Talleyrand were performing in their usual manner, while I felt, more than ever before, the futility of human endeavours, the shortcomings of men who are holding the destiny of the world in their hands ... The fine sounding inanities of these gentlemen shrouded my mind in a cloud of unreality.

Gentz, after hosting a dinner party, diary
entry of January 12, 1815, in Königswald's
Prussian Reader *(1966).*

The ceremony was in no way lacking, nor the pomp befitting the occasion, nor the choice of spectators, nor the pain which the event commemorated must always arouse ...

Talleyrand, to Louis XVIII, report of the
solemn service in memory of Louis XVI,
January 21, 1815, in Orieux's Talleyrand
(1970).

It is Alexander's fault that Napoleon is on the island of Elba. If they had listened to Talleyrand and me, he would have been deported 16,000 leagues away, to the Azores or even farther.

Viscount Castlereagh, Britain's foreign mini-
ster, to Prince Schwarzenberg, Vienna,
February 1815, in Orieux's Talleyrand
(1970).

The whole [French] nation is devoted to the Emperor, but it desires peace and he will be wise enough to be guided by public opinion in this matter; he has found out—the Bourbons are demonstrating it—that one may remain a sovereign only if one does not separate one's own cause from that of the people ... The people are eagerly awaiting to learn the intentions of Emperor Alexander; they think it is in his own interest to stay at peace with France, and that he has no reason to fear any difficulties on the question of Poland ... [Napoleon] has promised a liberal constitution and a free press, in short, he wants to please everybody and if he fails in this he cannot maintain his position ... If you are our friend, all will turn out to the best.

Hortense de Beauharnais, to Czar Alexander,
after Napoleon's return from Elba, letter of
March 1815, in Troyat's Alexander I *(1980).*

By assuming the title of King of Poland, I desired to meet the wishes of the nation. The kingdom of Poland will be united with the empire of Russia as provided by its own constitution which I want to be the basis of happiness for the country. Critical considerations for general peace make it impossible for all Poles to be united under the same rule, but at least I have attempted to soften the hardships of division as much as possible and to secure the realization of their nationality everywhere.

*Czar Alexander, to the president of the Polish
Senate, April 1815, in Troyat's* Alexander I
(1980).

Most of Germany's governments are despotic and hated by the people. Unless the duty to introduce fair constitutions is imposed upon them they will never do it. We [in Prussia], though, have made a beginning. If a good constitution is drafted soon and is given by the king to the people as a present ...

*General Count von Gneisenau (Prussia),
from the draft of a letter probably meant for
Chancellor Hardenberg, May 1815, in
Königswald's* Prussian Reader *(1966).*

The very unsatisfactory way the question of the German Constitution has been settled has grieved me very much, and I would have much preferred if Prussia had agreed on a strong and good one with a few well meaning princes, instead of this outcome [the German Federation].

*Von Humboldt, to his wife, letter of May 21,
1815, in Königswald's* Prussian Reader
(1966).

He [Blücher and his staff at St. Cloud] smokes where I have seen the court fully dressed up. Where the theater had been, the army tailors have now settled down ... This city and this sun will still look at each other when Napoleon, Blücher and myself will be nothing but memories ... Nature's unchanging laws will always be the same, but we poor creatures who are thinking so highly of ourselves conduct our lives only to present a little spectacle by our ceaseless activities, by our dabbling in mud and in the shifting sands.

*Prince Clemens Metternich, to his daughter
Marie, from occupied Paris, July 13, 1815, in
de Grunwald's* Life of Metternich *(1838).*

It is painful for me to talk to you about your sister. All people are in complete agreement on the way she has participated in the recent unhappy events ... That is what happens to most women of good will: When they mix into politics, they usually pick the wrong side and then cannot extricate themselves from their errors.

*Czar Alexander, to Eugène de Beauharnais,
on Hortense's siding with Napoleon, letter of
July 1815, in Palmer's* Alexander I *(1974).*

Dearest Papa, I hope we shall have a lasting peace now that the Emperor Napoleon will not be able to disturb it. I do hope that he will be treated with clemency and kindness, and, dearest Papa, I beg you to make sure that this will be done. This is the only request I dare make to you, and it will be the last time I shall trouble you about his fate, but I do owe him some gratitude for letting me live in calm indifference rather than making me unhappy. [A year earlier she had written to Napoleon: "I ... love you with all my heart."]

*Marie Louise of Austria, to her father,
Emperor Francis, on Napoleon's birthday, letter of August 15, 1815, in Lacour-Gayet's*
Napoleon *(1921).*

Metternich is unwilling to thwart the Emperor of Russia in a conception which, however wild, might save him and the rest of the world much trouble as long as it should last. In short, seeing no retreat, after making some verbal alterations the Emperor of Austria agreed to sign it.

*Castlereagh, to Prime Minister Lord Liverpool, on the czar's proposal of a Holy Alliance, report of September 20, 1815, in
Cheney's* Readings in English History
(1908).

I shall refuse to be the instrument of the ruin of my people, and I shall step down from my throne rather than consent to tarnishing its ancient splendor by an unprecedented humiliation.

*Louis XVIII, to Czar Alexander, after Prussia
asked for cession of several French provinces,
letter of September 23, 1815, Guizot's* History of France.

No human tribunal can pronounce a sentence heavy enough for such a criminal [Napoleon]. Not having been sufficiently punished by mortals, he will present himself drenched in the blood of nations before the terrible tribunal, in the face of God, when everyone will receive the award for his acts.

*Czar Alexander, after returning to Russia,
manifesto of January 1816, in Troyat's*
Alexander I *(1980).*

Appendix A
List of Documents

1. The Tennis Court Oath, June 20, 1789

2. The Royal Session of June 23, 1789

3. Declaration of the Intentions of the King, June 23, 1789

4. Decree of the Assembly, June 23, 1789

5. The Decrees of August 4, 1789

6. Documents upon the Constituent Assembly and the Church, November 2, 1789

7. Decree upon the Departments and Districts, December 22, 1789

8. Of the formation and organization of the administrative assemblies, December 22, 1789

9. Decree abolishing hereditary nobility and titles, June 19, 1790

10. Decree for Reorganizing the Judicial System, August 16, 1790

11. Circular letter of Louis XVI, June 20, 1791

12. Decree for the Arrest of the King, June 21, 1791

13. Decree for the Maintenance of Public Order, June 21, 1791

14. Decree in regard to Foreign Affairs, June 21, 1791

15. Decree for calling out the National Guards, June 21, 1791

16. Decree upon the Oath of Allegiance, June 22, 1791

17. Decree concerning the King, June 24, 1791

18. The Declaration of Pillnitz, August 27, 1791

19. Constitution of 1791 [Declaration of the Rights of Man], September 3, 1791

20. The King's Acceptance of the Constitution, September 13, 1791

21. Letter of Louis XVI to the King of Prussia, December 3, 1791

22. Declaration of War against Austria, April 20, 1792

23. Decree for the Deportation of the Non-Juring Priests, May 27, 1792

24. Manifesto of the Duke of Brunswick, July 25, 1792

25. Decree for Suspending the King, August 10, 1792

26. Decree for Electing the Convention, August 11, 1792

27. Decree upon Religious Policy, January 11, 1793

28. Decree upon the Non-Juring Priests, April 23, 1793

29. Decree upon Dangerous Priests, October 20-21, 1793

30. Decree upon Religious Freedom, December 8, 1793

31. Decree for Establishing the Worship of the Supreme Being, May 7, 1794

32. Decree upon Expenditures for Religion, September 18, 1794

33. Decree upon Religion, February 21, 1795

34. Declaration of the Regent of France, January 28, 1793

35. Decree for Establishing the Revolutionary Committees, March 21, 1793

36. Decree upon the Press, March 29, 1793

37. Decree for Establishing the Committee of Public Safety, April 6, 1793

38. Robespierre's Proposed Declaration of Rights, April 24, 1793

39. Decree for the Levée en Masse, August 23, 1793

40. The Law of Suspects, September 17, 1793

41. The Law of the Maximum, September 29, 1793

42. Treaty of Basle, April 5, 1795

43. Constitution of the Year III, August 22, 1795

44. The Brumaire Decree, November 10, 1799

45. Constitution of the Year VIII, December 13, 1799

46. Law for Reorganizing the Administrative System,
    February 17, 1800

47. Treaty of Lunéville, February 9, 1801

48. Treaty of Amiens, March 27, 1802

49. Constitution of the Year XII, May 18, 1804

50. Two Documents upon the Kingdom of Italy, March 17, 19, 1805

51. British Note to the Neutral Powers, May 16, 1806

52. The Berlin Decree, November 21, 1806

53. The Rambouillet Decree, March 23, 1810

54. Treaty for Establishing the Confederation (of the Rhine),
    July 12, 1806

55. Note of Napoleon to the Diet (of the German Empire),
    August 1, 1806

56. Abdication of (Emperor) Francis II, August 7, 1806

57. Treaty of Peace between France and Russia (of Tilsit), July 7, 1807

58. Imperial Decree for the Annexation of the Papal States,
    May 17, 1809

59. First Abdication of Napoleon, April 4, 1814

60. The Senate's Proposed Constitution, April 6, 1814

61. Proclamation of Napoleon, March 1, 1815

62. Declaration of the Powers against Napoleon, March 13, 1815

63. The Holy Alliance Treaty, September 26, 1815

64. Treaty of Paris, November 20, 1815

65. Treaty of Alliance against France, November 20, 1815

1. The Tennis Court Oath

June 20, 1789

The National Assembly, considering that it has been summoned to determine the constitution of the kingdom, to effect the regeneration of public order, and to maintain the true principles of the monarchy; that nothing can prevent it from continuing its deliberations in whatever place it may be forced to establish itself, and lastly, that wherever its members meet together, there is the National Assembly.

Decrees that all the members of this assembly shall immediately take a solemn oath never to separate, and to reassemble wherever circumstances shall require, until the constitution of the kingdom shall be established and consolidated upon firm foundations; and that, the said oath being taken, all the members and each of them individually shall ratify by their signatures this steadfast resolution.

2. Documents upon the Royal Session of June 23, 1789

1. The King wishes that the ancient distinction of the three orders of the state be preserved in its entirety, as essentially linked to the constitution of his kingdom; that the deputies, freely elected by each of the three orders forming three chambers, deliberating by order, and being able, with the approval of the sovereign, to agree to deliberate in common, can alone be considered as forming the body of the representatives of the nation. As a result, the king has declared null the resolutions passed by the deputies of the order of the Third Estate, the 17th of this month, as well as those which have followed them, as illegal and unconstitutional.

2. His Majesty declares valid all the credentials verified or to be verified in each chamber, upon which there has not been raised nor will be raised any contest; His Majesty orders that these shall be communicated by each order respectively to the other two orders.

As for the credentials which might be contested in each order, and upon which the parties interested would appeal, it will be enacted, for the present session only of the States-General, as will be hereafter ordered.

[Articles three to six set aside the instructions given to members in regard to their action upon the organization of the States-General and announced that imperative instructions would not be permitted in the future.]

7. His Majesty having exhorted the three orders, for the safety of the state, to unite themselves during this session of estates only, to deliberate in common upon the affairs of general utility, wishes to make his intentions known upon the manner of procedure.

8. There shall be particularly excepted from the affairs which can be treated in common, those that concern the ancient and constitutional rights of the three orders, the form of constitution to be given to the next States-General, the feudal and seignorial rights, the useful rights and honorary prerogatives of the first two orders.

9. The especial consent of the clergy will be necessary for all provisions which could interest religion, ecclesiastical discipline, the régime of the orders and secular and regular bodies.

11. If, with the view of facilitating the union of the three orders, they desire that the propositions that shall have been considered in common, should pass only by a majority of two-thirds of the votes, His Majesty is disposed to authorise this form.

12. Matters which shall have been decided in the assembly of the three orders united shall be taken up again the next day for deliberation, if one hundred members of the assembly unite to ask for it.

15. Good order, decency, and liberty of the ballot even, require that His Majesty prohibit, as he expressly does, that any person, other than the members of the three orders comprising the States-General, should be present at their deliberations, whether they deliberate in common or separately.

3. Declaration of the Intentions of the King

June 23, 1789

1. No new tax shall be established, no old one shall be continued beyond the term fixed by the laws, without the consent of the representatives of the nation.

2. The new taxes which will be established, or the old ones which will be continued, shall hold only for the interval which will elapse until the time of the following session of the States-General.

3. As the borrowing of money might lead to an increase of taxes, no money shall be borrowed without the consent of the States-General, under the condition, however, that in case of war, or other national danger, the sovereign shall have the right to borrow without delay, to the amount of one hundred millions: for it is the formal intention of the king never to make the safety of his realm dependent upon any person.

4. The States-General shall examine with care the situation of the finances, and they shall demand all the information necessary to enlighten them perfectly.

5. The statement of receipts and expenses shall be made public each year, in a form proposed by the States-General and approved by His Majesty.

6. The sums attributed to each department shall be determined in a fixed and invariable manner and the king submits to this general rule even the funds that are destined for the maintenance of his household.

7. The king wishes, in order to assure this [　] of the different expenses of the state, that provisions suitable to accomplish this object be suggested to him by the States-General; and His Majesty will adopt them if they are in accordance with the royal dignity and the indispensable celerity of the public service.

8. The representatives of a nation faithful to the laws of honor and probity, will make no attack on the public credit, and the king expects from them that the confidence of the creditors of the state will be assured and secured in the most authentic manner.

Reflect, gentlemen, that none of your projects, none of your dispositions can have the force of a law without my special approbation. So I am the natural guarantee of your respective rights, and all the orders of the state can depend upon my equitable impartiality. All distrust upon your part would be a great injustice. It is I, at present, who am doing everything for the happiness of my people, and it is rare, perhaps, that the only ambition of a sovereign is to come to an understanding with his subjects that they may accept his kindnesses.

I order you, gentlemen, to separate immediately, and to go tomorrow morning, each to the chamber allotted to your order, in order to take up again your sessions. I order, therefore, the grand master of ceremonies to have the halls prepared.

4. Decree of the Assembly

June 23, 1789

The National Assembly unanimously declares that it persists in its previous resolutions.

The National Assembly declares that the person of each of the deputies is inviolable; that any individuals, any corporations, tribunal, court or commission that shall dare, during or after the present session, to pursue, to seek for, to arrest or have arrested, detain or have detained, a deputy, by reason of any propositions, advice, opinions, or discourse made by him in the States-General: as well as all persons who shall lend their aid to any of the said attempts by whomsoever they may be ordered, are infamous and traitors to the nation, and guilty of capital crime. The National Assembly decrees that, in the aforesaid cases, it will take all the necessary measures to have sought out, pursued and punished those who may be its authors, instigators or executors.

5. The Fourth of August Decrees

August 4-11, 1789

1. The National Assembly completely abolishes the feudal regime. It decrees that, among the rights and dues, both feudal and *censuel*, all those originating in real or personal serfdom, personal servitude, and those which represent them, are abolished without indemnification; all others are declared redeemable, and that the price and mode of the redemption shall be fixed by the National Assembly. Those of the said dues which are not extinguished by this decree shall, nevertheless, continue to be collected until indemnification takes place.

2. The exclusive right to maintain pigeon-houses and dove-cotes is abolished; the pigeons shall be confined during the seasons fixed by the communities; and during that time, they shall be regarded as game, and every one shall have the right to kill them upon his own land.

3. The exclusive right to hunt and to maintain unenclosed warrens is likewise abolished; and every land-owner shall have the right to kill or to have destroyed upon his own land only, all kinds of game, observing, however, such police regulations as may be established with a view to the safety of the public.

All *capitaineries*, royal included, and all hunting reserves, under whatever denominations, are likewise abolished; and provision shall be made, in a manner compatible with the respect due to property and liberty, for maintaining the personal pleasures of the king.

The president of the assembly shall be commissioned to ask of the king the recall of those sent to the galleys or exiled simply for violations of the hunting regulations, as well as for the release of those at present imprisoned for offences of this kind, and the dismissal of such cases as are now pending.

4. All manorial courts are suppressed without indemnification; nevertheless the magistrates of these courts shall continue to perform their functions until such time as the National Assembly shall provide for the establishment of a new judicial system.

5. Tithes of every description and the dues which have been substituted for them, under whatever denomination they are known or collected, even when compounded for, possessed by secular or regular congregations, by holders of benefices, members of corporations, including the Order of Malta and other religious and military orders, as well as those impropriated to lay persons and those substituted for the *portion congruë*, are abolished, on condition, however, that some other method be devised to provide for the expenses of divine worship, the support of the officiating clergy, the relief of the poor, repairs and rebuilding of churches and parsonages, and for all establishments, seminaries, schools, academies, asylums, communities and other institutions, for the maintenance of which they are actually devoted. And

moreover, until such provision shall be made and the former possessors shall enter upon the enjoyment of an income on the new system, the National Assembly decrees that the said tithes shall continue to be collected according to law and in the customary manner. Other tithes of whatever nature they may be, shall be redeemable in such manner as the Assembly shall determine. Until such regulation shall be issued, the National Assembly decrees that these, too, shall continue to be collected.

6. All perpetual ground rents, payable either in money or in kind, of whatever nature they may be, whatever their origin, and to whomsoever they may be due, as to members of corporations, domanial apanagists, or to the Order of Malta, shall be redeemable; *champarts*, of every kind and under every denomination, shall likewise be redeemable at a rate fixed by the assembly. No due shall in the future be created which is not redeemable.

7. The sale of judicial and municipal offices shall be suppressed forthwith. Justice shall be dispensed gratis; nevertheless, the magistrates at present holding such offices shall continue to exercise their functions and to receive their emoluments until the assembly shall have made provision for indemnifying them.

8. The fees of the country *curés* are abolished; and shall be discontinued as soon as provision shall be made for increasing the minimum salary (*portion congrué*) for priests and for the payment to the curates; and there shall be a regulation drawn up to determine the status of the priests in the towns.

9. Pecuniary privileges, personal or real, in the payment of taxes are abolished forever. The assessment shall be made upon all the citizens and upon all property, in the same manner and in the same form; and plans shall be considered by which the taxes shall be paid proportionally by all, even for the last six months of the current year.

10. Inasmuch as a national constitution and public liberty are of more advantage to the provinces than the privileges which some of these enjoy, and inasmuch as the surrender of such privileges is essential to the intimate union of all parts of the realm, it is declared that all the peculiar privileges, pecuniary or otherwise, of the provinces, principalities, districts, cantons, cities and communes, are once for all abolished and are absorbed into the law common to all Frenchmen.

11. All citizens, without distinction of birth, are eligible to any office or dignity, whether ecclesiastical, civil or military; and no profession shall imply any derogation.

12. Hereafter no remittances shall be made for annates or for any other purpose to the court of Rome, the vice-legation at Avignon, or to the nunciature at Lucerne; but the clergy of the diocese shall apply to their bishops for all provisions in regard to benefices and dispensations, which shall be granted gratis, without regard to reservations, expectancies, and monthly divisions, all the churches of France enjoying the same freedom.

13. The rights of *deport*, of *côte-morte, dépouilles, vacat, censaux*, Peter's pence, and other dues of the same kind, under whatever denomination, established in favor of bishops, archdeacons, archpresbyters, chapters, *curés primitifs* and all others, are abolished, but appropriate provision shall be made for those benefices of archdeacons and archpresbyters which are not sufficiently endowed.

14. Pluralities shall not be permitted hereafter in cases where the revenue from the benefice or benefices held shall exceed the sum of three thousand livres. Nor shall any individual be allowed to enjoy several pensions from benefices, or a pension and a benefice, if the revenue which he already enjoys from such sources exceeds the same sum of three thousand livres.

15. The National Assembly shall consider, in conjunction with the king, the report which is to be submitted to it relating to pensions, favors and salaries, with a view to suppressing all such as are not deserved and reducing those which shall prove excessive; and the amount shall be fixed which the king may in the future disburse for this purpose.

16. The National Assembly decrees that a medal shall be struck in memory of the recent grave and important deliberations for the welfare of France, and that a *Te Deum* shall be chanted in gratitude in all the parishes and the churches of France.

17. The National Assembly solemnly proclaims the king, Louis XVI, the *Restorer of French Liberty*.

18. The National Assembly shall present itself in a body before the king, in order to submit to His Majesty the decree which has just been passed, to tender to him the tokens of its most respectful gratitude, and to pray him to permit the *Te Deum* to be chanted in his chapel, and to be present himself at this service.

19. The National Assembly shall consider, immediately after the constitution, the drawing up of laws necessary for the development of the principles which it has laid down in the present decree which shall be transmitted without delay by the deputies to all the provinces, together with the decree of the tenth of this month, in order that both may be printed, published, announced from the parish pulpits, and posted up wherever it shall be deemed necessary.

6. Documents upon the Constituent Assembly and the Church

November 2, 1789

The National Assembly decrees, 1st, that all the ecclesiastical estates are at the disposal of the nation, on condition of providing in a suitable manner for the expense of worship, the maintenance of its ministers, and the relief of the poor, under the supervision and following the directions of the provinces; 2d, that in the provisions to be made, in order to provide for the maintenance of the ministers of religion, there can be assured for the endowment of each curé not less than twelve hundred livres per annum, not including the dwelling and the gardens attached.

7. Decree upon the Departments and Districts

December 22, 1789

1. There shall be made a new division of the kingdom into *departments*, both for representation and administration. These departments shall be from seventy-five to eighty-five in number.

2. Each department shall be divided into *districts*, of which the number, which shall not be less than three nor more than nine, shall be determined by the National Assembly, according to the need and convenience of the department, after having heard the deputies of the provinces.

3. Each district shall be divided into divisions called *cantons*, of about four square leagues (common leagues of France).

5. There shall be established at the head-town of each department a higher administrative assembly, under the title of *department administration*.

6. There shall likewise be established at the head-town of each district a subordinate administrative assembly, under the title of *district administration*.

7. There shall be a municipality in each city, borough, parish or rural community.

8. Of the formation and organization of the administrative assemblies.

December 22, 1789

1. There shall be only one degree of election intermediate between the primary assemblies and the administrative assemblies.

2. After having selected the representatives to the National Assembly, the same electors in each department shall elect the members, to the number of twenty-six, who shall compose the *department administration*.

9. Decree abolishing hereditary nobility and titles

June 19, 1790

1. Hereditary nobility is forever abolished; in consequence the titles of prince, duke, count, marquis, viscount, vidame, baron, knight, *messire, écuyer, noble*, and all other similar titles, shall neither be taken by anyone whomsoever nor given to anybody.

2. A citizen may take only the true name of his family; no one may wear liveries nor cause them to be worn, nor have armorial bearings; incense shall not be burned in the temples, except in order to honor the divinity, and shall not be offered for any one whomsoever.

3. The titles of *monseigneur* and *messeigneurs* shall not be given to any society nor to any person, likewise the titles of excellency, highness, eminence, grace, etc.; nevertheless, no citizen, under pretext of the present decree, shall be permitted to make an attack on the monuments placed in the temples, the charters, titles and other tokens of interest to families or properties, nor the decorations of any public or private place; nevertheless, the execution of the provisions relative to the liveries and the arms placed upon carriages shall not be carried out nor demanded by any one whomsoever before the 14th of July for the citizens living in Paris and before three months for those who inhabit the country.

4. No foreigners are included in the provisions of the present decree; they may preserve in France their liveries and their armorial bearings.

10. Decree for Reorganizing the Judicial System

August 16, 1790

Title I. Of the Arbiters.

1. Arbitration being the most reasonable means for the termination of disputes between citizens, the legislature shall not make any provision which may tend to diminish either the popularity or the efficiency of the compromise.

Title II. Of the Judges in General.

1. Justice shall be rendered in the name of the king.

2. The sale of judicial offices is abolished forever; the judges shall render justice gratuitously and shall be salaried by the state.

3. The judges shall be elected by the justiciable.

4. they shall be elected for six years; at the expiration of this term a new election shall take place, in which the same judges may be re-elected.

12. They shall not make regulations, but they shall have recourse to the legislative body, whenever they think necessary, either to interpret a law or to make a new one.

13. The judicial functions are distinct and shall always remain separate from the administrative functions. The judges, under penalty of forfeiture, shall not disturb in any manner whatsoever the operations of the administrative bodies, nor cite before them the administrators on account of their function.

14. In every civil or criminal matter, the pleadings, testimony, and decisions shall be public, and every citizen shall have the right to defend his own case, either verbally or in writing.

15. Trial by jury shall occur in criminal matters; the examination shall be made publicly and shall have the publicity which shall be determined.

16. All privilege in matters of jurisdiction is abolished; all citizens, without distinction, shall plead in the same form and before the same judges in the same cases.

11. Circular Letter of Louis XVI to Foreign Courts

June 20, 1791

The king charges me to inform you that it is his most express wish that you should make known his sentiments upon the French revolution and constitution at the court where you reside. The ambassadors and ministers of France at all the courts of Europe are receiving the same directions, in order that there may not remain any doubt about the intentions of His Majesty, or about the free acceptance which he has given to the new form of government, or about his irrevocable oath to maintain it.

His Majesty convoked the States-General of the kingdom and determined in his council that the commons should have in it a number of deputies equal to that of the other two orders which then existed. This act of provisional legislation, which the obstacles of the moment did not permit to be made more favorable, announced sufficiently the desire of His Majesty to re-establish the nation in all of its rights.

The States-General met and took the title of *National Assembly*; soon a constitution, qualified to secure the welfare of France and of the monarch, replaced the former order of things, in which the apparent power of the kingship only concealed the actual power of certain aristocratic bodies.

The National Assembly adopted the form of representative government in conjunction with hereditary kingship. The legislative body was declared permanent; the election of clergymen, administrators, and judges was made over to the people; the executive power was conferred upon the king, the formation of the law upon the legislative body, and the sanction upon the monarch. The public force, both internal and external, was organized upon the same principles and in accordance with the fundamental basis of the distinction of the powers; such is the new constitution of the kingdom.

What is called the revolution is only the abolition of a multitude of abuses accumulated in the course of centuries through the error of the people or the authority of the ministers, which has never been the authority of the king. These abuses were not less disastrous to the monarch than to the nation; under wise reigns authority had not ceased to attack these abuses, but was not able to destroy them. They no longer exist; the sovereign nation has no longer any but citizens equal in right, no despot but the law, no organs except the public functionaries, and the king is the first of these functionaries: such is the French revolution.

It was bound to have as enemies all those who in the first moment of horror, on account of personal advantage, mourned for the abuses of the former government. From this comes the apparent division which has manifested itself within the kingdom, but which is enfeebled each day; from this, also, perhaps, come some severe and exceptional laws which time will correct: but the king, whose real power is inseparable from that of the nation, who has no other ambition than the welfare of the people, nor any real authority other than that which is delegated to him; the king was bound to agree without hesitation to a happy constitution which would regenerate at one and the same time his authority, the nation, and the monarchy. He has retained all his authority, except the redoubtable power to make the laws; he remains in charge of the negotiations with foreign powers, the task of defending the kingdom and of repulsing its enemies; but the French nation henceforth will not have any enemies abroad except its aggressors. It no longer has internal enemies except those who, still nourishing foolish hopes, believe that the will of 24,000,000 men entered again upon their natural rights, after having organized the kingdom in such a manner that only the memory of the old forms and former abuses remains, is not an immovable and irrevocable constitution.

The most dangerous of these enemies are those who seek to spread doubts as to the intentions of the monarch; these men are indeed culpable or blind; they believe themselves the friends of the king; they are the only enemies of the monarchy; they would have deprived the monarch of the love and confidence of a great nation, if his principles and probity had been less known. Ah! what has the king not done to show that he counts both the French revolution and the constitution among his titles to glory ...

Signed, Montmorin

12. Decree for the Arrest of the King

June 21, 1791

The National Assembly orders that the minister of the interior shall immediately send couriers into all the departments, with orders to all the public functionaries and the national guards or troops of the line of the kingdom, to arrest or cause the arrest of all persons whomsoever leaving the realm, as well as to prevent all removal of goods, arms, munitions of war, and every species of gold, silver, horses, vehicles and munitions of war; and, in case the said couriers should encounter any persons of the royal family and those who may have assisted in their removal, the said public functionaries or national guards and troops of the line shall be required to take all the necessary measures to stop the said removal, to prevent them from continuing their route, and to render account of everything to the legislative body.

13. Decree for the Maintenance of Public Order

June 21, 1791

The National Assembly declares to the citizens of Paris and to all the inhabitants of the kingdom, that the same firmness which it has exhibited in the midst of all the difficulties that have attended its labors will control its deliberations upon the occasion of carrying away the king and the royal family. It notifies all citizens that the maintenance of the constitution and the safety of the empire have never more imperatively demanded good order and public tranquility; that the National Assembly has taken the most energetic measures to follow the traces of those who have made themselves guilty of carrying away the king and the royal family; that, without interrupting its sittings, it will employ every means in order that the public interest may not suffer from that event; that all citizens ought to rely entirely upon it for the arrangements which the safety of the kingdom may demand; and that everything which may excite trouble, alarm individuals, or menace property, would be all the more culpable since thereby liberty and the constitution might be compromised.

It orders that the citizens of Paris hold themselves in readiness to act for the maintenance of public order and the defence of the fatherland, in accordance with the orders which will be given them in conformity with the decrees of the National Assembly.

It orders the department administrators and the municipal officers to cause the present decree to be promulgated immediately and to look with care to the public tranquility.

14. Decree in regard to Foreign Affairs

June 21, 1791

The National Assembly, the king absent, orders that the minister of foreign affairs shall make known to the ambas-sadors and ministers of foreign powers residing at present in Paris, as well as the ambassadors of France in foreign states and kingdoms, the desire of the French nation to continue with the said states and kingdoms the relation of friendship and good understanding which has existed up to the present and shall inform the said ambassadors and residents for the powers, that they ought to remit to M. Montmorin the official notes with which they are charged on the part of the respective princes and states.

15. Decree for calling out the National Guards

June 21, 1791

1. The national guards of the kingdom shall be called into service, according to the arrangements set forth in the following articles.

2-3. [Provided for calling out two to three thousand or more from each department.]

4. In consequence, all citizens and sons of citizens in condition to bear arms, and those who wish to take them for the defence of the state and the maintenance of the constitution, shall cause themselves to be enrolled immediately after the publication of the present decree, each in his municipality, which shall send at once the list of the enrolled to the commissioners whom the directory of the department shall appoint, either from among the members of the general council or the other citizens, in order to proceed to the formation.

16. Decree upon the Oath of Allegiance

June 22, 1791

The National Assembly decrees as follows:

1. That the oath ordered on June 11 and 13, the present month, shall be taken in the following form:

"I swear to employ the arms placed in my hands for the defence of the fatherland and to maintain against all its enemies within and without the constitution decreed by the National Assembly; to perish rather than to suffer the invasion of French territory by foreign troops, and to obey only the orders which shall be given in consequence of the decrees of the National Assembly."

2. That commissioners, taken from within the body of the assembly, shall be sent into the frontier departments in order to receive there the above-mentioned oath, a record of which shall be drawn up, and to concert there with the administrative bodies and the commanders of the troops the measures which they think suitable for the maintenance of public order and the security of the state, and to make for that purpose all the necessary requisitions.

17. Decree concerning the King

June 24, 1791

1. As soon as the king shall have arrived at the chateau of the Tuileries he shall temporarily be given a guard, which, under the orders of the commanding general of the Parisian national guard, shall look after his security and shall be responsible for his person.

18. Declaration of Pillnitz

August 27, 1791

His Majesty, the Emperor, and his Majesty, the King of Prussia, having given attention to the wishes and representations of *Monsieur* (the brother of the King of France), and of M. le Comte d'Artois, jointly declare that they regard the present situation of His Majesty the King of France, as a matter of common interest to all the sovereigns of Europe. They trust that this interest will not fail to be recognized by the powers, whose aid is solicited, and that in consequence they will not refuse to employ, in conjunction with their said majesties, the most efficient means in proportion to their resources to place the King of France in a position to establish, with the most absolute freedom, the foundations of a monarchical form of government, which shall at once be in harmony with the rights of sovereigns and promote the welfare of the French nation. In that case [*Alors et dans ce cas*] their said majesties the Emperor and the King of Prussia are resolved to act promptly and in common accord with the forces necessary to obtain the desired common end.

In the meantime they will give such orders to their troops as are necessary in order that these may be in a position to be called into active service.

Leopold.   Frederick William.

19. Constitution of 1791

September 3, 1791

Declaration of the Rights of Man and Citizen.

The representatives of the French people, organized in National Assembly, considering that ignorance, forgetfulness or contempt of the rights of man, are the sole causes of the public miseries and of the corruption of governments, have resolved to set forth in a solemn declaration the natural, inalienable, and sacred rights of man, in order that this declaration, being ever present to all the members of the social body, may unceasingly remind them of their rights and their duties; in order that the acts of the legislative power and those of the executive power may be each moment compared with the aim of every political institution and thereby may be more respected; and in order that the demands of citizens, grounded henceforth upon simple and incontestable principles, may always take the direction of maintaining the constitution and the welfare of all.

In consequence, the National Assembly recognizes and declares, in the presence and under the auspices of the Supreme Being, the following rights of man and citizen.

1. Men are born and remain free and equal in rights. Social distinctions can be based only upon public utility.

2. The aim of every political association is the preservation of the natural and imprescriptible rights of man. These rights are liberty, property, security, and resistance to oppression.

3. The source of all sovereignity is essentially in the nation; no body, no individual can exercise authority that does not proceed from it in plain terms.

4. Liberty consists in the power to do anything that does not injure others; accordingly, the exercise of the natural rights of each man has no limits except those that secure to the other members of society the enjoyment of these same rights. These limits can be determined only by law.

5. The law has the right to forbid only such actions as are injurious to society. Nothing can be forbidden that is not interdicted by the law, and no one can be constrained to do that which it does not order.

6. Law is the expression of the general will. All citizens have the right to take part personally, or by their representatives, in its formation. It must be the same for all, whether it protects or punishes. All citizens being equal in its eyes, are equally eligible to all public dignities, places, and employments, according to their capacities, and without other distinction than that of their virtues and their talents.

7. No man can be accused, arrested or detained, except in the cases determined by the law and according to the forms that it has prescribed. Those who procure, expedite, execute, or cause to be executed arbitrary orders ought to be punished: but every citizen summoned or seized in virtue of the law ought to render instant obedience; he makes himself guilty by resistance.

8. The law ought to establish only penalties that are strictly and obviously necessary, and no one can be punished except in virtue of a law established and promulgated prior to the offence and legally applied.

9. Every man being presumed innocent until he has been pronounced guilty, if it is thought indispensable to arrest him, all severity that may not be necessary to secure his person ought to be strictly suppressed by law.

10. No one should be disturbed on account of his opinions, even religious, provided their manifestation does not derange the public order established by law.

11. The free communication of ideas and opinions is one of the most precious of the rights of man; every citizen then can freely speak, write, and print, subject to responsibility for the abuse of this freedom in the cases determined by law.

12. The guarantee of the rights of man and citizen requires a public force; this force then is instituted for the advantage of all and not for the personal benefit of those to whom it is entrusted.

13. For the maintenance of the public force and for the expenses of administration a general tax is indispensable; it ought to be equally apportioned among all citizens according to their means.

14. All the citizens have the right to ascertain, by themselves or by their representatives, the necessity of the public tax, to consent to it freely, to follow the employment of it, and to determine the quota, the assessment, the collection, and the duration of it.

15. Society has the right to call for an account of his administration from every public agent.

16. Any society in which the guarantee of the rights is not secured, or the separation of powers not determined, has no constitution at all.

17. Property being a sacred and inviolable right, no one can be deprived of it, unless a legally established public necessity evidently demands it, under the condition of a just and prior indemnity.

FRENCH CONSTITUTION.

The National Assembly, wishing to establish the French constitution upon the principles which it has just recognized and declared, abolishes irrevocably the institutions that have injured liberty and the equality of rights.

There is no longer nobility, nor peerage, nor hereditary distinctions, nor distinctions of orders, nor feudal régime, nor patrimonial jurisdictions, nor any titles, denominations, or prerogatives derived therefrom, nor any order of chivalry, nor any corporations or decorations which demanded proofs of nobility or that were grounded upon distinctions of birth, nor any superiority other than that of public officials in the exercise of their functions.

There is no longer either sale or inheritance of any public office.

There is no longer for any part of the nation nor for any individual any privilege or exception to the law that is common to all Frenchmen.

There are no longer *jurandes*, nor corporations of professions, arts, and crafts.

The law no longer recognizes religious vows, nor any other obligation which may be contrary to natural rights or to the constitution ...

Title III, Chapter II. Section IV. Of the ministers.

1. The choice and dismissal of the ministers shall belong to the king alone.

2. The members of the present National Assembly and of the legislatures following, the members of the tribunal of cassation, and those who shall serve on the high jury, cannot be promoted to the ministry, nor receive any place, gift, pension, stipend, or commission from the executive power or from its agents, during the continuance of their functions, nor for two years after having ceased the exercise of them.

It shall be the same with those who are only enrolled upon the list of the high jury, during the time that their enrollment shall continue.

3. No one can enter upon the exercise of any employment either in the offices of the ministry or in those of the management or administration of the public revenues, nor in general any employment at the nomination of the executive power, without taking the civic oath, or without proving that he has taken it.

4. No order of the king can be executed unless it is signed by him and countersigned by the minister or administrator of the department.

5. The ministers are responsible for all the offences committed by themselves against the national security and the constitution;

For every attack upon property and personal liberty;

For all waste of monies appropriated for the expenses of their departments.

6. In no case can the order of king, verbal or in writing, shield a minister from his responsibility.

7. The ministers are required to present each year to the legislative body at the opening of the session an estimate of the expenditures to be made in their departments, to render account of the employment of the sums which were appropriated for them, and to indicate the abuses which may have been able to introduce themselves into the different parts of the government.

8. No minister, in office or out of office, can be prosecuted for any acts of his administration, without a decree of the legislative body.

Chapter III. Of the Exercise of the Legislative Power.

Section I. Powers and functions of the National Legislative Assembly.

1. The constitution delegates exclusively to the legislative body the following powers and functions:

1st. To propose and enact the laws; the king can only invite the legislative body to take the matter under consideration;

2d. To fix the public expenditures;

3d. To establish the public taxes, to determine the nature of them, the quota, the duration, and the mode of collection;

4th. To make the apportionment of the direct tax among the departments of the kingdom, to supervise the employment of all the public revenues, and to cause an account of them to be rendered;

5th. To decree the creation or suppression of public offices;

6th. To determine the title, weight, stamp, and denomination of the monies;

7th. To permit or forbid the introduction of foreign troops upon French soil and foreign naval forces in the ports of the kingdom; ...

Section IV. Relations of the Legislative Body with the King.

1. When the legislative body is definitely constituted, it sends to the king a deputation in order to inform him thereof.

The king can each year open the session and can bring forward the matters which he believes ought to be taken into consideration in the course of that session, without this formality, nevertheless, being considered necessary for the activity of the legislative body.

2. When the legislative body wishes to adjourn beyond fifteen days, it is required to notify the king thereof by a deputation, at least eight days in advance.

3. At least eight days before the end of each session, the legislative body sends to the king a deputation, in order to announce to him the day whereupon it proposes to terminate its sittings. The king can come to close the session.

4. If the king thinks it important for the welfare of the state that the session be continued, or that the adjournment should not occur, or that it should occur only for a shorter time, he can send a message to that effect, upon which the legislative body is required to deliberate.

5. The king shall convoke the legislative body during the intermission of its sessions, whenever the interests of the state appear to him to require it, as well as in the cases which have been provided for and determined by the legislative body before its adjournment.

6. Whenever the king repairs to the place of the sittings of the legislative body, he shall be received and conducted by a deputation; he cannot be accompanied within the interior of the hall except by the prince royal and the ministers.

7. In no case can the president make up part of a deputation.

8. The legislative body shall cease to be a deliberative body as long as the king shall be present.

9. The documents of the correspondence of the king with the legislative body shall always be countersigned by a minister.

10. The ministers of the king shall have entrance into the National Legislative Assembly; they shall have a designated place there.

They shall be heard, whenever they shall demand it, upon matters relative to their administrations or when they shall be required to give information.

They shall likewise be heard upon matters foreign to their administrations when the National Assembly shall grant them the word.

Chapter IV. Of the Exercise of the Executive Power.

1. The supreme executive power resides exclusively in the hands of the king.

The king is the supreme head of the general administration of the kingdom; the task of looking after the maintenance of public order and tranquility is confided to him.

The king is the supreme head of the army and navy.

The task of looking after the external security of the kingdom and of maintaining its rights and possessions is delegated to the king.

2. The king appoints the ambassadors and other agents of political negotiations.

He confers the command of the armies and fleets, and the grades of marshal and admiral.

He appoints two-thirds of the rear-admirals, half of the lieutenant generals, camp-marshals, ship-captains, and colonels of the national *gendarmerie*.

He appoints two-thirds of the colonels and lieutenant colonels, and a sixth of the ship-lieutenants.

All of these conforming to the laws upon promotion.

He appoints in the civil administration of the navy the managers, comptrollers, treasurers of the arsenals, heads of the works, under-chiefs of civil buildings, and half of the heads of administration and under-chiefs of construction.

He appoints the commissioners before the tribunals.

He appoints the officers-in-chief for the administrations of the indirect taxes and for the administration of the national lands.

He superintends the coining of monies, and appoints the officers charged with the exercise of this surveillance in the general commission and in the mints ...

20. The King's Acceptance of the Constitution

September 13, 1791

Gentlemen: I have examined attentively the constitutional act which you have presented to me for my acceptance; I accept it and shall cause it to be executed. This declaration might have sufficed at another time; today I owe it to the interests of the nation, I owe it to myself, to make known my reasons.

Let everyone recall the moment at which I went away from Paris: the constitution was on the point of completion, nevertheless the authority of the laws seemed to become enfeebled every day. Opinion, far from becoming fixed, was subdividing into a multitude of parties. The most extreme opinions alone seemed to obtain favor, the license of the press was at the highest pitch, no authority was respected. I could no longer recognize the mark of the general will in the laws which I saw everywhere without force and without execution. At that time, I am bound to declare, if you had presented the constitution to me, I should not have believed that the interest of the people (the constant and sole rule of my conduct) would permit me to accept it. I had only one feeling, I formed only one project: I wished to isolate myself from all the parties and to know what was truly the will of the nation.

The considerations which were controlling me no longer remain today; since then the inconveniences and evils of which I was complaining have impressed you as they did me; you have manifested a desire to re-establish order, you have directed your attention to the lack of discipline in the army, you have recognized the necessity of repressing the abuses of the press. The revision of your work has put in the number of the regulative laws several articles which had been presented to me as constitutional. You have established legal forms for the revision of those which you have placed in the constitution. Finally, the opinion of the people is to me no longer doubtful; I have seen it manifested both in their adhesion to your work and their attachment to the maintenance of the monarchical government.

I accept then the constitution. I take the engagement to maintain it within, to defend it against attacks from without, and to cause it to be executed by all the means which it places in my power. I declare that, instructed by the adhesion which the great majority of the people give to the constitution, I renounce the co-operation which I had claimed in that work; and that, being responsible only to the nation, no other, when I renounce it, has the right to complain thereof. I should be lacking in sincerity, however, if I said that I perceived in the means of execution and administration, all the energy which may be necessary in order to give motion to and to preserve unity in all parts of so vast an empire; but since opinions at present are divided upon these matters, I consent that experience alone remain judge therein. When I shall have loyally caused to operate all the means which have been left to me, no reproach can be aimed at me, and the nation, whose interests alone ought to serve as rule, will explain itself by the means which the constitution has reserved to it.

Signed, Louis.

21. Letter of Louis XVI to the King of Prussia

Paris, **December 3, 1791**

Monsieur my Brother, I have learned through M. du Moustier of the interest which Your Majesty had expressed not only for my person, but also for the welfare of my kingdom. The disposition of Your Majesty towards me in giving these proofs in all the cases where that interest might be useful for the welfare of my people, has warmly aroused my sensibility. I lay claim to it with confidence in this moment, wherein, despite the acceptance which I have made of the new constitution, the factions openly exhibit the project of destroying entirely the remnants of the monarchy. I have just addressed myself to the Emperor, the Empress of Russia, the kings of Spain and Sweden, and presented to them the idea of a congress of the principal powers of Europe, supported by an armed force, as the best manner to check the factions here, to give the means to establish a more desirable order of things, and to prevent the evil which afflicts us from being able to take possession of the other states of Europe. I hope that Your Majesty will approve of my ideas and that you will preserve the most absolute secrecy upon the step that I have taken with you. You will easily realize that the circumstances in which I find myself compel the greatest circumspection on my part. That is why only the Baron de Breteuil is informed of my projects, and Your Majesty can communicate to him what you

shall wish. I take this occasion to thank Your Majesty for the acts of kindness which you have shown to M. Heyman, and I experience a real delight in giving to Your Majesty the assurances of esteem and affection with which I am,

Louis.

22. Declaration of War against Austria

April 20, 1792

The National Assembly, deliberating upon the formal proposition of the king; considering that the court of Vienna, in contempt of the treaties, has not ceased to grant an open protection to the French rebels; that it has instigated and formed a concert with several powers of Europe against the independence and security of the French nation;

That Francis I, King of Hungary and Bohemia, has, by his notes of March 18 and April 7 last, refused to renounce this concert;

That, despite the proposition which has been made to him by the note of March 11, 1792, to reduce on both sides to the peace basis the troops upon the frontiers, he has continued and augmented hostile preparations;

That he has formally attacked the sovereignty of the French nation, in declaring his determination to support the pretentions of the German princes to possessions in France, for which the French nation has not ceased to offer indemnities;

That he has sought to divide the French citizens and to arm them against each other, by offering to the malcontents a support in the concert of the powers;

Considering, finally, that the refusal to reply to the last despatches of the King of the French leaves no longer any hope of obtaining, by way of an amicable negotiation, the redress of these different grievances and is equivalent to a declaration of war;

Decrees that there is urgency.

The National Assembly declares that the French nation, faithful to the principles consecrated in the constitution, *not to undertake any war with a view to making conquest, and never to employ its forces against the liberty of any people,* takes arms only to maintain its liberty and its independence;

That the war which it is forced to sustain is not a war of nation against nation, but the just defence of a free people against the unjust aggression of a king.

That the French will never confound their brothers with their real enemies; that they will neglect nothing in order to alleviate the scourge of war, to spare and preserve property, and to cause to return upon those alone, who shall league themselves against its liberties, all the miseries inseparable from war;

That it adopts in advance all foreigners, who, abjuring the cause of its enemies, shall come to range themselves under its banners and to consecrate their efforts to the defence of its liberty; that it will favor also, by all the means which are in its power, their establishment in France.

Deliberating upon the formal proposition of the King, and after having decreed urgency, [the National Assembly] decrees war against the King of Hungary and Bohemia.

23. Decree for the Deportation of the Non-Juring Priests

May 27, 1792

The National Assembly, after having heard the report of its committee of twelve, considering that the troubles excited within the kingdom by the non-juring ecclesiastics require that it should apply itself without delay to the means of suppressing them, decrees that there is urgency;

The National Assembly, considering that the efforts to overthrow the constitution, to which the non-juring ecclesiastics are continually devoting themselves, do not permit it to be supposed that these ecclesiastics desire to unite in the social compact, and that it would compromise the public safety to regard for a longer time as members of society the men who evidently are seeking to dissolve it; considering that the laws are without force against these men, who, operating upon the consciences in order to mislead them, nearly always conceal their criminal maneuvers from the attention of those who might be able to cause them to be repressed and punished; after having decreed urgency, decrees as follows:

1. The deportation of the non-juring ecclesiastics shall take place as a measure of public security and of general police, in the case and according to the forms herinafter set forth.

2. All those are considered as non-juring ecclesiastics, who, being liable for the oath prescribed by the law of December 26, 1790, may not have taken the oath; also those who, not being subject to that law, have not taken the civic oath subsequent to September 3 last, the day whereon the French constitution was declared completed; finally, those who shall have retracted either oath.

3. When twenty active citizens of the same canton shall unite to ask for the deportation of a non-juring ecclesiastic, the department directory shall be required to pronounce the deportation, if the opinion of the district directory is in conformity with the petition.

4. When the opinion of the district directory shall be in conformity with the petition, the department directory shall be required to cause the commissioners to ascertain by examination whether the presence of the ecclesiastic or ecclesiastics denounced is injurious to the public tranquility, and upon the opinion of these commissioners, if it is in conformity with the petition, the department directory shall be required to pronounce the deportation.

24. The Duke of Brunswick's Manifesto

July 25, 1792

Their Majesties, the Emperor and the King of Prussia, having committed to me the command of the united armies which they have caused to assemble on the frontiers of France, I have wished to announce to the inhabitants of this kingdom, the motives which have determined the measures of the two sovereigns and the intentions which guide them.

After having arbitrarily suppressed the rights and possessions of the German princes in Alsace and Lorraine, disturbed and overthrown good order and legitimate government in the interior; exercised against the sacred person of the king and his august family outrages and brutalities which are still carried on and renewed day by day; those who have usurped the reins of the administration have at last completed their work by declaring an unjust war against His Majesty the Emperor and by attacking his provinces situated in the Low Countries. Some of the possessions of the Germanic Empire have been enveloped in this oppression, and several others have only escaped the same danger by yielding to the imperious threats of the dominant party and of its emissaries.

His Majesty the King of Prussia, united with his Imperial Majesty by the bonds of a strict defensive alliance and himself the preponderant member of the Germanic body, could not excuse himself from marching to the help of his ally and his co-state; and it is under this double relationship that he takes up the defence of this monarch and of Germany.

To these great interests is added another aim equally important and very dear to the hearts of the two sovereigns; it is to put an end to the anarchy in the interior of France, to stop the attacks carried on against the throne and the altar, to re-establish the legal power, to restore to the king the security and liberty of which he is deprived, and to put him in a position to exercise the legitimate authority which is his due.

Convinced that the sound part of the French nation abhors the excesses of a faction which dominates it, and that the greatest number of the inhabitants look forward with impatience to the moment of relief to declare themselves openly against the odious enterprises of their oppressors. His Majesty the Emperor and His Majesty the King of Prussia, call upon them and invite them to return without delay to the ways of reason, justice, order and peace. It is in accordance with these views, that I, the undersigned, the General, commanding in chief the two armies, declare:

1. That, drawn into the present war by irresistible circumstances, the two allied courts propose to themselves no other aim than the welfare of France and have no intention of enriching themselves by conquests;

2. That they do not intend to meddle with the internal government of France, but that they merely wish to deliver the king, the queen and the royal family from their captivity, and to procure for His Most Christian Majesty the necessary security that he may make without danger or hindrance the conventions which he shall judge suitable and may work for the welfare of his subjects, according to his promises and as far as it shall depend on him;

3. That the combined armies will protect the towns, boroughs and villages and the persons and goods of those who shall submit to the king and who shall co-operate in the immediate re-establishment of order and of the police in the whole of France;

4. That the national guard will be called upon to watch provisionally over the peace of the towns and country districts, the security of the persons and goods of all Frenchmen, until the arrival of the troops of their Imperial and Royal Majesties, or until otherwise ordered, under pain of being personally responsible; that on the contrary, those of the national guard who shall fight against the troops of the two allied courts, and who shall be taken with arms in their hands, will be treated as enemies and punished as rebels to their king and as disturbers of the public peace;

5. That the generals, officers, under officers and troops of the French line are likewise summoned to return to their former fidelity and to submit themselves at once to the king, their legitimate sovereign;

6. That the members of the departments, of the districts and municipalities shall likewise answer with their heads and their goods for all offences, fires, murders, pillaging, and acts of violence, which they shall allow to be committed, or which they have not manifestly exerted themselves to prevent within their territory; that they shall likewise be required to continue their functions provisionally, until His Most Christian Majesty, being once more at liberty, may have provided for them subsequently or until it shall have been otherwise ordained in his name in the meantime;

7. That the inhabitants of the towns, boroughs and villages who may dare to defend themselves against the troops of their Imperial and Royal Majesties and fire on them either in the open country, or through windows, doors and openings of their houses, shall be punished immediately according to the strictness of the law of war, and their houses destroyed or burned. On the contrary, all the inhabitants of the said towns, boroughs and villages, who shall submit to their king, opening their doors to the troops of their Majesties, shall at once be placed under their immediate protection; their persons, their property, and their effects shall be under the protection of the laws, and the general security of all and each of them shall be provided for;

8. The city of Paris and all its inhabitants without distinction shall be required to submit at once and without delay to the king, to put that prince in full and perfect liberty, and to assure him as well as the other royal personages the inviolability and respect which the law of nations and men requires of subjects toward their sovereigns; their Imperial and Royal Majesties declare personally responsible with their lives for all events, to be tried by military law and without hope of pardon, all the member of the National Assembly, of the department, district, municipality and national guard of Paris, the justices of the peace and all others that shall be concerned; their said Majesties also declare on their honor and on their word as Emperor and King, that if the château of the Tuileries be entered by force or attacked, if the least violence or outrage be offered to their Majesties, the king, queen and royal family, if their preservation and their liberty be not immediately provided for, they will exact an exemplary and ever-memorable vengeance, by delivering the city of Paris over to a military execution and to complete ruin, and the rebels guilty of these outrages to the punishments they shall have deserved. Their Imperial and Royal Majesties, on the contrary, promise the inhabitants of Paris to employ their good offices with his Most Christian Majesty to obtain pardon for their misdeeds and errors, and to take the most vigorous measures to assure their lives and property, if they obey promptly and exactly all the above mentioned order.

Finally, their Majesties being able to recognize as laws in France only those which shall emanate from the king, in the enjoyment of a perfect liberty, protest beforehand against the authenticity of any declarations which may be made in the name of His Most Christian Majesty, so long as his sacred person, that of the queen, and those of the royal family shall not be really in security, for the effecting of which their Imperial and Royal Majesties beg His Most Christian Majesty to appoint the city in his kingdom nearest the frontiers, to which he would prefer to retire with the queen and his family under good and sufficient escort, which will be furnished him for this purpose, so that his most Christian Majesty may in all security summon such ministers and councillors as he may see fit, hold such meetings as he deems best, provide for the re-establishment of good order and regulate the administration of his kingdom.

Finally, I declare and bind myself, moreover, in my own private name and in my above capacity, to cause the troops entrusted to my command to observe a good and exact discipline, promising to treat with kindness and moderation all well intentioned subjects who show themselves peaceful and submissive, and only to use force against those who shall make themselves guilty of resistance and ill-will.

It is for these reasons that I call upon and exhort all the inhabitants of the kingdom in the strongest and most urgent manner not to oppose the march and the operations of the troops which I command, but rather to grant them everywhere a free passage and with every good will to aid and assist as circumstances shall require.

Given at the head-quarters at Coblentz, July 25, 1792.
Signed, Charles-William Ferdinand,
Duke of Brunswick-Lunebourg.

25. Decree for Suspending the King

August 10, 1792

The National Assembly, considering that the dangers of the fatherland have reached their height;

That it is for the legislative body the most sacred of duties to employ all means to save it;

That it is impossible to find efficacious ones, unless they shall ocupy themselves with removing the source of its evils;

Considering that these evils spring principally from the misgivings which the conduct of the head of the executive power has inspired, in a war undertaken in his name against the constitution and the national independence;

That these misgivings have provoked from different parts of the kingdom a desire tending to the revocation of the authority delegated to Louis XVI;

Considering, nevertheless, that the legislative body ought not to wish to aggrandize itself by any usurpation;

That in the extraordinary circumstances wherein events unprovided for by any of the laws have placed it, it cannot reconcile what it owes, in its unshaken fidelity to the constitution, with the firm resolve to be buried under the ruins of the temple of liberty rather than to permit it to perish, except by recurring to the sovereignty of the people and by taking at the same time the precautions which are indispensable, in order that this recourse may not be rendered illusory by treasons; decrees as follows:

1. The French people are invited to form a national convention; the extraordinary commission shall present tomorrow a proposal to indicate the method and the time of this convention.

2. The head of the executive power is provisionally suspended from his functions until the national convention has pronounced upon the measures which it believes ought to be adopted in order to assure the sovereignty of the people and the reign of liberty and equality.

3. The extraordinary commission shall present within the day a method for organizing a new ministry; the ministers actually in service shall continue provisionally the exercise of their functions.

4. The extraordinary commission shall present, likewise, within the day, a proposal for a decree upon the selection of a governor for the prince royal.

5. The payment of the civil list shall continue suspended until the decision of the national convention. The extraordinary commission shall present, within twenty-four hours, a proposal for a decree upon the stipend to be granted to the king during the suspension.

6. The registers of the civil list shall be deposited in the office of the National Assembly, after having been numbered and attested by two commissioners of the assembly, who shall repair for that purpose to the intendant of the civil list.

7. The king and his family shall reside within the precincts of the legislative body until quiet may be re-established in Paris.

8. The department shall give orders to cause to be prepared for them within the day a lodging at the Luxembourg, where they shall be put under the custody of the citizens and the law.

9. Every public functionary, every soldier, under-officer, officer, of whatever grade he may be, and general of an army, who, in these days of alarm shall abandon his post, is declared infamous and traitorous to the fatherland.

10. The department and the municipality of Paris shall cause the present decree to be immediately and solemnly proclaimed.

11. It shall be sent by extraordinary couriers to the eighty-three departments, which shall be required to cause it to reach the municipalities of their jurisdiction within twenty-four hours, in order to be proclaimed with the same solemnity.

26. Decree for Electing the Convention

August 11, 1792

The National Assembly, considering that it has not the right to submit to imperative regulations the exercise of the sovereignty in the formation of a national convention, and that, nevertheless, it is important for the public safety that the primary and electoral assemblies should form themselves at the same time, should act with uniformity, and that the national convention should be promptly assembled,

Invites the citizens, in the name of liberty, equality, and the fatherland, to conform themselves to the following regulations:

1. The primary assemblies shall select the same number of electors as they have selected in the last elections.

2. The distinction of Frenchmen into active and non-active citizens shall be suppressed; and in order to be admitted to them, it shall suffice to be French, twenty-one years of age, domiciled for a year, living from his income or the product of his labor, and not being in the status of a household servant. As to those who, meeting the conditions of activity, were summoned by the law to take the civic oath, they shall be bound, in order to be admitted, to give proof of the taking of that oath.

3. The conditions of eligibility demanded for the electors or for the representatives not being applicable to a national convention, it shall suffice, in order to be eligible as deputy or as elector, to be twenty-five years of age and to unite the conditions demanded by the preceding article.

4. Each department shall select the number of deputies and alternates which it has selected for the existing legislature.

5. The elections shall take place according to the same method as for the legislative assemblies ...

27. Decree upon Religious Policy

January 11, 1793

The National Convention, after having heard a deputation of the citizens of the departments of Eure, Orne and Eure-et-Loir, who ask in the name of more than a hundred thousand of their fellow citizens that they be not disturbed in the exercise of their worship, and who protest that they wish to live and die good catholics as well as good republicans, and upon the proposal of one of its members, passes to the order of the day, giving as the reason the existence of its decree of the 30th of November, in which it orders that a notification to the people shall be made in order to explain to them that the National Convention never had an intention of depriving them of the ministers of the catholic sect whom the Civil Constitution of the Clergy has given them ...

28. Decree upon the Non-Juring Priests

April 23, 1793

1. The National Convention decrees that all the secular and regular ecclesiastics and converts and lay brothers, who have not taken oath to maintain liberty and equality in conformity with the law of August 15, 1792, shall be embarked and transferred without delay to French Guiana.

2. Those who shall be denounced because of incivism by six citizens in the canton shall be subject to the same penalty.

5. Those deported in execution of articles 1 and 2 above who may return to the territory of the Republic shall be punished by death within twenty-four hours.

29. Decree upon Dangerous Priests

October 20-21, 1793 (29-30 Vendémiaire, Year II)

1. Priests subject to deportation and taken with arms in their hands, either upon the frontiers or in the country of the enemy;

Those who shall have been or shall be discovered in possession of permits or passports delivered by French émigré leaders, or by commanders of enemies' armies, or by leaders of the rebels;

And those who shall be provided with any counter-revolutionary symbols, shall be delivered within twenty-four hours to the executioner of condemned criminals and put to death, after the facts shall have been declared proven by a military commission formed by the officers of the staff of the division within the area of which they shall have been arrested.

2. Those who have been or who shall be arrested without arms in the countries occupied by the troops of the Republic shall be tried in the same form and punished by the same penalty, if they have been previously in the armies of the enemy or in the musters of émigrés or insurgents, or if they were there at the moment of their arrest.

5. Those of these ecclesiastics who shall return and those who have returned to the territory of the Republic shall be sent to the court house of the criminal tribunal of the department within the area of which they shall have been or shall be arrested; and, after having undergone examination, of which record shall be kept, they shall be delivered within twenty-four hours to the executioner of condemned criminals and put to death, after the judges of the tribunal shall have declared that the prisoners are convicted of having been subjects of deportation.

10. Those declared subjects for deportation, trial and punishment, as such, are the bishops, former archbishops, curés kept in place, vicars of these bishops, superiors and directors of seminaries, vicars of the curés, professors of seminaries and colleges, public instructors, and those who shall have preached in any churches whatsoever since the decree of February 5, 1791, who shall not have taken the oath prescribed by article 39 of the decree of July 24, 1790 ... or who have retracted it, although they may have taken it again since their retraction;

All secular or regular ecclesiastics and convert and lay brothers, who have not complied with the decrees of August 14, 1792, and April 21st, last, or who have retracted their oath;

And finally all those who have been denounced because of incivism, when the denunciation shall have been pronounced valid, in conformity with the decree of the said 21st day of April.

12. The ecclesiastics who have taken the oath prescribed by the decrees of July 24 and November 27, 1790, as well as that of liberty and equality, within the fixed time, and who shall be denounced because of incivism, shall be embarked without delay and transferred to the east coast of Africa from the twenty-third to the twenty-eighth degree south.

17. Priests deported voluntarily and with passports ... are reputed émigrés.

18. Every citizen is required to denounce the ecclesiastic whom he shall know to be subject to deportation, to arrest him or cause him to be arrested and conducted before the nearest police officer; he shall receive a hundred livres reward.

19. Every citizen who shall conceal a priest subject to deportation shall be condemned to the same penalty.

30. Decree upon Religious Freedom

December 8, 1793 (18 Frimaire, Year II)

1. All violence and measures in constraint of the liberty of worship are forbidden.

2. The surveillance of the constituted authorities and the action of the public force shall confine themselves in this

matter, each for what concerns it, to measures of police and public safety.

3. The National Convention, by preceding provisions, does not mean to derogate in any manner from the laws or precautions of public safety against the refractory or turbulent priests, or against all those who may attempt to take advantage of the pretext of religion to compromise the cause of liberty; no more does it intend to disapprove of what has been done up to this day in virtue of the orders of the representatives of the people, nor to furnish or for diminishing the free text for disturbing patriotism or for diminishing the free scope of the public spirit. The Convention invites all good citizens, in the name of the fatherland, to abstain from all disputes that are theological or foreign to the great interests of the French people, in order to co-operate by all methods in the triumph of the Republic and the ruin of all its enemies.

31. Decree for Establishing the Worship of the Supreme Being

May 7, 1794 (18 Floréal, Year II)

1. The French people recognize the existence of the Supreme Being and the immortality of the soul.

2. They recognize that the worship worthy of the Supreme Being is the practice of the duties of man.

3. They place in the first rank of these duties, to detest bad faith and tyranny, to punish tyrants and traitors, to relieve the unfortunate, to respect the weak, to defend the oppressed, to do to others all the good that is possible and not to be unjust to anyone.

4. Festivals shall be instituted to remind man of the thought of the divinity and of the dignity of his being.

5. They shall take their names from the glorious events of our revolution, from the virtues most cherished and most useful to man, and from the great gifts of nature.

6. The French Republic shall celebrate every year the festival of July 14, 1789, August 10, 1792, and May 31, 1793.

7. It shall celebrate on the days of *décadi* the list of festivals that follows: to the supreme being and to nature; to the human race; to the French people; to the benefactors of humanity; to the martyrs of liberty; to liberty and equality; to the republic; to the liberty of the world; to the love of the fatherland; to the hatred of tyrants and of traitors; to truth; to justice; to modesty; to glory and immortality; to friendship; to frugality; to courage; to good faith; to heroism; to disinterestedness; to stoicism; to love; to conjugal love; to paternal love; to maternal tenderness; to filial affection; to childhood; to youth; to manhood; to old age; to misfortune; to agriculture; to industry; to our forefathers; to posterity; to happiness.

8. The committees of public safety and of public instruction are charged to present a plan of organization for these festivals.

9. The National Convention summons all the talents worthy to serve the cause of humanity to the honor of contributing to its establishment by hymns and patriotic songs and by all the means which can enhance its beauty and utility.

10. The Committee of Public Safety shall confer distinction upon those works which seem the best adapted to carry on these purposes and shall reward their authors.

11. Liberty of worship is maintained, in conformity with the decree of 18 Frimaire.

12. Every gathering that is aristocratic and contrary to public order shall be suppressed.

13. In the case of disturbances of which any worship whatsoever may be the occasion or motive, those who may excite them by fanatical preaching or by counter-revolutionary insinuations, those who may provoke them by unjust and gratuitous violence, shall likewise be punished with all the severity of the law.

14. A special report upon the provisions of detail relative to the present decree shall be made.

15. A festival in honor of the Supreme Being shall be celebrated upon 20 Prairial next.

David is charged to present the plan thereof to the National Convention.

32. Decree upon Expenditures for Religion

September 18, 1794 (2 Sans-Culottides, Year II)

1. The French Republic no longer pays the expenses or salaries of any sect.

33. Decree upon Religion

February 21, 1795 (3 Ventôse, Year III)

1. In conformity with article 7 of the *Declaration of the Rights of Man* and with article 122 of the constitution, the exercise of any worship cannot be disturbed.

2. The Republic does not pay salaries for any of them.

3. It does not furnish an edifice, either for the exercise of worship or the lodging of the ministers.

4. The ceremonies of every worship are forbidden outside of the premises chosen for their exercise.

5. The law does not recognize any minister of religion: nobody can appear in public with garments, ornaments or costumes set apart for religious ceremonies.

6. Every gathering of citizens for the exercise of any worship is subject to the surveillance of the constituted

authorities. That surveillance confines itself to measures of police and public security.

7. No symbol peculiar to a religion can be put in or upon the outside of a public place, in any manner whatsoever. No inscription can designate the place which is set aside for it. No proclamation or public summons can be made in order to call the citizens there.

34. Declaration of the Regent of France

January 28, 1793

Louis-Stanislas-Xavier of France, son of France, uncle of the king, regent of the kingdom, to all those to whom these presents shall come, greeting.

Filled with horror upon learning that the most criminal of men have just reached the climax of their numerous outrages by the greatest of crimes, we have first implored heaven to obtain its assistance in surmounting the feelings of a profound grief and the impulses of our indignation, to the end that we may give ourselves up to the fulfilling of the duties which, under such grave circumstances, are the first in order of those which the immutable laws of the French monarchy impose upon us,

Our very dear and honored brother and sovereign lord, King Louis, the sixteen of that name, having died on the 21st of the present month of January, beneath the parricidal sword which the ferocious usurpers of the sovereign authority in France raised against his august person, we declare that the Dauphin Louis-Charles, born on the 27th day of March, 1785, is king of France and of Navarre, under the name of Louis XVII …

35. Decree for Establishing the Revolutionary Committees

March 21, 1793

1. There shall be formed in each commune of the Republic and in each section of the communes divided into sections, at the hour which shall be indicated in advance by the general council, a committee composed of twelve citizens.

2. The members of this committee, who cannot be chosen from the ecclesiastics, former nobles, former seigneurs of the locality, and agents of the former seigneurs, shall be chosen by ballot and by plurality of the votes.

4. The committee of the commune, or each of the committees of the sections of the commune, shall be charged to receive for its district the declarations of all the strangers actually residing within the commune or who may arrive there.

5. These declarations shall contain the names, age, profession, place of birth and means of existence of the declarer.

6. They shall be made within eight days after the publication of the present decree; the list thereof shall be printed and posted.

7. Every foreigner who shall have refused or neglected to make his declaration before the committee of the commune or of the section in which he shall reside, within the period above prescribed, shall be required to leave the commune within twenty-four hours and the territory of the Republic within eight days.

36. Decree upon the Press

March 29, 1793

The National Convention decrees:

1. Whoever shall be convicted of having composed or printed works or writings which incite to the dissolution of the national representation, the re-establishment of monarchy or of any other power which constitutes an attack upon the sovereignty of the people, shall be arraigned before the extraordinary tribunal and punished with death.

2. The vendors, distributors and hawkers of these works or writings shall be condemned to an imprisonment which shall not exceed three months, if they declare the authors, printers or other persons from whom they have obtained them; if they refuse this declaration, they shall be punished by two years in prison.

37. Decree for Establishing the Committee of Public Safety

April 6, 1793

The National Convention decrees:

1. There shall be formed, by the call of names, a committee of public safety, composed of nine members of the National Convention.

2. The committee shall deliberate in secret; it shall be charged to supervise and accelerate the action of the administration entrusted to the provisional executive council, of which it may even suspend the orders, when it shall believe them contrary to the national interest, subject to giving information thereof to the Convention without delay.

3. It is authorised to take, under urgent circumstances, measures of external and internal defence; and the orders signed by the majority of its deliberating members, which cannot be less than two-thirds, shall be executed without delay by the provisional executive council. It shall not in any case issue warrants of capture or arrest, except against the

executive agents, and subject to rendering an account thereof without delay to the Convention.

4. The National Treasury shall hold at the disposal of the committee of public safety [a sum of money] to the amount of a hundred thousand livres for secret expenses, which shall be disbursed by the committee and paid upon its commands, which shall be signed as are the orders.

5. It shall make each week in writing a general report of its operations and of the situation of the Republic.

6. A register of all its deliberations shall be kept.

7. This committee is established only for one month.

8. The national treasury shall remain independent of the committee of execution and subject to the immediate surveillance of the Convention, according to the method determined by the decrees.

38. Robespierre's Proposed Declaration of Rights

April 24, 1793

The representatives of the French people, met in National Convention, recognizing that human laws which do not flow from the eternal laws of justice and reason are only the outrages of ignorance and despotism upon humanity; convinced that neglect and contempt of the natural rights of man are the sole causes of the crimes and misfortunes of the world; have resolved to set forth in a solemn declaration these sacred and inalienable rights, in order that all citizens, being enabled to compare constantly the acts of the government with the purpose of every social institution, may never permit themselves to be oppressed and disgraced by tryanny; and in order that the people may always have before their eyes the foundations of their liberty and their welfare; the magistrate, the rule of his duties; the legislator, the purpose of his mission.

In consequence, the National Convention proclaims in the face of the world and under the eyes of the Immortal Legislator the following declaration of the rights of man and citizen.

1. The purpose of every political association is the maintenance of the natural and imprescriptible rights of man and the development of all his faculties.

2. The principal rights of man are those of providing for the preservation of his existence and his liberty.

3. These rights belong equally to all men, whatever may be the difference of their physical and mental powers.

4. Equality of rights is established by nature: society, far from impairing it, exists only to guarantee it against the abuse of power which renders it illusory.

5. Liberty is the power which belongs to man to exercise at his will all his faculties; it has justice for rule, the rights of others for limits, nature for principle, and the law for safeguard.

6. The right to assemble peaceably, the right to express one's opinion, either by means of the press or in any other manner, are such necessary consequences of the principle of the liberty of man, that the necessity to enunciate them supposes either the presence or the fresh recollection of despotism.

7. The law can forbid only that which is injurious to society; it can order only that which is useful.

8. Every law which violates the imprescriptible rights of man is essentially unjust and tyrannical; it is not a law.

9. Property is the right which each citizen has, to enjoy and dispose of the portion of goods which the law guarantees to him …

39. Decree for the Levée en Masse

August 23, 1793

1. From this moment until that in which the enemy shall have been driven from the soil of the Republic, all Frenchmen are in permanent requisition for the service of the armies.

The young men shall go to battle; the married men shall forge arms and transport provisions; the women shall make tents and clothing and shall serve in the hospitals; the children shall turn old linen into lint; the aged shall betake themselves to the public places in order to arouse the courage of the warriors and preach the hatred of kings and the unity of the Republic.

2. The national buildings shall be converted into barracks, the public places into workshops for arms, the soil of the cellars shall be washed in order to extract therefrom the saltpetre.

3. The arms of the regulation calibre shall be reserved exclusively for those who shall march against the enemy; the service of the interior shall be performed with hunting pieces and side arms.

4. The saddle horses are put in requisition to complete the cavalry corps; the draught-horses, other than those employed in agriculture, shall convey the artillery and the provisions.

5. The Committee of Public Safety is charged to take all the necessary measures to set up without delay an extraordinary manufacture of arms of every sort which corresponds with the ardor and energy of the French people. It is, accordingly, authorised to form all the establishments, factories, workshops and mills which shall be deemed necessary for the carrying on of these works, as well as to put in requisition, within the entire extent of the Republic, the artists and workingmen who can contribute to their success. For this purpose there shall be put at the disposal of the Minister of War a sum of thirty millions, to be taken out of the four hundred ninety- eight million two hundred thousand livres in *assignats* which are in reserve in the fund of the three keys. The central establishment of this extraordinary manufacture shall be fixed at Paris.

6. The representatives of the people sent out for the execution of the present law shall have the same authority in their respective districts, acting in concert with the Committee of Public Safety; they are invested with the unlimited powers assigned to the representatives of the people and the armies.

7. Nobody can get himself replaced in the service for which he shall have been requisitioned. The public functionaries shall remain at their posts.

8. The levy shall be general. The unmarried citizens and widowers without children, from eighteen to twenty-five years, shall march first; they shall assemble without delay at the head-town of their districts, where they shall practice every day at the manual of arms while awaiting the hour of departure.

40. The Law of Suspects

September 17, 1793

1. Immediately after the publication of the present decree all the suspect-persons who are in the territory of the Republic and who are still at liberty shall be placed under arrest.

2. These are accounted suspect-persons: 1st, those who by their conduct, their connections, their remarks, or their writings show themselves the partisans of tyranny or federalism and the enemies of liberty; 2d, those who cannot, in the manner prescribed by the decree of March 21st last, justify their means of existence and the performance of their civic duties; 3d, those who have been refused certificates of civism; 4th, public functionaries suspended or removed from their functions by the National Convention or its commissioners and not reinstated, especially those who have been or shall be removed in virtue of the decree of August 14th last; 5th, those of the former nobles, all of the husbands, wives, fathers, mothers, sons or daughters, brothers, or sisters, and agents of the *émigrés* who have not constantly manifested their attachment to the revolution; 6th, those who have emigrated from France in the interval from July 1, 1789, to the publication of the decree of March 30-April 8, 1792, although they may have returned to France within the period fixed by that decree or earlier.

3. The committees of surveillance established according to the decree of March 21st last, or those which have been substituted for them, either by the orders of the representatives of the people sent with the armies and into the departments, or in virtue of special decrees of the National Convention, are charged to prepare, each in its district, the list of suspect-persons, to issue warrants of arrest against them, and to cause seals to be put upon their papers. The commanders of the public force to whom these warrants shall be delivered shall be required to put them into execution immediately, under penalty of removal.

4. The members of the committee without being seven in number and an absolute majority of votes cannot order the arrest of any person.

5. The persons arrested as suspects shall be first conveyed to the jail of the place of their imprisonment: in default of jails, they shall be kept from view in their respective dwellings.

6. Within the eight days following they shall be transferred to the national building, which the administrations of the department, immediately after the receipt of the present decree, shall be required to designate and to cause to be prepared for that purpose.

7. The prisoners can cause to be transferred to these buildings the movables which are of absolute necessity to them; they shall remain there under guard until the peace.

8. The expenses of custody shall be at the charge of the prisoners and shall be divided among them equally; this custody shall be confided preferably to the fathers of families and the parents of the citizens who are upon or shall go to the frontiers. The salary for it is fixed for each man of the guard at the value of a day and a half of labor.

9. The committees of surveillance shall send without delay to the committee of general security of the National Convention the list of the persons whom they shall have caused to be arrested, with the reasons for their arrest and the papers which shall have been seized with them as suspect-persons.

10. The civil and criminal tribunals can, if there is need, cause to be arrested and sent into the above mentioned jails persons accused of offences in respect of whom it may have been declared that there was no ground for accusation, or who may have been acquitted of the accusations brought against them.

41. The Law of the Maximum

September 29, 1793

1. The articles which the Convention has decided to be of prime necessity and for which it has believed that it ought to fix the *maximum* or highest price are: fresh meat, salt meat and bacon, butter, sweet-oil, cattle, salt fish, wine, brandy, vinegar, cider, beer, fire-wood, charcoal, mineral coal, candles, combustible oil, salt, soda, sugar, honey, white paper, skins, iron, brass, lead, steel, copper, hemp, linen, wool, woolens, fabrics, the raw materials which serve for fabrics, sabots, shoes, cabbages and turnips, soap, potash, and tobacco.

2. For the articles included in the above list, the *maximum* price for fire-wood of the first quality, that of charcoal and of mineral coal, are the same as in 1790, plus a twentieth of the price. The decree of August 19th upon the determination by the departments of the prices of fire-wood, coal and peat is repealed.

The *maximum* or highest price of tobacco in rolls is twenty *sous* per pound, *poids de marc*; in that of smoking tobacco is ten *sous*; that of salt per pound is two *sous*; that of soap is twenty five *sous*.

3. The *maximum* of the price of all the other commodities and articles of merchandise included in article 1 for the whole extent of the Republic, until the month of September next, shall be the price which each fo them had in 1790, such as is established by the official price-lists or the market price of each department, and a third over and above this same price, deduction being made of fiscal and other duties to which they were then subject, under whatever denomination they may have existed.

7. All persons who may sell or purchase the articles of merchandise included in article 1 above the *maximum* of the price settled and posted in each department shall pay by way of the municipal police a fine, for which they shall be jointly and severally liable, of double the value of the article sold and payable to the informer: they shall be enrolled upon the list of suspected persons and treated as such. The purchaser shall not be subject to the penalties provided above, if he denounces the offence of the seller; and each merchant shall be required to have a list displayed in his shop, bearing the *maximum* or highest price of his merchandise.

8. The *maximum* or highest price belonging to salaries, wages, and manual labor by the day in each place, shall be fixed, to commence from the publication of this law until the month of September next, by the general councils of the communes at the same amount as in 1790, to which there shall be added half of that price in addition.

9. The municipalities shall put into requisition and punish, according to circumstances, with three days' imprisonment the workingmen, factory operatives and various laboring persons who may refuse without legitimate reasons to engage in their accustomed labors.

17. During the war all exportation of articles of merchandise or commodities of prime necessity, under any name or commission whatsoever, is prohibited upon all the frontiers, salt excepted.

42. Treaty of Basle

April 5, 1795 (16 Germinal, Year III)

The French Republic and the King of Prussia, equally prompted by the desire to put an end to the war which divides them, by a firm peace between the two nations,

1. There shall be peace, amity and good understanding between the French Republic and the King of Prussia, considered as such and in the capacity of Elector of Brandenburg and of co-state of the Germanic Empire.

2. Accordingly, all hostilities between the two contracting powers shall cease, dating from the ratification of the present treaty; and neither of them, dating from the same time, shall furnish against the other, in any capacity or by any title whatsoever, any assistance or contingent, whether in men, in horses, provisions, money, munitions of war, or otherwise.

3. Neither of the contracting powers shall grant passage over its territory to troops of the enemies of the other.

4. The troops of the French Republic shall evacuate, within the fifteen days which follow the ratification of the present treaty, the parts of the Prussian states which they may occupy upon the right bank of the Rhine.

5. The troops of the French Republic shall continue to occupy the part of the states of the King of Prussia situated upon the left bank of the Rhine. All definitive arrangement with respect to these provinces shall be put off until the general pacification between France and the German Empire.

11. The French Republic shall accept the good offices of His Majesty the King of Prussia in favor of the princes and states of the Germanic Empire who shall desire to enter directly into negotiation with it, and who, for that purpose, have already requested or shall yet request the intervention of the king. The French Republic, in order to give to the King of Prussia a signal proof of its desire to co-operate for the re-establishment of the former bonds of amity which have existed between the two countries, consents not to treat as hostile countries, during the space of three months after the ratification of the present treaty, those of the princes and states of the said empire situated upon the right bank of the Rhine and in favor of whom the king shall interest himself.

SEPARATE AND SECRET ARTICLES.

2. If at the general pacification between the Germanic Empire and France, the left bank of the Rhine remains with France, His Majesty, the King of Prussia, will come to an agreement with the French Republic upon the method of the cession of the Prussian States situated upon the left bank of this river, in exchange for such territorial indemnification as shall be agreed upon. In this case the king shall accept the guarantee which the Republic offers him for this indemnification.

43. Constitution of the Year III

August 22, 1795 (5 Fructidor, Year III)

Declaration of the Rights and Duties of Man and Citizen.

The French people proclaim in the presence of the Supreme Being the following declaration of the rights of man and citizen:

Rights.

1. The rights of man in society are liberty, equality, security, property.

2. Liberty consists in the power to do that which does not injure the rights of others.

3. Equality consists in this, that the law is the same for all, whether it protects or punishes.

Equality does not admit of any distinction of birth, nor of any inheritance of authority.

4. Security results from the co-operation of all in order to assure the rights of each.

5. Property is the right to enjoy and to dispose of one's goods, income, and the fruit of one's labor and industry.

6. The law is the general will expressed by the majority of the citizens or their representatives.

7. That which is not forbidden by the law cannot be prevented.

No one can be constrained to do that which it does not ordain.

8. No one can be summoned into court, accused, arrested, or detained except in the cases determined by the law and according to the forms which it has prescribed.

9. Those who incite, promote, sign, execute, or cause to be executed arbitrary acts are guilty and ought to be punished.

10. Every severity which may not be necessary to secure the person of a prisoner ought to be severely repressed by the law.

11. No one can be tried until after he has been heard or legally summoned.

12. The law ought to decree only such penalties as are strictly necessary and proportionate to the offence.

13. All treatment which increases the penalty fixed by the law is a crime.

14. No law, either civil or criminal, can have retroactive effect.

15. Every man can contract his time and his services, but he cannot sell himself nor be sold; his person is not an alienable property.

16. Every tax is established for the public utility; it ought to be apportioned among those liable for taxes, according to their means.

17. Sovereignty resides essentially in the totality of the citizens.

18. No individual nor assembly of part of the citizens can assume the sovereignty.

19. No one can without legal delegation exercise any authority or fill any public function.

20. Each citizen has a legal right to participate directly or indirectly in the formation of the law and in the selection of the representatives of the people and of the public functionaries.

21. The public offices cannot become the property of those who hold them.

22. The social guarantee cannot exist if the division of powers is not established, if their limits are not fixed, and if the responsibility of the public functionaries is not assured.

TITLE V. LEGISLATIVE POWER.

General Provisions.

44. The legislative body is composed of a Council of Ancients and a Council of the Five Hundred.

45. In no case can the legislative body delegate to one or several of its members, nor to anybody whomsoever, any of the functions which are assigned to it by the present constitution.

46. It cannot itself or by delegates discharge the executive or the judicial power.

47. The position of member of the legislative body and the discharge of any other public function, except that of archivist of the Republic, are incompatible.

48. The law determines the method of permanently or temporarily replacing the public functionaries who have been elected members of the legislative body.

49. Each department contributes, in proportion to its population alone, to the selection of the members of the Council of Ancients and of the members of the Council of the Five Hundred.

50. Every ten years the legislative body, according to the lists of population which are sent to it, determines the number of members of each council which each department shall furnish.

51. No change can be made in this apportionment during this interval.

52. The members of the legislative body are not representatives of the department which has selected them, but of the entire nation, and no instructions can be given to them.

53. Both councils are renewed every year by a third.

54. The members retiring after three years can be immediately re-elected for the three following years, after which there must be an interval of two years before the can be elected again.

55. No one in any case can be a member of the legislative body during more than six consecutive years.

56. If through extraordinary circumstances either of the two councils finds itself reduced to less than two-thirds of its members, it gives notice thereof to the Executive Directory, which is required to convoke without delay the primary assemblies of the departments, which have members of the legislative body to replace through the effect of these circumstances: the primary assemblies immediately select the electors, who proceed to the necessary replacements.

57. The newly elected members for both of the councils meet upon 1 Prairial of each year in the commune which has been indicated by the preceding legislative body, or in the same commune where it has held its last sittings, if it has not designated another.

58. The two councils always reside in the same commune.

59. The legislative body is permanent; nevertheless, it can adjourn for periods which it designates.

60. In no case can the two councils meet in a single hall.

61. Neither in the Council of Ancients nor in the Council of the Five Hundred can the functions of president and secretary exceed the duration of one month.

62. The two councils respectively have the right of police in the place of their sittings and in the environs which they have determined.

63. They have respectively the right of police over their members; but they cannot pronounce any penalty more severe than censure, arrests for eight days, or imprisonment for three.

64. The sittings of both councils are public: the spectators cannot exceed in number half of the members of each council respectively.

The minutes of the sittings are printed.

65. Every decision is taken by rising and sitting; in case of doubt, the roll call is employed, but in that case the votes are secret.

66. Upon the request of one hundred of its members each council can form itself into secret committee of the whole but only in order to discuss, not to resolve.

67. Neither of these councils can create any permanent committee within its own body.

But each council has the power, when a matter seems to it susceptible of a preparatory examination, to appoint from among its members a special commission, which confines itself exclusively to the matter that led to its formation.

This commission is dissolved as soon as the council has legislated upon the matter with which it was charged.

68. The members of the legislative body receive an annual compensation; it is fixed for both councils at the value of three thousand myriagrams of wheat (six hundred and thirty quintals, thirty-two pounds).

69. The Executive Directory cannot cause any body of troops to pass or to sojourn within six myriameters (twelve common leagues) of the commune where the legislative body is holding its sittings, except upon its requisition or with its authorisation.

70. There is near the legislative body a guard of citizens taken from the reserve national guard of all the departments and chosen by their brothers in arms.

This guard cannot be less than fifteen hundred men in active service.

71. The legislative body fixes the method of this service and its duration.

72. The legislative body is not to be present at any public ceremony nor does it send deputations to them.

COUNCIL OF THE FIVE HUNDRED.

73. The Council of the Five Hundred is unalterably fixed at that number.

74. In order to be elected a member of the Council of the Five Hundred it is necessary to be fully thirty years of age and to have been domiciled upon the soil of France for the ten years which shall have immediately preceded the election.

The condition of thirty years of age shall not be required before the seventh year of the Republic. Until that date the age of twenty-five shall be sufficient.

75. The Council of the Five Hundred cannot deliberate, unless the sitting is composed of at least two hundred members.

76. The proposal of the laws belongs exclusively to the Council of the Five Hundred.

77. No proposition can be considered or decided upon in the Council of the Five Hundred, except in observance of the following forms.

There shall be three readings of the proposal; the interval between two of these readings cannot be less than ten days.

The discussion is open after each reading; nevertheless, the Council of the Five Hundred can declare that there is cause for adjournment, or that there is no occasion for consideration.

Every proposal shall be printed and distributed two days before the second reading.

After the third reading the Council of the Five Hundred decides whether or not there is cause for adjournment.

78. No proposition, which after having been submitted to discussion, has been definitely rejected after the third reading, can be renewed until after a year has elapsed.

79. The propositions adopted by the Council of the Five Hundred are called *Resolutions.*

80. The preamble of every resolution states:

1st. The dates of the sittings upon which the three readings of the proposition shall have occurred;

2d. The act by which after the third reading it has been declared that there was not cause for adjournment.

81. The propositions recognized as urgent by a previous declaration of the Council of the Five Hundred are exempt from the forms prescribed by article 77.

This declaration states the motives for urgency and mention shall be made of them in the preamble of the resolution.

COUNCIL OF THE ANCIENTS.

82. The Council of Ancients is composed of two hundred and fifty members.

83. No one can be elected a member of the Council of Ancients,

Unless he is fully forty years of age;

Unless, moreover, he is married or a widower;

And unless he has been domiciled upon the soil of the Republic for the fifteen years which shall have immediately preceded the election.

84. The condition of domicile required by the preceding article and that prescribed by article 74 do not affect the citizens who are away from the soil of the Republic upon a mission of the government.

85. The Council of Ancients cannot deliberate unless the sitting is composed of at least one hundred and twenty-six members.

86. It belongs exclusively to the Council of Ancients to approve or reject the resolutions of the Council of the Five Hundred.

87. As soon as a resolution of the Council of the Five Hundred has reached the Council of Ancients the president directs the reading of the preamble.

88. The Council of Ancients refuses to approve the resolutions of the Council of the Five Hundred which have not been taken in the forms prescribed by the constitution.

89. If the proposition has been declared urgent by the Council of the Five Hundred, the Council of Ancients decides to approve or reject the act of urgency.

90. If the Council of Ancients rejects the act of urgency it does not pass upon the matter of the resolution.

91. If the resolution is not preceded by an act of urgency there shall be three readings of it: the interval between two of these readings cannot be less than five days.

The debate is open after each reading.

Every resolution is printed and distributed at least two days before the second reading.

92. The resolutions of the Council of the Five Hundred adopted by the Council of Ancients are called *Laws.*

93. The preamble of the laws states the dates of the sittings of the Council of Ancients upon which the three readings have occurred.

94. The decree by which the Council of Ancients recognizes the urgency of a law is adduced and mentioned in the preamble of that law.

95. The proposition for a law made by the Council of the Five Hundred embraces all the articles of a single project: the council shall reject them all or approve them in their entirety.

96. The approval of the Council of Ancients is expressed upon each proposition of law by this formula signed by the president and the secretaries: *The Council of Ancients approves …*

97. The refusal to adopt because of the omission of the forms indicated in article 77 is expressed by this formula, signed by the president and the secretaries: *The Constitution annuls …*

98. The refusal to approve the principle of law is expressed by this formula, signed by the president and secretaries: *The Council of Ancients cannot adopt …*

99. In the case of the preceding article, the rejected project of law cannot be again presented by the Council of the Five Hundred until after a year has elapsed.

100. The Council of the Five Hundred, nevertheless, can present at any date whatsoever a project of law which contains articles included in a project which has been rejected.

101. The Council of Ancients within the day sends the laws which it has adopted to the Council of the Five Hundred as well as to the Executive Directory.

102. The Council of Ancients can change the residence of the legislative body; it indicates in this case a new place and the date at which the two councils are required to repair thence.

The decree of the Council of Ancients upon this subject is irrevocable.

103. Upon the day of this decree neither of the councils can deliberate any further in the commune where they have until then resided.

The members who may continue their functions there make themselves guilty of an attempt against the security of the Republic.

PROMULGATION OF THE LAWS.

128. The Executive Directory causes the laws and other acts of the legislative body to be sealed and published within two days after their reception.

129. It causes to be sealed and promulgated, within a day, the laws and acts of the legislative body which are preceded by a decree of urgency.

130. The publication of the law and the acts of the legislative body is prescribed in the following form:

"In the name of the French Republic, (law) or (act of the legislative body) … the Directory orders that the above law or legislative act shall be published, executed, and that it shall be provided with the seal of the Republic."

131. Laws whose preambles do not attest the observation of the forms prescribed by articles 77 and 91 cannot be promulgated by the Executive Directory, and its responsibility in this respect lasts six years.

Laws are excepted for which the act of urgency has been approved by the Council of Ancients.

TITLE VI. EXECUTIVE POWER.

132. The executive power is delegated to a Directory of five members appointed by the legislative body, performing then the functions of an electoral body in the name of the nation.

133. The Council of the Five Hundred forms by secret ballot a list of ten times the number of the members of the Directory to be appointed and presents it to the Council of Ancients, which chooses, also by secret ballot, within this list.

134. The members of the Directory shall be at least forty years of age.

135. They can be taken only from among the citizens who have been members of the legislative body or ministers.

The provision of the present article shall be observed only commencing with the ninth year of the Republic.

136. Counting from the first day of the Year V of the Republic the members of the legislative body cannot be elected members of the Directory or ministers, either during the continuance of their legislative functions or during the first year after the expirations of these same functions.

137. The Directory is renewed in part by the election of one new member each year.

During the first four years, the lot shall decide upon the order of retirement of those who shall have been appointed for the first time.

138. None of the retiring members can be re-elected until after an interval of five years.

139. The ancestor and the descendant in the direct line, brothers, uncle and nephew, cousins of the first degree, and those related by marriage in these various degrees, cannot be at the same time members of the Directory, nor can they succeed them until after an interval of five years.

140. In case of the removal of one of the members of the Directory by death, resignation or otherwise, his successor is elected by the legislative body within ten days at the latest.

44. The Brumaire Decree

November 10, 1799 (19 Brumaire, Year VIII)

The Council of the Five Hundred, considering the situation of the Republic, approves the act of urgency and the following resolution:

1. The Directory is no more, and the following named persons, owing to the excesses and the crimes in which they have constantly engaged, and especially as regards the majority of them in the session of this morning, are no longer members of the national representation … [Here follow the names of sixty-one persons.]

2. The legislative body creates provisionally a consular executive commission, consisting of Citizens Siéyès, Roger-Ducos, and General Bonaparte, who shall bear the name of Consuls of the French Republic.

3. This commission is invested with the plentitude of directorial power and is particularly charged to organize order in all parts of the administration, to re-establish internal tranquility, and to procure honorable and enduring peace.

4. It is authorized to send out delegates having powers which are fixed and are within the limits of its own [powers].

5. The legislative body adjourns to the following 1 Ventôse [Feb. 20, 1800]; it shall reassemble of full right upon that date in its palace at Paris.

6. During the adjournment of the legislative body the adjourned members preserve their indemnity and their consitutional guarantee.

7. Without loss of their character as representatives of the people, they can be employed as ministers, diplomatic agents, delegates of the consular executive commission, and in all other civil functions. They are even invited in the name of the public welfare to accept these [employments].

8. Before its separation and during the sitting, each council shall appoint from its own body a commission consisting of twenty-five members.

9. The commissions appointed by the two councils with the formal and requisite proposal of the consular executive commission, shall decide upon all urgent matters of police, legislation, and finance.

10. The commission of the Five Hundred shall exercise the initiative; the commission of the Ancients, the approval.

11. The two commissions are further charged, in the same order of labor and co-operation, to prepare the changes to be brought about in the organic arrangements of the constitution of which experience has made known the faults and inconveniences.

45. Constitution of the Year VIII

December 13, 1799

TITLE I. OF THE EXERCISE OF THE RIGHTS OF CITIZENSHIP.

1. The French Republic is one and indivisible.

Its European territory is divided into departments and communal districts.

2. Every man born and residing in France fully twenty-one years of age, who has caused his name to be inscribed upon the civic register of his communal district and has since lived for one year upon the soil of the Republic, is a French citizen.

3. A foreigner becomes a French citizen when, after having reached the full age of twenty-one years and having declared his intention to settle in France, he has resided there for ten consecutive years.

4. The title to French citizenship is lost:

By naturalization in a foreign country;

By the acceptance of appointments or pensions tendered by a foreign government;

By affiliation with any foreign corporation which may imply distinctions of birth;

By condemnation to afflictive or infamous punishments.

5. The exercise of the rights of French citizenship is suspended by the state of bankruptcy or of direct inheritance, with gratuitous title, to the succession, in whole or in part, of a bankrupt;

By the condition of domestic service for wages, either for a person or a household;

By the condition of judicial interdiction, of accusation, or of contempt of court.

6. In order to exercise the rights of citizenship in a communal district, it is necessary to have acquired domicile there by one year of residence and not to have lost it by one year of absence.

7. The citizens of each communal district designate by their votes those among them whom they believe the most fit to conduct public affairs. Thus the result is a list of the trustworthy, containing a number of names equal to one-tenth of the number of citizens having the right to co-operate there. It is from this first communal list that the public functionaries of the district must be taken.

8. The citizens included in the communal lists of a department designate likewise a tenth of themselves. Thus there results a second list, known as the departmental list, from which the public functionaries of the department must be taken.

9. The citizens comprised in the departmental list designate in like manner a tenth of themselves: thus there results a third list which comprises the citizens of that department eligible to the national public functions.

10. The citizens who have the right to co-operate in the formation of one of the lists mentioned in the three preceding

articles, are called upon every three years to provide for replacing those of the enrolled who have died or are absent for any other cause than the exercise of a public function.

11. They can, at the same time, remove from the lists the enrolled whom they judge unfit to remain there, and replace them by other citizens in whom they have greater confidence.

12. No one is removed from a list except by the votes of the majority of the citizens who have the right to co-operate in its formation.

13. No one is removed from a list of eligibles by the mere fact that he is not kept upon another list of higher or superior degree.

14. Inscription upon a list of eligibles is necessary only with reference to those of the public officers for which that condition is expressly required by the constitution or the law. The list of eligibles shall be formed for the first time during the course of the Year IX.

Citizens who shall be selected for the first formation of the constituted authorities, shall form a necessary part of the first lists of eligibles.

TITLE II. OF THE CONSERVATIVE SENATE.

15. The Conservative Senate is composed of eighty members, irremovable and for life, of at least forty years of age.

For the formation of the Senate, there shall at first be chosen sixty members: that number shall be increased to sixty-two in the course of the Year VIII, to sixty-four in the Year IX, and it shall thus be gradually increased to eighty, by the addition of two members in each of the first ten years.

16. Appointment to the place of senator is made by the Senate, which chooses among three candidates presented, the first by the Legislative Body, the second by the Tribunate, the third by the First Consul.

It chooses between only two candidates if one of them is proposed by two of the three presenting authorities: it is required to admit that one who may be proposed at the same time by the three authorities.

17. The First Consul, upon leaving his place, either by expiration of his office or by resignation, becomes a senator *ipso facto* and necessarily.

The other two consuls, during the month following the expiration of their duties, can take seats in the Senate, but they are not required to make use of this right.

They do not have it if they leave their consular duties by resignation.

18. A senator is forever ineligible to any other public office.

19. All the lists made in the departments, in virtue of article 9, are despatched to the Senate: they constitute the national list.

20. It chooses from this list the legislators, the tribunes, the consuls, the judges of cassation, and the commissioners of accounts.

21. It sustains or annuls all the acts which are referred to it as unconstitutional by the Tribunate or the government: the lists of eligibles are included among these acts.

22. Fixed revenues from the national domains are set apart for the expenses of the Senate. The annual stipend of each of its members is taken from these revenues, and is equal to a twentieth of that of the First Consul.

23. The sittings of the Senate are not public.

24. Citizens Siéyès and Roger-Ducos, retiring consuls, are appointed members of the Conservative Senate: they shall join to themselves the second and third consuls appointed by the present constitution. These four citizens appoint the majority of the Senate, which then completes itself and proceeds to the elections that are entrusted to it.

TITLE III. OF THE LEGISLATIVE POWER.

25. New laws shall be promulgated only when the project for them shall have been proposed by the government, communicated to the Tribunate, and decreed by the Legislative Body.

26. The projects that the government proposes are drawn up in articles. In any stage of the discussion of these proposals, the government can withdraw them; it can reproduce them in modified form.

27. The Tribunate is composed of one hundred members, at least twenty-five years of age; they are renewed by a fifth each year and are indefinitely re-eligible as long as they remain upon the national list.

28. The Tribunate discusses the projects for laws: it votes for their adoption or their rejection.

It sends three orators taken from its own body, by whom the grounds for the view that it has taken upon each of these proposals are set forth and defended before the Legislative Body.

It refers to the Senate, on account of unconstitutionality only, the lists of eligibles, the acts of the Legislative Body and those of the government.

29. It expresses its opinion upon the laws made and to be made, the abuses to be corrected, and the improvements to be undertaken in all parts of the public administration, but never upon civil or criminal matters pending before the tribunals.

The opinions that it expresses by virtue of the present article have no necessary consequence and do not compel any constituted authority to a deliberation.

30. When the Tribunate adjourns, it can appoint a commission of from ten to fifteen of its members, charged to convoke it if it deems expedient.

31. The Legislative Body is composed of three hundred members of at least thirty years of age; they are renewed each year by a fifth.

It must always contain at least one member from each department of the Republic.

32. A member retiring from the Legislative Body cannot re-enter it until after an interval of one year; but he can be immediately elected to any other public office, including that of tribune, if he is otherwise eligible to it.

33. The session of the Legislative Body commences each year upon I Frimaire, and continues only four months; it can

be convoked in extraordinary session during the other eight months by the government.

34. The Legislative Body makes a law by deciding through secret ballot, and without any discussion on the part of its members, upon the projects of law discussed before it by the orators of the Tribunate and the government.

35. The sittings of the Tribunate and those of the Legislative Body are public; the number of spectators at either of them cannot exceed two hundred.

36. The annual stipend of a tribune is fifteen thousand francs; that of a legislator, ten thousand francs.

37. Every decree of the Legislative Body is promulgated by the First Consul the tenth day after its passage unless within that period it has been referred to the senate upon the ground of unconstitutionality. This recourse cannot be taken against promulgated laws.

38. The first renewal of the Legislative Body and of the Tribunate shall take place only in the course of the Year X.

TITLE IV OF THE GOVERNMENT.

39. The government is confided to three Consuls appointed for ten years and indefinitely re-eligible.

Each of them is elected individually with the distinguishing title of First, Second or Third Consul.

The constitution appoints as First Consul, Citizen Bonaparte, former provisional consul; as Second Consul, Citizen Cambacérès, former minister of justice; and as Third Consul, Citizen Lebrun, former member of the commission of the Council of the Ancients.

For this time the Third Consul is appointed only for five years.

40. The First Consul has special duties and prerogatives in which he is temporarily replaced by one of his colleagues, when there is need.

41. The First Consul promulgates the laws; he appoints and dismisses at will the members of the Council of State, the ministers, the ambassadors and other foreign agents of high rank, the officers of the army and navy, the members of the local administrations, and the commissioners of the government before the tribunals. He appoints all criminal and civil judges, other than the justices of the peace and the judges of cassation, without power to remove them.

42. In the other acts of the government, the Second and Third Consuls have a consultative voice: they sign the register of these acts in order to attest their presence; and if they wish, they there record their opinions; after that the decision of the First Consul suffices.

43. The stipend of First Consul shall be five hundred thousand francs in the Year VIII.

46. Law for Reorganizing the Administrative System

February 17, 1800 (28 Pluviôse, Year VIII)
TITLE I. DIVISION OF THE TERRITORY.

1. The European territory of the Republic shall be divided into departments and communal districts, in conformity with the table annexed to the present law. [This table made but one change in the existing departments.]

TITLE II. ADMINISTRATION.

Section I. Department administration.

2. There shall be in each department a prefect, a council of prefecture, and a department general council, which shall discharge the functions now performed by the administrations and department commissioners.

[The remainder of the article provides for the number of members in the councils of prefecture and the department general councils. The former have three, four, or five members; the latter have sixteen, twenty, or twenty-four members.]

3. The prefect alone shall be charged with the administration.

4. The council of prefecture shall pronounce:

Upon the requests of individuals seeking to obtain the discharge or the reduction of their share of the direct taxes;

Upon disputes which may arise between the contractors for public works and the administration over the meaning or execution of articles in their contracts;

Upon the claims of individuals who shall complain of injuries and damages proceeding from the personal acts of the contractors and not the acts of the administration;

Upon requests and contests over indemnities due to individuals by reason of lands taken or excavated for the making of roads, canals, and other public works;

Upon disputes which may arise in the matter of the great highway commission;

Upon requests which shall be presented by city, town or village communities to be authorised to litigate;

Finally, upon litigation over the national lands.

5. When the prefect shall attend the council of prefecture, he shall preside; in case of equal division, he shall have the casting vote.

6. The department general council shall meet each year; the time of its meeting shall be determined by the government; the duration of its session cannot exceed fifteen days.

It shall appoint one of its members for president, another for secretary.

It shall make the division of the direct taxes among the communal districts of the department.

It shall decide upon the requests for reductions made by the councils of the districts, cities, towns, and villages.

It shall determine, within the limits fixed by the law, the number of additional centimes, the imposition of which shall be requested for the expenses of the department.

It shall hear the annual account which the prefect shall render of the employment of the additional centimes which shall have been set aside for these expenses.

It shall express its opinion upon the condition and the needs of the department and shall address it to the minister of the interior.

7. A general secretary for the prefecture shall have the custody of the papers and shall sign the documents.

Section II. Communal administration.

8. In each communal district there shall be a sub-prefect and a district council composed of eleven members.

9. The sub-prefect shall discharge the functions now performed by the municipal administrations and the cantonal commissioners, with the exception of those which are assigned hereafter to the district council and the municipalities.

10. The district council shall meet each year: the time of its meeting shall be determined by the government; the duration of its session cannot exceed fifteen days.

It shall appoint one of its members for president and another for secretary.

It shall make the division of the direct taxes among the cities, towns, and villages of the district.

It shall give its opinion, with a statement of reasons, upon the requests for discharge which shall be formulated by the cities, towns and villages.

It shall hear the annual account which the sub-prefect shall render of the employment of the additional centimes set apart for the expenses of the district.

It shall express an opinion upon the condition and the needs of the district and shall address it to the prefect.

11. In the communal districts in which the head-town of the department shall be situated, there shall not be any sub-prefect.

SECTION III. MUNICIPALITIES.

12. In the cities, towns, and other places for which there are now a municipal agent and deputy, and whose population shall not exceed two thousand five hundred inhabitants, there shall be a mayor and a deputy; in the cities or towns of two thousand five hundred to five thousand inhabitants, a mayor and two deputies; in the cities of five thousand to ten thousand inhabitants, a mayor, two deputies, and a commissioner of police; in the cities whose population shall exceed ten thousand inhabitants, besides the mayor, two deputies and a commissioner of police, there shall be a deputy for each twenty thousand inhabitants in excess and a commissioner for each ten thousand in excess.

13. The mayors and deputies shall discharge the administrative functions now performed by the municipal agent and the deputy: in relation to the police and the civil state, they shall discharge the functions now performed by the municipal administrations of the canton, the municpal agents, and the deputies.

47. Treaty of Lunéville

February 9, 1801 (20 Pluviôse, Year IX)

His Majesty the Emperor, King of Hungary and of Bohemia, and the First Consul of the French Republic, in the name of the French people, induced by a common desire to put an end to the evils of war, have resolved to proceed to the conclusion of a definitive treaty of peace and amity. His said Imperial and Royal Majesty desiring no less sincerely to extend the benefits of peace to the German Empire, and the existing conditions not affording the necessary time for consulting the Empire, or permitting its representatives to take part in the negotiations, has resolved, in view of the concessions made by the deputation of the Empire at the recent Congress of Rastadt, to treat in the name of the German body, as has happened before under similar circumstances.

1. Peace, amity and a good understanding shall hereafter exist forever between His Majesty the Emperor, King of Hungary and of Bohemia, acting both in his own name and in that of the German Empire, and the French Republic; His Majesty agreeing that the said Empire shall ratify the present treaty in due form. The contracting parties shall make every effort to maintain a perfect agreement between themselves, and to prevent the commission of any acts of hostility by land or sea upon any ground or pretence whatsoever; striving in every way to maintain the concord thus happily re-established. No aid or protection shall be given either directly or indirectly to any one attempting to injure either of the contracting parties.

2. The cession of the former Belgian Provinces to the French Republic, stipulated in Article 3 of the treaty of Campo Formio, is renewed here in the most solemn manner. His Majesty the Emperor and King therefore renounces for himself and his successors, as well on his own part as on that of the German Empire, all right and title to the above specified provinces, which shall be held in perpetuity by the French Republic in full sovereignty and proprietary right, together with all territorial possessions belonging to them.

His Imperial and Royal Majesty cedes likewise to the French Republic, with the due consent of the Empire:

1. The county of Falkenstein with its dependencies.

2. The Frickthal and all the territory upon the left bank of the Rhine between Zurzach and Basle belonging to the House of Austria; the French Republic reserving the future cession of this district to the Helvetian Republic.

3. Moreover, in confirmation of Article 6 of the treaty of Campo Formio, His Majesty the Emperor and King shall possess in full sovereignty and proprietary right the countries enumerated below, to wit:

Istria, Dalmatia and the islands of the Adriatic, formerly belonging to Venice, dependent upon them; the mouths of the Cattaro, the city of Venice, the Lagunes, and the territory included between the hereditary States of His Majesty the Emperor and King, the Adriatic Sea and the Adige from the point where it leaves Tyrol to that where it flows into the

Adriatic, the thalweg of the Adige forming the boundary line. And since by this line the cities of Verona and Porto-Legnago are separated into two parts, draw-bridges indicating the frontier shall be established in the middle of the bridges connecting the two parts of the said towns.

4. Article 18 of the treaty of Campo Formio is likewise renewed, whereby His Majesty the Emperor and King agrees to cede to the Duke of Modena, as an indemnity for the territory which this prince and his heirs possessed in Italy, the Breisgau, which he shall possess upon the same conditions as those upon which he held Modena.

5. It is further agreed that His Royal Highness the Grand Duke of Tuscany shall renounce for himself, his successors or possible claimants, the Grand Duchy of Tuscany and that part of the island of Elba belonging to it, as well as all rights and titles resulting from the possession of the said states, which shall hereafter be held in full sovereignty and proprietary right by His Royal Highness the Infante Duke of Parma. The Grand Duke shall receive a complete and full indemnity in Germany for the loss of his state in Italy …

6. His Majesty the Emperor and King consents not only on his part but upon the part of the German Empire, that the French Republic shall hereafter possess in full sovereignty and proprietary right the territory and domains lying on the left bank of the Rhine and forming a part of the German Empire, so that, in conformity with the concessions granted by the deputation of the Empire at the Congress of Rastadt and approved by the Emperor, the thalweg of the Rhine shall hereafter form the boundary between the French Republic and the German Empire from that point where the Rhine leaves Helvetian territory to the point where it reaches Batavian territory.

In view of this the French Republic formally renounces all possessions whatsoever upon the right bank of the Rhine and agrees to restore to their owners the following places: Düsseldorf, Ehrenbreitstein, Philippsburg, the fortress of Cassel and other fortifications across from Mainz on the right bank of the stream, and the fortress of Kehl and Alt Breisach, under the express provision that these places and forts shall continue to exist in the condition in which they are left at the time of evacuation.

7. Since the consequence of this cession made by the Empire to the French Republic various princes and states of the Empire find themselves individually dispossessed in part or wholly of their territory, while the German Empire should collectively support the losses resulting from the stipulations of the present treaty, it is agreed between His Majesty the Emperor and King (both on his part and upon the part of the German Empire) and the French Republic that, in accordance with the principles laid down at the congress of Rastadt, the Empire shall be bound to furnish the hereditary princes who have lost possession upon the left bank of the Rhine an indemnity within the Empire, according such arrangements as shall be determined later in accordance with the stipulations here made.

11. The present treaty of peace … is declared to be common to the Batavian, Helvetian, Cisalpine and Ligurian republics. The contracting parties mutually guarantee the independence of the said republics and the freedom of the inhabitants of the said countries to adopt such form of government as they shall see fit.

12. His Majesty the Emperor and King renounces for himself and for his successors in favor of the Cisalpine Republic all rights and titles depending upon such rights, which His Majesty might assert over the territories in Italy which he possessed before he war and which, according to the terms of article 8 of the treaty of Campo Formio, now form a part of the Cisalpine Republic which shall hold them in full sovereign and proprietary right together with all the territorial possessions dependent upon them.

13. His Majesty the Emperor and King confirms both in his own name and in the name of the German Empire the sanction already given by the treaty of Campo Formio to the union of the former imperial fiefs to the Ligurian Republic and renounces all claims and titles resulting from these claims upon the said fiefs.

48. Treaty of Amiens

March 27, 1802

His Majesty the King of the United Kingdom of Great Britain and Ireland, and the First Consul of the French Republic, in the name of the French people, being animated with an equal desire to put an end to the calamities of war, have laid the foundation of peace in the preliminary articles signed at London the 1st of October 1801 (9 Vendémaire, Year X); …

1. There shall be peace, friendship and good understanding, between His Majesty the King of the United Kingdom of Great Britain and Ireland, his heirs and successors, on the one part; and the French Republic, His Majesty the King of Spain, his heirs and successors, and the Batavian Republic, on the other part …

3. His Britannic Majesty restores to the French Republic and her allies, namely, His Catholic Majesty and the Batavian Republic, all the possessions and colonies which belonged to them respectively, and which had been occupied or conquered by the British forces in the course of the war, with the exception of the island of Trinidad, and the Dutch possessions in the island of Ceylon.

4. His Catholic Majesty cedes and guarantees, in full right and sovereignty to his Britannic Majesty, the island of Trinidad.

5. The Batavian Republic cedes and guarantees in full right and sovereignty to his Britannic Majesty, all the possessions and establishments in the island of Ceylon, which belonged before the war to the Republic of the United Provinces, or to their East India company.

6. The Cape of Good Hope remains in full sovereignty to the Batavian Republic, as it was before the war …

7. The territories and possessions of Her Most Faithful Majesty [of Portugal] are maintained in their integrity, such as they were previous to the commencement of the war …

8. The territories, possessions and rights of the Ottoman Porte, are hereby maintained in their integrity, such as they were previous to the war.

9. The Republic of the Seven Islands is hereby acknowledged.

10. The islands of Malta, Gozo and Comino, shall be restored to the order of St. John of Jerusalem, and shall be held by it upon the same conditions on which the order held them previous to the war, and under the following stipulations:

4th. The forces of his Britannic Majesty shall evacuate the island and its dependencies within three months after the exchange of ratifications, or sooner if it can be done. At that period the island shall be delivered up to the order in the state in which it now is, provided that the grand master, or commissioners, fully empowered, according to the statutes of the order, be upon the island to receive possession, and that the force to be furnished by His Sicilian Majesty, as hereafter stipulated, be arrived there.

18. The branch of the House of Nassau, which was established in the republic, formerly called the Republic of the United Provinces, and now the Batavian Republic, having suffered losses there, as well in private property as in consequence of the change of constitution adopted in that country, an adequate compensation shall be procured for the said branch of the House of Nassau for the said losses.

19. The present definitive treaty of peace is declared common to the Sublime Ottoman Porte, the ally of His Britannic Majesty and the Sublime Porte shall be invited to transmit its act of accession thereto in the shortest delay possible.

49. Constitution of the Year XII.

May 18, 1804 (28 Floréal, Year XII)
TITLE I.

1. The government of the French Republic is entrusted to an emperor, who takes the title of EMPEROR OF THE FRENCH.

Justice is administered in the name of the Emperor by the officers whom he appoints.

Napoleon Bonaparte, present First Consul of the Republic, is Emperor of the French.

TITLE II. OF THE INHERITANCE.

3. The imperial dignity is hereditary in the direct natural and legitimate lineage of Napoleon Bonaparte, from male to male, by order of primogeniture, and to the perpetual exclusion of women and their descendants.

4. Napoleon Bonaparte can adopt the children or grandchildren of his brothers, provided they have fully reached the age of eighteen years, and he himself has no male children at the moment of adoption.

His adopted sons enter into the line of his direct descendants.

If, subsequently to the adoption, male children come to him, his adopted sons can be summoned only after the natural and legitimate descendants.

Adoption is forbidden to the successors of Napoleon Bonaparte and their descendants.

5. In default of a natural and legitimate heir or an adopted heir of Napoleon Bonaparte, the imperial dignity is devolved and bestowed upon Joseph Bonaparte and his natural and ligitimate descendants, by order of primogeniture, from male to male, to the perpetual exclusion of women and their descendants.

6. In default of Joseph Bonaparte and his male descendants, the imperial dignity is devolved and bestowed upon Louis Bonaparte, and his natural and legitimate descendants by order of primogeniture from male to male to the perpetual exclusion of women and their descendants.

7. In default of a natural and legitimate heir and of an adopted heir of Napoleon Bonaparte;

In default of natural and legitimate heirs of Joseph Bonaparte and his male descendants;

Of Louis Bonaparte and his male descendants;

An organic senatus-consultum, proposed to the Senate by the titular high dignitaries of the Empire and submitted for the acceptance of the people, appoints the emperor and controls in his family the order of inheritance, from male to male, to the perpetual exclusion of women and their descendants.

8. Until the moment in which the election of the new emperor is completed, the affairs of the state are directed by the ministers, who form themselves into a council of government and who make their decisions by a majority of votes. The secretary of state keeps the register of the deliberations.

TITLE III. OF THE IMPERIAL FAMILY.

9. The member of the imperial family within the order of inheritance bear the title of *French Princes.*

The eldest son of the Emperor bears that of *Prince Imperial.*

10. A senatus-consultum regulates the manner of the education of the French princes.

11. They are members of the Senate and of the Council of State when they have reached their eighteenth year.

12. They cannot marry without the authorisation of the Emperor.

The marriage of a French prince made without the authorisation of the Emperor entails deprivation of all right of inheritance, both for him who contracts it and for his descendants.

Nevertheless, if there is no child from this marriage, and it becomes dissolved, the prince who had contracted it recovers his rights of inheritance.

13. The documents which attest the birth, marriages, and decease of the members of the imperial family, are transmitted upon an order of the Emperor to the Senate, which orders their transcription upon its registers and their deposit in its archives.

14. Napoleon Bonaparte establishes by statutes, to which his successors are required to conform:

1st. The duties of the persons of both sexes, members of the imperial family, towards the Emperor.

2d. An organization of the imperial palace in conformity with the dignity of the throne and the grandeur of the nation.

15. The civil list remains as it has been regulated by articles 1 and 4 of the decree of May 26-June 1, 1791.

The French princes, Joseph and Louis Bonaparte, and, for the future, the younger natural and legitimate sons of the Emperor, shall be treated in conformity with articles 1, 10, 11, 12 and 13 of the decree of December 21, 1790-April 6, 1791.

The Emperor can fix the jointure of the Empress and assign it out of the civil list; his successors can change none of the dispositions which he shall have made in this respect.

16. The Emperor visits the departments: in consequence, imperial palaces are established at the four principal points of the Empire.

These palaces are designated and their appointments determined by a law.

TITLE IV. OF THE REGENCY.

17. The Emperor is a minor until he has fully completed eighteen years; during his minority there is a regent of the Empire.

18. The regent must be at least fully twenty-five years of age.

Women are excluded from the regency.

19. The Emperor designates the regent from among the French princes who are of the age required by the preceding article, and in default of them, from among the titular grand dignitaries of the Empire.

20. In default of designation on the part of the Emperor, the regency is bestowed upon the prince the nearest in degree in the order of inheritance, who has fully completed twenty-five years.

21. If, the Emperor not having designated the regent, none of the French princes have fully completed twenty-five years, the Senate elects the regent from the titular grand dignitaries of the Empire.

22. If, by reason of the minority in age of the prince summoned to the regency in the order of heredity, it has been bestowed upon a more remote kinsman, or upon one of the titular grand dignitaries of the Empire, the regent who has entered upon his functions continues until the majority of the Emperor.

23. No organic senatus-consultum can be issued during the regency, nor before the end of the third year which follows the majority.

24. The regent exercises, until the majority of the Emperor, all the attributes of the imperial dignity ...

50. Two Documents upon the Kingdom of Italy

March 17, 1805

A. CONSTITUTIONAL STATUTE.

The Council of State, in view of the unanimous desire of the united council and the deputation of the 15th instant:

In view of article 60 of the constitution, upon the constitutional initiative;

Decrees:

1. The emperor of the French, Napoleon I, is King of Italy.

2. The crown of Italy is hereditary in his direct and legitimate lineage, natural or adopted, from male to male, and to the perpetual exclusion of women and their descendants, provided, nevertheless, that his right of adoption cannot be extended over any other person than a citizen of the French Empire or of the Kingdom of Italy.

3. At the moment in which foreign armies shall have evacuated the state of Naples, the Ionian Islands, and the island of Malta, the Emperor Napoleon shall transmit the hereditary crown of Italy to one of his legitimate, natural or adopted children.

4. Dating from that time, the crown of Italy shall no longer be united with the crown of France upon the same head, and the successors of Napoleon First in the Kingdom of Italy shall be obliged to reside constantly upon the territory of the Italian Republic.

5. Within the course of the present year, the Emperor Napoleon, with the advice of the Council of State and the deputations of the electoral colleges, shall give to the Italian monarchy constitutions founded upon the same bases as those of the French Empire, and upon the same principles as the laws which he has already given to Italy.

Signed, Napoleon.

Melzi, Mareschalchi, Caprara, Paradisi, Fenaroli, Costabili, Luosi, Guiccardi.

March 19, 1805

B. PROCLAMATION OF THE KINGDOM.

The Council of State to the Peoples of the Kingdom of Italy.

A new State, created in the midst of political commotions, could not arrive all at once at a degree of perfection, consistency and strength, capable of assuring forever its existence, its repose and its prosperity. The genius of the founder, however gigantic, however bold it might be, was bound to pause before insurmountable obstacles, and his wisdom exhibited itself in not going beyond what circumstances would permit. Such was the lot of our republic, when, for the first time, it appeared suddenly upon the political horizon of Europe.

It took a great step, when in the comitia of Lyons, under the auspices and under the direction of its creator, it gave itself a new constitution and proclaimed for its head the man whose power and enlightenment could elevate it most rapidly to the degree of consideration and welfare to which its destinies would permit it to aspire.

But this second organization could be only provisional, for it was then necessary to conform to the circumstances of the time and to wait for the result of the lessons of experience. Soon, indeed, experience proved that many things were lacking for the completion fo the edifice; that its foundations were not solid enough; and the conduct of affairs, however skillful, however unsullied might be the hands which guided them, was so slow and so embarrassed that one could not but perceive that the means which might be made use of were not sufficiently effective.

Finally, the great example given by France served to carry conviction to all minds, and its happy results apprised us that the time had come to imitate it …

51. British Note to the Neutral Powers

Downing Street, **May 16, 1806.**

The undersigned, His Majesty's principal Secretary of State for Foreign Affairs, has received His Majesty's commands to acquaint Mr. Monroe, that the king, taking into consideration the new and extraordinary means resorted to by the enemy for the purpose of distressing the commerce of his subjects, has thought fit to direct that the necessary measures should be taken for the blockade of the coast, rivers and ports, from the river Elbe to the port of Brest, both inclusive; and the said coast, rivers and ports are and must be considered as blockaded; but that His Majesty is pleased to declare that such blockade shall not extend to prevent neutral ships and vessels laden with goods not being the property of His Majesty's enemies, and not being contraband of war, from approaching the said coast, and entering into and sailing from the said rivers and ports (save and except the coast, rivers and ports from Ostend to the river Seine, already in a state of strict and rigorous blockade, and which are to be considered as so continued), provided the said ships and vessels so approaching and entering (except as aforesaid), shall not have been laden at any port belonging to or in the possession of any of His Majesty's enemies; and that the said ships and vessels so sailing from said rivers and ports (except as aforesaid) shall not be destined to any port belonging to or in possession of any of His Majesty's enemies, nor have previously broken the blockade.

Mr. Monroe is therefore requested to apprise the American consuls and merchants residing in England, that the coasts, rivers and ports above mentioned, must be considered as being in a state of blockade, and that from this time all the measures authorised by the law of nations and the respective treaties between His Majesty and the different neutral powers, will be adopted and executed with respect to vessels attempting to violate the said blockade after this notice.

The undersigned requests Mr. Monroe, etc.

C.J. Fox.

52. The Berlin Decree

From our Imperial Camp at Berlin, **November 21, 1806.**

Napoleon, Emperor of the French and King of Italy, in consideration of the fact:

1. That England does not recognize the system of international law universally observed by all civilized nations;

2. That she regards as an enemy every individual belonging to the enemy's state, and consequently makes prisoners of war not only of the crews of armed ships of war but of the crews of ships of commerce and merchantmen, and even of commercial agents and of merchants travelling on business;

3. That she extends to the vessels and commercial wares and to the property of individuals the right of conquest, which is applicable only to the possessions of the belligerent power;

4. That she extends to unfortified towns and commercial ports, to harbors and the mouths of rivers, the right of blockade, which, in accordance with reason and the customs of all civilized nations, is applicable only to fortified places;

That she declares places in a state of blockade, before which she has not even a single ship of war, although a place may not be blockaded except it be so completely guarded that no attempt to approach it can be made without imminent danger. That she declares also in a state of blockade places which all her united forces would be unable to blockade, such as entire coasts and the whole of an empire.

5. That this monstrous abuse of the right of blockade has no other aim than to prevent communication among the nations and to raise the commerce and the industry of England upon the ruins of that of the continent.

6. That, since this is the obvious aim of England, whoever deals on the continent in English goods, thereby favors and renders himself an accomplice of her designs.

7. That this policy of England, worthy of the earliest stages of barbarism, has profited that power to the detriment of every other nation.

8. That it is a natural right to oppose such arms against an enemy as he makes use of, and to fight in the same way that it fights; when it disregards all ideas of justice and every high sentiment, due to the civilization among mankind.

We have resolved to apply to her the usages which she has sanctioned in her maritime legislation.

The provisions of the present decree shall continue to be looked upon as embodying the fundamental principles of the Empire until England shall recognize that the law of war is one and the same on land and sea, and that the rights of war cannot be extended so as to include private property of any kind or the persons of individuals unconnected with the profession of arms; and that the right of blockade should be restricted to fortified places actually invested by sufficient forces.

We have consequently decreed and do decree that which follows:

1. The British Isles are declared to be in a state of blockade.

2. All commerce and all correspondence with the British isles are forbidden. Consequently letters or packages directed to England or to an Englishman or written in the English language shall not pass thorough the mails and shall be seized.

3. Every individual who is an English subject, of whatever state or condition he may be, who shall be discovered in any country occupied by our troops or by those of our allies, shall be made a prisoner of war.

4. All warehouses, merchandise or property of whatever kind belonging to a subject of England shall be regarded as lawful prize.

5. Trade in English goods is prohibited, and all goods belonging to England or coming from her factories or her colonies are declared lawful prize.

6. Half of the product resulting from the confiscation of the goods and possessions declared lawful prize by the preceding articles shall be applied to indemnify the merchants for the losses they have experienced by the capture of merchant vessels taken by English cruisers.

7. No vessel coming directly from England or from the English colonies or which shall have visited these since the publication of the present decree shall be received in any port.

8. Any vessel contravening the above provision by a false declaration shall be seized, and the vessel and cargo shall be confiscated as if it were English property.

9. Our court of prizes at Paris shall pronounce final judgment in all cases arising in our Empire or in the countries occupied by the French army relating to the execution of the present decree. Our court of prizes at Milan shall pronounce final judgment in the said cases which may arise within our Kingdom of Italy.

10. The present decree shall be communicated by our minister of foreign affairs to the kings of Spain, of Naples, of Holland and of Etruria, and to our other allies whose subjects, like ours, are the victims of the unjust and barbarous maritime legislation of England.

11. Our ministers of foreign affairs, of war, of the navy, of finance and of the police and our directors-general of the port are charged with the execution of the present decree so far as it affects them.

Signed, Napoleon.

53. The Rambouillet Decree

March 23, 1810

Napoleon ... considering that the government of the United States, by an act dated March 1, 1809, which forbids the entrance of ports, harbors and rivers of the said states to all French vessels, orders:

1st. That, dating from the 20th of May following, the vessels under the French flag which shall arrive in the United States shall be seized and confiscated, as well as their cargoes;

2d. That, after the same date, no merchandise and productions coming from the soil or manufactures of France or of its colonies can be imported into the said United States from any port or foreign place whatsoever, under penalty of seizure, confiscation and fine of three times the value of the merchandise;

3d. That American vessels cannot repair to any port of France, its colonies or dependencies,

We have decreed and do decree as follows:

1. That all vessels navigating under the flag of the United States, or possessed in whole or in part by any citizen or subject of that power, which, dating from May 20, 1809, may have entered or shall enter into the ports of our Empire, our colonies or the countries occupied by our armies, shall be seized, and the products of the sales shall be deposited in the surplus fund.

Vessels which may be charged with despatches or commissions of government of the said states and which have not cargo or merchandise on board are excepted from this provision.

2. Our grand judge, minister of justice, and our minister of finance, are charged with the execution of the present decree.

54. Treaty for Establishing the Confederation (of the Rhine)

July 12, 1806

His Majesty, the Emperor of the French, King of Italy, of the one part, and of the other part their Majesties the Kings of Bavaria and of Wurtemburg and their most Serene Highnesses the Electors, the Archchancellor of Baden, the Duke of Berg and of Cleves, the Landgrave of Hesse-Darmstadt, the princes of Nassau-Usingen and Nassau-Weilburg, the princes of Hohenzollern-Heckingen and Hohenzollern-Sigmaringen, the princes of Salm-Salm and Salm-Kirburg, the Prince of Isneburg-Birstein, the Duke of Aremberg and the Prince of Lichtenstein, and the Count of Leyen, wishing, by suitable stipulations, to assure the internal peace of the south of Germany, for which experience for a long time past, and again quite recently, has shown that the Germanic constitution can no longer offer any sort of guarantee ...

1. The states of ... [names of the parties of the second part] shall be forever separated from the territory of the Germanic Empire and united among themselves by a separate confederation, under the name of the Confederated States of the Rhine.

3. Each of the kings and confederated princes shall renounce those of his titles which express any relations with the Germanic Empire; and on the 1st of August next he shall cause the diet to be notified of his separation from the Empire.

4. His Most Serene Highness the Archchancellor shall take the titles of Prince Primate and Most Eminent Highness. The title of prince primate does not carry with it any prerogative contrary to the plenitude of sovereignty which each of the confederates shall enjoy.

6. The common interests of the confederated states shall be dealt with in a diet, of which the seat shall be at Frankfort, and which shall be divided into two colleges, to wit: the college of kings and the college of princes.

12. His Majesty the Emperor of the French shall be proclaimed Protector of the Confederation, and in that capacity, upon the decease of each prince primate, he shall appoint the successor of that one.

[Articles 13-34 provide for a large number of territorial changes, principally consolidations in the interests of the larger states of the confederation.]

35. There shall be between the French Empire and the Confederated States of the Rhine, collectively and separately, an alliance in virtue of which every continental war which one of the high contracting parties may have to carry on shall immediately become common to all the others.

38. The contingent to be furnished by each of the allies in case of war is as follows: France shall furnish 200,000 men of all arms; the Kingdom of Bavaria 30,000 men of all arms; the Kingdom of Wurtemburg 12,000; the Grand Duke of Baden 8,000; the Grand Duke of Berg 5,000; the Grand Duke of Darmstadt 4,000; Their Most Serene Highnesses the Dukes and the Princes of Nassau, together with the other confederated princes, shall furnish a contingent of 4,000 men.

39. The high contracting parties reserve to themselves the admission at a later time into the new confederation of other princes and states of Germany whom it shall be found for the common interest to admit thereto.

55. Note of Napoleon to the Diet (of the German Empire)

August 1, 1806

The undersigned, *chargé d'affaires* of His Majesty the Emperor of the French and King of Italy at the general diet of the Germanic Empire, has received orders from His Majesty to make the following declarations to the diet:

Their Majesties the Kings of Bavaria and of Wurtemberg, the sovereign princes of Regensburg, Baden, Berg, Hesse-Darmstadt and Nassau, as well as the other leading princes of the south and west Germany have resolved to form a confederation between themselves which shall secure them

against future emergencies, and have thus ceased to be states of the Empire.

The position in which the treaty of Pressburg has directly placed the courts allied to France, and indirectly those princes whose territory they border or surround, being incompatible with the existence of an empire, it becomes a necessity for those rulers to reorganize their relations upon a new system and to remove a contradiction which could not fail to be a permanent source of agitation, disquiet and danger.

France, on the other hand, is directly interested in the maintenance of peace in southern Germany and yet must apprehend that, the moment she shall cause her troops to recross the Rhine, discord, the inevitable consequence of contradictory, uncertain and ill-defined conditions, will again disturb the peace of the people and reopen, possibly, the war on the continent. Feeling it incumbent upon her to advance the welfare of her allies and to assure them the enjoyment of all the advantages which the treaty of Pressburg secures them and to which she is pledged, France cannot but regard the confederation that they have formed as a natural result and a necessary sequel to that treaty.

56. Abdication of Francis II

August 7, 1806

We, Francis the Second, by the Grace of God Roman Emperor Elect, Ever August, Hereditary Emperor of Austria, etc., King of Germany, Hungary, Bohemia, Croatia, Dalmatia, Slavonia, Galizia, Lodomeria and Jerusalem; Archduke of Austria, etc.

Since the peace of Pressburg all our care and attention has been directed towards the scrupulous fulfillment of all engagements contracted by the said treaty, as well as the preservation of peace so essential to the happiness of our subjects, and the strengthening in every way of the friendly relations which have been happily re-established. We could but await the outcome of events in order to determine whether the important changes in the German Empire resulting from the terms of the peace would allow us to fulfill the weighty duties which, in view of the conditions of our election, devolve upon us as the head of the Empire. But the results of certain articles of the treaty of Pressburg, which showed themselves immediately after and since its publication, as well as the events which, as is generally known, have taken place in the German Empire, have convinced us that it would be impossible under these circumstances farther to fulfill the duties which we assumed by the conditions of our election. Even if the prompt readjustment of existing political complications might produce an alteration in the existing conditions, the convention signed at Paris, July 12th, and approved later by the contracting parties, providing for the complete separation of several important states of the Empire and their union into a separate confederation, would entirely destroy any such hope.

Thus, convinced of the utter impossibility of longer fulfilling the duties of our imperial office, we owe it to our principles and to our honor to renounce a crown which could only retain any value in our eyes so long as we were in a position to justify the confidence reposed in us by the electors, princes, estates and other members of the German Empire, and to fulfill the duties devolving upon us.

We proclaim, accordingly, that we consider the ties which have hitherto united us to the body politic of the German Empire as hereby dissolved; that we regard the office and dignity of the imperial headship as extinguished by the formation of a separate union of the Rhenish states, and regard ourselves as thereby freed from all our obligations toward the German Empire; herewith laying down the imperial crown which is associated with these obligations, and relinquishing the imperial government which we have hitherto conducted.

We free at the same time the electors, princes and estates, and all others belonging to the Empire, particularly the members of the supreme imperial courts and other magistrates of the Empire, from the duties constitutionally due to us as the lawful head of the Empire. Conversely, we free all our German provinces and imperial lands from all their obligations of whatever kind, towards the German Empire, in uniting these, as Emperor of Austria, with the whole body of the Austrian state we shall strive, with the restored and existing peaceful relations with all the powers and neighboring states, to raise them to the height of prosperity and happiness, which is our keenest desire, and aim of our constant and sincerest efforts.

Done at our capital and royal residence, Vienna, August 6, 1806, in the fifteenth year of our reign as Emperor and hereditary ruler of the Austrian lands.

Francis.

57. Treaty of Peace between France and Russia (Treaty of Tilsit)

July 7, 1807

His Majesty the Emperor of the French, King of Italy, Protector of the Confederation of the Rhine and His Majesty the Emperor of all the Russias, being prompted by an equal desire to put an end to the calamities of war …

1. There shall be, dating from the day of the exchange of the ratifications of the present treaty, perfect peace and amity beween His Majesty the Emperor of the French, King of Italy, and His Majesty the Emperor of all the Russias.

4. His Majesty the Emperor Napoleon, out of regard for His Majesty the Emperor of all the Russias, and wishing to give a proof of his sincere desire to unite the two nations by

the bonds of an unalterable confidence and friendship, consents to restore to His Majesty the King of Prussia, the ally of His Majesty the Emperor of all the Russias, all the conquered countries, cities and territories denominated herinafter …

5. The provinces which on the 1st of January, 1772, made us part of the former Kingdom of Poland and which have since passed at different times under Prussian domination, with the exception of the countries that are named or designated in the preceding article and those specified in article 9 herinafter, shall be possessed in complete ownership and sovereignty by His Majesty the King of Saxony, under the title of the Duchy of Warsaw, and shall be governed by constitutions which, while assuring the liberties and privileges of the peoples of this duchy, are consistent with the tranquility of the neighboring states.

58. Imperial Decree for the Annexation of the Papal States

May 17, 1809

Napoleon, Emperor of the French, King of Italy, Protector of the Confederation of the Rhine, etc., in consideration of the fact that when Charlemagne, Emperor of the French and our august predecessor, granted several counties to the bishops of Rome he ceded these only as fiefs and for the good of his realm and Rome did not by reason of this cession cease to form a part of his empire; farther that since this association of spiritual and temporal authority has been and still is a source of dissensions and has but too often led the pontiffs to employ the influence of the former to maintain the pretensions of the latter, and thus the spiritual concerns and heavenly interests which are unchanging have been confused with terrestrial affairs which by their nature alter according to circumstances and the policy of the time; and since all our proposals for reconciling the security of our armies, the tranquility and the welfare of our people and the dignity and integrity of our Empire, with the temporal pretensions of the popes have failed, we have decreed and do decree what follows:

1. The Papal States are reunited to the French Empire.

2. The city of Rome, so famous by reason of the great memories which cluster about it and as the first seat of christianity, is proclaimed a free imperial city. The organization of the government and administration of the said city shall be provided by a special statute.

3. The remains of the structures erected by the Romans shall be maintained and preserved at the expense of our treasury.

4. The public debt shall become an imperial debt.

59. First Abdication of Napoleon

April 4, 1814

The allied powers having proclaimed that the Emperor Napoleon was the sole obstacle to the re-establishment of peace in Europe, the Emperor Napoleon, faithful to his oath, declares that he is ready to descend from the throne, to leave France and even to lay down his life for the welfare of the fatherland, which cannot be separated from the rights of his son, those of the regency of the Empress, and the laws of the Empire.

> Done at our palace of Fontainebleau, April 4, 1814.
>
> Napoleon.

60. The Senate's Proposed Constitution

April 6, 1814

The Conservative Senate, deliberating upon the project of a constitution which has been presented to it by the provisional government, in execution of the act of the Senate of the 1st of this month.

After having heard the report of a special commission of seven members,

Decrees as follows:

1. The French government is monarchical and hereditary from male to male, by order of primogeniture.

2. The French people freely summon to the throne of France Louis-Stanislas-Xavier of France, brother of the late king, and, after him, the other members of the house of Bourbon in the old order.

3. The old nobility resume their titles: the new retain theirs hereditarily. The Legion of Honor is maintained with its prerogatives; the king shall determine the decoration.

4. The executive power belongs to the king.

5. The king, the Senate and the Legislative Body co-operate in the formation of the laws.

Projects of law can be proposed both in the Senate and in the Legislative Body.

Those relative to taxes can be proposed only in the Legislative Body.

The king can likewise invite the two bodies to occupy themselves with matters which he deems in need of consideration.

The sanction of the king is necessary for the completion of the law.

6. There are at least one hundred and fifty senators and two hundred at most.

Their rank is irremovable and hereditary from male to male, by order of primogeniture. They are appointed by the king.

The present senators, with the exception of those who may renounce the attribute of French citizenship, are retained and make part of that number. The present endowment of the Senate and of the senatorships belong to them. The revenues thereof are likewise divided among them and pass to their successors. In case of the death of a senator without direct male posterity, his portion returns to the public treasury. The senators who shall be appointed in the future cannot have part in this endowment.

61. Proclamation of Napoleon

March 1, 1815

Frenchmen, the defection of the Duke of Castiglione delivered Lyon without defence to our enemies; the army, of which I had confided to him the command was, by the number of its battalions, and the bravery and patriotism of the troops who composed it, in a condition to fight the Austrian army which was opposing it and to reach the rear of the left flank of the hostile army which was threatening Paris.

The victories of Champ-Aubert, Montmirail, Château-Thierry, Vauchamp, Mormans, Montereau, Craone, Reims, Arcy-sur-Aube and Saint-Dizier, the rising of the brave peasants of Lorraine, Champagne, Alsace, Franche-Comté and Bourgogne, and the position which I had taken at the rear of the hostile army, separating it from its magazines, its reserve parks, its convoys and all its equipment, had placed it in a desperate position. Frenchmen were never at the point of being more powerful, and the flower of the hostile army was lost beyond recovery; it would have found its grave in the vast countries which it has so pitilessly plundered, but that the treason of the Duke of Raguse gave up the capital and disorganized the army. The unexpected conduct of these two generals, who betrayed at one and the same time their fatherland, their prince and their benefactor, changed the destiny of the war.

62. Declaration of the Powers against Napoleon

March 13, 1815

The powers who have signed the treaty of Paris reassembled in congress at Vienna having been informed of the escape of Napoleon Bonaparte, and of his entrance into France with an armed force, owe to their dignity and the interest of social order a solemn declaration of the sentiments which that event has inspired in them.

In thus violating the convention which established him in the island of Elba, Bonaparte destroyed the only legal title for his existence. By reappearing in France with projects of disorder and destruction, he has cut himself off from the protection of the law and has shown in the face of the world that there can be neither peace nor truce with him.

Accordingly, the powers declare that Napoleon Bonaparte is excluded from civil and social relations, and, as an enemy and disturber of the tranquility of the world, that he has incurred public vengeance.

At the same time, being firmly resolved to preserve intact the treaty of Paris of May 30, 1814, and the arrangements sanctioned by that treaty, as well as those which have been or shall be arranged hereafter in order to complete and consolidate it, they declare that they will employ all their resources and will unite all their efforts in order that the general peace, the object of the desires of Europe and the constant aim of their labors, may not be again disturbed, and in order to secure themselves from all attempts which may threaten to plunge the world once more into the disorders and misfortunes of revolutions.

And although fully persuaded that all France, rallying around its legitimate sovereign, will strive unceasingly to bring to naught this last attempt of a criminal and impotent madman, all the sovereigns of Europe, animated by the same feeling and guided by the same principles, declare that if, contrary to all expectation, there shall result from that event any real danger, they will be ready to give to the King of France and the French nation or to any government which shall be attacked, as soon as shall be required, all the assistance necessary to re-establish the public tranquility, and to make common cause against all who may attempt to compromise it.

The present declaration, inserted in the protocol of the Congress assembled at Vienna, March 13, 1815, shall be made public.

63. The Holy Alliance Treaty

September 26, 1815

In conformity with the words of the Holy Scriptures which command all men to look upon each other as brothers, the three contracting monarchs shall remain united by the bonds of a true and indissoluble fraternity and, considering themselves as compatriots, on all occasions and in all places they shall lend each other assistance, help and aid; regarding themselves as fathers of their subjects and armies, they shall guide them in this same spirit of fraternity by which they themselves are animated so as to protect religion, peace and justice ... They are delegated by Providence to govern the three branches of a single family ...

64. Treaty of Paris

November 20, 1815

In the Name of the Most Holy and Undivided Trinity.

The allied powers having by their united efforts, and by the success of their arms, preserved France and Europe from the convulsions with which they were menaced by the late enterprise of Napoleon Bonaparte, and by the revolutionary system reproduced in France, to promote its success: participating at present with His Most Christian Majesty in the desire to consolidate, by maintaining inviolate the royal authority, and by restoring the operation of the Constitutional Charter, the order of things which had been happily re-established in France, as also in the object of restoring between France and her neighbours those relations of reciprocal confidence and good will which the fatal effects of the revolution and of the system of conquest had for so long a time disturbed; persuaded, at the same time, that this last object can only be obtained by an arrangement framed to secure to the allies proper indemnities for the past and solid guarantees for the future, they have, in concert with His Majesty the King of France, taken into consideration the means of giving effect to this arrangement; and being satisfied that the indemnity due to the allied powers cannot be either entirely territorial or entirely pecuniary, without prejudice to France in one or other of her essential interest, and that it would be more fit to combine both the modes, in order to avoid the inconvenience which would result, were either resorted to separately, their Imperial and Royal Majesties have adopted this basis for their present transactions; and agreeing alike as to the necessity of retaining for a fixed time in the frontier provinces of France, a certain number of allied troops, they have determined to combine their different arrangements, founded upon these bases, in a definitive treaty.

1. The frontiers of France shall be the same as they were in the year 1790, save and except the modifications on one side and on the other, which are detailed in the present article.

[This line is indicated in the maps facing p. 350 of Hertslet, *Map of Europe by Treaty*.]

4. The pecuniary part of the idemnity to be furnished by France to the allied powers is fixed at the sum of 700,000,000 francs ...

5. The state of uneasiness and fermentation, which after so many violent convulsions, and particularly after the last catastrophe, France must still experience, notwithstanding the paternal intentions of her king, and the advantages secured to every class of his subjects by the Constitutional Charter, requiring for the security of the neighbouring states, certain measures of precaution and of temporary guarantee, it has been judged indispensable to occupy, during a fixed time, by a corps of allied troops certain military positions along the frontiers of France, under the express reserve, that such occupation shall in no way prejudice the sovereignty of His Most Christian Majesty, nor the state of possession, such as it is recognized and confirmed by the present treaty. The

number of these troops shall not exceed 150,000 men ... As the maintenance of the army destined for this service is to be provided by France, a special convention shall regulate everything which may relate to that object ... The utmost extent of the duration of this military occupation is fixed at 5 years. It may terminate before that period if, at the end of 3 years, the allied sovereigns, after having, in concert with His Majesty the King of France, maturely examined their material situation and interests, and the progress which shall have been made in France in the re-establishment of order and tranquility, shall agree to acknowledge that the motives which led them to that measure have ceased to exist. But whatever may be the result of this deliberation, all the fortresses and positions occupied by the allied troops shall, at the expiration of 5 years, be evacuated without further delay, and given up to His Most Christian Majesty, or to his heirs and successors.

11. The treaty of Paris of the 30th of May, 1814, and the final act of the Congress of Vienna of the 9th of June, 1815, are confirmed, and shall be maintained in all such of their enactments which shall not have been modified by the articles of the present treaty.

65. Treaty of Alliance against France

November 20, 1815

In the Name of the Most Holy and Undivided Trinity.

The purpose of the alliance concluded at Vienna the 25th day of March, 1815, having been happily attained by the re-establishment in France of the order of things which the last criminal attempt of Napoleon Bonaparte had momentarily subverted; Their Majesties the King of the United Kingdom of Great Britain and Ireland, the Emperor of Austria, King of Hungary and Bohemia, the Emperor of all the Russias, and the King of Prussia, considering that the repose of Europe is essentially interwoven with the confirmation of the order of things founded on the maintenance of the royal authority and the Constitutional Charter, and wishing to employ all their means to prevent the general tranquility (the object of the wishes of mankind and the constant end of their efforts), from being again disturbed; desirous moreover to draw closer the ties which unite them for the common interests of their people, have resolved to give to the principles solemnly laid down in the treaties of Chaumont of the 1st March, 1814, and of Vienna of the 25th of March, 1815, the application the most analogous to the present state of affairs, and to fix beforehand by a solemn treaty the principles which they propose to follow, in order to guarantee Europe from dangers by which she may still be menaced; ...

1. The high contracting parties reciprocally promise to maintain, in its force and vigour, the treaty signed this day with His Most Christian Majesty, and to see that the stipulations of the said treaty, as well as those of the particular conventions which have reference thereto, shall be strictly and faithfuly executed in their fullest extent.

2. The high contracting parties, having engaged in the war which has just terminated for the purpose of maintaining inviolably the arrangements settled at Paris last year, for the safety and interest of Europe, have judged it advisable to renew the said engagements by the present act, and to confirm them as mutually obligatory, subject to the modifications contained in the treaty signed this day with the plenipotentiaries of His Most Christian Majesty, and particularly those by which Napoleon Bonaparte and his family in pursuance of the Treaty of the 11th of April, 1814, have been forever excluded from supreme power in France, which exclusion the contracting powers bind themselves, by the present act, to maintain in full vigour, and, should it be necessary, with the whole of their forces. And as the same revolutionary principles which upheld the last criminal usurpation, might again, under other forms, convulse France, and thereby endanger the repose of other states; under these circumstances, the high contracting parties solemnly admitting it to be their duty to redouble their watchfulness for the tranquility and interests of their people, engage, in case so unfortunate an event should again occur, to concert among themselves, and with His Most Christian Majesty, the measures which they may judge necessary to be pursued for the safety of their respective states, and for the general tranquility of Europe ...

Appendix B

Biographies of Major Personalities

Alexander I (1777-1825): Czar of Russia. Son of Paul I in whose murder he may have taken an indirect part. First inclined toward liberalism, which he gradually dropped and completely abandoned after 1813. Allied with Austria in 1805 and Prussia in 1806-7 against Napoleon, he joined the latter's blockade against England in 1807. After 1812, leader of the anti-French coalition and after 1815 of the reactionary "Holy Alliance." At the Congress of Vienna, he put through the personal union with Poland and made Russia the foremost power of continental Europe. In his last years a religious mystic, and completely reactionary, thereby causing the formation of secret political clubs (Decembrists).

Arndt, Ernst Moritz (1769-1860): German poet, historian and politician. Fled from Napoleon because of his main work, *Geist der Zeit* (Spirit of the Age). Secretary of the Baron vom Stein 1812-15.

Artois, Charles Philippe Duc d' (1757-1836): Younger brother of Louis XVI. Even more royalist than Louis; foe of all reforms, one of the leaders of the emigrants. Became king of France, ruling from 1824 to 1830, as Charles X. Overthrown by the July revolution of 1830.

Augereau, Charles Pierre Francois d' (1757-1816): Successful general under Bonaparte in Italy; carried out the coup d'état of the 18th Fructidor. Napoleon made him marshal, then Duke of Castiglione. Fought at Jena, Eylau, in Spain and at Leipzig. In 1814, he went over to the Bourbons.

Babeuf, Francois Noel (1760-97): Radical revolutionary and publicist, with Communist tendencies. Through the secret Club of the Equals, he tried to overthrow the Directory; the plot was discovered and B. was executed, after a long trial. Advocated equal distribution of goods.

Bailly, Jean Sylvain (1736-93): Astronomer and politician; 1789, president of the National Assembly, 1789-91, mayor of Paris. Executed during the July 1793 massacres.

Barère de Vieuzac, Bertrand (1755-1841): Delegate of the National Assembly, first a moderate, then a radical member of the Committee of Public Safety. Follower of Robespierre, but turned against him on the 9th Thermidor. Then in prison for several years; after his release, hiding. Later a secret agent for Napoleon. Banished as *régicide* in 1815, returned to France under Louis Philippe.

Barnave, Antoine Pierre Joseph Marie (1761-1793): Leader of the Jacobins in the National Assembly; participated in the arrest of the royal family in June of 1791, then joined the Feuillants. Developed a theory of revolution; in 1793 condemned to death by the Revolutionary Tribunal, and executed.

Barras, Paul Francois Jean Nicolas, Vicomte de (1755-1829): Radical Jacobin and terrorist (in Toulon). Turned against Robespierre on 9th Thermidor, then commander of Paris; suppressed the royalist uprising on October 5, 1795 (13th Vendemiaire), then a leading member of the Directory. His corruptibility was well known. Supported Napoleon at his 1799 coup d'état, but played no important role after that.

Barthélemy, Balthazar Francois, Marquis de (1747-1830): Negotiated the peace of Basle 1795; then a member of the Directory. Arrested during the coup d'état of September 4, 1797 (18th Fructidor), and banished to Guyana. Escaped from there, returned and supported Napoleon. In 1814, he went over to the Bourbons.

Beauharnais, Alexander Francois Vicomte de (1760-1794): French general during the American war of independence, then commander of the Army of the Rhine in 1792. Was made responsible for the capitulation of Mayence and guillotined shortly before the end of the Reign of Terror. First husband of Josephine, the later empress.

Beaumarchais, Pierre Auguste Caron de (1732-1799): Successful writer of comedies, also secret arms merchant for France in the American war of independence. Fled to London in 1792 and returned to France after the end of the Reign of Terror.

Bernadotte, Jean Baptiste Jules (1763-1844): French general, fought under Napoleon in Italy, then minister of war. Participated in the battle of Austerlitz. In 1810, he was adopted by the king of Sweden, and fought as the Swedish Crown Prince against Napoleon in 1813. Ruled as Charles XIV, king of Sweden and Norway, 1818-1844.

Berthier, Louis Alexandre (1753-1815): French general in the American war of independence, then with Napoleon in Italy, Egypt and on many other campaigns. Was made marshal and Prince of Neuchatel. Died by a fall from a window of the Bamberg castle, probably a suicide.

Besenval, Pierre Joseph, Baron de (1721-1794): Commander of Parisian troops during the storming of the Bastille, which succeeded because of his indecisiveness. Shortly thereafter he retired and died of natural causes during the Reign of Terror.

Beyle, Marie Henri (Stendhal) (1783-1842): French writer, served in the French army 1800-02 and in 1812; began his literary career after the Napoleonic wars.

Billaud-Varenne, Jacques Nicolas (1756-1819): Fanatic anti-monarchist in the Convention. Member of the Committee of Public Safety, became president of the Convention. Participated in the conspiracies against Danton and Robespierre. After 9th Thermidor banished to Guyana as former terrorist. He did not accept Napoleon's offer of amnesty and died in Haiti.

Blücher, Gebhardt Leberecht, Prince of Walstatt (1741-1819): Prussian field marshal, fought the French in 1806 and became a leader in the war of 1813-14. Participated in the battle of Leipzig, then crossed the Rhine and led his troops to Paris. In the 1815 campaign, he was beaten by Napoleon at Ligny, but arrived at Waterloo in time to save the day for the Allies.

Bonaparte, Jérôme (1784-1860): Youngest brother of Napoleon; king of Westphalia, 1807-13.

Bonaparte, Joseph (1768-1844): Elder brother of Napoleon; king of Naples 1806-08, king of Spain 1808-13. Forced to leave Spain in 1813.

Bonaparte, Letizia (1750-1836): Née Ramolino, mother of Napoleon. Was given the title "Madame Mère" but continued her simple life throughout the empire.

Visited Napoleon in Elba. After his downfall she found refuge in Rome.

Bonaparte, Lucien (1775-1840): Younger brother of Napoleon; at the time of the coup d'état, president of the Council of 500. Later critical of his brother's policies, tried to flee to America in 1810, but was interned by the English. Returned to France during the 100 Days.

Bonaparte, Napoleon (1769-1821): General, consul, emperor and dictator of France. (See text for details.)

Bourbon: For the French branch of this dynastic royal family *see* Artois, Louis XVI, Louis XVII, Louis XVIII, Orléans.

Bourrienne, Louis Antoine Fauvelet de (1769-1834): Diplomat and secretary of Napoleon 1797-99; ambassador in Hamburg 1804-14; later a minister of Louis XVIII.

Brissot, Jacques-Pierre (1754-1793): Revolutionary journalist and leader of the Girondists. After the king's flight in 1791 he fought the monarchy and advocated the war against the Allies. Very influential in foreign politics, but lost influence when he argued against the overthrow of the monarchy in July of 1792. Adversary of Robespierre and the Montagnards. Arrested in June of 1793 and executed in October.

Brune, Guillaume Marie Ann (1763-1815): Captain of the National Guard in 1789 and friend of Danton. As a general, he fought in Holland, Italy and Switzerland. Marshal in 1804; later in disgrace with Napoleon. Was probably murdered by royalists.

Brunswick (Braunschweig), Duke Karl Wilhelm Ferdinand (1735-1806): Prussian field marshal, successful during the Seven Years War. In 1792, as supreme commander of the Prussian army in France, beaten at Valmy, but victorious at Kaiserslautern and Pirmasens in 1793. In 1806 he was beaten by Davout, and mortally wounded, at Auerstedt.

Burke, Edmund (1729-1797): British political writer and statesman, originally with liberal tendencies. Advocated generosity toward the American colonies and India. Of his many essays, the highly critical one on the French Revolution (1790) is best known. In his later years he approached the conservative point of view.

Byron, George Gordon Noel, Lord (1788-1824): British poet and satirist. Fought with the Greeks in their war of independence and died of a fever at Missolonghi.

Cadoudal, Georges (1771-1804): A leader of the counter-revolutionaries in the Vendée. Made several attempts to assassinate Napoleon. During the attempt of 1804, undertaken with Pichegru and Moreau, he was arrested by Fouché and executed.

Calonne, Charles Alexandre de (1734-1802): Minister of finance under Louis XVI; first tried a policy of big spending, then adopted Turgot's reform program. Defeated by the Notables, he was dismissed in 1787 and fled to England to escape indictment. From London, he supported the emigrant cause.

Cambacérès, Jean Jacques Régis de (1753-1824): Revolutionary legislator at the Convention, kept out of sight during the Reign of Terror. After 9th Thermidor member of the Committee of Public Safety, then in the Chamber of the 500. Second Consul under Napoleon, where he played an important part in the creation of the Civil Code.

Campan, Jeanne Louise Henriette (1752-1822): Reader at the royal court and chambermaid of Marie Antoinette.

Carnot, Lazare Nicolas Marguerite (1753-1823): Montagnard and military expert, minister of war in 1793 and known as the "organizer for victory." One of the leaders in the overthrow of Robespierre and a leader in the Directorate. There he turned moderate and was pushed aside by Barras. Ousted by the coup d'état of September 1797, he went abroad. Napoleon called him back, but he did not last as minister of war, as he was not submissive enough. Napoleon thought highly of his military writings; fought again for Napoleon in 1814-15. After the Restoration he was exiled for life.

Carrier, Jean Baptiste (1756-94): Extreme Jacobin, responsible for the Terror at Nantes; executed in 1794.

Caulaincourt, Armand Augustin Louis, Marquis de (1772[3?]-1827): General and diplomat, created Duke of Vicenza by Napoleon. Was his aide-de-camp and ambassador to Russia, and accompanied him on the Russian campaign and his rapid return to Paris. Foreign minister in 1814 and during the Hundred Days.

Championnet, Jean Etienne (1762-1800): Commander of the Army of Italy; conquered Naples in 1799, but was recalled because of a dispute with the Directory. He was acquitted and then commanded the Army of the Alps, with little success.

Charette, François Athanase (1763-1796): Leader of the rioters in the Vendée after the original commanders Cathelineau and d'Elbée had fallen. He was abandoned by the Bourbons living in England, betrayed and handed over to the republicans. He was shot at Nantes.

Charles IV (1748-1819): King of Spain 1788-1808. Made war on France from 1793 to 1795, then allied Spain with France, after which his navy suffered major defeats by the British, in particular at Trafalgar in 1805. Napoleon forced him and his son to abdicate in 1808.

Charles (1771-1824): Archduke of Austria, brother of Emperor Francis II; the ablest Austrian commander in the revolutionary and Napoleonic wars, but often handicapped by unwise decisions of the Vienna court. Minister of war in 1805; defeated Napoleon at Aspern in 1809, but was beaten by him at Wagram two months later.

Chateaubriand, Francois René, Vicomte de (1768-1848): French writer and diplomat, in 1791 immigrated to North America. In 1803-04 ambassador of Napoleon; later opposed him. Representative of early French romanticism.

Chaumette, Pierre Gaspard (1763-1794): Called "Anaxagoras," member of the Cordeliers Club and follower of Hébert; tried to introduce the worship of reason. One of the leaders of the Paris Commune; arrested and executed with the Hébertists.

Chénier, André Marie de (1762-1794): Famous poet, at first a sympathizer of the revolution, then disillusioned by the Jacobin excesses. He was arrested by Robespierre's orders and executed three days before the Terror ended.

Chénier, Marie Joseph (1764-1811): Brother of André; also a poet and dramatist, famous for some revolutionary songs. Stayed in the service of the Republic, then worked for Napoleon.

Chouan: see Cottereau.

Clausewitz, Carl von (1780-1831): Prussian general, friend of Scharnhorst and Gneisenau; 1812, in Russian service; later, director of the Berlin War Academy and chief of the general staff. His main publication, *On War*, was highly regarded all over the world, even by Engels and Lenin.

Cloots, Jean Baptiste (1755-1794): Called "Anacharsis"; born near Cleves, Germany. Sacrificed his fortune for his humanistic and liberal ideas; advocated war against all of Europe. Called himself "orator of the human race." Indicted by Saint-Just as an atheist and Hébertist, and executed.

Collot d'Herbois, Jean Marie (1749-1796): Actor and dramatist, then radical enemy of the Girondists and wild terrorist at the reconquered Lyons. Member of the Committee of Public Safety and participant in the overthrow of Robespierre. Exiled to Guyana; tried to revolutionize the Negroes, was again arrested and died of a fever.

Condorcet, Jean Antoine Nicolas de Caritat, Marquis de (1743-1794): Important mathematician and philosopher. Elected to the Convention, he voted mostly with the Girondists against the extremism of the Jacobins. He was indicted as an enemy of the republic, escaped, but was finally found and imprisoned, where he poisoned himself.

Constant de Rebecque, Henri Benjamin (1767-1830): French-Swiss politician and writer, close friend of Madame de Staël. Defended the Directory and then an advocate of a constitutional monarchy. Went into exile with de Staël, but supported Napoleon after his return from Elba.

Corday, Charlotte (1768-1793): Descendant of the poet Corneille and sympathizer with the Girondists. When their persecution began, she left her native Normandy and went to Paris where she assassinated Marat. She was arrested and executed.

Cottereau, Jean (1767-1794): Called Jean Chouan; salt-smuggler, then one of the leaders in the uprisings in Maine and Normandy. He was killed just before the end of the Terror; his whole family died during the fighting in the Vendée.

Couthon, Georges Auguste (1755-1794): Member of the Convention and the Committee of Public Safety; follower of Robespierre. Though crippled, he was extremely active during the retaking of Lyons, where he proved to be more humane than his successor Collot. He was executed together with Robespierre.

Custine, Adam Philippe, Comte de (1740-1793): Soldier in the Seven Years War and the American war of independence. As a general in the War of the First Coalition he conquered Worms, Mayence and Frankfort, but became suspect because of his delaying tactics in 1793. After the defeat of the Gironde, he was indicted by the Hébertists and executed.

Danton, Georges Jacques (1759-1794): Parisian lawyer, leader of hte Cordeliers party, great orator; worked for the overthrow of the monarchy. As Jacobin minister of justice, involved in the September massacres of 1792. Called passionately for national defense against the Allied invasion in the same year. First president of the Committee of Public Safety. In 1793 he pleaded for moderation against the extreme terror under Robespierre, who had him arrested and executed in April of 1794.

Daunou, Pierre Claude Francois (1761-1840): Moderate delegate at the Convention, responsible for the founding of the National Institute in October of 1795. Promoted education and sciences in post-revolutionary France.

David, Jacques Louis (1748-1825): Prominent painter of the classicistic style, and, during the revolutionary years, art and fashion dictator for the whole country. Follower of Robespierre, later of Napoleon. Under Louis XVIII exiled as a regicide.

Desaix de Veygoux, Louis Charles Antoine (1768-1800): General under Jourdan and Moreau, excelled during Napoleon's Egyptian campaign. He decided Napoleon's victory at Marengo in 1800, where he was killed.

Desmoulins, Camille (1760-1794): French journalist and revolutionary. His speeches helped to bring about the storming of the Bastille. In the National Convention, he fought the Gironde, and after their overthrow called for moderation. As friend of Danton's, arrested and executed in April of 1794.

Diderot, Denis (1713-1784): Philosopher of the Enlightenment, coeditor (with d'Alembert) of the *Encyclopédie*. In his later years, he enjoyed the patronage of Empress Catherine of Russia.

Drouet, Jean Baptiste (1763-1824): Postmaster of Sainte-Menehould; became famous when he recognized Louis XVI during his flight from Paris, and arranged for his arrest. Then soldier of the Army of the North, captured by the Austrians and exchanged for Madame Royale. Member of the Council of Five Hundred. In 1815 he was exiled as a regicide.

Ducos, Pierre Roger (1754-1816): Member of the Convention and the Council of Five Hundred. Supported Napoleon and became vice president of his senate. Considered to have been without talent and unqualified for the high positions he held.

Dumont, Etienne (1759-1829): Swiss citizen who lived in France during the Revolution, met Robespierre and later wrote his memoirs.

Dumouriez, Charles Francois (1739-1823): French general under Louis XV; minister of foreign affairs in 1792, later in the year commander of French army as successor of Lafayette; victor at Valmy. After his defeat at Neerwinden, in 1793, he deserted to the Austrians.

Duport, Adrien (1759-1798): Learned jurist. As advocate in the Paris Parlement he opposed Calonne and Loménie. Then, member for Paris at the Estates-General, representing the nobility. Formed the so-called triumvirate with Barnave and Lameth after Mirabeau's death. Left the Jacobins and joined the Feuillants. Arrested during the insurrection of August 10, 1792, he escaped with Danton's help. Returned after 9th Thermidor, but in exile again after the coup d'état of 18th Fructidor.

Elbée, Maurice Joseph Louis Gigost d' (1752-1794): First a supporter of the Revolution, then, because of the anti-priest legislation, its enemy. One of the most prominent leaders in the Vendée uprising, first under Cathelineau, then independently. Won several battles in 1793, but at the battle of Cholet wounded, captured and shot.

Enghien, Louis Antoine Henri, Duke of (1772-1804): Member of the French royal family, suspected of participating in Cadoudal's conspiracy; illegally kidnapped, court-martialed and shot at Vincennes.

Fabre d'Eglantine, Philippe Francois (1750-1794): Poet and dramatist. At the Convention, follower of Danton. He invented the names of the months of the revolutionary calendar. Involved in the East India scandal. Indicted and executed with Danton.

Ferdinand I (1751-1828): Spanish-Bourbon king of Naples, 1799-1805 and 1815-16, then king of the Two Sicilies, 1816-25. Joined the Second Coalition against France in 1798 and the Third against Napoleon in 1805. Fled to Sicily in 1806. Reactionary ruler whose government provoked an insurrection in 1820. This forced him to grant a constitution, which he soon repudiated.

Ferrières de Marsay, Charles Elie Marquis de (1741-1804): Delegate of the noblemen at the National Assembly, pupil of Rousseau and prolific writer. He left Paris in 1792 and returned after the end of the Terror.

Fersen, Count Hans Axel (1755-1810): Swedish officer and diplomat; at the court in Versailles, a favorite of the queen. He prepared and aided the royal couple during their flight from Paris and attempted, in vain, to arrange for their escape from the Temple. After his return to Sweden he was accused of having tried to poison the crown prince and was killed by a mob.

Fouché, Joseph (1759-1820): At the Convention, a supporter of Robespierre, then a terrorist at Lyons. Then opposed Robespierre because of his Cult of the Supreme Being. Minister of police under the Directory. Supported Napoleon's coup d'état and made himself indispensable to the consul and emperor. He managed to survive even the Bourbon Restoration and became ambassador to Dresden.

Fouquier-Tinville, Antoine Quentin (1746-1795): Relative of Camille Desmoulins who furthered his career. Became public prosecutor to the Revolutionary Tribunal, superintending all political executions during the Reign of Terror. After a long trial, he was executed in May of 1795.

Francis II, of Austria (1768-1835): The last Holy Roman Emperor; succeeded his father, Leopold II, in 1792. Declared himself emperor of Austria in 1804 and resigned as Holy Roman Emperor after the establishment of the Confederation of the Rhine in 1806. Ruled then as Francis I in Austria, but left most political affairs to his chancellor, Metternich. Father of Napoleon's second wife, Marie Louise.

Frederick William II (1744-1797): King of Prussia, nephew of Frederick the Great. Entered the alliance against France, but concluded a separate peace at Basel in 1795. Acquired large parts of Poland during the second and third partitions.

Frederick William III (1770-1840): King of Prussia, son of Frederick William II. Passive attitude toward Napoleon; approved only reluctantly the reforms of Stein and Hardenberg. Pushed into the national uprising in 1813, he was an ardent advocate of "restauration," after 1815, and suppressed liberal and national movements.

Fréron, Louis Marie Stanislas (1754-1802): First radical journalist in his *Orateur du peuple* (Orator of the people), then a wild terrorist at Toulon and Marseilles. Involved in the overthrow of Robespierre, after which he turned royalist. Became one of the leaders of the Jeunesse Dorée. Had an affair with Pauline, Napoleon's favorite sister. In 1799 he went as a commissioner to Saint Domingue, where he died.

Garat, Dominique Joseph (1749[?]-1832): Political and historical writer, successor of Danton as minister of justice, then minister of the interior. Twice arrested during the Terror, then again in the diplomatic service; welcomed Napoleon's coup d'état and served in his senate.

Gentz, Friedrich von (1764-1832): German political theorist, influenced by Edmund Burke; fought against the Revolution and Napoleon. Since 1810 under Metternich's influence.

George III (1738-1820): King of Great Britain and Ireland; elector, later king, of Hanover. Under him, the American colonies were lost. Became permanently insane in 1810.

George, Canvas (1797-?): Wrote novels, short stories and historical works, as well as his memoirs of the Napoleonic era. Little is known about his life.

Gobel, Jean Baptiste Joseph (1727-94): Was elected bishop of Paris in March of 1791 but, because of abuses of his authority, forced to retire in November of the same year. Was then indicted as an atheist and executed with the Hébertists.

Gneisenau, August Count Neidhart von (1760-1831): Prussian field marshal, collaborated with Scharnhorst. Dismissed in 1807 on Napoleon's initiative. Blücher's chief of staff in the campaigns of 1813-14 and 1815.

Goethe, Johan Wolfgang von (1749-1832): German poet, accompanied the duke of Weimar during the 1792 campaign in France; met Napoleon at the Congress of Erfurt.

Grégoire, Henri (1750-1831): Prelate and revolutionary. As deputy of the clergy to the Estates-General he cooperated with the Third Estate and worked for the abolition of Negro slavery. Opposed the abolition of the monarchy and the trial of the king, also Napoleon's coup d'état. In 1814, he proposed the deposition of Napoleon. Died unreconciled with the church.

Grouchy, Emanuel Marquis de (1766-1847): General of the revolutionary and Napoleonic wars; made a marshal after Napoleon's return from Elba. Has been held responsible for Napoleon's defeat at Waterloo through his failure to prevent the Prussians from joining the English forces.

Guadet, Marguerite Elie (1759-1794): Prominent Girondin administrator, president of the criminal tribunal in 1791. Opposed the Paris Commune and, in March of 1793, negotiated with Danton about a reconciliation between Girondists and Montagnards. Guillotined during the Reign of Terror.

Guillotin, Joseph Ignace (1738-1814): Physician and influential delegate of the Third Estate during the first months of the National Assembly. Proposed the use of a decapitation machine invented by Schmitt and Dr. Antoine Louis. The first execution by the "Guillotine" took place in April of 1792. Guillotin was imprisoned during the Terror. After his release he returned to medicine and founded the Académie de Médicine.

Hardenberg, Karl August, Baron von (1750-1822): Prussian statesman; minister of foreign affairs in 1803-06 and 1807, then dismissed upon Napoleon's demand; chancellor from 1810, continued Stein's reforms.

Hébert, Jacques René (1757-1794): Radical journalist, one of the leaders of the Paris Commune, editor of the *Père Duchesne* and dominant at the Cordeliers Club. Atheist, he favored maximum prices, laws against suspects and the cult of Reason during the Terror. Opposed by Danton and Robespierre, he attempted an uprising in March of 1794, after which he and his followers were arrested and executed.

Hegel, Georg Wilhelm Friedrich (1770-1831): German philosopher, lecturer at Jena 1801-07; school director at Nürnberg 1808-16; professor at Heidelberg University 1816-21, then at Berlin.

Hérault de Séchelles, Marie Jean (1759-1794): Lawyer, writer and favorite of the queen. First a member of the Feuillant, then of the Gironde party, finally a Montagnard. One of the authors of the 1793 constitution, cofounder of the Revolutionary Tribunal, member of the Committee of Public Safety, and on many diplomatic missions. Accused of treason and condemned to death with Danton.

Hoche, Louis Lazare (1768-1797): Successful general on Rhine and Moselle, then denounced by his rival Pichegru and imprisoned from April 1794 until the overthrow of Robespierre. After his release, commander of the Vendée army; frustrated the royalist landings at Quiberon Bay. Led an abortive expedition on Ireland and against the British. The Directory refused to appoint him war minister because of his youth. Died suddenly at Wetzlar, Germany, from tuberculosis (or poisoning?). Napoleon declared him the only revolutionary general equal to himself.

Humboldt, Wilhelm von (1767-1835): German statesman, diplomat and scholar, friend of Schiller and Goethe; founder of the Berlin University, reformer of the school system; retired from state service in protest against the prevailing spirit of reaction. A leader of neo-humanism.

Isnard, Maximin (1755-1825): Leading Girondist, from Var; in the Legislative Assembly and the Convention, radical foe of the emigrants. Tried to reduce the influence of the Commune and helped to protect the king from the mob on June 20, 1792. Instrumental in establishing the Committee of Nine, which, in April of 1793, became the Committee of Public Safety. He was hiding during the Terror, but was then elected to the Convention in 1795. Active as persecutor of terrorists. Napoleon made him a baron.

Josephine (1763-1814): Empress of the French, wife of Napoleon Bonaparte. Née Marie Josephe Rose Tascher de la Pagerie, widow of Alexandre de Beauharnais, from whom she had two children, Eugène and Hortense. Napoleon had the marriage annulled in 1809 because of her alleged sterility; retired at Malmaison.

Joubert, Barthélemy Catherine (1769-1799): Successful general in Italy in 1793, then general under

Napoleon in 1796 in Italy and the Tyrol. Then commander in Holland, on the Rhine and again in Italy. Defeated and killed at the battle of Novi in August of 1799.

Jourdan, Jean Baptiste (1762-1833): Fought in the American war of independence. Victorious at Neerwinden and Jemappes, also defeated Coburg at Wattignies. His army invaded Germany in 1796 and occupied Frankfort and Bavaria, but then had to retreat across the Rhine. Defeated by Archduke Charles at Stockach in March of 1799, thereafter member of the Council of 500. Napoleon made him marshal in 1804 and governor of Naples in 1806. Wellington defeated him at Vittoria in 1813. He supported the Bourbons in 1814 and the revolution of 1830.

Kellermann, Francois Etienne Christophe (1735-1820): Born in Strasbourg, fought in the Seven Years War. Under Dumouriez, the real victor at Valmy in September of 1792. Accused by Custine of treason and dismissed by Robespierre. Then commander of the Army of the Alps. Under the Empire, he was made marshal and duke. Reconciled with Louis XVIII in 1815 and them member of the House of Peers.

Kléber, Jean Baptiste (1753-1800): Fought under Custine then in the Vendée and with the Army of the Rhine. Victor in the battles of Fleurus and Cholet. Went with Napoleon to Egypt where he was critically wounded, then left in charge when Napoleon left Egypt. While negotiating a treaty with the Turks and British, he was assassinated by a Moslem fanatic.

Kleist, Heinrich von (1777-1811): German dramatic poet, served 1792-1799 in the army, 1805-07 in civil service; temporarily arrested by the French in 1807; in his last years, journalist in Berlin. Committed suicide.

Kutusov, Michail Ilarionovich (1745-1813): Russian general and field marshal, fought repeatedly against the Turks, and at Austerlitz. Replaced Barclay de Tolly as commander against Napoleon's invasion. After the bloody battle of Borodino he retreated behind Moscow, then pursued Napoleon's army relentlessly when he was forced to turn back. Was made prince of Smolensk for a victory late in 1812. Hesitated to cross the border into Germany and was overruled by the Russian emperor.

Lafayette, Marie Joseph Paul Yves Roch Gilbert du Motier, Marquis de (1757-1834): Soldier and politician, fought in the American colonies 1777-79 and became a friend of Washington. Later active in the defense of Virginia and at the battle of Yorktown. Then liberal delegate of the nobles in the National Assembly of 1789 and commander of the National Guard. Helped to design the Declaration of Human Rights and tried to restrain the mob of Paris and to protect the king after his flight. In 1792 he became commander of the Army of the East. His operations failed and he fled to the Austrians who imprisoned him. Liberated by Napoleon, served in the Chamber of Deputies after the emperor's fall, and was active in the revolution of 1830. He introduced the modern French flag.

Lameth, Alexandre Theodore Victor de (1760-1829): Participated in the American war of independence. As deputee of the nobles he joined the Third Estate. Opposed Mirabeau's alliance with the royal court and after Lafayette's decline formed the so-called "triumvirate" with Duport and Barnave. Tried to mediate between aristocracy and Third Estate; went over to the Austrians with Lafayette and was imprisoned by them for three years. Returned after Napoleon's coup d'état, and was made a baron.

Las Cases, Emanuel, Comte de (1766-1842): French historian, accompanied Napoleon into exile to St. Helena, where the emperor dictated part of his memoirs to him.

La Reveillière-Lépeaux, Louis Marie de (1753- 1824): At first close to the Girondists, hiding during the Reign of Terror. First president of the Council of the Ancients, then a director, where he took a position at the center. Anti-Catholic, tried to substitute for the Christian religion a new cult called "théophilanthropie." Retired in June of 1799.

La Rochejaquelein, Henri de (1772-1794): Led the Royalists in the Vendée and defeated the republican armies, but was beaten in December of 1793 and later killed at Nouaillé.

Launay, Bernard René Jourdan, Marquis de (1740-1789): Commander of the Bastille on July 14, 1789. After its fall, he was captured by the crowd and killed at the Place de Grève.

Le Chapelier, Isaac René Guy (1754-1794): Delegate of the Third Estate and founder of the Breton Club. Known by the law of June 1791 named after him, which prohibited meetings and associations of workers and employers and made strikes illegal. This laws was not completely repealed until 1884. After the king's flight he left the Jacobins and joined the Feuillants. Executed during the Terror.

Loménie de Brienne, Etienne Charles de (1727-1794): Archbishop of Toulouse, then of Sens. Friend of Turgot and foe of Calonne whom he succeeded as controller of finances in 1787. He then adopted Calonne's reform program, but was resisted by the parlement of Paris. He resigned in August of 1788 and was made cardinal. He accepted the Civil Constitution of the Clergy, which was, however, repudiated by the pope. Arrested in 1793, died in prison.

Louis XVI (1754-93): Grandson and successor of Louis XV, king of France from 1774. Dismissed Finance Minister Turgot in 1776, and supported the reforms attempted by his successor Necker until 1781. Called back Necker in 1788. Tried to prevent joint action of the Estates-General. His second dismissal of Necker led to the storming of the Bastille. Forced to return to Paris after he refused to approve the abolition of feudal rights; after his attempt to escape, forced to accept the constitution of 1791, which deprived him of all power. Imprisoned in August 1792, then tried as traitor before the National Convention, because of his attempts to make contact with foreign governments. Executed on January 21, 1793.

Louis XVII (1785-1795): Titular king of France 1793-95; became dauphin after his brother died in June of 1789. Imprisoned with his father, Louis XVI, in August of 1792; is supposed to have died as a result of neglect and ill-treatment, in June of 1795. Later, over 30 people claimed to be the dauphin.

Louis XVIII (1755-1824): King of France 1814-1824, younger brother of Louis XVI, known as the Comte de Provence. After the death of the dauphin, he was recognized as king by the emigrants. Lived in exile on the continent and in England, restored as the legitimate king by the Allies in 1814. Fled when Napoleon returned from Elba and returned after the battle of Waterloo.

Luckner, Baron Nikolas von (1722-1794): Born in Bavaria, then general of the Army of the Rhine. After some setbacks he was dismissed, then indicted for treason and executed.

Luise (1776-1810): Queen of Prussia, from the ducal house of Mecklenburg-Strelitz; married the later king Frederick William III in 1793; supported the Prussian reforms and the alliance with Russia.

Macdonald, Etienne Jacques Joseph Alexandre (1765-1840): Fought at Jemappes under Dumouriez, and in 1798 replaced Championnet as commander of the Army of Naples. His friendship with Moreau made him suspicious to Napoleon, who, however, made him duke of Taranto after the battle of Wagram. Also fought in Russia and at Leipzig, and served again under Louis XVIII.

Mack von Leiberich, Baron Karl von (1752-1828): Austrian general, occupied Rome with Neapolitan troops in November of 1797, then defeated by Championnet and captured. Breaking his word of honor, he escaped from Paris in 1800. Had to capitulate at Ulm in 1805 and was condemned to death by the Austrians but then pardoned.

Malesherbes, Guillaume Chrétien de Lamoignon de (1721-1794): Tolerant censor of the press during the Old Regime, permitted the publication of the *Encyclopédie* of d'Alembert and Diderot. Retired when Turgot was dismissed. Defended the king before the Convention. Was executed during the Reign of Terror, together with his daughter and his grandchildren.

Marat, Jean Paul (1743-93): Radical French revolutionary. In his journal, *L'Ami du Peuple*, he attacked Necker, Mirabeau, Lafayette and, finally the king. Twice exiled, from 1792 a member of the National Convention; instigated the September massacres of 1792. Murdered by Charlotte Corday.

Maréchal, Pierre Sylvain (1750-1803): Follower of Babeuf, coauthor of the "Manifesto of the Equals." Also wrote a hymn to the Supreme Being for Robespierre, designed a republican calendar and wrote a dictionary of atheists. Indicted after Babeuf's conspiracy, but acquitted.

Marie Antoinette (1755-1793): Daughter of Emperor Francis I and Maria Theresa, married the later Louis XVI in 1770. Compromised by the "diamond necklace" affair. Attempted secret negotiations with European royalties to save the monarchy. Executed on October 16, 1793.

Marie Louise (1791-1847): Daughter of Emperor Francis II of Austria, second wife of Napoleon (1810); was made duchess of Parma after Napoleon's overthrow.

Marwitz, Friedrich August Ludwig v.d. (1777-1837): Prussian officer, represented the "old-Prussian" party, opposed Stein and Hardenberg violently. Organized the Prussia militia in 1813.

Masséna, André (1758-1817): Served under Louis XVI, then for the republic in Italy. General in 1793, victorious at Zurich in 1799. Later, marshal of the empire; fought in most of Napoleon's campaigns, but was not successful against the British in Spain and Portugal. Later, he was made duke of Rivoli and prince of Essling. Among Napoleon's generals, he was one of the most indiscriminate plunderers.

Merda, Charles André (1770-1812): Gendarme in the National Guard, wounded Robespierre on the chin on 9th Thermidor, 1794. Napoleon made him a colonel and baron. He was killed in a battle near Moscow.

Metternich, Clemens Wenzel Lothar Nepomuk, Prince of (1775-1859): Austrian statesman. After the war of 1809 allied with Napoleon, but joined the anti-French coalition in summer of 1813. As foe of national German endeavors, he became the founder of the Germanic Federation, in which Austria was predominant. Cofounder of the Holy Alliance, anti-liberal, legitimacy-oriented; depended on a rigid police and censorship system. Forced to abdicate and flee from Vienna in 1848.

Mirabeau, Honoré Gabriel Riqueti, Comte de (1749-1791): During his youth repeatedly imprisoned, once even condemned to death for abduction, and rejected by the nobles. Became a delegate of the Third Estate in 1789. Great orator and leader of the Assembly during the first months. Tried for a constitution formed after the English example and hoped to become prime minister. Was rejected by the National Assembly, and also by the court, particularly the queen, although he was in the pay of the court from May of 1790. After his early death there was little chance for the monarchy to survive.

Montesquieu, Charles Louis de Secondat (1689-1755): Political philosopher of the Enlightenment, famous for his *Persian Letters* (1721) and *The Spirit of the Laws* (1748), also for his history of the Romans. Admirer of English institutions and analyst of the various types of government.

Morris, Gouverneur (1752-1816): American politician and diplomat, went to France on his own in 1789, became the American ambassador in 1792. Tried to help the Royalists and participated in an attempt to free the king. In February of 1793 the French government asked for his recall. But he returned to the United States only in 1798 and became senator of the state of New York. Known for his diary of the French Revolution.

Murat, Joachim (1767-1815): Supported Napoleon against the uprising of the 13th Vendémiaire (1795) and fought with him in Italy and Egypt. He married Napoleon's sister Caroline in 1800. Became marshal and king of Naples, also fought in the Russian campaign, taking over its command when Napoleon left. Negotiated with the Allies in 1813 to save his throne, and tried to rally support for Napoleon. In 1815, he tried to start a revolt in Calabria, but was captured by King

Ferdinand's men and shot. A brave and dashing cavalry officer, but without strategic or political insight.

Necker, Jacques (1732-1804): Swiss banker in London and Paris, also director of the East India Company; became famous by his writings on Colbert and against the free grain trade advocated by Baron de Turgot. Director of finances in 1777. Both he and the salon of his wife were very popular in Paris. His report on the finances of the state (1781) was slanted, his attempts at reforms frustrated by the nobility. Dismissed in 1781, highly critical of his successor Calonne. Called back in 1788. His second dismissal in July of 1789 was one of the reasons for the storming of the Bastille. The king was forced to call him back, but, disillusioned by the events and having lost much of his popularity, he resigned finally in September of 1790 and retired to Geneva. Father of Germaine de Staël.

Nelson, Horatio (1758-1805): British seaman and admiral, lost an eye in his fight against the French garrison at Calvi in 1794, and his right arm in 1797. Decided Napoleon's campaign in Egypt by destroying the French fleet at Aboukir Bay in 1798, also successful at the battle of Copenhagen. Lover of Lady Emma Hamilton after 1798. Mortally wounded in the battle of Trafalgar, which established British naval superiority once and for all (1805). Became a national hero.

Ney, Michel (1769-1815): French general and marshal, defeated the Austrians at Ulm in 1805, excelled in the Russian campaign of 1812-13. In 1814, he put himself at the disposal of the Bourbons, but joined Napoleon after his return from Elba. After Waterloo, he was shot as a traitor.

Orléans, Louis Philippe Joseph, Duc d' (1747-1793): Called Philippe Egalité. Descendant of a brother of Louis XIV, one of the richest property owners in France. Opposed to the policies of the court, admirer of England and ardent freemason. Joined the Third Estate in 1789 and for some time made himself very popular with the people. He voted for the death of the king. When his son, the later King Louis-Philippe (1830-48) joined the Austrian armies, following General Dumouriez, Philippe was arrested in April of 1793 and executed in November.

Paine, Thomas (1737-1809): English radical and American Quaker, became famous for his pamphlet of 1776, "Common Sense," which argued for the independence of the colonies. Back in England he wrote a reply to Burke's "Reflections on the Revolution in France." He had to leave England and was triumphantly received in Paris. As a member of the Convention, he sided with the Girondists and proposed to offer the king an asylum in the United States. This aggravated Robespierre, and in 1794 he was imprisoned for 11 months. He completed his *Age of Reason* in prison; it antagonized many of his followers because of its anti-biblical tendencies. He regained his seat in the Convention, but became disillusioned with developments in France and returned to the United States in 1802.

Palm, Johann Philipp (1768-1806): Bookseller in Nuremberg, published an anonymous anti-French pamphlet in 1806. Since he would not reveal the name of the author, Napoleon had him shot.

Paoli, Pascal (1725-1807): Corsican patriot, opposed the acquisition of the Island by the French in 1768. Fled to England, but was appointed governor of Corsica by the revolutionary government. When he strove again for independence and called in the British, he was dismissed and returned to England. Foe of the Bonaparte family.

Paul I, Czar of Russia (1754-1801): Ascended the throne in 1796 and joined the second coalition against France in 1798. After the defeat at Zurich he quarreled with his Austrian and English allies and became an admirer of Napoleon. Retired from the coalition in 1799 and was assassinated two years later.

Percy, Pierre Francois (1754-1825): Chief medical officer of the Grande Armée, wounded several times. Appointed member of the Academy of Sciences by the Prussian king, in recognition of his aid for Prussian wounded.

Pétion de Villeneuve, Jérôme (1756-1794): Lawyer from Chartres, successor of Bailly as mayor of Paris in 1791; also first president of the Convention. Helped to bring back the royal family from Varennes. Voted for the death of the king. Arrested as a Girondist in June of 1793, but escaped. His body was found near Saint-Emilion. He had probably committed suicide.

Pichegru, Jean Charles (1761-1804): Jacobin general, commander of the Army of the Rhine in 1793. Together with Hoche he conquered Holland and the Austrian Netherlands, also helped to suppress the uprising of April 1, 1795. Again with the Army of the Rhine he caused Jourdan's defeat by his inactivity, and established contact with the émigrés. Was dismissed, but later elected into the Council of Five Hundred, becoming its president. Exiled to Guayana after the coup d'état of 18th Fructidor. Escaped to London and joined in

Cadoudal's conspiracies against Napoleon. Arrested in Paris in 1804 and found strangled in the Temple prison.

Pitt, William (the Younger) (1759-1806): British statesman; prime minister from 1783 to 1801 and again from 1804 to 1806. He became the soul of the first three coalitions against revolutionary and Napoleonic France.

Pius VI (Gian Angelo Braschi) (1717-1799): Pope from 1775 to 1799. Condemned the civil constitution of the clergy and joined the first coalition against France. He sued for peace after Napoleon's Italian campaign. When the French General Duphot was killed in a riot in December of 1797, General Berthier invaded Rome, and since Pius would not recognize the newly proclaimed republic, he was taken prisoner. He died in Valence in August 1799.

Pius VII (Barnaba Gregorio Chiaramonti) (1740-1823): Pope from 1800, negotiated the Concordat with France. He performed the ceremony of Napoleon's consecration as emperor at Notre Dame in Paris in December of 1804. The Papal States were again occupied by the French in 1808-9 and Pius taken to Fontainebleau, where he had to sign a new concordat which he disavowed after the battle of Leipzig. He returned to Rome in triumph in 1814 and the Papal States were restored at the Vienna Congress.

Reubell, Jean-Francois (1747-1807): Delegate of the Third Estate from Alsace, fought for an independent Alsace and against the emancipation of the Jews. Member of the Committee for Public Safety after 9th Thermidor, then influential as a director, advocating an aggressive policy in the Rhineland. One of the men of the "triumvirate" of 18th Fructidor (September 1797). With 18th Brumaire, his career came to an end.

Rivarol, Antoine (1755-1801): French journalist, essayist and critic. He criticized king and nobility, but tried to save them. After the September massacres of 1792, he fled to Brussels.

Robespierre, Augustin Bon Joseph (1763-94): Younger brother of Maximilien. Member of the Convention, followed his brother's policies. Sent to the south to counteract the agitation of the Fédérés. Met and supported Bonaparte at Toulon. On 9th Thermidor he declared that he wanted to share the fate of his brother. After his arrest he threw himself from the window of the Paris City Hall. Executed with his brother.

Robespierre, Maximilien de (1758-94): Lawyer from Arras, member of the Jacobin club, leader of the mountain party, carried out the overthrow of the Girondists and the condemnation of Louis XVI. Brought the Terror to its climax during which he held a dictator-like position. Overthrown by his own followers on July 27 (9th Thermidor) of 1794 and guillotined.

Rochambeau, Jean Baptiste Donatien de Vimeur, Comte de (1725-1807): Soldier since 1742, sent to Rhode Island in 1780, supported the American army at the capture of Yorktown in 1781. Commander of the Army of the North in 1791. Arrested during the Reign of Terror.

Roederer, Pierre Louis Comte de (1754-1835): Delegate of the Third Estate, Jacobin and attorney general for Paris. Went into hiding after the coup of 18th Fructidor, assisted in Napoleon's coup d'état of 18th Brumaire. Editor of several journals and member of the Institute. Lost his positions during the Restoration, but regained them after 1830.

Rohan-Guémenée, Cardinal (1734-1803): Involved in the necklace scandal of 1785. Sent to the Bastille and released through the Paris parlement in 1786. Then delegate of the clergy in the National Assembly. He refused the oath of loyalty and went into exile in 1791.

Roland, Manon Jeanne Philippon (1754-1793): Wife of the Girondist minister of the interior. Her salon in Paris wielded considerable political influence. Disciple of Rousseau and violent opponent of Danton and Robespierre. After the fall of the Gironde she was arrested and condemned to death. Her last words at the guillotine became famous.

Roland de la Platière, Jean Marie (1734-1793): Inspector of manufactures before the Revolution. Became acquainted with the leading Girondists and was appointed minister of the interior in March of 1792. Was apparently involved in the preparations for the king's flight. Dismissed by the king in favor of the Feuillants, recalled after the king was imprisoned. Hated by the Jacobins for his protest against the massacres of September 1792. Stepped down after the king's execution and escaped arrest during the Terror, but committed suicide at the news of his wife's execution.

Rouget de Lisle, Claude Joseph (1760-1836): Officer at the Strasbourg garrison. In April of 1792, he wrote the text and composed the famous song later known as the "Marseillaise." Later imprisoned for his loyalty to the king and released after 9th Thermidor. Wounded in the battle of Quiberon, lived in great poverty from then on. Finally, Louis Philippe granted him a pension.

Rousseau, Jean Jacques (1712-1778): French writer and philosopher of Swiss descent who exercised a tremendous influence over the thinking of his age and the following generations. He saw in civilization the source of all evil and demanded a return to nature, as well as a total reorganization of society based on the voluntary surrender of the individual under the will of the collective. Among his disciples were many French revolutionaries and many thinkers and poets of the Romantic age.

Roux, Jacques (1752-1794): Priest, then radical revolutionary. Member of the Paris Commune and the Convention. Leader of the Enragés who declared that only the rich had profited from the Revolution. Organized hunger revolts in February and March of 1793. Arrested in September of 1793 and condemned to death by the Revolutionary Tribunal. Committed suicide in prison. Many consider him the first spokesman for the underprivileged masses.

Saint-Just, Louis de (1767-1794): As member of the Convention he made a name for himself through his wild attacks on Louis XVI. Fanatic follower of Robespierre, who sent him to supervise the armies fighting at the fronts. He contributed to several important victories. During the Terror he brought about the downfall of the Hébertists, then the Dantonists. Arrested and executed on 9th Thermidor. His character is as controversial as that of Robespierre.

Sapinaud de Boishuguet, Madame de. Widow of one of the early leaders of the Vendée uprising, wrote interesting *Mémoires*. The exact dates of her life are not known.

Savary, Anne Jean Marie René (1774-1833): French general, made Duke of Rovigo by Napoleon. Minister of police from 1810 to 1814, as successor of Fouché.

Sanson, Charles-Henri (1739-1806): Official executioner in Paris. Under his supervision, Louis XVI, Marie Antoinette, Danton, Hébert, Robespierre, Fouquier-Tinville and many other revolutionaries were decapitated. His so-called memoirs are spurious.

Santerre, Antoine Joseph (1752-1809): Rich Paris brewer, took part in the storming of the Bastille and became commander of the National Guard in August of 1792. Conducted Louis XVI to the guillotine. Was then appointed general in the Army of the Vendée, but proved an utter failure. Recalled and imprisoned, released after 9th Thermidor.

Scherer, Barthélemy Louis Joseph (1747-1804): Soldier in the Austrian army, wounded at Torgau (1760), then general of the Army of the Rhine, also in Spain and Italy. Rejected Napoleon's plan of an Italian campaign in 1796. He was dismissed, but restored in Italy during the Egyptian campaign. Beaten in the battle of Magnano by the Austrian General Kray, April of 1799.

Schill, Ferdinand von (1776-1809): Prussian officer. After the Austrian uprising against Napoleon in 1809, he tried to make Prussia join Austria by leading his regiment from Berlin via Magdeburg to Stralsund, constantly fighting French units. He was killed in street fighting at Stralsund.

Schiller, Johann Christoph Friedrich von (1759-1805): German poet. First welcomed the Revolution and was made honorary citizen of the French Nation, but soon turned against the excess of the Revolution.

Schwarzenberg, Karl Philipp, Prince of (1771-1820): Austrian field marshal and supreme commander of the Allied armies in the wars of liberation, 1813-1815.

Ségur, Paul Philippe de (1780-1873): French brigadier general and adjutant of Napoleon, participated in his campaigns; later became a writer on military matters.

Sieyès, Emanuel-Joseph (1748-1836): Known as Abbé Sieyès. Attained fame by his pamphlet "What Is the Third Estate" (February 1789) and other publications. One of the leading personalities in the National Assembly, coauthor of the Declaration of Human Rights and the constitution of 1791, also influential in the division of the country into 83 departements. Voted for the king's death, then retreated from public life and returned only after 9th Thermidor. He then entered the Directory and became its leading man. Supported the coup d'état of Napoleon, who, however, changed Sieyès' draft of a new constitution radically. He gave up his consulship. Exiled at the Restoration and returned to Paris only in 1830.

Simon, Antoine (1735-1794): Parisian shoemaker who was made custodian of Louis XVI's young son. He probably did not treat him as inhumanly as has been assumed for sometime. Fanatic follower of Robespierre, was arrested on 10th Thermidor and executed.

Soult, Jean de Dieu (1769-1851): Called Nicolas. Officer in the Army of the Moselle, excelled at the battle of Fleurus (June of 1794), also at Stockach and in Switzerland. Great career under Napoleon as duke of Dalmatia. Became minister of war under the Bourbons and prime minister under Louis-Philippe.

Staël-Holstein, Germaine, Baronne de (1766-1817): Daughter of Finance Minister Necker, left France in 1792 and returned during the Directory. Center of a political salon, banned by Napoleon in 1803, then head of a literary circle at Coppet, Switzerland. Threatened by the French police, after publication of her main work

De l'Allemagne (*On Germany*), she fled to Russia and England; she returned to Coppet in 1815. Had great influence on the romantic movement in France.

Talleyrand-Périgord, Charles Maurice de (1754-1838): Bishop of Autun in 1789, then deputy of the clergy at the National Assembly, siding with the Revolution. Advocated the expropriation of church property and the civil constitution of the clergy. Sent to England on a diplomatic mission in 1792. Went into exile after the fall of the monarchy and lived in England and America until 1795 when his friend, Madame de Staël, arranged for his return. Almost penniless, he supported the Directory and was made minister for foreign affairs by Barras in 1797. He resigned in July of 1799, then supported Napoleon who made him foreign minister and prince of Benevento (1806). Intrigued against Napoleon when he sensed his forthcoming downfall, served then under Louis XVIII and had his greatest triumphs during the Vienna Congress.

Tallien, Jean Lambert (1767-1820): Jacobin journalist and politician, involved in the attack on the Tuileries and the September massacres of 1792. Member of the Convention and then of Committee of General Security; worked on the destruction of the Gironde. Radical advocate of the Terror, particularly at Bordeaux in 1793. Attacked by Robespierre in June of 1794, he helped to overthrow him one month later. Under the Directory, his influence declined. Accompanied Napoleon to Egypt and was captured by the British on his return voyage. Died in poverty.

Tolly, Prince Mikhail Barclay de (1761-1818): Russian field marshal, retreated continuously during Napoleon's Russian campaign. After the battle of Smolensk in August of 1812, he was replaced by Kutusov.

Treilhard, Jean-Baptiste (1742-1810): Delegate of the Third Estate, then member of the Committee of Public Safety. Against the revolts in Bordeaux he proceeded less ruthlessly than his successor Tallien. Later president of the Council of 500 and director, but Sieyès had his election declared invalid. Worked for Napoleon and assisted in the creation of the Civil Code. His ashes were interred at the Pantheon.

Vadier, Marc Guillaume Alexis (1736-1828): Delegate at the Convention and member of the Committee of Public Safety, participated in the intrigues against Danton and Robespierre. Persecuted as a terrorist, he went into hiding after 9th Thermidor. Arrested as a participant in Babeuf's conspiracy. Pardoned during the Consulate.

Vergennes, Charles Gravier, Comte de (1717-87): From 1774 foreign minister under Louis XVI, arranged France's participation in the American war of independence. Opposed Necker, but supported Calonne's attempts to reform.

Vergniaud, Pierre Victurnien (1753-1793): Lawyer and leader of the Girondists, great orator. Voted for war against Austria and for the king's death, which he pronounced as president of the Convention. Arrested with the other Gironde leaders, and executed in October of 1793.

Voltaire (Francois Marie Arouet) (1694-1778): Writer and philosopher, most important representative of French Enlightenment. Admirer of English institutions and advocate for tolerance and human rights.

Wellington, Arthur Wellesley, Duke of (1769-1852): British field marshal and statesman, fought the French in Spain 1808-13; commanded the British at Waterloo. Tory prime minister 1828-30, minister for foreign affairs under Peel in 1834-35.

Westermann, Francois Joseph (1751-1794): Cavalry officer, worked with Danton and played an important part at the fighting around the Tuileries in August of 1792. Fought against the Austrians and in the Vendée where he was beaten by La Rochejacquelein in December of 1793. He got his revenge at Le Mans and Savenay soon after and decimated the population cruelly. Was then indicted as an "indulgent" and executed together with Danton and Desmoulins.

Wurmser, Dagobert Sigismund, Count of (1724-1797): Born in the Alsace; then an Austrian general, forced the capitulation of Mayence by the French in 1793. Fought with little success against Pichegru in the Alsace and was thoroughly beaten by Napoleon in Italy. He surrendered Mantua in 1797 and died during the same year.

Appendix C

France in 1789

showing provinces and principal centers of administration

AUSTRIAN NETHERLANDS

BOULONNAIS

Lille • Douai
• Valenciennes
Arras
FLANDERS & HAINAULT

Amiens
ARTOIS

PICARDIE

Caen
Rouen ⊙
Soissons

NORMANDIE
ILE DE
FRANCE
Paris ⊙
Châlons •
Verdun •
⊙ Metz
Strasbourg
LORRAINE
CHAMPAGNE
Nancy ⊙
ALSACE

Alençon

BRETAGNE
Rennes ⊙
MAINE

Orléans •
ORLÉANAIS
FRANCHE
COMTÉ
Dijon •
⊙ COLMAR
Besançon

ANJOU
Tours •
NIVERNAIS
BOURGOGNE

TOURAINE
Bourges •
Poitiers •
BERRY

POITOU
Moulins •
BOURBONNAIS

La Rochelle •
MARCHE
Lyons •
Trevoux

AUNIS
SAINTONGE
&
ANGOUMOIS
Limoges •
Riom •
LYONNAIS

LIMOUSIN
AUVERGNE
Grenoble ⊙

Bordeaux ⊙
DAUPHINÉ
VENAISSIN

BÉARN

GUYENNE & GASCOGNE
LANGUEDOC
AVIGNON ■

Auch •
Montauban •
Montpellier •
PROVENCE

Pau ⊙
Toulouse ⊙
Aix ⊙

BÉARN

FOIX
Perpignan

SPAIN
ROUSSILLON

N

0   100 Miles
0   100 Kms

Pays d'états: lands claiming
preserved privileges

⊙ Sièges des parlements — centers of legal administration

■ Conseils souverains

• Other centers of royal administration

Departments of France in 1790

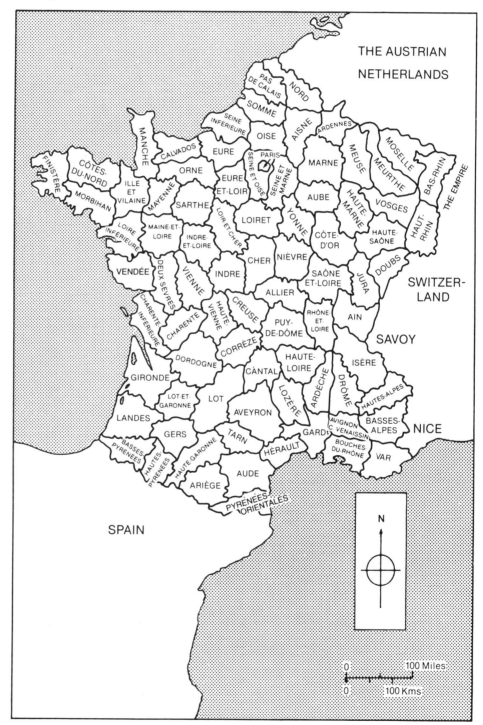

Paris at the Time
of the Revolution

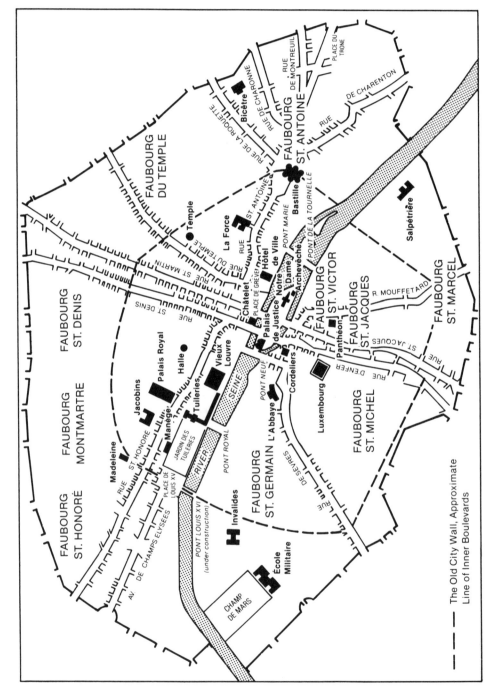

The Old City Wall, Approximate

Line of Inner Boulevards

The Sections of Paris

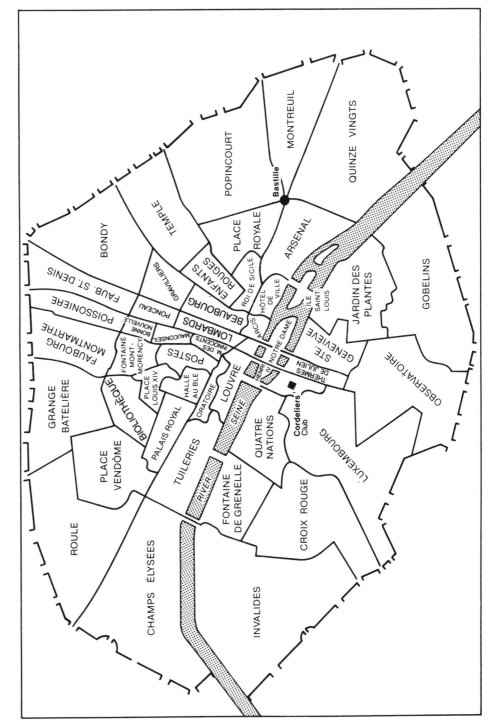

Napoleonic Europe, 1815

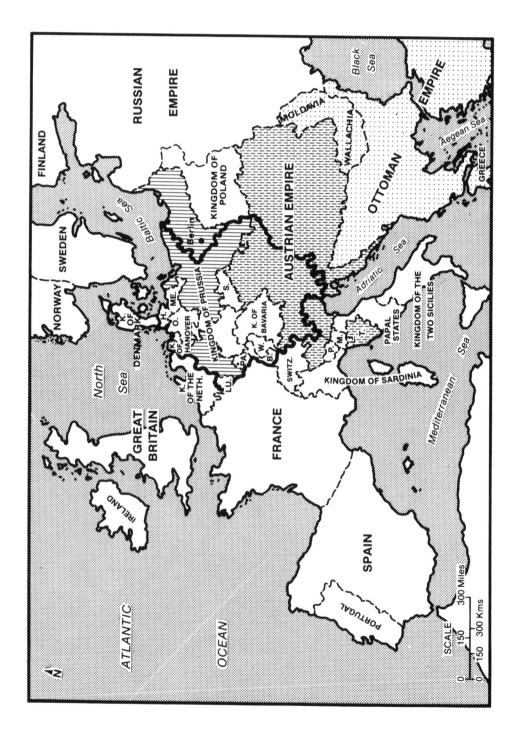

Europe after Congress of Vienna, 1815

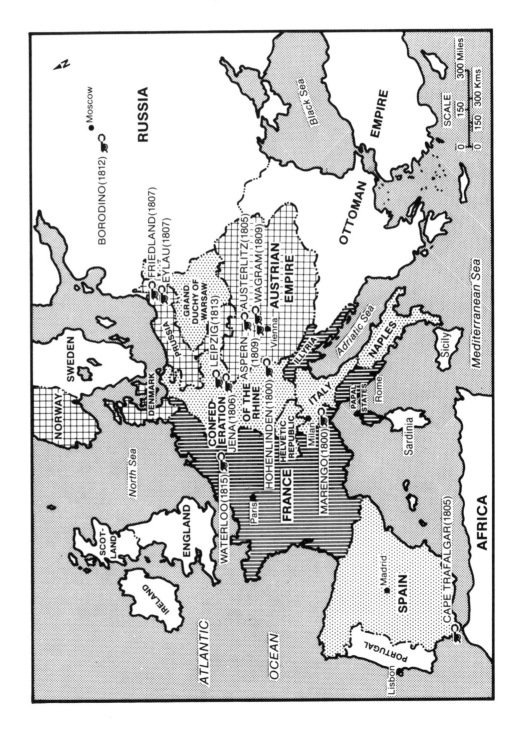

Bibliography

For Czar Alexander I, see works by A. Palmer, H. Troyat. For his predecessor, Empress Catherine II, see Beer and Brueckner. For Napoleon I, see Bourrienne, Castelot, Goodrich, Lacroix, Lacour-Gayet, Las Cases, Lévy, Masson, Méneval, Mereschkowskij, Montholon, O'Meara, Stendhal. For Rouget de L'Isle, see Tiersot. For Sidney Smith, see Barrow. For Kerversau, see Two Friends of Liberty. For Burke, see Hoffman and Levack.

Anderson, Frank Maloy (ed.), *The Constitutions and Select Documents Illustrative of the History of France, 1789-1907*. Minneapolis: H.W. Wilson, 1908.

Anonymous (ed.), *Collection Des Mémoires relatifs a la révolution Francaise*. Paris: 1820-26. (Includes, among others: Bailly, Besenval, Campan, Desmoulins, Ferrières, Freron, Méda, Rivarol, Roland, Sapinaud.)

Anonymous (ed.), *Copies of Original Letters from the Army of General Buonaparte in Egypt, intercepted by the Fleet under Admiral Lord Nelson*. London: J. Wright, 1798.

Anonymous (ed.), *Correspondance intime du Comte de Vaudreuil et du Comte d'Artois*. Paris: 1889.

Anonymous, *Horrors of the Prisons of Arras*. London: 1926.

Arnault, Antoine Vincent, *Les souvenirs et les regrets*. Paris: Leclerc, 1861.

Arndt, Ernst Moritz, *Geist der Zeit*, 1806-1818.

Babeuf, Francois Noel, *Textes Choisies*. Paris: Editions Sociales, 1950.

Baden, Carl Friedrich von, *Brieflicher Verkehr mit Mirabeau und Dupont*. Heidelberg: Winter, 1892.

Bailly, Jean Sylvain, *Mémoires d'un Témoin de la Revolution ou Journal des faits qui se sont passés sous ses yeux*. Paris: Baudoin Frères, 1804.

Barante, Baron de, *Souvenirs du Baron de Barante*, 5 vols. Paris: C. Levy, 1890-95.

Barère, Bertrand de Vieuzac, *Mémoires*. Brussels: Meline, Lans & Cie., 1842.

Barrow, John, *The Life and Correspondence of Admiral Sir William Sidney Smith*, 2 vols. London: R. Bentley, 1848.

Beer, Adolf, *Leopold II, Franz II und Katharina: Ihre Korrespondenz*. Leipzig: Duncker & Humblot, 1874.

Besenval, Baron de, *Mémoires*, 2 vols. Paris: Baudoin Frères, 1821.

Beugnot, Comte, *Mémoires*, ed. A Beugno. Paris: 1868.

Bonaparte, Joseph, *Mémoires*. Paris: Perrotin, 1853-54.

Bonaparte, Lucien, *Memoirs*, 3 vols. London: Saunders & Otley, 1836.

Borcke, Johann von, *Kriegerleben, 1806-1815*. Berlin: Mittler, 1888.

Bourrienne, Louis Antoine Fauvelet de, *Mémoires sur Napoleon*, 10 vols. Paris: 1829-30.

Boyen, Hermann von, *Erinnerungen*, ed. Chr. Coler. Berlin: Rütten & Loening, 1953.

Brinton, Crane (ed.), *The Portable Age of Reason Reader*. New York: Viking, 1956.

Brissot de Warville, Jacques Pierre, *Correspondance et Papiers*. Paris: A. Picard, 1912.

Broc, Vicomte de, *Dix ans de la vie d'une femme pendant l'Emigration*. Paris: 1893. (Includes memoirs of the Marquise de Falaiseau.)

Brueckner, A., *Katharina II*. Berlin: G. Grote, 1883.

Byron, George Gordon, Lord, *The Complete Poetical Works of Lord Byron* (Cambridge Edition). Boston: Houghton Mifflin, 1905.

Calonne, Charles Alexandre de, *Les Papiers*, ed. Chr. de Parrel Cavaillon. Paris: Mistral, 1932.

Campan, Jeanne Louise Henriette, *Mémoires sur la vie privée de Marie Antoinette*. Paris: Baudouin Frères, 1823.

Carrichon, Abbé, "Exécution des dames de Noailles," *La Nouvelle Revue* (January-February 1888).

Castelot, André, *Bonaparte*. Paris: Perrin, 1967.

Caulaincourt, Louis, Marquis de, *Mémoires*. Paris: Plon, 1933.

Chateaubriand, Vicomte Francois René de, *Mémoires d'outretombe*, ed. E. Biré. Paris: Garnier Frères, 1899.

Cheney, Edward P. (ed.), *Readings in English History*. Boston: Ginn, 1908.

Chronique de Paris (April 25, August 20, 1792; July 16, 1793).

Cléry, Jean Baptiste (Hanet), *Journal de ce qui s'est passé a la tour de Temple pendant la captivité de Louis XVI*. London: Baylis, 1798.

Constant de Rebecque, Henri Benjamin de, *Oeuvres*. Paris: Gallimard, 1957.

Convention Nationale, *Journal des Débats et de Décrets, 1-1139*, 37 vols. Paris: Imprimerie Nationale, 1792- 95.

Damas, Comte R. de, *Mémoires*, ed. J. Rambaud. Paris: Plon-Nourrit, 1922.

Dampierre, Maréchal de, "Rélation de la Conduite des troupes ... de l'armée de Belgique," in C. de la Jonquière's *La Bataille de Jemappes*. Paris: 1902.

Danton, Georges Jacques, *Oeuvres*, ed. A. Vermorel. Paris: A. Faure, 1867.

Daudet, Ernest, *Histoire de L'Emigration*. Paris: Hachette, 1905.

Daudet, Ernest, "La Princesse de Lieven," *Revue des deux Mondes*, 5(1901).

Denon, Baron Dominique Vivant, *Voyages dans la Basse et la Haute Egypte ... en 1798 et 1799*, 2 vols. London: Bagoter, 1809.

Desmoulins, Camille, *Le Vieux Cordelier*, ed. M. Matton. Paris: Ebrard, 1834.

Desvernois, Nicolas Philibert, Baron, *Mémoires*. Paris: E. Plon, Nourrit & Cie., 1898.

Drouet, Jean Baptiste, *Mémoir justificatif*. Paris: Imprimerie Nationale, 1796.

Dumas, Comte Guillaume Mathieu, *Memoirs of His Own Time, Including the Revolution and the Restoration*, 2 vols. Philadelphia: Lea & Blanchard, 1839.

Dumont, Pierre Etienne Louis, *Recollections of Mirabeau and of the First Two Assemblies*. Philadelphia: Carey & Lea, 1833.

Dupuis, V., *Les opérations militaires sur la Sambre en 1794*. Paris: 1891.

Durant, Will and Ariel, *The Age of Napoleon*. New York: Simon and Schuster, 1975.

Eckermann, J.P., *Gespräche mit Goethe*, 2 vols. Leipzig: Diederichs, 1902.

Elisabeth de France, *Correspondance*, ed. Feuillet de Conches. Paris: 1867.

Fabre d'Eglantine, Philippe Francois Nazaire, *Oeuvres politiques*, ed. C. Velley, Paris: Charpentier, 1914.

Ferrières, Marquis Charles Elie, *Mémoires*, 2 vols. Paris: Firmin-Didot, 1880.

Fersen, Count Hans Axel, *Diary and Correspondence Relating to the Court of France*. New York: Boston: Hardy, Pratt & Co., 1902.

Fisher, John, *Six Summers in Paris*. New York: Harper & Row, 1966.

Fluehe, Ludwig von der, "Rélations de la prise de la Bastille, le 14 juillet 1789, par un ses défenseurs," *Revue Rétrospective*, vol. 4, ed. M.J. Taschreau. Paris: Paulin, 1834.

Fouché, Joseph, *Mémoires*, 2 vols. Paris: Le Rouge, 1824.

Fox, Charles James, *Memorials and Correspondence*, 4 vols., ed. John Russell. New York: AMS Press, 1970.

Furet, Francois and Denis Richet, *The French Revolution*. New York: Macmillan, 1970.

Gazette Francaise (Paris), 1793.

Gentz, Friedrich von, *Ausgewählte Schriften*, 5 vols., ed. W. Weick. Stuttgart: Rieger, 1836-38.

Gentz, Friedrich von and Johannes von Mueller, *Correspondence*, 5 vols., ed. G. Schlesier. Mannheim: 1840.

George, Canvas, *Erinnerungen eines Preussen.* Grimma: 1840.

Goethe, Johann Wolfgang von, *Sämtliche Werke*, 6 vols. Stuttgart: Cotta, 1854. (See also J.P. Eckermann.)

Gontaut, Madame la Duchesse de, *Mémoires.* Paris: E. Plon, Nourrit & Cie., 1893.

Goodrich, Frank B., *The Court of Napoleon*, New York: Derby & Jackson, 1857.

Gourgaud and Montholon: see Montholon.

Gouvion Saint-Cyr, Laurent, Marquis de *Mémoires pour servir a l'histoire militaire sous le directoires, le consulat et l'empire.* Paris: Anselin, 1831.

Gower, Earl Granville Leveson (later known as the Duke of Sutherland), *Despatches.* Cambridge: University Press, 1885.

Grab, Walter (ed.), *Die Französische Revolution, Eine Dokumentation.* Munich: Nymphenburger, 1973.

Granier, H. (ed.), *Berichte aus der Berliner Franzosenzeit, 1807-1809. Leipzig: S. Hirzel, 1913.*

Greenlaw, Ralph W. (ed.), *The Economic Origins of the French Revolution* ("Problems in European Civilization" series). Boston: Heath, 1958.

Griesheim, Philippine, *Briefe einer Braut ... der Freiheitskriege.* Berlin: 1905.

Grunwald, C. de, *La Vie de Metternich.* Paris: Calman-Lévy, 1938.

Guizot, Francois and Mme. Guizot de Witt, *The History of France*, vols. 6-8, tr. Robert Black. New York: J.B. Alden, 1885.

Herold J. Christopher, *Bonaparte in Egypt.* New York: Harper & Row, 1966.

Hoffman, Ross J. and Paul Levack (eds.), *Burke's Politics.* New York: Knopf, 1949.

Houssaye, Henri, *La premiére abdication.* Paris: Perrin & Cie., 1905.

———, *La seconde abdication.* Paris: Perrin & Cie., 1905.

Hugo, Victor, *Quatre-vingt-treize.* Paris: Michael Lévy Frères, 1874.

Humboldt, Wilhelm von, *Gesammelte Schriften*. Berlin: Akademie der Wissenschaften, 1903.

Jefferson, Thomas, *Writings*, 9 vols. New York: Derby & Jackson, 1859.

Journal Officiel (Paris), 1796.

Kircheisen, F.M. (ed.), *Fürstenbriefe an Napoleon*, 2 vols. Stuttgart: J.G. Cotta, 1929.

Koch, W.A. (ed.), *Briefe deutscher Romantiker*. Leipzig: Dieterich, 1938.

Koenigswald, Harald von, *Preussisches Lesebuch*. Munich: Biederstein, 1966.

Lacour-Gayet, Georges, *Napoleon*. Paris: Hachette, 1921.

Lacroix, Paul, *Directoire, Consulat et Empire*. Paris: Firmin-Didot, 1884.

————, *Histoire de Napoleon*. Paris: 1902.

Lafayette, Marie Paul, Marquis de, *Mémoires publiés par sa famille*. Brussels: Société Belge de Lib., 1837- 39.

La Rochejacquelein, Marie Louise de Donissan (Henri de La R.'s widow), *Memoirs*. London: Routledge, 1933.

La Varende, Jean de, *Mademoiselle de Corday*. Rouen: Defontaine, 1946.

Las Cases, Comte Emanuel de, *Mémorial de Sainte-Hélène*, 2 vols. Paris: Gallimard, 1956-57.

Lefèbvre, Georges, *The Coming of the French Revolution*. New York: Vintage, 1958.

————, *The French Revolution*. New York: Vintage, 1968.

————, *The Thermidorians and the Directory*. New York: Random House, 1964.

Lettow-Vorbeck, Oscar von, *Der Krieg von 1806 und 1807*, 2 vols. Berlin: E.S. Mitter & Sohn, 1891.

Lévy, Arthur, *Napoléon intime*. Paris: E. Plon, 1893.

Longford, Elizabeth, *Wellington*. New York: Harper, 1969.

Louis XVI, *Journal*. A manuscript held in the National Archives, Paris.

———, *Oeuvres*, 2 vols. Paris: Desloges, 1864.

MacManus, Seumas, *The Story of the Irish Race*. New York: Devin-Adair, 1946.

Maillane, Durand de, *Histoire de la Convention Nationale*. Paris: 1825. Contains minutes for sessions of 9th Thermidor.

Mallet du Pan, Jacques, *Memoirs and Correspondence*, 2 vols., ed. by A. Sayous. London: 1852.

Marat, Jean Paul, *Textes choisies*, ed. M. Vovelle. Paris: Editions Sociales, 1963.

Marie Antoinette, *Correspondance inédite*, ed. P.V. d'Hunolstein. Paris: 1864.

Marie-Thérèse Charlotte de France (Madame Royale), *Mémoire sur la captivité de prince et princesse ses parents, depuis le 10 aout 1792 jusqu'a la mort de son frère, arrivée le 9 juin 1795*. Paris: E. Plon, Nourrit & Cie., 1892.

Marmont, Auguste Frederic Louis Viesse de, *Mémoires*, 9 vols. Paris: 1856-57.

Marmontel, Jean Francois, *Memoirs*, 4 vols., London: H.S. Nichols, 1895.

Marwitz, F.A.L. von der, *Ein märkischer Edelmann*. Munich: A. Langen-Müller, 1939.

Masson, Frédéric, *Napoléon, Manuscrits inédits*. Paris: P. Ollendorff, 1910.

Méda, Charles André, *Précis historique*. Paris: 1825.

Meister, Henri, *Souvenirs de mon dernier voyage à Paris (1795)*. Paris: A. Picard, 1910.

Melito, Comte Mio de, *Memoirs*. Paris: 1858.

Ménéval, Claude Francois de, *Memoirs of Napoleon*, 3 vols. New York: D. Appleton, 1894.

Mercier, Louis Sebastien, *Tableau de Paris*, 12 vols. Amsterdam: 1783-89.

Mereschkowskij, Dmitri, *Napoleon*. Berlin: Th. Knaur, 1928.

Metternich, Clemens, Fürst von, *Mémoires, Documents et écrits divers*, 8 vols., ed. by his son. Paris: E. Plon & Cie., 1880-84. (See also Grunwald and Palmer.)

Miles, William Augustus, *Correspondence on the French Revolution, 1789-1817*, 2 vols. London: Longmans, Green & Co., 1890.

Millet, P., *Le Chasseur P. Millet: Souvenirs de la Campagne d'Egypte*. Paris: 1903.

Mirabeau, Honoré Gabriel Rìqueti, Comte de, *Oeuvres*, 3 vols., Paris: E. Fasquelle, 1912-21.

Moniteur, *Reimpressions de l'ancien Moniteur la Réunion des Etats-Généraux jusqu'au Consulat*. Paris: 1840-1845.

Montholon, Charles Jean Tristan, Marquis de, and General Baron Gaspard Gourgaud, *Mémoires, pour servir a l'histoire de France sous Napoléon, écrits a Sainte-Hélène*. Paris: Didot, 1823-25. Vols. 1-2: Gourgaud; vols. 3-8: Montholon.

Moore, John, *A Journal*. Boston: B. Larkin, 1794.

Mornet, D. *French Thought in the Eighteenth Century*. Hamden, Conn.: Archon Books, 1969.

Morris, Gouverneur, *The Diary and Letters of Gouverneur Morris*, 2 vols., ed. Anne C. Morris. New York: Scribners, 1888.

Mundhencke, H. (ed.), *Hannover, ein Tagebuch*, vol. 14. Hanover: 1960.

Napoléon I, *Correspondance, publiée par l'ordre de l'empereur Napoléon III*, 8 vols. Paris: 1858-61.

Necker, Jacques, *De la Révolution Francaise*, 2 vols., Paris: Maret, 1797.

Nelson, Viscount Horatio, *Dispatches and Letters*. London: H. Colburn, 1845-46.

Nicol, John, *The Life and Adventures of John Nicol, Mariner*. Edinburgh: W. Blackwood, 1822.

Niebuhr, Barthold Georg, *Briefe*. Berlin: De Gruyter & Cie., 1926.

Nostitz, General Count von, *Tagebuch des Generals Grafen von Nostitz*. Greifswald: H. Adler, 1908.

O'Meara, Barry Edward, *Napoleon in Exile, or A Voice from St. Helena*, 2 vols. New York: Worthington, 1890.

Orieux, Jean, *Talleyrand*. Paris: Flammarion, 1970.

Paine, Thomas, *The Political Works of Th. Paine*. London: W. Dugdale, 1844.

Palmer, Alan, *Alexander I*. New York: Harper and Row, 1974.

————, *Metternich*. New York: Harper and Row, 1972.

Palmer, R.R., *Twelve Who Ruled*. Princeton: Princeton University Press, 1941.

Percy, Pierre Francois, "Journal des campagnes," in *Revue des questions hist*. (Paris), 80(1903).

Perlet, Charles Frédéric, *Journal de Perlet du 12 Thermidor, an II*. Published by author.

Pétion, Jérôme, *Mémoires*, ed. C.A. Dauban. Paris: H. Plon, 1866.

Pinel, Philippe, *Letters*. Paris: 1859.

Pitt, William, *The War Speeches of William Pitt the Younger*, selected by R. Coupland. Oxford: Clarendon Press, 1940. (See also O.W. Wilson.)

Prudhomme, Louis Marie, *Les Revolutions de Paris*. Paris: Imprimerie des Révolutions, 1789-94.

Rémusat, Claire Elisabeth, Comtesse de Vergennes, *Mémoires 1802-1808*. Paris: C. Levy, 1881.

Rivarol, Comte de (Antoine Rivaroli), *Mémoires*. Paris: Didier, 1852.

Robespierre, Maximilien Marie Isidore de, *Oeuvres complètes*, 8 vols., Paris: E. Leroux, 1910-67.

Robinet, Jean Francois E., *Dictionnaire historique et biographique de la révolution et de l'empire*, 2 vols. Paris: Librairie Historique, 1899.

Roederer, Pierre Louis, *Chronique de cinquante jours du 20 juin au 10 aout 1792*. Paris: H. Gautier, 1896.

Romains, Comte Felix de, *Souvenir d'un officier royaliste*. Paris: 1824.

Roux, Jacques, *Scripta et Acta*. Berlin: Akademie Verlag, 1969.

Saint-Just, Antoine Louis Léon de, *Oeuvres*. Paris: 1834.

Sapinaud, Mme. de, *Mémoires historiques sur la Vendée*. Paris: Horizons de France, 1942.

Schiller, Friedrich von, *Werke*. Stuttgart: J.G. Cotta, 1847.

Schmidt, O.E. (ed.), *Berichte über die Leipziger Schlacht*. Leipzig: Reclam #5526, n.d.

Schoeps, H.J. (ed.), *Aus den Jahren preussicher Not, 1805-20*. Berlin: Haude & Spener, 1963.

Sciout, L., *Le Directoire*, 4 vols. Paris: Firmin & Didot, 1895-97.

Ségur, Philippe-Paul de, *Histoire de Napoléon et de la Grande Armée pendant l'année 1812*. Paris: Baudoin Frères, 1825.

————, *Mémoires*, 3 vols. Paris: 1827.

Sieburg, Friedrich, *Im Licht und Schatten der Freiheit*. Stuttgart: Deutsche Verlagsanstalt, 1964.

Sieyès, Emanuel Joseph, *Qu'est de que le tiers état*, ed. E. Champion. Paris: Au siège de la Societé, 1888.

Simon, E.T. (ed.), *Correspondance de l'Armée Francaise en Egypte*. Paris: Garnery, 1799-1800.

Simpkin & Marshall, Editors of, *The Reign of Terror, A Collection of Authentic Narratives Written by Eyewitnesses*. London: W. Simpkin & R. Marshall, 1826.

Smith, Page, *The Shaping of America*, vol. 3. New York: McGraw-Hill, 1980.

Soboul, Albert, *Précis de l'histoire de la revolution francais*. Paris: Editions Sociales, 1962.

Staël, Mme. Germaine de, *Choix de textes*. Paris: Klindsieck, 1974.

Stendhal (Marie Henri Beyle), *Selected Letters*, ed. A. Schurig. Berlin: 1923.

————, *Vie de Napoleon*. Paris: 1843.

Talleyrand-Périgord, Charles Maurice de, *Mémoires*, 5 vols., ed. A. de Broglie. Paris: C. Lévy, 1891- 92. (See also Orieux.)

Thibaudeau, Antoine Claire, *Mémoires sur la Convention et le Directoire*, 2 vols. Paris: Plon-Nourrit, 1913.

Thiébault, Général Charles Francois Adrien Henri Dieudonné, *Mémoires*. Paris: Hachette, 1962.

Thiers, Louis Adolphe, *History of the Consulate and the Empire of France*, 12 vols. Philadelphia: J.B. Lippincott, 1893.

Thompson, J.M. (ed.), *English Witnesses to the French Revolution*. London: Blackwell, 1938.

Thurman, Louis, *Bonaparte en Egypte*. Paris: 1902.

Tiersot, Julien, *Rouget de l'Isle*. Paris: C. Delagrave, 1892.

Tourzel, Louise Elisabeth, Duchesse de, *Mémoires*, 2 vols. Paris: Plon & Cie., 1883.

Troyat, Henri, *Alexandre I*. Paris: Flammarion, 1980.

Tulard, J., J.F. Fayard and A. Fierro, *Histoire et Dictionnaire de la Revolution Francaise*. Paris: Robert Laffon, 1987.

Turreau, Baron Louis Marie de Linières, *Mémoires pour servir a l'histoire de la guerre de la Vendée*. Paris: Baudoin Frères, 1824.

Two Friends of Liberty, *Histoire de la Révolution de France de 1789*, 3 vols. Paris: Clavelin, 1790-93.

Varenne, Maton de la, *Les Crimes de Marat et des autres égorgeurs ou une résurrection*. Paris: 1795.

Varnhagen von Ense, Karl August, *Denkwürdigkeiten*. Berlin: Verlag der Nation, 1954.

Vergniaud, Pierre Victurnien, *Histoire Parlementaire de Vergniaud*. Paris: 1847.

Vertray, Captain C.F., *Journal d'un officier de l'armée d'Egypte*. Paris: G. Charpentier, 1883.

Vidal, Pierre, *Histoire de la Révolution francaise*. Paris: 1885-89. Includes Cassanyès' memoirs.

Vilate, Joachim, *Causes secrètes de la Révolution du 9 au 10 Thermidor*. Paris: 1825.

Vossische Zeitung (Berlin), 1794(#97).

Warner, Oliver, *The Battle of the Nile*. New York: Macmillan, 1960.

Weber, Joseph, *Mémoires*, 2 vols. Paris: Firmin- Didot, 1847. Weber was Marie Antoinette's foster brother.

Wellington, Arthur Wellesley, Duke of, *Memoirs of the Duke of Wellington*. London: Longman, 1852. (See also Longford.)

Williams, Helen Maria, *Letters Containing a Sketch ... during the Tyranny of Robespierre*. London: G.G. & J. Robinson, 1795.

Wilson, O.W., *William Pitt the Younger*. Garden City, N.Y.: Doubleday, 1930.

Wordsworth, William, *The Poetical Works*. New York: Worthington, 1886.

Young, Arthur, *Travels in France*, ed. M. Betham-Edwards. London: Bell, 1890.

INDEX

A

Abdication of Emperor Francis II (Aug. 7, 1806) 298, 332

Abolition of the Monarchy 22, 54-67

Acts of the Apostles (journal) 26

Adams, Abigail (1744-1818) 142

Adams, John (1797-1801) 135, 142

Adhemar, Count d' 13

Administrative Assemblies, Of the Formation and Organization of the (Dec. 22, 1789) 296, 304

Alexander I, Czar of Russia (1777-1825) 205, 209, 238

    Biography **337**

    Congress of Vienna 287-295

    Napoleon's Conquest of Europe (1805-1807) 219-235

    Russian Campaign Apr-Dec 1812 252-261

    War of Jan 1813-May 1814 262-274

Alvinzi, Gen. Josef 167

American Colonies—*See United States of America*

Ami des Citoyens, L' (journal) 44

Ami du Peuple, L' (journal) 21, 25, 28, 55

Ami du Roi, L' (journal) 22, 27

Amiens, Treaty of (Mar. 27, 1802) 206, 298, 327

Anglas, Comte Francois Boissy d' 121

Annexation of the Papal States, Imperial Decree for the (May 17, 1809) 298, 333

Aristocracy—*See Second Estate*

Arnault, Antoine Vincent 173

Arndt, Ernst Moritz (1769-1860) 233, 238, **337**

Arrest of the King, Decree for the (June 21, 1791) 296, 305

Artenteau, Mercy d' 132

Artois, Charles Philippe Duc d' (1757-1836) 5, 9, 19-21, 23, 26, 68, 72, 80, 112, 150, 263, 278, **337**

Arts and Science, National Institute for 112

Assembly, Decree of the (June 23, 1789) 296, 302

Assembly of Notables 4, 5, 8

Assignats 21, 23, 26-28, 42, 45, 81, 85, 86, 88, 96, 99, 103, 113-115, 118, 146

Augereau, Charles Pierre Francois d' (1757-1816) 123, 138, 153, 162, **337**

August 4, 1789, The Decrees of 19, 20, 25, 296, 302

Aulard, Alphonse xii, 15, 97

Austerlitz, Battle of 223, 237

Austria

    Congress of Vienna 287-295

    Franco War 1795-98 134-144

    Napoleonic Relations 1808-1812 235-251

    Napoleon's Conquest of Europe (1805-1807) 219-235

    Russian Campaign Apr-Dec 1812 252-261

    War of the First Coalition 43, 68-70, 73, 123-133

B

Babeuf, Francois Noel (1760-97) viii, 112, 114, 115, 119, 121, 145, 150-152, 156

    Biography **337**

    Illustration 146

Bailly, Jean Sylvain (1736-93) 14, 18-21, 24, 25, 33, **337**

Bank of France 204, 209

Barbe-Marbois, Francois 152

Barere de Vieuzac, Bertrand (1755-1841) 88, 97, 103, 114, 115, 127, 131, **337**

Barnave, Antoine Pierre Joseph Marie (1761-93) 23, 41, 50, 100, **337**

Barras, Paul Francois Jean Nicolas, Vicomte de (1755-1829) 88, 97, 113, 114, 116, 117, 143, 146, 150, 165

    Biography **337**

    Coup d'Etat and Consulate 203-218

    Directory, The (1795-99) 145-160

    Illustration 145

Barruel, Abbe 159

Barthelmy, Balthazar Francois, Marquis de (1747-1830) 129, 152, **337**

Basle, Treaty of (Apr. 5, 1795) 123-133, 124, 129, 298, 319

Bastille, The Storming of the xviii, xix, 20, 22, 25, 27

Batavian Republic—*See Holland*

Beauharnais, Alexander Francois Vicomte de (1760-94) 103, **337**

Beauharnais, Eugene 254

Beauharnais, Hortense de 215, 294

Beauharnais, Josephine—*See Josephine*

Beaumarchais, Pierre Auguste Caron de (1732-1799) **338**

Beethoven, Ludwig van (1770-1827) 245

Belgium

    Franco War 1795-98 134-144

    War of the First Coalition 70, 71, 123-133

Bellerophon (British warship) 279

Beresford, William Carr 243

Berlin, Treaty of 73

Berlin, University of 238

Berlin Decree, The (Nov. 21, 1806) 298, 330

Bernadotte, Jean Baptiste Jules (1763-1844) 154, 179, 265, 267

    Biography **338**

    Napoleonic Power 1808-1812 237-251

Berthier, Louis Alexandre (1753-1815) 166, 178, 183, 237, 261, **338**

Bertier, Louis Benigne de 25

Besenval, Pierre Joseph, Baron de (1721-94) 11, 18, 31, 32, 77, **338**

Beugnot, Jacques Claude 106

Beurnonville, Pierre de 126, 150

Beyle, Marie Henri (Stendhal) (1783-1842) **338**

Billaud-Varenne, Jacques Nicolas (1756-1819) 84, 88, 97, 103, 114-116, **338**

Blake, William (1757-1827) 42

Blucher, Gebhardt Leberecht, Prince of Walstatt (1741-1819) 225

Biography **338**
Illustration 275
War of Jan 1813-May 1814 263-274
Waterloo, Battle of 276-286
Bohnsack, August H. 227
Bonaparte, Charles Joseph 236
Bonaparte, Jerome (1784-1860)
Biography **338**
Napoleonic Power 1808-1812 236-251
Bonaparte, Joseph (1768-1844) 160, 186, 275
Biography **338**
Napoleonic Power 1808-1812 235-251
Bonaparte, Josephine—*See Josephine*
Bonaparte, Letizia (1750-1836) 237, 281
Biography **338**
Illustration 236
Bonaparte, Lucien (1775-1840) 120, 121, 276
Biography **338**
Coup d'Etat and Consulate 202-218
Illustration 202
Napoleonic Power 1808-1812 235-251
Bonaparte, Napoleon (1769-1821) viii, xx, 49, 101, 113, 114, 117-119, 136, 138, 141, 143, 146
Background 160-174
Biography **338**
Centralization of Power (Jan 1808-July 1812) 235-251
Conquest of Europe (Mar 1805-Dec 1807) 219-235
Coup d'Etat and Consulate 202-218
Egyptian Campaign 187-201
Elba to St Helena 275-286
Illustration 153, 165, 170, 211, 281
Russian Campaign Apr-Dec 1812 252-262
War of Jan 1813-May 1814 262-274
War of the Second Coalition 175-187
Bonchamp, Charles Melchior 86
Borghese, Pauline 240
Bouchotte, Jean Baptiste Noel 124
Bouille, Francois Claude, Marquis de 40
Bourdic, Gaston 82
Bourrienne, Louis Antoine Fauvelet de (1769-1834) 52, 195, 197, 201, **338**
Bouthillier, Marquis de 77
Boyen, Hermann von 231
Bread
Riots 3, 4, 8, 20, 23, 26, 59, 86
Breteuil, Louis Auguste, Baron de 40
Brienne, Lomenie de 5, 6, 8, 9
Brissot, Jacques-Pierre (1754-93) 25, 41, 44, 50, 51, 53, 59, 65, 80, 87, 99, 100
Biography **338**
Illustration 41

British Note to the Neutral Powers (May 16, 1806) 298, 330
Broglie, Victor Francois, Duc d' 18
Brottier, (Abbe) Charles 145, 146, 151
Brueys, Francois Paul 175, 190
Brumaire Decree, The (Nov. 10, 1799) 298, 323
Brune, Guillaume Marie Ann (1763-1815) 117, 139, 154, 177, 180, **338**
Brunswick (Braunschweig), Duke Karl Wilhelm Ferdinand (1735-1806) 43, 70, 73, 221, 224, **338**
Bulgaria 243
Buonarotti, Philippe Michel 151
Burke, Edmund (1729-97) ix, 55, 68, 72, 74, 75, **338**
Buulow, Friedrich Wilhelm von 266
Byron, George Gordon Noel, Lord (1788-1824) 285, **338**

C

Cabarrus, Theresa 102, 114, 148
Illustration 115
Cacault, Baron Jean Baptiste 183
Cadoudal, Georges (1771-1804) 205, 211, **338**
Calling Out the National Guard, Decree for (June 21, 1791) 296, 306
Calonne, Charles Alexandre de (1734-1802) xv, 4, 5, 8, 68, **339**
Cambaceres, Jean Jacques Regis de (1753-1824) 133, 155
Biography **339**
Coup d'Etat and Consulate 203-218
Napoleonic Power 1808-1812 237-251
Cambon, Pierre Joseph 74, 80, 130
Campan, Jeanne Louise Henriette (1752-1822) 11, 13, 38, **339**
Campo Formio, Treaty of (Oct. 17, 1797) 138, 162, 168
Canning, George 225
Caprara, Jean Baptiste 216
Carnot, Lazare Nicolas Marguerite (1753-1823) 83, 84, 88, 97, 102, 103, 115, 129, 134-144, 145, 146, 150, 151, 165, 276
Biography **339**
Illustration 150
Carrichon, Abbe 108
Carrier, Jean Baptiste (1756-94) 95, 102, 114, **339**
Carteaux, Jean Baptiste Francois 117, 164
Cassanyes, Jacques Jospeh Francois 108
Castlereagh, Robert Stewart 268, 290, 295
Cathelineau, Jacques 82
Catherine II (Catherine The Great), Czarina of Russia (1762-96) 68, 75, 132

War of the First Coalition 124
Catholicism 2, 27, 96, 100, 111, 147, 205, 237, 288
Caulaincourt, Armand Augustin Louis, Marquis de (1772-1827)
Biography **339**
Russian Campaign Apr-Dec 1812 252-261
Ceylon 287
Chalier, Joseph 87
Champ de Mars Massacre 44
Championnet, Jean Etienne (1762-1800) 123, 136, 176, 178, 180, **339**
Champollion, Jean Francois 189
Charette, Francois Athanase (1763-96) 88, 117, 151, **339**
Charles, Archduke of Austria (1771-1824) 134-144, 137, 142, 162, 167, 223
Biography **339**
Illustration 175
Napoleonic Power 1808-1812 238-251
War of the Second Coalition 175-187
Charles IV (1748-1819) King of Spain **339**
Chateaubriand, Francois Rene, Vicomte de (1768-1848) 78, 239, 273, **339**
Chaumette, Pierre Gaspard (1763-94) 102, **339**
Chenier, Andre Marie de (1762-94) 103, **339**
Chenier, Marie Joseph (1764-1811) **339**
Chouan, Jean (1767-94)—*See Cottereau, Jean*
Chouans 55, 59
Coup d'Etat and Consulate 202-218
Circle of Constitutionals 152
Circular Letter of Louis XVI to Foreign Courts (June 20, 1791) 296, 305
Clarke, Henri Jacques Guillaume 234
Clausewitz, Karl von (1780-1831)
Biography **339**
Napoleonic Power 1808-1812 238-251
Claviere, Etienne 58
Clergy—*See First Estate*
Clery, Jean-Baptiste Antoine 66, 67
Cloots, Jean Baptiste (1755-94) 55, 96, 100, 102, **339**
Club Breton—*See Jacobins*
Cobenzl, Jean Philippe de 143
Coburg, Duke Frederick de 126
Code Civil—*See Code Napoleon*
Code Napoleon xxii, 204, 211, 223
Coignet, Jean-Roch 233
Colbert, Jean Baptiste xiv
Coleridge, Samuel Taylor (1772-1834) 42
Collot d'Herbois, Jean Marie (1749-96) 84, 88, 95, 97, 103, 114-116, **339**
Committee of Public Safety 81, 82, 84,

86-88, 95, 114, 127, 164
Terror, Reign of 95-110
Committee of Public Safety, Decree for Establishing the (Apr. 6, 1793) 297, 316
Committee of Twelve 86
Common Sense (pamphlet) 55
Compte rendu 4, 8
Conde, Louis Joseph de, Prince 19, 23, 69, 72
Condorcet, Jean Antoine Nicolas de Caritat, Marquis de (1743-1794) 340
Confederation of the Rhine 220, 221, 266
Congress of Erfurt (1808) 237, 240
Congress of Rastatt 175
Consalvi, Ercole 186, 215, 288
Conspiracy for Equality, Secret Committee of 146, 151
Constant de Rebecque, Henri Benjamin (1767-1830) 151, 158, 239, 276, 278
    Biography **340**
    Coup d'Etat and Consulate 203-218
    Illustration 205
Constituent Assembly and the Church, Documents upon the (Nov. 2, 1789) 296, 303
Constitution of 1791 (Sept. 3, 1791) 297, 307
Constitution of the Year III (Aug. 22, 1795) 298, 319
Constitution of the Year VIII (Dec. 13, 1799) 298, 323
Constitution of the Year XII (May 18, 1804) 298, 328
Consulate, The 19
Continental System 242, 243
Convention of Cintra (1808) 240
Convention of Paris (1808) 240
Corday, Charlotte (1768-93) 50, 81, 83, 87, 93, **340**
Cordeliers 21, 27, 41, 46, 96
Cordeliers Club—*See Cordeliers*
Cottereau, Jean (1767-94) 55, 99, **340**
Council of Ancients 117, 145, 203
Council of Five Hundred 117, 145, 203
Couthon, Georges Auguste (1755-94) 95, 98, 103, 111, **340**
Crisis of the Old Regime, The Jan 1774-May 1789 1-15
Custine, Adam Philippe, Comte de (1740-93) 73, 83, 87, 88, 124, 127, 131, 136, **340**

D

Dampiere, August Picot, Marquis de 79
Dangerous Priests, Decree upon (Oct. 20-21, 1793) 297, 314
Danican, Louis Michel 113
Danton, Georges Jacques (1759-94) viii, 21, 82, 86, 87, 89, 91, 93, 94, 126, 162

Biography **340**
Second Revolution 54-67
Terror, Reign of 95-110
Daunou, Pierre Claude Francois (1761-1840) 150, **340**
David, Jacques Louis (1748-1825) 103, 115, 149, **340**
Davout, Louis Nicolas 265
    Napoleon's Conquest of Europe (1805-1807) 220-235
Declaration of Pillnitz, The (Aug. 27, 1791) 42, 69, 70, 72, 297, 307
Declaration of the Intentions of the King (June 23, 1789) 296, 301
Declaration of the Powers against Napoleon (Mar. 13, 1815) 299, 334
Declaration of the Regent of France (Jan. 28, 1793) 297, 316
Declaration of the Rights of Man (Aug. 26, 1789) 19, 25, 27, 297, 310
Delacroix, Jean Francois 102
De Lesseps, Ferdinand 189
Democracy in America (book) xii
Denmark 225
    Napoleonic Relations 1808-1812 237-251
Denon, Baron Dominique Vivant 193, 198, 199, 200
Departments and Districts, Decree upon the (Dec. 22, 1789) 296, 304
Deportation of the Non-Juring Priests, Decree for the (May 27, 1792) 297, 311
Desaix de Veygoux, Louis Charles Antoine (1768-1800) 136, 185
    Biography 181, **340**
    Egyptian Campaign 187-201
    Illustration 187
Descartes, Rene (1596-1650) 99
Desmoulins, Camille (1760-94) 18, 21, 25, 32, 34, 96, 100-102, 105, 107
    Biography **340**
    Illustration 26
Dessalines, Jean Jacques 212
Desvernois, Baron Nicolas Philibert 195, 199
Dickens, Charles (1812-70) xii
Diderot, Denis (1713-84) x, xi, 3, **340**
Diebitsch, Hans Karl von 256
Dietrich, Luise 51
Directory, The xx, 16, 134, 161
    Oct 1795-Oct 1799 145-160
Douai, Philippe Antoine Merlin de 150, 153
Drouet, Jean Baptiste (1763-1824) 48, 150, **340**
Ducos, Jean Francois
    Coup d'Etat and Consulate 203-218
Ducos, Pierre Roger (1754-1816) 183, **340**
Dumas, Comte Guillame Mathieu 61
Dumont, Etienne (1759-1829) 30, 34, 36, 109, **340**
Dumouriez, Charles Francois (1739-

1823) 42, 43, 45, 70, 73, 76, 82, 86, 123, 126, 130, 131, 136
    Biography **340**
    Illustration 123
Duphot, Maturin Leonard 178
Du Pont de Nemours, Samuel Pierre 11, 121
Duport, Adrien (1759-98) 16, 23, 41, **340**
Duval, Georges 119

E

Egalite, Philippe—*See Orleans, Louis Philippe Joseph, Duc d' (1747-93)*
Egypt 139, 168, 176, 177
    Napoleon's Campaign 187-201
Egyptian Campaign, The 187-201
Egyptian Institute for Sciences and Arts 189, 190
18th Brumaire (Nov. 9, 1799) 203, 208
18th Fructidor (Sept. 4, 1797) 153, 202
Elba, Isle of 137
    Napoleon's Exile 275-286
Elbee, Maurice Joseph Louis Gigost d' (1752-1794) 86, 101, **340**
Electing the Convention, Decree for (Aug. 11, 1792) 297, 313
Elliott, Sir Gilbert 165
Emmett, Robert 211
Enghien, Louis Antione Henri, Duke of (1772-1804) 205, 211, **340**
Enrages 59, 81, 85, 87
Establishing the Worship of the Supreme Being, Decree for (Sept. 18, 1794) 297, 315
Estates-General xv, xviii, 5, 6, 8, 9, 24
Execution of Louis XVI 62
Expenditures for Religion, Decree upon (Feb. 21, 1794) 297, 315

F

Fabre d'Eglantine, Philippe Francois (1750-94) 101, **341**
Faipoult, Guillaume Charles 179
Falaiseau, Marquis de 77
Favras, Thomas de Mahy, Marquis 26, 40
Feraud, Jean Bertrand 116
Ferdinand I (1751-1828), King of Naples 74, **341**
Ferrieres de Marsay, Charles Elie Marquis de (1741-1804) 30, 34, 37, 52, 61, 64, **341**
Fersen, Count Hans Axel (1755-1810) 14, 34, 40, **341**
Fesch, Joseph 243
Feuillants 41, 42, 44, 45, 54, 56
Fichte, Johann Gottlieb 238
Finland 221, 241
First Abdication of Napoleon (Apr. 4, 1814) 299, 334
First Coalition, War of the—*See War of the First Coalition*

First Estate xviii, 2, 16, 17
First Treaty of Paris (May 30, 1814) 268
Fluhe, Ludwig von der 33
Fontainebleau Decrees 243
Food
  Riots xx, 42, 81, 85
Foreign Affairs, Decree in Regard to (June 21, 1791) 296, 306
Foreign Policy
  War of the First Coalition 68-80, 123-133
  War of the Second Coalition 175-187
  Wars 1795-1798 134-144
Forster, Georg 74
Fouche, Josiph (1759-1820) viii, 95, 97, 103, 109, 117, 155, 203, 205, 208, 213, 276
  Biography **341**
  Illustration 237
  Napoleonic Power 1808-1812 237-251
Foulon, Joseph Francois 25
Fouquier-Tinville, Antoine Quentin (1746-95) 85, 114, 116
  Biography **341**
  Illustration 96
Fox, Charles James 33, 42, 68, 72, 80, 119, 205, 210, 224, 231
Foy, Maximilien Sebastien 284
France, Marie-Therese Charlotte de (madame royale) 62, 66, 93, 120
France Libre, La (pamphlet) 25
Francis, Sir Philip 217
Francis II, of Austria (1768-1835) 69, 73, 217
  Biography **341**
  Napoleonic Power 1808-1812 238-251
  War of Jan 1813-May 1814 262-274
Frederick William II, King of Prussia (1744-97) 69, **341**
Frederick William III, King of Prussia (1770-1840) 227
  Biography **341**
  War of Jan 1813-May 1814 262-274
Freedom of Religion 19, 25
Freron, Louis Marie Stanislas (1754-1802) 88, **341**
Friends of the Constitution, Society of the—*See Jacobins*
Friends of the Rights of Man and of the Citizen, Society of the—*See Cordeliers*
Funck-Brentano, Frantz xiii

G

Galles, Bonaventure Morard de 137
Garat, Dominique Joseph (1749-1832) 59, 85, 152, **341**
Gaxotte, Pierre xiii
Gazette Francaise (journal) 93
General Assembly 2
Gentz, Friedrich von (1764-1832) ix,

294, **341**
George, Canvas (1797-?) 341
George III, King of Great Britain (1738-1820) 217
  Biography **341**
  Napoleon's Conquest of Europe (1805-1807) 219-235
Gerry, Elbridge (1744-1814) 135
Girondists 41-43, 45, 55-57, 57, 59, 69, 73
  Civil War Jan-Sept 1793 81-94
Gleim, Ludwig 42
Gneisenau, August Count Neidhart von (1760-1831) 295
  Biography **342**
  Napoleonic Power 1808-1812 238-251
  Waterloo, Battle of 277-286
Gobel, Jean Baptiste Joseph (1727-94) 102, **341**
Godoy, Manuel de 237
Goerres, Joseph von 273
Goethe, Johan Wolfgang von (1749-1832) 78, 79, 131, 141, 143, 189, 201, 231, 238, 272, 285, **342**
Gontaut, Duchesse de 34
Good, J. Bonifaci 61
Gourgaud, Gaspard 280
Grain—*See Bread*
Grain Famine (1788-89) 5
Grande Arme 255, 256
Great Britain
  Congress of Vienna 287-295
  Egyptian Campaign 187-201
  Franco War 1795-98 134-144
  Napoleonic Relations 1808-1812 235-251
  Napoleon's Conquest of Europe (1805-1807) 219-235
  Russian Campaign Apr-Dec 1812 252-261
  War of Jan 1813-May 1814 262-274
  War of the First Coalition 68, 71, 123-133
  War of the Second Coalition 175-187
Great Fire of Moscow (Sept. 1812) 255
Gregoire, Henri Baptiste (1750-1831) 114, **342**
Grenville, William Wyndham, Lord 80
Griesheim, Philippine von 260
Grouchy, Emanuel Marquis de (1766-1847)
  Biography **342**
  Waterloo, Battle of 277-286
Guadet, Marguerite Elie (1759-94) 41, **342**
Guillotin, Joseph Ignace (1738-1814) 20, 26, **342**
Guillotine, The 58, 95

H

Haiti 44, 210

Hamilton, Alexander (1755-1804) 55
Hanriot, Francois 83
Hardenberg, Karl August, Baron von (1750-1822) 238, 290, **342**
Hebert, Jacques Rene (1757-94) 83, 84, 86, 96, 100-102, 124, **342**
Hegel, Georg Wilhelm Friedrich (1770-1831) 72, 232, **342**
Herault de Sechelles, Marie Jean (1759-1794) 342
Histoire de la Revolution Francaise (book) xi
Hoche, Louis Lazare (1768-97) 83, 88, 112, 116, 134-144, 146, 151, 152
  Biography **342**
  Illustration 69
Hoelderlin, Friedrich 42, 72
Hofer, Andreas 238, 241, 242
Holland
  Franco War 1795-98 134-144
  Napoleon's Conquest of Europe (1805-1807) 220-235
  War of the First Coalition 123-133
Holy Alliance Treaty, The (Sept. 26, 1815) 291, 299, 335
Hotel de Ville 20
Houchard, Jean Nicolas 124
Hugo, Victor xii
Humbert, Gen. Jean Joseph 139
Humboldt, Wilhelm von (1767-1835) 249, 290, 293, 295, **342**
Hundred Days 277

I

Ireland 135, 137, 152, 211
  Egyptian Campaign 187-201
Isnard, Maximin (1755-1825) 75, **342**, 445
Italy
  Franco War 1795-98 134-144

J

Jacobins xx, 10, 21, 23, 26, 41, 44, 56, 59, 74, 96, 100, 103, 111, 113, 115-117, 124, 127, 145, 147, 178, 276, 279
  Civil War Jan-Sept 1793 81
  Coup d'Etat and Consulate 202-218
Jansenists 111
Jaures, Jean xii, xiii
Jay, John (1754-1829) 135
Jefferson, Thomas (1743-1826) 35, 206
Jeunesse doree 112, 114, 115, 117
Jews 26, 44, 178
Josephine (1763-1814) 103, 148, 165, 242, 263, 278
  Biography **342**
  Illustration 160
  Napoleonic Power 1808-1812 235-251
Joubert, Barthelemy Catherine (1769-99) 176, **342**

Jourdan, Jean Baptiste (1762-1833) 83, 88, 97, 128, 129, 134-144, 154, 159, 176, 343

Journal de la Liberte 114

Judicial System, Decree for Reorganizing the (Aug. 16,1790) 296, 304

Junot, Andoche 226, 240

K

Kant, Immanuel (1724-1804) 67

Kellermann, Francois Etienne Christophe (1735-1820) 70, 73, 88, 166, 343

Kerversau, T. M. 32, 33

King, Decree Concerning the (June 24, 1791) 297, 307

Kingdom of Italy, Two Documents Upon the (Mar. 17 and 19, 1805) 298, 329

King's Acceptance of the Constitution, The (Sept. 13, 1791) 297, 309

Kleber, Jean Baptiste (1753-1800) 99, 123, 128, 181, 188, 191, 198
    Biography 343
    Illustration 188

Kleist, Heinrich von (1777-1811) 232, 238, 343

Klopstock, Friedrich Gottlieb 42

Korsakov, Alexander 180

Kosciousko, Tadeusz 55

Krajova, Paul Kray von 179

Kutusov, Michail Ilarionovich (1745-1813) 223
    Biography 343
    Illustration 262
    Russian Campaign Apr-Dec 1812 253-261
    War of Jan 1813-May 1814 262-274

L

Labrousse, C. E. xiii

Lacretelle, Charles de 119

Lafayette, Marie Joseph Paul Yves Roch Gilbert du Motier, Marquis de (1757-1834) viii, xvii, 16, 19-22, 25, 40, 41, 44-46, 52, 56, 62, 69, 70, 73, 76, 82, 123, 136, 285
    Biography 343
    Illustration 28

Lameth, Alexandre Theodore Victor de (1760-1829) 23, 41, 343

LaMotte, Comtesse de 4

Lanarque, Francois 158

Lanjuinais, Jean Denis, Comte 16, 276

Lannes, Jean 181, 241, 249

LaReveilliere-Lepeaux, Louis Marie de (1753-1824) 146, 150, 153, 343

La Rochejaquelian, Henri, Comte de (1772-94) 86, 101, 343

La Rochejaquelian, Marie Louise de 92, 108

Las Cases, Emanuel, Comte de (1766-1842) 343

Launay, Bernard Rene Jourdan, Mar-

quis de (1740-89) 18, 343

Laurent, Marquis de Gouvion-Saint-Cyr 184

Law for Reorganizing the Administrative System (Feb. 17, 1800) 298, 325

Law of Suspects, The (Sept. 17, 1793) 95, 99, 111, 150, 298, 318

Law of the Maximum, The (Sept. 29, 1793) 298, 318

Le Bon, Guislain Francois 95

Lebrun, Charles Francois
    Coup d'Etat and Consulate 203-218
    Napoleonic Power 1808-1812 237-251

Lebrun-Tondu, Pierre Marie 58

Le Chapelier, Isaac Rene Guy (1754-94) 16, 23, 102, 343

LeClerc, Victor Emanuel 209, 236

Lefebvre, Georges (1874-1959) xiii

Legendre, Louis 114

Legislative Assembly 44, 58

Leibniz, Gottfried Wilhelm x

Leipzig, Battle of 267

Leopold II (Emperor of Austria) 23, 68, 72, 75

Le Peletier de Saint-Fargeau, Louis Michel 59

Letourneur, Louis Francois 150, 152

Letter of Louis XVI to the King of Prussia (Dec. 3, 1791) 297, 310

Letters de cahet 21, 26

Levasseur, Rene 131

Levee en Masse, Decree for the (Aug. 23, 1793) 83, 123, 298, 317

Levinson, Granville, Earl 50

Lieven, Princess Charlotte de 183

Lindet, Robert Thomas 155

Linieres Turreau, Baron Louis-Marie de 93

Locke, John (1632-1704) x

Lomenie de Brienne, Etienne Charles de (1727-1794) 343

Louisiana 211

Louis XVI (1754-93) ix, xv
    Biography 344
    Crisis of the Old Regime 1-10
    Flight and Capture 40-53
    Illustration 12, 44
    Letter to King of Prussia 72
    Rise of the National Assembly 16-29
    Trial and Execution 54-67
    War of the First Coalition 68

Louis XVII (1785-95) 85, 116, 344

Louis XVIII (1755-1824) 112, 116, 210, 214
    Biography 344
    Congress of Vienna 287-295
    Elba to St Helena 276-286
    Illustration 287
    War of Jan 1813-May 1814 263-274

L'Ouverture, Francois Dominique Toussaint 210

Lowe, Sir Hudson 280

Luckner, Baron Nikolas von (1722-94) 69, 72, 73, 344

Luise, Queen of Prussia (1776-1810) 344

Luneville, Treaty of (Feb. 9, 1801) 177, 182, 298, 326

Luxembourg 129

M

Macdonald, Etienne Jacques Joseph Alexandre (1765-1840) 177, 180, 182, 266, 344

Mack von Leiberich, Baron Karl von (1752-1828) 178, 184
    Biography 344
    Napoleon's Conquest of Europe (1805-1807) 220-235

Madison, James (1751-1836) 55

Maillane, Durand de 110

Maillard, Stanislas Marie 20

Maintenance of the Public Order, Decree for the (June 21, 1791) 296, 306

Maistre, Joseph de 157

Malesherbes, Guillame Chretien de Lamoignon de (1721-94) xv, 102, 344

Malet, C. F. de 254, 256, 260

Malmesbury, Lord 141

Malta 168, 181, 287
    Egyptian Campaign 187-201

Mamelukes, The 190, 240

Mandats territoriaux 151

Manifesto of the Duke of Brunswick (July 25, 1792) 297, 311

Manifesto of the Enraged 87

Marat, Jean Paul (1743-93) viii, 81-84, 86, 87, 89, 387
    Biography 344
    Illustration 54, 61, 85
    Rise of The National Assembly 21-39
    Second Revolution 49-67
    Terror, Riegn of 100-115

Marceau, Francois Severin 99

Marechal, Pierre Sylvain (1750-1803) 151, 156, 344

Maria Theresa (Empress of Austria) 1

Marie Antoinette (1755-93) 1, 4, 27, 50, 53, 66, 99, 344
    Illustration 13, 64

Marie Louise (1791-1847) 344

Marmont, Auguste Frederic 193, 201

Marmontel, Jean Francois 11, 32

Marseillaise, La (anthem) x, 45, 117

Marshall, John (1755-1835) 135

Marwirtz, Friedrich August Ludwig (1777-1837) 344

Massena, Andre (1758-1817) 162, 166, 167, 170, 223, 243
    Biography 344
    Illustration 176
    Napoleonic Power 1808-1812 235-251

War of the Second Coalition 176-187

Mathiez, Albert xii, xiii, 97

Maupeou, Rene Nicolas de 3

Maurepas, Jean Frederic Phelippeause, Comte de 3, 4

Mazarin, Jules xiv

Meda, Charles Andre 110

Meier, Friedrich 230

Meister, Henri 121

Melas, Michael 176

Menou, Jacques Francois 116, 191, 192

Mercier, Louis Sebastien 12

Merda, Charles Andre (1770-1812) 345

Metternich, Clemens Wenzel Lothar Nepomuk, Prince of (1755-1859) 241
    Biography **345**
    Congress of Vienna 287-295
    Illustration 257
    War of Jan 1813-May 1814 262-274

Meurthe, Boulay de la 158

Michelet, Jules xi, xii

Miles, William Augustus 77

Mirabeau, Honore Gabriel Riqueti, Comte de (1749-91) viii, ix, xvii, 9, 16, 18, 19, 21, 23, 24, 27, 28, 31, 33-35, 38, 95, 100
    Biography **345**
    Illustration 17

Monaco 123, 126

Moniteur, Le (journal) 204, 209

Monotholon, Charles Jean Tristan de 236

Montagnards 42, 54-56, 112, 113, 116, 145, 151
    Civil War Jan-Sept 1793 81-94

Montesquieu, Charles Louis de Secondat (1689-1755) x, 1, **345**

Montholon, Charles Jean Tristan de 280

Moore, Sir John 241

Moreau, Jean Victor 6, 123, 134-144, 152, 177, 185, 186, 211

Morris, Gouverneur (1752-1816) 30-32, 34, **345**

Mounier, Jean Joseph 17, 35

Mountain Party 87

Mueffling, Friedrich C. F. von 231

Mueller, Johannes von 227, 233

Murat, Joachim (1767-1815) 116, 236, 237, 240, 254, 256, 279
    Biography **345**
    Coup d'Etat and Consulate 203-218
    Napoleon's Conquest of Europe (1805-1807) 220-235
    War of Jan 1813-May 1814 263-274

N

Naples, Kingdom of
    Napoleon's Conquest of Europe (1805-1807) 219-235
    War of the Second Coalition 175-187

Napoleon II 245, 279

National Assembly xi, xviii, 24, 41, 46, 69, 72
    May 1789-June 1791 16-39

National Convention xx, 55, 56, 58, 70, 83-85, 95, 96
    Final Months 111-122

National Guard 19, 20, 23, 25, 28, 40, 41, 44, 46, 54, 56, 116

Necker, Jacques (1732-1804) viii, xv, xviii, 3-6, 8, 9, 16-19, 21, 23-25, 28
    Biography **345**
    Illustration 13

Nelson, Horatio (1758-1805) 178, 209, 220
    Biography **345**
    Egyptian Campaign 187-201

Neufchateau, Nicolas Louis Francois de 153, 154, 158

Ney, Michel (1769-1815) 256, 266
    Biography **345**
    Napoleon's Conquest of Europe (1805-1807) 220-235
    Waterloo, Battle of 276-286

Nicol, John 197

Niebuhr, Barthold Georg 233, 258

Ninth of Thermidor 97, 98, 117

Nivose, Incident of 209

Nobility and Titles, Decree Abolishing Hereditary (June 19,1790) 296, 304

Non-Juring Priests, Decree upon (April 23, 1793) 297, 314

Northumberland, H.M.S. (British warship) 279

Nostitz, Karl von 231

Note of Napoleon to the Diet (of the German Empire) (Aug. 1, 1806) 298, 332

November 27, Decree of 28

O

Oath of Allegiance, Decree upon the (June 22, 1791) 296, 306

Order of the Legion of Honor 210

Orleans, Louis Philippe Joseph, Duc d' (1747-93) xvii, 41, 44, 58, 82, 86, 100, 126, 203, **345**

Oudinot, Charles Nicholas 256

P

Pache, Jean-Nicolas 85, 86, 102

Paine, Thomas (1737-1809) ix, 55, 74, 96, **345**

Palm, Johann Philipp (1768-1806) 224, **346**

Pan, Jacques Mallet du 106, 121

Pantheon Club 150

Paoli, Pascal (1725-1807) 87, 101, 127, 160, 163, **346**

Papal States
    Napoleon's Conquest of Europe (1805-1807) 219-235

Paris

Jan-Sept 1793 81-94
    Riots 25, 45, 112, 115

Paris Commune 56, 64, 83, 86, 97

Parlements xiv, 2, 4, 6, 9

Pasquier, Etienne Denis 158

Patriote Francois, Le (newspaper) 25

Patterson, Elizabeth 236

Paul I, Czar of Russia (1754-1801) 177, 180, 181, 184, 190, 205, 209, **346**

Percy, Pierre Francois (1754-1825) 232, 245, **346**

Pere Duchesne, Le (journal) 124

Perthes, Friedrich Christoph 251

Pestalozzi, Johann Heinrich 55, 282

Petion de Villeneuve, Jerome (1756-94) 43, 45, 49, 53, 59, 87, 91, **346**

Phelipeaux, Louis 188

Philippeaux, Pierre Nicolas 102

Pichegru, Jean Charles (1761-1804) 97, 116, 123, 127-129, 134-144, 152, 211, 218, **346**

Pinckney, Charles Cotesworth (1746-1825) 135

Pinel, Philippe 67

Pitt, William (the Younger) (1759-1806) ix, 68, 71, 130, 133, 184, 206, 209, 211, 220, 230, **346**

Pius VI, Pope (Gian Angelo Braschi) (1717-99) 27, 28, 151, 161, 166, 178, 184, 235, **346**

Pius VII, Pope (Barnaba Gregorio Chiaramonti) (1740-1823) 206, 212
    Biography **346**
    Napoleonic Power 1808-1812 238-251

Poland 225, 264
    Congress of Vienna 290
    Russian Campaign Apr-Dec 1812 252-261
    War of the First Coalition 123-133

Portugal 222
    Congress of Vienna 290
    Napoleonic Relations 1808-1812 237-251
    War of the Second Coalition 175-187

Press 19, 25, 146

Press, Decree upon the (Mar. 29, 1793) 297, 316

Priestley, Joseph (1733-1804) 55

Priests 45, 118, 146

Prieur, Claude Antoine 88

Proclamation of Napoleon (Mar. 1, 1815) 299, 334

Protestantism 2, 9, 21, 26, 288

Provinces
    Jan-Sept 1793 81-94

Prudhomme, Louis Marie 104

Prussia
    Congress of Vienna 287-295
    Napoleon's Conquest of Europe (1805-1807) 219-235
    Russian Campaign Apr-Dec 1812 252-261

War of Jan 1813-May 1814 262-274
War of the First Coalition 43, 68-70, 73, 123-133

Q

Quadruple Alliance 291

R

Rambouillet Decree, The (Mar. 23, 1810) 298, 331
Ramel, Dominique Vincent 153
Rapp, Jean 258
Recamier, Juliette
    Illustration 252
Reding, Aloys von 139
Reflections on the French Revolution (book) 72
Reiche, Ludwig von 231
Religion, Decree upon (Feb. 21, 1795) 297, 315
Religious Freedom, Decree upon (Dec. 8, 1793) 297, 314
Religious Policy, Decree upon (Jan. 11, 1793) 297, 314
Remusat, Claire Elisabeth de 239, 245
Republican Calender 58, 96, 99
Reubell, Jean-Francois (1747-1807) 146, 152, 162, **346**
Reveil du Peuple, Le (hymn) 115, 117
Revolutionary Committees, Decree for Establishing the (Mar. 21, 1793) 297, 316
Revolutionary Tribunal 81, 83, 103, 114, 116
Rheinbund—*See Confederation of the Rhine*
Rhenisch National Convention 126
Richelieu, Armand Manuel de 291
Riding Academy (Manege) 21, 26
Rights of Man, Declaration of the—*See Declaration of the Rights of Man*
Rivarol, Antione de, Comte (1755-1801) 31, 50, **346**
Robespierre, Augustin Bon Joseph (1763-94) 169, **346**
Robespierre, Maximilien de (1758-94) viii, xi, xx, 82, 84, 88, 111, 114, 132, 146, 148, 160, 164
    Biography **346**
    Illustration 59
    Rise of the National Assembly 16-39
    Second Revolution 42-67
    Terror, Reign of 95-110
Robespierre's Proposed Declaration of Rights (Apr. 24, 1793) 298, 317
Rochambeau, Jean Baptiste Donatien de Vimeur, Comte de (1725-1807) 69, 72, 73, **347**
Roederer, Pierre Louis Comte de (1754-1835) 61, 218, **347**
Rohan-Guemenee, Cardinal (1734-1803) 2, 4, **347**

Roland, Manon Jeanne Philippon (1754-93) 100, **347**
Roland de la Platiere, Jean Marie (1734-93) 43, 45, 56, 81, 85, 91, 100, **347**
Romains, Felix Comte de 76
Ronsin, Charles Phillipe 88
Rosetta Stone (artifact) 189
Rossignol, Jean Antoine 87
Rostopchin, Feodor Vasilyevich 259
Rouget de Lisle, Claude Joseph (1760-1836) 46, **347**
Rousseau, Jean Jacques (1712-78) xi, 95, 102, 114
    Biography **347**
    Illustration 2
Roux, Jacques (1752-94) viii, 59, 65, 67, 81, 83-85, 87-89, 91, 92, 102, **347**
Royal Council 20
Royal Session of June 23, 1789, The 296, 301
Russia
    Congress of Vienna 287-295
    Napoleonic Relations 1808-1812 235-251
    Napoleon's Campaign Apr-Dec 1812 252-261
    Napoleon's Conquest of Europe (1805-1807) 219-235
    War of Jan 1813-May 1814 262-274
    War of the First Coalition 68
    War of the Second Coalition 175-187

S

Saint-Just, Louis de (1767-94) viii, xi, 56, 81, 84, 90, 111, 124, 128, 130, 132
    Biography **347**
    Illustration 55, 61
    Second Revolution 59-67
    Terror, Reign of 97-110
Saliceti, Christophe 161
Salles, Jean Baptiste 59
Salon Francais 27, 40
Salt Tax (Gabelle) xix, 22, 27
Sansculottes 45, 54, 83, 88, 95, 96, 112, 114-116, 124
Sanson, Charles-Henri (1739-1806) **347**
Santerre, Antoine Joseph (1752-1809) 46, 58, **347**
Sapinaud de Boishuguet, Madame de **347**
Sardinia, Kingdom of 126
    War of the First Coalition 68
Savary, Anne Jean Marie Rene (1774-1833) 281, **347**
Savary, Louis Jacques 250
Scandal of the Diamond Necklace, The (1785) 1, 2, 4, 8
Scharnhorst, Gerhard Johann von 226
    Napoleonic Power 1808-1812 238-251
Schauenberg, Baron Alexis Henry An-

toine Balthasar de 139, 143
Schelling, Friedrich Wilhelm Joseph 72
Scherer, Barthelemy Louis Joseph (1747-1804) 134-144, 153, **348**
Schill, Ferdinand von (1776-1809) 241, **348**
Schiller, Johann Christoph Friedrich von (1759-1805) 93, **348**
Schlegel, August Wilhelm 270, 272
Schopenhauer, Johanna 232
Schwarzenberg, Karl Philip, Prince of (1771-1820) 255
    Biography **348**
    War of Jan 1813-May 1814 263-274
Second Coalition, War of the—*See War of the Second Coalition*
Second Directory 147
Second Estate xviii, 16, 17
Second Revolution, The (June 1791-August 1792) 40-53, 54-67
Second Treaty of Paris (Nov. 1815) 277, 280, 299, 335
Seguier, Louis Antoine 14
Segur, Paul Philippe, de (1780-1873) 228, 257-260, **348**
Senate's Proposed Constitution, The (Apr. 6, 1814) 299, 334
September Massacres, The (1792) 55, 58
Serfdom 8, 17
Sieyes, (Abbe) Emanuel-Joseph (1748-1836) xvii, 9, 15-17, 19, 116, 147, 150, 152
    Biography **348**
    Coup d'Etat and Consulate 202-218
    Illustration 16
Simon, Antoine (1735-1794) **348**
Simoneau, Jacques Guillaume 45
Slavery 22, 28, 44, 101, 265, 268
Smith, Sir Sidney 191, 200, 201, 212
Soult, (Nicolas) Jean de Dieu (1769-1851) 181, 241
    Biography **348**
    Napoleon's Conquest of Europe (1805-1807) 220-235
Spain
    Congress of Vienna 290
    Napoleonic Relations 1808-1812 235-251
    Napoleon's Conquest of Europe (1805-1807) 220-235
    War of Jan 1813-May 1814 262-274
    War of the First Coalition 68, 123-133
St. Helena, Island of 277, 279
Stael-Holstein, Germaine, Baronne de (1766-1817) 12, 23, 37, 38, 90, 119, 121, 148, 159, 185, 211, 239, 250, 253, 284
    Biography **348**
    Illustration 111
Staps, Friedrich 242
Stein, Baron Karl von 226, 238, 290
    Illustration 253
    Russian Campaign Apr-Dec 1812

253-261
Stofflet, Jean-Nicolas 82, 101, 150
Supreme Being 102, 103
Suspending the King, Decree for (Aug. 10, 1792) 297, 313
Suvorov, Alexander Wasilievitch 176, 177, 179, 180
Sweden
    Congress of Vienna 290
    Napoleonic Relations 1808-1812 237-251
    Napoleon's Conquest of Europe (1805-1807) 219-235
    Russian Campaign Apr-Dec 1812 252-261
    War of Jan 1813-May 1814 262-274
    War of the First Coalition 68
Swinburne, Henry 157
Swiss Guards 54, 58
Switzerland
    Franco War 1795-98 134-144
    War of the First Coalition 71

T

Taine, Hippolyte xii
Tale of Two Cities, A (book) xii
Talleyrand-Perigord, Charles Maurice de (1754-1838) viii, 11, 16, 22, 73, 135, 143, 148, 152, 157, 264, 273, 274
    Biography **348**
    Congress of Vienna 287-295
    Coup d'Etat and Consulate 203-218
    Egyptian Campaign 187-201
    Elba to St Helena 275-286
    Napoleon's Conquest of Europe (1805-1807) 220-235
Tallien, Jean Lambert (1767-1820) 44, 95, 97, 99, 102, 103, 110, 114, 117, 121, 148, 152, **348**
Talma, Francois Joseph 238
Tauentzien, Bogislaw Emanuel 266
Taxation 2, 4-6, 8, 17, 21, 28, 244
Tennis Court Oath, The (June 20, 1789) 17, 24, 296, 301
Terror, Reign of xx, 16, 82-84
    Sept 1793—July 1794 95-110
Thermidoreans 112, 114
Thibaudeau, Antoine Claire 90, 104, 108, 109, 110, 119
Thiebault, Paul, Baron de 35, 61

Third Coalition 223
Third Estate xiv, xvii, xviii, xx, 6, 9, 16-18, 24
Thouret, Jacques Guillaume 102
Three Emperors, Battle of the—*See Austerlitz, Battle of*
Thurman, Louis 194
Tilsit, Treaty of (July 8-9, 1807) 221, 225, 240, 252, 298, 333
Tocqueville, Alexis de xii, xiii
Tolly, Prince Mikhail Barclay de (1761-1818) 255, **348**
Tone, Theobald Wolfe 139, 141, 156
Tourzel, Louise Elizabeth, Duchess de 48, 49
Trafalgar, Battle of (1805) 220, 229
Treaty for Establishing the Confederation (of the Rhine) (July 12, 1806) 298, 331
Treaty of Alliance against France (Nov. 20, 1815) 299, 336
Treilhard, Jean-Baptiste (1742-1810) **348**
Tricolor 19, 20, 26-28, 99
Turgot, Anne Robert Jacques xv, 3, 8
Turkey 191
    Napoleonic Relations 1808-1812 238-251
    Napoleon's Conquest of Europe (1805-1807) 219-235
    War of the Second Coalition 175-187
Tuscany, Grand Duchy of 125
22nd Floral (May 11, 1798) 202

U

Ultramontanists 111
United States of America 3, 4, 8, 135, 211

V

Vadier, Marc Guillaume Alexis (1736-1828) 115, **348**
Varenne, Maton de la 64
Varennes, Capture of Louis XVI at 40-53
Varlet, Jean 83, 86
Vendee, Rebellion of the xx, 145-159
Vergennes, Charles Gravier, Comte de (1717-87) 349
Vergniaud, Pierre Victurnien (1753-

93) 41, 53, 59, 66, 87, 90-92, 100
    Biography **349**
    Illustration 47
Versailles, Palace of 2, 20
Victor, Claude 181, 256
Vienna, The Congress of (Sept. 1814-Nov. 1815) 275, 287-295
Vilatte, Joachim 108
Villaret, Louis Thomas de 137
Villeneuve, Pierre de 212, 220, 229
Voltaire (Francois Marie Arouet) (1694-1778) x, xi, 5, 11, 29, **349**

W

Walewska, Marie 278
War of the First Coalition 43, 123-133
War of the Second Coalition 175-187
Washington, George (1732-99) 55, 209
Waterloo, Battle of (June 18, 1815) 278-286
Weber, Joseph 11, 12, 49
Wellington, Arthur Wellesley, Duke of (1769-1852) 266, 290
    Biography **349**
    Illustration 276
    Napoleonic Power 1808-1812 237-251
    Waterloo, Battle of 276-286
Westermann, Francois Joseph (1751-94) 87, **349**
What is the Third Estate? (pamphlet) 9
Wieland, Christoph Martin 238
Wilberforce, William 42, 55
Williams, Helen Maria 109, 119
Wittgenstein, Ludwig Adolf Peter 265
Women 20, 26, 27, 98
Wordsworth, William (1770-1850) 42, 174
Wurmser, Dagobert Sigismund, Count of (1724-97) 161, 166, 167, **349**

X

XYZ Affair 136, 138

Y

York, Johann David von 255, 256
    War of Jan 1813-May 1814 262-274
Young, Arthur 12, 14, 34